The New Chess Player

Le Nouveau Joueur d'Échecs

Der neue Schachspieler

De Nieuwe Schaakspeler

Den nye Schackspelare

Il Nuovo Giocatoré di Scacchi

El Nuevo Ajedrecista

Новый Шахматист

2

1978

B

PITMAN

PITMAN PUBLISHING LIMITED
39 Parker Street, London WC2B 5PB

Associated Companies
Copp Clark Limited, Toronto
Fearon-Pitman Publishers Inc., Belmont, California
Pitman Publishing New Zealand Ltd., Wellington
Pitman Publishing Pty Ltd., Melbourne

Distributed in Italy by
Edizioni Scholastiche APE SpA
Via Tanaro 14, 20128 Milano

© The Chess Player Ltd 1978

First published in Great Britain 1978

Printed and bound in England by
Billing & Son Ltd., Guildford

ISBN 0 273 01264 9

Contents

+ = white stands slightly better   les blancs
ont jeu un peu meilleur   Weiss steht
etwas besser   wit staat er iets beter voor
vit står något bättre   il bianco sta un po'
meglio   el blanco está algo mejor
белые стоят немного лучше

= + black stands slightly better   les noirs ont
jeu un peu meilleur   Schwarz steht etwas
besser   zwart staat er iets beter voor svart
står något bättre   il nero sta un po' meglio
el negro está algo mejor   черные стояат
немного лучше

± white has the upper hand   les blancs ont
le meilleur jeu   Weiss steht besser   wit
staat beter   vit står bättre   il bianco sta
meglio   el blanco está mejor   белые
стоят лучше

∓ black has the upper hand   les noirs ont
le meilleur jeu   Schwarz steht besser
zwart staat beter   svart står bättre   il
nero sta meglio   el negro está mejor
черные стоят лучше

+ − white has a decisive advantage   les blancs
ont un avantage décisif   Weiss hat entscheidenden vorteil   wit heeft een beslissend voordeel   vit har avgörande fördel
il bianco è in vantaggio decisivo   el
blanco tiene una ventaja decisiva   белые
имеют решающее преимущество

− + black has a decisive advantage   les noirs
ont un avantage décisif   Schwarz hat
entscheidenden vorteil   zwart heeft een
beslissend voordeel   svart har avgörande
fördel   il nero è in vantaggio decisivo
el negro tiene una ventaja decisiva   черные
имеют решающее преимущество

= the game is even   le jeu est égal   das
Spiel ist ausgeglichen   de stellingen zÿn
gelÿkwaardig   spelet är jamnt   giuoco
pari   el juego está equilibrado   игра равна

≈ approximately equal   plus où moins égal
ungefähr gleich   ongeveer gelÿkwaardig
narmelsevis jämnt   piu o meno eguale
más o menos igual   приблизительно равно

∝ the position is unclear   le jeu est incertain
das Spiel ist unklar   de posities zÿn
onduidelÿk   ställningen är oklar   il giuoco
è poco chiaro   la posición no es clara
неясная позиция

! a very good move   un tres bon coup
ein sehr guter Zug   een zeer goede zet
ett bra drag   una buona mossa   una
jugada muy buena   очень хороший ход

!! an excellent move   un excellent coup
ein ausgezeichneter Zug   een uitstekende
zet   ett utmärkt drag   una mossa ottima
una jugada excelente   отличный ход

? a mistake   un coup faible   ein schwacher
Zug   een fout   ett dåligt drag   una moss
debole   una mala jugada   плохой ход

?? a blunder   une grave erreur   ein grober
Fehler   een ernstige fout   ett grovt fel
un grave errore   un gran error   грубая
ошибка

!? a move deserving attention   un coup qui
mérite l'attention   ein beachtenswerter
Zug   een zet die de aandacht verdient
ett drag som fortjäner uppmärksamhet
una mossa degna di considerazione   una
jugada que merece atención   ход,
заслуживающий внимания

?! a dubious move   un coup d'une valeur
douteuse   ein Zug von zweifelhaftem
wert   een dubieuze zet   ett tvivelaktigt
drag   una mossa dubbia   una jugada de
dudoso valor   ход, имеющий
сомнительную ценность

Δ with the idea . . .   avec l'idée . . .   mit
der Idee . . .   met het idee om . . .   med
idén . . .   con l'idea . . .   con idea . . .
с идеей...

N a novelty   une innovation   eine Neuer-
ung   een nieuwtje   en nyhet   un'innova-
zione   una novedad   новинка

Contributors

A. Adorjan	GM	R. Maric	IM
U. Andersson	GM	A. Miles	GM
J. Banas		E. Mednis	IM
R. Bellin	IM	T. Petrosian	GM
G. Botterill		J. Plachetka	IM
V. Ciocaltea	IM	J. Pribyl	IM
F. Gheorghiu	GM	K. Pytel	IM
A. Gipslis	GM	D. Rajkovic	GM
E. Gufeld	GM	D. Sahovic	GM
P. Hardicsay		L. Shamkovich	GM
K. Honfi	IM	G. Sigurjonsson	GM
Z. Ilic		R. Snyder	
A. Kapengut		A. Suetin	GM
R. Keene	GM	E. Sveshnikov	GM
J. Konikowski		J. Tompa	
A. Kuligowski		M. Tukmakov	GM
B. Kurajica	GM	L. Vadasz	GM
B. Larsen	GM	L. Vogt	GM
B. Malich	GM	M. Vukic	GM
		S. Webb	IM
		K. Wicker	

Journals

Ajedrez, British Chess Magazine, Butlleti D'Escacs, Ceskoslovensky Sach, Chess, Chess Bulletin (Canada), Chess in Australia, Chess Life and Review, Deutsche Schachblatter, Deutsche Schachzeitung, Europe Echecs, Fernschach, Jaque, Jaque Mate, Le Courrier Des Echecs, L'Italia Scacchistica, Magyar Sakkelet, Modern Chess Theory, Revista Romana de Sah, Rochade, Sahovski Glasnik, Scacco, Schaakbulletin, Schach, Schach-Echo, Schack nytt, Schakend Nederland, Shahmat, Shakhmatna Mis'l, Skakbladet, South African Chessplayer, Suomen Shakki, Szachy, Tidskrift for Schack, 64 Шахматы Шахматный Бюллетень, Шахматы в СССР.

Bulletins

1977: Barcelona, Innsbruck (World Junior Championship), New York, Rome
1978: Budapest (women), Belgrade (women), Bugojno, Dortmund, Eeklo (junior), Lone Pine, Reggio Emilia, Reykjavik, Sarajevo, Vrn. Banja, Valletta, Wellington

Novelties

3	Vadasz	— Honfi
13	Mihalchishin	— Chekhov
14	Uhlmann	— Alburt
23	Lipinski	— Schinzel
30	Uhlmann	— Bellon
40	Gligoric	— Miles
65	Vukic	— Kovacevic
70	Hort	— Byrne
89	Youngworth	— Shamkovich
125	F.Portisch	— Georgiev
136	Miles	— Vukic
137	Pinter	— F.Portisch
149	Reicher	— Troys
155	Pytel	— Gralka
177	Kapengut	— Terentiev
193	Kalinichev	— Timoshenko
208	Kapengut	— Juferov
215	Korsunsky	— Konoval
222	Beljavsky	— Ubilava
225	Gufeld	— Osnos
238	Eingorn	— Vaisman
249	Ivanovic	— Kurajica
267	Kapengut	— Shereshevsky
268	Tunik	— V.Zhuravlev
273	Tseshkovsky	— Beljavsky
274	Kupreichik	— Shereshevsky
284	P.Toth	— Perenyi
290	Kurajica	— Kloric
300	Stein	— E.Kristiansen
313	Banas	— Prandstetter
317	Arbakov	— Gurevich
321	M.Tseitlin	— Feishter
343	Mednis	— Soltis
346	Shamkovich	— Mednis
358	Pribyl	— Swic
363	Acers	— Soltis

Combinations

4	Larsen	— Westerinen
5	Borowiec	— Chatelain
8	Balashov	— Dorfman
25	Sunye	— Shamkovich
29	Goodman	— Nunn
34	Tompa	— Farago
40	Gligoric	— Miles
42	Podgaets	— Svedchikov
45	Gheorghiu	— Bisguier
55	Timman	— Karpov
77	Szmetan	— Vaisman
82	Dzieciołowski	— Holm
84	Ripley	— Denman
94	Kruger	— Iskov
98	Farago	— Pokojowczyk
104	Balashov	— Romanishin
108	Ivkov	— Pokojowczyk
120	Knaak	— Uhlmann
164	Chechelian	— Podgaets
165	Peresipkin	— Grigorian
179	Lipski	— Kruszynski
181	Spassky	— Hort
186	Sax	— Sveshnikov
198	Kuzmin	— Dorfman
207	Perenyi	— A.Schneider
220	Gusenov	— Korsunsky
226	Malevinsky	— N.Popov
234	Plachetka	— Jankovec
235	Velimirovic	— Rajkovic
251	Korsunsky	— Sharif
291	Sax	— Sanz
300	Stein	— E.Kristiansen
301	Tatai	— Kraidman
304	Vogt	— Mohring
316	Chikovani	— Liutian
330	Wagman	— Bukal
337	Olafsson	— Larsen
345	Christiansen	— Seirawan
358	Pribyl	— Swic
361	Portisch	— Bilek
379	Chiburdanidze	— Alexandria
383	E.Vladimirov	— Vaganian

1.v.78

Name	Title	ELO
J. Adamski	IM	2470
Adorjan	GM	2515
Alburt	GM	2515
U. Andersson	GM	2545
Anikaev	IM	2455
Antoshik		*2450
Antoshin	GM	2440
Arapovic		2415
J. Arnason		2470
Asmundsson		2405
Augustin	IM	2430
Averbach	GM	2520
Averkin	IM	2455
Baczynsky		*2400
Bagirov	IM	2505
Baikov		2400
Balashov	GM	2590
Balinas	GM	2440
Balshan		2415
Barcza	GM	2420
Barczay	GM	2465
Barle	IM	2425
Basagic		2400
Beljavsky	GM	2530
Bellin		2420
P. Benko	GM	2485
Bernat		2405
Y. Bernstein		2425
Bertok	IM	2415
Bilek	GM	2445
Birnboim		2465
Bisguier	GM	2425
Biyiasis	IM	2450
Bjelalac		2415
Bleiman	IM	2440
Bobotsov	GM	2405
Boey		2415
Bogdanovic	IM	2430
H. Bohm	IM	2410
Bohosjan		2425
Bojkovic		2415
J. Bonin		*2425
Bonsch	IM	2490
Borik		2400
Borkowski		2400
Botterill		2400
Brkljaca		*2450
D. Bronstein	GM	2570
L. Bronstein		2400
Buchman		2430
Bukal	IM	2410
Bukic	GM	2500
Buljovcic	IM	2445
Byrne	GM	2550
Calvo	IM	2455
O. Castro	IM	2425
Cebalo		2450
Charitonoy		*2460
Chekhov	IM	2470
Cherepkov		2425
Chernikov		2465
Chiong		*2400
Christiansen	GM	2490
Ciocaltea	IM	2455
Ciric	GM	2430
Cleghorn		*2405
Commons	IM	2485
Cosulich		2430
Csom	GM	2510
Cuartas	IM	2415
Cuasnicu		2400
Czeshkovsky	GM	2550
Damjanovic	GM	2455
Darga	GM	2510
Debarnot	IM	2425
De Firmian		*2405
Deli	IM	2445
Dementjev		2490
Didishko		2415
Diesen	IM	2440
Diez del Corral	GM	2490
Doda	IM	2405
Dolmatov		*2495
A. Donchenko		2405
O. Donchenko		2400

Name	Title	Rating
Donner	GM	2490
Donoso		2425
Doroshkevich		2420
Dricta		*2405
Duckstein	IM	2425
Dueball	IM	2450
Dvoretzky	IM	2525
Dzibuan		*2440
Dzindzindihashvili	GM	2550
Eliskases	GM	2430
Enklaar	IM	2400
Ermenkov	GM	2520
Ermolinsky		*2450
L. Espig	IM	2470
Estrin	IM	2430
Etruk		2400
L.D. Evans		2440
L. Evans	GM	2530
Faibisovich		2460
Farago	GM	2510
Fedder		2400
Filip	GM	2485
I. Fischer		2405
Flesch	IM	2435
Forintos	GM	2435
Formanek	IM	2410
Frias		2400
Furman	GM	2525
Gaprindashvili	IM	2425
Guil. Garcia		2535
R. Garcia	IM	2430
S. Garcia	GM	2435
Garcia-Padron		2415
Garriga		*2400
E. Geller	GM	2590
T. Georgadze	GM	2535
Georgiev	IM	2415
Gerusel	IM	2410
Gheorghiu	GM	2520
Ghinda		2445
Ghitescu	IM	2450
Ghizdavu		2415
Gik		2400
Gipslis	GM	2540
Gligoric	GM	2565
Godes		2405
Gofshtein		2400
Goichberg		*2530
Gonzales-Mestrez		*2400
Gouveia		*2405
Govedarica		2405
Grefe	IM	2430
K. Grigorjan		2520
L. Grigorjan		2480
R. Grinberg		2405
Gruchacz		*2425
Gufeld	GM	2525
B. Gulko	GM	2565
Gurgenidze	GM	2500
V. Gusev		2410
L. Gutman		2420
Gutop		*2430
Haag	IM	2430
Haik	IM	2425
Hamann	IM	2470
Hartoch	IM	2405
Hartston	IM	2475
J. Hase		2410
Hazai	IM	2455
Hecht	GM	2480
Hennings	IM	2445
Hermann		2425
R. Hernandez	IM	2465
P. Hesse		2415
Holz		*2410
K. Honfi	IM	2420
Hort	GM	2620
T. Horvath		2410
Hubner	GM	2595
Hug	IM	2460
Hulak	GM	2525
Ignatiev		2400
Ilijevsky		2420
Inkjov	IM	2450
I. Ivanov		2415
B. Ivanovic	IM	2460
Ivkov	GM	2515
O. Jakobsen	IM	2400

R.M. Jamieson	IM	2420	Kurajica	GM	2530
Janosevic	GM	2455	Kuzmin	GM	2560
Jansa	GM	2505	Langeweg	IM	2450
Jelen		2420	Larsen	GM	2620
S. Johannessen	IM	2400	Lechtynski	IM	2420
I.R. Johannsson	IM	2440	Lederman	IM	2405
S. Joksic		2405	Lehmann	IM	2405
A. Jusupov	IM	*2450	Lein	GM	2505
S. Kagan	IM	2465	L. Lengyel	GM	2430
Kaiszauri	IM	2410	Lerner		2445
Kakageldiev		2415	Liberson	GM	2555
Kaldor	IM	2420	Liebert	IM	2420
Kapengut		2465	Ligterink	IM	2440
Kaplan	IM	2460	S.H. Lim		2430
Karaklaic	IM	2460	Ljubojevic	GM	2605
V. Karasev	IM	2465	Lombard	IM	2400
H. Karner		2425	Lombardy	GM	2540
Karpov	GM	2725	P. Lukacs	IM	2460
Kavalek	GM	2570	Lukin		2460
Keene	GM	2480	Lutykov	GM	2540
Kelecevic		2410	Magerramov		*2435
D. Keller	IM	2410	Makarichev	GM	2495
Kestler	IM	2405	G. Makarov		*2400
Khassin	IM	2405	Malevinsky		*2440
Kholmov	GM	2550	Malich	GM	2535
Kirov	GM	2465	Marangunic	IM	2470
Y. Klovan	IM	2490	Maric	IM	2420
Knaak	GM	2520	Mariotti	GM	2475
M. Knesevic	GM	2505	Marjanovic	IM	2450
Kochijev	GM	2555	Marovic	GM	2455
B. Kogan		2400	Martinovic	IM	2460
Kolarov	IM	2435	Martz	IM	2405
P. Kondratiev		2450	Matanovic	GM	2505
Korchnoi	GM	2665	Matera	IM	2415
Vl. Koslov		2445	Matulovic	GM	2525
Kotov	GM	2470	Mechkarov		*2420
Kovacevic	GM	2505	Mecking	GM	2630
L.M. Kovacs	IM	2400	Mednis	IM	2460
Kraidman	GM	2455	Meduna		2425
Krnic	IM	2420	Menakov		*2450
Krogius	GM	2550	Messing	IM	2420
Kuindsky		2435	Mestel	IM	2450
Kuijpers	IM	2415	Mestrovic	IM	2435
Kupreichik	IM	2530	A. Mihaljcicin	IM	2460

9

Mikadze		2425	A. Petrosian		2415
Miles	GM	2565	T. Petrosian	GM	2620
Minic	IM	2425	Pfleger	GM	2530
Mishuchkov		2410	Piasetski	IM	2410
Mnazakanian		2415	Pilnik	GM	2435
Mochjalov		2450	J. Pinter	IM	2430
Mohring	IM	2405	Plachetka	IM	2470
Mohrlock	IM	2440	Planinc	GM	2430
M. Mukhin	IM	2470	Plaskett		2410
Muratov		2415	Platonov		2455
Y. Murey		2420	Podgaetz		2450
E. Nagy		2405	Polugaevsky	GM	2620
Najdorf	GM	2525	Pomar	GM	2420
Navarovsky	IM	2400	L. Popov	IM	2435
Nei	IM	2500	N. Popov		2420
I. Nemet	IM	2425	P. Popovic		2400
Nicevsky	IM	2400	F. Portisch	IM	2450
Nikolac	IM	2495	L. Portisch	GM	2630
Novopashin		*2435	E. Poulsson		2430
Jos. Nun	IM	2405	Poutiainen	IM	2425
J. Nunn	IM	2440	Prandstetter		2405
Ogaard	IM	2435	Pribyl	IM	2455
O'Kelly	GM	2460	Pritchett	IM	2405
F. Olafsson	GM	2530	L. Psachis		*2480
H. Olafsson		2420	Quinteros	GM	2480
Ornstein	IM	2425	Radashkovich	IM	2425
Ostermeyer		2400	Radovici	IM	2410
Ostojic	GM	2420	Radulov	GM	2490
Pablo		*2450	Raiashenok		2420
Pachman	GM	2515	V. Rajcevic	GM	2450
Padevsky	GM	2455	D. Rajkovic	GM	2490
Palatnik	IM	2490	Rajna	IM	2410
Panchjenko	IM	2495	Rakic		2410
Panno	GM	2580	Rantanen	IM	2420
Parma	GM	2540	Rashkovsky	IM	2500
Partos	IM	2420	Rath		2405
Pavicic		*2450	Razuvaev	GM	2465
M. Pavlov	IM	2405	Ree		2500
Peev	IM	2420	Regan		2430
Penrose	IM	2420	Renman		*2400
Peressypkin		2430	Reshevsky	GM	2490
J. Peters		2430	Reshko		2425
Petkevich		2445	Ribli	GM	2585
Pal. Petran	IM	2400	Robatsch	GM	2430

Name	Title	Rating	Name	Title	Rating	Name	Title	Rating
A. Rodriguez	GM	2495	Soltis	IM	2460			
O. Rodriguez	IM	2485	Soos	IM	2425			
R. Rodriguez		2415	Sosonko	GM	2575			
I. Rogers		*2400	Spassky	GM	2630			
Rogoff	IM	2520	Spassov	GM	2450			
Rogulj	IM	2420	Speelman		2410			
Rohde	IM	2425	Spiridonov	IM	2405			
Romanishin	GM	2610	Spraggett	IM	*2450			
Rossetto	GM	2405	Stean	GM	2510			
Rotov		2400	Stoica	IM	2420			
Rubinetti	IM	2430	Stolyar		2435			
Rukavina	IM	2435	Suba	IM	2430			
Rusakov		2435	Suetin	GM	2535			
A. Sacharov	IM	2460	Suttles	GM	2470			
Y. Sacharov		2475	Sveshnikov	GM	2565			
Sahovic	IM	2490	L. Szabo	GM	2515			
Saidy	IM	2430	P. Szekely		2435			
Sanguineti	IM	2485	L. Szell		*2435			
Savon	GM	2550	P. Szilagyi		2405			
Sax	GM	2550	J. Szmetan	IM	2420			
Schiffer		2435	Sznapik	IM	2430			
Schinzel		2400	Taimanov	GM	2505			
L. Schmid	GM	2520	Tal	GM	2625			
B. Schmidt		2420	Tarjan	GM	2510			
W. Schmidt	GM	2505	Tatai	IM	2455			
L.A. Schneider	IM	2430	Taulbutt		2405			
Schweber	IM	2450	T. Taylor		*2460			
Seirawan		*2455	Terentov		2415			
Shamkovich	GM	2485	Teschner	IM	2425			
Shashin		2425	J. Timman	GM	2585			
Sheliandinov		2425	Timoshenko	IM	2530			
Shereshevsky		2460	Todorcevic	IM	2425			
Shmit		*2420	Tompa		2400			
Shpilker		*2480	Toran	IM	2445			
Shuralev		2490	E. Torre	GM	2490			
G. Sigurjonsson	GM	2500	B. Toth	IM	2480			
Sikora		2415	Trabattoni		*2435			
C. Silva		2405	Tringov	GM	2480			
Sisniega		2455	Trois		2405			
Skrobek		2460	Tukmakov	GM	2570			
Smejkal	GM	2555	Ubilava		2430			
Smyslov	GM	2575	Uddenfeldt		2405			
Sofrevski	IM	2435	Uhlmann	GM	2575			
S. Sokolov		2435	Ungureanu		2410			

Unzicker	GM	2525	S. Webb	IM	2445
Vadasz	GM	2505	N. Weinstein	IM	2475
Vaganian	GM	2555	Westerinen	GM	2450
Vaisman	IM	2400	Wibe	IM	2420
Valvo		*2560	Wirthensohn	IM	2410
Van der Sterren		2400	Wockenfuss		2400
Hzak Vainger		*2470	Yanofsky	GM	2420
Van Wijgerden		2435	M. Yudovich		2400
Varlamov		*2460	Yuferov		2450
Varnusz		2410	I. Zaichev	GM	2490
Vasjukov	GM	2555	G. Zaichik		2485
Velikov	IM	2430	M. Zeitlin		2480
Velimirovic	GM	2520	Mik. Zeitlin		2510
Veselovsky		*2420	V. Ziangori		*2410
Vilela	IM	2450	Zilberstein		2455
Vitolinshy		2415	L. Zivkovic		2425
B. Vladimirov	IM	2445	Zlotnik		2430
E. Vladimirov		2445	Zsidkov		2520
L. Vogt	GM	2520	Zuckerman	IM	2475
Vorotnikov		2410	Zuidema	IM	2450
Vukcevich		2460	Zwaig		2450
Vukic	GM	2480			

Theory

English

1 c4 ♘f6 2 ♘c3 d5 3 cxd5 ♘xd5 4 ♘f3 g6 5 e4 ♘xc3 6 dxc3! ♛xd1+ 7 ♚xd1 ♘d7

8 ♗f4 8 ♗c4 ♗g7 (8...f6! Euwe 9 ♚c2 e5 10 ♗e3 ♗c5 11 ♖he1 ♚e7 12 ♖ad1 ♗xe3 13 ♖xe3 ♘b6= Dizdarevic-Kirov, Sarajevo 1978) 9 ♖e1 c6 10 ♚c2 0-0 11 ♗e3 h6 12 a4 a5 13 e5! e6 14 ♖ad1 ♖e8 15 ♗d4 b6 16 ♗e3± Romanishin-Grigorian, USSR Final 1976

8...c6 8...♘c5 9 ♘d2! c6 10 ♗e3 e5 11 b4 ♘a4 12 ♚c2 b5 13 a3 ♗e6 14 ♘b3 a6 15 ♗e2 ♗e7 16 ♖hd1 += Larsen-Hubner, Biel 1976

9 a4 9 ♚c2 ♗g7 (9...f6 △ e5, ♗c5= Book-Najdorf, Saltsjobaden 1948) 10 ♘d2 0-0 11 f3 ♖e8 12 ♘c4 b6 13 ♖d1 ♘f8 14 ♘e5! ♗xe5 15 ♗xe5 f6 16 ♗g3 ♗e6 17 ♗a6!± Commons-Mihaljcisin, Primorsko 1976

9...♗g7 10 ♗c4 0-0 10...♘c5 11 ♖e1 f6 12 ♘d2 e5 13 ♗e3 ♘e6 14 a5 h5 15 ♚c2 ♗h6 16 ♗xh6 ♖xh6 17 b4 ♚e7= Tukmakov-Grigorian, Erevan 1976

11 ♚c2 ♘c5 12 ♘d2 e5 13 ♗e3 ♘e6 14

h4! ♘c7 15 ♗c5 ♖d8 16 ♗e7 ♖d7 17 ♗g5 += Nikitin-Rosenberg, Moscow 1977

1 d4 b6

1 d4 1 c4 b6 2 ♘c3 ♗b7 3 e4 e6 4 ♘f3 ♗b4 5 ♛b3 ♗xc3 6 ♛xc3 ♗xe4 7 ♛xg7 ♛f6 8 ♛xf6 ♘xf6 9 ♗e2 ♖g8 10 d3 ♗b7 11 ♖g1 ♘c6= Smejkal-Miles, Reykjavik 1978 **1...e6 2 c4 b6 3 d5**

3 ♘c3 ♗b7 4 ♘f3 ♗b4 5 ♗d3 ♘f6 6 ♛e2 d5 7 e5 ♘e4 8 ♗d2 ♘xd2 9 ♛xd2 ♗e7?!∞ Janssen-Goodman, Innsbruck 1977

3 e4 ♗b7 4 ♘c3 ♗b4 5 f3 f5 6 e5 ♘h6 7 a3 ♗xc3+ 8 bxc3 ♘c6 9 ♘h3 ♘f7 10 ♘f4 ♛h4+ 11 g3 ♛e7 12 ♗e2 ♗a6 13 ♛a4 ♘a5 =+ Kraidman-Keene, Netanya 1977; 5 ♛c2 ♛h4! 6 ♗d3 f5 7 g3 ♛h5 8 ♗e2 ♛f7 9 f3 fxe4 10 fxe4 ♘f6 11 d5 0-0 12 ♘f3 ♛g6 13 ♗d3 ♛h5 14 0-0 ♘a6∓ Farago-Miles, Hastings 1976/77; 5 ♗d3 f5 6 ♛h5+ (6 ♛e2 ♘f6 7 ♗g5 fxe4 8 ♗xe4 ♗xc3+ 9 bxc3 ♗xe4 10 ♗xf6 ♛xf6 11 ♛xe4 ♘c6 12 ♘f3 0-0 13 0-0 ♛f4!= Garces-Keene, Lausanne 1977) 6...g6 7 ♛e2 ♘f6 8 ♗g5 (8 f3 ♘c6!) 8...h6 N (8...fxe4 9 ♗xe4 ♘c6 10 0-0-0 ♗xc3 11 bxc3 ♛e7∓ Rodriguez-Keene, Alicante 1977) 9 ♗xf6 ♛xf6 10 ♘f3 c5 11 0-0 ♗xc3 12 bxc3 0-0 13 ♖fe1 ♛g7 14 ♖b1 ♘a6 15 e5± Toth-Forintos, Rome 1977

3 a3 ♗b7 4 d5 ♛h4?! 5 ♘c3 ♛xc4 6 e4 ♛c5 7 ♗e3 ♛e7 8 ♘b5± Larsen; 3...d5?! 4 cxd5 exd5 5 ♘c3 ♗b7 6 g3 ♘f6 7 ♗g2 ♗e7 8 ♘f3 0-0 9 0-0 ♘bd7 10 ♗f4 a6 11 ♘e5+= Gheorghiu-Hartston, Moscow 1977

3 a3 c5 4 d5 exd5 5 cxd5 ♗a6 6 ♘f3 d6 7 g3 g6 8 ♗h3 (8 ♗g2 ♗g7 9 0-0 +=)

13

8...♗g7 9 ♕a4+? b5 10 ♕c2 ♘f6 11
0-0 0-0 =+ Zuodar-Keene, Lausanne
1977
3 a3 ♘f6 4 ♘c3 ♗b7 5 d5! ♗d6!
(5...♗e7 6 g3 b5 7 ♘xb5 exd5 8
♗f4 d6 9 c5 0-0 10 cxd6 cxd6 11 ♘d4
♘c6 12 ♘gf3 ♘e4∞ Petrosian-Keene,
Bath 1973) 6 ♘f3 0-0 (6...exd5
7 cxd5 0-0 8 ♗g5 ♖e8 9 e3 ♗e7 10
♗c4 h6 11 ♗f4 ♘h5 12 ♗e5 ♗f6 13
♗d4 ♗a6 14 ♗xa6 ♘xa6 15 0-0 c5 16
♗xf6 ♘xf6 17 ♕d3± Karpov-Miles,
Las Palmas 1977) 7 ♗g5 (7 e4 exd5
8 exd5 c6 9 ♗e2 cxd5 10 cxd5 ♘a6 11
0-0 ♖e8 12 ♗g5 h6 13 ♗h4 ♖c8 14
♘d4 ♘c5= Petrosian-Planinc, Moscow
1975) 7...♗e7 8 ♗f4 ♘h5 9 ♗g3 ♗f6
10 ♘d4 c5 11 ♘db5 ♘xg3 12 hxg3
h6 13 e3 exd5 14 ♘xd5 ♗xb2 15
♖b1 a6 16 ♘bc7 ♗xd5? (16...♗c3+
17 ♔e2 ♖a7∞) 17 ♘xd5 ♗xa3 18
♗d3± Sosonko-Planinc, Ljubljana
1977
3...♕h4!? 4 ♘c3 4 e3 ♘f6 5 a3 ♗b7 6
♘f3 ♕h5 7 dxe6 fxe6 8 ♗e2 ♕g6 9
♘h4 ♕h6 10 ♗f3 ♘c6 11 g3 g5 −+
Ogaard-Miles, Reykjavik 1978

**4...♗b4 5 ♗d2 ♘f6 6 e3 ♗xc3 7 ♗xc3
♘e4 8 ♕c2 ♘xc3 9 ♕xc3 0-0 10 g3
♕e4! 11 f3 ♕g6 12 ♘e2 ♗b7 13
0-0-0 d6 14 g4 ♘d7 15 h4 ♕f6 16
♕xf6 ♘xf6=** Karpov-Miles, Bugojno

1978

Queen's Gambit Accepted

1 d4 d5 2 c4 dxc4 3 ♘f3
3 e3 ♘f6 (3...e5=) 4 ♗xc4 e6 5 ♘f3 c5
6 0-0 ♘c6 7 ♘c3 ♗e7 8 a3!? (8 ♕e2
0-0 9 ♖d1 cxd4 10 exd4 ♘a5! 11 ♗d3
b6 12 ♗g5 ♗b7 13 ♘e5 ♖c8= Gulko-
Lombard 1976) 8...cxd4 9 exd4 0-0
10 ♖e1 b6 11 ♕d3 ♗b7 12 ♗a2 ♖c8
(12...♕c7) 13 ♗f4! ♖e8? (13...♕d7
14 ♖ad1 ♘d5 15 ♗b1 g6 16 ♗h6 ♖fe8=
Najdorf-Reshevsky, 1953) 14 ♖ad1
♗f8 15 d5!± Wirthensohn-Niklasson,
Reggio Emilia 1977/78
3 e4 e5 4 ♘f3 ♗b4+ 5 ♗d2 (5 ♘bd2?!;
5 ♘c3 exd4 6 ♕xd4 ♕xd4 7 ♘xd4
♘f6 8 f3 a6 9 ♗xc4 0-0 10 ♗f4 b5 11
♗e2 ♗c5= Tukmakov-Romanishin,
USSR 1970) 5...♗xd2+ 6 ♘bxd2 exd4
7 ♗xc4 ♘c6 8 0-0 ♘f6 9 e5 ♘g4 10
h3 ♘h6 11 ♘b3 0-0 12 ♘bxd4 ♘xd4
13 ♕xd4 (13 ♘xd4 ♕h4 14 ♖c1 +=
Forintos-Mihaljcisin, Sarajevo 1965)
13...♕e7 14 ♕f4 N (14 ♖fd1 ♗f5 15
♕f4 += Bukic-Matulovic, Vrsac 1975)
14...♗e6= Disdarevic-Osmanovic,
Sarajevo 1978
3...♘f6 4 e3 ♗g4 4...e6 5 ♗xc4 c5 6
0-0 a6 7 a4 ♘c6 8 ♕e2 cxd4 9 ♖d1
♗e7 10 exd4 0-0 11 ♘c3 ♘d5! 12
♗d3 ♘cb4 13 ♗b1 b6 14 a5 bxa5!
N (14...♗d7 15 ♘e5 bxa5 16 ♖a3
f5 17 ♘xd5 ♗xd5 18 ♘xd7 ♕xd7 19
♖xa5± Gligoric-Portisch, Jugoslavia
v Hungary 1971) 15 ♘e4 ♗d7 16
♘e5 (16 ♘c5 ♗b5 17 ♕e4 ♘f6 18
♕h4 ♗xc5 19 ♗g5∞) 16...♗b5 17
♕h5 f5∓ Gligoric-Portisch, Bugojno
1978
5 ♗xc4 e6 6 ♘c3
6 h3 ♗h5 7 ♘c3 ♘bd7 8 ♗e2 ♗d6 9
e4 ♗b4 10 e5 ♘d5 11 ♕b3 c5 12 0-0

14

♗xc3 13 bxc3 ♛b6= Gligoric-Matulovic, Novi Sad 1976
6 0-0 ♘bd7 7 ♘c3 ♗d6 8 h3 (8 e4 e5 9 dxe5 ♘xe5 10 ♗e2 0-0 11 ♗g5 h6 12 ♗h4 ♘g6 13 ♗g3 ♗xf3 14 ♗xf3 ♗xg3 15 hxg3 += Pfleger-Bellon, Rome 1977) 8...♗h5 9 e4 e5 10 ♗e2 0-0 11 dxe5 ♘xe5 12 ♘d4 ♗c5 N (12... ♘g6 13 ♗g5 ♖e8 14 ♘db5 ♘c6 15 ♘xd6 cxd6 16 f3± Portisch-Spassky (8) 1977) 13 ♘b3 ♛xd1 14 ♗xd1 ♗b6 15 a4 ♗xd1 16 ♖xd1 c6 17 a5 ♗c7 18 f4 ♘g6 19 e5± Portisch-Miles, Lone Pine 1978

6...♘bd7 7 ♗e2 ♗d6 8 e4 ♗b4 9 ♗g5 h6 10 ♗xf6 ♗xc3+ 11 bxc3 ♘xf6 12 ♘e5 ♗xe2 13 ♛xe2 0-0 14 0-0 c5 =+ Gligoric-Miles, Bugojno 1978

1 d4 d5 2 c4 dxc4 3 ♘f3 ♘f6 4 ♘c3 a6 5 e4 b5 6 e5 ♘d5 7 a4 7 ♘g5 ♘xc3 8 bxc3 f6∓ 7...♘xc3 8 bxc3 ♛d5
8...♗b7 9 e6! fxe6 (9...f6 10 g3 ♛d5 11 ♗g2 ♛xe6+ 12 ♗e3±) 10 ♗e2 ♛d5 11 ♘g5 ♛xg2 12 ♖f1 ♗d5 13 axb5 axb5 14 ♖xa8 ♗xa8 15 ♗f4± Bronstein-Ljavdanski, USSR Final 1964; 10 ♘g5 ♛d5 11 ♕g4!? ♛f5 12 ♕g3 e5 13 ♕xe5 ♛xe5+ 14 dxe5 += Bronstein-Chikovani, Spartakiad 1967
9 g3 ♗e6 9...♗b7 10 ♗g2 ♛d7 11 ♘h4

(11 ♗a3 e6 12 ♗xf8 ♔xf8 13 0-0∞ Bronstein-Korchnoi, Moscow 1964) 11...c6 12 f4 e6 13 f5 exf5 14 0-0 g6 15 ♗g5± Kavalek-Miles, Wijk aan Zee 1978
10 ♗g2 ♛b7 11 0-0 11 ♘h4 ♗d5 12 ♗xd5 ♛xd5 13 0-0 e6 14 ♘g2 ♘d7 15 ♘f4 ♛b7 16 ♕g4± Sosonko-Schammo, Ostende 1975

11...♗d5 12 e6! N 12 ♗a3 e6 (12... ♘d7 13 ♘e1 [13 ♘h4 N e6 14 ♗xf8 ♘xf8 15 ♛b1 ♗xg2 16 ♘xg2 ♖b8∓ Szilagyi-Osmanovic, Sarajevo 1978] 13...♘b6 14 axb5 axb5 15 f4 ♗xg2 16 ♘xg2 ♘d5 17 ♕f3 e6∓ Pachman-Lehmann, Marianske Lazne 1965) 13 ♗xf8 ♔xf8 14 ♘h4 ♗xg2 15 ♘xg2 ♘d7 16 ♘e3 g6 17 f4 ♘b6 18 ♛b1 ♘d5∓ Ivkov-Filep, Zagreb 1965
12...♗xe6 12...fxe6 13 ♖e1 ♘d7 14 axb5 axb5 15 ♖xa8+ ♛xa8 16 ♕e2 g6 17 ♗f4 ♗g7∞; 13 ♘h4∞ Hartston
13 ♘g5 ♗d5 14 ♗xd5 ♛xd5 15 axb5 axb5? 15...h6 16 ♘h3 e6 17 ♘f4 ♛d7∞; 15...e6; 16 ♖xa8 ♛xa8 17 ♕g4! ♘c6 18 ♕f3 f6 19 ♘e6 ♛b7 20 ♛d5 +- Balashov-Miles, Bugojno 1978

Catalan

1 d4 d5 2 c4 e6 3 g3 ♘f6 4 ♗g2 ♗e7

5 ♘f3 0-0 6 0-0

6 ♘c3 dxc4 7 0-0 ♘c6 8 e4 ♖b8 9 ♖e1 b5 10 e5 ♘d5 11 ♘e4 ♘cb4 12 ♘fg5 h6 13 ♘h3 ♘d3 14 ♗xh6!? gxh6 15 ♕g4+ ♔h7 16 f4 α/± Kavalek-Geller, Wijk aan Zee 1977; 7 ♘e5 c5 8 dxc5 ♕xd1+ 9 ♘xd1 ♗xc5! 10 ♘xc4 ♘c6 11 ♗e3 ♗b4+! 12 ♗d2 ♗xd2+ 13 ♘xd2 ♗d7 14 ♘c4 ♖fd8 15 ♘c3 ♔f8= Korchnoi-Petrosian (9) 1977

6...dxc4 7 ♕c2

7 ♘e5 ♘c6! 8 ♘xc6 bxc6 9 ♘c3 (9 ♗xc6 ♖b8 10 ♘c3 ♘d5 11 ♕a4 ♘b4 12 ♗g2 ♖b6 13 a3 ♖a6 14 ♕b5 ♘c2 15 ♖b1 ♗xd4 16 ♕xc4 c5 17 b4!± Ivkov-Donner, Amsterdam 1976; 12... ♗d7 13 ♕xa7 ♖b6!) 9...♖b8 10 ♕c2!? ♘d5 11 ♕a4 c5 12 dxc5 ♘xc3 13 bxc3 ♗xc5 14 ♕xc4 ♕d6 (14...♕e7) 15 ♗f4 e5 16 ♖ad1 ♗a6 17 ♕e4 ♕e6 18 ♗e3 ♗xe3 19 ♕xe3 α/+= Webb-Tisdall, Hastings 1977/78

7...a6 7...b5? 8 a4; 7...c5 8 dxc5 ♕c7 9 ♘a3±

8 a4!? 8 ♕xc4 b5 9 ♕c2 ♗b7 10 ♗f4 ♘d5 (10...♗d6 11 ♘bd2 ♘bd7 12 a4 ♕b8? [12...♕e7] 13 ♖fc1 ♖c8 14 ♘e5! ♗xg2 15 ♔xg2 ♘b6 16 ♘c6 ♕b7 17 ♘e4! ♘bd5 Sosonko-Rogoff, Biel 1976 18 ♘xf6+ ♗xf6 19 e4±) 11 ♘c3!? ♘xf4 12 gxf4 g6 13 ♖fd1 ♗d6

14 e3 ♗xf3 15 ♗xf3 ♖a7 16 a4 b4 17 ♘e4 ♘d7 18 ♕c6 ♘f6 19 ♘c5 ♕e8 20 a5± Csom-Barczay, Kecskemet 1975

8...c5

8...♗d7 9 ♕xc4 (9 ♘e5 ♗c6 10 ♘xc6 ♘xc6 11 ♗xc6 bxc6 Liebert-Barczay, Szolnok 1975, 12 ♕xc4 +=) 9...♘c6 10 ♗f4 += Mednis-Barczay, Szolnok 1975

8...b6!? 9 ♘e5! ♖a7 10 ♖d1 ♗b7 11 e4 ♘c6 12 ♘xc6 ♗xc6 Adamski-Luczak, Poland Final 1977, 13 ♗g5! h6 14 ♗xf6 ♗xf6 15 ♕xc4 ♗a8 16 ♘c3±

9 dxc5 ♘c6! 10 ♕xc4 e5 11 ♗e3 h6 12 ♕c1 ♗e6 13 ♘a3 ♘a5 14 ♖d1 ♕c7 15 ♕c3 ♘d5! 16 ♕xe5 ♕xe5 17 ♘xe5 ♘xe3 18 fxe3 ♗xc5 19 ♔f2 ♘b3 20 ♖ab1 ♖ae8 21 ♘d3 ♗a7 22 ♗xb7 ♗d7!∓ Mihalchishin-Kuzmin 1977

Benoni

1 d4 ♘f6 2 c4 c5 3 d5 e6 4 ♘c3 exd5 5 cxd5 d6 6 ♘f3 g6 7 e4 ♗g7 8 ♗e2 0-0 9 0-0 ♗g4

10 ♗f4

(1) 10 ♗g5 a6 11 ♘d2 ♗xe2 12 ♕xe2 ♘bd7 13 f4 ♖e8 14 ♕f3 ♕c7 15 ♖ae1 c4 16 ♔h1 += Rabar-Gligoric, Zagreb

1955; 14 ♖ae1 b5 15 ♕f3 c4 16 ♔h1 ♕c7 17 ♗xf6 ♗xf6 18 e5! dxe5 19 fxe5 ♗xe5 20 ♕xf7+ +− Uhlmann-Dely, Sarajevo 1964; 12...♖e8 13 a4 ♘bd7 14 f4 (14 f3 h6 15 ♗h4 ♕c7 16 g4 ♖ac8 17 a5 ♘e5 18 ♗g3 c4!?≈ Panno-Rodriguez 1972; 14 ♖ad1 h6 15 ♗h4 ♕c7 16 f4 c4! Savon) 14... ♕c7 15 ♕f3 (15 ♖ae1 b5 16 axb5 axb5 17 ♘xb5 [17 ♕xb5 ♖ab8 18 ♕c6 += Gligoric] 17...♕b6 18 ♔h1 ♘xd5! 19 ♘a3 ♘b4 20 ♘ac4 ♕c6= Gligoric-Ree, Amsterdam 1971; 15... h6 16 ♗xf6 ♗xf6 17 e5! dxe5 18 f5 e4! Spassky-Balashov, Moscow 1971) 15...c4 16 ♔h1 ♖ab8 (16...b6 17 ♖ae1 h6? 18 ♗xf6 ♘xf6 19 e5! ♘h7 20 ♘de4 dxe5 21 f5!± Gligoric-Hartoch, Amsterdam 1971; 16...♖ac8 17 ♖ae1 ♕b8 18 ♗xf6 ♘xf6 19 e5 dxe5 20 f5 ♕c7 21 ♘de4 ♘xe4 22 ♘xe4 ♕d7!= Gligoric-Pfleger, Hastings 1971/72) 17 ♖ae1 b5 18 axb5 axb5 19 e5 dxe5 20 f5! (20 ♗xf6 ♘xf6 21 f5 b4! 22 ♘ce4 ♘xd5 23 ♖c1 gxf5 24 ♕xf5 ♘e3∓ Amos-Piasetski, Canada 1972) 20...♖f8?! (20...e4 Δ ♘e5 Bukic) 21 ♘de4 ♖b6 22 ♖d1 ♘xe4 23 ♘xe4 f6 24 ♗e3± Timman-Nunn, London 1975

(2) 10 ♗g5 h6! 11 ♗h4 ♕b6! 12 ♖b1 ♘bd7 13 ♘d2 ♗xe2 14 ♕xe2 ♖ae8 15 ♘c4 ♕a6 16 ♗g3 ♘xe4! 17 ♘xe4 f5; 15 ♖fe1 ♘h5 16 ♕f1 ♘e5 17 ♘c4 ♕a6 18 ♘xe5 ♕xf1+ 19 ♖xf1 ♗xe5 20 f3 ♘f4∓; 15 ♔h1 ♘xe4!? 16 ♘cxe4 f5 17 ♗g3 fxe4 18 ♖fe1 e3! =+ Peshina-Kapengut, Vilnius 1977

(3) 10 h3 ♗xf3 11 ♗xf3 ♘bd7 (11... ♖e8 12 ♗f4; 11...a6 12 ♗f4 b5 13 e5! dxe5 14 d6 ♖a7 15 ♗xe5; 11... ♘a6 12 ♗f4 ♕e7 13 ♖e1 ♘d7 14 ♕d2 ♘c7 15 ♗e2 a6 16 a4 ♖ab8 17 ♗f1 ♖fc8 18 ♗g5 ♗f6 19 ♗xf6 ♕xf6

20 e5!± Toprovev-Bleshtsin, Leningrad 1972) 12 ♗f4 ♘e8 13 a4 (13 ♕d2 a6 14 ♗g5 ♗f6 15 ♗h6 ♗g7 16 ♗g5 ♗f6 17 ♗xf6 ♘exf6 18 ♖ae1 ♖e8 19 ♘d1 b5 20 ♘c2 c4 21 f4 b4 22 ♘a4± Gligoric-Matulovic, Palma 1967; 14 ♗e2 b5 15 a4 b4 16 ♘d1 ♕e7 17 f3 ♘ef6= Hartoch-Browne, Amsterdam 1972) 13...a6 14 ♗e2 (14 ♗h2 ♕c7 [14...♖b8 15 ♗e2 ♗d4 16 ♔h1 ♕e7 17 f4 f5 18 exf5 gxf5 19 ♗d3 ♘g7=] 15 ♖c1 ♖b8 16 b3 ♘ef6 17 ♕c2± Smyslov-Filep, Baden-Baden 1957; 14 ♖e1 ♖c8 15 ♕c2 c4 16 ♗g4 ♖c7 17 ♗xd7 ♕xd7 18 a5 ♖c5 19 ♕a4 ♕e7 20 ♕b4 ♘f6 21 ♕b6 ♖d8 22 ♗xd6!± Sanguinetti-Malich, Lugano 1968) 14...♕e7 (14...♕c7 15 ♖c1 c4 16 b3 cxb3 17 ♕xb3 ♘c5 18 ♕a3± Boleslavsky; 15 ♕c2 b6 16 ♗h2 ♘c7 17 f4 ♖ae8 18 ♗f3 b5 19 axb5 axb5 20 ♖a7 ♕d8 21 e5!± Polugaevsky-Tomson, Spartakiad 1962) 15 ♕d2 ♘c7 16 ♖fe1 ♖fb8 17 ♗f1 ♕f8 18 ♔h1 b6 19 ♗h2 ♖b7 20 f4 f6 21 e5!±

(3) 10 ♘d2 ♗xe2 11 ♕xe2 ♖e8 (11... ♘bd7 12 ♘c4 ♘b6 13 ♘xb6 ♕xb6 14 a4 a6 15 ♗e3 Garcia-Rodriguez, Havana 1974, 15...♖ae8! 16 f3 ♘d7 Δ f7-f5) 12 ♘c4 (12 ♕f3 ♘bd7 13 ♘c4 ♘b6 14 ♘xb6 ♕xb6 15 ♖b1 Fernandez-Gulfdanarsson, Dresden 1969, 15...♕b4 16 ♗f4 ♘xe4 17 ♘xe4 ♕xe4 18 ♕xe4 ♖xe4 19 ♗xd6 ♖d8 20 ♗xc5 b6=; 12 f3 ♘a6 13 ♘c4 ♘c7 14 ♗g5 b5 [14...♕d7! 15 ♘e3 h6 16 ♗h4 ♘h5!] 15 ♘e3· ♕d7 16 a4 bxa4 17 ♕c2!± Nemet-Planinc, Jugoslavia 1975) 12...b5 (12...♕e7 13 ♗f4 ♘xe4 14 ♖ae1 f5 15 ♘xd6±; 12...♘xe4 13 ♘xe4 f5 14 ♘cxd6 ♕xd6 15 ♘xd6 ♖xe2 16 ♘xb7±) 13 ♘xb5 ♘xe4 14 ♕c2 a6 15 ♘c3 ♘xc3 16

bxc3 ♕f6∞ Bagirov-Karasev 1974
10...♖fe8 11 ♘d2 11 h3 ♗xf3 12
♗xf3 a6 (12...b5 13 ♘xb5 ♘xe4 14
♗xe4 ♖xe4 15 ♕f3 ♖b4 16 ♘xd6
♕f6 17 ♘e4 ♕f5 18 ♖fe1 ♘d7 19
♖ad1 ♗d4 20 d6± Matsuri-Kertes,
Rumania Final 1974; 12...♕b6 13 ♔c2
♘a6 14 b3 ♘d7 15 a3! ♗d4 16 ♖ad1
♘e5 17 ♗e2 ♖ac8 Balashov-Savon,
USSR Final 1971, 18 ♔h1 += Savon)
13 ♖e1! ♘fd7!? 14 a4 ♘e5 15 ♗e2
♘bd7 16 ♕d2 ♘b6= Friedstein-
Swilga, USSR 1957; 14 ♗xd6! ♕b6
15 ♗xb8 ♕xb2∞
**11...♗xe2 12 ♕xe2 ♘h5 13 ♗e3
♘d7 14 g4 ♘hf6**

15 h3
(9...a6 10 a4) 16 f3 ♕c7 17 ♗f4 ♘e5 18
♗g3 ♖ac8 19 a5 c4 20 ♗xe5 ♖xe5
21 ♔h1 h5 22 h3 hxg4 23 hxg4 ♕d8
24 ♖f2 b5 25 axb6 ♕xb6 =+ O'Kelly-
Miles, Malaga 1973; 16 a5 h5 17 h3
hxg4 18 hxg4 ♘e5 19 f3 ♖c8 20
♖a4 ♕d7 21 ♔g2 ♘h7 22 ♖aa1 f5 23
g5 ♕f7 24 f4 ♘g4 25 ♗g1 ♗xc3! 26
bxc3 ♕xd5 =+ Ree-Portisch, Teesside
1972
**15...♘b6 16 ♖ae1?! ♕d7 17 ♕f3
h5!∓** Didishko-Kapengut, Minsk
1978

Nimzo Indian

1 d4 ♘f6 2 c4 e6 3 ♘c3 ♗b4 4 e3
(1) 4 ♘g5 h6 5 ♗h4 c5 6 d5 ♗xc3+
(6...b5 7 e3 [7 e4 g5 8 ♗g3 ♘xe4 9
♕f3 ♗xc3+ 10 bxc3 exd5 11 0-0-0
♕a5 12 ♖xd5 ♕a3+ 13 ♔c2 ♕xa2+
= Bronstein-Unzicker, Tallinn 1977]
7...♗b7 8 dxe6 fxe6 9 cxb5 0-0 10
♘f3 ♕a5 11 ♗xf6 ♖xf6∞ Timman-
Ligterink, Wijk aan Zee 1977) 7 bxc3
d6 8 e3 e5 9 f3 ♗f5 (9...♕a5 10
♕c2 ♘bd7 11 ♖b1 a6 12 a4 g5 13
♗g3 ♘b6 14 ♗d3 ♘xa4= Timman-
Sosonko, Wijk aan Zee 1977) 10 ♕b3
b6 11 h3 ♘bd7 12 g4 ♗h7 13 ♘e2
g5 14 ♗f2 h5 15 h4 e4!∓ Timman-
Djindihashvili, Geneva 1977
(2) 4 g3 c5 5 ♘f3 ♘e4!? (5...d5 6
cxd5 ♘xd5 7 ♗d2 cxd4 [7...♘c6 8
♘xd5 ♗xd2+ 9 ♕xd2 ♕xd5 10 dxc5
♕xc5 11 ♖c1± Liptay-Kluger,
Budapest 1968] 8 ♘xd4 [8 ♘xd5!
♗xd2+ 9 ♕xd2 ♕xd5 10 ♕xd4 ♕a5+
11 b4±] 8...0-0 9 ♗g2 ♘xc3 N [9...
♘b6 10 ♘cb5 ♗xd2 11 ♕xd2 a6 12
♘a3 e5 13 ♘b3 ♕xd2 14 ♘xd2±
Romanishin-Sydor, Dortmund 1976]
10 bxc3 ♗e7 11 0-0 e5 12 ♘b3 ♕c7
13 c4 ♘c6 =+ Green-Chandler, Wellington 1978) 6 ♕d3 ♕a5 7 ♕xe4 ♗xc3+
8 ♗d2 ♗xd2+ 9 ♘xd2 0-0 (9...♘c6
10 d5 ♘d4 11 ♗g2 ♘b3∞ Romanishin)
10 a3?! N (10 dxc5 ♕xc5 11 ♗g2
f5 12 ♕d3 ♘c6 13 0-0± Golz-Sliwa,
Dresden 1956) 10...cxd4 11 ♕xd4
d5 Green-Sharif, Wellington 1978,
12 b4! ♕b6 13 ♕b2 +=
4...c5
(1) 4...0-0 5 ♘e2 d5 6 a3 ♗d6 7
c5 ♗e7 8 b4 b6 9 ♘f4 c6 N (9...bxc5
10 bxc5 ♗a6 11 ♗xa6 ♘xa6 12 0-0
♘b8 13 ♗d2 ♘c6 14 ♕a4 += Saidy-
Fischer, USA Final 1960; 9...a5
10 ♗b2 bxc5 11 bxc5 ♗a6 12 ♗xa6
♖xa6 13 0-0 += Taimanov-Krogius,

USSR Final 1961) 10 ♘d3 ♘bd7 11 f4
a5 12 ♗d2 ♘e4 13 ♘xe4 dxe4 14 ♘b2
axb4 15 axb4 ♖xa1 16 ♕xa1 b5 17
♘d1 f5 18 ♘c3 g5!?≈ Lombardy-
Larsen, Reykjavik 1978
(2) 4...b6 5 ♘e2 ♗a6 6 a3 ♗xc3+ 7
♘xc3 d5 8 b4 (8 cxd5 ♗xf1 9 ♔xf1
exd5 10 f3 0-0 11 b4 ♖e8 12 ♖a2
♘c6= Tukmakov-Timman, Reykjavik
1972) 8...0-0 (8...♗xc4 9 ♗xc4 dxc4
10 ♕e2 a5! [10...c5 11 dxc5 bxc5
12 ♕xc4 cxb4 13 axb4 0-0 14 ♗b2
+= Portisch-Kluger, Budapest 1961]
11 b5 ♘d5 12 ♕xc4 ♘xc3 13 ♕xc3
♕d5 14 0-0 ♕xb5 15 ♕xc7 ♕c6=)
9 b5 (9 ♗b2 ♘bd7 10 cxd5 ♗xf1 11
♔xf1 exd5= Szabo-Larsen, Winnipeg
1967) 9...♗b7 10 cxd5 ♘xd5 11 ♘xd5
♕xd5 12 f3 a6 13 ♗d3 (13 e4 ♕d7
14 a4 axb5 15 ♗xb5 ♗c6=) 13...f5 14
a4 axb5 15 ♗a3 b4 16 ♗xb4 ♖f7 17
♖c1 ♗a6 =+ Portisch-Hubner, Bugojno
1978

5 ♗d3 5 ♘e2 cxd4 6 cxd4 0-0! 7 a3
♗e7 8 d5 exd5 9 cxd5 ♗c5 10 ♘g3=
Gligoric
5...d5 6 ♘f3 0-0 7 0-0 b6 8 cxd5
exd5 9 ♘e5 ♗b7
9...♖e8 10 ♗d2 ♗a6 11 ♗xa6 ♘xa6
12 ♕a4 ♕c8 13 ♖ac1 ♕b7 14 ♕c6
♖ab8= Portisch-Spassky (14) 1977
10 ♗d2 ♘c6 11 a3 ♗xc3 11...♘xe5

12 dxe5 ♗xc3 13 ♗xc3 ♘e4 14 ♗xe4
dxe4 15 ♕g4 ♕e7 16 ♖fd1 ♕e6 17
♕h4 ♗d5 18 ♖d2 += Gligoric-Szabo,
Jugoslavia v Hungary 1960
12 ♗xc3 ♖e8 N 12...♕e8= Gligoric-
Govedarica, Vrbas 1977 13 ♘xc6
13 f4 ♘xe5 14 dxe5 ♘e4 15 ♗xe4
dxe4 16 ♕g4 +=
13...♗xc6 14 ♖c1 c4! 15 ♗b1 b5 16
♖e1 ♘e4 17 f3 ♘xc3 18 ♖xc3 ♕b6∓
Gligoric-Spassky, Bugojno 1978

1 d4 ♘f6 2 c4 e6 3 ♘c3 ♗b4 4 e3
c5 5 ♗d3 0-0 6 ♘f3 d5 7 0-0 ♘c6 8
a3 ♗xc3 9 bxc3 ♕c7

10 cxd5
(1) 10 ♕e2? dxc4 11 ♗xc4 e5 12
♘xe5 ♘xe5 13 dxe5 ♕xe5 14 f3 ♗d7
15 a4 ♕xc3! 16 ♗b2 ♕a5 17 ♗xf6
gxf6 18 ♖fd1 ♕c7 −+ Fraguela-
Byrne, Torremolinos 1976
(2) 10 ♕c2 ♘a5 11 ♘d2 b6 12 cxd5
exd5 13 dxc5 bxc5 14 c4 dxc4 15
♘xc4 ♘xc4 16 ♗xc4 ♘g4 17 f4 ♗b7
18 e4∞ Vaganian-Sacherev, Voronesh
1969; 10...exd5 11 ♘h4 ♗e7 12
a4 ♖e8 12...c4 Unzicker-Byrne, Haifa
1976 13 ♗b1 △ ♖a2-e2, f3 +=
13 ♗a3 c4 14 ♗c2 ♘g6 15 ♘f5 ♘e4
16 ♗xe4 ♖xe4 17 ♘g3 ♖e8 18 ♕h5
♕d7 N 18...♕c6 19 a5 ♘f8= Panno-
Korchnoi, Palma 1969

19

19 a5 f5 20 ♕f3 ♕f7 21 ♗d6 ♗e6 22
♖ab1 ♖ad8 23 ♗f4 h6∞ Portisch-
Byrne, Bugojno 1978

Queen's Indian

1 d4 ♘f6 2 c4 e6 3 ♘f3 b6 4 g3 ♗b7
4...♗a6 5 b3 (5 ♕a4 c6 6 ♘c3 b5 7
cxb5 cxb5 8 ♘xb5 ♕b6 9 ♘c3 ♗b4
10 ♗g2 ♘c6 [10...0-0 11 0-0 ♗xc3
12 bxc3 ♗xe2 13 ♖e1 ♗b5 14 ♕b3=
Vukic-Bronstein, Sarajevo 1971] 11
0-0 ♗xc3 12 bxc3 ♗xe2 13 ♖e1 ♗b5
N [13...♕a6 c4 ♕xa6 ♗xa6 15 ♘e5
+= Karner-Bronstein, Parnu 1971]
14 ♕a3 ♖c8 15 ♘h4!? ♘e7 16 ♖b1
♕a6 17 ♕b4 ♗d3= Ristic-Ornstein,
Vrnjacka Banja 1978) 5...♗b4+ (5...d5
6 ♗g2 c5 [6...♗b4+ 7 ♗d2 ♗xd2+
8 ♘bxd2 0-0 9 0-0 ♘bd7 10 ♖e1 c5
11 e4 dxe4 12 ♘xe4 ♘xe4 13 ♖xe4
♗b7= Sahovic-Bohm, Lone Pine 1978]
7 0-0 ♘c6 8 ♗b2 ♖c8 9 cxd5 exd5
10 ♘c3 ♗e7 11 dxc5 bxc5 12 ♖c1
0-0= Romanishin-Fernandez, Cienfuegos 1977) 6 ♗d2 ♗e7 7 ♗g2
c6 8 0-0 d5 9 ♘e5 0-0 10 ♘c3 ♘fd7
11 ♘xd7 ♘xd7 12 ♘d2 ♖c8 13 e4 N
(13 ♖e1 f5 14 a4 ♘f6 15 e3 ♖c7 16
a5 ½-½ Korchnoi-Petrosian (8) 1971)
13...dxc4! 14 bxc4 b5 15 ♕c2 bxc4
16 ♖fd1 ♘f6 17 ♖ab1= Bukic-Tal,
Bugojno 1978
5 ♗g2 ♗e7 6 ♘c3 0-0 7 0-0 d5 7...
♘e4 8 ♕c2 ♘xc3 9 ♕xc3 d6 10 ♕c2
♕c8 11 e4 ♘d7 12 ♖e1 ♖e8 13 ♗d2
c5 14 d5 ♗f6 15 ♖ad1 ♕c7 16 ♗f4
exd5 17 exd5 ½-½ Bukic-Hort, Bugojno
1978; 9...f5 10 b3 ♗f6 11 ♗b2 ♘c6 12
♖ad1 ♕e7 13 ♕d2 ♘d8 14 d5 ♗xb2
15 ♕xb2 d6 16 dxe6 ♘xe6 Miles-
Korchnoi, Wijk aan Zee 1978 17 e3!
g5!?≈; 9...c5
(1) 10 b3 ♗f6 11 ♗b2 cxd4 12 ♘xd4

♗xg2 13 ♔xg2 ♘c6 (13...d5 Pomar-
Karpov, Montilla 1976, 14 ♖fd1!
dxc4 15 ♕xc4 ♕c8 16 ♕d3 ♕b7 17
♕f3 ♕xf3+ 18 ♔xf3 +=) 14 ♕d2 ♗xd4
15 ♗xd4 d5 Pachman-Djindihashvili,
Geneva 1977, 16 ♗b2! dxc4 17 ♕c3
f6 18 ♖fd1 ♕e7 19 ♕xc4±
(2) 10 ♖d1 d6 11 b3 (11 ♗f4 ♘d7!
12 dxc5 ♘xc5 13 ♖ac1 ♖c8 14 b4
♘e4 15 ♕b3 ♕c7 16 ♘d4 ♕b8 17
♕e3 ♕a8 (Bukic-Jelen, Portoroz-
Ljubljana 1977, 18 ♗xe4! ♗xe4 19
f3 ♗b7 20 ♘g5 +=) 11...♕c7 (11...
♗f6 12 ♗b2 ♕e7 13 ♖d2
[13 ♕c2 ♘c6 14 e4 g6! 15 d5 ♘b4 16
♗xf6 ♕xf6 17 ♕d2 exd5 18 exd5
♘c8 19 a3 ♘a6
(1) 20 ♖e1 ♘c7 21 ♕h6 ♗f5 22 ♘g5
♕g7 23 ♕xg7+ ♔xg7= Polugaevsky-
Mecking 1977; 21 ♘g5 ♗f5 22 ♕f4
♕g7 23 g4 h6 24 ♘xf7 ♖xf7 25 gxf5±;
(2) 20 ♘g5 ♗f5 21 ♕f4 ♔g7 22 g4
h6 23 h4 ♗xg4 – 23...♖ae8 24 gxf5
hxg5 25 hxg5 ♕xf5 26 ♕xd6 ♕xg5
27 ♖e1± Mihalchishin-Toth, Rome
1977 – 24 ♕xg4 hxg5 25 hxg5 ♕xf5
26 ♕g3± Grigorian-Makarichev,
Moscow Final 1978]
13...♘c6 14 ♕c2 ♘b4 15 ♕b1 ♖ac8
16 e4 e5 17 d5 g6 18 ♗h3 ♖c7=
Hort-Korchnoi, Hastings 1976/76) 12
♗b2 ♗f6 13 ♕c2 ♘d7 14 ♖ac1 N
(14 e4 ♖fd8 15 ♕e2 ♖ac8 16 ♖d2
♕c6 17 ♖e1 ♖e8 18 ♕d1 ♖cd8 19 h4!
+= Karpov-Pomar, Las Palmas 1977)
14...♖fd8 15 e3 ½-½ Hort-Balashov,
Bugojno 1978

Diagram

8 ♘e5 8 cxd5 exd5 (8...♘xd5 9
♘xd5 ♗xd5 [9...exd5 10 ♘e1 △
♘d3± Ivkov] 10 ♕c2 c5 [10...♘c6]
11 e4 ♗b7 12 ♖d1 cxd4 13 ♘xd4

20

♕c8 14 ♕xc8 ♖xc8 15 ♗f4± Ivkov-Radulov, Porec 1974) 9 ♘e5 c6 10 ♗g5 N (10 e4 dxe4 11 ♘xe4 ♘d5 12 ♘c3 ♘a6 13 ♘xd5 cxd5 14 ♗e3 f6 15 ♘d3± Rubinetti-Anelli, Buenos Aires 1971) 10...c5 11 ♖c1 ♘e4 12 ♗e3 ♖c8 13 ♗h3!± Rajkovic-Ornstein, Vrnjacka Banja 1978

8...♞a6 8...♘bd7 9 cxd5 ♘xd5 10 ♘xd5 exd5 11 ♘d3 ♖e8 12 b4 ♘f6 13 ♗f4 ♗d6 14 ♗g5± Ivkov-Damjanovic, Banja Luka 1974

9 ♗g5

(1) 9 a3 c5 10 dxc5 bxc5 11 ♕a4 ♕e8 12 ♕xe8 ♖fxe8 13 ♖d1 ♘c7 14 ♗f4 ♖ac8 15 cxd5 exd5 16 ♘d3 ♘e6 17 ♗e5 ♘e4= Gutman-Vaiser, Beltsi 1976

(2) 9 cxd5 exd5 10 b3 c5 11 ♗b2 ♘c7 12 dxc5 bxc5 13 ♖e1 ♖e8 14 ♖c1 ♗f8 15 ♘d3 ♘e6= Palatnik-Charitonov, Beltsi 1976

(3) 9 ♗e3 c5 10 ♖c1 ♘e4 11 cxd5 exd5 12 ♘xe4 dxe4 13 dxc5 ♗xc5 14 ♗xc5 ♘xc5 15 b4 ♘e6= Browne-Tal, Las Palmas 1977

(4) 9 ♕a4 ♕e8 10 ♕xe8 ♖fxe8 11 ♖d1 ♘e4 12 ♗e3 ♘xc3 13 bxc3 c6 14 cxd5 cxd5 15 c4 ♖ac8= Kochiev-Karpov, Leningrad 1977

9...c5 10 e3 10 ♖c1 ♘e4 11 ♗xe7 ♕xe7 12 dxc5 ♘axc5 13 ♘xe4 dxe4

14 ♘g4 (14 b4 ♖ad8 15 ♕c2 ♕g5 16 bxc5 ♕xe5 17 cxb6 axb6 18 ♖b1 ♕a5= Petrosian-Tal, Sochi 1977) 14...f5 15 ♘e3 a5 =+ Garcia-Padron-Karpov, Las Palmas 1977

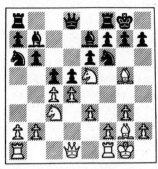

10...♞e4 11 ♗xe7 ♕xe7 12 cxd5 exd5 13 ♕a4

(1) 13 ♖c1 ♘c7 14 ♕a4?! (14 ♘d3=) 14...♖fe8 15 ♖fd1 ♘xc3 16 ♖xc3 c4! =+ Smejkal-Byrne, Biel 1976

(2) 13 ♘d3 ♘c7 14 ♘f4 ♖fd8 15 ♖e1 ♘e8 16 ♕c2 ♘8f6 17 dxc5 ♕xc5 18 ♖ac1 ♕e7 19 ♖ed1± Beljavsky-Kopec, Mexico 1977

13...♖fe8! 13...♕e8?! 14 ♗xe4 ♕xa4 15 ♗xh7+ ♔xh7 16 ♘xa4 c4 17 ♘c3 ♘c7 18 b4 += Ivkov-Hubner, Bugojno 1978

14 ♘xd5 ♗xd5 15 ♕xa6 cxd4 16 exd4 ♕e6 17 ♕b5 17 ♖ae1 ♘d2 18 ♘f3 ♘xf3+ 19 ♗xf3!

17...♖ed8 18 ♖fc1 ♗g5 19 ♗c6? 19 ♖c6 ♗xc6 20 ♕xc6 ♖ac8 21 ♕xe6 ♘xe6 22 ♘c6 ∝/∓

19...♗xg2 20 ♘xd8 ♕e4 21 h3 ♗f3+ 0-1 Hubner-Timman, Bugojno 1978

Grunfeld

1 d4 ♘f6 2 c4 g6 3 ♘c3 d5 4 cxd5 ♘xd5 5 e4 5 ♕b3 ♘xc3 6 bxc3 ♗g7 7 ♗a3 N 0-0 8 ♖d1 b6 9 e3 ♖e8 10

♘f3 ♗b7 11 ♗e2 e6 12 0-0 ♘bd7= Popov-Forintos, Sarajevo 1978

5...♘xc3 6 bxc3 ♗g7 7 ♗c4 0-0 8 ♘e2 c5

(1) 8...b6?! 9 h4 (9 0-0 ♗b7 10 f3 ♘c6 11 ♗e3 e6 12 ♕d2 ♘a5 13 ♗d3 c5?! 14 dxc5 ♕d7 15 cxb6 ♖fd8 16 ♖fd1± Nikolac-Jansa, Vrnjacka Banja 1978) 9...♘c6! 10 ♗d5 N (10 h5 ♘a5 11 ♗d3 e5 12 hxg6 fxg6 13 ♗e3 ♗b7 14 ♕d2 ♕e7 15 d5 c6 16 c4 cxd5 17 cxd5 ♗xd5 18 exd5 e4 19 ♖d1= Larsen) 10...♕d7 11 h5 ♗a6? (11...e6 12 ♗b3 +=) 12 hxg6 hxg6 13 ♘f4 e6 14 ♕g4± Spassky-Timman (3) 1977

(2) 8...♘c6 9 0-0 b6 10 ♗e3 ♗b7 11 h4 ♘a5 12 ♗d3 ♕d7 13 h5 ♖fd8 14 hxg6 hxg6 15 f3 c5= Debarnot-Palau, Barcelona 1977

9 0-0 ♘c6 10 ♗e3 ♘a5!?

(1) 10...cxd4 11 cxd4 ♗g4 12 f3 ♘a5 13 ♗d5 ♗d7 14 ♖b1 a6 15 ♗xb7 ♖a7 16 ♗d5 ♗b5 17 a4 ♗xe2 18 ♕xe2 e6 19 ♗c4 ♗xd4 20 ♖fd1 ♗xe3+ 21 ♕xe3 ♖d7 22 ♗e2 ♖xd1+ 23 ♖xd1 ♕c8 24 ♕c1 N (24 ♖c1 ♕b7 25 ♔f2 ♕b4= Polugaevsky-Mecking (5) 1977) 24...♕b7 25 ♕c5 ♘b3 26 ♕e3 ♘a5= Spassky-Timman, Bugojno 1978

(2) 10...♕c7 11 ♖c1 ♖d8 12 ♗f4 ♕d7 13 d5! ♘a5 14 ♗b3! N (14 ♗d3 b5 15 ♗e3 e6! 16 ♘f4 c4 17 ♗e2 ♕e7= Najdorf-Gheorghiu, Manila 1973) 14...b5 15 ♗e3 ♕c7 16 c4!± Ree-Rajna, Budapest 1977

11 ♗d3 b6 12 ♖c1!

(1) 12 dxc5 bxc5 13 ♗xc5 ♕c7 14 ♗d4 e5 15 ♗e3 ♘c4 =+ Ritov-Averkin, USSR 1966

(2) 12 f4 cxd4 13 cxd4 f5 14 ♕e1 e6 15 ♖d1 ♗b7∓ Holm-Pribyl, Primorsko 1974

(3) 12 ♕d2 ♗b7 13 ♗h6 cxd4 14 cxd4 e6 15 ♖ad1 ♖c8 16 ♗xg7 ♔xg7 17 ♖fe1 ♕e7= Gligoric-Smejkal, Leningrad 1973

12...e6!? N

(1) 12...♗b7 13 d5! c4 14 ♗b1 e6 15 dxe6 fxe6 16 ♕xd8 ♖axd8 17 ♘d4 += Knaak-Smejkal, Halle 1974

(2) 12...cxd4 13 cxd4 e6 14 ♕d2 ♗b7 15 ♗h6 ♕e7 16 ♗xg7 ♔xg7 17 ♕e3 (17 ♕b2!? Gheorghiu, 17...♖ac8 18 d5+ ♔g8 19 ♘f4±) 17...♖ac8 18 ♕g3 ♖fd8 19 h4 ♘c6 20 h5!± Ghitescu-Pavlov, Sinai 1975

13 dxc5 ♕c7 14 cxb6 axb6 15 c4 ♗a6 16 ♘d4 ♘xc4!= Polugaevsky-Korchnoi (10) 1977

1 d4 ♘f6 2 c4 g6 3 ♘c3 d5 4 ♘f3 ♗g7 5 ♕b3 dxc4 6 ♕xc4 0-0 7 e4 ♗g4 7...a6 8 ♕b3 b5 9 e5 ♘fd7 10 a4 (Boleslavsky; 10 ♗e3 ♘b6 11 ♗d3 ♗e6 12 ♕c2 ♘c6 13 a3 ♘a5 14 0-0=) **10...b4!! 11 ♕xb4 c5 12 dxc5 ♘c6 13 ♕h4 ♘dxe5 14 ♘xe5 ♘xe5 15 ♕g3 ♗g4∓** Ramazzotti-Sorri, corr. 1977/78 **8 ♗e3 ♘fd7 9 ♕b3 ♘b6 10 ♖d1 ♘c6 11 d5 ♘e5 12 ♗e2 ♘xf3+ 13 gxf3 ♗h5** 13...♗h3 14 ♖g1 ♕c8 15 f4 ♗d7 16 f5 ♔h8 17 fxg6 fxg6 18 h4 += Mikenas-Vaganian, USSR 1967 **14 ♖g1! ♕b8? N**

(1) 14...♕d7 15 ♖g3 ♔h8 (15...c6 16

22

dxc6 ♕xc6 17 ♘b5! ♖fc8 [17...
♘c8 18 ♖d5 ♔h8 19 ♖c5± Portisch-
Gheorghiu, Manila 1974] 18 ♘xa7
♖xa7 19 ♗xb6± Keene-Tarjan,
Torremolinos 1975) 16 ♘b5 f5 17 ♗d4
fxe4 18 ♗xg7+ ♔xg7 19 ♘d4 exf3∝
Sosonko-Timman, Amsterdam 1975
(2) 14...♕c8 15 ♖g3 c6 N (15...♔h8?
16 ♘b5 f5 17 ♗d4 f4? 18 ♗xg7+ ♔xg7
19 ♖g5± Sosonko-Nikolac, Wijk aan
Zee 1977) 16 a4 ♗e5 17 a5! ♘d7
18 dxc6 bxc6 19 f4± Popov-Szilagyi,
Sarajevo 1978
15 f4! N 15 ♖g3 c6 16 a4 cxd5 17
a5 ♘c4 18 ♘xd5 ♘xe3 19 ♘xe7+
♔h8 20 fxe3 += Botvinnik
**15...♗xe2 16 ♘xe2 c6 17 dxc6 bxc6
18 h4!±** Ivkov-Timman, Bugojno
1978

**1 d4 ♘f6 2 c4 g6 3 ♘c3 d5 4 ♘f3
♗g7 5 ♗g5 ♘e4 6 cxd5** 6 ♗h4 c5 (6...
♘xc3 7 bxc3 dxc4!? 8 e3 b5 9 a4 c6
10 ♗e2 a6 11 ♘d2 0-0 12 ♗f3 ♖a7
∝ Lengyel-Gulko, Sombor 1974) 7
cxd5 ♘xc3 8 bxc3 ♕xd5 9 e3 cxd4
10 cxd4 ♘c6 11 ♗e2 0-0 12 0-0 b6
13 ♕a4 N ♗b7 14 ♖ac1 ♖ac8 15
♗b5 e5 16 ♗xc6 ♗xc6 17 ♕xa7 g5!
18 ♗g3 g4 19 ♖xc6 ♕xc6 20 ♘xe5
♗xe5 21 ♗xe5∝ Mihalchishin-
Vaganian, Rome 1977
6...♘xg5 7 ♘xg5 e6
(1) 7...e5 8 ♘f3 exd4 9 ♘xd4 c5 10
♘f3 b5 11 ♕d2 b4 12 ♘e4± Tatai-
Fletzer, Venice 1966
(2) 7...c6!? (Korchnoi) 8 ♘f3 cxd5
9 e3 0-0 10 ♗e2 ♘c6 11 0-0 e6 12
♖c1 ♕e7= Petrosian-Korchnoi, USSR
Final 1973; 8 ♕b3 e6 9 dxc6 ♘xc6
10 ♘f3 ♘xd4 11 ♘xd4 ♗xd4 12 e3
♗xc3+ 13 ♕xc3 0-0= Sahovic-Gutman,
USSR 1970
(3) 7...c6!? 8 dxc6 ♘xc6 9 d5 ♘e5

(9...e6 10 ♘xf7 ♔xf7!?∝) 10 e4 0-0
11 ♗e2 e6 12 ♘f3 ♘xf3+ 13 ♗xf3
exd5 14 ♕xd5 ♗e6 15 ♕xd8 ♖fxd8≈
Minev

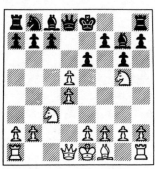

8 ♘f3 exd5 9 b4 N 9 e3 0-0 10 ♗d3
c6 11 0-0 ♗g4 12 h3 ♗xf3 13 ♕xf3
♕d6 14 ♖ab1 f5 15 ♘e2 ♘d7= Mista-
Cibulka, CSSR 1966
9...♘c6 9...♘c6 10 a3 0-0 11 e3 ♘e7
12 ♗e2 ♗e6 13 0-0 c6 14 ♖c1 ♕d6
15 ♘a4 b6 16 ♕b3 ♗g4!?∝ Green-
Sutton, Wellington 1978

**1 d4 ♘f6 2 c4 g6 3 ♘c3 d5 4 ♘f3
♗g7 5 ♗f4 c5! 6 dxc5** 6 ♗xb8?!
♖xb8 7 ♕a4+ ♗d7 8 ♕xa7 cxd4 9
♕xd4 dxc4 10 ♕xc4 0-0∝
**6...♕a5 7 cxd5 ♘xd5 8 ♕xd5 ♗xc3+
9 ♘d2 ♗e6!** N 9...♗xd2+ 10 ♕xd2
♕xc5 (10...♕xd2+ 11 ♘xd2 0-0 12
e3 ♗e6 13 ♗b5!± A.Zaitsev-Szilagyi,
Albena 1970) 11 ♖c1 ♕f5 12 ♘d4
♕d7 13 ♕h6 ♘c6 14 ♘xc6 bxc6 15
♕g7± Timman-Littlewood, Holland
v England 1969
10 ♕xb7 10 ♗xc3 ♕xc3+ 11 ♕d2
♕xc5 12 ♖c1 +=
10...♗xd2+ 11 ♘xe2 0-0 12 b4 12
♕xa8 ♖d8 13 ♖d1 ♗d5 14 b4 ♕a3
–+

Diagram

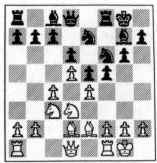

12...♕a4! 13 e4 13 ♕xa8 ♘c6 14 ♕b7 ♘xb4 15 ♖c1 ♘c2+! 16 ♖xc2 ♕xc2 17 ♕b1 ♕c3 18 e3 ♖d8 19 ♕d1 ♗xa2 (△ ♗b3) 20 c6 ♕xc6∝

13...♘d7 14 ♕b5 ♕a3 15 c6 ♘f6 16 ♗e2 Grigorian-Tseshkovsky, Baku 1977 **16...♕c3 17 ♖d1 ♖fd8! 18 f3** a5! 19 bxa5 ♖xa5 20 ♕b6 ♖d6∓; **18 c7 ♕xc7 19 0-0 ♕c2 20 ♕b7** ♕xa2 =+

King's Indian

1 d4 ♘f6 2 c4 g6 3 ♘c3 ♗g7 4 e4 d6 5 ♘f3 0-0 6 ♗e2 e5 7 0-0 ♘c6 8 d5 ♘e7 9 ♘e1 ♘d7 10 ♘d3 f5 11 ♗d2 ♘f6 11...fxe4 12 ♘xe4 ♘f6 13 ♗f3 ♘f5 (13...c6 14 dxc6 bxc6 15 ♗g5 ♗f5 16 ♗xf6 ♗xf6 17 ♘b4 ♖b8 18 ♕a4 ♗d7= Pribyl-F.Portisch, Zalaegerszeg 1977) 14 ♘xf6+ ♕xf6 (14...♗xf6 15 ♗e4 ♘d4 16 ♗c3 ♗f5 17 ♖e1 c5= Panno-R.Garcia, Mar del Plata 1968) 15 ♗e4 ♗d7 16 ♕b3 N (16 ♖e1 ♖ae8 17 ♖c1 += Sosonko-Gligoric, Ljubljana/Portoroz 1977) 16...b6 17 ♖ae1 ♖ae8 18 ♕d1 a5 19 ♕c1 += Miles-Byrne, Bugojno 1978

Diagram

12 f3 f4 12...♔h8 13 ♖c1 c5 14 g4 += Ftacnik-Geller, Sochi 1977

13 c5 g5 14 ♖c1 ♘g6 15 cxd6 cxd6 16 ♘b5 ♖f7 17 ♕c2 17 ♘f2!? a6! 18 ♘a3 b5 19 ♘c2 ♗f8 =+ Sosonko-Kavalek, Amsterdam 1975

17...♘e8 18 a4 h5 19 ♘f2 ♗f8 19... ♗d7 20 h3 ♗f8 21 ♕b3 ♖g7 22 ♖c2 += Ftacnik-Ligterink, Amsterdam 1977

20 ♘xa7 ♖c7 21 ♗a5 ♖xc2 22 ♗xd8 ♖xe2 23 ♘xc8 ♖xa4 N 23...♖xb2 24 a5± Stean

24 ♘d3 g4 25 ♖f2 ♖e3 26 ♘e1 ♖a8 27 ♖fc2 += Miles-Vukic, Bugojno 1978

1 d4 ♘f6 2 c4 g6 3 ♘c3 ♗g7 4 e4 d6 5 ♘f3 0-0 6 ♗e2 e5 7 0-0 ♘bd7 8 ♖e1 c6 9 ♗f1 a5

10 ♖b1 10 ♗e3!? exd4 (10...♘g4 11 ♗g5 f6 12 ♗h4 [12 ♗c1] 12...♘h6 13 ♘a4 ♘f7 14 dxe5 dxe5 15 c5 ♕e7∝ Kuzmin-Dvoretsky, USSR Final

24

1976) 11 ♘xd4 ♖e8 12 f3 d5 13 cxd5
cxd5 14 ♘db5 N (14 exd5 ♘b6 15
d6! [15 ♗f2 ♖xe1 16 ♕xe1 ♘fxd5 17
♘xd5 ♘xd5 18 ♖d1 +=] 15...♘bd5
16 ♘xd5 ♘xd5 17 ♗f2 ♖xe1 18 ♕xe1
♕xd6 19 ♖d1 += Janosevic-Matulovic,
Skopje 1970) 14...dxe4 15 ♘d6 ♖f8
16 ♘cxe4 ♘xe4 17 ♘xe4 a4 18 ♗d4
♘f6!= Dorfman-Kochiev, USSR Final
1977

10...exd4 11 ♘xd4 ♖e8 12 f3
12 h3 ♘c5 13 f3 ♘h5 14 ♗e3 ♗e5
15 ♕d2 ♕f6 =+ Nemet-Ivkov, Jugoslavia Final 1976
(2) 12 ♗f4 ♘c5 13 ♕c2 ♘g4 14 ♖bd1
♗e5 15 ♗xe5 dxe5 16 ♘b3 ♕h4=
Smejkal-Kochiev, Dortmund 1977
**12...d5 13 cxd5 cxd5 14 ♘db5 dxe4
15 ♘d6 exf3!? 16 ♘xe8 ♘g4 17 gxf3!**
N 17 ♘e4 ♕h4 18 h3 f2+ 19 ♘xf2
♕xf2+ 20 ♔h1 ♗d4= Polugaevsky-
Kochiev, USSR Final 1977
17...♕b6+ 17...♕h4 18 fxg4 ♘c5 Δ
♗xg4∞ **18 ♗e3! ♘xe3 19 ♕d6! +−**
Heinicke-Schutze, Hamburg 1978

1 d4 ♘f6 2 c4 g6 3 ♘c3 ♗g7 4 e4 d6
5 ♘f3 0-0 6 ♗e2 ♗g4 7 0-0
(1) 7 ♗e3 ♘c6 (7...♘fd7 8 h3 ♗xf3
9 ♗xf3 ♘c6 10 d5 ♘a5 11 ♗e2 ♘b6
N [11...♗xc3+ 12 bxc3 e5 13 dxe6
fxe6 14 0-0 b6 15 f4 ♕e7 16 ♕c2 +=
Bukic-Stull, Pula 1975] 12 ♗d4 ♗xd4
13 ♕xd4 c5 14 dxc6 ♘xc6 15 ♕d2
e5!?≈ Panno-Hug, Biel 1977)
(2) 7 ♗e3 ♘c6 8 d5 ♗xf3 9 ♗xf3 ♘e5
N (9...♘a5 10 ♗e2 c5 11 0-0 ♘d7
12 ♕d2 a6 13 ♖b1 ♖b8 14 b3 +=)
10 ♗e2 c6 11 0-0 ♕a5 12 a3 cxd5
13 cxd5 ♖fc8 14 b4 ♕d8 15 ♕b3±
Schmidt-Barlov,   Vrnjacka   Banja
1978

Diagram

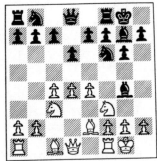

7...♘fd7 8 ♗e3 8 d5 ♘a6! N (8...♘b6
9 ♘g5 ♗xe2 10 ♕xe2 h6 11 ♘h3
♘8d7 12 ♗d2 c6 13 ♖ae1 ♕c7 14
b3 += Wade-Bilek, Havana 1965)
9 ♗e3 ♘ac5 10 ♗d4 ♗xf3 11 ♗xf3
♗xd4 12 ♕xd4 e5 13 dxe6 fxe6 14
b4 ♘e5! 15 bxc5 ♖xf3∓ Robatsch-
Hug, Biel 1977
8...♘c6 9 d5 ♗xf3 10 ♗xf3 ♘a5 11
♕a4 11 ♗e2 ♗xc3 12 bxc3 e5 13
dxe6 fxe6 14 f4 ♕e7 15 ♕a4 +=
Cuellar-Tal, Leningrad 1973
11...♗xc3 12 bxc3 c6 N 12...b6 13
♗e2 e5 14 g3 ♘c5 15 ♕c2 ♕d7 =+
Hamann-Geller, Copenhagen 1960
13 ♗e2 ♖c8 14 ♖ab1 b6 15 ♕d1 ♕c7
16 ♗h6 ♖fe8= Golubovic-Martinovic,
Nis 1977

1 d4 ♘f6 2 c4 g6 3 ♘c3 ♗g7 4 e4 d6
4...0-0 5 f3 c5 6 dxc5 b6 7 ♗d3 N
(7 ♗e3 bxc5 8 ♗xc5 ♘c6 9 ♕d2 ♖b8
10 ♖c1 ♕a5= Raisa-Balcerowski,
Varna 1962) 7...♘c6 8 ♗e3 bxc5 9
♗xc5 ♕a5 10 ♗e3 ♖b8 11 ♖b1 ♘e5 12
♘e2 ♗a6 13 0-0 ♗xc4∓ Brasket-
Whitehead, Lone Pine 1978
5 f3 0-0 5...a6 6 ♗e3 c6 7 ♕d2 (7 ♗d3
b5 8 e5 ♘fd7 9 exd6 N [9 f4 0-0 10
♘f3 ♘b6 11 b3 ♘8d7 12 a4 bxc4 13
bxc4 c5 14 a5 cxd4 15 ♘xd4 +=
Portisch-Kavalek, Wijk aan Zee 1975]
9...exd6 10 ♘ge2 ♘b6 11 cxb5 axb5

12 0-0 0-0 13 ♕d2 ♖e8= Dezso-Vasyukov, Zalaegerszeg 1977) 7...b5 8 0-0-0 ♕a5 9 e5 (9 ♔b1 ♘bd7 10 ♗h6 ♗xh6 11 ♕xh6 ♗b7 12 ♕d2 0-0-0 13 d5 b4 14 ♘ce2 cxd5 15 cxd5 Gheorghiu-Byrne, Monte Carlo 1968, 15...♕b6!=) 9...b4 10 exf6 bxc3 11 fxg7 cxd2+ 12 ♗xd2 ♕xd2+ 13 ♖xd2 ♖g8= (Razuvaev) 14 ♘e2 ♖xg7 15 ♘c3 ♗d7 16 ♗d3 c5 17 ♗e4 ♖a7 18 ♖e1 += Balashov-Byrne, Bugojno 1978

6 ♗e3 ♘c6 6...b6 7 ♗d3 ♗b7 8 ♘ge2 (8 ♘h3 e5 9 d5 ♗c8 10 ♘g1! N [10 g4? ♘h5! Bobotsov-Vukic, Sarajevo 1971] 10...♘h5 11 ♕d2 f5 12 0-0-0 f4 13 ♗f2 ♗f6 14 ♘ge2 ♗h4 15 ♗g1 a5 16 ♔b1 += Portisch-Vukic, Bugojno 1978) 8...c5 9 d5 ♘bd7!? N (9...e6 10 ♗g5 ♘bd7 11 f4 a6 12 a4 ♕c7 13 h3 += Popov-Bukic, Skopje 1967) 10 ♗g5! (10 ♗c2 a6 11 a4 ♘e5 12 b3 e6 13 ♕d2 exd5 14 exd5 ♘h5!= Green-Suradiradja, Wellington 1978) 10...♘e5 11 f4 ♘xd3+ 12 ♕xd3 a6 13 0-0 b5 14 b3 ♕d7 15 ♖ad1 e6? 16 dxe6 fxe6 17 ♗xf6 ♗xf6 18 ♕xd6 ♗d4+? 19 ♖xd4 1-0 Quinteros-Suradiradja, Wellington 1978

7 ♘ge2 a6 7...♖b8 8 ♘c1 e5 9 ♘b3 exd4 10 ♘xd4 ♖e8 11 ♗e2 N (11 ♕d2 d5!= Gligoric-Kavalek, Manila 1974) 11...♘h5 12 ♘xc6 bxc6 13 ♕d2 ♕h4+ 14 ♗f2 ♕f4 15 ♗e3 ♕h4+ 16 ♗f2 ♕f6 17 ♗xa7 ♖xb2!=+ Eperjesi-F.Portisch, Budapest 1977

8 ♕d2 ♖b8

Diagram

9 ♘c1

(1) 9 ♖b1 ♖e8 (9...b5! 10 cxb5 axb5 11 b4 e5 12 d5 ♘e7 13 ♘c1 ♗d7 14 ♘b3 ♘h5=) 10 b4 e5?! N (10...b5

11 cxb5 axb5 12 d5 ♘e5 13 ♘d4 += Boleslavsky) 11 d5 ♘d4 12 ♘xd4 exd4 13 ♗xd4 c5 14 bxc5 dxc5 15 ♗e3 ♘h5 16 ♗d3 ♕h4+ 17 ♗f2 ♕f6 18 ♘e2± Green-Shirazi, Wellington 1978 (2) 9 h4 h5 10 ♗h6 N (10 0-0-0 ♖e8 11 ♗h6 b5 12 g4 bxc4 13 ♘g3 e5 14 ♗xg7 ♔xg7 15 dxe5 ♖xe5 16 g5 ♘d7 17 f4± Gheorghiu-Westerinen, Torremolinos 1974) 10...b5 11 ♗xg7 ♔xg7 12 d5 ♘a5 13 cxb5 axb5 14 b4 ♘c4 15 ♕c1 e6 16 ♘d4 ♗d7 17 dxe6 fxe6 18 ♘cxb5 c5 19 bxc5 dxc5 20 ♘b3 Ornstein-Martinovic, Nis 1977, 20...♗xb5 21 ♗xc4 ♘xe4! ∝/∓

9...e5 10 d5 ♘d4 11 ♘b3 ♘xb3 12 axb3 c5 13 b4 cxb4 14 ♘a4 ♘e8 N 14...b5 15 cxb5 axb5 16 ♕xb4 ♘e8 17 ♘c3 ♗h6! 18 ♗f2 ♕g5 =+ Bobotsov-Ivkov, Beverwijk 1966

15 ♕xb4 ♗h6 16 ♕b6 ♕h4+ 17 g3 ♗xe3 18 ♕xe3 ♕e7 19 ♘b6 f5= Milicevic-Mednis, Kragujevac 1977

1 d4 ♘f6 2 c4 g6 3 g3 ♗g7 4 ♗g2 0-0 5 ♘f3 d6 6 0-0 ♘c6 7 ♘c3 a6 7...♗g4 8 d5 ♘a5 9 ♕d3 c5 10 h3 ♗xf3 N (10...♗d7 11 e4 e5 12 dxe6 ♗xe6 13 b3 a6 14 ♗f4 ♘e8 15 ♖ad1 b5 16 ♘d5 bxc4= Filip-Unzicker, Vienna 1957) 11 exf3! a6 12 ♖b1 ♘d7 13 b3 ♖b8 14 a4± Tatai-Marjanovic, Dortmund 1978

8 d5 8 b3 ♖b8 9 ♗b2 b5 10 d5 (10 cxb5 axb5 11 ♖c1 ♗d7 12 ♘e1 ♘a5 13 ♘d3 += Csom-Liberzon, Bad Lauterberg 1977) 10...♘a5 11 cxb5 axb5 12 ♘d4 b4 13 ♘cb5 N (13 ♘a4 e5 14 ♘c2 ♗d7 15 ♕e1 c5 16 dxc6 ♘xc6 =+ Olafsson-R.Byrne, Moscow 1971) 13... e5?! 14 dxe6 c5 15 ♘c6 ♘xc6 16 exf7+ ♔xf7 17 ♗xc6 ♖b6 18 ♘xd6 ♖xc6 19 ♘xf7 ♕xd1 20 ♖fxd1 ♔xf7 ∞ Raicevic-Schmidt, Vrnjacka Banja 1978

8...♘a5 9 ♘d2! c5 10 ♕c2 ♖b8 11 b3 b5 12 ♗b2 bxc4 13 bxc4 ♗h6 14 f4 e5 15 dxe6 ♗xe6 15...fxe6 16 ♘ce4 ♗g4 17 ♘b3 ♘xb3 18 axb3 ♗g7 19 ♗xg7 ♔xg7 20 ♕c3+ ♔g8 21 ♖fd1 +– Portisch-Van der Sterren, Wijk aan Zee 1978
16 ♘d5 ♗xd5 17 cxd5 ♗g7 N 17...♘g4 18 ♗c3 ♘e3 19 ♕a4 ♖b5 20 ♖fb1 ♗g7 21 ♗xg7 ♖xb1+ 22 ♖xb1 ♔xg7 23 ♕a3± Csom-Ghitescu, Moscow 1977
18 ♗c3 ♖e8 19 e4 ♘d7 20 ♗xg7 ♔xg7 21 ♕c3+ ♔g8 22 ♖ab1 ♕c7 23 ♗h3 ♗b7 Portisch-Timman, Bugojno 1978, 24 e5! dxe5 25 ♗xd7 ♕xd7 26 ♘e4 ♕e7 27 fxe5 +–

Sicilian

1 e4 c5 2 ♘c3 ♘c6 2...e6 3 g3 d5 4 exd5 exd5 5 ♗g2 ♘f6 6 ♘ge2 d4 7 ♘e4 ♘xe4 8 ♗xe4 ♘d7= Spassky-Korchnoi 1968
3 g3 g6 4 ♗g2 ♗g7 5 d3 d6 6 f4 e5 7 ♘h3! ♘ge7 7...exf4 8 ♗xf4 ♘ge7 9 0-0 h6 10 ♖b1 0-0 11 a3 ♗e6 12 ♗e3 ♘e5 13 ♘f4 ♗d7 14 ♔h1 ♖c8 15 ♕d2 ♔h7 16 a3 += Spassky-Portisch (13) 1977
8 0-0 ♘d4 8...0-0? 9 f5! gxf5 10 exf5 ♗xf5 11 ♖xf5 ♘xf5 12 ♗e4 ♘fd4 13 ♕h5 +– Bilek-Gheorghiu, Bucharest 1968
9 f5 gxf5 10 ♕h5! N 10 ♗g5 f6! 11 ♕h5+ ♔d7 12 exf5 ♘xc2 13 ♖ac1 ♘d4 14 ♘e4 ♕f8 =+ Trapl-Pribyl, Czechoslovakia 1972

10...h6 10...♗e6 11 ♘g5 ♕d7 12 ♘xe6 ♕xe6 13 exf5±; 10...♘xc2 11 ♘g5 ♖f8 12 ♘xh7 Δ 12...♘xa1 13 ♗h6 ♗xh6 14 ♘f6
11 ♖f2 ♗e6 12 ♗e3 ♕d7 13 ♖af1 0-0-0 14 ♘d5 fxe4 15 ♗xe7+ ♕xe7 16 ♗xd4 cxd4 17 ♖xf7!± Spassky-Hort, Bugojno 1978

1 e4 c5 2 ♘f3 ♘c6 3 ♗b5 ♘f6 3...g6 4 0-0 ♗g7 5 c3 (5 ♖e1 ♘f6 6 e5 ♘d5 7 ♘c3 ♘c7 8 ♗xc6 dxc6 9 d3 ♘e6 10 h3 b6 11 ♘e4 0-0= Trapovic-Osmanovic, Sarajevo 1978) 5...♘f6 6 d4 cxd4 7 cxd4 ♘xe4 (7...♕b6 8

27

♘c3 ♘xe4 9 ♘xe4 ♕xb5 10 d5 ♘d8
11 d6 e6 12 ♗g5± Lutikov-Sazonov,
USSR 1975) 8 d5 ♘d6 9 ♘a3 a6 10
♗a4 N (10 ♕a4? ♘e5 11 ♘xe5 ♗xe5
12 ♖e1 ♗f6 13 ♗d3 0-0 =∓ Barle-
Matulovic, Jugoslav Final 1976) 10...
♘e5 11 ♘xe5 ♗xe5 12 ♖e1 ♗f6 13
♗h6 ♘f5 14 ♕f3 ♗xb2 15 ♘c4 ♘xh6
16 ♘xb2 0-0∓ Evans-Zaltsman, New
York 1977

4 ♘c3 a6

(1) 4...e6 5 0-0 ♗e7 6 ♗xc6 bxc6 7
d3 d5 8 ♗g5 += Lein-Lengyel, Cein-
fuegos 1972

(2) 4...g6 5 h3 ♗g7 6 e5 ♘g8 7 ♗xc6
dxc6 8 d3 ♘h6 9 g4!? f5 10 exf6
exf6 11 ♕e2+ ♕e7 12 ♕xe7+ ♔xe7
13 ♗e3 += Kuzmin-Timoshenko, Baku
1977

(3) 4...♘d4 5 e5 ♘xb5 6 ♗xb5 ♘d5 7
0-0 a6 8 c4! N (8 ♘c3 ♘xc3 9 dxc3
d5 10 exd6 ♕xd6 11 ♕xd6 exd6 12
♖e1+ ♗e6= Parma-Taimanov, Jugoslavia v USSR 1973) 8...♘b6 9 ♘c3
d5 10 d4 e6 11 ♗g5 ♕d7 12 cxd5
♘xd5 13 ♘xd5 ♕xd5 14 dxc5 ♗xc5
15 ♕c2 0-0 16 ♖fd1± Sax-
Sveshnikov, Hastings 1977/78

5 ♗xc6 dxc6 6 h3 N 6 0-0 g6 7 ♖e1
♗g7 8 e5 ♘d5 9 ♘e4 b6 10 d4 cxd4
11 ♘xd4± Dueball-Schiffer, Berlin
1971

6...g6 7 0-0 ♗g7 8 d3 0-0 9 ♗e3 ♘d7
10 ♕d2 e5 11 ♗h6 ♕e7 11...f5 12
exf5 gxf5 13 ♗xg7 ♔xg7 14 ♕g5+
♕xg5 15 ♘xg5 +=; 11...f6!?
12 ♘h2 ♖d8 13 ♗xg7 ♔xg7 14 f4±
Gipslis-Wirthensohn, Dortmund 1978

**1 e4 c5 2 ♘f3 e6 3 d4 cxd4 4 ♘xd4
a6 5 ♗d3**

(1) 5 ♘d2 ♘e7 6 ♗c4 N △ ♘d6 mate!
(6 ♗d3 b5 7 0-0 ♗b7 8 a4 bxa4 9
♖xa4 ♘g6 10 ♘2b3 ♘c6 11 ♖e1

♘xd4 12 ♘xd4 ♗d6 13 ♕h5 ♘f4
14 ♗xf4 ♗xf4 15 ♘b3± Vasyukov-
Savon, USSR 1965) 6...d5 7 exd5
♘xd5 8 a4 ♗c5 9 c3 ♕f6 10 ♗e2
♘c6 11 ♘f3 h6 12 0-0 0-0 13 ♗d3
♖d8 14 ♕e2 ♗f8 15 ♗e4 ♖b8 16
♘fe5± Radulov-Covic, Sarajevo 1978
(2) 5 c4 ♘f6 6 ♘c3 ♗b4 7 ♗d3 ♘c6 8
♗c2 ♕c7 (8...♘e5?! 9 0-0 ♘xc4 10
♕e2 ♘e5 11 ♔h1 d6 12 f4 ♘g6 13 f5!
♘e5 14 ♗a4+!± Mestel-Shamkovich,
Hastings 1977/78) 9 0-0 ♘e5 N 10
f4 ♘xc4 11 e5 ♗xc3 12 bxc3 ♘d5
13 ♖f3 b5 14 ♕e1 ♗b7 15 a4 b4∞
Fedorowicz-Meyer, Lone Pine 1978

5...♘c6

(1) 5...♘f6 6 0-0 d6 (6...♕c7 7 c4 g6
8 ♘c3 ♗g7 9 ♗e3 d6 10 ♖c1 0-0 11
♖e1 ♘bd7 12 f3 b6 13 ♗f1 ♗b7 14
♕d2 ♘h5 [14...♖ac8 15 ♔h1 ♖fd8 16
♕f2 ♕b8 17 ♖ed1 += Weinstein-
Meyer, Lone Pine 1978] 15 b3 ♖ae8
16 ♖ed1 f5? 17 exf5 gxf5 18 ♘de2±
Mednis-Watson, New York 1977)
7 c4 ♗e7 (7...g6 8 b3 ♗g7 9 ♗b2 0-0
10 ♘c3 b6 11 ♕e2 ♗b7 12 ♖ad1 ♕c7
13 ♗b1 ♘bd7 14 ♖fe1 ♖ac8 15 f3
♖fe8= Spassky-Hubner, Bugojno
1978) 8 ♘c3 0-0 (8...b6 N 9 ♘f3 ♗b7
10 ♕g3 0-0 11 ♗h6 ♘e8 12 ♗e3 ♘d7
13 f4 ♘c5 14 ♗c2 ♘f6 15 e5±
Matulovic-Popov, Sarajevo 1978) 9

♗e3 (9 ♕e2 ♗d7 10 f4 ♘c6 11 ♘c2 e5 12 f5± Murei-Bikov, USSR 1967) 9...b6 10 ♖c1 ♗b7 11 a3 (11 ♕e2 ♘bd7 12 ♖fd1 ♖c8 13 b3 +=) 11... ♘bd7 12 b4 ♖c8 13 f4! += Bangiev-Terentev, Kiev 1977

(2) 5...g6 6 c4 ♗g7 7 ♗e3 ♘e7 (7...d6 8 ♘c3 ♘f6 9 0-0 0-0 10 ♖c1 [10 f3 ♘bd7 11 ♖e1 ♖e8 12 ♗f2 b6 13 ♗f1 ♗b7 14 ♘c2 ♕c7 15 ♕d2 += Covic-Popov, Sarajevo 1978] 10...b6 11 ♕e2 ♗b7 12 ♖fd1 ♘bd7 13 ♗b1 ♕c7 14 f3 ♖ac8 15 b3 += Timman-Hubner, Tilburg 1977) 8 ♘c3 0-0 9 0-0 d6 10 ♖c1 ♘d7 11 ♗b1 d5 12 cxd5 exd5 13 ♘b3 ♘f6 14 exd5 ♘exd5 15 ♘xd5 ♘xd5= Byrne-Hubner, Bugojno 1978

6 ♘xc6 6 ♗e3 ♘f6 7 0-0 ♕c7 8 ♘bd2 ♗e7 9 f4 ♘xd4 10 ♗xd4 ♗c5 11 ♗xc5 ♕xc5+ 12 ♔h1 d6 13 c4 += Gaprindashvili-Hartston, Belgrade 1978

6...dxc6 7 0-0
(1) 7 f4 e5 8 f5 ♘f6 N (8...b5 9 a4 ♗b7 10 ♗e3 ♘f6 11 ♘d2 ♕c7 12 ♕e2 += Matulovic-L.Popov, Zagreb 1973) 9 ♗e3?! ♘xe4 10 ♕f3 ♗b4+ 11 ♔e2 ♘f6 12 a3 ♗d6 13 ♘c3 0-0 14 g4∞ Jakobsen-Cebalo, Barcelona 1977

(2) 7 ♘d2 e5 8 ♘c4 ♗e7 9 ♗e3 ♘g6 10 ♘b6 ♖b8 11 ♘xc8 ♖xc8 12 ♕g4 N (12 g3 += Gipslis-Moiseiev, USSR 1971) 12...♗d6 13 0-0-0 0-0 14 ♗c4 ♕c7 15 h4 b5 16 ♗e6 ♖cd8 17 h5 ♘f4 18 ♗f5 ♖fe8≈ Timman-Miles, Bugojno 1978

Diagram

7...e5 8 ♘d2 ♗d6 8...♘e7 9 ♘c4 ♘g6 10 ♗e3 N (10 ♕h5 ♕c7 11 ♗e3 ♗e7 12 a4± Atanasov-Spasov, Bulgaria 1971) 10...♗e6 11 ♘b6 ♖b8 12 a4 += Erenska-Hartston, Belgrade 1978

9 ♘c4 ♗c7 10 b3 N 10 ♗e3 ♗e6 11 ♕e1 b5 12 ♘d2 ♘f6 13 ♘b3 ♗xb3 14 axb3 += Kaplan-Bobotsov, Skopje 1972
10...♘e7 11 ♕h5 ♘g6 12 ♗a3 b5 13 ♗e3 ♘f4 14 ♕f3 ♗d6 15 ♗xd6 ♕xd6 16 ♖fd1 ♕c5= Rohde-Miles, Lone Pine 1978

1 e4 c5 2 ♘f3 d6 3 d4 cxd4 4 ♘xd4 ♘f6 5 ♘c3 g6 6 ♗e2 6 ♗e3 ♗g7 7 f3 ♘c6 8 ♕d2 0-0 9 ♗c4 ♗d7 10 h4 ♖c8 11 ♗b3 ♘e5 12 h5 ♘xh5 (12...♘c4 13 ♗xc4 ♖xc4 14 0-0-0 ♕c7 15 hxg6 fxg6 16 ♗h6 ♘xe4! 17 ♕e3! ♘xc3 18 ♗xg7 ♖f7 19 ♖xh7 ♘e2+!! 20 ♘xe2 ♖xc2+ 21 ♔b1 ♖xe2 22 ♖h8+ ♔xg7 23 ♕h6+ ♔f6 24 ♕h4+ ½-½ Fleck-Doncevic, Berlin 1977) 13 g4 ♖c4? (Keene; 13...♘f6 14 ♘d5!) 14 gxh5 (14 ♗xc4 ♘xc4 15 ♕e2 ♘xe3 16 ♕xe3 ♘f6= Keene) 14...♖xd4 15 ♕e2! N ♖b4 16 hxg6 hxg6 17 0-0-0 Δ ♕h2 +− Whitehead-Fleck, Eeklo 1978
6...♗g7 7 ♗e3 7 ♘b3 0-0 8 0-0 ♘c6 9 ♗g5 ♗e6 10 ♔h1 ♘a5?! 11 ♘d4 ♗c4 12 f4 h6 13 ♗h4 a6 14 f5 g5 15 ♗f2± Schussler-Pirisi, Eeklo 1978
7...0-0 8 0-0 ♘c6 9 ♘b3 ♗e6 10 f4 b5?! N
(1) 10...♘a5 11 f5 ♗c4 12 ♘xa5 (12 ♗d3! += Spielmann) 12...♗xe2

13 ♕xe2 ♕xa5 14 g4 ♖ac8! 15 g5
♖xc3 16 gxf6 ♖xe3 17 ♕xe3 ♗xf6
18 c3 b5 N 19 a3 ♕c7 20 ♖ad1 a5
=+ Corden-Miles, Birmingham 1973
(2) 10...♕c8 11 h3 ♖d8 12 ♘f3 ♗c4
13 ♖f2 e5 14 ♖d2 ♕e6 15 ♘d5 exf4
16 ♘d4 ♘xd4 17 ♗xd4 ♗xd5 18
exd5 ♕f5= Rolland-Larsen, Le Havre
1966
11 f5 11 ♗xb5 ♘g4 **11...b4** 11...♗xb3
12 axb3 b4 13 ♘d5 ♘xe4 14 ♖a6!
**12 fxe6 bxc3 13 exf7+ ♔h8 14 bxc3
♘e5** 14...♘xe4 15 ♗f3 ♘xc3 16 ♕d2
△ ♘d4±
**15 ♗d4! ♘xe4 16 ♗f3! ♘xf3+ 17
♕xf3 ♘f6 18 ♖ad1±** Spassky-Miles,
Bugojno 1978

1 e4 c5 2 ♘f3 d6 3 d4 cxd4 4 ♘xd4
♘f6 5 ♘c3 a6 6 ♗g5 6 a4 g6 (6...♘c6
7 ♗e2 e5 8 ♘xc6 [8 ♘b3 ♗e7 9 0-0
0-0 10 f4 b6 11 f5 ♗b7 12 ♘d5!?
♘xe4 13 ♗e3!∝ Gaprindashvili-Hasin,
USSR 1977] 8...bxc6 9 f4 ♗e7 10
fxe5 dxe5 11 ♕xd8+ ♗xd8 12 a5 ♗e6
13 ♖a4 0-0 14 ♗e3 ♗c7= Larsen-
Bukic, Bugojno 1978) 7 ♗e2 ♗g7 8
♗e3 0-0 9 0-0 ♘c6 10 f4 ♗d7 11 ♘b3
♖c8 12 ♗f3 ♗e6 13 ♘d5!± Tal-Byrne,
Bugojno 1978

6...e6 7 f4 ♗e7
(1) 7...♕b6 8 ♕d2 (8 ♘b3 ♗e7 9 ♕f3

♘bd7 10 0-0-0 ♕c7 11 ♗e2 h6 12
♕h3 b5 13 ♗f3 ♗b7 14 ♗xf6 ♗xf6
15 e5 dxe5 16 ♗xb7 ♕xb7 17 f5∝
Chandler-Quinteros, Wellington 1978)
8...♕xb2 9 ♖b1 ♕a3 10 e5 (10 f5
♘c6 11 fxe6 fxe6 12 ♘xc6 bxc6 13
e5 dxe5 14 ♗xf6 gxf6 15 ♘e4 ♕xa2
N 16 ♖d1 [16 ♘xf6+ ♔f7 17 ♖d1
♕b2! 18 ♘e4 ♗b4+ 19 c3 ♕xd2+
20 ♖xd2 ♗e7 21 ♗e2 ♖b8∓] 16...
♗e7 17 ♗e2 0-0 18 0-0 f5 19 ♕h6
♕xc2∓ Soler-Engel, corr. 1976/78)
10...dxe5 11 fxe5 ♘fd7 12 ♗c4 ♕a5
13 0-0 (13 ♘xe6 fxe6 14 ♗xe6 ♕xe5+
15 ♕e3 ♕xe3+ 16 ♗xe3 ♘c6∓
Mazzoni-Fischer, Monte Carlo 1967)
13...♘xe5 14 ♗xe6 (14 ♖be1 ♘xc4
15 ♕f4 ♘d6 16 ♘e4 ♕c7∝; 14...
♘bc6!) 14...♗xe6 15 ♘xe6 fxe6 16
♖xf8+ ♖xf8 17 ♕d6 ♘f3+! −+
Nieuwelink-Stempin, Eeklo 1978
(2) 7...b5 8 e5 (8 a3 ♘bd7 9 ♕e2
♕b6 10 0-0-0 ♗b7 11 g4 ♖c8 12
♗xf6 gxf6 13 f5 ♖xc3∝ Andre-Tatai,
Dortmund 1978) 8...dxe5 9 fxe5 ♕c7
10 exf6 ♕e5+ 11 ♗e2 (11 ♕e2 ♕xg5
12 g3?! N [12 ♘e4 ♕e5 13 0-0-0
♖a7! 14 ♘f3 ♕f4+ 15 ♔b1 ♖d7∓
Stein-Saharov, USSR 1960] 12...gxf6
13 ♗g2 ♖a7 14 ♘e4 ♕e5 15 0-0-0
♗e7 16 ♖he1 ♖d7∓ Sampouw-
Quinteros, Wellington 1978) 11...♕xg5
12 ♕d3 ♕xf6 13 ♖f1 ♕g6 (13...♕e5
14 0-0-0 − 14 ♖d1 ♗d7 [14...♗b7??
15 ♘c6 ♕d6 16 ♕f3 +− Matulovic-
Bogdanovic, Sarajevo 1976] 15 ♘f3
♕c7 16 ♘e5! ♗e7 17 ♘xf7 0-0 18
♘d6 += Ljubojevic-Polugaevsky,
Hilversum 1973; 14 ♘f3 ♗c5 15 0-0-0
♗e7 16 ♘e4 ♕c7 17 ♘fg5! f5 18
♕h3!± Gusev-Juferov, 1976 [14...
♖a7 15 ♘f3 ♕f4+ 16 ♘d2] 16 ♔b1
♖d7∝; 16...♕c7! 17 ♘h5 g6 18 ♕d4
e5 19 ♕f2 ♗c5 20 ♕f6 0-0 21 ♘d5

♗e7!∓ Gheorghiu-Ljubojevic, Amsterdam 1975; 13...♕g5 14 ♘e4 ♕e5 15 ♖d1 ♗b4+ 16 c3 ♗e7 17 ♘f3 ♕c7 18 ♘eg5 ♗f6 19 ♘xh7 ♘d7 20 ♘xf6+ ♘xf6 21 ♘e5 0-0! 22 ♕g3 ♘e4 23 ♕f4 f5∞ Gufeld-Bronstein, Vilnius 1975) 14 ♕e3 ♗c5 15 ♗f3 ♖a7 16 ♘e4 ♗b4+ 17 c3 ♗e7 18 ♘xe6! ♕xe6 19 ♕xa7 ♘c6 20 ♕c7 f5 21 0-0-0 fxe4 22 ♖fe1! N (22 ♗h5+ g6 23 ♗g4 ♕xg4 24 ♕xc6+ ♗d7 25 ♖xd7 ♕xd7 26 ♕a8+= Matulovic-Polugaevsky, Belgrade 1974) 22...0-0? (22...♕h6+ 23 ♔b1 ♗f5 24 ♗xe4 ♗xe4 25 ♖xe4 +=) 23 ♗xe4± Matulovic-Bohmfeldt, Dortmund 1977

8 ♕f3 ♕c7 8...h6 9 ♗h4 g5 10 fxg5 ♘fd7 11 ♘xe6 fxe6 12 ♕h5+ ♔f8 13 ♗b5 ♖h7 14 0-0+ ♔g8 15 g6 ♖g7 16 ♖f7 ♗xh4 17 ♕xh6 ♕f6!? 18 ♖xf6 ♗xf6 19 ♗e2 ♘e5 20 ♖f1 ♖xg6 21 ♕d2∞ Radev-Inkiov, Bulgaria Final 1976

9 0-0-0 ♘bd7 10 ♗d3 h6 11 ♗h4 g5!?

12 e5 12 fxg5 ♘e5 13 ♕e2 ♘fg4 (13...♘h7 14 ♘f3 hxg5 15 ♗f2 ♘f8 16 ♗e3 ♖g8 17 ♘xe5 dxe5 18 ♕f3!± Hort-Bobotsov, Wijk aan Zee 1970) 14 ♘f3 hxg5 15 ♗xg5?! (15 ♗g3 ♘xf3 16 gxf3 ♘e5 17 f4 gxf4 18 ♗xf4 ♗d7 19 ♖df1 ♖h7 20 h4 0-0-0 21 h5 += Minic) 15...♗xg5+ 16 ♘xg5

♕c5 17 ♘f3!? (17 ♘h3 ♗d7 18 ♕d2 0-0-0 19 ♗e2 ♘e3 =+ Litvinov-Zidkov, USSR 1973) 17...♘f2 18 ♘xe5 dxe5 (18...♘xd1 19 ♘xf7 ♘xc3 ?0 ♕f3 ♖f8 21 ♖f1 ♘xa2+ 22 ♔b1 ♘b4 23 e5 ♘xd3! 24 ♘xd6+ ♔xd6 25 e5 ♘xd3! 24 ♘xd6+ ♕xd6 25 ♕h5+ ♔d7 26 exd6 ♖xf1+ 27 ♔a2 ♘c1+ 28 ♔a3 ♔xd6 −+; 24 ♕xd3 ♖xf7! 25 ♕g6 ♔d7 −+; 24 exd6 ♔d7 25 cxd3 ♕f5! 26 ♕e2 ♖xf7! 27 ♖xf5 ♖xf5 −+; 24 ♕f6 ♕c7 25 ♕g6 ♕xf7! −+;) 19 ♘a4 ♕a7 (∓ Geller) 20 ♗b5+ axb5 21 ♕xb5+ ♔e7 22 ♕b4+ ♔f6 23 ♘b6! ♘xd1? (23...♘xh1!) 24 ♖f1+ ♔g6 25 ♕e7 f5 26 exf5+ exf5 Ivanovic-Bukic, Jugoslav Final 1978, 27 ♖f3! f4 28 ♘c4! +−; 27...♘f2 28 ♕d6+ ♔g5 29 ♖a3 ♕xa3 30 bxa3 ♖a6 31 ♕d2+ ♔f6 32 ♕xf2 ♗e6 33 ♕c5! +−; 28...♔h5 29 g4+! ♘xg4 30 ♖h3+ ♔g5 31 ♖xh8 ♕xa2 32 ♘d5 ♕xd5 33 ♕xd5 ♖a1+ 34 ♔d2 ♖d1+ 35 ♔xd1 ♘e3+ 36 ♔d2 ♘xd5 37 ♖xc8 +−

12...gxh4 13 exf6 ♗xf6 14 f5 e5 15 ♘de2 ♗d7 16 ♘e4 16 ♗e4 ♘c6 17 ♘d5 ♗xd5 18 ♗xd5 ♘xd5 19 ♖xd5 ♗g5+ 20 ♔b1 0-0-0 21 ♖hd1 ½-½ Ikonic-Osmanovic, Sarajevo 1978

16...d5! N 16...♘c6 17 ♘xf6+ ♗xf6 18 ♗e4 0-0-0 19 ♘c3± Parma-Bukic, Ljubljana/Portoroz 1977

17 ♘xf6+ ♗xf6 18 ♕xd5 ♘c6 19 ♕b3 19 ♕c5 0-0-0 △ ♖d5∓ **19... 0-0-0 20 ♗c4 ♗xg2∓** Parma-Bukic, Jugoslav Final 1978

1 e4 c5 2 ♘f3 ♘c6 3 d4 cxd4 4 ♘xd4 ♘f6 5 ♘c3 d6 6 ♗g5 e6 7 ♕d2 a6 8 0-0-0 ♗d7 9 f4 ♗e7 9...h6 10 ♗h4 ♘xe4 11 ♕e1 ♘f6 12 ♘f5 ♕a5 13 ♘xd6+ ♗xd6 14 ♖xd6 0-0-0 15 ♖d2 ♘e7 16 ♕e5 ♕xe5= Matulovic-

31

Szilagyi, Sarajevo 1978
10 ♘f3 b5 11 ♗xf6 gxf6 11...♗xf6
12 ♕xd6 ♖a7 13 e5 ♗e7 14 ♕d3 ♕a5
15 ♘d4 ♘b4! 16 ♕e3 ♖c7 17 ♔b1
♖xc3 18 ♕xc3 ♕xa2+ 19 ♔c1 ♘d5
20 ♕b3 ♕a1+ = Hardicsay-Mista,
Olomouc 1977

12 g3 12 f5 ♕b6 13 ♔b1 0-0-0 14 g3
♔b8 15 fxe6 fxe6 16 ♗h3 ♗c8 17
♕e1!± Karpov-Liberzon, Bad Lauterberg 1977
12...♕b6 13 ♗h3 0-0-0 14 f5 ♔b8 15
fxe6 fxe6 16 ♘e2? ♘e5! 17 ♘fd4
♘c4 18 ♕d3 f5! 19 exf5 e5!∓
Matulovic-Ivanovic, Jugoslav Final
1978

1 e4 c5 2 ♘f3 e6 3 d4 cxd4 4 ♘xd4
♘c6 5 ♘c3 ♕c7 6 ♗e2 ♘f6 7 0-0 a6
8 ♔h1 ♗e7 9 f4 d6 10 ♗e3 0-0 11
♕e1 ♗d7 12 ♕g3 ♔h8!? (Larsen)
12...b5 13 a3 ♘xd4 14 ♗xd4 ♗c6 15
♗d3 (15 e5 dxe5 16 ♗xe5 ♕b7 17 f5
exf5 18 ♖xf5 ♘e8= Polugaevsky-
Matulovic, Havana 1966) 15...e5 16
fxe5 ♘h5 17 ♕h3 dxe5 18 ♗xe5 ♕xe5
19 ♖f5 Kovacs-Wagman, Reggio Emilia
1978, 19...♕d4 20 ♖xh5 g6! 21
♖xh7∞
13 ♖ad1 13 a3 b5 14 ♘xc6 ♗xc6 15
♗d4 ♕b7 16 ♗d3 b4 17 axb4 ♕xb4
18 ♘e2 ♕b7 19 ♘c3 ♕b4 20 ♘e2 ♕b7

21 e5 dxe5 22 ♘xe5 ♗e4 23 ♗xe4
♕xe4 24 ♘d4 ♗c5!= Valenti-Wagman,
Reggio Emilia 1978

13...b5 14 e5! 14 a3 b4 (14...♖ac8
15 ♘xc6 ♗xc6 16 ♗d4 ♕b7 17 ♗d3
♖ce8? 18 e5 dxe5 19 ♗xe5± Wagman-
Valenti, Il Ciocco 1976) 15 axb4
♘xb4 16 e5 dxe5 17 fxe5 ♘fd5 18
♘xd5 ♘xd5 19 ♗c1 ♗c5= O'Kelly-
Larsen, Dundee 1967
14...dxe5?! 14...♘e8! Larsen **15 fxe5**
♘e8 15...♘xe5? 16 ♗f4 ♗d6 17 ♘b3±;
15...♕xe5 16 ♗f4 ♕c5 17 ♗e3 ½-½
Torre-Spassky, Manila 1976; 17 ♘b3
♕a7 18 ♗e3 ♕b7 19 ♘c5 ♗xc5 20
♗xc5 ♖g8! 21 ♕g5!?∞ Larsen
16 ♘f3 ♗c8 17 ♘e4 ♕g8 18 ♗f4 ♗b4
19 ♘f6+ +− Larsen-Hort, Bugojno
1978

Caro-Kann

1 e4 c6 2 d4 d5 3 ♘c3 dxe4 4 ♘xe4
♘f6 5 ♘xf6+ exf6 5...gxf6
(1) 6 ♗e2 ♗f5 7 ♘f3 ♕c7 8 0-0 e6
9 c4 ♘d7 10 ♗e3 ♗d6 11 c5 ♗e7 12
♘d2 0-0 13 f4 ♗g6 14 f5 ♗xf5 15
♖xf5 exf5 16 ♗d3± Browne-Bellon,
Las Palmas 1977
(2) 6 ♗c4 ♗f5 7 ♗f4 ♕b6 N 8 ♗b3
a5 9 a4 ♘d7 10 ♘f3 ♕a6 11 ♘h4!
+= Tal-Larsen Las Palmas 1977

32

(3) 6 c3 ♕d5 7 ♗e3 N (7 ♘f3 ♗f5 8 ♗e2 △ 0-0, c4±) 7...♖g8 8 ♘f3 ♘d7 9 ♕b3 ♘b6 10 c4 ♕h5 11 0-0-0 ♘h6 12 ♖e1 ♗e6! =+ Kagan-Basman, Birmingham 1977
(4) 6 c3 h5!? N 7 h4 ♗g4 8 ♕b3 ♕c7 9 ♗c4 e6 10 ♘e2 ♗f5! △ b5 11 ♗f4?! e5! 12 ♘g3 b5 13 ♘xf5 bxc4 14 ♕xc4 ♕d7! 15 ♕d3 exf4 −+ Suradiradja-Shirazi, Wellington 1978

6 ♗c4
(1) 6 c3 ♗d6 7 ♗d3 0-0 8 ♕c2 g6 9 h4!±; 8...h6!?
(2) 6 g3 ♗e6 (6...♕d5 7 ♘f3 ♗d6 8 ♗g2 0-0 9 0-0 ♕h5 10 c4 ♗g4= Boleslavsky; 6...♗d6 7 ♗g2 0-0 8 ♘f3 ♕a5+ 9 c3 ♖e8+ 10 ♗e3 ♕h5?! 11 ♘d2 += Samadov-Karpov, USSR 1966) 7 ♗g2 ♗e7 8 ♘e2 ♗d5 9 ♗xd5 cxd5 10 ♘f4 ♘c6 11 c3 ♕d7 12 ♕f3! 0-0-0 13 h4 += Vasyukov-Rodriguez, Quito 1976

6...♕e7+!
(1) 6...♗d6 7 ♕e2+! ♕e7 8 ♕xe7+ ♔xe7 9 ♘e2 ♗e6 10 ♗d3 ♖e8 N (10...♘d7 11 ♗f4 ♘b6 12 ♗xd6+ ♔xd6 13 b3 ♔c7 14 c4 += Matulovic-Smyslov, Siegen 1970) 11 ♗f4 ♗xf4 12 ♘xf4 g6 13 h4 ♔f8 14 0-0-0 += Vujic-Kovacevic, Belgrade 1978
(2) 6...♗e7 7 ♘e2 0-0 8 0-0 ♘d7 9 ♗b3 ♖e8 10 ♗f4 += Boleslavsky

7 ♕e2 ♗e6 8 ♗xe6 8 ♘b3!? Gipslis
8...♕xe6 9 ♗f4 ♘a6 10 c3 10 0-0-0 0-0-0 11 ♕xe6+ fxe6 12 ♘e2 ♘b4 13 c3 ♘d5= Schmit-Bronstein, Moscow 1970
10...0-0-0 11 ♕xe6+ fxe6 12 ♘e2 c5! 13 ♗e3 ♗d6 14 0-0-0 ♖he8 15 ♔c2 ♗f8= Gaprindashvili-Andersson, Dortmund 1978

1 e4 c6 2 d4 d5 3 ♘c3 dxe4 4 ♘xe4 ♘d7 5 ♘f3 5 ♗c4
(1) 5...♘df6 6 ♘g5 ♘h6 7 ♘1f3 ♗g4 8 c3 e6 9 h3 ♗xf3 10 ♕xf3 ♘d5 11 ♗d2 ♕f6 12 ♕e2± Vasyukov-Livshin, USSR 1956, 6 ♘g3 ♘d5 7 ♘f3 ♘gf6 8 0-0 e6 9 ♗b3 ♗e7 10 ♕e2 b5 11 ♘e5 ♕b6 12 ♖e1 0-0 13 ♗g5 c5= Balashov-Hubner, Bugojno 1978
5...♘gf6
(2) 6 ♘g5 e6 7 ♕e2 ♘b6 8 ♗d3 (8 ♗b3 h6 9 ♘5f3 a5! [9...c5 10 ♗e3 a6 11 0-0-0 c4?! 12 ♗xc4 ♘xc4 13 ♕xc4 b5 14 ♕e2 ♗b7 15 ♔b1± Matulovic-Kelecevic, Sarajevo 1978; 14 ♕f1! ♗b7 15 ♘e2 ♖c8 16 ♔b1 ♕c7 17 ♖c1 ♗d6∞ Tseshkovsky-Razuvaev, Baku 1977] 10 a3 a4 11 ♗a2 c5 12 ♗e3 ♘bd5 13 c3 ♗e7 14 ♘e5 0-0 15 ♘gf3 ♕c7= Liberzon-Smyslov, Biel 1976) 8...h6 (8...c5 9 dxc5 ♗xc5 10 ♘1f3 ♕c7 N 11 ♗b5+ ♗d7 12 ♗xd7+ ♘bxd7 13 ♘xf7 +− Bednarski-Holmov, Balashikha 1977) 9 ♘5f3 c5 10 dxc5 (10 ♗e3 ♘bd5 11 ♘e5 a6 12 ♘gf3 ♕c7 13 0-0 ♗d6 14 c3 b6 15 ♖ad1 0-0 16 ♗c1 ♗b7 17 ♖fe1 += Karpov-Balashov, Tilburg 1977) 10...♗xc5 (10...♘bd7 11 ♘e5 ♘xe5 12 ♕xe5 ♘d7 13 ♕e2 ♘xc5 14 ♗b5+ ♗d7 15 ♗xd7+ ♕xd7 16 ♘f3 += Chiburdanidze-Kushmir (4) 1978) 11 ♘e5 ♘bd7 12 ♘gf3 ♕c7 (12...♘xe5 13 ♘xe5 0-0 14 0-0 b6 15 b4! N

33

[15 ♗f4 ♗b7 16 ♖ad1 ♕e7 17 c3
♖fd8 = Mecking-Hort, Las Palmas
1975; 15 ♖ad1 ♕e7 16 g4?! ♘d7!
=+ Ciocaltea-Christiansen, Torremolinos 1976] 15...♘xb4 16 ♘c6 ♕d6 17
♘xb4 ♕xb4 18 ♕f3 ♗d7 19 ♗a3 ♕a4
20 ♗xf8 ♗c6 21 ♕e2± Medina-Buxade,
Barcelona 1977) 13 0-0 (13 ♗d2?
♘xe5 14 ♘xe5 ♗xf2+! Suetin-Holmov,
Budapest 1976, Ikonic-Kelecevic,
Sarajevo 1978!) 13...0-0 (13...♗d6 14
♖e1 ♘xe5 15 ♘xe5 0-0 16 ♗d2 b6 17
h3 ♗b7= Radulov-Kelecevic, Sarajevo
1978) 14 ♗f4 += Jansa-Holmov,
Budapest 1976

5...♘gf6 6 ♘xf6+ 6 ♘g3 e6 7 ♗d3 c5
(7...♗d6 8 0-0 ♕c7 9 b3 b6 10 c4 ♗b7
11 ♗b2 0-0 12 ♘e4 ♘xe4 13 ♗xe4
♘f6 14 ♗c2± Ermenkov-Spiridonov,
Bulgaria Final 1976) 8 0-0 cxd4
(8...♗e7 9 b3 N 0-0 10 ♗b2 b6 11
♕e2 ♗b7 12 c4 ♖e8 13 ♖ad1 ♕c7=
Martin-Eslon, Barcelona 1977) 9 ♘xd4
♗c5 10 ♘f3 0-0 11 b3 (11 a3 N a5
12 b3 b6 13 ♗b2 ♗b7 14 c4 ♕c7
15 ♕e2 ♖fd8 16 ♖ad1 ♕c6= Martin-
Palau, Barcelona 1977) 11...b6 12
♗b2 ♗b7 13 ♕e2 ♕c7= Spassky-
Filip, Nice 1974
6...♘xf6 7 ♘e5 7 ♗c4 e6 8 0-0 ♕c7
9 ♖e1 ♗e7 10 ♘g5 0-0 11 ♕e2 b6
12 ♖ad1 ♗b7 13 ♘e5 ♖ad8 14 ♘xf7

♖xf7 15 ♗xe6∞ Ristic-Nikolac,
Vrnjacka Banja 1978
7...♗f5
(1) 7...♘e6 8 ♗e2 (8 c3 g6 9 ♗d3
♗g7 10 0-0 0-0 11 ♕e2 c5 12 dxc5
♕c7= Timoshenko-Rasuvaev, USSR
1971) 8...g6 9 0-0 ♗g7 10 c4 0-0
11 ♗e3 ♕c8 12 ♗f3 ♖d8 13 ♕e2 ♘d7
14 ♘g4 += Browne-Rogoff, USA
1975;
(2) 7...♘d7 N 8 ♗f4 ♘xe5 9 ♗xe5
♕b6 10 ♗d3! f6 (10...♕b4+ 11 c3
♕xb2 12 d5!) 11 ♗g3 ♗e6 12 ♕e2
♗f7 13 0-0± Larsen-Rogoff, Lone
Pine 1978
8 c3 e6 8...♘d7 9 ♘xf7 ♔xf7 10
♕f3 e6 11 g4 ♕f6 12 gxf5 ♕xf5 13
♕e3± Kavalek-Barcza, Caracas 1971,
13 ♕xf5+ exf5 14 ♗c4+ ♔f6 15
♖g1 +− Boleslavsky

9 g4 ♗g6 10 h4 h5?! N 10...♗d6!?
11 ♕e2! c5 (11...♘xe5 12 dxe5 ♕d5
13 ♖h3 ♘xg4 14 ♕xg4 ♕xe5+ 15
♖e3 +− Mecking-Miles, Wijk aan Zee
1978) 12 ♗g2! cxd4 13 h5! +−
11 g5 ♘d5 12 ♘xg6 fxg6 13 ♕c2!
♕f7 14 ♖h3 ♗e7 15 ♗c4 ♘f5 16 ♖f3
♕d7 17 ♖xf5+! +− Karpov-Hort,
Bugojno 1978

1 e4 c6 2 d4 d5 3 ♘c3 dxe4 4 ♘xe4
♗f5 5 ♘g3 ♗g6 6 h4

(1) 6 ♗c4 e6 7 ♘1e2 ♘f6 8 h4 h6 9 ♘f4 ♗h7 10 0-0 ♗d6 11 ♘xe6 fxe6 12 ♗xe6 ♕c7 N (12...♘bd7 13 ♖e1 ♕c7 14 ♗g8+ ♔f8 15 ♗xh7 ♖xh7 16 ♘f5 Tal-Botvinnik 1960; 16...g6! 17 ♗xh6+ ♔g8 18 ♘xd6 ♕xd6 19 ♗g5 ♖e7= Botvinnik) 13 ♘h5 ♖f8 Tal-Vukic, Bugojno 1978, 14 f4! ♗g6 15 ♘xf6+ ♖xf6 16 f5 ♗h7 17 ♗g5 hxg5 18 hxg5 ♖xe6 19 fxe6 ♗g6 20 ♕f3± Kondratiev

(2) 6 ♘f3 ♘d7 7 h4 (7 ♗d3 ♕a5+? N [7...e6 8 0-0 ♘gf6 9 c4 ♗d6 10 b3 0-0 11 ♗b2 ♕c7 12 ♗xg6 hxg6 13 ♕e2 ♖fe8 14 ♘e4 += Spassky-Karpov, Candidates 1974] 8 ♗d2 ♕c7 9 ♗xg6 hxg6 10 ♕e2 e6 11 ♘e4 0-0-0 12 g3 c5?! 13 ♗f4 ♕c6 14 0-0-0 ± Spassky-Larsen, Bugojno 1978) 7...h5 8 ♗d3 ♗xd3 9 ♕xd3 e6 N [9...♘gf6 10 ♗d2 e6 11 0-0-0 ♕c7 13 ♘e4 ♘xe4 13 ♕xe4 ♗e7 14 ♔b1 ♘f6 15 ♕e2 ♘g4= Matulovic-Hort, Skopje 1968] 10 ♘e4! ♕a5+ 11 ♗d2 ♕f5 12 0-0-0 0-0-0 13 ♗e3 ♘h6 14 ♘eg5 ♕xd3 15 ♖xd3 += Karpov-Larsen, Bugojno 1978

6...h6 7 ♘f3 ♘d7 8 h5 ♗h7 9 ♗d3 ♗xd3 10 ♕xd3

10...e6 10...♘gf6 11 ♗d2 ♕c7 12 c4 e6 13 ♕e2 ♗d6 14 ♘f5?! 0-0! N (14...♗f4 15 ♗xf4 ♕xf4 16 ♘e3 ♕c7

17 0-0-0 += Spassky-Karpov 1974; 14...0-0-0 15 ♘xd6+ ♕xd6 16 ♗a5 ♖de8 17 ♘e5 += Karpov-Pomar, Nice 1974) 15 ♘xd6 ♕xd6 16 ♗c3 N (16 ♖h4? b5!∓ Lanka-Kasparov, Riga 1977) 16...b5! 17 cxb5 cxb5 18 ♕xb5 ♘d5∓ Beljavsky-Bagirov, Baku 1977; 12 ♕e2 e6 13 0-0-0 ♗d6 14 ♘f5 ♗f4 15 ♗xf4 (15 ♘e3 ♘e4!= Buljovcic-Vukic, Novi Sad 1976) 15...♕xf4+ 16 ♘e3 0-0-0 17 g3 ♕c7 18 ♘c4 ♖he8= Mihaljcisin-Nikolac, Vrnjacka Banja 1978

11 ♗f4 ♕a5+ 12 ♗d2 ♕c7 13 ♕e2 ♘gf6 14 c4 ♗d6 15 ♘f5 ♗f4 16 ♗xf4 ♕xf4 17 ♘e3 c5! N 17...♕c7 18 0-0-0 b5 19 cxb5 cxb5 20 ♔b1 0-0 21 g4 += Spassky-Karpov, 1974
18 ♘d5 ♘xd5 19 cxd5 0-0 20 dxe6 ♖fe8 21 0-0 ♖xe6= Tal-Portisch, Bugojno 1978

4♘

1 e4 e5 2 ♘f3 ♘c6 3 ♘c3 ♘f6 4 d4 ♗b5
(1) 4...♗c5 5 0-0 0-0 6 ♘xe5 ♘d4 7 ♘d3 N (7 ♗c4 d6 8 ♘f3 ♗g4 9 ♗e2 ♘xe2+ 10 ♕xe2 ♖e8 11 d3±) 7...♗b6 8 e5 ♘e8 9 ♗c4 d6 10 ♘d5 dxe5 11 ♘xb6 axb6 12 ♘xe5± Maslesa-Plachetka, Sarajevo 1978
(2) 4...♘d4 5 ♗a4 ♘xf3+ (5...♗c5=) 6 ♕xf3+ c6 7 0-0 d6 8 ♘d5 N (8 d3 ♗e6 9 ♕e2 ♘d7 10 ♗b3 ♘c5 11 f4 ♘xb3 12 axb3 exf4 13 ♗xf4 ♗e7 14 d4 0-0 15 d5 += Pachman-Gligoric, Madrid 1960) 8...♘d7 9 ♘e3 ♘c5 10 ♗b3 ♘xb3 11 axb3 g6 12 ♕g3 ♗g7 13 d3 0-0 14 ♗d2 d5 15 exd5 cxd5 16· ♖a5 ♗e6∓ Nikolic-Ornstein, Vrnjacka Banja 1978
(3) 4...♗b4 5 0-0 0-0 6 d3 ♗xc3 7 bxc3 d6 8 ♗g5 ♕e7 9 ♗xc6 (9 ♖e1

♞d8 10 d4 ♗g4 11 h3 ♗h5 12 g4
♗g6 13 ♘h4 h5 14 ♘h2 c6 15 ♗c4
♘e6= Ivkov-Portisch, Santa Monica
1966) 9...bxc6 10 ♘d2 h6 11 ♗h4
♕e6 12 ♗xf6 ♕xf6 13 ♖b1 c5= Hort-
Portisch, Bugojno 1978

4...exd4 4...♗b4 5 ♘xe5 ♘xe4 6 ♕g4
♘xc3 7 ♕xg7 ♖f8 8 a3 ♘xd4 (8...
♕h4? 9 ♘xc6 dxc6 10 axb4 +−
Drimer-Littlewood, Hastings 1969/70)
9 axb4 ♘xc2+ 10 ♔d2 ♘xa1 11 ♔xc3
a5 12 bxa5 N (12 ♗c4 axb4+ 13 ♔d3
d5 14 ♗b5+ c6 15 ♘xc6 ♗f5+ 16 ♔d2
bxc6 17 ♗xc6+ ♔e7 18 ♗xa8
Angantysson-Polgar, Dresden 1969,
18...♘b3+ −+) 12...♖xa5 13 b4 ♖a2
14 ♗h6 ♖c2+ 15 ♔d3 ♕e7 16 ♕xf8+
♕xf8 17 ♗xf8 ♔xf8 18 ♗e2 d6 19
♗g4 ♗xg4 20 ♘xg4 ♖a2 ∓/−+
Bellon-Toth, Rome 1977

5 ♞d5 d6?! 5...♗e7 6 ♗f4 d6 7 ♘xd4
♘xd5 8 exd5 ♘xd4 9 ♕xd4 ♗f6 10
♕b4 ♕e7+ N (10...0-0 11 0-0-0 ♗f5
12 f3 Δ g4 += Bellon-Szmetan, Wijk
aan Zee 1977) 11 ♔d2 0-0 12 ♖e1
♕d8 13 ♔c1 ♗f5 14 f3 += Szmetan-
Amado, Buenos Aires 1977

6 ♞xd4 ♞xe4? 7 ♞b5 ♗e6 8 ♞bxc7+?
8 ♘dxc7+! +− **8...♕d7 9 ♞xa8 ♕a5+
10 ♞c3 ♞xc3 11 bxc3 ♕xc3+ 12 ♗d2
♕e5+ 13 ♗e2 ♞d4** Valenti-Passerotti,
Reggio Emilia 1977/78, 14 ♗c3

♘f3+?! 15 ♔f1 ♕xc3 16 ♗xf3 +−;
14...♕xe2+ 15 ♕xe2 ♘xe2 16 ♔xe2
+−

Spanish

1 e4 e5 2 ♞f3 ♞c6 3 ♗b5 a6 4 ♗a4
d6 5 ♗xc6+ 5 c4 ♗g4 6 h3 ♗xf3 7
♗xc6+ N bxc6 8 ♕xf3 g6 9 ♘c3 ♗g7
10 d3 ♕d7 11 ♗e3 ♘e7= Ikonic-
Knezevic, Sarajevo 1978

5...bxc6 6 d4 f6 6...exd4 7 ♕xd4
♘e7 N (7...f6 8 ♘c3 g6 9 ♗f4 Δ 0-0-0±
Ozsvath-Smejkal, Hungary 1970) 8
0-0 c5 9 ♕c3 f6 10 ♖e1 ♘g6 11 ♕c4
♕d7 12 ♘c3± v.d.Mije-Petronic,
Belgrade 1978

7 ♞c3 7 ♗e3 g6 8 ♕d2 ♗g7 9 ♘c3 a5!?
10 0-0-0 ♘e7 11 ♗h6 ♗xh6 12 ♕xh6
exd4 13 ♘xd4 ♔f7 14 h4±
Chiburdanidze-Eretova, Budapest
1978

7...♞e7 7...g6 8 ♕d3 ♘h6 9 dxe5
fxe5 10 ♗g5 ♕d7 11 0-0-0 (11 ♗f6
♗g7 12 ♗xg7 ♕xg7=; 11 ♕c4) 11...
♕e6 12 ♔b1 ♘f7 13 h4 ♗g7 14 h5 h6
15 ♗c1 g5∓ Rohde-Westerinen, New
York 1977

8 ♕d3 a5 8...♘g6 9 ♗e3 ♗e7 10 h4
h5 11 0-0-0 ♗e6!? 12 d5! cxd5 13
♘xd5! N ♕c8?! 14 ♘d2 ♗d8 15 ♘c4
♘e7 16 ♘db6! ♗xc4 17 ♘xc4±

36

Horton-Giu, corr. 1978
9 ♗e3 ♗a6 10 ♕d2 ♘g6 11 h4 h5 12 0-0-0 ♕c8 13 dxe5 fxe5 14 ♖h3 ♗e7 15 ♖g3± Rodriguez-Medina, Barcelona 1977

1 e4 e5 2 ♘f3 ♘c6 3 ♗b5 a6 4 ♗a4 ♘f6 5 0-0 ♘xe4 6 d4 b5 7 ♗b3 d5 8 dxe5 ♗e6 9 ♕e2 9 c3 ♗c5 10 ♘bd2 0-0 11 ♗c2 f5 12 exf6 ♘xf6 13 ♘b3 ♗b6 14 ♗g5 (14 ♘g5 ♕d7 15 ♘xe6 ♕xe6 16 ♘d4 ♘xd4 17 cxd4 ♖ae8= Larsen) 14...♕d7 15 ♕d3 ♘e4 16 ♗e3 N ♗xe3 17 ♕xe3 ♖ae8 18 ♘fd4 Δ f3 α/+= Mednis-Golubovic, Nis 1977

9...♗e7 10 ♖d1 0-0 10...♘c5 11 ♘c3 ♘xb3 12 cxb3 ♘a5? N (12...0-0 13 ♗e3 ♕d7 14 ♖d2 f6 15 exf6 ♗xf6 16 ♖ad1 ♗xc3 17 bxc3 ♖ad8= Ivkov-Suetin, Jugoslavia v USSR 1963) 13 b4! ♗xb4 14 ♘xb5 ♗e7 15 ♘bd4 c5 16 ♘xe6 fxe6 17 b4!± Ostojic-Passerotti, Rome 1977

11 c4 bxc4 12 ♗xc4 ♕d7 13 ♘c3 ♘xc3 14 bxc3 ♘a5 15 ♗d3! ♖fd8 N 15...c5 16 h3 h6 17 ♘h2 Δ ♕h5 Korchnoi **16 ♘g5 ♗f5?! 17 ♕f3 ♗xg5 18 ♗xf5 ♕e7 19 ♗xh7+ ♔f8 20 ♗xg5 ♕xg5 21 ♖xd5 +−** Jansa-Golubovic, Nis 1977

1 e4 e5 2 ♘f3 ♘c6 3 ♗b5 a6 4 ♗a4 ♘f6 5 0-0 ♗e7 6 ♖e1 b5 7 ♗b3 d6 8 c3 0-0 9 h3 ♘a5 9...♗b7 10 d4 ♖e8 11 ♘bd2 ♗f8 12 a3 (12 ♗c2 g6 13 b3 ♘b8 14 a4 ♘bd7 15 ♗d3 c6 16 ♗b2 ♗g7 17 ♕c2 ♖b8= Byrne-Karpov, Bugojno 1978) 12...g6 13 ♗a2 ♗g7 14 d5 ♘b8 15 ♘f1 ♘bd7 16 ♘g3 ♕e7 17 b3 c6 18 c4 bxc4 19 bxc4 cxd5 20 cxd5 += Karpov-Gligoric, Bugojno 1978
10 ♗c2 c5 11 d4 ♕c7 12 ♘bd2 cxd4 13 cxd4 ♘c6 14 ♘b3 a5 15 ♗e3 15 ♗d2 ♗d7 16 d5 ♘d8 17 ♖c1 ♘b7 18 ♕e2 ♕b8= Geller-Kuzmin, USSR Final 1977

15...a4 16 ♘bd2 ♘b4 17 ♗b1 ♗d7 18 a3 ♘c6 19 ♗a2 19 ♗d3 ♘a5 20 ♖c1 ♕b8 21 ♖c2 (21 ♕e2 ♖e8 22 ♖c2 ♗d8 23 dxe5 dxe5= Tal-Kuzmin, Leningrad 1977) 21...♖e8 22 ♘f1 ♗e6 23 d5 ♗d7 24 ♗d2 ♗d8≈ Beljavsky-Kuzmin, Leningrad 1977
19...♖ac8 20 ♖c1 ♕b8 21 ♕e2 h6 22 dxe5 dxe5 23 ♘h4 ♖fd8 24 ♕f3 b4! =+ Tal-Spassky, Bugojno 1978

French

1 e4 e6 2 d4 d5 3 e5 c5 3...b6 4 c3 ♕d7
(1) 5 ♘f3 ♘e7 6 ♗d3 ♗a6 7 ♗xa6 ♘xa6

37

8 ♕d3? ♘b8 9 ♘bd2 ♘bc6 10 0-0
♘g6 11 ♖e1 f6! =+ Hedman-
Romanishin, Cienfuegos 1977
(2) 5 ♘h3 c5 6 ♘a3 cxd4 7 cxd4
♗a6 8 ♗xa6 ♘xa6 9 0-0 ♗xa3 10 bxa3
♘e7= Mohrlock-Ivkov, Vrnjacka
Banja 1977
(3) 5 a4! a5 6 f4! h5 7 ♘d2 ♘e7 8
♘df3 ♗a6 9 ♗xa6 ♘xa6 10 ♗e3 ♘f5
11 ♗f2 ♗e7 12 ♘e2 += Kupreichik-
Korchnoi, USSR 1970
4 c3 ♘c6 4...♕b6 5 ♘f3 ♗d7 6 ♗e2
♗b5 7 c4!? ♗xc4 (7...dxc4?! 8 d5!
exd5 9 ♕xd5 ♘e7 10 ♕e4 ♘bc6 11
♘c3 ♗a6 12 ♗xc4 ♗xc4 13 ♕xc4
♕b4 14 ♕e2± Erenska-Pihajlic, Gosa
1977) 8 ♗xc4 ♕b4+ 9 ♘bd2 dxc4 10
a3 ♕b5 11 ♕e2 N (11 0-0 ♘c6 12
dxc5 ♗xc5 13 ♕e2 ♘ge7 14 b4 ♘d4≈
Stean-Forintos, Moscow 1975) cxd4
12 ♘xd4 ♕d5 13 ♘4f3 ♗d7 [13...b5
14 a4!?] 14 ♘xc4 ♖c8 15 ♘e3 ♕e4
16 b4 ♘xe5 17 ♘xe5 ♕xe5 18 ♗b2
α/± Pinter-Ornstein, Budapest 1977
5 ♘f3 ♕b6 6 a3 6 ♗d3 cxd4 7 cxd4
♗d7 8 0-0 ♘xd4 9 ♘xd4 ♕xd4 10
♘c3 a6 11 ♕e2 ♘e7 12 ♔h1 ♘c6 13
f4 ♘b4? (13...g6) 14 ♖d1 ♘xd3 15
♖xd3 ♕c4 16 b3 ♕c7 17 ♗b2±
Mohring-Casper, Frankfurt 1977
6...c4 6...a5 7 ♗d3 ♗d7 8 0-0 cxd4
9 cxd4 ♘xd4 10 ♘xd4 ♕xd4 11
♘c3 ♕b6 12 ♕e2 ♗c5 13 ♗d2 a4 14
♘b5 ♘e7 15 ♖ac1 ♗xb5 16 ♗xb5+
♘c6 Halasz-Soreghy, corr. 1970, 17
♖xc5! ♕xc5 18 ♗b4 ♕b6 19 ♖c1α
7 ♘bd2 ♘a5

Diagram

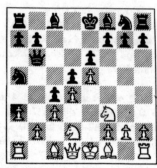

8 g3
(1) 8 b4!? cxb3 9 ♗b2 ♗d7 10 ♖c1
♗b5! 11 c4 dxc4 12 ♗xc4 ♘xc4 13
♘xc4 ♗xc4 14 ♖xc4 ♘e7 15 ♖b4

Remisov-Ilinski, USSR 1975, 15...
♕c6!=+
(2) 8 ♗e2 ♗d7 9 0-0 ♘e7 10 ♖b1 h6
11 ♘h4 0-0-0 12 g3 ♔b8 (12...f5 13
exf6 gxf6 14 ♗g4 e5 15 b3! cxb3 16
♘xb3 f5 17 ♗h3 ♗a4 18 ♘xa5!±
Zaitsev-Farago, Szolnok 1975) 13 ♗h5
g6 14 ♗e2 ♕c7 15 ♘g2 ♗c6 16 h4
♕d7 17 h5 ♗a4= Timman-Liberzon,
Venice 1974
8...♗d7 9 ♗h3 ♗e7
(1) 9...f6? 10 exf6 gxf6 11 0-0 0-0-0
12 ♖e1 ♗g7 13 ♖b1 ♔b8 14 b4!
cxb3 15 ♘xb3 ♘xb3 16 ♖xb3 ♗a4?
17 ♖xb6 ♗xd1 18 ♖bxe6 +– Zaitsev-
Pokojowczyk, Sochi 1976
(2) 9...h6!? 10 0-0 0-0-0 11 ♘e1 f5
12 exf6 gxf6 13 ♘ef3 ♘e7 14 ♖e1
♘g6 15 ♖b1 f5 16 ♕e2 ♕c7 17 b3±
Ivanov-Suetin, USSR 1978
**10 0-0 h5 11 ♘e1 0-0-0 12 ♘g2 g6
13 ♘e3 ♘h6 14 b4!? cxb3 15 ♗b2
♘f5 16 c4! ♘xc4 17 ♘dxc4 dxc4
18 ♘xc4 ♕a6 19 d5!** α/± Vitolins-
Zelinsky, USSR 1978

Alekhine

1 e4 ♘f6 2 e5 ♘d5 3 d4 d6 4 ♘f3
♗g4 5 ♗e2 e6 5...c6 6 0-0 ♗xf3 7
♗xf3 dxe5 8 dxe5 e6 9 ♕e2 ♘d7
10 ♖e1 ♕c7 11 a3 ♗c5 N (11...♘e7
12 b3 ♘g6 13 ♗b2 0-0-0 14 g3 ♗e7

=+ Kotkov-Kopylov, Volograd 1964)
12 c3 a5 13 b3 0-0 14 罝a2 罝fd8 15
g3± Evans-Shamkovich, Lone Pine
1978

6 h3 6 0-0 ♗e7 7 c4 ♘b6 8 ♘c3 0-0
9 ♗e3 d5!? 10 c5 ♗xf3 11 gxf3! ♘c8
12 f4! (12 b4!? a6 13 f4 ♕d7 14 ♗d3
♗d8 15 a4 c6 16 ♘e2 f5 17 ♔h1±
Matanovic-Vukic, Jugoslavia Final
1978) 12...a5 13 f5! ♗g5 14 f4 ♗h6
15 fxe6 fxe6 16 ♗g4± Shamkovich-
Vukic, New York 1976

6...♗h5 7 0-0 ♗e7 8 c4 ♘b6 9 ♗e3
9 exd6 cxd6 10 ♘bd2 ♘c6 11 b3
d5 12 c5 ♘d7 13 ♗b2 0-0 14 ♗c3!
b6 15 b4± Kapengut-Ivanov, USSR
1976

9...0-0 10 ♘c3 d5 11 c5 11 cxd5
exd5 12 ♗d3 ♘c6 13 g4 ♗g6 14 ♗f5
♕e8 15 ♘e2 f6= Gulko-Bagirov,
Baku 1977

11...♗xf3 12 gxf3 ♘c8 13 f4 f5!=
Byrne-Vukic, Bugojno 1978

**1 e4 ♘f6 2 e5 ♘d5 3 d4 d6 4 ♘f3 g6
5 ♗c4 ♘b6 6 ♗b3 ♗g7 7 ♘g5 7 ♕e2**
Geller

7...d5 8 0-0 ♘c6 8...0-0 9 罝e1 ♘c6 10
c3 f6 11 exf6 exf6 12 ♘e6 ♗xe6 13
罝xe6 += Parma-Gheorghiu, Skopje
1968

9 c3 ♗f5?!

(1) 9...h6 10 ♘f3 Δ ♘h4, f4, f5;
(2) 9...f6 10 exf6 exf6 11 罝e1+ ♘e7
12 ♘e6 ♗xe6 13 罝xe6 ♕d7 14 罝e1
0-0 15 ♘d2 ♔h8 16 ♘f3 Δ a4-a5 +=
Olafsson

10 g4! ♗xb1? 10...♗c8 **11 ♕f3 0-0
12 罝xb1 ♕d7 13 ♗c2 ♘d8 14 ♕h3!
h6 15 f4! +−** Olafsson-Larsen,
Reykjavik 1978

Pirc

1 e4 d6 2 d4 ♘f6 3 ♘c3 3 ♗d3 g6 4
c3 ♗g7 5 f4 e5 6 fxe5 N dxe5 7
dxe5 ♘g4 8 ♗b5+ c6 9 ♕xd8+ ♔xd8
10 ♗g5+ ♔c7 11 ♗e2 ♘xe5 12 ♘d2
♗e6 =+ Vujic-Stadler, Belgrade 1978
3...g6 4 f4 ♗g7 5 ♘f3 c5 5...0-0 6
♗d3 (6 ♗e3 ♘a6 7 e5 ♘g4 8 ♗g1 c5
9 ♗xa6?! N cxd4 10 ♗xd4 dxe5 11
fxe5 bxa6 12 ♕e2 罝b8 13 罝d1 ♕a5
14 b3 ♗b7∓ Mitchell-Horton, corr.
1977) 6...♘c6 7 0-0 (7 e5 dxe5 8
dxe5 ♘d5 9 ♗d2 ♗e6 10 0-0 N [10
♕e2 ♕d7 11 ♘xd5 ♕xd5 12 ♗c3
♗h6 13 ♕e3 ♗f5 14 ♗xf5 gxf5 15
0-0 罝ad8= Matanovic-Darga, Winnipeg
1967] 10...♕d7 11 ♘e4 ♘cb4 12
♘c5 ♕c6 13 ♘xe6 fxe6! 14 ♘g5
♘xd3 15 cxd3 ♗h6∓ Rejaibi-Dur,
Innsbruck 1977) 7...e5 8 fxe5 dxe5
9 d5 ♘e7 10 ♘xe5 ♘xe4?! 11 ♗xe4
N (11 ♘xg6! ♘xc3 12 ♘xe7+ ♕xe7
13 bxc3±) 11...♗xe5 12 ♗f4 ♗xf4
13 罝xf4 ♘f5 14 ♗xf5 ♗xf5 15 ♕d2
♕d6= Bisguier-Timman, Lone Pine
1978

6 dxc5 6 ♗b5+ ♗d7 7 e5 ♘g4 8 e6
♗xb5 9 exf7+ ♔d7 10 ♘xb5 ♕a5+
11 ♘c3 cxd4 12 ♘xd4 ♗xd4 13
♕xd4 ♘c6 14 ♕c4 罝ac8 15 h3 ♘h6
16 ♗d2 ♘f5 17 ♘d5 ♕d8 18 ♗c3 +−
Small-Torre, Wellington 1978
6...♕a5 7 ♗d3 ♕xc5 8 ♕e2

39

(3) 11 ♘d5? ♛a5+ 12 ♗d2 ♛d8 13 ♛f2 ♗xb2

(4) 11 ♛d2 ♗xc3 12 bxc3 ♘g3 (12...e5!∓) 13 ♖g1 f5?!∞ Levacic-Tonoli, Eeklo 1978

9 ♗e3 ♛a5 10 0-0 0-0 11 h3 11 ♛e1!?

11...♗xf3 12 ♛xf3 ♘c6 13 a3 ♘d7 14 ♗d2 ♛b6+ 15 ♚h1 ♘c5 16 b4!? 16 ♖ab1 ♘xd3 17 cxd3 e6!= Spassky-Bronstein, Tallinn 1973

16...♘xd3 16...♘d4!? 17 ♛g3! ♘xd3 18 ♛xd3 ♖fc8 19 ♘d5 ♛d8 20 c4± Hort-Suttles, Zagreb 1973

17 cxd3? 17 ♛xd3 △ ♘d5, c4 **17...a5 18 b5 ♘d4∓** Fleck-Coppini, Eeklo 1978

8...♗g4! 8...0-0 9 ♗e3 ♛c7 10 h3? N (Keene/Botterill) 10...♘h5!

(1) 11 ♚f2 ♗xc3 12 bxc3 e5!

(2) 11 ♚f2 ♗xc3+ 12 bxc3 ♛xc3+ 13 ♚e2 ♛f6 14 g3 e5

Mexico City ii-iii.78

				1	2	3	4	5	6	7	8	9	0	1	2	3	4	
1	Shamkovich	GM	2485	x	1	½	½	1	1	1	½	½	½	1	1	1	1	10½
2	J.Fernandez	IM	2370	0	x	½	½	½	½	½	½	1	1	1	1	1	1	9
3	Fedorowicz		2360	½	½	x	½	0	½	½	1	1	1	1	½	½	1	8½
4	Armas		2385	½	½	½	x	½	½	1	0	0	1	1	½	1	1	8
5	Boudy	IM	2395	0	½	1	½	x	½	½	1	0	½	1	½	1	1	8
6	Lebredo	IM	2385	0	½	½	½	½	x	½	1	½	1	½	½	1	1	8
7	Frey	IM	2390	0	½	½	0	½	½	x	½	½	½	1	1	1	1	7½
8	Campos	IM	2355	½	½	0	1	0	0	½	x	1	½	0	1	+	1	7
9	Sisniega		2455	½	0	0	1	1	½	½	0	x	0	0	½	1	1	6
10	Villarreal		2325	½	0	0	0	½	0	½	½	1	x	½	1	1	½	6
11	Acevedo		2370	0	0	0	0	0	½	0	1	1	½	x	1	1	1	6
12	Morales			0	0	½	½	½	½	0	0	½	0	0	x	½	½	3½
13	A. Anguiano			0	0	½	0	0	0	0	−	0	0	0	½	x	½	1½
14	Winter		2340	0	0	0	0	0	0	0	0	0	0	½	0	½	½	x	1½

Category 5 (2358)   IM = 8½

Wellington 5-19.iv.78

				1	2	3	4	5	6	7	8	9	0	1	2	3	
1	Quinteros	GM	2480	x	0	½	½	1	1	1	1	1	1	1	1	1	10
2	Torre	GM	2490	1	x	½	1	0	½	1.	½	0	1	½	1	1	8
3	Sarapu	IM	2290	½	½	x	½	½	½	½	0	1	½	½	1	1	7
4	Mascarinas		2355	½	0	½	x	½	½	½	1	½	1	1	0	1	7
5	Small			0	1	½	½	x	½	½	0	½	0	1	½	1	6
6	Sharif	IM	2380	0	½	½	½	½	x	½	½	1	0	½	1	½	6
7	Green			0	0	½	½	½	½	x	1	½	½	½	1	½	6
8	Chandler	IM	2390	0	½	1	0	1	½	0	x	1	1	½	0	0	5½
9	Sampouw		2315	0	1	0	½	½	0	½	0	x	0	½	1	½	4½
10	Suradiradja	IM	2330	0	0	½	0	1	1	½	0	1	x	½	0	0	4½
11	Sutton			0	½	½	0	0	½	½	½	½	½	x	1	0	4½
12	Shirazi		2285	0	0	0	1	½	0	0	1	0	1	0	x	1	4½
13	Cardoso	IM	2320	0	0	0	0	0	½	½	1	½	1	1	0	x	4½

Category 3 (2325)   IM = 8½

Dortmund 11-22.iv.78

				1	2	3	4	5	6	7	8	9	0	1	2	
1	Andersson	GM	2545	x	½	0	½	½	1	½	1	1	1	1	1	8
2	Keene	GM	2480	½	x	½	½	½	½	1	½	½	1	1	1	7½
3	Gaprindashvili	IM	2425	1	½	x	½	½	½	0	½	1	1	1	1	7½
4	Farago	GM	2510	½	½	½	x	½	0	½	1	1	1	½	1	7
5	Gipslis	GM	2525	½	½	½	½	x	½	1	½	½	½	1	1	7
6	Tatai	IM	2455	0	½	½	1	½	x	½	1	1	½	1	½	7
7	Wirthensohn	IM	2410	½	0	1	½	0	½	x	½	½	½	½	1	5½
8	Borngasser		2370	0	½	½	0	½	0	½	x	1	½	0	½	4
9	Marjanovic	IM	2450	0	½	0	0	½	0	½	0	x	1	½	1	4
10	Tomic			0	0	0	0	½	½	½	½	0	x	1	0	3
11	Andre		2360	0	0	0	½	0	0	½	1	½	0	x	½	3
12	Kierzek			0	0	0	0	0	½	0	½	0	1	½	x	2½

Category 7 (2411)   GM = 8   IM = 6½

Kiel 12-23.iv.78

				1	2	3	4	5	6	7	8	9	0	1	2	
1	Smejkal	GM	2555	x	½	1	½	0	½	1	1	1	1	1	1	8½
2	Parma	GM	2540	½	x	½	½	½	½	1	1	1	1	1	1	8½
3	Mortensen		2365	0	½	x	1	1	½	0	1	½	1	1	1	7½
4	Radulov	GM	2490	½	½	0	x	½	½	½	1	1	1	1	1	7½
5	Csom	GM	2510	1	½	0	½	x	1	1	0	½	1	1	1	7½
6	Ogaard	IM	2435	½	½	½	½	0	x	½	½	1	1	1	1	7
7	S.Hamann	IM	2470	0	0	1	½	0	½	x	1	1	½	1	1	6½
8	G.Hamann			0	0	0	0	1	½	0	x	0	1	½	1	4
9	Neumann			0	0	½	0	½	0	0	1	x	½	0	½	3
10	Schramm			0	0	0	0	0	0	½	0	½	x	1	½	2½
11	Brendel			0	0	0	0	0	0	0	½	1	0	x	1	2½
12	Firnhaber			0	0	0	0	0	0	0	0	½	½	0	x	1

			1	2	3	4	5	6	7	8	9	0	1	2	3	4	
1	Gligoric	GM	2565	x	½	½	½	½	1	½	1	1	½	½	1	½	1	9
2	Adorjan	GM	2515	½	x	½	½	½	½	1	1	½	½	½	1	1	1	9
3	Kurajica	GM	2530	½	½	x	1	½	½	½	1	½	1	1	0	½	½	8
4	Velimirovic	GM	2520	½	½	0	x	1	½	½	½	0	½	1	1	1	1	8
5	Sax	GM	2550	½	½	½	0	x	0	½	1	1	0	½	1	1	1	7½
6	Tringov	GM	2480	0	½	½	½	1	x	½	½	½	1	½	½	1	½	7½
7	Ivkov	GM	2515	½	0	½	½	½	½	x	½	½	½	1	½	1	1	7½
8	Koshanski		2360	0	0	0	½	0	½	½	x	1	1	1	½	½	1	6½
9	Marovic	GM	2455	0	½	½	1	0	½	½	0	x	½	½	1	½	1	6½
10	Smederevac	IM	2335	½	½	0	½	1	0	½	0	½	x	½	1	½	1	6½
11	Diesen	IM	2440	½	½	0	0	½	½	0	0	½	½	x	½	½	1	5
12	Calvo	IM	2455	0	0	1	0	0	½	½	½	0	0	½	x	½	1	4½
13	Hulak	GM	2525	½	0	½	0	0	0	0	½	½	½	½	½	x	1	4½
14	Pocucu			0	0	½	0	0	½	0	0	0	0	0	0	0	x	1

Category 9 (2460)   GM = 8½   IM = 6½

			1	2	3	4	5	6	7	8	9	0	1	2	3	4	
1	Torre	GM	2490	x	½	½	½	½	½	1	1	1	1	1	1	1	1	10½
2	Quinteros	GM	2480	½	x	½	0	1	1	½	1	1	1	1	1	1	1	10½
3	Sharif	IM	2380	½	½	x	1	½	½	½	½	1	½	1	1	1	1	9½
4	Mascarinas		2355	½	1	0	x	½	1	½	1	½	½	1	½	1	1	9
5	Bachtiar		2335	½	0	½	½	x	½	½	½	½	1	1	0	1	½	7
6	Chiong		2400	½	0	½	0	½	x	½	0	1	1	1	½	0	1	6½
7	O'Kelly	GM	2460	0	½	½	½	½	½	x	1	½	0	0	1	0	1	6
8	Laird			0	0	½	0	½	1	0	x	0	1	1	½	½	1	6
9	Shirazi		2285	0	0	0	½	½	0	½	1	x	0	½	1	1	1	6
10	Chandler	IM	2390	0	0	½	½	0	0	1	0	1	x	½	0	1	1	5½
11	Ardijansjah	IM	2330	0	0	0	0	0	0	1	0	½	½	x	1	1	1	5
12	Sampouw		2315	0	0	0	½	1	½	0	½	0	1	0	x	1	0	4½
13	Hon			0	0	0	0	0	1	1	½	0	0	0	0	x	0	2½
14	Suradiradja	IM	2330	0	0	0	0	½	0	0	0	0	0	0	1	1	x	2½

Category 5 (2354)   GM = 10   IM = 8½

43

Zamardi 2-13.v.78

			1	2	3	4	5	6	7	8	9	0	1	2	
1	F.Portisch	IM	2450	x	½	1	½	0	1	1	½	½	1	1	1	8
2	Mohring	IM	2405	½	x	1	½	½	0	½	1	1	½	1	1	7½
3	Ujtelky	IM	2280	0	0	x	1	1	½	½	½	1	0	1	1	6½
4	Bielczyk		2380	½	½	0	x	½	½	½	½	½	1	1	1	6½
5	Pinter	IM	2430	1	½	0	½	x	0	1	1	½	1	0	½	6
6	Georgiev	IM	2415	0	1	½	½	1	x	0	0	½	1	½	1	6
7	Varasdy			0	½	½	½	0	1	x	1	½	½	½	1	6
8	Marosi		2380	½	0	½	½	0	1	0	x	½	½	½	1	5
9	G.Szabo		2355	½	0	0	½	½	½	½	½	x	½	½	1	5
10	Szell		2435	0	½	1	0	0	0	½	½	½	x	½	0	3½
11	Budinszky			0	0	0	0	1	½	½	½	½	½	x	0	3½
12	Kaikamdzsozov		2330	0	0	0	0	½	0	0	0	0	1	1	x	2½

Category 5 (2361)   IM = 7½

Varna 14-29.v.78

			1	2	3	4	5	6	7	8	9	0	1	2	3	4	
1	Donchev		2350	x	½	½	1	½	½	½	1	½	1	1	1	1	1	10
2	Peev	IM	2420	½	x	½	1	0	1	1	0	½	0	1	1	1	1	8½
3	Pribyl	IM	2455	½	½	x	½	½	½	½	½	½	1	½	1	1	1	8½
4	Suba	IM	2430	0	0	½	x	0	1	0	1	1	1	1	1	0	1	7½
5	P.Atanasov		2305	½	1	½	1	x	0	½	½	½	1	½	½	0	½	7
6	Bruggemann		2310	½	0	½	0	1	x	1	½	1	½	0	0	1	1	7
7	Spiridonov	IM	2405	½	0	½	1	½	0	x	½	0	½	1	1	1	½	7
8	Nogueiras	IM	2385	0	1	½	0	½	½	½	x	½	½	1	½	1	½	7
9	Szymczak	IM	2390	½	½	½	0	½	0	1	½	x	½	½	½	½	½	6
10	Hazai	IM	2455	0	1	0	0	0	½	½	½	½	x	0	1	½	1	5½
11	Radev	IM	2395	0	0	½	0	½	1	0	0	½	1	x	0	1	½	5
12	Dobrev			0	0	0	0	½	1	0	½	½	0	1	x	1	½	5
13	Semkov		2355	0	0	0	1	1	0	0	0	½	½	0	0	x	½	3½
14	Ajanski		2355	0	0	0	0	½	0	½	½	½	0	½	½	½	x	3½

Category 5 (2372)   IM = 8½

Albena vi.78

			1	2	3	4	5	6	7	8	9	0	1	2	3	4	
1	Skalkotas		2285	x	½	½	½	½	½	1	½	½	1	1	1	½	1	9
2	N.Popov		2420	½	x	½	1	½	½	½	½	½	½	1	1	1	1	9
3	Tonchev			½	½	x	½	½	½	½	½	½	½	1	1	1	1	8½
4	Ornstein	IM	2425	½	0	½	x	½	1	½	½	½	½	1	1	1	1	8½
5	Ciocaltea	IM	2455	½	½	½	½	x	0	½	½	1	½	1	1	1	1	8½
6	Prodanov		2335	½	½	½	0	1	x	½	0	½	1	1	1	1	1	8½
7	Spiridonov	IM	2405	0	½	½	½	½	½	x	½	½	1	1	1	1	1	8½
8	Bielczyk		2380	½	½	½	½	½	1	½	x	½	½	0	1	½	1	7½
9	Hazai	IM	2455	½	½	½	½	0	½	½	½	x	½	½	1	1	1	7½
10	Kaikamdzosov		2330	0	½	½	½	½	0	0	½	½	x	0	½	1	1	5½
11	Spirov		2360	0	0	0	0	0	0	0	1	½	1	x	0	1	1	4½
12	Paoli	IM	2280	0	0	0	0	0	0	0	0	0	½	1	x	½	1	3
13	Dankov		2350	½	0	0	0	0	0	0	½	0	0	0	½	x	0	1½
14	Savov		2380	0	0	0	0	0	0	0	0	0	0	0	0	1	x	1

Category 5 (2361)   IM = 8½

Sao Paulo vi.78

			1	2	3	4	5	6	7	8	9	0	1	2	3	4	
1	Smyslov	GM	2575	x	½	½	½	½	1	½	1	1	1	½	1	1	½	9½
2	Dorfman	IM	2550	½	x	½	½	½	½	½	1	1	1	½	1	1	½	9
3	Ivkov	GM	2515	½	½	x	½	½	0	½	1	1	1	1	0	1	1	8½
4	Quinteros	GM	2480	½	½	½	x	½	1	½	½	½	0	1	1	1	1	8½
5	Sosonko	GM	2575	½	½	½	½	x	1	1	½	½	½	½	0	½	1	7½
6	O.Castro	IM	2425	0	½	1	0	0	x	½	½	0	½	1	1	1	1	7
7	Najdorf	GM	2525	½	½	½	½	0	½	x	½	½	½	½	1	1	0	6½
8	L.Evans	GM	2530	0	0	0	½	½	½	½	x	0	1	1	1	½	1	6½
9	G.van Riemsdyk		2375	0	0	0	½	½	1	½	1	x	½	½	1	0	½	6
10	Segal	IM	2395	0	0	0	1	½	½	½	0	½	x	½	½	½	½	5
11	Sunye		2360	½	½	0	0	½	0	½	0	½	½	x	0	1	1	5
12	Filguth		2350	0	0	1	0	1	0	0	0	0	½	1	x	½	½	4½
13	Camara	IM	2325	0	0	0	0	½	0	0	½	1	½	0	½	x	1	4
14	C.van Riemsdyk			½	½	0	0	0	0	1	0	½	½	0	½	0	x	3½

Category 8   GM = 9   IM = 7

45

Maspalomas v-vi.78

				1	2	3	4	5	6	7	8	9	0	1	2	
1	Csom	GM	2510	x	½	½	½	1	1	½	½	1	1	1	1	8½
2	Olafsson	GM	2530	½	x	½	1	½	1	½	1	½	1	1	1	8½
3	O.Rodriguez	IM	2485	½	½	x	½	1	½	½	1	1	1	1	1	8½
4	Garcia Padron		2415	½	0	½	x	0	½	1	1	½	1	1	1	7
5	Westerinen	GM	2450	0	½	0	1	x	0	½	½	½	1	1	1	6
6	Medina	IM	2350	0	0	½	½	1	x	½	½	½	0	½	1	5
7	Tatai	IM	2455	½	½	½	0	½	½	x	1	½	0	1	0	5
8	Rubio		2250	½	0	0	0	½	½	0	x	1	1	½	½	4½
9	Gonzalez Mestres		2400	0	½	0	½	½	½	½	0	x	½	0	1	4
10	O.Perez			0	0	0	0	0	1	1	0	½	x	½	1	4
11	Cabrera		2205	0	0	0	0	0	½	0	½	1	½	x	0	2½
12	Lezcano		2285	0	0	0	0	0	0	1	½	0	0	1	x	2½

Category 6 (2378) GM = 8½ IM = 7

Smed Palanka 3-18.vi.78

				1	2	3	4	5	6	7	8	9	0	1	2	3	4	
1	S.Nikolic	IM	2350	x	½	½	½	½	0	1	1	½	1	1	1	1	1	9½
2	Jansa	GM	2505	½	x	½	1	½	½	1	½	½	1	½	1	½	1	9
3	Despotovic		2355	½	½	x	½	½	½	½	½	½	1	½	½	1	1	8
4	Cebalo		2450	½	0	½	x	½	½	1	½	½	1	½	½	1	1	8
5	Filip	GM	2485	½	½	½	½	x	½	½	½	0	½	0	1	1	1	7
6	Padevsky	GM	2455	1	½	½	½	½	x	½	½	½	½	½	0	½	1	7
7	Martinovic	IM	2460	0	0	½	0	½	½	x	½	1	1	1	1	1	0	7
8	W.Schmidt	GM	2505	0	½	½	½	½	½	½	x	½	½	½	½	1	½	6½
9	Rajkovic	GM	2490	½	½	½	½	1	½	0	½	x	0	0	½	1	1	6½
10	Ljubisavljevic			0	0	0	0	½	½	0	½	1	x	1	1	1	1	6½
11	Inkiov	IM	2450	0	½	½	½	1	½	0	½	1	0	x	0	½	½	5½
12	Janosevic	GM	2455	0	0	½	½	0	1	0	½	½	0	1	x	0	½	4½
13	Gajic		2270	0	½	0	0	0	½	0	0	0	0	½	1	x	½	3
14	Ristic			0	0	0	0	0	0	1	½	0	0	½	½	½	x	3

Category 7 (2402) GM = 9½ IM = 7½

Niksic 6-20.vi.78

			1	2	3	4	5	6	7	8	9	0	1	2	
1	Timman	GM	2585	x	½	1	½	1	½	1	½	½	½	1	1	8
2	Gulko	GM	2565	½	x	½	1	1	1	½	1	½	1	½	½	8
3	Vaganian	GM	2555	0	½	x	½	½	1	½	½	½	½	1	1	6½
4	Hort	GM	2620	½	0	½	x	0	1	½	½	½	½	1	1	6
5	Portisch	GM	2630	0	0	½	1	x	½	½	½	½	½	1	1	6
6	Gligoric	GM	2565	½	0	0	0	½	x	½	½	1	1	½	1	5½
7	Ribli	GM	2585	0	½	½	½	½	½	x	0	½	1	1	½	5½
8	Uhlmann	GM	2575	½	0	½	½	½	½	1	x	0	1	0	1	5½
9	Andersson	GM	2545	½	½	½	½	½	0	½	1	x	½	½	0	5
10	Ljubojevic	GM	2605	½	0	½	½	½	0	0	0	½	x	1	1	4½
11	Velimirovic	GM	2520	0	½	0	0	0	½	0	1	½	0	x	1	3½
12	B.Ivanovic	IM	2460	0	½	0	0	0	0	½	0	1	0	0	x	2

Category 13 (2567)   GM = 5½

Warsaw 30.v-10.vi.78

			1	2	3	4	5	6	7	8	9	0	1	2	
1	Kuligowski		2310	x	1	½	½	1	1	0	½	½	1	1	1	8
2	Webb	IM	2445	0	x	½	1	1	½	1	1	1	0	½	1	7½
3	Schinzel		2400	½	½	x	1	0	½	1	1	1	½	0	1	7
4	Filipowicz	IM	2360	½	0	0	x	0	½	1	1	1	½	1	1	6½
5	Sliwa	IM	2370	0	0	1	1	x	0	1	½	½	1	½	1	6½
6	Nun	IM	2405	0	½	½	½	1	x	½	0	½	½	1	½	5½
7	Rajna	IM	2410	1	0	0	0	0	½	x	1	0	1	1	1	5½
8	Gromek		2370	½	0	0	0	½	1	0	x	½	1	1	½	5
9	Bernard		2360	½	0	0	0	½	½	1	½	x	½	0	1	4½
10	Witkowski	IM	2365	0	1	½	½	0	½	0	0	½	x	1	½	4½
11	B.Balogh		2280	0	½	1	0	½	0	0	0	1	0	x	0	3
12	Bohling		2450	0	0	0	0	0	½	0	½	0	½	1	x	2½

Category 7 (2378)   IM = 7

Philippines i.78

			1	2	3	4	5	6	7	8	
Torre	GM	2490	1	½	½	1	1	1	1	1	7
Balinas	GM	2440	0	½	½	0	0	0	0	0	1

Warsaw 15-21.v.78

				1	2	3	4	
1	Kuligowski		2310	x	0 ½	½ 1	1 1	4
2	Skrobek		2460	1 ½	x	0 1	½ 0	3
3	Sznapik	IM	2430	½ 0	1 0	x	½ ½	2½
4	W.Schmidt	GM	2505	0 0	½ 1	½ ½	x	2½

Lodz 13-30.iv.78

				1	2	3	4	5	6	7	8	9	0	1	2	3	4	5	6	
1	Inkiov	IM	2450	x	1	½	½	½	½	½	½	0	½	½	1	½	1	1	1	9½
2	Helmers		2345	0	x	0	1	½	0	½	½	1	1	½	1	1	1	½	½	9
3	Lukacs	IM	2460	½	1	x	½	½	½	½	½	½	½	0	½	½	1	½	1	8½
4	Luczak			½	0	½	x	½	½	½	1	1	1	½	½	½	0	½	1	8½
5	Barczay	GM	2465	½	½	½	½	x	½	½	½	½	½	1	0	½	½	1	½	8
6	Kirov	GM	2465	½	1	½	½	½	x	½	½	½	½	½	½	½	½	½	½	8
7	Lengyel	GM	2430	½	½	½	½	½	½	x	½	½	½	½	1	½	½	½	½	8
8	Adamski	IM	2470	½	½	½	0	½	½	½	x	½	0	½	0	1	½	½	1	7
9	Espig	IM	2470	1	0	½	0	½	½	½	½	x	0	½	0	1	½	½	1	7
10	Pribyl	IM	2455	½	0	½	0	½	½	½	1	1	x	1	0	½	½	0	½	7
11	Swic			½	½	1	½	0	½	½	½	½	0	x	½	½	½	½	½	7
12	Sznapik	IM	2430	0	0	½	½	1	½	0	1	1	1	½	x	½	0	½	0	7
13	Ghitescu	IM	2450	½	0	½	½	½	½	½	0	0	½	½	½	x	1	½	½	6½
14	Skrobek		2460	0	0	0	1	½	½	½	½	½	½	½	1	0	x	1	0	6½
15	Witkowski	IM	2365	0	½	½	½	0	½	½	½	½	1	½	½	½	0	x	½	6½
16	Pokojowczyk		2385	0	½	0	0	½	½	½	0	0	½	½	1	½	1	½	x	6
17	Niklasson		2340			½				½	0			0						1

Category 7 (2406) IM = 9 GM = 10½

Lvov iv.78

				1	2	3	4	5	6	7	8	9	0	1	2	3	4	5	
1	Balashov	GM	2590	x	½	1	1	½	½	½	½	½	½	1	0	1	½	1	9
2	Vaganian	GM	2570	½	x	½	0	½	½	½	1	1	1	½	½	½	1	½	8½
3	Kuzmin	GM	2535	0	½	x	½	½	½	½	½	½	1	1	½	½	½	1	8
4	Romanishin	GM	2610	0	1	½	x	½	½	½	½	1	½	1	½	0	1	½	8
5	Tseshkovsky	GM	2570	½	½	½	½	x	1	½	1	½	0	½	1	0	1	½	8
6	Tukmakov	GM	2560	½	½	½	½	0	x	½	0	1	1	½	½	1	0	1	7½
7	Bagirov	IM	2495	½	½	½	½	½	½	x	0	½	0	½	½	½	1	1	7
8	Beljavsky	GM	2545	½	0	½	½	0	1	1	x	½	½	1	½	½	½	0	7
9	Gulko	GM	2575	½	0	½	0	½	0	½	½	x	½	½	1	1	½	1	7
10	Smyslov	GM	2575	½	0	0	½	1	0	1	½	½	x	0	1	1	½	½	7
11	Dorfman	IM	2550	0	½	0	0	½	½	½	0	½	1	x	½	½	1	1	6½
12	Kochiev	GM	2555	1	½	½	½	0	½	½	½	0	0	½	x	½	½	1	6½
13	Savon	GM	2560	0	½	½	1	1	0	½	½	0	0	½	½	x	½	1	6½
14	Sveshnikov	GM	2565	½	0	½	0	0	1	0	½	½	½	0	½	½	x	½	5
15	Geller	GM	2590	0	½	0	½	½	0	0	1	0	½	0	0	0	½	x	3½

V. Banja 6-24.iv.78

				1	2	3	4	5	6	7	8	9	0	1	2	3	4	5	6	
1	Nikolac		2495	x	½	1	½	1	1	½	½	½	½	½	1	1	½	½	1	10½
2	Mihaljcisin	IM	2380	½	x	1	½	0	1	0	½	½	1	1	1	1	1	1	½	10½
3	Jansa	GM	2505	0	0	x	1	1	½	½	½	½	½	1	0	1	1	1	1	9½
4	Ermenkov	GM	2520	½	½	0	x	½	1	½	½	1	1	½	½	0	½	1	1	9
5	Ornstein	IM	2425	0	1	0	½	x	½	0	½	1	0	1	½	1	1	1	1	9
6	Martinovic	IM	2460	0	0	½	0	½	x	½	½	1	½	½	1	1	1	1	1	9
7	Duric		2350	½	1	½	½	1	½	x	½	½	½	½	½	0	0	1	1	8½
8	Schmidt	GM	2505	½	½	½	½	½	½	½	x	½	½	½	0	½	1	½	1	8
9	Todorcevic	IM	2435	½	½	½	0	0	0	½	½	x	½	1	½	1	½	1	1	8
10	Rajkovic	GM	2490	½	0	½	0	1	½	½	½	½	x	½	1	½	½	½	½	7½
11	Padevsky	GM	2455	½	0	0	½	0	½	½	½	0	½	x	1	1	½	½	½	6½
12	Raicevic	GM	2450	0	0	1	½	½	0	½	1	½	0	0	x	½	½	1	½	6½
13	S.Nikolic	IM	2350	0	0	0	1	0	0	1	½	0	½	0	½	x	1	0	1	5½
14	Joksic		2410	½	0	0	½	0	0	1	0	½	½	½	½	0	x	0	1	5
15	Ristic			½	0	0	0	0	0	0	½	0	½	½	0	1	1	x	0	4
16	Barlov		2310	0	½	0	0	0	0	0	0	0	½	½	½	0	0	1	x	3

Category 7 (2421) GM = 10½ IM = 9

Las Palmas iv-v.78

				1	2	3	4	5	6	7	8	9	0	1	2	3	4	5	6	
1	Sax	GM	2550	x	1	½	0	½	½	1	½	½	½	1	1	1	1	½	1	10½
2	Tukmakov	GM	2570	0	x	½	1	½	1	½	½	1	½	½	1	½	1	1	1	10½
3	Olafsson	GM	2530	½	½	x	½	0	0	½	1	½	½	1	1	1	1	1	1	10
4	Stean	GM	2510	1	0	½	x	½	0	1	0	1	½	½	1	1	1	1	½	9½
5	Miles	GM	2565	½	½	1	½	x	1	0	½	1	½	1	0	1	1	½	½	9½
6	Larsen	GM	2620	½	0	1	1	0	x	½	1	½	½	½	½	1	0	1	1	9
7	Westerinen	GM	2450	0	½	½	0	1	½	x	½	½	½	1	½	½	1	1	1	9
8	Csom	GM	2510	½	½	0	1	½	0	½	x	1	1	0	½	0	1	1	1	8½
9	Mariotti	GM	2475	½	0	½	0	0	½	½	0	x	1	1	½	1	1	1	1	8½
10	Del Corral	GM	2490	½	½	½	½	½	½	½	0	0	x	0	½	½	½	1	1	7
11	Panchenko	IM	2495	0	½	0	½	0	½	0	1	0	1	x	½	1	1	0	1	7
12	O.Rodriguez	IM	2485	0	0	0	0	1	½	½	½	½	½	½	x	½	½	1	1	7
13	Sanz		2330	0	½	0	0	0	0	½	1	0	½	0	½	x	½	1	0	4½
14	Garcia-Padron		2415	0	0	0	0	0	1	0	0	0	½	0	½	½	x	1	½	4
15	Medina	IM	2350	½	0	0	0	½	0	0	0	0	0	1	0	0	0	x	1	3
16	Dominguez		2285	0	0	0	½	½	0	0	0	0	0	0	0	1	½	0	x	2½

Category 10 (2477) GM = 9 IM = 7

Jurmala vi 78

				1	2	3	4	5	6	7	8	9	0	1	2	3	4	5	6	
1	Bronstein	GM	2570	x	½	1	½	½	1	½	½	½	½	½	1	0	1	1	1	10
2	Gufeld	GM	2525	½	x	0	½	0	1	½	½	½	½	1	1	½	½	1	1	9
3	Knaak	GM	2520	0	1	x	½	1	0	½	½	½	1	½	1	½	1	1	0	9
4	Taimanov	GM	2505	½	½	½	x	½	½	½	0	½	½	½	1	1	½	½	1	8½
5	Ermenkov	GM	2520	½	1	0	½	x	0	1	½	½	½	1	0	½	½	1	½	8
6	Lutikov	GM	2540	0	0	1	½	1	x	1	½	½	0	1	1	½	½	0	½	8
7	Sahovic	IM	2490	½	½	½	½	0	0	x	1	1	0	1	1	½	½	0	1	8
8	Vitolins		2415	½	½	½	1	½	½	0	x	½	1	0	0	½	1	0	1	7½
9	Gipslis	GM	2540	½	½	½	½	½	½	0	½	x	½	½	0	½	1	1	½	7½
10	Klovan	IM	2490	½	½	0	½	½	1	1	0	½	x	½	½	1	½	½	0	7½
11	Kirpichnikov			½	0	½	½	0	0	0	1	½	½	x	½	½	1	0	1	6½
12	Lanka			0	0	0	0	1	0	0	1	1	½	½	x	1	½	½	½	6½
13	Ligterink	IM	2440	1	½	½	0	½	½	½	½	½	0	½	0	x	0	½	1	6½
14	Nogueiras	IM	2385	0	½	0	½	½	½	½	0	0	½	0	½	1	x	1	1	6½
15	Westerinen	GM	2450	0	0	0	½	0	1	1	1	0	½	1	½	½	0	x	0	6
16	Schneider	IM	2430	0	0	1	0	½	½	0	0	½	1	0	½	0	0	1	x	5

Category 9 (2451) GM = 10 IM = 7½

Kiev vi.78

				1	2	3	4	5	6	7	8	9	0	1	2	3	4	5	6	
1	Beljavsky	GM	2530	x	0	1	0	½	½	1	1	1	1	½	1	1	½	1	1	11
2	Kuzmin	GM	2560	1	x	1	½	½	½	1	½	0	0	0	½	1	½	1	1	9
3	Palatnik	IM	2490	0	0	x	½	1	½	½	½	½	½	1	1	½	1	1	1	9
4	Savon	GM	2550	1	½	½	x	1	½	½	½	1	½	½	½	½	½	½	½	9
5	Alburt	GM	2515	½	½	0	0	x	½	1	0	1	1	1	½	0	½	1	1	8½
6	Knezevic	GM	2505	½	½	½	½	½	x	½	½	1	0	½	½	½	0	1	1	8
7	Lerner		2445	0	0	½	½	0	1	x	½	½	1	0	1	1	0	1	1	8
8	Peresipkin		2430	0	½	½	½	1	½	½	x	½	½	½	0	½	1	½	1	8
9	Romanishin	GM	2610	0	1	½	0	0	0	½	½	x	½	1	1	1	0	1	1	8
0	Farago	GM	2510	0	1	½	½	0	1	0	½	½	x	½	½	½	1	½	1	8
1	Velikov	IM	2430	½	1	0	½	0	½	½	½	0	½	x	½	½	1	½	½	7
2	Adamski	IM	2470	0	½	0	½	½	½	0	1	0	½	½	x	½	½	½	1	6½
3	Platonov		2455	0	0	½	½	1	½	0	½	0	½	½	½	x	½	½	1	6½
4	Ftacnik	IM	2380	½	½	½	½	½	½	1	0	1	0	0	½	½	x	0	½	6½
5	Ree	IM	2500	0	0	0	½	0	½	0	½	0	½	½	½	½	1	x	½	5
6	Lehmann	IM	2405	0	0	0	½	0	0	0	0	0	0	½	0	0	½	½	x	2

Category 10 (2486) GM = 9 IM = 7

USA Final vi.78

		1	2	3	4	5	6	7	8	9	0	1	2	3	4	5	
1	Kavalek	x	0	½	1	1	1	½	1	½	½	1	½	½	1	1	10
2	Tarjan	1	x	1	½	1	0	½	0	1	½	1	½	1	½	½	9
3	Shamkovich	½	0	x	1	½	½	½	½	0	1	1	½	1	1	0	8
4	Mednis	0	½	0	x	½	½	½	1	1	½	½	1	½	1	½	8
5	Byrne	0	0	½	½	x	½	½	1	½	½	½	½	½	1	1	7½
6	Lein	0	1	½	½	½	x	½	½	½	1	½	½	½	0	1	7½
7	Weinstein	½	½	½	½	½	½	x	½	½	½	½	½	1	½	½	7½
8	Rogoff	0	1	½	0	0	½	½	x	1	½	½	½	1	½	½	7
9	Lombardy	½	0	1	0	½	½	½	0	x	½	1	½	0	½	1	6½
10	Benko	½	½	0	½	½	0	½	½	½	x	½	½	1	½	½	6½
11	Soltis	0	0	0	½	½	½	½	½	0	½	x	1	1	½	½	6
12	Zuckerman	½	½	½	0	½	½	½	½	½	½	0	x	½	½	½	6
13	Christiansen	½	0	0	½	½	½	0	0	1	0	0	½	x	1	1	5½
14	Commons	0	½	0	0	0	1	½	½	½	½	½	½	0	x	½	5
15	Regan	0	½	1	½	0	0	½	½	0	½	½	½	0	½	x	5

London 23-29.iii.78

1	Haik	IM	2425	7½
2	Franklin		2315	7½
3	Hartston	IM	2475	7
4	Diesen	IM	2440	7
5	Soos	IM	2425	7
6	Nunn	IM	2440	6½
7	Ornstein	IM	2425	6½
8	Bailey		2325	6½
9	Mestel	IM	2450	6
10	S. Webb	IM	2445	6
11	Bellin		2415	6
12	Botterill		2400	6
13	Basman		2395	6
14	Law		2345	6
15	Supancic		2335	6
16	Garbett		2310	6
17	Nicholson		2290	6
18	Silman		2360	6
19	Kinlay		2300	6
20	T. Bennett		2270	6
21	Ligterink	IM	2440	5½
22	Speelman		2410	5½
23	Valvo			5½
24	Goodman		2320	5½
25	Crouch		2300	5½
26	Baczynskyj		2370	5½
27	Shapiro			5½
28	Short		2225	5½
29	Macdonald-Ross		2265	5½
30	Cafferty		2300	5½
31	Britton		2235	5½
32	King			5½
33	Fuller		2390	5
34	P. Littlewood		2345	5
35	Whiteley		2385	5
36	Werner		2255	5
37	Lobo		2370	5
38	Wicker		2305	5
39	Pettersson			5
40	Povah		2350	5
41	Macpherson		2315	5
42	Carleton		2280	5
43	Pagden		2235	5
44	Quigley			5
45	Goichberg		2525	4½
46	T. Kristiansen		2320	4½
47	Johnsen		2280	4½

. . . . (72)

Fredrikstad 19-26.iii.78

1	Pytel	IM	2390	6½
2	Schussler		2365	6
3	Stein		2260	6
4	Wedberg		2360	6
5	Doda	IM	2405	6
6	Wiedenkeller			5½
7	Helmers		2345	5½
8	Niklasson		2340	5½
9	Johannessen	IM	2400	5
10	Ekstrom		2360	5
11	Rorvall		2350	5
12	Kaiszauri		2420	5
13	Gulbrandsen		2350	4½
14	Ulrichsen		2315	4
15	Lundin	IM	2375	4
16	Paulsson		2340	4
17	Haugli			4

. . . . (24)

Gausdal 28.iii-2.iv.78

1	Ogaard	IM	2435	7½
2	Pytel	IM	2390	7
3	Schussler		2365	7
4	Ekstrom		2360	6½
5	Beijar			6½
6	Doda	IM	2405	6½
7	Estrin	IM	2430	6½
8	E. Kristiansen		2350	6
9	Vanman			6
10	Berg		2240	6
11	Orseth			6
12	Nordstrom			6
13	L. Karlsson		2360	6
14	Heiberg		2225	6
15	Hoen		2380	6
16	A. Jensen		2245	6

. . . . (117)

Lone Pine 2-12.iv.78

#	Name	Title	Rating	Score
1	Larsen	GM	2620	7½
2	Polugaevsky	GM	2620	7
3	Portisch	GM	2630	6½
4	Lein	GM	2505	6½
5	Peters		2430	6½
6	Petrosian	GM	2620	6
7	Rogoff	IM	2520	6
8	Evans	GM	2530	6
9	Ree	IM	2500	6
10	Zaltsman			6
11	Timman	GM	2585	5½
12	Miles	GM	2565	5½
13	Benko	GM	2485	5½
14	Sahovic	IM	2490	5½
15	Ligterink	IM	2440	5½
16	Biyiasas	IM	2450	5½
17	Panno	GM	2580	5
18	Browne	GM	2550	5
19	Lombardy	GM	2540	5
20	Gheorghiu	GM	2520	5
21	Stean	GM	2510	5
22	Reshevsky	GM	2490	5
23	Shamkovich	GM	2485	5
24	Janosevic	GM	2455	5
25	Mestel	IM	2450	5
26	Bisguier	GM	2425	5
27	Formanek	IM	2410	5
28	Taulbut		2405	5
29	Angantysson		2350	5
30	Petursson		2350	5
31	Commons	IM	2485	4½
32	Christiansen	GM	2490	4½
33	Westerinen	GM	2450	4½
34	Mestrovic	IM	2435	4½
35	H.Olafsson		2420	4½
36	Speelman		2410	4½
37	Seirawan		2400	4½
38	Taylor		2380	4½
39	Sunye		2360	4½
40	Meyer		2350	4½
41	Tarjan	GM	2510	4
42	Weinstein	IM	2475	4
43	Bogdanovic	IM	2430	4
44	Bohm	IM	2410	4
45	Van der Sterren		2400	4
46	Henley		2340	4
47	Van Riemsdyk		2375	4
48	P.Whitehead			4
49	Odendahl			4
50	Garcia-Palermo		2385	3½
51	Loftsson		2335	3½
52	Coudari		2285	3½
53	Filguth		2350	3½
54	Donaldson			3½
55	Morris		2325	3½
56	Balinas	GM	2440	3
57	Rohde	IM	2425	3
58	Fedorowicz		2360	3
59	Brasket		2370	3
60	Verduga	IM	2355	3
61	Gruchacz		2400	3
62	J.Whitehead		2245	3
63	Youngworth		2215	3
64	Gild.Garcia		2365	2½
65	Arnason		2350	2
66	Erlingsson		2270	1

Mexico City 2

#	Name	Rating	Score
1	Navarro	2300	8½
2	Aldrete	2310	8
3	B. Ramirez	2255	7
4	Leal		7
5	A. Belmont		6½
6	Lara	2230	6
7	Ocampo	2230	5
8	R. Anguiano		4½
9	Ferriz		4
10	Estrada	2205	4
11	Monray		3½
12	Ruiz	2250	2

1 b3

1 Petkevich-Bangiev USSR 77

**1 ♘f3 d5 2 b3 ♘f6 2...♗g4!= 3 ♗b2
♗f5 4 g3 e6 5 ♗g2 ♗e7 6 0-0 h6 7
d3 0-0 8 e3 ♘bd7 9 ♕e2 ♗h7 10 ♘c3!?**
10...♘bd2 **c6** 10...c5 11 e4 += **11
e4 dxe4! 12 dxe4 ♕c7 13 ♔h1** 13
e5 ♘d5 14 ♘e4 ♖fd8 15 ♖fd1 ♗b4!
16 a3 ♗c3! =+; 15 a3 a5! △ ♘c5∞
a5 14 a4 ♖fd8 14...e5 15 ♘d2 △ f4∞
15 ♘d2 ♘f8? 15...♘c5! 16 f4 ♖d7
17 ♘c4 ♖ad8= **16 ♘c4** △ e5, ♘e4
**♘6d7 17 f4 ♘c5 18 ♕g4! f6 19 ♖ae1
♔h8?!** 19...♖d7 **20 ♕e2! ♖d7 21 e5!**
f5 21...♖ad8 22 exf6 ♗xf6 23 ♖d1 +=
22 ♗a3! ♖ad8? 22...♗g6 23 ♕e3 b6
24 ♖d1 ♗e8 25 ♘d6! += **23 ♕e3!**
b6 23...♘a6 24 ♘d6!± **24 ♘xa5 bxa5**
24...♘d3?! 25 ♗xe7 ♘xe1 26 ♗xd8
♘xg2 27 ♕xb6!± **25 ♗xc5 ♗xc5 26
♕xc5± ♖c8 27 ♖d1 ♗g6 28 ♘b1 ♗e8
29 ♘d2 ♕a7 30 ♕xa7 ♖xa7 31 ♘c4
♖b8 32 ♖d6 +- ♖c8 33 ♖fd1 ♔g8
34 ♗f3 ♖a6 35 ♖d8 ♖xd8 36 ♖xd8
♗d7 37 ♘d6! +- ♖a7 38 h4 g6 39
♔g1 ♔g7 40 ♔f2 g5 41 h5! gxf4 42
gxf4 ♖a6 43 ♔e3 1-0 Gufeld**

2 Balashov-Kochiev Lvov 78

**1 ♘f3 ♘f6 2 c4 g6 3 b3 ♗g7 4 ♗b2
0-0 5 g3 d6 6 d4 ♘bd7 7 ♗g2 e5 8
dxe5 dxe5 9 0-0 9 ♘xe5? ♘g4 −+
e4?!** 9...♖e8!? **10 ♘e1 ♕e7 11 ♘c2
♖d8 12 ♘c3 ♘c5 13 ♕c1 c6 14 ♘e3
+= a5 15 ♖d1 15 ♕c2!? ♖xd1+ 16
♕xd1 ♘g4 17 ♕d2 a4! 18 b4 ♘xe3
19 ♕xe3 a3∓ 20 ♘d5 20 ♗c1 ♘a4
cxd5 21 ♗xg7 ♔xg7 22 bxc5 22
♕xc5 ♕xc5 23 bxc5 dxc4 24 ♗xe4;
23...♗e6! dxc4 23 ♖c1 ♗f5 24 ♖xc4
♕e5 25 ♖c3 25 ♕c1 ♕d5 26 g4 ♗xg4
27 ♖xa3 ♕d1+ 28 ♗f1 ♗xe2! 0-1
Pytel**

3 Vadasz-Honfi Subotica 78

**1 ♘f3 ♘f6 2 g3 g6 3 b3 ♗g7 4 ♗b2
0-0 5 ♗g2 d6 6 d4 a5 7 0-0 ♘bd7 8
♘bd2** 8 c4 c5! N **9 c4 cxd4 10 ♘xd4
♘c5 10...a4!? 11 a3 ♗d7 12 ♖b1!
♕b6 13 ♗a1 ♖fc8?!** 13...e5!? 14 ♘c2
♗c6=; 14 b4 axb4 15 axb4 ♘e6 16
c5= **14 b4 axb4 15 axb4 ♘e6 16 c5!
♕a7! 17 ♘xe6 ♗xe6 18 cxd6 exd6 19
♘b3 ♗f5 20 ♗d4 ♕a3 20...♕a4? 21
♘a5± 21 ♗xb7 ♖xb1 22 ♕xb1 ♕xb4
23 ♗xc8 ♖xc8 24 ♕a1 ½-½ Honfi**

4 Larsen-Westerinen USA 78

**1 ♘f3 ♘f6 2 g3 g6 3 b3 ♗g7 4 ♗b2
0-0 5 ♗g2 d6 6 d4 ♗f5 7 c4 ♕c8 8
h3 ♕d8 9 ♘c3 e5 10 dxe5 dxe5 11
♘d2 ♘c6! 12 ♗xc6!** 12 e4 ♗e6 13
♘d5 ♘d7! bxc6 13 g4 ♗e6 14 ♕c2
a5 15 ♘a4 ♘d7 16 ♘e4 f6 17 f3 ♕b8
18 h4 ♕b4+ 19 ♗c3 ♕e7 20 0-0-0
♖fb8 21 h5 f5? 21...g5! 22 h6 ♗f8
△ ♘b6 **22 ♘g3 ♕a3+ 23 ♗b2! 23
♔b1?? ♕xa4 ♕xa2 24 hxg6 fxg4**
24...hxg6 25 gxf5 gxf5 26 ♖dg1
♔f7 27 ♘xf5 +- **25 ♖xh7 ♘f6**

26 ♖xg7+ ♔xg7 27 ♘h5+! ♔f8 27...
♘xh5 28 ♗xe5+ △ ♕xa2 **28 ♘xf6
♕xb3 29 ♕xb3 ♖xb3 30 ♘c5 ♖b4
31 ♘xe6+ ♔e7 32 ♘xc7** 32 ♘a3
♔xf6 33 ♗xb4 axb4 34 ♘c5 +-
♖xc4+ 32...♖c8 33 ♘cd5+ +- **33**

♕b1 ♖c8 34 ♘xg4 ♖xc7 35 ♘xe5
♖b4 36 g7 ♖b8 37 f4 ♕e6 38 e4
38 ♖g1 ♖g8 39 ♘c4 ♖xg7 39 f5+ 1-0

1 b4

5 Borowiec-Chatelain Corresp. 78
1 b4 e5 2 ♗b2 f6 3 b5 3 e4!? **d5**
4 e3 ♗e6 5 ♘f3 ♗d6 5...c5!? 6 d4
e4 7 ♘fd2 c4 **6 d4 e4 7 ♘fd2 f5 8**
c4 c6 9 a4 9 ♘c3 **♘f6 10 ♗e2 0-0**
11 0-0 11 ♘c3 **♘bd7 12 ♘a3 f4 13**
♘c2 f3! −+ **14 gxf3 ♗h3 15 ♖e1**
♘h5 16 f4 16 ♗f1 ♕g5+ 17 ♔h1
♘f4 18 ♗xh3 (18 exf4 ♕xf4 −+)
♘xh3 19 ♖f1 ♕h4 20 f4 ♘xf4! −+;
19 ♕e2 ♕h4 20 f4 ♘xf2+ 21 ♔g2
♘d3 △ ♖f6

16...♘xf4! 17 exf4 ♖xf4 18 ♘f1
♖xf2! **19 ♘ce3** 19 ♔xf2 ♕h4+ 20
♔g1 (20 ♘g3 ♖f8+) ♗xh2+!! 21 ♔h1
♗xf1 −+; 21 ♘xh2 ♕g3+; 21 ♔xh2
♗xf1+ 22 ♔g1 ♕g3+! 23 ♔xf1 ♖f8+
24 ♗f3 exf3 −+ **♕h4 0-1 Konikowski**

6 Alexandria-Chiburdanidze (2) 77
1 d4 ♘f6 2 ♘f3 g6 3 b4 ♗g7 4 ♗b2
0-0 5 ♘bd2 d6 6 e3 c5 7 dxc5 dxc5
8 b5 ♕a5 8...♗f5!? **9 ♗d3 ♖d8 10 0-0**
c4!? 11 ♗xc4 11 ♘xc4 ♕xb5= **♘e4**
12 ♗xg7 ♔xg7 12...♘xd2? 13 ♘xd2
♖xd2 14 ♕f3 +− **13 ♘b3** 13 ♗d3

♘c3 14 ♕c1 ♖xd3! **♕c7 14 ♗d3 ♗g4**
15 ♕c1?! 15 ♘bd4! ♗xf3 16 gxf3
♘c3! 17 ♖e1 ♘d7 18 ♗f1 18 f4 e5!
♘e5 19 ♗g2 ♘xb5?! 19...♘c4!∓
△ ♖d1 **20 a4 ♘c3 21 ♕a3= ♖ac8**
22 ♘d4 e6?! 22...♕c5= **23 f4 ♘g4**
24 h3 24 ♘c6! bxc6 25 ♕xc3+ ♔g8 26
♖ab1 += **♘f6 25 ♕b2** 25 ♘c6!? **♖d7**
26 ♖a3 ♔g8 27 ♘c6?! 27 ♘b5 ♘xb5
28 axb5 ♘d5= **♘cd5?!** 27...♘ce4!
28 ♘xa7? 28 ♘e5 += **♕a5∓ 29 ♘xc8**
♕xe1+ 30 ♗f1 ♘e4 31 c4 ♘dc3 31...
♘xf4 −+ **32 ♖a1 ♘e2+!** −+ **33 ♕xe2**
♕xa1 34 c5 ♖d1 35 ♕b5 ♔g7 36
♘d6 ♘d2 37 ♕e8 ♖xf1+ 38 ♔h2
♖xf2+ 0-1 Gufeld

7 Alexandria-Chiburdanidze (4) 77
1 d4 ♘f6 2 ♘f3 g6 3 b4 ♗g7 4 e3 0-0
5 ♗c4?! d6 6 0-0 e5!= 7 c3 e4 8 ♘fd2
♖e8 8...♗g4!? **9 a4 ♘bd7 10 ♕b3**
♕e7 11 ♗a3 ♘f8 12 b5 ♗f5 13 ♗e2
h5 14 c4 ♘g4!? 15 h3 ♘h6 16 ♘c3
♕h4 17 ♖fe1 ♘e6 18 ♗f1 ♘g5 19
♘d5 19 g3 ♘xb3+ −+ **♗xh3 20 gxh3**
♘xh3+ 21 ♗xh3 ♕xh3 22 ♘f4 ♕g4+
23 ♘g2 23 ♔f1 ♗xd4 **♕h3 24 ♘f4**
♕f5? 24...♕g4+ = **25 ♘f1 h4** 25...
♗xd4? 26 ♘g3 ♕g4 27 exd4 ♕xf4
28 ♗c1 +− **26 ♘h2!** += **♘g4 27 ♕d1!**
♘xh2 28 ♔xh2 g5 29 ♘h3?! 29 ♕h5!
♗xd4 30 ♖g1± g4 30 ♘f4 ♗h6 31
♗c1 ♕h7 32 ♖g1 ♖g8 33 ♖g2 ♖g7
34 ♖a2! ♖ag8 35 ♕f1 ♗xf4+ 36 exf4
♕h5≈ 37 ♖a3! ♖g6 38 ♕e2 f5 39
♔g1 ♕h6 40 ♗d2 g3 41 fxg3 41 ♔h1
♖g4 42 f3 h3! 43 ♖g1 ♖xf4!! 44
fxe4 ♗f2! 45 ♗xh6 ♖xe2 46 ♖axg3
♖xg3 47 ♖xg3 ♔xh6 48 exf5 ♗f2=;
44 ♕e3? h2 45 ♖g2 exf3 −+; 43...g2+
44 ♔h2 ♖g3 45 ♖e3! ♕h4 46 ♕f2!!±;
46 fxe4?? ♕xf4 −+; 45...♕xf4 46
♖xe4 +−; 42 ♖g1!? ♕h5! 43 ♖e3
♕h6!=; 43 f3? g2+ 44 ♔h2 ♖g3∓

h3 42 Rh2! 42 Rf2 Rxg3+ 43 Rxg3
Rxg3+ 44 Kh1 Kg6 **Rxg3+ 43 Rxg3**
Rxg3+ 44 Kh1 Kg6 45 Wf1= 45 Re3
Wg4 46 Wxg4 fxg4 47 Re2 Kg6 48
Kh2 Rf3 49 c5 d5 50 a5 (△ b6! +−)
b6 51 axb6 axb6 52 c6! Kh5 53 Bf2!=
e3?! 54 Bg3! Kg6 55 f5+! Kxf5 56
Re1!!±; 54 Rxe3? Kh4 −+ Wg4 46
Re2 Rf3 47 Rf2 Rd3 ½-½ Gufeld

1 c4 c5

8 Balashov-Dorfman Lvov 78
**1 c4 Nf6 2 Nc3 c5 3 Nf3 d5 4 cxd5
Nxd5 5 d4 Nxc3 6 bxc3 g6 7 e3 Bg7
8 Bd3 0-0 9 0-0 Wa5?!** 9...Wc7 △ b6,
Bb7, Nc6 **10 Bb2 cxd4? 11 cxd4±
Nc6 12 Nd2 Bf5 13 Nb3 Wd5 14
Ba3 Rfc8 15 Rc1 Bxd3 16 Wxd3 e6
17 Rfd1 Na5 18 e4 Wh5 19 d5 Nc4?**

20 dxe6 Nxa3 20...fxe6 21 Wd7 **21
Rxc8+ Rxc8 22 Wd7 Ra8** 22...Rf8
23 e7 **23 Wxf7+ Kh8 24 Rd7 Be5 25
g3 1-0 Pytel**

9 Stefanov-Nacht
Rumania Final 77
**1 Nf3 Nf6 2 c4 c5 3 Nc3 d5 4 cxd5
Nxd5 5 e4 Nb4 6 Bb5+? 6 Bc4!? Bd7**
6...N8c6 7 0-0 a6 8 Ba4 b5 9 a3 Nd3
10 Nxb5 axb5 11 Bxb5 Wd6 12
Wb3 Ba6!∓ Tukmakov-Tal, USSR 77;

7 a3 Nd3+ 8 Ke2 Nf4+ 9 Kf1 Ne6
10 d3= Polovoj-Kapengut, USSR 76
7 Bc4 7 a3?! Bxb5 8 axb4 Bd3!? 9
Ne5 Nc6 =+ Mochalov-Palatnik, USSR
77 **Be6 8 Bxe6 Nd3+ 9 Wf1 fxe6 10
Ng5** 10 Ne1?! Nc6 11 Nxd3 Wxd3+
12 We2 Wd7 13 d3! =+ O'Kelly-
Palatnik, BRD 76 **Wd7 11 Wf3!?**
11 Wg4 e5 12 Ne6 Nf4 13 Nxg7+
Bxg7 14 Wxg7 Wf8∓; 12 Wxd7+ =;
11...Nc6 12 Nxe6 Nd4 13 Nxg7+ Bxg7
14 Wxg7 0-0-0∓; 12 Wxe6 Wxe6
Nxe6 Kd7 14 Nxf8+ Baxf8 15 f3
g5∓; 11 Wh5+ g6 12 Wh3 Ne5 12 Wh3
Nbc6!? 12...Wd3+ 13 Wxd3 Nxd3
14 Ke2 Nf4+! 15 Kf3 e5 +=; 14...
Nxc1+? 15 Raxc1 Kd7 16 d4!±
Stefanov-Neamtu, Rumania 77 **13
Nxe6 Rc8 14 Nxc5?!** 14 f4! Wxh3
15 gxh3 b6 16 Nb3? 16 Ne6 Nd3 17
We2 Nce5= 18 Nd4 g6 19 Nd5 Rc4!
20 f4 20 Ke3!? **Rxd4 21 fxe5 Bg7
22 Rf1 Bxe5∓ 23 We3 Nc5 24 Nc3
Rd3+ 25 We2 Rxh3 26 Rf2 Nd3 27
Rf3 Rxf3 28 Wxf3 Ne1+ 29 We2 Nc2
30 Rb1 Nd4+ 31 We3 Rf8 −+ 32 Wd3
b5 33 Nd5 Rf1 34 b3 h5 35 a4 a6 36
h4 e6 37 Ne3 Rh1 38 axb5 axb5
Ra1 Nxb3 40 Ra8+ Kd7 41 Ba3 Rc1+
42 Kc2 Be2 43 Ra7+ Kc6 44 Ra6+
Kb7 45 Ra5 Nd4+ 46 Kd3 Bc7 0-1
Ciocaltea**

10 Gheorghiu-Peters Lone Pine 78
**1 c4 Nf6 2 Nc3 c5 3 Nf3 d5 4 cxd5
Nxd5 5 e4 Nb4 6 Bc4 e6!?** 6...Be6!?∞;
6...Nd3+ **7 0-0 N8c6 8 d3 Na5 9
Bb5+!± Nbc6 10 d4! cxd4** 10...a6!?
11 Bxc6+ Nxc6 12 d5!± **11 Nxd4
Bd7 12 Bf4 a6 13 Be2 Wf6!? 14
Nxc6 14 Be3! Ne5 15 b3 Rc8 16
Rc1 Ba3 17 Rc2 △ f4± Nxc6 15
Wd2!?** 15 Be3! △ f4, e5± **Wd4! 16
Rad1 Wxd2 17 Rxd2 Bc5 18 Rfd1**

0-0-0!∝ 18...罝d8? 19 ♗c7 +− **19 ♞a4 ♗a7 20 ♗d6 ♞d4!! +=**

21 ♞c3 ♞xe2+ 22 ♞xe2 ♗c6 23 e5 ♗b8 24 ♞d4!? 24 ♗xb8 罝xd2 25 罝xd2 ♚xb8 26 ♞f4! += **♗xd6 25 ♞xc6 bxc6 26 罝xd6 罝xd6 27 罝xd6 ♚c7! 28 罝d3 罝d8 29 罝xd8 ♚xd8 30 ♚f1 ♚c7 31 ♚e2 ♚b6 32 ♚d3 ♚c5 33 ♚c3! g5** 33...♚d5?! 34 ♚b4! +− **34 ♚b3! ♚b5!= ½-½ Gheorghiu**

11 Benko-Seirawan Lone Pine 78

1 ♞f3 ♞f6 2 c4 c5 3 ♞c3 d5 4 cxd5 ♞xd5 5 e4 ♞xc3 5...♞b4 6 ♗c4 ♞e6!?; 6...♞d3+ 7 ♚e2 ♞f4+!? 8 ♚f1± Benko-Peters, Lone Pine 78 **6 dxc3! += ♛xd1+ 7 ♚xd1 ♞c6 8 ♗e3 e6 9 ♚c2 b6 10 ♗b5 ♗d7 11 a4! a6 12 ♗e2 ♗d6 13 ♞d2** Δ ♞c4 **♞a5 14 罝hb1 0-0** 14...罝c8 15 ♗xa6 **15 b4 cxb4 16 cxb4 ♞c6 17 b5 axb5 18 axb5 ♞b4+ 19 ♚b3 ♗c5 20 罝c1! 罝xa1 21 罝xa1 罝d8** 21...罝c8 22 ♗xc5± **22 ♗xc5 bxc5 23 ♚c3 ♚f8 24 ♚b3 +− 罝c8 25 罝a7 ♚e7 26 ♚c4 ♞c2 27 ♞xc5 罝d8 28 ♞xd7 罝xd7 29 罝xd7+ ♚xd7 30 ♚c3! +− 1-0** 30...♞e1 31 g3 Δ ♚d2; 30...♞a3 31 ♗d3 Δ ♚b4 **Gheorghiu**

12 Meyer-Portisch Lone Pine 78

1 ♞f3 ♞f6 2 g3 c5 3 c4 d5 4 cxd5 ♞xd5 5 ♗g2 ♞c6 6 ♞c3 ♞c7 7 a3!? g6! 8 b4 ♗g7 9 罝b1 9 bxc5 ♞e6 =+ **♗f5 10 罝b2 c4 11 b5 ♞a5 12 ♛a4 b6 13 ♞h4 罝c8 14 ♞xf5 gxf5 15 ♚c2 ♛d7 16 ♗b4 0-0 17 0-0 罝fd8 18 a4 e6 19 罝d1 ♞e8** Δ ♞d6∓ **20 ♞a2 ♛d6 21 ♗b2?** 21 罝b1 c3!∓

22 ♗a3 cxd2 23 ♛b1 ♛c7 24 罝f4 ♛c2! 25 ♛xc2 罝xc2 26 ♞b4 罝c3 27 罝f3 ♞c4 28 ♞c6 罝d7 29 ♞b8 罝c7 30 ♞a6 罝c8 31 罝xc3 ♗xc3 32 ♗b4 ♗xb4 33 ♞xb4 罝d8 34 ♞d3 e5! −+ 35 f3 ♞f6 Δ e4 **36 ♗h3 ♞d5 37 ♞xe5 ♞de3! 38 ♞xc4 ♞xd1 39 ♗xf5 ♞c3 0-1 Gheorghiu**

13 Mihalchishin-Chekhov USSR 77

1 c4 c5 2 ♞f3 ♞f6 3 ♞c3 d5 4 cxd5 ♞xd5 5 g3 5 d3 ♞c6 5...g6!? **6 ♗g2 ♞c7 7 ♛a4** 7 d3 e5 8 ♞d2!? **♛d7** 7...♗d7 8 ♛e4 ♞e6 9 e3 g6 10 d4 += Romanishin-Tal, USSR 76 **8 0-0 g6 9 ♚c4 b6 10 b4! ♗g7** 10...♞xb4 11 ♞e5; 10...cxb4 11 ♞g5 ♞e5 12 ♛f4 **11 bxc5 b5 12 ♚e4!** N 12 ♛b3 b4 13 ♞g5 0-0∝ **b4 13 ♞g5 ♗b7** 13...bxc3 14 ♛xc6 cxd2 15 ♗xd2 ♗xa1 16 罝xa1 罝b8 17 ♗f4! **14 罝b1 h6**

Diagram

English: 1...c5

15 ♖xb4 ♞xb4 **16** ♕xb7 hxg5 **17**
♕xb4 ♖c8 **18** c6± ♔e6?! 18...♕d4!±
19 d4 ♕g4 **20** ♖d1 f5 **21** h3 ♕h5 **22**
♕c4! g4 **23** h4 ♕h7 **24** ♗f4 +– ♕g8
25 ♞d5! ♞e6 **26** c7 ♔f7 **27** ♞b6!!
1-0 27...♖xc7 **28** ♕xe6+ ♔xe6 **29**
♗d5+ ♔f6 **30** ♗g5 mate **Gufeld**

14 Uhlmann-Alburt Bucharest 78
1 c4 c5 **2** ♞f3 ♞f6 **3** ♞c3 d5 **4** cxd5
♞xd5 **5** g3 5 e3 ♞xc3 6 bxc3 g6 7
♕a4+ ♞d7 8 ♗a3?! ♕c7 9 ♗e2 ♗g7
10 0-0 0-0= Uhlmann-S.Garcia, Madrid
73; 7 ♗c4?!; 5 d4 ♞xc3 6 bxc3 g6 7
e3 ♗g7 8 ♗d3 0-0 9 0-0 ♕c7 10 ♖b1
♖d8 += Tal-Vaganian, Leningrad 77;
5 e4 ♞b4 6 ♗b5+?!; 6 ♗c4!; ♞c6
5...g6 6 ♕b3 ♞b4 7 ♞e4 ♗g7!; 6...
♞b6?! 7 ♞e5! e6 8 ♗g2 ♗g7 9 ♕b5+
♞8d7 10 ♞xd7 ♞xd7 11 a4 +=
Cvetkovic-Ftacnik, Stary Smokovec 77
6 ♗g2 g6 **7** d3 ♗g7 **8** ♗d2 8 ♞xd5
♕xd5 9 0-0 0-0 10 ♗e3 ♗d7 11 ♕d2
♕d6 12 ♗h6 ♖ac8 13 a3 b6= Larsen-
Miles, England 77 **0-0 9** ♕c1!? N **b6?!**
9...♞f6!?; 9...♞c7 **10** ♗h6 ♗b7 **11** h4
♞f6 **12** h5 ♞d4 12...♞xh5? 13 ♖xh5!
+– **13** hxg6 ♞xf3+ **14** ♗xf3 ♗xh6!
14...♗xf3 15 gxh7+ **15** ♕xh6 ♗xf3
16 exf3 16 gxf7+!? fxg6 17 ♞e4 ♕d7!
18 0-0-0 e5 += **19** ♕g5? 19 ♞g5!
♞xe4 **20** dxe4 ♕e6 **21** ♕h6 ♖f7 **22**

♖d5 ♖af8 **23** g4! ♕f6 **24** ♖h3 ♕e7
25 ♕d2 ♕e6 **26** ♕c3 ♖e8 **27** ♕h1 ♕f6
28 ♖d3 ♖ee7 **29** ♖d8+ ♕g7 **30** ♕e3
♕f4= **31** ♕xf4 ♖xf4 **32** ♖h3 ♖ef7
33 ♖d3 c4 **34** ♖c3 h6 **35** ♔d2 ♖d7+
36 ♔e2 b5 **37** a4 a6 **38** axb5 axb5
39 b3 ♖d4 **40** bxc4 bxc4 **41** ♖h1 ♖f7
42 ♖b1 ♖a7 **43** ♔e3 ♖ad7 **44** ♖b4
♖d3+ **45** ♖xd3 ♖xd3+ **46** ♔e2 ♖c3
47 ♖b7+ ♔f6 **48** ♖b6+ ♔f7 **49** ♖b7+
½-½ **Ciocaltea**

15 Tukmakov-Platonov USSR 77
1 ♞f3 c5 **2** c4 ♞f6 **3** ♞c3 e6 **4** g3 d5
4...b6 **5** cxd5 ♞xd5 5...exd5 6 ♗g2
♞c6 7 0-0 ♗e7 8 d4 0-0 9 e4 += ♞b6
10 d5 exd5 11 exd5 ♞b4 12 ♞e5?!
12 ♞e1! c4 13 a3 ♞a6 14 ♗f4 ♗d6 15
♗xd6 ♕xd6 16 ♕d4 += Gulko-Alburt,
USSR 75 **♗f6 13** f4 **♗f5!=** 14 a3 ♞c2
15 ♖a2 ♖c8 **16** g4?! 16 b3 ♞d4 17
♗e3 ♖e8!= **♗xe5!** =+ **17** fxe5 ♗g6
18 b3 ♞d4 **19** ♗f4 ♖e8 **20** ♖d2 ♞d7
21 e6! 21 ♖e1 ♕b6! ♞b6 21...fxe6
22 dxe6 += **22** a4 a5 **23** d6 fxe6
24 ♗xb7 e5 **25** ♗xc8 ♞xc8 =+ Zeitnot
½-½ 26 ♗g3 ♞xd6 27 ♖e1 ♕g5 28
♖f2 h5!∓ **Gufeld**

16 Malich-Bueno Leipzig 77
1 ♞f3 c5 **2** c4 ♞c6 **3** ♞c3 g6? **4** e3
♗g7 **5** d4 cxd4 **6** exd4 d6 **7** h3 ♞f6
8 d5 ♞b8 **9** ♗e3 0-0 **10** ♗e2 ♞bd7 **11**
0-0 a6 **12** ♖c1 ♞c5 **13** ♖e1?! 13 b4!
♞ce4 14 ♞a4! +–; 13...♞fe4 14 ♗d4
+– ♞fe4 **14** ♗d4 ♗h6!? **15** ♖c2 ♞xc3
16 ♖xc3 ♞e4 **17** ♖c2 e5 **18** dxe6
♗xe6 **19** ♗f1 d5 **20** c5 ♖c8 **21** b4
♞d7 **22** ♖b2 ♕e8 **23** ♞d3 23 ♕b3!?
♗a4 **24** ♕b1 f5 **25** ♖be2 ♖f7 **26**
a3 ♖e7 **27** ♕a2 ♗c6 **28** ♗f6 ♖e6 **29**
♗a1 ♖c7 **30** ♞d4 ♖ee7

Diagram

58

31 ♘xc6? 31 a4! ♗xa4 32 ♕xd5+ ♕f7 33 ♗c4 ♘e8 34 ♘xf5! gxf5 35 ♕d4 +− **bxc6 32 ♗xa6 ♗d2 33 ♖f1?** 33 ♖xd2 ♘xd2 34 ♖xe7 ♖xe7 35 ♕b2 ♘e4 36 f3! ♘g3 37 ♕h8+ ♔f7 38 ♕g7+ ♔e6 39 ♕f6+ ♔d7 40 ♕d6 mate; 35...♘c4!≈; 33 ♖xe4! ♗xe1 34 ♕b2!! ♖xe4 35 ♕h8+ ♔f7 36 ♕g7+ ♔e6 37 ♕f6+ ♔d7 38 ♕d6 mate **♖a7 34 ♖xd2** 34 ♗d3 ♗xb4 35 ♕b2 ♗xc5 36 ♗xe4 ♖xe4 37 ♕h8+ = **♘xd2 35 ♕xd2 ♖xa6 36 ♕c3 h5?** 36...♖aa7 37 g4!? fxg4 38 hxg4 h5?! 39 gxh5 gxh5 40 ♕h8+ ♔f7 41 ♕xh5+ ♔e6 42 ♕h3+ ♔f7 43 ♕h1≈ **37 b5!** cxb5 37...♖a8 38 ♕h8+ ♔f7 39 ♕g7+ ♔e6 40 ♕f6+ ♔d7 41 ♕xc6+ +− **38 ♕h8+ ♔f7 39 ♕g7+ ♔e6 40 ♕f6+ ♔d7 41 ♕xa6 1-0 Malich**

17 Pytel-Seniepik Poland 78

1 c4 ♘f6 2 ♘c3 c5 3 g3 g6 4 ♗g2 ♗g7 5 e3 0-0 6 ♘ge2 d6 7 d4 ♘a6? 7...♘c6 8 0-0 ♖b8 9 b3 ♗d7 10 ♗b2 ♘c7 11 ♕d2 cxd4 12 ♘xd4 +− a6 **13 ♖ac1 b5?** 13...♘e6 **14 ♘d5! ♘fe8** 14...bxc4 15 ♘xc7 ♕xc7 16 ♖xc4 +− **15 ♘b4** Δ ♘c6 **♗xd4 16 ♕xd4 ♘f6 17 cxb5 ♖xb5 18 ♖fd1 a5 19 ♘c6 ♗xc6 20 ♖xc6 ♘e6 21 ♕d3 ♖f5** 21...♖b8 22 ♗xf6 +− **22 e4 ♖c5 23 ♖xc5 ♘xc5 24 ♕c4 ♘cd7 25 e5!**

♘e8 25...dxe5 26 ♗c6 ♕b6 27 ♗xd7 ♖d8 28 ♗g4 **26 ♗h3! ♘b8 27 ♕d4 f6 28 ♖c1! fxe5 29 ♕d5+ ♔g7 29...♔h8 30 ♗xe5+ ♘f6 31 ♖c8 30 ♕b7 a4 31 b4!? a3 32 ♗a1 d5 33 ♗xe5+ 1-0 Pytel**

18 Pytel-Wentman Gausdal 78

1 c4 ♘f6 2 ♘c3 c5 3 g3 ♘c6 4 ♗g2 g6 5 e3 ♗g7 6 ♘ge2 d6 7 d4 0-0 8 0-0 ♗d7 8...♗g4 9 h3 ♗xe2 10 ♘xe2 cxd4 11 exd4 d5 12 c5 b6 13 ♗e3 bxc5 14 dxc5 ♖c8 15 f4 ♘e4 16 ♖b1 +− R.Byrne-Balcerowski, Varna 62; 9...♗d7 10 b3 a6 11 ♗b2 ♖b8 12 ♕d2 cxd4 13 exd4 b5 14 cxb5 axb5 15 d5! ♘a7 16 ♘d4 ♕b6 17 ♖fe1 ♖fe8 18 a3 ♕b7 19 ♖e2 ♖bc8 20 ♖ae1 ♔f8 21 ♘a2! ♘xd5? 22 ♘b4 e6 23 ♘dc6! +− Ornstein-Schmidt, Budapest 77 **9 b3** 9 f4?! a6 10 d5 ♘a5 11 ♕d3 b5! 12 b3 ♖b8 13 ♗d2 b4 14 ♘a4 ♘xc4! 15 ♘xc5 ♘xd2 16 ♘xd7 ♘xd7 17 ♘d4? ♗xd4 18 ♕xd4 ♘f1 0-1 Djordjevic-Pytel, Kikinda 76 **a6 10 ♗b2 ♖b8 11 ♕d2 cxd4** 11...b5 12 cxb5 axb5 13 dxc5 dxc5 14 ♖fd1 ♕b6 15 ♘f4 e6 16 ♘e4 ♘xe4 17 ♗xe4 ♗xb2 18 ♕xb2 +− Pytel-Kupke, Zagreb 77 **12 exd4 b5 13 cxb5 axb5 14 d5 ♘a5 15 ♘d4 +− ♕b6 16 ♖fe1 ♖fe8 17 ♖ac1 ♗f8?!** 18 ♘ce2 ♖ec8 19 ♘f4 Δ ♘d3-b4 **♘e8 20 ♘c6 ♘xc6?!** 20...♗xc6!? 21 dxc6 e6 22 ♘xe6!! fxe6 23 ♖xe6 ♗g7 24 ♗d5!! ♔h8 25 ♖xg6 ♘xc6!? 26 ♖xg7 ♘xg7 27 ♗xg7+ ♔xg7 28 ♕g5+ ♔f8 29 ♕f6+ ♔e8 30 ♕f7+ ♔d8 31 ♕f6+ ♔c7 32 ♕e7 mate **21 dxc6 ♗xc6 22 ♖xc6! ♖xc6 23 ♘d5 ♕d8 24 ♘xe7+ ♗xe7 25 ♗xc6 +− ♘f6 26 ♕e2** 26 ♕d4 d5!? **♗f8 27 ♖xb5 ♗g7 28 ♗c4 ♕d7 28...♕a5 29 ♗xf6 Δ ♖d1 29 ♕f3 ♕b7 30 ♕xb7**

Rxb7 31 Rd1 Rd7 32 a4 d5 33 ♗b5
Rd8 34 ♗c6 Rd6 35 ♗b5 Rd8 36
f3 Rd6 37 a5 Rd8 38 a6 ♘e8 39 ♗xg7
♕xg7 40 ♗xe8 Rxe8 41 Rxd5 Re1+
42 ♔f2 Ra1 43 Rd6 1-0 Pytel

19 Palatnik-Kapengut USSR 77

1 ♘f3 ♘f6 2 c4 c5 3 d4 cxd4 4 ♘xd4
a6!? 5 ♘c3 5 g3 d5 6 ♗g2 e5 7 ♘f3
e4! 8 ♘d2 e3! =+ d5 5...e6 6 g3 ♕c7
7 ♕d3 +=; 6 ♗g5 ♘c6 7 e3 ♗e7 8 ♗e2
♕a5 9 ♗f4∝ 6 cxd5 ♘xd5 7 ♘db5
♘b4! 8 ♕xd8+ ♔xd8 9 ♘a3 b5 9...e5!?
10 g3 ♗e6 11 ♗g2 ♘8c6 12 0-0 f6=
10 e4 e6? 10...e5! 11 ♗e3 ♗e6 12
0-0-0+ ♘d7 13 ♔b1 Rc8 14 f4 exf4
15 ♗xf4 f6 16 ♗e2 ♔e8 17 h3 Rxc3!
Karasev-Tseshkovsky, USSR 76 11
♗e3 ♘d7 12 Rd1?! 12 0-0-0 ♘c6 13
♘c2 ♗b4 14 f4 △ e5± ♗b7 13 ♗e2
♘c6 14 ♘c2 ♗e7= 15 0-0 ♔c8 16 a3
Rd8 17 b4 ♔c7? 17...♗f6! 18 ♘d4
♘xd4 19 ♗xd4

18 a4!± bxa4 19 ♘xa4 ♗xb4 20 ♘xb4
♗xb4 21 Rd4 ♗a5 22 Rc1+ ♔b8 23
Rb1 e5 24 Rd5 ♗c7 25 Rxd7 Rxd7
26 ♘c5 Re7 27 ♘xb7 1-0 Gufeld

20 N.Popov-Tseshkovsky USSR 77
1 d4 ♘f6 2 c4 c5 3 ♘f3 cxd4 4 ♘xd4
e6 5 ♘c3 ♗b4 6 g3 ♕c7?! N 6...♘e4
7 ♕d3 ♕a5 8 ♘c2 ♘xc3 9 ♘xb4∝/+=;

8...♗xc3+ 9 bxc3 ♘c5!? 7 ♕b3
♘d2!? ♗c5 8 ♗e3 a6 9 ♘c2 9 ♘a-
♘g4 10 ♘xe6 ♕a5+! 11 ♗d2 ♗xf2-
12 ♔d1 ♕e5∝ b6 10 ♗g2 ♘c6 1
♘a4 ♗xe3 12 ♘xe3 Rb8 13 ♕c3?
0-0 14 0-0 b5! 15 cxb5 axb5 16
♗xc6 bxa4! 16...dxc6?± 17 ♗xa-
♕a7 ∝/=+ 18 ♗c2 d5 19 ♕e5 ♗a
20 ♗d3?! ♘d7 21 ♕d6 ♗xd3 22 exd3
♘c5 23 Rfc1 ♘xd3 24 Rc7 ♕d4
25 Rd1 ♕e4 26 b3 Ra8 27 a3 ♘e5 28
h4 h5 -+ 29 a4 Rab8 30 ♕a3 d-
31 ♘c2 ♘f3+ 32 ♔f1 d3 33 ♘e3 ♘xh
34 ♔g1 ♘f3+ 35 ♔f1 Rxb3! 36 ♕d
36 ♕xb3 ♘d2+ -+ ♘e5 37 ♔g1 Rb
0-1 Gufeld

21 Gheorghiu-Bogdanovic
Lone Pine 78
1 d4 ♘f6 2 c4 c5 3 ♘f3 cxd4 4 ♘xd
e6 5 ♘c3 ♗b4 5...♘c6 6 g3 += 6 g
0-0 6...♘e4 7 ♕d3 ♕a5∝ 7 ♗g2 d
8 cxd5 ♘xd5 9 ♗d2 ♗xc3 9...♘xc
10 bxc3 ♗e7+ 10 bxc3 e5 11 ♘b
♘c6 12 c4 ♘b6 13 Rc1 ♗f5 13...♗e
14 ♘c5!± 14 0-0 Rc8 15 ♗e3 ♕c7?
16 c5!± ♘d7 16...Rfd8? 17 cxb6 +-
17 ♘d2! △ ♘c4-d6 Rcd8 18 ♕a4 ♗f
19 ♘c4 ♗e4 20 f3 ♗d5 21 ♘d6 ♘e
22 Rfd1! ♘d4 22...♘xd6 23 cxd
Rxd6 24 ♗c5 23 ♗xd4 exd4 24 e4
+- ♗e6 24...♗c6 25 ♕xd4 +-; 24.
dxe3!? 25 ♘xe8 Rfxe8 26 Rxd5
+- 25 ♘b5 ♕c6 26 ♕a5! d3 Zeitno
27 ♕xd8 ♕xb5 28 ♕xd3 1-
Gheorghiu

22 Sakharov-Czar Corr. 76/77
1 c4 c5 2 ♘f3 ♘f6 3 ♘c3 ♘c6 4
d4 cxd4 5 ♘xd4 e6 6 ♘db5 6 g3! +=
♗c5 7 ♗f4 7 ♘d6+ ♔e7 8 ♘de4 ♘xe
9 ♘xe4 ♗b4+ 10 ♗d2 d5 11 cxd
exd5 12 a3 ♗xd2+ 13 ♘xd2 Re8
12 ♗xb4 ♘xb4 13 ♕d2 ♕a5 14 ♘c

Rd8 =+ e5! 8 ♗g5 ♗xf2+! 8...♕b6 9
e3 a6 10 ♗xf6 axb5!∝; 9 ♗xf6! ♗xf2+
10 ♔d2 gxf6 11 ♘d5 ♕a5+ 12 ♔c1
0-0 13 e3±; 10...♕e3+ 11 ♔c2 gxf6
12 ♘c7+? ♔d8 13 ♘xa8 ♘d4+ 14
♔b1 d5 15 a4 ♗f5+ 16 ♔a2 ♗c2 17
♕c1 ♗b3+ 18 ♔a3 dxc4∓; 12 ♘d5
♕e4+ 13 ♕d3± 9 ♕xf2 ♘g4+ 10 ♕e1
♕xg5 11 ♘c7+ ♔d8 12 ♘xa8 ♗e3?
12...♕e3? 13 ♕d3!±; 12...♕f4 13
♕d2 ♕f2+ 14 ♔d1 ♘e3+ 15 ♔c1
♘xf1∝; 13 ♕d6 ♕f2+ 14 ♔d2 ♕e3+
15 ♔d1? ♘f2+ 16 ♔e1 ♘b4!∓; 15
♔e1!= 13 ♕d2 ♘d4 14 ♖c1 b6 15 ♘d5
1-0 15...♘df5 16 ♘ac7 ♕h4+ 17 g3
♘xg3 18 ♕xe3 ♘xh1+ 19 ♔d2 +−
Gufeld

23 Lipinski-Schinzel Poland 77
1 ♘f3 c5 2 c4 ♘f6 3 d4 cxd4 4 ♘xd4
e6 5 ♘c3 ♘c6 6 g3 ♕b6!? 6...♗c5!?;
6...♗b4 7 ♘db5!? N ♗c5 7...♘e5!
8 ♗g2!! ♗xf2+? 9 ♔f1 ♘g4 10 ♕d6!!
♖b8 10...♗c5 11 ♘c7+ ♔d8 12 ♘xa8
+−; 10...♘e3+ 11 ♗xe3 ♗xe3 12
b4 +−: 10...♗g1 11 e3! 11 ♘a4!
♕a5 12 ♗d2 1-0 Pytel

24 Gulko-Diesen Polanica 77
1 c4 ♘f6 2 ♘c3 e6 3 e4 c5 4 e5 ♘g8
5 ♘f3 ♘c6 6 d4 cxd4 7 ♘xd4 ♘xe5
8 ♘db5 a6 9 ♘d6+ ♗xd6 10 ♕xd6 f6
11 ♗e3 ♘e7!? 11...♘f7 12 ♗b6 12
♕a3 0-0 13 ♗c5?! ♖e8 14 ♘a4 d5
15 ♘b6 ♖b8 16 ♗d6 ♕xb6= Pytel-
Pokojowczyk, Poland 77 ♘f5 13
♗xd8 ♘xd6 14 ♗c7 ♕e7 14...♘dxc4
15 b3 15 c5 ♘e8 16 ♗b6 d5 17 cxd6+
♕xd6? 17...♘xd6! 18 0-0-0 ♘ec4
19 ♗xc4 ♘xc4 20 ♗c5+ ♔f7 21 ♖d4
b5 22 b3 e5 23 ♖d5 ♘a5 24 ♗b6
♗b7 25 ♖hd1∓ ½-½ Miles-Hubner,
Tilburg 77 18 f4 ♘d7 19 ♗d8 ♘c7?
20 ♘e4+ ♔d5 21 ♘xf6+ gxf6 22

♗xc7 +− ♘c5 23 ♗e2 ♕c6 24 ♗a5
♗d7 25 0-0 ♕d6 26 ♖fd1+ ♕e7 27
♗f3 ♗b5 28 ♗b4 ♖ac8 29 a4 1-0
Pytel

25 Sunye-Shamkovich
Lone Pine 78
1 ♘f3 g6 2 c4 ♗g7 3 ♘c3 c5 4 g3
♘c6 5 ♗g2 e6 6 0-0 ♘ge7 7 d3 0-0
8 a3 b6 9 ♖b1 d5!? 9...h6 10 ♗d2
d5 10 cxd5 exd5 11 ♗f4 h6 12 ♕c1
12 e4!? g5! 13 ♗d2 ♗e6 =+ 14 b4?!
d4 15 ♘a4 15 ♘e4 f5! cxb4 16 axb4
♖c8∓ 17 b5? 17 ♕b2!? ♘e5 18 ♕a3
♗xf3+ 19 ♗xf3 ♘d5 20 e3? 20 ♖fc1
♕d7; 20 ♘b2? ♘c3 21 ♗xc3 dxc3 −+
dxe3 21 fxe3 ♖c2! 22 ♖f2 ♕d7 23
♗d1

23...♖xd2 24 ♖xd2 ♗xe3 25 ♗f3
♗d4 26 ♖f2 26 ♔h1 ♗d5! −+ ♘c2
27 ♕c1 ♗xf2+ 28 ♔xf2 ♕d4+ 29
♔g2 ♕xa4 30 ♗d1 ♘e3+! 0-1
Shamkovich

26 Sliwa-Pytel Poland 77
1 c4 e6 2 ♘c3 c5 3 ♘f3 ♘f6 4 e4
♘c6 5 d3 5 d4 cxd4 6 ♘xd4 ♗b4 7
♘xc6 dxc6! =+ ♗e7!? 6 e5 ♘g4 7
♗f4 g5! 8 ♗g3 8 ♘xg5 ♘gxe5 9 ♕h5
♘g6≈ h5 9 h3 ♘h6 10 ♕d2 ♘f5 11
♘e4 ♖g8 12 ♘d6+ ♗xd6 13 exd6
g4?! 13...f6!? 14 hxg4 hxg4 15 ♘g5!

15 Nh2? Nxg3 16 fxg3 f5∓ Bxg3
16 fxg3 f5 17 Bh7 Rg6 18 0-0-0?!
18 Qf4! Δ Qf2, Be2∓ Qa5!!

19 Qf4! Qxa2 20 Ng5 Rg8 20...Kf8
21 d4!? Qa1+ 22 Kc2 Bb4+ 23 Kd2
Qxb2+ 24 Ke1 Qc3+ 25 Kf2 cxd4!
26 Rxd4 Nc6 26...Rxg5 27 Qe5 Rg8
28 Rh8 27 Rh7! Rxg5 27...Qxd4+??
28 Qxd4 Nxd4 29 Re7+ +- 28 Qxg5
Qxd4+ 29 Qe1 ½-½ 29...Qa1+ =; 29...
Qxd6 30 Rh8+ Kf8 31 Qg6+! Ke7 32
Qg5+ = Pytel

1 c4 e5

27 Pytel-Seret Montpelier 77/78
1 c4 e5 2 Nc3 Nc6 3 Nf3 f5 4 d4 e4
5 Bg5 Nf6 6 Nd2 Be7 7 e3 0-0 7...h6?
8 Bxf6 Bxf6 9 g4! +- 8 Be2 Qe8 9
h4!? d6 10 a3 Nd8 11 Bxf6 Bxf6
12 Nd5 f4?! 13 Qc2! fxe3 14 fxe3
c6! 15 Nxf6+ Rxf6 16 Nxe4 Rf8 17
0-0-0?! 17 Kd2!? +- d5 18 Ng5
Qxe3+ 19 Kb1 Bf5 20 Bd3 Bxd3 21
Rxd3 Qe8?? 21...Qf2= 22 cxd5 cxd5
23 Rf3 +- g6 24 Qc7 Nf7 25 Rhf1
1-0 Pytel

28 Roizman-Gulko USSR 78
1 c4 Nc6?! 2 d4 e5 3 dxe5 3 d5 +=
Nxe5 4 e3!? Nf6 5 Nc3 Bb4 6 Bd2
0-0 7 Be2 d6 8 Nf3 += Be6 9 b3 c6

10 0-0 Qa5!? 10...Qc7?! 11 Nb5! +-
11 Qe1 Bxf3+ 12 Bxf3 Qe5 Δ Ng4
13 Be4! Ng4?! 13...Nxd2 14 Nxf6+
Qxf6 15 Qxd2 Rfd8 += 14 Bxg4
Bxd2 15 Qxd2 Bxg4 16 f3 Rad8 17
Rad1 +- d5!? 18 Nc3! Be6 19 cxd5
Bxd5

20 e4! Bxb3 21 Qxd8 Bxd1 22 Qd3
+- Qc5+ 23 Kh1 Bxf3 24 gxf3 24
Rxf3 Qg5 Qa3 25 Rd1 b5 26 Nd5
Qxa2 27 Nf6+! 1-0 27...gxf6 28
Rg1+ Kh8 29 Qd6 +- Gufeld

29 Goodman-Nunn England 78
1 c4 e5 2 Nc3 Nf6 3 Nf3 Nc6 4 e3
Bb4 5 Qc2 0-0 6 Nd5 Re8 7 Qf5!
d6 8 Nxf6+ gxf6? 8...Qxf6! 9 Qxf6
gxf6 += Keene-Ljubojevic, Moscow
77 9 Qh5! 9 Qc2? Keene-Timman,
Bad Lauterberg 77 d5 10 a3 Bf8
11 d4! Be6 11...exd4 12 Nd3 h6 13
0-0! Be6 14 exd4 dxc4 15 Be4! 12
Bd3 e4 13 Bc2 Ne7 14 Nd2 f5?
14...c6 15 cxd5 Qxd5 16 f3 Qc6?
16...f4!

Diagram

17 Nxe4!! Qxc2 18 Nf6+ Kg7 19
e4!! +- Qxc1+ 20 Rxc1 Bxf6 21
Qxh7 Ng6 22 e5+ Kg5 23 h4+ Kf4
24 Kf2 1-0 Keene

30 Uhlmann-Bellon Bucharest 78

1 c4 e5 2 ♘c3 ♘f6 3 ♘f3 e4?! 4 ♘g5
b5 5 d3! ♗b7 5...bxc4? 6 dxe4± 6
♘gxe4 bxc4 7 g3! N 7 ♘xf6+ ♕xf6
8 dxc4 ♗c5 cxd3 8 exd3 ♗b4 8...♗e7
9 ♗g2 ♘xe4 10 dxe4 ♕f6 11 0-0 ♗xc3
12 bxc3 0-0 12...♕xc3?! 13 ♖b1
13 ♗f4! ♕c6 14 ♖b1 ♘a6 15 ♕d5
♘c5 15...♖fb8 16 ♖b5 ♕xd5 17 exd5
♗c8 18 ♖fb1 d6 19 ♗e3 16 c4 d6
17 e5! ♕xd5 18 cxd5 ♗a6 19 exd6!
♗xf1 20 ♗xf1 g5 20...cxd6 21 ♗xd6
♖fc8 22 ♗h3 +− 21 dxc7! 21 ♗xg5
cxd6 22 ♗e7 ♖fb8 23 ♖xb8+ ♖xb8
24 ♗xd6 ♖c8 25 ♗h3 +−; 22...♖fd8
gxf4 22 d6 f3 22...♘e6 23 ♗a6 fxg3
24 hxg3 ♔g7 25 ♖c1 ♘xc7 26 dxc7
♖ac8 27 ♔g2 ♔f6 28 ♗xc8 ♖xc8 29
♔f3 +− 23 ♖c1 ♘d7 24 ♗b5 ♘b6 25
d7 ♔g7 26 ♗c6! ♖ad8 27 cxd8♕
♖xd8 28 ♖e1 +− ♖b8 29 h4 29 ♖e8??
♘xd7 ♕f6 30 g4 1-0

31 Bilek-Skalkotas Kallithea 77

1 c4 e5 2 g3 c6 3 ♗g2 d5 4 cxd5 cxd5
5 d4 e4 5...exd4!? 6 ♘c3 ♘c6 7 ♘h3
♗b4 8 0-0 ♘ge7 9 e3 ♗f5? 9...0-0
10 f3! += exf3 11 ♕xf3 ♗xc3 12 bxc3
0-0 13 ♘f2 ♕a5 13...♕d7 △ ♖ac8
14 ♗d2± ♗e6 15 a4 ♕c7 16 e4 ♘a5
17 ♖ae1 ♘c4 18 ♗g5 dxe4 19 ♘xe4

♗d5 20 ♕h5 ♘xe4 21 ♗xe4 ♘g6 22
♕f3 ♘d6 23 ♗d5 ♖ac8 24 c4 b6?
24...♘xc4!? 25 ♖c1 ♕a5!≈ 25 h4! +−
h5 26 ♔h2! ♖ce8 27 ♖xe8 ♖xe8 28
♕xh5 ♘f8 29 ♗f4 ♖d8 30 ♗xd6 1-0
Pytel

32 Szabo-Tompa Hungary 78

1 c4 e5 2 g3 ♘f6 3 ♗g2 c6 4 d4 exd4
5 ♕xd4 d5 6 ♘c3 ♗e6! 7 cxd5 cxd5
8 ♘f3 8 ♗g5 ♗e7 9 ♘f3 0-0 10 ♖d1
♕a5 11 0-0 ♘c6 12 ♕d2 ♖fd8 =+
Madsen-Jezek corr. 59; 8 ♗f4? ♘c6
9 ♕a4 ♗b4 10 ♖c1 0-0 11 a3 ♗xc3+
12 ♖xc3 ♘e4 13 ♖c1 ♕b6 14 ♗e3
d4 =+ Puc-Pirc 57 ♘c6 9 ♕a4 ♗c5
9...♗e7 10 ♘e5 ♕b6 11 0-0 0-0=
12 ♘xc6 bxc6 13 b3 ♗b4! 14 ♗b2
♖ab8 15 ♖fc1 ♖fc8 16 e3 ♘d7 −+
Sotkin-Ravinsky, Leningrad 66 10
♕b5 N 10 0-0 0-0 11 ♗g5 h6 12 ♗xf6
♕xf6 13 e4 dxe4 14 ♘xe4 ♕e7 15
♘xc5 ♕xc5 16 ♖fd1 ♖fd8= Pirc-
Keres 56 ♗b6 11 0-0 a6 11...0-0
12 ♘a4 ♗c7 += 12 ♕a4 h6 12...0-0
13 ♗g5 h6 14 ♗xf6 ♕xf6 15 ♕b3 +=
13 ♗f4 0-0 14 ♖ad1 ♕e7 15 ♘e5
♖ac8 16 ♕b3?! 16 ♘xc6 ♖xc6 17
♘xd5 ♘xd5 18 ♗xd5 ♗xd5 19 ♖xd5
♕xe2 20 ♖d2= ♗xf2+! 17 ♖xf2 17
♔xf2? ♕xe5 18 ♗xe5 ♘g4+ d4 18
♘xc6 bxc6 19 ♕c2 19 ♕b6? dxc3
20 ♗d6 c2 −+ dxc3 20 ♕xc3 20
♗d6 ♕a7 21 ♗xf8 ♘g4∓ ♘d5 20...
♗d5?! 21 ♗xh6! ♗xg2 22 ♔xg2 ♕e4+
23 ♔g1 ♕g6 24 ♖xf6! +− 21 ♕a5
♖fd8 22 ♖c1 ♕a7 23 a3 23 ♕c5?
♕xc5 24 ♖xc5 ♘xf4 △ ♖d1+, ♖d2∓
♘e3?! 23...c5! 24 e4 ♘xf4 25 gxf4
♗b3 =+ 24 ♗xe3 ♕xe3 25 ♕c3 ♕b6?
25...♕xc3 26 ♖xc3 ♖d1+ 27 ♖f1
♖d2= 26 b4 ♖d6 27 ♕c5 ♕d8 28
♗e4 ♖a8? Zeitnot 28...♖d1+ = 29
a4 ♗d5 30 ♖d1 += ♖d7 31 ♗f5 ♗e6

**32 ⌶df1! ♗xf5 33 ⌶xf5 ⌶b8? 34
♕xc6 ⌶xb4 35 ♕xa6 ⌶bb7 36 a5 ⌶a7
37 ♕b6 ♕a8 38 ⌶e5 ⌶db7 39 ♕e3
⌶b8 40 ♕c5 ⌶c8 41 ♕b4 ⌶e8! 42
⌶ff5?!** 42 ⌶xe8+!? ♕xe8 43 ♕b6
⌶a8 41 ⌶a1!? ♕xe2? 45 a6±; 44...
♕e5! 45 ⌶a2 ♕d5= **g6! 43 ⌶xe8+
♕xe8 44 ⌶d5 ♕e3+ 45 ♔f1 ⌶a8 46
♔f4 ♕e6 47 ⌶b5 ⌶e8 48 ♕f3 ♕c4=
49 ♕d3** 49 ⌶b7 ⌶e5! **♕c1+ 50 ♔g2**
50 ♔f2 ♕h1≈ **♕e1 51 ⌶b2 ♕xa5 52
♕f3 ½-½ Tompa**

33 Petursson-Gheorghiu
Lone Pine 78

**1 c4 e5 2 ♘c3 ♘c6 3 g3 g6 4 ♗g2
♗g7 5 e3 ♘ge7 6 ♘ge2 0-0 7 0-0 d6
8 a3** 8 d4 exd4 9 exd4 ♗g4!= **♗e6
9 ♘d5! ♕d7 10 d3 ⌶ae8 11 ♕a4?**
11 ♘ec3 **♘d4!∓ 12 ♕d1 ♗xe2+
13 ♕xe2 ♘f5 14 b4 c6 15 ♘c3 d5 16**
cxd5 cxd5 **17 ♗b2** 17 ♘xd5?! ♗xd5
18 e4 ♘d4∓; 18...♗e6∓ **⌶d8 18
⌶fd1 ⌶fe8 19 ⌶ac1 b6 20 ♗a1 ⌶c8 21
♕d2 d4! 22 ♘e4 dxe3 23 fxe3 ⌶ed8
24 ♘f2 h5 25 ⌶xc8 ♕xc8 26 ♗h3!
♘d6 27 ⌶c1 ♕d7 28 ♗xe6 ♕xe6 29
⌶c6 h4 30 ♕c2 hxg3?!** 30...♕f5!∓
**31 e4 ♕f3; 31 ♔g2 h3+! 32 ♘xh3
e4 -+; 31 ♕e2 e4! -+ 31 hxg3 ♗h6
32 e4 ♗g5 33 ♔g2 ♕g7 34 ♕e2 ♕e8
35 ⌶c2 ♘b5 36 ♕g4 ♕e7 37 ♗b2
♗e3 38 ⌶c8 ♗d4! 39 ♗xd4 ♘xd4 40
⌶c4 a5!? 41 bxa5 bxa5 42 ♕h4 f6!?=**
Zeitnot **43 a4 ♘e6 44 ♕g4 ♗g5 45
♕d1 ♘e6 46 ♕d2 ⌶a8 47 ♕c3= ½-½
Gheorghiu**

1 c4 f5

34 Tompa-Farago Hungary 78

**1 c4 f5 2 e4!? fxe4 3 ♘c3 ♘f6 4 d3
d6?!** 4...e5 5 dxe4 ♗b4= **5 dxe4
e5 Δ** c5, ♘c6, ♘d4 **6 f4! exf4 7**
♗xf4 ♗e7 8 ♘f3 0-0 9 c5! ♕h8 9...
dxc5 10 ♕b3+ ♔h8 11 ♘g5 ♕e8 12
♗c4± **10 cxd6 cxd6 11 ♕d2 ♘h5?!**
11...♘c6 12 0-0-0 ♕a5 13 ♗xd6≈
12 ♗e3 ♗g4 13 0-0-0 ♘c6 13...♗xf3
14 gxf3 ⌶xf3 15 ♔b1!±; 13...⌶xf3
14 gxf3 ♗xf3 15 ♗e2 ♗xh1 16 ⌶xh5
+- **14 ♗e2 ♕a5 15 ♔b1 ♗f6 16 ♘d4?!**
♗xe2 17 ♕xe2 d5!? 18 ♘e6 ⌶fc8 19
♘xd5? 19 exd5 ♘b4 20 ♗d4 ⌶xc3
21 bxc3 ♘bxd5 22 c4 ♘c3+ 23 ♗xc3
♕xc3 24 ⌶c1 +- **♗xd5 20 exd5 ♘b4
21 a3 ♘xd5 22 ♗d4 ♗f6 23 ♕g4?**
Zeitnot 23 ♗xf6 ♘xf6 24 g4 ⌶e8
25 ⌶he1 +=; 23 ♕e4! ♗xd4 24 ♕xd4
♘f6 25 ⌶hf1±; 23 ⌶c1!? **♕a4! 24
♕g3?** 24 ⌶c1!=

**24...♘c3+!! 25 ♗xc3 ⌶xc3 26 bxc3
♕b3+ 27 ♔c1 ⌶c8?** 27...♕xa3+ 28
♔c2 ♕a2+ 29 ♔c1 ♕xe6∓ **28 ⌶d8+!
⌶xd8 29 ♘xd8 ♕xa3+ 30 ♔c2 ♕a2+
31 ♔d3 ♕d5+ 32 ♔c2 ♕a2+ 33 ♔d3
♕d5+ 34 ♔c2 ½-½ Tompa**

35 Mohring-Enders
DDR Final 78

**1 c4 f5 2 ♘f3 ♘f6 3 b3 e6 4 ♗b2
♗e7 5 g3 0-0 6 ♗g2 c6 7 0-0 d5 8 ♕c2
♘bd7 9 ♘d4** 9 cxd5 exd5 10 ♕xf5
♘e4 11 ♕g4 ♗f6 12 ♘c3 ♘e5 -+;
9 d3!? Δ ♘bd2, e4± **♘c5 10 cxd5
exd5 11 ♘xf5** 11 b4!? **♗xf5 12 ♕xf5**

♞fe4 13 ♕g4 ♗f6 14 d4? 14 ♘c3 ♘xd2 15 ♖fd1 ♕e8 △ h5 +- 15 e3 15 ♗xe4 ♘xe4 16 e3 ♘xf2! 17 ♖xf2 ♕xe3 18 ♕e2 ♗xd4 -+; 18 ♘a3 ♗g5 19 ♖af1 ♖xf2 20 ♖xf2 ♕e1+ 21 ♔g2 ♗e3 22 ♖e2 ♕g1+ 23 ♔h3 ♕f1+ 24 ♖g2 ♖e8 25 ♘c2 ♗d2≈ ♞xf2 16 ♖xf2 ♘d3 17 ♕e2 17 ♖e2 ♘xb2 18 ♖xb2 ♕xe3+ ♞xf2 18 ♕xf2 ♗g5 19 ♕e1 ♕xe3+ 20 ♕xe3 ♗xe3+ 21 ♔h1 ♖f2 22 ♗c3 ♖c2 23 ♗f1 ♖f8 24 ♗d3 ♖c1+ 25 ♔g2 ♖f2+ 26 ♔h3 ♖h1 **0-1 Malich**

1 c4 ♘f6

36 Christiansen-Brasket
Lone Pine 78

1 c4 ♘f6 2 ♘c3 e6 3 e4 c5 4 e5 ♘g8 5 ♘f3 ♘c6 6 d4 cxd4 7 ♘xd4 ♘xe5 8 ♘db5 f6 9 ♗e3 b6?! 9...a6 10 ♘d6+ ♗xd6 11 ♕xd6 ♘e7 12 ♗b6 ♘f5! 10 f4!± ♘c6 11 f5 ♘e5 11...exf5?? 12 ♘d5 +- 12 ♕h5+ g6 13 fxg6 ♘xg6 14 ♗d3 ♗g7 15 0-0 a6 16 ♘d6+ ♔f8

17 c5! +- bxc5 18 ♗xc5 ♘8e7 1-0 19 ♘ce4 +- **Gheorghiu**

37 Adorjan-Jvenekilde Denmark 78
1 c4 ♘f6 2 ♘c3 e6 3 e4 d5!? 4 e5 ♘fd7 5 cxd5 ♘xe5 6 d4 ♘g6 7 dxe6

♗xe6 8 d5 += ♗c8 9 g3 ♗e7 10 ♗g2 0-0 11 ♘ge2 ♘d7 12 0-0 ♖e8 13 h3 ♘f6 14 b3?! 14 ♘f4 += a6! 15 ♗b2 ♗d6 16 ♕d2 ♗d7 17 ♖ae1 ♕c8 18 ♔h2?? ♗h4!∓ 19 ♘g1 ♖xe1 20 ♖xe1 ♘xg2 21 ♔xg2 c6! 22 ♘e4 22 ♔h2 ♘xe4 23 ♖xe4 cxd5 24 ♗xg7 ♗f5! 24...♔xg7? 25 ♕g5+ =; 24...dxe4?? ♕g5 +- 25 ♖h4 ♗e7 25...♔xg7? 26 ♕h6+ +- 26 ♗b2 ♗xh4 27 ♕d4 f6! 28 ♕xh4 ♗e4+ 29 ♔h2 ♕f5! 30 ♕xf6 ♕xf6 31 ♗xf6 ♖c8 32 a4 ♖c2 33 ♗d4 ♖d2 34 ♗e3 ♖d1 0-1

38 Gheorghiu-Garcia Palermo
Lone Pine 78

1 c4 ♘f6 2 ♘c3 e6 3 ♘f3 ♗b4 4 ♕c2 b6 5 a3 ♗xc3 6 ♕xc3 ♗b7 7 b4! += d6 8 ♗b2 ♘bd7 8...e5 9 d4± 9 e3 0-0 10 ♗e2 e5 11 d4 ♗e4! 12 ♕c2 ♕e7 13 d5!± f5 14 0-0 ♘df6 15 ♘h4!? 15 ♘e1! △ ♘d3/f3± g6 16 f3 ♗g5 17 ♖ae1 c6 18 dxc6 ♗xc6 19 ♕b3 ♕e6 20 e4! fxe4?! 20...f4∝ 21 f4!± exf4 22 ♖xf4 ♘d7 23 ♗g4!? 23 ♕g3! ♖xf4 24 ♕xf4 ♘f7 25 ♗g4 ♕e7 26 ♗xd7 ♕xd7 27 ♕f6 ♘e5 28 ♖d1!±; 26...♗xd7 27 ♖xe4± ♕e7 24 ♖xf8+ 24 c5+ d5 ♖xf8 25 c5+ d5 26 ♗xd7 ♕xd7 27 ♕c3 d4!! 28 ♕xd4 ♕xd4+ 29 ♗xd4 ♘e6! 30 ♗f2 30 ♗e3 g5 -+ bxc5 31 bxc5 ♘f4 31...g5 32 ♘f3 32 ♗e3 g5 33 ♗xf4 ♖xf4 34 g3 ♖f6 35 ♘g2 ♖f5! 36 ♖c1 ♖f3 37 a4 ♔f7 38 a5 ♔e6 39 ♖d1! ♗d5 40 a6 ♖c3 41 ♖b1∝ Zeitnot ♖xc5 42 ♖b8 ♖a5 43 ♘e3 ♖a1+ 44 ♔f2 ♖a2+ 45 ♔g1 ♖e2 46 ♘xd5 ♔xd5 47 ♖b7!= ½-½ **Gheorghiu**

39 Korchnoi-Kraidman Beersheva 78
1 c4 ♘f6 2 ♘c3 e6 3 ♘f3 b6 4 e4 ♗b7 5 ♗d3! ♗b4?! 5...c5! 6 e5 ♘g8 7 ♗e4 ♗xe4 8 ♘xe4 d5 9 exd6 ♗xd6 10

0-0 ♘f6 11 ♗xf6+ ♕xf6 12 ♕a4+?!
12 d4 += c6 13 d4 0-0 14 ♗g5 ♕f5
15 ♖fe1 b5! 16 ♕a5! 16 cxb5 cxb5=
h6 16...bxc4 17 ♕xf5 exf5 18 ♖ac1±
17 ♗d2 ♘d7 18 c5 ♗f4 19 ♗xf4 ♕xf4
20 a4 ♖fb8 21 ♖e2 ♖b7 22 h3 bxa4
23 ♕xa4 ♕c7 24 ♕a6 ♖ab8 25 ♖a2
g6 26 ♕a5 ♕g7 26...♕xa5 27 ♖xa5
♖c7 Δ ♖bb7 += 27 ♕e1 ♕f4 28
♕a1! e5! 28...♕c7 29 ♘d2 Δ ♘c4
29 ♘xe5 ♘xe5 30 dxe5 ♖e8 31 b4
♖e6 32 ♖xa7 ♖xb4 33 ♖d7 ♕c4?
33...♖e4! 34 ♖xe4 ♕xe4 35 ♖d6
♕xe5 36 ♕xe5+ ♖xe5 37 ♖xc6 ♖e1+
38 ♔h2 ♖c1 += 34 ♖e3! ♕c2 35 ♖f3
♖b1+ 36 ♔h2 g5 36...♖xa1 37 ♖dxf7+
+- 37 ♕a8 ♕e4 38 ♖dxf7+ ♔g6 39
♕g8+ ♔h5 40 ♖7f5 ♕e1 41 ♖xg5+!
1-0 Keene

1 d4 d5 2 c4 dxc4

40 Gligoric-Miles Bugojno 78
1 d4 d5 2 c4 dxc4 3 ♘f3 ♘f6 4 e3
♗g4 5 ♗xc4 e6 6 ♘c3 ♘bd7 7 ♗e2
♗d6 8 e4 ♗b4 9 ♗g5 N 9 e5 ♘d5 10
♕b3 c5 h6 9...c5?! 10 e5 h6 11
exf6 hxg5 12 fxg7 ♖g8 13 0-0±
10 ♗xf6 ♗xc3+ 11 bxc3 ♘xf6 12
♘e5 ♗xe2 13 ♕xe2 0-0 14 0-0 c5=
15 ♖ad1 cxd4 16 cxd4 ♖c8 17 ♖d3
♕a5 18 ♖g3 ♖c3! 19 ♘d3?! ♖d8 =+
19...♕h5!? 20 ♕e1!≈ 20 ♕e3 ♘e8!
21 d5 21 ♕xh6? ♖xd3 -+ exd5
22 e5 d4 22...♕xa2?! 23 ♕xh6! ♖xd3?
24 ♕h4! 23 ♕e2 ♕a6 24 f4 f5! 24...
♖dc8?! 25 f5 Δ ♕h5, f6 25 exf6 25
e6!? ♘f6!? 26 ♕e5 ♘h5 ♕xf6 25...
♘xf6?? 26 ♖xg7+ 26 f5 ♕f7 27 ♕d2
27 ♘e5 ♕c7 28 f6 ♘xf6 29 ♖xf6
♖xg3 30 hxg3 d3 -+; 28 ♘g6 ♘f6
♘f6 28 ♖e1 ♖e8 29 ♘e5 ♕d5 30
♘g4!? 30 ♖xc3 dxc3 31 ♕xc3 ♘e4
32 ♕c4 ♖xe5 ∓/-+; 32 ♘g6 ♕xf5!

♖xe1+ 31 ♕xe1 ♘e4! 32 ♘xh6+
32 ♕xe4 ♖c1+ 33 ♔f2 ♕xa2+ -+;
32 ♖xc3 dxc3 -+ ♔h7!? 32...♔f8
33 ♖g4 33 ♖g4

33...d3! -+ Δ d2, ♕c5+ 34 ♕xe4
♕xe4 35 ♖xe4 d2 36 ♖d4 ♖c1+ 37
♔f2 d1♕ 38 ♖xd1 ♖xd1 39 ♘f7
♖d2+ 40 ♔f3 ♖xa2 41 h4 a5 42
♘d6 a4 43 g4 a3 44 g5 ♖d2 45 ♘e4
0-1 Miles

1 d4 d5 2 c4 c6

41 Zaltsman-Bohm Lone Pine 78
1 c4 c6 2 ♘f3 d5 3 d4 ♘f6 4 ♘c3 dxc4
5 a4 ♗f5 6 e3 e6 7 ♗xc4 ♗b4 8 0-0
♘bd7 9 ♕e2 ♗g6 10 ♖d1 10 e4!?
♗xc3 11 bxc3∝ ♕c7 11 ♗d3 ♗xd3
12 ♖xd3 e5 13 e4 0-0-0 14 ♗g5!
exd4 15 ♖xd4 ♗xc3 16 bxc3 h6 17
♗h4 ♖he8 18 ♖ad1 ♘c5 19 e5 g5 20
♖xd8+ ♖xd8 21 ♖xd8+ ♕xd8 22
♘xg5!± hxg5 23 ♗xg5 ♘xa4 24 ♗xf6
♕d7 25 h4 ♘xc3 26 ♕f3 ♕d2 27
♔h2 ♘e2 28 ♗g5 ♕e1 29 e6! 1-0
29...fxe6 30 ♕f8+ Δ ♕d8+ Gheorghiu

42 Podgaets-Svedchikov USSR 77
1 d4 d5 2 c4 c6 3 ♘f3 ♘f6 4 ♘c3
dxc4 5 a4 ♗f5 6 e3 e6 7 ♗xc4 ♗b4 8
0-0 0-0 9 ♕e2 9 ♘h4 ♗g6 10 f3 ♘h5
11 g4 += ♗g4 10 ♖d1 ♘bd7 11 e4 ♖c8

12 h3 &xf3 13 ♕xf3 e5 14 ♘e2 ♕e7 15 ♘g3 exd4 16 ♖xd4 ♘e5 17 ♕e2 &c5 18 ♘f5 ♕e8? 18...♕c7

19 &e3!! &xd4 20 &xd4 ♖d8 21 &c3! 21 &c5?! ♘g6 21...♘xc4 22 &xf6 +− 22 ♕f3 ♘h5?! 22...♘xe4 23 ♖e1 +−; 22...♕xe4 23 ♘h6+ ♔h8 24 ♕xf6 +−; 22...♘e5 23 ♕g3 ♘g6 24 ♕g5 ♘xe4 25 ♕h6! +− 23 ♕xh5 ♕xe4 24 ♕h6! 1-0 Gufeld

43 Pachman-Hermann
BRD Final 78

1 d4 d5 2 c4 c6 3 ♘f3 ♘f6 4 ♘c3 dxc4 5 a4 &f5 6 e3 e6 7 &xc4 &b4 8 0-0 0-0 9 ♘h4 9 ♕e2 ♘bd7 10 e4 &g6 11 &d3 &h5! 12 e5 ♘d5 ♘bd7 9...&g4 10 f3 &h5 11 g4 &g6 12 ♘xg6 hxg6 13 ♕b3 ♕e7 14 g5 ♘d5 15 e4 Karpov-Portisch, Portoroz 75 10 f3 &g6 11 e4?! 11 ♘xg6 hxg6 12 ♕c2! a5 13 ♖d1 ♕b6 14 ♔h1 ♖ac8 15 ♖b1! e5?! 11...♕a5 12 ♘a2 ♘b6 13 &e2 ♖fd8 △ ♖xd4 12 ♘xg6?! 12 dxe5! ♘xe5 13 &e2 hxg6 13 &e3 exd4? 13...♕e7; 13...♕b6! 14 &xd4 &c5 15 &xc5 ♘xc5 16 e5! ♘fd7 17 ♕e2 ♕e7 18 f4! ♖ad8? 18...b6 △ a6, b5 19 ♔h1 a5 20 ♘e4 ♘xe4 21 ♕xe4 ♘b6 21...♘c5? 22 ♕xg6 22 &b3 ♘d5 23 ♖ad1 ♕e6 24 ♖d4 ♖d7 25 h3 ♖fd8 26 ♔h2 f5 27 ♕e1 b6 28

♕g3 ♘f8 29 ♖fd1 ♕e8 30 ♕g5 ♕e6 31 ♖4d3 ♘f7 32 ♔g1 ♕e7 33 ♕g3 ♕c5+ 34 ♔h1 ♕e7 35 ♕f2 ♕b4 36 ♕g3 ♕e7 37 ♕e3 ♕e6 38 ♕f3 ♔f8 39 ♖1d2 ♕e7 40 ♔g1 ♔f8 41 ♕g3 ♕e8 42 ♕h4! ♔f7 43 ♕h7 ♕e6 44 h4! ♖g8 45 ♖g3 ♖dd8 46 h5 gxh5 47 ♖g5 ♖d7 48 ♖xh5 ♔e8 49 ♕xf5 ♕xf5 50 ♖xf5 ♘e7 51 ♖xd7 ♔xd7 52 ♖f7 ♖b8 53 ♖xg7 b5 54 f5 bxa4 55 &e6+ ♔d8 56 f6 1-0

44 Keene-Birnboim Beersheva 78
1 d4 d5 2 c4 c6 3 ♘f3 ♘f6 4 ♘c3 dxc4 5 a4 &f5 6 ♘e5! ♘bd7 6...e6 7 f3! &b4 8 e4 ♘xe4 9 fxe4 ♘xe4 10 &d2 += 7 ♘xc4 e6 8 f3 &b4 9 ♕b3?! 9 e4! ♘xe4? 10 fxe4 ♕h4+ 11 ♔d2 ♕xe4 12 ♘d6+ +− a5 10 e4 &g6 11 &g5 ♕b8 12 &e2 0-0 13 0-0 b5 14 axb5 cxb5 15 ♘e3 e5 16 d5 ♕b6 17 ♔h1 ♘c5 17...h6 18 &xf6 ♕xe3 19 ♘h4 &xc3 20 &xb5! 18 ♕c2 &xc3 19 ♕xc3 19 bxc3 ♘fxe4 20 fxe4 ♘xe4 21 ♘f5 ♘xg5 22 h4 &xf5 23 ♖xf5 ♕h6 &fxe4 20 fxe4 ♘xe4 21 ♕c6! ♕xc6? 21...♕a7!∝ 22 dxc6 ♘xg5 23 ♘d5± ♘e6 24 c7 ♘d4 25 ♘e7+ ♔h8 26 &f3 ♖ae8 26...♘xf3 27 gxf3 ♖ae8 28 ♖fc1 +− 27 ♘xg6+ hxg6 28 &b7 ♘b3 29 ♖ae1 ♘d2 30 ♖f2 ♘c4 31 &a6 ♘b6 32 ♖d2 ♖a8 33 &xb5 ♖ac8 34 ♖c1 ♘a8 35 ♖dc2 ♘xc7 36 ♖xc7 ♖xc7 37 ♖xc7 ♖d8? 38 ♖xf7 +− ♖b8 39 &d3 ♖d8 40 &c4 ♖d4 41 b3 1-0 Keene

45 Gheorghiu-Bisguier
Lone Pine 78
1 d4 ♘f6 2 c4 e6 3 ♘f3 d5 4 ♘c3 c6 5 &g5 h6 5...dxc4 6 e4 b5 7 e5 h6 8 &h4 g5 9 ♘xg5 hxg5 10 &xg5 ♘bd7∝ 6 &xf6 ♕xf6 7 ♕b3 7 e3 += ♘d7 8 e3 &d6 9 &d3 0-0 10 0-0 ♕e7 11

♖ad1! dxc4 12 ♗xc4 e5 13 ♘e4!±
♗c7 13...exd4 14 ♘xd6 ♕xd6 15
♖xd4 △ ♖fd1 14 d5 cxd5 15 ♗xd5
♖d8 16 ♖c1 ♗b6 17 ♖fd1 ♘f6 18
♘xf6+ ♕xf6 19 a4! ♖b8 20 h3 ♗d7
21 ♕b4!± △ a5 ♖e8 22 a5 ♗d8 23
a6! ♗e7 23...♕xa6 24 ♗xf7+ ♖xd7
+− 24 ♕e4 ♗f5 25 ♕xe5 bxa6 26
♖c6! +− ♗e6 27 ♗xe6 fxe6 28 ♖xe6
♕xe5 29 ♘xe5 ♗f6 30 ♖xe8+ ♖xe8
31 ♘c4! ♖b8 32 ♖d7 32 ♖d6 +−
♖b4 33 ♖c7 ♘h7 34 g3 ♗d8 35 ♖c6
a5 36 ♔f1 a4 37 e4 ♗b6 38 e5 ♗d4
39 ♔g2

39...♖xb2! 40 ♘xb2 a3 41 ♘c4 a2
42 ♖a6 a1♕ 43 ♖xa1 ♗xa1 44 f4
♗c3 45 ♔f3 a5 46 ♘b6! ♗d4 47 e6
♔g8 48 ♘a4! h5 44 ♔e4 ♗f2 50
g4 hxg4 51 hxg4 ♔f8 52 f5 ♔e7 53
♔d5 ♗h4 54 ♘c5 g6!? 55 fxg6 ♔f6
56 ♔d6!? Zeitnot 56 ♘e4+! ♔xg6
57 g5! +− ♔xg6 57 ♔d7 57 ♘e4!
a4 58 g5 ♗e1 59 ♔d7 ♗b4 60 ♘d6 +−
♔g7!! 58 ♘e4 a4 59 g5 ♗xg5 60 ♘xg5
a3 61 e7 a2 62 ♘e6+ ♔h6 63 e8♕
a1♕ 64 ♕f8+ ♔g6 65 ♕g8+ ♔f5 66
♕h7+ ♔g4 67 ♕e4+ ♔g3 68 ♕e3+
♔h2 69 ♕e2+ ♔h1 70 ♕f3+ ♔g1 71
♘f4 ♕a7+ 72 ♔e6 ♕b6+ 73 ♔f7 ♕c7+
74 ♔g6 ♕d6+ 75 ♔h5 ♕e5+ 76 ♔g4
♕g7+ ½-½ Gheorghiu

46 Manin-Shabanov USSR 77
1 ♘f3 ♘f6 2 d4 d5 3 c4 c6 4 cxd5
cxd5 5 ♘c3 ♘c6 6 ♗f4 e6! 6...♗f5
7 e3 e6 8 ♗b5 ♗d7 9 ♕a4! ♕b6 10
♘h4! +=; 9...♖c8 10 0-0 a6 11 ♗xc6
♖xc6 12 ♖fc1 △ ♘e2 += 7 e3 ♗d6
7...♗e7?! 8 ♗g3 0-0 8...♗e4?! 9 ♘xe4
dxe4 10 ♘d2 ♗xg3 11 hxg3 e5?!
12 dxe5 ♕a5 13 ♕b3 += 9 ♗d3 g6!?
9...♖e8 10 ♘e5 ♗xe5 11 dxe5 ♘d7
12 f4 ♘c5 13 ♗b1 b6 14 ♘b5 ♗a6
15 ♘d6 ♘b4 16 ♗xh7+ ♔xh7 17 ♕h5+
♔g8 18 ♕xf7+ ♔h7 19 ♕h5+ ½-½
Silva-Durao (6) 78 10 ♖c1 += ♗xg3
11 hxg3 ♕b6 12 ♕e2 ♗d7 13 a3 ♖fc8!
13...♖ac8 14 0-0! += 14 b4?! 14 ♘g5?!
♔g7 15 ♕f3 ♗e8 △ h6 =+; 14 ♖c2!?
♗e8! 15 0-0 ♘a5 16 ♘e5 += ♖c7!
15 ♘g5?! 15 ♘a4 ♘xd4 16 ♘xb6
♖xc1+ 17 ♕d1 ♘xf3+ 18 gxf3 ♖xd1+
19 ♔xd1 axb6∓; 15 ♘b5!? ♖cc8!=
♘xb4! 15...♘e8!? 16 ♘a4 ♘xd4! =+;
16 ♗b1 ♘a6? 16...♗e8 17 axb4 ♕xb4
18 ♕d3 ♖ac8 19 ♔d2 ♘e4+! 20 ♘xe4
dxe4 21 ♕c2 ♗b5∓ 17 ♕f3! ♖xc3
17...♔g7 18 ♖xh7+! 18 ♕xf6! ♖xc1+
19 ♔e2 ♖xh1 20 ♕xf7+ ♔h8 21
♕f6+ ♔g8= 22 ♗xg6? △ ♗f7+ ♕d8!∓
22...hxg6 23 ♕xg6+ ♔h8 24 ♘f7 mate
23 ♗f7+ ♔f8 24 ♕f4 ♔g7 25 ♕g4
♗b5+ 0-1 Gufeld

1 d4 d5 2 c4

47 Portisch-Sosonko
Wijk aan Zee 78
1 ♘f3 d5 2 d4 ♘f6 3 c4 c5 4 cxd5
cxd4 5 ♕xd4 ♕xd5 6 ♘c3 ♕xd4
7 ♘xd4 a6 8 g3 8 ♗g5!? ♗d7 9 ♗g2
e5 10 ♘c2 10 ♗xb7?? ♖a7 ♗c6 11 0-0
+= ♗xg2 12 ♔xg2 ♘bd7 13 ♖d1 ♖c8
14 ♘e3 ♗c5 15 ♘ed5 ♗d4 16 ♗e3!
♗xc3 17 ♘xc3 ♗e7 18 ♖d2 ♖c6 19
♖ad1 ♘b6 20 ♗xb6 ♖xb6 21 f4 exf4

22 gxf4 ♜c8 23 ♚f3 ♚e6 24 ♜d3! ♚e7 24...♖xb2? 25 ♖e3+ ♔f5 26 ♖g1 **25 ♜1d2± ♚e8 26 e4 ♞g8 27 ♞d5 ♜bc6 28 a4 ♞f6 29 ♞e3 g6 30 ♜b3 b6 31 ♜bd3 ♞g8 32 ♞d5 ♞e7 33 ♞c3 ♜6c7 34 ♚e2 ♜c4 35 ♜h3! h5 36 ♜hd3 ♜b4 37 ♚f3 f5 38 ♜d7** Δ ♖xe7+ **♜xb2 39 ♜xe7+ ♚xe7 40 ♞d5+ ♚d6 41 e5+!** 41 ♖xb2 fxe4+ 42 ♔xe4 ♖c4+ = **♚e6 42 ♜xb2 ♚xd5 43 ♜d2+!?** 43 ♖xb6 ♖c3+ = **♚e6 44 ♜d6+ ♚f7 45 ♜f6+ ♚g7?** 45...♔e7! **46 ♜xb6 ♜c3+ 47 ♚g2 ♜c4 48 ♜xa6 ♜xf4 49 ♜a7+ ♚f8 50 a5 ♜a4 51 a6 1-0** 51...♔e8 52 e6! ♔f8 53 e7+ ♔e8 54 ♖a8+ ♔xe7 55 a7 Δ ♖h8 +− **Pytel**

48 Heinig-Starck
DDR Final 78

1 d4 d5 2 c4 e5 3 dxe5 d4 4 ♞f3 c5?! 4...♘c6 5 g3 **5 e3 ♞c6 6 exd4 cxd4 7 ♝d3 ♞ge7** 7...♗g4 8 0-0 ♘ge7 9 ♗f4 ♘g6 10 ♗g3 ♘gxe5 11 ♗xe5 ♘xe5 12 ♕e1!; 10...♗xf3 11 ♕xf3 ♘gxe5 12 ♖e1 ♗d6 13 ♗xe5 ♘xe5 14 c5! **8 h3! ♞g6 9 0-0 ♝e7 10 ♜e1 0-0 11 ♞bd2 ♝b4** 11...♗e6 12 ♘b3 ♕d7 13 ♗xg6 hxg6 14 ♘fxd4 ♘xd4 15 ♕xd4 ♕xd4 16 ♘xd4 ♗xc4 17 ♗e3 **12 a3 ♝xd2 13 ♝xd2 ♜e8 14 ♛c2! ♝e6 15 b4 ♛d7 16 ♜ad1 ♜ac8 17 ♝c1 b5 18 c5 ♝d5 19 ♝xg6 ♝xf3** 19...hxg6 20 ♘xd4 ♘xe5 21 ♘xb5 **20 ♝xh7+ ♚h8 21 ♛f5!** 21 gxf3 g6! 22 ♗xg6 fxg6 23 ♕xg6 **♜e6 22 ♛xf3 ♚xh7 23 ♝b2 ♚g8 24 ♜e4 ♞xe5?! 25 ♛g3 ♞c6 26 ♜exd4 1-0** 26...♘xd4 27 ♖xd4 ♖e1+ 28 ♔h2 ♕c7 29 ♖d8+

49 Portisch-Holm Denmark 78

1 c4 c5 2 ♞f3 e6 3 ♞c3 d5 4 cxd5 exd5 5 d4 ♞c6 6 g3 c4!? 7 ♝g2 ♝b4 8 0-0 ♞ge7 9 e4 dxe4 10 ♞xe4 ♝g4 11 a3! ♝a5 12 ♝f4 0-0 13 ♞d6!? ♝c7 14 ♞xb7 ♛b8 15 ♝xc7 ♛xc7 16 d5 ♛xb7 17 dxc6 ♞xc6? 17...♕xb2

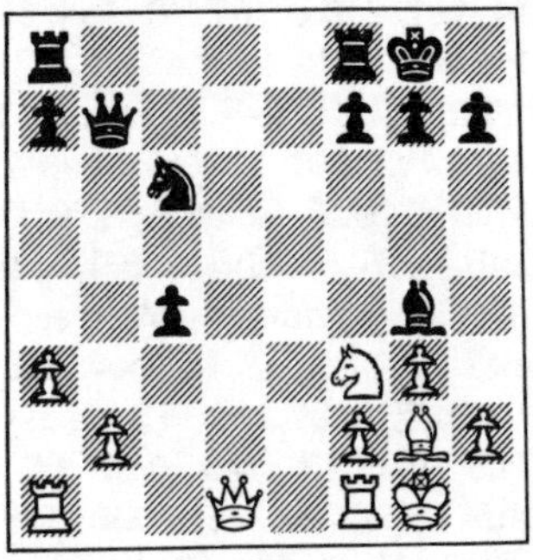

18 ♛a4! +− ♝d7 19 ♛xc4 ♛xb2 20 ♜ad1 ♝e8 21 ♞g5! ♜c8 22 ♛e4 g6 23 ♛h4 ♛g7 24 ♜fe1 h6 25 ♞e4 g5 26 ♛h3 ♜c7 27 ♛f5 +− ♜e7 28 ♞f6+ ♚h8 29 ♞xe8 ♜fxe8 30 ♜xe7 ♞xe7 31 ♛d7 1-0

50 Farago-Marjanovic Dortmund 78

1 d4 d5 2 c4 e6 3 ♞c3 c5 4 e3 ♞f6 5 ♞f3 ♞c6 6 a3 a6 6...♘e4! **7 b3 ♝e7 8 ♝b2 0-0 9 ♝d3 b6 10 0-0 ♝b7 11 ♜c1 ♜e8?!** 11...cxd4! **12 cxd5 exd5 13 dxc5 ♝xc5** 13...bxc5 14 ♘a4! **14 ♞e2 ♝d6 15 b4 ♞e4 16 ♞g3 ♞e5? 17 ♞xe5 ♝xe5 18 ♝xe5 ♜xe5 19 ♝xe4! dxe4 20 ♛xd8+ ♜xd8 21 ♜c7± ♜b8 22 ♞e2 ♚f8 23 ♜fc1 a5 24 ♞d4 axb4 25 axb4 ♝d5 26 ♚f1 ♜a8 27 ♜d7 b5 28 ♞xb5 ♝e6 29 ♜a7 ♜xa7** 29...♖b8! **30 ♞xa7 ♜d5 31 ♚e1 ♜d3 32 ♜b1 ♜a3 33 ♞c6 ♝c4 34 b5 ♜a2 35 ♞d4 ♝d3 36 ♜b3 ♜a1+ 37 ♚d2 ♜a2+ 38 ♚c3! +− ♜xf2 39 b6 ♝a6 40 ♜a3 ♝b7 41 ♜a7 ♝d5 42 ♜d7 ♜f6 43 ♜d8+ ♚e7 44 ♜xd5 1-0 Keene**

51 Kavalek-Andersson (5) 78

1 c4 c5 2 ♞f3 ♞f6 3 ♞c3 e6 4 e3

d5 5 d4 ♘c6 6 cxd5 ♘xd5 7 ♗d3 7 ♘c4
cxd4 8 exd4 ♗e7 9 0-0 0-0 10 ♖e1
Botvinnik-Alekhine, AVRO 38 **cxd4
8 exd4 ♗e7 9 0-0 0-0 10 ♖e1** 10 a3
♘f6 11 ♗g5 h6? 12 ♗h4 ♔h8 13 ♘c2
g5 14 ♗g3 g4 15 ♗e5! Kavalek-Grefe,
USA Final 73 **♗f6 11 ♗e4** 11 a3 ♘xc3
12 bxc3 b6 **♕d6 12 ♗c2** 12 ♕d3 h6
13 ♗xd5 exd5 14 ♘b5 ♕b8 15 g3 ♗g4
16 ♗f4 Miles-Andersson, Wijk aan Zee
78 **♘ce7** 12...♘db4? 13 ♘e4 ♕e7 14
♘xf6+ ♕xf6 15 ♗g5; 12...♘cb4 13
♗e4; 13 ♗b1 **13 ♘e5 ♘g6 14 ♘g4
14 ♕h5!?** ♕e7 **♗e7 15 ♘e5 ♗f6 16
♘e4 ♕b6 17 ♘xf6+ ♗xf6 18 ♗g5!
♘d5** 18...♕xb2 19 ♗xf6 gxf6 20
♘g4 f5 21 ♘f6+ ♔g7 22 ♘h5+ ♔h8
23 ♕d2; 20...♔g7 21 ♕d2 **19 ♗b3
♕d6 20 ♕f3 b6 21 ♗xd5 ♕xd5** 21...
exd5 22 ♘xg6 hxg6 23 ♗e7 **22 ♕xd5
exd5 23 ♘xg6 hxg6 24 ♖e7 ♗f5 25
♖c1 ♖fc8 26 ♖cc7 ♖xc7 27 ♖xc7
♕f8 28 ♖b7 ♖e8 29 ♗d2 ♖a8 30
h4 ♗c8 31 ♖c7** 31 ♗b4+ ♔g8 32 ♖e7
♗e6 33 ♗d6!? **♗e6 32 f3 32** ♗b4+
♕e8 **33 g4 ♗d7 34 ♗f4 ♕e7 35 ♖b7
♕e6 36 b3** 36 ♖b8 ♖xb8 37 ♗xb8
a6 38 ♗e5 f6 39 ♗c7 b5 40 ♗a5 ♗c6
37 ♖c7 ♗d7 38 ♕f2 b5 38...a6 39
♖b7 b5 40 ♖b6+ **39 ♕e3 a5 40 ♖b7
♗c6 41 ♖c7 ♗d7 42 ♖b7 ♗c6 43 ♖b8
43** ♖b6 ♔d7 44 ♖b8! a4?! 45 b4 a3
46 ♔d3 ♖a4 47 ♔c3; 44...b4; 44
♖b8 ♖xb8 45 ♗xb8 **♖xb8 44 ♗xb8
a4 45 ♕d2 axb3 46 axb3 ♗e8 47
♗a7 f6 48 ♗b6 g5 49 h5 ♗d7 50 ♕c3
f5 51 ♗d8 fxg4 52 fxg4 ♕d6 ½-½**

52 Miles-Ljubojevic Bugojno 78

1 c4 c5 2 ♘f3 ♘f6 2 ♘c3 e6 4 e3
d5 5 d4 ♘c6 6 cxd5 exd5 7 ♗e2
♗d6 8 0-0 0-0 9 b3 9 ♘b5!? **cxd4
10 ♘xd4 ♘xd4 11 ♕xd4 ♖e8** 11...
♕c7?! 12 ♘b5 ♗xh2+ 13 ♔h1 ♕b8

14 g3±; 14 f4!?; 13...♕e5 14 ♘a3
♖fd8 15 g3 ♗xg3 16 fxg3 ♕xg3 17
♖f3 **12 ♗b2 ♗e5 13 ♕d2 ♗g4!? 14
♗xg4 ♗xh2+?** 14...♘xg4 15 h3 +=
15 ♕xh2 15 ♔h1?! ♘xg4 16 g3 ♕g5
17 ♔g2 ♗xg3 18 fxg3 ♘xe3+ 19 ♔h1
♕xg3 ∓/-+ **♘xg4+**

16 ♕h3! 16 ♔g3 ♕g5 **17 ♕d4!?** 17 g3
♕h5+ 18 ♔g2 ♕h2+ 19 ♔f3 ♘xe3;
17 ♖h1 d4! (17...♖d8 Δ d4≈) 18
♕xd4 ♘xf2+ 19 ♔h2 ♕h5+ Δ ♘xh1;
18 ♘d1 dxe3 **♕h5+** 17...f5 18 g3!
**18 ♕g3 ♘h6 19 ♖h1 ♗f5+ 20 ♕f4
♕g6** 20...♕xh1 21 ♖xh1 ♘xd4 22
exd4 ±/+- **21 ♕xd5 ♖e6 22 ♕xf5**
22 g4 ♘e7 23 ♕h5? ♕c2! Δ ♕xb2/
♕xf2+; 23 ♕d2 ♖f6+ 24 ♔g3 ♘f5+
25 ♔h3 h5≈; 22 ♔f3 ♖ae8 23 ♘d1
±/+- **♖f6 23 g4?!** 23 ♕xf6 ♕xf6+
24 ♔g3 **♖xf5+ 24 gxf5 ♕g2 25 ♖af1**
25 ♘e4?? ♖e8 26 ♘f6+ gxf6 27 ♖ag1
♖e4 mate **g5+ 26 fxg6** 26 ♔e5?!
♖e8+ 27 ♔f6 h6! 28 e4 ♕f3! Δ ♖e6
mate; 28 ♖xh6 ♕xf1 29 ♘d5 ♕xf2
**fxg6 27 e4 ♖f8+ 28 ♕e3 ♕f3+ 29
♕d2 ♖d8+ 30 ♕c2 ♕d3+ 31 ♕c1
♖c8 32 ♖d1 ♕xe4?** 32...♖xc3+ 33
♗xc3 ♕xc3+ 34 ♔b1 ♕f3 35 ♖d8+
♔g7 36 ♖d7+ ♔f6 37 ♖hxh7 ♕xe4+
38 ♔c1 ♕e1+ 38 ♔b2 ♕e5+ 39 ♔c2
♕e2+ 40 ♖d2 ±/+-; 35 ♖he1 ♕xf2
36 e5 ♕f5+ 37 ♔b2 ♕e6 (37...♕xf2+

38 ♔a1) 38 ♖d6 (38 a4!? △ ♔a3)
♕f5 39 ♖f6 ♕g4≈; 37 ♔a1 ♕e6;
37 ♔c1 ♕f4+ 38 ♔b2; 37...♕e6 38
♖d6 ♕e7 33 ♖d8+ ♔g7 34 ♖d7+ ♔f6
35 ♖hxh7 ♕e1+ 36 ♔c2 ♕xf2+ 37
♔b1 ♕f1+ 38 ♖d1 ♕g2 39 ♘d5+
♔g5 40 ♗f6+ 1-0 Miles

53 Gheorghiu-Voiculescu
Rumania 78

1 c4 ♘f6 2 ♘c3 e6 3 ♘f3 d5 4 d4
♗b4 5 ♗g5 h6 6 ♗xf6 ♗xc3+ 6...♕xf6
7 ♕a4+ ♘c6 8 ♖c1 += 7 bxc3 ♕xf6
8 g3!± 8 e3 += 0-0 9 ♗g2 ♘d7 10
cxd5 exd5 11 0-0 ♕d6 12 ♘d2! △
e4, c4 ♘b6 12...♘f6 13 c4± 13 e4!
dxe4 14 ♘xe4 ♕d8 15 ♘c5 c6 16 ♕b3
♕c7 17 ♖fe1 ♖b8 18 a4! ♘d7 19
♘e4± b6 20 ♕a3 20 c4 ♗b7 21 ♖ad1±
c5 21 d5 ♘e5 22 d6! ♕d8 23 f4
♘g4 23...♘d3 24 ♖e3± 24 ♖ad1
♗d7 25 a5 25 c4 △ ♘c3-d5± ♘f6
26 axb6 axb6 27 ♕a7 ♗g4 28 ♖d2
♘xe4 29 ♖xe4 ♕f6 30 ♖e5! ♖be8=
31 ♖xe8 31 h3 ♖xe5 32 fxe5 ♕xe5
△ ♕e1+∓ ♖xe8 32 d7 ♖d8 33 h3!
♕e7 34 ♕c7 ♗f5 35 ♕xb6 ♖xd7=
36 ♖xd7 ♗xd7 37 ♔f2 ♗f5 38 ♔b8+
♔h7 39 ♕e5 ♕xe5 40 fxe5 ♗e6 41
h4 ♔g8 42 ♔e3 ♔f8 ½-½ Gheorghiu

54 Knaak-Petkevich Zabrze 77

1 d4 d5 2 c4 e6 3 ♘c3 ♗e7 4 cxd5
exd5 5 ♗f4 ♘f6 5...c6 6 e3 ♗f5=
6 e3 c6 7 ♗d3 0-0 8 ♕c2 a5?! 9
♘f3 ♘a6 10 a3 ♘c7? 11 ♗g5!± g6
11...h6?? 12 ♘h7 ♘xh7 13 ♗xh7+
♔h8 14 ♗xc7 ♕xc7 15 ♘xd5 +−
12 h4 ♘e6 13 ♗e5! ♘g7 14 0-0-0
h5 15 f3 ♗f5 16 g4 ♗xd3 17 ♕xd3
b5 17...hxg4!? 18 ♖dg1 b4 19 ♘a4!
bxa3 20 bxa3 hxg4 21 h5 ♘fxh5
22 fxg4! ♗xg5 23 gxh5 f6 24 ♖xg5
fxe5 24...fxg5 25 ♕xg6 ♖f7 26 h6

25 ♖xg6 e4 26 ♕e2 ♘h7 27 ♕g4 ♕e7
28 ♖h6+ ♔g8 29 ♘c5 ♖f3 30 ♖g6
♕h8 31 ♖g1 ♕f8 32 ♖h6+ ♔g8 33
♕e6+! +− ♕f7 34 ♕xf7+ ♖xf7 35
♘e6 ♖aa7 36 ♖g2 ♖ab7 37 ♔c2 ♖be7
38 ♔b3 ♖d7 39 ♔a4! ♖a7 40 ♖hg6
♕h8 41 ♘xg7 ♖xg7 42 ♖xg7 ♖xg7
43 ♖xg7 ♔xg7 44 ♔xa5 c5 45 dxc5
d4 46 ♔b4 1-0 Pytel

55 Timman-Karpov Bugojno 78

1 c4 e6 2 ♘c3 d5 3 d4 ♗e7 4 cxd5
exd5 5 ♗f4 ♘f6 5...c6 6 e3 ♗f5 6
e3 0-0 7 ♕c2 c6 8 ♗d3 ♖e8 9 ♘f3
♘bd7 10 0-0-0 ♘f8 11 h3 ♗e6 12
♔b1 ♖c8 13 ♘g5!? b5? 13...c5!?
14 ♗e5! △ ♗xf6 h6 15 ♘xe6 ♘xe6
16 g4 ♘d7 17 h4!± b4 17...♗xh4!?
18 ♘e2 ♗xh4? 19 f4 c5 19...♘xe5
20 dxe5 c5 21 ♗c4!±; 19...f6 20
f5 fxe5 21 fxe6 ♖xe6 22 ♗f5 20
♗a6 ♗e7 20...♖c6 21 ♗b5 21 ♗xc8
♕xc8 22 ♘g3 f6

23 ♖xh6! ♘ef8 23...gxh6 24 ♕g6+
♔f8 25 ♘f5; 23...fxe5 24 ♕h7+ ♔f8
25 ♖xe6 24 ♖h3 c4 25 ♘f5 fxe5
26 fxe5 ♕c6 27 ♖dh1 ♘g6 28 ♘d6?!
28 ♘xg7 ♔xg7 29 ♖h7+ ♔g8 30 ♖h8+
♘xh8 31 ♕h7+ +− ♘df8 29 ♘xe8
♕xe8 30 ♖h5 ♕c6 31 ♕f5 a5 31...
♕e6 32 e4 32 e6! ♕xe6 33 ♕xd5
+− a4 34 ♖c1 c3 35 bxc3 bxc3 36

♖xc3 ♕xd5 37 ♖xd5 ♞e6 38 ♔c2
♕f7 39 ♖a5 ♞g5 40 ♖c6 ♞e4 41
♖xa4 41 ♖xg6 ♔xg6 42 ♖e5 ♞f6 42
♖a7 ♞d5 43 ♖xg6 ♔xg6 44 e4 ♞b4+
45 ♔b3 ♗f8 46 ♖b7 1-0 Pytel

56 Grigorian-A.Petrosian
Kiev 77

1 d4 ♞f6 2 c4 e6 3 ♞c3 d5 4 ♞f3 ♗e7
5 e3!? 0-0 6 b3 b6 7 ♗b2 ♗b7 8
♗d3 ♞bd7 9 0-0 c5= 10 ♖c1!? 10
♕e2 △ ♖fd1, ♖ac1 cxd4 11 exd4
♞e4! 12 ♞e2? 12 ♕e2= ♖c8 =+ 13
♖c2 ♗d6 14 ♕c1 ♖e8 15 a3 dxc4
16 ♗xc4 a6! 17 a4 ♞df6 18 ♞f4 18
♞g3? ♞xg3 19 hxg3 ♗e4∓ b5 19
axb5 axb5 20 ♗d3 20 ♗xb5 ♖xc2
21 ♕xc2 ♗xf4 22 ♗xe8 ♕xe8∓ ♖xc2
21 ♗xc2 ♕a5! 22 ♗b1 ♕b4 23 ♕e3
23 ♗c2 ♖c8∓ ♗xf4 24 ♕xf4 ♕xb3
25 ♗a1 ♗d5∓ 26 ♞e5 ♞c3 27 ♗d3
27 ♗xc3 ♕xc3 28 g4? h6 29 h4 ♕h3
30 f3 ♕xh4∓; 28 ♖c1 ♕a3∓ ♗e4!
28 ♕d2 ♗xd3 29 ♕xd3 ♖c8 30 ♕f3
♕d5 31 ♗xc3 ♕xf3 32 gxf3 ♖xc3 33
♖b1 ♞d5! 34 ♖xb5 g5! 35 ♔g2
35 ♖b8+ ♔g7! 36 ♖b7? ♖c1+ 37
♔g2 ♞f4+∓ f6 35...♖c1 36 h4!= 36
♞d7 ♔g7 37 ♖b7 ♔g6! 38 ♞f8+ ♔f5
39 ♖xh7 ♞f4+ 40 ♔g3 g4! 41 h3
♖xf3+ 42 ♔h2 ♖xf2+ 0-1 Gufeld

57 Petkevich-Ubilava USSR 77
1 d4 d5 2 c4 e6 3 ♞c3 ♗e7 4 ♞f3 4
cxd5 △ ♗f4 += ♞f6 5 ♗g5 5 cxd5
0-0 6 e3 ♞bd7 7 ♖c1 c6 8 ♕c2 8 ♗d3
h6 8...♖e8 9 ♗d3 += 9 ♗h4 ♞e4 10
♗xe7 ♕xe7 11 cxd5 11 ♞xe4 dxe4
12 ♕xe4 ♕b4+ 13 ♞d2 ♕xb2 △ e5=;
12 ♞d2 f5=: exd5 12 ♗d3 ♞df6 12...f5!=
13 0-0 ♖e8 14 ♞e5 ♞d7 14...♞g4 15
♞xg4 ♗xg4 16 ♖ce1! ♗f5 17 f3
♞xc3 18 bxc3 ♗xd3 19 ♕xd3 c5 20
e4 += 15 f4 ♞xc3 16 bxc3 ♞f6 17

h3 ♗d7 18 g4 ♞e4 19 c4 ♖ad8 20
cxd5 cxd5 21 ♗xe4 dxe4 22 f5 +=
♗b5 23 ♖fe1 ♗a6 24 ♕f2 ♖c8 25
h4 ♗d3 25...f6 26 ♞g6 ♕d6 27 ♞f4
♗c4 += 26 ♕g3 ♕a3 27 ♖xc8 ♖xc8
28 g5 ♕d6 29 gxh6 ♕xh6 30 ♞g4
△ f6 ♕b6 31 f6 ♕h7 32 ♕e5 ♕b5
33 d5! +− ♕b4 34 ♕h5+ ♔g8 35 ♞h6+
1-0 Gufeld

58 Petkevich-Izvozchikov
USSR 77

1 d4 d5 2 c4 e6 3 ♞c3 ♞f6 4 ♞f3
♗e7 5 ♗g5 ♞bd7 6 e3 0-0 7 ♖c1 ♖e8?!
7...c6 △ a6, dxc4, b5, c5 8 ♗d3 dxc4?!
8...c6 += 9 ♗xc4 c5 10 0-0 cxd4
10...b6 11 exd4 ♞b6 11...b6!? 12 ♗d3
12 ♗b3?! ♞bd5= ♞bd5 13 ♞e5! +=
♕b6 13...♞d7!? 14 ♖e1 g6 14...♕xb2
15 ♞xd5 ♞xd5 16 ♗xh7+; 15...exd5
16 ♗xf6 +−

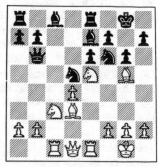

15 ♕f3!± ♔g7 15...♕xd4 16 ♞xd5
♕xd5 17 ♕f4 ♔g7 18 ♖c7 +− 16
♞xd5 exd5 17 ♞c6! ♞e4 17...♗g4
18 ♕f4 +− 18 ♗xe7 bxc6 19 ♖xe4!
+− dxe4 20 ♕f6+ ♔g8 21 ♗c4 ♖xe7
22 ♕xe7 ♕b7 23 ♕e8+ ♔g7 24 ♕xe4
♗f5 24...♕xb2 25 ♖b1 +− 25 ♕e5+
f6 26 ♕d6 ♕d7 27 ♕xd7 ♗xd7 28 d5!
cxd5 28...♖c8 29 ♗a6 ♖c7 30 ♗b5 +−
29 ♗xd5 ♖d8 30 ♖c7 ♔h8 31 ♖xa7
♗e6 32 ♖a8 1-0 Gufeld

59 Browne-Hort Reykjavik 78

**1 d4 d5 2 c4 e6 3 ♘c3 ♘f6 4 ♗g5 ♗e7
5 ♘f3 0-0 6 e3 h6 7 ♗h4 b6 8 ♖c1
♗b7 9 ♗xf6 ♗xf6 10 cxd5 exd5 11
b4 c6 12 ♗e2 ♕d6** 12...♘d7 13 0-0 a5
14 b5 c5= Korchnoi-Spassky (7) 77
**13 ♕b3 ♘d7 14 0-0 a5 15 a3 ♖fe8
16 ♖fd1 ♗e7 17 ♖b1** 17 e4 axb4 18
e5 ♕e6 19 axb4 b5! △ f6 **♗f8 18 ♘e1
♖a7 19 ♘d3 ♖ea8 20 ♗f3 axb4 21
axb4 ♖a3 22 ♕b2 ♘f6?** 22...b5 23 e4
dxe4 24 ♘xe4 ♕g6 25 ♘c3

23 b5! g5? 23...c5 24 dxc5 bxc5 25
♘f4 **24 bxc6 ♖xc6 25 ♘e5 ♘e4?**
25...♗e8 26 ♘b5 **26 ♗xe4! dxe4 27
♘c4! 1-0**

1 d4 d5

**60 Alexandria-Chiburdanidze (8)
USSR 77**

**1 d4 ♘f6 2 ♘c3 d5 3 ♘f3 g6 4 ♗f4
♗g7 5 ♕d2 0-0 6 ♗h6 ♘e4 7 ♘xe4
dxe4 8 ♗xg7 ♔xg7 9 ♘g5 ♕d5 10 h4?!**
10 c4!? ♕xc4 11 ♘xe4 e5 12 e3 ♕d5
13 ♘c3 ♕d6 14 ♘b5 ♕e7= **h6 11 ♘h3
e5?!** 11...♗xh3! 12 ♖xh3 ♖d8 13 e3
c5 =+ **12 e3 ♖d8 13 c4 ♕d6 14 0-0-0=
♘c6 15 d5 ♘e7** 15...♘b4!? **16 f3
exf3 16**...♗xh3!? **17 gxf3 b5** 17...
♗xh3!? **18 ♘f2 += ♕a6?!** 18...bxc4
19 ♗xc4 ♗a6 20 ♘b3 += **19 ♕c3 f6**

19...♕xa2?! **20 ♕xe5+ ♔f8± 20 a3?!**
20 ♔b1± **bxc4 21 ♗xc4 ♕b6 22
♖he1?!** 22 ♖d2! **♗b7= 23 f4 ♗xd5
24 fxe5 ♗xc4 25 ♘g4 ♘g8!** 25...♕b3
26 exf6+ ♔f7 27 ♕e5!± **26 exf6+
♘xf6 27 ♘xf6 ♕xf6 28 ♕xc4 ♕e5!
29 ♖d3 ♖ab8 30 ♖e2 ♖xd3 31 ♕xd3
♖f8 32 ♔c2 ♖f6 33 ♕d4?! ♖c6+ 34
♔b1?!** 34 ♔b3! **♕xd4 35 exd4 =+
♔f6 35**...g5! **36 ♖f2+ ♔e6 37 ♖f4
g5 38 hxg5 hxg5 39 ♖f8! ♖d6?!**
39...♖c4!?; 39...♔e7 **40 ♖c8! ♖d7
41 ♔c2 ♖g7?** 41...♔f5! =+ ½-½ 42
♔d3 g4 43 ♔e2= **Gufeld**

**61 Szyszko-Bohusz — Hochej
Poland 77**

**1 d4 d5 2 ♘c3 ♘f6 3 ♗g5 h6!? 4 ♗xf6
exf6 5 e3!?** 5 e4 ♗b4!∞ ♗e7 5...c6
**6 ♗d3 c6 7 ♘ge2 0-0 8 ♘g3 ♕b6 9
♖b1 g6? 10 h4!± ♕g7 11 h5 ♗e6**
11...f5!? **12 hxg6 fxg6 13 ♗xg6!
♔xg6 14 ♕h5+ ♔g7 15 ♕xh6+ ♔f7
16 ♕h5+ ♔g7 17 ♕h7 mate 1-0 Pytel**

62 Rashkovsky-Beljavsky USSR 77

**1 d4 d5 2 ♘f3 ♗f5?! 3 c4 e6 4 ♘c3
4 ♕b3 ♘c6!?** ∝/+= **c6 5 ♕b3 ♕b6 6
c5 ♕xb3** 6...♕c7 7 g3± **7 axb3** △ b4-5
± **♘a6 8 ♗f4!±** 8 e4 ♘b4 9 ♖a4 ♘c2+
10 ♔d1 dxe4 11 ♘h4 ♘xd4 12 ♖xd4
♗xc5∝ **f6 9 e3 ♗b4 10 ♔d2 e5 11 ♗g3
exd4 12 ♘xd4** 12 exd4? g6 **♘h6 13
♘a4 b5 14 cxb6** 14 ♘b6 ♖d8 15 ♗c7
axb6? 16 cxb6 ∝/±; 15...a6!! **16
♗xd8 ♔xd8∝ axb6 15 ♗e2 ♗e7 16
♘xb6 ♖xa1 17 ♖xa1 0-0 18 ♖a7 ♗c5
19 ♖b7 ♖e8 20 ♘xf5 ♘xf5 21 ♘a4
♗f8 22 ♖b8 ♔f7 23 ♖xe8 ♔xe8 24
♖b8 ♘d6 25 f3 ♘b7 26 ♗d3 g6 27 g4
♔d7 28 ♗g3** 28 ♗f4!? △ h4, h5 ♗h6
**29 f4?! ♘xd3 30 ♔xd3 f5! += 31
gxf5 gxf5 32 ♗e1 ♗f8 33 ♗c3 ♔e6
34 ♗d4 ♗e7 35 ♔c3 ♗h4 36 b4 ♗e1+**

37 ♕b3 ♕d7 38 ♘c3 ♖xc3! 39 bxc3
♖d6 40 ♕c2 ♘e4 41 ♕d3 ♘f2+ 42 ♕e2
♘e4 43 ♗g7 h5!= 44 h4 44 ♔d3 h4!
45 ♔d4 ♔e6 46 ♗e5 h3 c5 ½-½ 45
♔d3 ♔c6 46 ♔c2 c4!= **Gufeld**

Catalan

63 Ftacnik-Plachetka
ICSSR Final 78

1 ♘f3 d5 2 d4 ♘f6 3 c4 e6 4 g3
♗b4+ 5 ♗d2 a5!? 5...♗e7 Polugaevsky-
Korchnoi (8) 77 6 ♗g2 ♘c6 Δ dxc4!
7 a3 ♗e7 7...♗xd2 8 ♘bxd2± 8 ♕c2
0-0 9 0-0 ♖e8?! 9...♘d7!? 10 ♖d1
+= ♗d7 11 b3 a4 12 b4 dxc4 13 ♕xc4
♘a7 14 ♘c3 ♗c6! Δ ♘e4!= 15 ♕d3!
15 b5 ♗d5 16 ♕xa4 ♘c6 17 ♕c2
♘xd4!= ♘d5 16 e4 ♗xc3 17 ♗xc3
♗f6 18 ♕c2 ♘b5 19 ♗b2 g6! Δ ♕e7,
♖ed8 20 ♘e5 ♗xe5 21 dxe5 ♕e7 22
♖d2

22...♖ec8! 22...♖ed8 23 ♖ad1 ♖xd2
24 ♕xd2± 23 f4 ♗e8 24 f5 c5 24...
♕g5 25 ♖e1! ♖d8 26 ♖f2 Δ ♗h3±;
24...b6!? 25 f6 ♕f8 26 bxc5 ♕xc5+
27 ♕xc5 ♖xc5 28 ♖ad1 ♕f8 29 ♗f1
♘c3 30 ♗xc3 ♖xc3= 31 ♖d8 ♖cc8 32
♖xc8 ♖xc8 33 ♕f2 ♗c6 34 ♔e3 ♔e8
35 ♖b1 ♔d7 36 ♗b5 ♗xb5 37 ♖xb5
♔c6 38 ♖b1 b5 Δ ♔b6∓ 39 ♖c1+
♔b7 40 ♖xc8 ♔xc8 41 ♔d4 ♔b7

41...b4!? 42 axb4 ♕b7 43 ♔c3 ♔b6
44 ♔b2 ♔a6 45 ♔a2= 42 ♕c5 ♕a6 43
♕d6!! += 43 ♔c6?! b4! 44 axb4 a3
45 b5+ ♔a7! 46 ♔c7 a2 47 b6+
♔a6 48 b7 a1♕ 49 b8♕ ♕xe5+ 50
♔c8 ♕xf6 =+ b4 44 axb4 a3 45
♕e7 a2 46 ♕xf7 a1♕ 47 ♕g8 ♕xe5
48 f7 ♕xe4 49 f8♕ ♕d5!= 50 ♕xh7
e5 51 ♕e8 e4 52 ♕xg6 ♕b6! 53 ♕b8+
♕c6 54 b5+ ♕c5 54...♕xb5? 55 ♕e8+
+- 55 ♕e8 ♕d4 56 b6 56 ♕h8+ ♔d3!
57 ♕b2 e3 ♕d6+ 57 ♕f5 ♕c5+ 58
♕f4 ♕d6+ 59 ♕f5 ♕c5+ ½-½ **Plachetka**

64 Alburt-Geller
USSR Final 77

1 d4 d5 2 c4 e6 3 ♘f3 ♘f6 4 g3 ♗e7
5 ♗g2 0-0 6 0-0 dxc4 7 ♘e5 ♘c6
8 ♘xc6 bxc6 9 ♘a3 ♗xa3 10 bxa3
♖a6! 10...♘d5 11 ♕a4 ♘b6 12 ♕xc4
♖b8 13 ♕c5 ♗a6 14 ♗f4 ♘d5 15
♕xa7 ♖b6 16 ♗xd5 ♕xd5 17 ♗xc7
♗b7 18 f3 ♖b2 19 ♖ab1 ♖a8 20 e4
♕b5 21 ♕b6± Palatnik-Razuvaev 73
11 ♗xc6 ♖b8 12 ♕a4 ♕c8 13 ♗g5
♘d5 14 e4 ♘b6 15 ♕a5 ♗b7!= 16
♕c5 ♗xc6 17 ♕xc6 ♕a6 18 ♗e7
♖fe8 19 ♗b4 ♖ed8 20 ♖fd1 ♕a4 21
♕xa4 ♘xa4 22 ♖ac1 ♖b5 23 ♗c3
f6 24 ♔g2 a6 25 ♗a1 ♘b6 26 ♗c3
♘a4 27 ♗a1 ♘b6 28 ♗c3 ½-½ **Petrosian**

65 Vukic-Kovacevic
Jugoslavia Final 78

1 ♘f3 ♘f6 2 c4 e6 3 g3 d5 4 ♗g2
♗e7 5 0-0 0-0 6 d4 ♘bd7 7 ♕c2 c6
8 b3 ♘e4!? 8...b6 9 ♗b2 f5 10 ♘e1
♘f6!? N 10...♗g5 11 ♕d3!?; 10...a5!?=
Pachman 11 ♘d3 g5 12 f3 ♘d6 13
c5 Δ e4 ♘b5 14 e3 ♕e7 Δ e5 15 a4
♘c7 16 ♕c3 16 e4?! e5! ♖e8 17 f4
g4= 18 ♘a3 ♗g7 19 ♖fb1 ♘f6 20 b4
♘e4 21 ♕c2 a6 22 ♗c3 h5! 22...♗d7
23 ♘e5 ♗xe5?! 24 dxe5 a5 25 ♗xe4

dxe4 26 ♘d4±; 23 ♘f2 ♘xf2 24 ♕xf2
≈ 23 b5 axb5 24 axb5 cxb5 25 ♘xb5
♖xa1 26 ♗xa1 ♘xb5 27 ♖xb5 h4 28
♗xe4 dxe4 29 ♘f2?! 29 ♘e5≈ hxg3
30 hxg3 ♗f6 31 ♗c3 ♕d7! 31...♔h7?!
32 ♕b3 ♔g7?! 33 ♖b6 Δ d5 +- 32
♕b3 ♗f7?? 32...♔h7!≈ 33 c6! +-
bxc6 34 ♖xf5 ♕b7 35 ♕a2 35 ♕xb7+
♗xb7 36 ♖a5 +- ♔g6 36 ♖a5 ♖h8
37 ♕c2 37 ♖a7 ♔f7 38 ♘xe4 ♔e7
39 ♘g5+ 39 d5! ♗xg5 40 ♖xg5 ♖h6
41 d5 ♕a6 42 ♖g7+ 42 dxc6! +- ♕xc6
43 ♗b4+ ♔d7 44 ♖g7+ ♔e8 43 d6 c5
44 ♖e7+ ♔d8 45 ♕d3 45 ♗e5 ♖h1+!!
46 ♔xh1 ♕f1+ 47 ♔h2 ♕h3+ 48 ♔g1
♕xg3+ 49 ♔g2 (49 ♔f1?? ♗a6) ♕e1+
50 ♔f1 ♕g3+ 51 ♔h1 ♕h4+ 52 ♔g2
♕h3+ 53 ♔f2 ♕h4+ = ♖h1+! 45...
♕xd3? 46 ♗a5 mate 46 ♔xh1 46
♔f2?? ♕a2+ ♗b7+ 47 ♔g1 ♖xb7
♕xd3 48 ♗a5+ ♔c8 49 d7+ ♔xb7 50
d8♕ ♕f1+ = ♕xd3 48 ♗a5+ ♔c8
49 d7+ ♕xd7 50 ♖xd7 ♕xd7 ½-½
Bellin

66 Petrosian-Panchenko Sochi 77
1 d4 e6 2 ♘f3 d5 3 g3 ♘f6 4 ♗g2
♘bd7 5 0-0 5 c4 b5!? 6 ♗g5 ♗b7 7
♘bd2 ♗e7 8 c3 Δ b4, ♘b3-c5 c5!
9 ♘e5 ♘xe5 10 dxe5 ♘d7 11 ♗xe7
♕xe7 12 e4 0-0 12...♘xe5 13 exd5
Δ d6, ♖e1 13 exd5?! 13 f4= ♗xd5!
14 ♗xd5 exd5 15 ♖e1 ♘b6 16 ♘f3 a6
17 ♕d3 h6 18 ♖e2?! 18 ♘h4 Δ f4
♖fd8! 19 ♘h4 ♕e6 20 ♘g2 d4! 21 ♘f4
dxc3!! 22 ♕xc3 22 ♕xd8+ ♖xd8
23 ♘xe6 cxb2 24 ♖xb2 fxe6∓ ½-½
Petrosian

Old Indian

67 Uhlmann-Espig
DDR Final 78
1 c4 ♘f6 2 ♘c3 d6 3 d4 ♘bd7 4 ♘f3

e5 5 e4 ♗e7 5...g6 6 ♗e2 0-0 7 0-0
♘c6 8 ♗e3 a6 9 ♕c2 ♕c7 10 b4 ♖e8
11 ♖fd1 exd4 12 ♘xd4 ♗f8 13 ♘f5
♗e5 14 ♗g5! ♗xf5 15 exf5 ♗e7 16
♖d2 ♘d5! 17 ♗xe7 17 ♘xd5 cxd5
18 ♗xe7 ♕xe7 19 ♖xd5 ♘c6 Δ ♘xb4=
♘xc3 17...♘xe7 18 f6! 18 ♗xd6
♘xe2+ 19 ♔f1 ♕b6 20 ♗c5 20 ♖xe2
♕d4 21 ♗xe5 ♖xe5 ♕c7 21 ♖xe2?

21...♘f3! 22 g3 b6 23 ♗e3 c5 24
♖d1 cxb4! 25 ♗f4! 25 ♖d5 ♕c6 26
♖d1 cxb4! 25 ♗f4! 25 ♖d5 ♕c6 26
♔g2 b5! ♕c6 26 ♖d6 ♘xh2+ 27 ♔g1
♘f3+ 28 ♔f1 ♕b7 29 ♖d5 Δ ♖xe8+,
♕e4 h6! 30 ♕d3 30 ♕d1 ♘h2+ 31 ♔g1
♘g4 32 ♖d7 ♕xd7! 33 ♕xd7 ♖xe2
34 ♕d1 ♖ae8 35 ♗e3 ♖8xe3! 36 fxe3
♖g2+! 0-1

Dutch

68 Webb-Pahtz Jelenia Gora 78
1 d4 f5 2 ♘c3 ♘f6 3 ♗g5 d5 4 ♗xf6
exf6 5 e3 c6 5...♗e6 6 ♗d3 g6 7 ♕f3
c6 8 ♘ge2 ♘d7 9 h3 ♕b6 10 g4±
Browne-Byrne, USA Final 77 6 ♗d3
b5?! 7 ♕f3 g6 8 ♘ge2 b4 9 ♘b1 ♗e6
10 h3 h5 11 g4!? fxg4 12 ♗xg6+
♔d7 13 hxg4 hxg4 14 ♕g2 += ♗d6
15 ♘d2 ♘a6? 15...♖xh1+ 16 ♕xh1
♘a6 += 16 0-0-0! f5 17 ♖xh8 ♕xh8
18 ♖h1 ♕g8 18...♕f6 19 ♖h7+ ♗e7
20 ♘f4±; 19...♔c8 20 ♗e8! 19 ♖h6
♘c7 20 ♕h1± ♖f8 21 ♕h4! ♘e8 22
♘b3! ♔c8 23 ♘c5 ♗xc5 24 dxc5 ♗d7

25 ♘d4 f4!? 26 ♗d3! ♛b7 37 exf4 ♖xf4

28 ♘xc6! +− ♗xc6 29 ♛e7+ ♘c7 30 ♗a6+ ♔xa6 30...♔b8 31 ♖h7 ♕xh7 32 ♕d8 mate; 31...♘xa6 32 ♕xa7+ ♔c8 33 ♕xa6+ ♔d8 34 ♕b6+ **31 ♛xc7 ♛e8 32 ♖xc6+ ♔b5 33 a4+! 1-0** 33...bxa3 34 ♕b7+ ♔c4 35 ♕b3+ ♔d4 36 ♕c3+ ♔e4 37 ♕e3+ **Webb**

69 Webb-Rajna Warsaw 78
1 d4 d5 2 c4 e6 3 ♘c3 f5?! 4 ♗f4! ♘f6 5 e3 c6 6 ♗d3 ♗e7 7 ♘f3 0-0 8 ♘e5 ♘bd7 9 ♛c2 ♘e4 10 f3 ♘xc3 11 bxc3 ♘xe5 12 ♗xe5± ♗d6 13 ♗xd6 ♛xd6 14 0-0 14 f4± e5!? **15 cxd5 cxd5 16 ♛b3 b6 17 ♛b4 ♛f6 18 a4 f4!? 19 dxe5?** 19 ♖fe1± ♛xe5 **20 ♗xh7+ ♔xh7 21 ♛xf8 fxe3 22 f4!** 22 ♛b4 ♗a6 23 ♖fe1 ♗c4∓ ♛xc3 **23 ♖ac1 e2!** 23...♛d2 24 ♖xc8 ♖xc8 25 ♛xc8 e2= ; 24 ♖c7! ♗d7! 25 ♛xa8 e2 −+ **24 ♖fe1 ♛e3+** 24...♛d2!? **25 ♔h1 ♛d2?** 25...♛f2! **26 ♛e8 ♗g4 27 ♛xa8 ♗f3=** ; 26 ♛f7 ♗g4 27 ♛xd5≈ **26 ♛e8! ♛xf4 27 ♛h5+ ♛h6 28 ♛xd5 ♗b7** 28...♖b8 29 ♛e5 +− **29 ♛xb7 ♖e8 30 ♛c6 ♖e6 31 ♛c2+ ♔g8 32 ♛f5 ♖e8 33 ♖c8 ♛e3 1-0 Webb**

70 Hort-Byrne Bugojno 78
1 c4 e6 2 ♘f3 f5 3 g3 ♘f6 4 ♗g2 ♗e7

5 0-0 0-0 6 d4 d5 6...c6!? 7 b3 a5; 7... ♛e8 8 ♗a3 d6 **7 b3 b6!?** N **8 ♛c2 c6** 8...♗b7? 9 cxd5 exd5 10 ♛xf5 ♘e4 11 ♛e6+ ♔h8 12 ♘e5±; 9... ♘/♗xd5± **9 ♗a3 ♗b7 10 ♘e5 ♗xa3** 10...♘bd7 11 cxd5 cxd5 12 ♘c6 ♗xc6 13 ♛xc6 +− **11 ♘xa3 ♛d6?** 11...♛e7 12 ♛b2 ♘bd7 13 ♘d3 a5!?≈ **12 ♛b2 ♘bd7 13 ♖ac1 ♖ac8 14 b4 ♛e7 15 ♘d3 += a6?!** 15...♘e4; 15... ♘g4!? **16 ♘b1 b5 17 c5± a5?! 18 bxa5 ♖a8 19 a4 ♖xa5 20 ♘c3 ♘e4 21 axb5 ♘xc3 22 bxc6 ♗xe2+ 23 ♛xe2 ♗xc6 24 ♖fe1 ♗a4** 24...♗b5?? **25 ♗xd5 +− 25 ♘f4 ♖e8 26 ♗xd5 ♗xd5 27 ♘xd5 ♛d8 28 c6! +− ♘f8 29 c7 ♛xd5 30 c8♛ ♖xc8 31 ♖xc8 ♖xd4** 31...♛f7 32 ♛h5+ g6 33 ♛h6 ♛d6 34 ♖b1 +− **32 ♛xe6+ ♛xe6 33 ♖xe6 ♔f7 34 ♖e5 g6** 34...♔f6? 35 f4 ♔g6 36 ♖c6+ **35 ♖c7+ ♘d7 35...♔f6 36 ♖e8; 35...♔g8 36 ♖e8 36 ♖a5 ♖d6 37 ♖a8 ♘e6 38 ♖e8+ ♔f6 39 ♖d8 ♔e6** 39...♔e7 40 ♖h8 h5 41 ♖h7+ ♔e6 42 ♖g7 ♘f8 43 ♖ce7+ ♔d5 44 ♖ef7 +−; 41...♔d8 42 ♖a7 +− **40 ♔g2 h5 41 ♔h3 ♔e7 42 ♖dx d7+!! ♖xd7 43 ♖xd7+ ♔xd7 44 ♔h4 ♔e6 45 ♔g5 ♔f7 46 f4! ♔g7 47 h3! ♔h7** 47...♔f7 48 ♔h6 ♔f6 49 ♔h7 ♔f7 50 h4 ♔f6 51 ♔g8 +− **48 ♔f6 h4** 48...♔h6 49 ♔f7 ♔h7 50 h4 ♔h6 51 ♔g8 +− **49 gxh4 ♔h6 50 ♔f7 1-0 Bellin**

71 Pytel-Wiedenkeller
Fredrikstad 78
1 c4 f5 2 d4 ♘f6 3 g3 e6 4 ♗g2 ♗e7 5 ♘f3 0-0 6 0-0 ♛e8?! 7 b3 d6 8 ♗b2 ♘e4? 8...♛h5; 8...a5 **9 ♘fd2!± d5** 9...♘d2!? **10 ♘xe4 dxe4 11 f3! exf3 12 exf3 c5?! 13 d5 exd5 14 cxd5 f4 15 ♘d2 fxg3 16 hxg3 ♗f6 17 ♗xf6 ♖xf6** 17...♛e3+ 18 ♖f2 ♖xf6 19 ♘c4

+− 18 ♘e4 ♖g6 19 ♖e1 ♕f8 20 d6
♗f5 21 ♕d5+

21...♔h8 21...♕f7? ♘g5!! +− 22 ♘xc5
♘d7 23 ♘xd7 ♗xd7 24 ♖e7 ♗c6 25
♕e5 ♕f6 26 ♕xf6 gxf6 27 ♔f2 f5
28 ♖h1 h6 29 ♖d1 ♖d8 30 d7! +−
♖g7 31 ♖xg7 ♔xg7 32 f4 ♖xd7 33
♖xd7+ ♗xd7 34 ♗xb7 ♔f6 35 ♔e3
♔e6 36 ♔d4 ♔d6 37 b4 ♔c7 38 ♗d5
♔d6 39 ♗b3 a6?! 40 ♗c4 ♗c8 41 ♗d3
♗e6 42 a4 ♗d7 43 a5 ♗c8 44 ♗c4
♗b7 45 ♗e2 1-0 Pytel

72 Uhlmann-Lutikov Leipzig 77

1 c4 f5 2 ♘c3 ♘f6 3 ♘f3 g6 4 g3
♗g7 5 ♗g2 0-0 6 0-0 d6 7 d4 c6 8
d5 e5 9 dxe6 ♗xe6 10 b3 10 ♕d3
♘a6 11 ♘g5 ♖e8 12 ♗f4 ♕b6 13 b3
♖ad8 14 ♖ad1 ♘c5 15 ♕c2 h6 16
♘xe6 ♘xe6≈ Smejkal-Lutikov,
Leipzig 77 ♘a6 10...♘e4?! 11 ♗b2
11 ♗e3 ♕e7 12 ♖c1 h6 13 ♕d2 ♔h7
14 ♖fd1 ♖fd8 15 ♗d4 ♗g8 16 ♕c2
♘c5 17 h3 ♘e6≈ A.Petrosian-Casper,
Leipzig 77 ♕e7 11...♔h8!?; 11...h6!?
12 ♘g5 ♘c5 13 ♕c2 13 ♘xe6≈ ♗d7
13...a5!? 14 ♖ad1 ♖ad8 15 b4 +=
♘e6 16 ♘f3 ♗c8 17 e3 ♕f7?! 17...
♔h8!?; 17...♘c7!? 18 ♖fe1 ♘c7 19
♘e2 h6 20 h4 ♔h7 20...♘e6 21 ♘f4
♗xd4?! 22 ♘xg6± 21 ♗d4! ♗e6 22
♖c1 a6 22...b6 23 c5! 23 ♘f4 ♘e4

23...♖c8!? 24 ♗b6 24 ♗xg7! ♔xg7
25 ♘d4 ♗c8 26 g4!±; 25...d5 26 b5!
axb5 27 cxb5 c5 28 ♘dxe6+ ♘xe6
29 ♘xe6+ ♕xe6 30 ♗xe4± ♖de8
25 ♖ed1 25 ♗xc7! ♕xc7 26 h5 g5
27 ♘xe6 ♖xe6 28 g4!± ♗c8 26 ♘e1
♘e6 27 ♗xe4 27 ♘xe6 ♖xe6≈ fxe4
28 ♕xe4 ♘xf4 29 ♕xf4 ♕e6 30
♕xd6 ♕h3 31 ♗d4 ♖xf2!! 32 ♔xf2
♕h2+ 33 ♘g2 ♗h3 34 ♖g1 34 ♕c7??
♕xg2+ 35 ♔e1 ♕f1+ 36 ♔d2 ♕f2+
37 ♔c3 ♕xe3+ ♖f8+ 35 ♕xf8 ♗xf8
36 ♗c5 36 c5!? += ♗g7 37 ♗d4 ♗f8 38
♗c5 ♗g7 39 ♗d4 ½-½ Bellin

73 Reshevsky-Formanek
Lone Pine 78

1 d4 f5 2 g3 ♘f6 3 ♗g2 g6 4 c4 ♗g7
5 ♘c3 0-0 6 ♘f3 d6 7 0-0 7 d5 e5 8
dxe6 ♕e7? 9 ♘d5+; 8...♗xe6 9 ♘d4±;
8...c6∞ ♘c6 8 d5 ♘a5 8...♘e5 9 ♘xe5
dxe5 10 e4 += 9 ♕d3 c5 10 ♘g5!?
10 ♘d2± ♖b8 11 ♖b1 a6 12 h3 h6
13 ♘f3 13 ♘e6 ♗xe6 14 dxe6 +=
b5 14 ♗d2! bxc4 15 ♘xc4 ♘xc4 16
♕xc4 ♖b4 17 ♕d3 ♗b7 17...♕b6
18 a3 ♖b3 19 ♕c2 ♕b6 20 e4! fxe4
21 ♘xe4 ♘xd5?! 21...♘xe4 22 ♗xe4
g5±; 22 ♕xe4! 22 ♘d2! ♖b5 23 ♕xg6
♖f6 24 ♕g4 ♔h8 25 ♘e4 +− ♗c8??
25...♖f8 26 ♕g6 △ ♗xh6 +− 26 ♕xc8+
1-0 Gheorghiu

Benko Gambit

74 Marjanovic-Gaprindashvili
Dortmund 78

1 d4 ♘f6 2 c4 c5 3 d5 b5 4 a4 bxc4
5 ♘c3 d6 6 e4 g6 6...♗a6 7 f4 e6 8
♘f3 exd5? 9 e5! d4 10 exf6 dxc3
11 ♕d5! ♕c7 12 ♗xc4 ♗xc4 13 ♕xa8±
Vaisman-Knaak, Halle 76 7 ♘f3
♗g4! 8 ♗xc4 ♘bd7 9 h3 ♗xf3 10
♕xf3 ♗g7 11 a5 0-0 12 ♕e2 12 0-0

♘e5 13 ♕e2 ♘xc4 14 ♕xc4 ♖b8∓
♗e5 13 ♗a6 ♖b8 14 ♘b5 14 0-0
♖b4 △ ♕c7, ♖fb8 **c4! 15 0-0 ♕d7 16**
♘a3 16 ♘d4 **♘d3 17 ♗xc4** 17 ♘xc4
♘c5! **♘c5 18 f3 ♘b3 19 ♗e3 ♘h5!**
19...♘xa1 20 ♖xa1≈ **20 ♗xb3 ♖xb3**
21 ♘c4 ♕b5!∓ 22 ♖f2 ♖c8?! 22...
♘g3! 23 ♕c2 ♖c8! 24 ♘xd6 (24 ♖c1
♖xe3) ♖xc2 25 ♘xb5 ♘e2+! −+ 26
♔f1 ♖xe3 −+; 26 ♖xe2 ♖xe2 −+;
26 ♔h2 ♖xe3 −+ **23 ♘d2 ♖xb2**
24 ♕xb5 ♖xb5 25 ♖a2 a6∓ 26 ♘f1
26 g4 ♘f6 △ ♘d7∓ **f5! 27 g4 f4?!**
27...♘f6∓ **28 ♗b6?!** Zeitnot 28 ♗d2!
♘f6 29 ♗xf4; 28...♘g3 29 ♗xf4 ♘xf1
30 ♔xf1≈ **♘f6 29 ♖fc2 ♖xc2 30**
♖xc2 ♘d7 31 ♗d8 ♗d4+ 32 ♔g2 ♔f7
33 g5 33 ♖c7 ♖b2+ 34 ♔h1 ♔e8
♗c5 34 ♘d2 ♔e8 35 ♗c7 ♖b7 36
♗b6 ♘xb6 37 ♖b2 ♖b8 38 axb6
♖xb6 39 ♖a2 ♔d7 40 ♔f1 ♔c7 41
♔e2 ♔b7 −+ **42 ♔d3** 42 ♘c4 ♖b4
43 ♔d3 ♖b3+ 44 ♔e2 ♖c3 −+ **♖b5**
43 ♖a1 ♖b2 44 ♖a4 ♗b4 45 ♘c4
♖b3+ 46 ♔e2 ♔a7! 47 e5 dxe5 48
♘xe5 ♔b6 △ ♔b5, a5 **49 ♘d3 ♔b5**
50 ♖a1 ♗d6 −+ **51 ♔d2 a5 52 ♔c2**
a4 **53 h4 ♗b4 54 ♘xf4 ♖c3+ 55 ♔b1**
♖xf3 56 ♘e6 ♖f1+ 57 ♔a2 ♖f2+
58 ♔b1 a3 59 ♘d4+ ♔c4 60 ♘c2
♔c3! 0-1 Gipslis

75 Kozlov-Alburt
USSR 78

1 d4 ♘f6 2 c4 c5 3 d5 b5 4 ♘f3 d6
5 cxb5 a6 6 e3 g6 7 ♘c3 ♗g7 8 a4 0-0
9 ♖a3 9 e4 axb5 10 ♗xb5 ♗a6 11
♗d2 ♘e8 12 0-0 ♘c7 13 ♕e2 ♘d7 14
h4 += F.Portisch-Barlov, Belgrade 75;
9...♘fd7 10 ♗d2 ♘e5 11 ♘xe5 ♗xe5
12 ♗c4 ♘d7 13 0-0 ♗d4 14 ♔h1 f5±
Juferov-Mochalov, USSR 77; 9...e6!?
♘bd7 9...axb5 10 ♗xb5 ♗a6 11 0-0
♘c7 12 ♘d2 ♘d7 13 ♗xd7 ♗xd7

14 ♘c4 ♖a6 15 e4 ♕b8 16 ♕c2 ♕b4
17 ♘a2 ♕b7 18 ♗d2 ♖fa8 19 a5 +−
Petrosian-Alburt, USSR 77 **10 h3?!**
10 e4 ♕c7 11 ♗e2 axb5 12 ♘xb5
♕b8 13 ♕c2 ♗a6 14 0-0 ♖c8 15 ♗d2
♘e8 16 ♖b3 ♕b6 17 a5 ♖d8 18 ♗c4
♘c7 +− Razuvaev-Tukmakov, USSR
77 **♘e8 11 ♗e2 axb5 12 ♘xb5 ♗a6**
13 0-0 ♘c7 14 ♘xc7 ♕xc7 15 b3
♕b7 16 e4 ♕b4 17 ♗xa6 ♖xa6 18
♘d2 ♘b6= 19 ♕e2 ♖fa8 20 ♖a2 c4!
21 ♘xc4 21 bxc4 ♖xa4 22 ♖xa4
♖xa4 △ ♘xc4= **♕xb3 22 ♘xb6 ♕xb6**
23 ♕c2 ♕c5 24 ♕xc5 dxc5 25 ♗g5
f6 25...♔f8 26 ♖c1 ♖xa4 27 ♖xa4
♖xa4 28 ♖xc5 f6 29 ♗e3 ♖xe4;
26 ♗e3 ♖xa4 27 ♖xa4 ♖xa4 28
♗xc5 ♖xe4 29 ♖b1 ♗d4 **26 ♗e3 ♖xa4**
27 ♖xa4 ♖xa4 28 ♗xc5 ♖xe4 29
d6 exd6 30 ♗xd6 ♖e6 ½-½ Kapengut/
Artishevsky

Benoni

76 Dorfman-Tal
USSR 77

1 d4 ♘f6 2 ♘f3 c5 3 d5 g6 4 ♘c3 ♗g7
5 e4 d6 6 ♗b5+ ♗d7 6...♘bd7?! +=
7 a4 0-0 8 0-0 ♘a6 9 ♗xa6 bxa6 10
♗d2 ♖b8! 10...e6 11 ♘c4 exd5 12
exd5 += **11 ♕e2** 11 ♘c4 ♖b4 12
b3 e6 **e6 12 ♕xa6** 12 dxe6 ♗xe6 13
♕xa6 d5! **exd5 13 ♕xd6!** 13 exd5
♗f5∓ **d4** 13...dxe4 14 ♕xc5∝ **14**
♘b5! ♖e8 15 ♕xc5 ♘xe4 16 ♘xe4
♖xe4 17 ♗g5 ♕b6 18 ♕xb6 ♖xb6 19
♖ad1! 19 c3? ♗xb5 20 axb5 ♖xb5
21 ♗c1 dxc3 22 bxc3 a5∓ **a6** 19...
♗xb5 20 axb5 ♖xb5 21 ♗c1 ♖e8
22 c3!= **20 f3 ♖e8** 20...♖e5 21 ♗d8!
♖b7; 21...♖b8 22 ♗c7 **21 ♘xd4 ♖xb2**
22 a5 ♗a4 23 ♗h4! ♗xc2 24 ♘xc2!
24 ♖d2? ♖b4! **♖xc2 25 ♖fe1 ♖ec8**
26 ♗d8 ♗c3 27 ♖e4 ♗g7 ½-½ Gufeld

Benoni

77 Szmetan-Vaisman Iasi 77

1 d4 c5 2 d5 e5 3 c4 3 e4 d6 4 ♘c3!?
d6 4 e4 ♘e7 5 ♘c3 ♗g5 5...♘f6 **6 ♗f3**
6 g3 ♗xc1 7 ♖xc1 ♘e7 8 ♗g2 0-0 9
♘ge2 f5 10 ♕d2 a6 11 a3 ♕e8 12 b4±
Nisman-Vaisman, Sandomierz 76 **♗xc1**
**7 ♖xc1 ♘f6 8 g3 ♘a6 9 a3 0-0 10
♗g2 ♗g4 11 0-0 ♕d7 12 ♕d2 ♗xf3
13 ♗xf3 ♖fc8 14 ♔g2 ♘c7 15 ♘d1!?**
a6?! 15...b6 16 ♗a4; 15...b5 16 cxb5
♘xb5 17 ♗a4 a6 18 f4! exf4 19 ♖xf4
♕b7 20 ♖cf1± **16 ♘a4! ♘xe4 17**
**♕e3 ♘f6 18 ♘b6 ♕e7 19 h3 ♖e8 20
♘xa8 ♘xa8 21 b4 ♖c8 22 ♗b3 ♘b6?!**
22...b6!? **23 a4! ♘c7 24 b5 ♘bd7?!**
24...a5!? **25 ♕c3 ♖e8 26 a5 axb5
27 cxb5 ♖a8 28 ♖a1 +−** e4 29 b6
♕c8 30 ♗c4! ♘b8 31 a6! bxa6 32
♖fb1 ♕b7 33 ♕b3 h6 34 ♖a2 ♘fd7
35 ♕e3 f5 36 ♕f4 ♘e5

37 ♕xf5! 37 ♗e2 ♕xd5; 37 ♗b3 ♕f7
♘xc4 38 ♕e6+ ♕f7 38...♔h8 39 ♕e8+
♔h7 40 ♕xe4+; 38...♔f8 39 ♖a4 ♘e5
40 ♕xd6+ ♕e7 41 b7!; 39...♘d2 40
♖b2 **39 ♕c8+ ♕f8 40 b7! ♖a7 41
♖e2 1-0 Ciocaltea**

78 Ghitescu-Ciocaltea
Rumania Final 77

1 d4 g6 2 c4 c5 3 d5 e5 4 e4 4 dxe6
dxe6 5 ♕xd8+ ♔xd8 6 ♘c3 ♘h6! **♘h6!**
7 g3 ♗d7 8 ♗g2 ♗c6 9 ♘f3 ♔e7 10

0-0 ♘d7= Vaganian-Romanishin,
Leningrad 77 **d6 5 ♘c3 a6** 5...♗g7 6
♗e2 f5 7 exf5 gxf5 8 ♗h5+ ♔f8 9
♘f3 ♘f6! 10 g4?! e4! Bagirov-
Razuvaev, USSR 77 **6 a3 ♘d7 7 ♘f3**
f6?! 7...♘gf6 **8 ♗e2 ♗h6 9 ♗xh6 ♘xh6
10 h4 += 0-0 11 ♕d2 ♔g7 12 h5 g5
13 ♘d1 ♖b8 14 a4 ♖f7 15 ♖a3 ♘f8
16 ♘e3 ♗d7** 16...f5 17 ♘xg5! ♕xg5
18 ♘xf5+ ♖xf5 19 ♖g3 ♕xg3 20 fxg3
♖f6≈ **17 a5 b6 18 axb6 ♖xb6 19 0-0
♗c8 20 ♖fa1 ♖fb7 21 ♖1a2 ♖b8 22
♕c2 ♕e7! 23 ♘d2 g4?** 23...♘g8!?;
23...♕f7 △ f5

**24 ♘xg4 ♗xg4 25 ♗xg4 ♘xg4 26
♖g3 ♔h8** 26...f5 27 exf5 ♕h4 28 ♘f3
♕xh5 29 ♕e4 ♖xb2 30 ♖xb2 ♖xb2
31 ♖xg4+ ♔h8! 32 ♖h4! +− **27
♖xg4 ♕f7 28 ♘f1?!** ♕xh5 29 ♕e2
♘g6 30 ♕f3! ♖f8 31 ♘g3 ♕h6 32
♘f5 ♕c1+? 32...♕h5! 33 ♖g3 ♕xf3
34 ♖xf3 ♖fb8 35 ♖fa3± **33 ♕h2
♕xc4 34 ♕h3! +−** ♖g8 34...♕xa2
35 ♖xg6 ♖b7 36 ♕h6 ♖ff7 37 ♖xf6
**35 ♕h6 ♖bb8 37 ♖a3! ♕b5 38 ♕xh7+
1-0**

79 Farago-Quinteros Polanica 77

**1 d4 ♘f6 2 c4 c5 3 d5 e5 4 ♘c3 d6 5
e4 ♘bd7 6 ♘f3 g6** 6...♗e7 **7 ♗e2
♗g7 8 0-0 0-0 9 ♗g5 h6 10 ♗h4 a6**
10...g5 11 ♗g3 ♘h5 12 ♘d2 ♘f4 13

79

♗g4 11 ♘e1 ♕c7 12 ♕d2 ♘h7 13 ♘c2
♚h8 14 g4 ♘df6 15 f3± ♘g8 16 ♘g3
♕d8 17 ♘e3 ♗f6 18 ♘g2 b6 19 a4
♖a7 20 a5! bxa5 21 ♘d1 ♖b7 22
♕xa5 ♕xa5 23 ♖xa5 ♖b3 24 ♗e1
♘g5 25 ♗c3 ♘h3+ 26 ♚h1 ♖e8 27
♘f2 ♘f4 28 ♗d1 ♖b8 29 ♗a4 ♖e7
30 ♘xf4 exf4 31 ♗xf6+ ♗xf6 32
♘d3 g5 33 ♖e1 ♚g7 34 e5! dxe5 35
♖xe5 ♖xe5 36 ♘xe5 ♖xb2 37 ♖xc5
♖e2 38 ♖xc8 ♖xe5 39 d6 1-0 Pytel

80 Sahovic-Henley
Lone Pine 78

1 d4 ♘f6 2 c4 e6 3 ♘f3 c5 4 d5 exd5
5 cxd5 d6 6 ♘c3 g6 7 ♘d2 ♘bd7 8
e4 ♗g7 9 ♗e2 0-0 10 0-0 ♖e8 11 f4
a6 12 a4 c4!? 13 e5! 13 ♗xc4 ♘c5
14 ♕f3 ♘g4∓ dxe5 14 ♘xc4 ♘b6 15
fxe5 ♘fxd5 16 ♘d6 ♘xc3 17 bxc3
♗e6!? 17...♖xe5 18 ♘xf7 ♚xd1 19
♗xd1 △ ♘b3 18 ♘xe8 ♕xe8 19 ♕d4
♘d7 20 ♗f4 ♖c8 21 ♗f3? 21 ♖ab1
♘c5 22 a5± ♖c4 22 ♕e3 ♕c8 23 a5
♕c7∝ 24 ♖fb1 ♖xf4!! 25 ♕xf4
♗xe5 26 ♚h6 ♘c5 27 ♖d1 ♗xc3 28
♖ac1 ♗xa5 29 ♕g5 ♗b6 29...b6?
30 ♕f6 +− 30 ♚h1 ♚g7 31 ♗d5 ♗f5
32 ♕e3 h5 33 ♕d4+ f6 34 ♗xb7 ♕xb7
35 ♖xc5 h4? Zeitnot 36 ♕b2! +−
♗e4 37 ♖c3! ♗c6 38 ♖d6 ♗b5 39
♖f3 ♕e4 40 ♕xf6+ ♚h6 41 ♕h8+ ♚g5
42 ♕f6+ ♚h6 43 ♖xb6? Zeitnot
43 ♕xg6+! ♕xg6 44 ♖ff6 +− ♕e1+
44 ♖f1 ♕xf1+ 45 ♕xf1 ♗xf1 46 ♚g1
♗b5 47 ♚f2 ♚g5 48 ♚e3 ♚f5 49
♚d4 g5? 49...♗f1 50 ♖b8 ♗c6 51
♖b2 ♗b5 52 ♖f2+ ♚g4 53 ♚e5 +−
♗c6 54 ♖c2 ♗b5 55 ♚f6 h3 56 g3!
♗f1 57 ♖c5 ♗e2 58 ♖xg5+ ♚f3 59
♖e5!! ♚f2 60 ♚g5 ♗f1 61 ♖a5! ♚g2
62 ♖a2+ ♚g1 63 ♚h4 ♗g2 64 g4 ♚xh2
65 ♚g5 ♚g1 66 ♚g3 ♗f1 67 ♖a1!
1-0 Sahovic

81 Podgaets-Gofshtein USSR 77

1 d4 ♘f6 2 c4 c5 3 d5 e6 4 ♘c3 exd5
5 cxd5 d6 6 e4 g6 7 ♘f3 ♗g7 8 ♗e2
0-0 9 0-0 a6!? 10 a4 ♗g4 10...♘bd7
11 ♗g5!? h6 12 ♗h4 ♕e7 13 ♘d2 g5
14 ♗g3 ♘e5 15 ♕c2 += Polugaevsky-
Kapengut, USSR 75 11 ♗f4 11 ♘d2!?;
11 ♗g5! ♘bd7 12 ♘d2! +=; 11...♗xf3
12 ♗xf3 ♘bd7 13 ♕c2 ♖e8 14 ♗e2
h6 15 ♗h4 g5 16 ♗g3 ♕e7 17 ♖ae1
+= ♖e8 12 ♘d2! 12 h3? ♘xe4!∓
♗xe2 13 ♕xe2 ♘h5 14 ♗e3 ♘d7
15 a5 += ♖b8 16 ♖a4 ♕f6 17 g3 ♕e7
18 ♖c1 ♘e5?! 19 f4 ♘d7 20 g4 ♘f6
21 ♘f1?? 21 ♖e1! b5 22 axb6 ♘xb6
23 ♖xa6± b5!∓ 22 axb6 ♘xb6 23
♖xa6 ♘xe4 24 ♗d2 ♗d4+ 25 ♚g2
♗xc3 26 ♗xc3 ♕b7?! 26...♘xd5!
27 ♕f3 ♕b7 27 ♕b5 ♘xc3 28 bxc3
♕xd5+ 29 ♚g1 ♘c4 30 ♕c6 ♕xc6
31 ♖xc6 ♘e4 −+ 32 ♘g3 ♖xf4 33 h3
♖b2 34 ♖f1 ♖xf1+ 35 ♚xf1 ♚g7
0-1 Gufeld

82 Dzieciolowski-Holm Zabrze 77

1 d4 ♘f6 2 c4 c5 3 d5 e6 4 ♘c3
exd5 5 cxd5 d6 6 ♘f3 g6 7 e4 ♗g7
8 ♗e2 0-0 9 0-0 ♖e8 10 ♘d2 ♘bd7
11 a4 ♘e5 12 ♖a3?! 12 ♕c2 g5 13
♕c2 g4 14 ♗b5?! =+ ♖f8 15 ♖e1
♘h5 16 ♘f1 f5 17 ♘g3 ♘xg3 18 hxg3
♕f6 19 ♗e3 ♕g6 20 ♗f4 a6 21 ♗f1
fxe4!∓ 22 ♘xe4 ♗f5 23 ♖ae3 b5!
24 ♕b3 bxa4 25 ♕xa4 ♘f7 26 b4
♗d4! 27 ♖3e2 ♗xe4 28 ♖xe4 ♘g5
29 ♖e7

Diagram

29...♖xf4! 30 gxf4 g3 31 ♖e8+ ♚g7!!
31...♖xe8? 32 ♕xe8+ ♚g7 33 ♖e7+
+− 32 ♖1e7+ ♘f7 33 ♕d7 33 ♖xf7+
♕xf7 34 ♖xa8 ♗xf2+ 35 ♚h1 ♚h5
mate ♖xe8 34 ♖xe8 ♗xf2+ 35 ♚h1

Benoni

♕h5+ 36 ♕h3 ♕d1 0-1 Pytel

83 Beljavsky-Gavrikov USSR 78

**1 d4 ♘f6 2 c4 c5 3 d5 e6 4 ♘c3 exd5
5 cxd5 d6 6 e4 g6 7 ♘f3 ♗g7 8 ♗e2
0-0 9 0-0 ♖e8 10 ♘d2 ♘bd7 11 a4**
11 h3 g5 12 ♘c4 ♘xe4 13 ♘xe4
♖xe4 14 ♗d3 ♖h4 15 ♘xd6 ♘e5 16
♘f5 c4?! 17 ♗c2 ♗xf5 18 ♗xf5 ♖d4
19 ♕c2 ♘d3 Donner-Hartoch, Wijk
aan Zee 72; 16...♘xd3 17 ♕xd3
♗xf5 18 ♕xf5 ♖d4 19 ♗xg5 ♕xd5=;
17 ♘xh4 ♕xd5 18 ♘f3 h6= **♘e5**
11...a6 12 h3 g5 13 ♕c2 ♘e5 14 ♘d1
♘fd7 15 ♘e3 ♘f8 16 ♘dc4 ♘fg6
17 a5 ♘xc4 18 ♘xc4 ♕e7 Donner-
Najdorf, IBM 73 **12 h3 g5 13 ♘f3
♘xf3+ 14 ♗xf3 h6 15 ♖b1 a6?!**
15...b6 16 b4 ♘d7 17 ♘e2 cxb4
18 ♖xb4 ♘c5 △ ♗a6; 17 ♗d2 cxb4
18 ♖xb4 ♘e5 19 ♗g4 ♘d3 20 ♖b1
♘c5; 19 ♗e2 f5; 15...♘d7!? 16 ♗g4
♘f8 17 f4 ♘g6 **16 b4! ♘d7 17 ♘e2
cxb4 18 ♖xb4 += ♘c5 19 ♘g3 ♗d7
20 ♗g4 a5 21 ♖c4 b5 22 ♗xd7 bxc4?!**
22...♕xd7! 23 axb5 ♕xb5 **23 ♗xe8
♕xe8 24 ♕g4 ♘d3 25 ♘f5 ♕e5 26 h4!
♖b8 27 ♗e3** 27 hxg5 ♘f4 28 g3!
28 ♗d4? ♕xe4 29 ♗xg7 ♘e2+ 30
♔h2 ♕xg4 31 ♘xh6+ ♔xg7 32 ♘xg4
c3∓ **♘g6 29 hxg5 hxg5 30 ♗d4 ♕xd4
+- 31 ♘xd4 ♗xd4 32 ♕xg5 c3 33
♔g2 ♖b2 34 ♕d8+ ♔g7 35 ♕xd6**

**♘e5 36 ♕e7 ♘c4 37 ♕g5+ ♔f8 38
d6 ♖d2 39 ♖b1 ♗b6 40 ♖xb6 1-0
Kapengut/Artishevsky**

84 Ripley-Denman London 78

**1 d4 ♘f6 2 c4 c5 3 d5 e6 4 ♘c3 exd5
5 cxd5 d6 6 ♘f3 g6 7 e4 ♗g7 8 ♗g5
a6!?** 8...h6 9 ♗h4 g5 10 ♗g3 ♘h5
11 ♗b5+ ♔f8 12 e5! **9 ♘d2 h6 10 ♗h4
b5 11 a4 b4 12 ♘cb1 ♕e7!?** N 12...0-0
13 ♗d3 ♘bd7 14 0-0 14 f4 g5 15
fxg5 ♘h7 **♘e5** 15 ♗e2 g5 16 ♗g3
♘g6 16...0-0 **17 ♘c4 ♘xe4!** 18 ♗d3
18 ♘b6 ♖b8 19 ♘xc8 ♖xc8 20 ♗xa6;
18...0-0!? 19 ♘xa8 ♕b7∞ **♗xg3 19
♖e1 ♘e5 20 hxg3 0-0! 21 f4?** 21
♘bd2 gxf4 22 gxf4

**22...♘f3+!! 23 gxf3 ♗d4+ 24 ♔g2
♕h4∓ 25 f5 ♔h8 26 ♖e4 ♕f2+ 27
♔h1 ♗xf5 28 ♕f1 ♕xf1+ 29 ♗xf1
♖xe4 30 fxe4 f5! 31 ♘bd2 fxe4 32
♘xe4 ♖f4 33 ♖e1** 33 ♘cxd6 ♖g8
34 ♗h3 ♖h4 35 ♘f7+ ♔g7 -+; 33
♘exd6 ♖g8 34 ♗h3 ♖h4 35 ♔h2 ♗f2
-+ **♖g8 34 ♗h3 ♖h4 35 ♔h2 ♖e8
36 ♘cd2 ♗e5+ 0-1 Keene**

85 Gulko-Savon Lvov 78

**1 d4 ♘f6 2 c4 e6 3 ♘c3 c5 4 d5 exd5
5 cxd5 d6 6 e4 g6 7 f4 ♗g7 8 ♗b5+
8 e5 ♘fd7 9 ♘b5∞ ♘fd7 9 a4 0-0
10 ♘f3 ♘a6 11 0-0 ♘c7 12 ♗d3**

a6 12...b6 △ ♗a6 **13 ♕e1! ♖b8 14 e5 ♘b6 15 f5 dxe5 16 fxg6 fxg6** 16...hxg6 17 ♗g5 f6 18 ♕h4 ♕e8!; 17 ♘g5 f6 18 ♕e4 fxg5 19 ♕xg6 ♖xf1+ 20 ♗xf1 ♕f6; 19 ♖xf8+ ♔xf8 20 ♕xg6 ♕f6 **17 ♗g5 ♕d6 18 ♕h4 ♘cxd5 19 ♖ad1 c4 20 ♘xd5 cxd3?** 20...♘xd5!? 21 ♗xc4 ♗e6 22 ♔h1 ♕c6 23 ♗h6 ♗xh6 24 ♘xe5 ♕c7; 22 ♖xd5 ♗xd5 23 ♗e7 ♕b6+; 22 ♗e7 ♕xe7 23 ♗xd5 ♗f6; 21 ♗e4 ♗e6 22 ♔h1 ♕c5 23 ♗xd5 ♗xd5 24 ♗e7 ♕c6 25 ♗xf8 ♖xf8; 20...♕xd5 21 ♗xg6 ♕c5+ 22 ♔h1 hxg6 23 ♗e7 △ ♘g5 **21 ♘e7+ ♔h8**

22 ♘xe5! ♗f5 23 ♖xf5! ♗xe5 23... ♖xf5 24 ♘5xg6+ ♔xg6 25 ♘xg6+ ♔g8 26 ♘e7+ △ ♘xf5 **24 ♖xe5! 1-0 Pytel**

---

86 Butnorus-Bangiev USSR 77
1 d4 ♘f6 2 c4 c5 3 d5 e6 4 ♘c3 exd5 5 cxd5 d6 6 e4 g6 7 f4 ♗g7 8 ♗b5+ 8 e5!? **♘fd7! 9 a4!?** 9 ♗d3 += **0-0 10 ♘f3 ♘a6!** 10...♘f6 11 0-0 ♗g4 12 h3 ♗xf3 13 ♕xf3 a6 14 ♗d3 ♘bd7 +=; 10...a6 11 ♗d3 ♕c7!? **11 0-0 ♘b4** 11...♘c7 12 ♗c4! += **12 ♔h1 ♘f6** 12... ♕c7 △ c4; 12...a6!? 13 ♗c4 ♘b6 14 ♕e2? ♘xc4 15 ♕xc4 b5!α; 14 ♗b3 c4! **13 f5!** 13 e5? dxe5 14 fxe5 ♘fxd5 =+ **a6** 13...♘g4!? 14 ♗g5 ♗f6; 14 h3

♘e5 15 ♘xe5 ♗xe5 16 ♗h6?! ♕h4! 17 ♗xf8 ♕g3 18 ♔g1 **14 ♗c4 ♘g4** **15 ♗g5 ♗f6 16 ♗xf6 ♕xf6 17 ♕d2!** += gxf5?! **18 ♖ae1** 18 h3 ♕h6! 19 ♕xh6α; 18 exf5 ♕xf5 19 h3 += **f4** **19 e5!? ♕h6?** 19...dxe5! 20 ♘e4 ♕g7 21 ♘xc5 a5 **20 ♘e4! dxe5?!** 20... ♘e3!? **21 ♘xc5 ♕b6** 21...a5 22 ♖xe5 ♘xe5 23 ♘xe5± **22 ♘xe5 ♕xc5 23 ♕xf4! f6! 24 ♕xg4 ♗xg4 25 ♘x g4+?!** 25 ♖e7!! ♗h5 26 ♖c7!! ♕b6 27 d6+ +- **♔h8** += **26 d6 ♗c6! 27 ♗a2** Zeitnot **♘e5 28 ♕e4 ♕xd6 29 h3 ♕c7 30 ♗d5 ♖ab8 31 ♖f5 b5 32 ♖ef1 ♕g7 33 ♕h4 ♘g6 34 ♕h5**α **½-½ Gufeld**

---

87 Vukic-Rajkovic
Jugoslavia Final 78
1 d4 c5 2 d5 ♘f6 3 c4 g6 4 ♘c3 ♗g7 5 ♘f3 d6 6 e4 0-0 7 ♗f4 b5? 7... ♘h5! 8 ♗g5 h6 9 ♗d2 e5 10 dxe6 ♗xe6 11 ♗e2 ♘c6= Tal-Velimirovic, Moscow 77 **8 cxb5 a6 9 ♗d2!±** axb5 10 ♗xb5 ♕a5 10...♗a6 11 a4! **11 ♘c4 ♕c7 12 0-0** 12 h3! ♘h5 13 ♗h2 **♘h5 13 ♗e3 ♘a6 14 ♖c1 ♖b8 15 a4 ♘b4 16 ♖e1 ♗d7 17 h3! ♖bd8 18 g4 ♘f6 19 ♗f4 ♕b7 20 ♕d2 ♘e8 21 ♔h1 ♘c7 22 ♗xd7 ♖xd7 23 ♗g3 ♕a6 24 b3 ♖b8 25 ♖cd1?!** 25 ♖b1! **♕b7 26 ♖b1 ♗d4 27 ♘e2 ♗g7 28 ♖ed1** 28 f4? e6! **♕a6 29 ♘c3 ♗d4 30 f3 ♖f8 31 ♗f2 ♗g7 32 ♗e3 ♖fd8 33 ♗g5 ♗d4 34 h4! ♖e8 35 ♘e2 ♗g7 36 ♗e3 ♘a8 37 ♘c3 ♘c7** 37...♘b6 38 ♘xb6 ♕xb6 39 ♘b5! **38 ♘e2 ♖dd8 39 ♗g5 ♖d7 40 ♗e3 ♖dd8 41 ♔g2 e6 42 ♘f4!** 42 dxe6? fxe6 △ d5 =+ **♗f8** 42...exd5 43 ♘xd5 ♘bxd5 44 exd5 △ ♗f4± **43 ♗f2 ♘h6 44 g5 ♗f8 45 ♘e3 e5 46 ♘h3 ♖e7 47 ♘c4 ♗g7 48 ♗e3 ♘e8 44 ♘f2 ♖b7 50 ♗g4 ♕a8 51 ♖h1 ♕c8 52 ♕e2 ♖e7 53 h5**

♕c7 54 ♖h3 ♖b8 55 ♔g3 ♘a6 56
♗d2 ♘b4 57 ♗e3 ♖d7 58 ♖bh1 ♗h8
59 ♔h2 +− ♘d3 60 hxg6 fxg6 61
♖h6!! ♘f4 61...♖g7? 62 ♘f6+ ♘xf6 63
gxf6 ♖f7 64 ♖xg6+ +− **62 ♗xf4 exf4+
63 ♔g2!** ♗d4 64 e5! ♗xe5 65 ♘gxe5
dxe5 66 ♖xg6+ ♔f8 67 d6 ♕d8 67...
♘xd6? 68 ♕h6+ ♔e7 69 ♖e6+ +− **68
♘xe5 1-0** 68...♘xd6 69 ♕xf4+ ♘f7
70 ♖xh7 +− **Vukic**

♖fe8 21 ♗c7 ♗b5 22 d6 22 ♖ed1!?
♖xe1+ 23 ♖xe1 ♖e8!∓ 24 ♖a1?
♗xb2! 25 ♖b1 ♗d7 −+ 26 ♗d5 26
♖xb2? ♖e1+ 27 ♗f1 ♗h3 −+ ♗d4
27 ♗c4 ♔f8 28 ♗d3 ♖e6 29 ♔f1 ♖f6
30 f4 g5! 0-1 **Shamkovich**

88 Akopov-Grigorian USSR 77

1 d4 ♘f6 2 c4 c5 3 d5 3 dxc5 g6
4 ♘c3 ♗g7 5 ♘f3 0-0 6 g3 d6 7 ♗g2
**e6 8 0-0 exd5 9 cxd5 a6 10 a4 ♘bd7
11 ♘d2 ♖e8 12 h3 ♖b8 13 ♘c4 ♘e5**
13...♘b6!? **14 ♘a3 ♘h5 15 e4 f5 16
exf5 ♗xf5 17 g4 ♗xg4 18 hxg4 ♕h4
19 gxh5 ♖f8** 19...♘g4 20 ♗f4 **20
h6 ♗h8 21 ♘e4 ♘g4 22 ♕xg4 ♕xg4
23 ♘c4 b5 24 axb5 axb5 25 ♘cxd6
♗e5 26 ♖a7 ♕h4! 27 ♖g7+ ♔h8!∓
28 f4 ♗d4+ 29 ♖f2 ♕xh6 30 ♘f7+
♖xf7 31 ♖xf7 ♖a8** 31 ♕h5!? **32
♔f1 ♖a1 33 ♖c2 ♕h2 34 ♘f2 ♕g3**
−+ △ ♖xc1+ ♔g1 **35 ♗xf2+ ♖xf2
36 ♖xc1+ ♖f1 37 ♖c2 0-1 Gufeld**

89 Youngworth-Shamkovich
Lone Pine 78

**1 d4 ♘f6 2 c4 e6 3 g3 c5 4 d5 exd5
5 cxd5 d6 6 ♘c3 g6 7 ♗g2 ♗g7 8 ♘f3
0-0 9 0-0 ♘a6 10 ♘d2 ♘c7 11 ♘c4
♘fe8!** N 11...b5 12 ♘xd6! ♕xd6 13
♗f4 ♕d8 14 d6± **12 a4 b6 13 ♕b3
♗a6** △ ♗xc4, a6, ♕d7, b5 **14 ♘b5
♕d7**

Diagram

15 ♗f4? 15 ♘xc7 ♘xc7 =+; 15 ♘ba3!?
♘xb5 **16 axb5 ♕xb5 17 ♕xb5 ♗xb5
18 ♘xd6** 18 ♘xb6 ♖b8∓ **♗xe2 19
♖fe1 ♘xd6 20 ♗xd6** 20 ♖xe2 ♖fd8∓

90 Karsa-Honfi Hungary 77

**1 d4 ♘f6 2 c4 c5 3 d5 e6 4 ♘c3 exd5
5 cxd5 d6 6 ♘f3 g6 7 g3 ♗g7 8 ♗g2
0-0 9 0-0 ♘a6 10 h3 ♗d7!? 11 a4
c4 12 ♗f4** 12 ♗e3? ♖e8 13 ♘d2
♘h5 14 ♘de4 f5 15 ♘xd6 ♖xe3∓
Padevsky-Honfi, Majdanpek 76 **♖e8!?**
12...♕b6!? **13 ♘d2 ♘h5 14 ♗xd6**
14 ♗e3? ♘xg3 −+; 14 ♘xc4 ♘xf4
15 gxf4 ♕h4∓ 16 ♘xd6? ♕xf4 17
♘xe8 ♗e5 18 ♘f6+ ♔g7 19 ♖e1
♕h2+ 20 ♔f1 ♗xh3 −+ **♗xh3 15
♗xh3 ♕xd6 16 ♘de4** 16 ♘xc4? ♕c5
△ ♘xg3 −+ **♕e5 17 f4 ♕d4+ 18 ♕xd4
♗xd4+ 19 ♔h2 f5 20 ♖ad1 ♗g7 21
♘d6 ♗xc3!?** 21...♖e7 22 e4 fxe4
23 ♘xc4≈ **22 ♘xe8 ♗b4** 22...♗xb2?
23 ♘d6 c3 24 ♘c4 c2 25 ♘xb2 cxd1♕
26 ♖xd1 += **23 e4! fxe4** 23...♖xe8?!
24 e5≈ **24 ♗e6+ ♔f8 25 g4 ♖xe8 26
gxh5 e3 27 f5! gxh5!** 27...e2? 28
fxg6+ exf1♕ 29 ♖xf1+ ♔g7 30 ♖f7+
♔h6 31 ♖xh7+ ♔g5 32 g7 +− **28
♖fe1 ♖xe1 29 ♖xe1 ♘c7?** Zeitnot
29...♔e7! 30 ♖xe3 ♘c7∓ **30 d6!
♘xe6 31 d7 ♖d8 32 fxe6 ♔e7 33**

♖xe3 ♖g8 34 ♖e2 34 ♔h3? ♖g4 △
♖d4∓ **b6** 34...♖g4 35 ♖d2 ♔d8??
36 e7+ +− **35 ♔h3 a6 36 ♔h4 ♖g4+
37 ♔xh5 ♖d4 38 ♔h6 b5 39 axb5
axb5 40 ♔xh7 b4 41 ♔g6 c3 ½-½**
Honfi

---

91 Azmajparashvili-Dvojris USSR 78
**1 c4 ♘f6 2 d4 c5 3 d5 e6 4 ♘c3 exd5
5 cxd5 d6 6 ♘f3 g6 7 g3 ♗g7 8 ♗g2
0-0 9 0-0 ♖e8! 9...a6 10 a4 ♖e8 11
♗f4!? ♕e7 12 ♖e1 ♘bd7 13 h3 +=**
Mijushkovich-Sibarevich, Jugoslavia
76; 11...♘e4!=; 10...♘bd7 11 ♘d2
♖e8 12 h3 ♖b8 13 ♘c4 ♘b6 14 ♘e3
♘bd7 15 ♘c4 ♘b6 16 ♘e3 ♘fd7!?
Pachman-Mecking, Manila 76; 9...
♕e7!?; 9...♗g4!? **10 ♘d2** 10 ♗f4 a6
11 a4 ♗g4 12 ♕d2 ♗xf3 13 ♗xf3
♕c7 14 ♖fc1 ♘bd7 15 b4! +=
Sosonko-Smejkal, Biel 76; 10...♘h5!
11 ♗g5 ♕b6! 12 ♕d2 ♘a6 13 h3 f6
14 ♗e3 f5 15 ♖ab1 ♗d7= I.Ivanov-
Kapengut, USSR 77 **♘bd7 11 a4 a6
12 ♘c4** 12 a5 b5 **♘b6 13 ♘a3** 13
♘e3 ♗d7! **14 ♕b3 ♘xa4! 15 ♘xa4
b5 16 ♘c3 b4 17 ♘ab1 bxc3 18 ♘xc3
♕c7 =+ 19 e4 ♘g4! 20 ♕c2 c4 21
♗f3?!** 21 h3 =+ **♘e5 22 ♗e2 f5 23
♗e3 ♘d3!∓ 24 ♗xd3 cxd3 25 ♕xd3
fxe4 26 ♕d2 ♗g4** △ ♗f3 **27 ♗d4 ♗f3
28 ♗xg7 ♕xg7 29 ♘e2 ♖e5! 30 ♘f4
♕h6** △ ♖h5! **−+ 31 h4 ♖h5! 32 ♖a3
♖f8 33 ♖c1 ♖hf5 34 ♖c4 ♖xf4!
35 ♖xf3 exf3 36 ♖xf4 ♖xf4 37 gxf4?!**
37 ♕xf4!? ♕f8? **38 ♕xf8+ ♔xf8 39
g4 ♔e7 40 g5** +−; 37...♕xf4 38 gxf4
♔g7 39 ♔h2 ♔h6 40 ♔g3 ♔h5 41 b4=;
39...♔f6 40 ♔g3 ♔f5 41 ♔xf3 a5 42
b3 h6 43 ♔e3 ♔g4 44 ♔e4 h5 −+
**♕xh4 38 ♕e3 ♕g4+ 39 ♔f1 ♔f8 40
♕d4 ♔f7 41 ♔e1 g5! 42 ♕a7+ ♔g6
43 ♕xa6 ♕xf4 44 ♕d3+ ♕f5 −+ 45
♕d4 ♕c2 46 ♕d2 ♕xd2+ 47 ♔xd2**

♕f5 48 ♕d3 ♕e5 0-1 49 ♔c4 g4 50
b4 g3 −+ **Gufeld**

Nimzo-Indian

92 Grigorian-Savon USSR 77
1 d4 ♘f6 2 c4 e6 3 ♘c3 ♗b4 4 ♕c2 d6
4...c5 5 dxc5 0-0 6 a3!? ♗c5 7 ♗f4 +=
5 g3 e5!? 6 ♘f3 6 ♕a4+?! ♘c6 7 d5
♗xc3+ 8 bxc3 ♗d7 e4 **7 ♘d2 ♘c6 8**
♘dxe4 ♘xd4 9 ♕d3 9 ♕a4+ ♗d7
♗f5 10 ♗g2 ♕e7 11 0-0 ♗xe4? 11...
♗xc3 12 bxc3 ♗xe4 13 ♗xe4 +=
12 ♕xd4? 12 ♘xe4 ♘c6 13 ♗g5±
13 ♘xf6+ ♕xf6 14 ♕b3!; 12...c5
13 ♘xf6+ gxf6 14 e3 ♘c6 15 ♕b3
♗a5 16 ♕a4 ♔c7 17 a3 0-0 18 b4±
12...♗xe4 13 ♕xd4 f5 14 ♕d5± **c5**
13 ♕d2 ♗xg2 14 ♔xg2 0-0-0 15 ♘d5
♕e4+ 16 f3 ♗xd2 16...♕xc4 17 ♘xb4
cxb4 18 a3 b3 19 ♕a5; 17...♕xb4
18 ♕xb4 cxb4 19 ♗d2≈ **17 fxe4 ♗xc1**
18 ♖axc1 ♘xd5 19 exd5 ♖d7 =+
20 ♖f3 ♖e8 21 ♔f2 ♖de7 21...♖e5
22 ♖e3! 23 ♖c2 f6 23 ♖f4 ♖e5
24 ♖h4 h6 25 ♖f4 ♕d7 25...♔c7!?
(△ a6, b5) **26 a4?! ♔b6** △ ♔a5 **26**
♖d2 f5 27 ♖c2 g5 28 ♖f3 ♔e7?!
29 ♖a3 ♖a8 30 ♖b3 ♖b8 31 ♖cc3
♔f6 32 ♖e3 f4 33 gxf4 gxf4 34
♖xe5 ♔xe5 35 ♖h3 b5 36 b3 bxc4
37 bxc4 ♔d4 38 ♖xh6 ♖d8 39 ♖h4
♔xc4 40 ♖xf4+ ♔xd5 41 ♔e3 ♖g8
42 h4 ♖g1 43 h5 ♖h1 44 ♖f5+ ♔c6
45 ♔d3 ♖h4 46 e4 ♔b5 47 e5 ♖h3+
48 ♔c2 ♖h2+ 49 ♔b3 ♖h3+ 50 ♔c2
dxe5 51 ♖xe5 ♔b4 52 ♖e4+ c4 53
a3+ **♔c5 54 ♖e7 a5 55 ♖e5+ ♔d4**
56 ♖xa5 ♖h2+ 57 ♔d1 c3 ½-½ Gufeld

---

93 Kraidman-Keene Beersheva 78
1 d4 e6 2 c4 ♘f6 3 ♘c3 ♗b4 4 e3 b6
5 ♗d3 ♗b7 6 ♘f3 ♘e4?! 6...0-0 7
0-0 c5 8 ♘a4 ♕e7!? **7 ♕c2 7 0-0 f5**

Nimzo-Indian

8 d5! f5 8 0-0 ♗xc3 9 bxc3 0-0 10 ♗b2
10 ♘e1: 10 ♘d2 c5 11 ♖ad1 d6 12
d5?! 12 ♘e1= exd5 13 cxd5 ♗xd5
14 c4 ♗b7 15 ♗xe4?! fxe4! 16 ♕c3
♕e7 17 ♘h4 ♖f7∓ 18 g3 ♘c6 19 ♖d2
♘e5 20 ♖fd1 ♖af8 21 ♗a1 ♘d3 22
♖f1 ♗a6 23 ♕b3 ♕e6 24 ♖c2 b5!
25 ♕a3 25 cxb5 ♕xb3 26 axb3 27
♗xb5 −+ ♕c8 26 ♘g2 bxc4 27 ♘f4
♘xf4 28 exf4 d5 29 ♖e1 d4? 30
♖xe4 ♗b7 31 ♖e5 ♕c6 32 f3 c3 33
♖f2 ♖f5 34 ♖e7 ♖5f7 Zeitnot 35
♖e5 ♖c8 36 ♕b3 c4 37 ♕d1 ♖d7 38
♕e1 h6 39 f5 ♖f8 40 g4 c2 41 ♕d2
♕a4! 42 ♕xc2 ♕xc2 43 ♖xc2 c3 0-1
44 ♗xc3 ♖c8! Keene

94 Kruger-Iskov Dortmund 78

1 d4 ♘f6 2 c4 e6 3 ♘c3 ♗b4 4 e3
b6 5 ♘ge2 ♗a6 6 ♘g3 0-0 7 e4 ♘c6
8 ♗d3 e5 9 d5! 9 0-0? ♘xd4 10 ♕a4
♗xc3+ 11 bxc3 ♘e6 12 ♗a3 ♗b7 13
♗xf8 ♕xf8 =+; 12 ♕xa6 ♘c5 −+
♗xc3+ 10 bxc3 ♘a5? 10...♘e7!∝
11 ♕e2 d6 12 ♗g5 h6 13 ♗d2 ♘d7
14 ♘f5 ♕f6? 14...♔h7 15 g4 ♗c5 16
g5± 15 h4 +− ♘c5

16 ♗g5!! hxg5 17 hxg5 ♕xg5 18
♕h5! ♗xd3+ 18...♕xh5 19 ♘e7+
♔h7 20 ♖xh5 mate 19 ♔f1 ♕xg2+
20 ♔xg2 ♘f4+ 21 ♔f3 1-0 Keene

95 Farago-Kuzmin Polanica 77

1 d4 ♘f6 2 c4 e6 3 ♘c3 ♗b4 4 e3
b6 5 ♘e2 ♘e4 6 ♕c2 ♗b7 7 a3 ♗xc3+
8 ♘xc3 ♘xc3 9 ♕xc3 0-0 10 f3?
10 b4 += ♕h4+! 11 g3 ♕h5 12 e4 f5!
13 ♗g2 fxe4 14 fxe4 ♘c6 15 ♗e3 d5
16 cxd5 exd5 17 e5 ♗a6 −+ 18
♕d2 ♔h8 19 b4 ♖ae8 20 ♗f1?

20...♘xe5! 21 dxe5 ♕xe5 22 ♖c1
♕e4 23 ♖g1 ♕f3! 24 ♗xa6 ♖xe3+
0-1 Pytel

96 Vaiser-Sturua USSR 78

1 d4 ♘f6 2 c4 e6 3 ♘c3 ♗b4 4 e3
0-0 5 ♗d3 c5 6 a3 ♗xc3+ 7 bxc3 b6!=
8 e4 ♗b7? 8...♘e8!= 9 ♗g5 +=/± d6
10 f4 10 e5? dxe5 11 dxe5 ♘e4!∓
h6 11 h4!± ♖e8 12 e5 dxe5 13 dxe5
♘e4 13...hxg5 14 hxg5 ♘e4 15 ♕h5
♔f8 16 ♖d1! +− ♘g3 17 ♕h8+ ♔e7
18 ♕xg7 ♘xh1 19 ♗g6 +−; 18...♖g8
19 ♕f6+ ♔e8 20 ♕xd8+ ♔xd8 21
♖h3 +−; 16...♘d7 17 g6 +− 14 ♖h3!
hxg5 15 hxg5 ♗xd3 16 gxf6 16
♖xd3? ♘fd7 17 ♕f3 ♘c6 18 ♕xc6
♘xe5! ♗g6 16...♗f5 17 ♕h5 ♗xh3
18 ♕g5 +− 17 ♕g4 gxf6 18 ♕h4 ♔f8
19 exf6 1-0 Gufeld

97 Szmetan-Suba Rumania 78

1 d4 ♘f6 2 c4 e6 3 ♘c3 ♗b4 4 e3
0-0 5 ♗d3 d5 6 ♘f3 c5 7 0-0 dxc4

7...b6?!; 7...♘c6 **8** ♗xc4 ♘bd7 8... cxd4 9 exd4 b6; 8...♕e7 **9** a3 9 ♕e2!?; **9** ♗d3 **cxd4 10** axb4 10 ♘b5= dxc3 **11** bxc3 ♕c7 **12** ♕b3! 12 ♕e2 ♘b6 13 ♗d3 e5! =∓ ♘b6 13 ♗e2 e5 **14** ♖a5 N 14 c4 ♗e6 15 ♖a5 Timman-Keene, Reykjavik 76 ♗e6 **15** ♕a3 15 c4 ♗xc4 16 ♕c3 ♘fd7 **16** ♘d2 a6 **17** ♗b2 ♘c4 **18** ♘xc4 ♗xc4 **19** ♗xc4 ♕xc4= **20** b5 ♘c5 **21** bxa6 b6 **22** ♕a2 ♕d3 **23** ♖a3 ♖xa6 **24** ♖xa6 ♘xa6? 24...♕xa6!= **25** c4 ♘b4 **26** ♕b1? 26 ♕a4! ♕xc4 27 ♖c1 △ ♗a3± ♕e4; 26...♘c2 27 ♖c1 ♘xe3 28 fxe3 ♕xe3+ 29 ♔h1± **f6 27** ♗xe5 ♕xb1 **28** ♖xb1 ♘d3 **29** ♗d4 ♖c8 ½-½ **Ciocaltea**

98 Farago-Pokojowczyk
Polanica 77

1 d4 ♘f6 2 c4 e6 3 ♘c3 ♗b4 4 e3 c5 5 ♗d3 0-0 6 ♘f3 d5 7 0-0 dxc4 8 ♗xc4 ♘bd7 9 ♕e2 b6 10 d5! ♗xc3 10...exd5 **11** ♘xd5± **11 dxe6 ♘e5!** 11...♗a5 12 exd7± **12 exf7+ ♔h8 13** bxc3 ♗g4 **14** e4 ♕e7 **15** ♖e1 b5?! **16** ♗xb5 ♕e6? 16...♘h5!= Knaak-Holmov, Balashikha 77

17 ♘g5!! ♗xe2 17...♕b6 18 f3 c4+ 19 ♗e3 ♕xb5 20 fxg4 +− **18** ♘xe6 ♗xb5 **19** ♘xf8 ♖xf8 **20** ♗a3 ♖xf7 20...♘d3 **21** e5 ♗xc5 ♘d3 **22**

♖eb1 ♗c6 23 ♖b8+ ♘g8 24 ♗e3 ♗xe4 25 f3 ♗c6 26 ♖d8 ♗b5 27 ♖d1 ♘f4 28 ♗xf4! ♖xf4 29 ♖1d4 ♖xd4 30 ♖xd4 h6 31 c4 ♗a6 32 c5 ♘e7 33 ♖a4 1-0 **Pytel**

99 O.Rodriguez-Olafsson
Las Palmas 78

1 d4 ♘f6 2 c4 e6 3 ♘c3 ♗b4 4 e3 c5 5 ♗d3 0-0 6 ♘f3 d5 7 0-0 ♘c6 8 a3 ♗xc3 9 bxc3 dxc4 **10** ♗xc4 ♕c7 **11 ♖e1?!** e5 **12** d5 ♘a5 **13** d6?! ♕d8 **14 ♘xe5 ♘xc4 15 ♘xc4 ♗e6 16** ♕d3 16 ♕e2!? ♘g4! 16...♗xc4= **17** ♖e2? 17 h3 ♘xf2 18 ♔xf2 ♕h4+ 19 g3 ♕xc4 =∓ ♗xc4 **18 ♕xc4 ♕xd6∓ 19** g3 ♘e5 **20** ♕a2 ♕g6 **21** e4 ♖ad8 **22** ♗f4 ♘f3+ **23** ♔g2 ♕g4 −+ **24** h3 ♘h4+ **25** ♔h2 ♕f3 **26** ♖g1

26...♕g2+! 0-1 27 ♖xg2 ♘f3+ 28 ♔h1 ♖d1+ −+ **Larsen**

101 Ghitescu-Schneider Roskilde 78
1 d4 ♘f6 2 c4 e6 3 ♘c3 ♗b4 4 e3 c5 5 ♘ge2 d5 5...cxd4 6 exd4 0-0 7 a3 ♗e7 8 g3 d5 9 cxd5 ♘xd5= Gligoric-Sosonko, Bad Lauterberg 77; 9 c5 b6 10 b4 a5 11 ♖b1 axb4 12 axb4 ♘e4 13 ♗g2± Ivanov-Kosikov, USSR 76; 8 ♘f4 d5 9 ♗e3 ♘c6 10 cxd5 ♘xd5 11 ♘cxd5 exd5 12 ♗e2 ♗g5= Ree-Olafsson, Wijk aan Zee 76;

5...d6!?; 5...b6 6 a3 ♗a5 7 ♖b1 ♕e7
8 ♗d2 ♘c6 9 ♘g3 cxd4 10 exd4
♗xc3!=   Guil.Garcia-Romanishin,
Cienfuegos 77; 5...♘e4?! 6 ♕c2 cxd4
7 exd4 d5 8 a3 ♘xc3 9 ♘xc3 ♗xc3+
10 ♕xc3 += Cvetkovic-Augustin,
Stary Smokovec 76 6 a3 ♗a5 6...
♗xc3+?! 7 ♘xc3 cxd4 8 exd4 dxc4
9 ♗xc4 ♘c6 10 ♗e3 0-0 11 0-0 b6
12 ♕d3 ♗b7 13 ♖ad1 ♕d7= Moiseev-
Hollis, corr 76 7 dxc5 7 g3 ♘e4 8
♕c2 ♘xc3 9 ♘xc3 cxd4 10 exd4 ♘c6
11 ♗e3 e5 =+ Gligoric-Ivkov,
Amsterdam 71 dxc4 8 ♕xd8+ ♔xd8
9 ♗d2 e5 9...♘bd7 10 ♘g3 ♘xc5 11
♗xc4 += Ivkov-Donner, Amsterdam 71
10 ♘g3 10 ♘e4!? ♘c6 11 ♘2g3 ♘xe4?
(11...♗xd2+!)   12 ♘xe4± Hort-
R.Garcia, Leipzig 73 ♗e6 11 ♘ce4
♗xd2+ 12 ♔xd2 ♘xe4+ 13 ♔xe4
♔e7 14 ♖c1 ♖d8+ 15 ♔c3 ♗d5! 16
♘d6 ♘a6 17 e4? 17 ♖d1!? =+ ♘xc5
18 ♘f5+ ♔f6 19 exd5 ♘e4+ 20 ♔b4
a5+! −+ 21 ♔a4 b5+ 22 ♔xb5 ♖ab8+
0-1 23 ♔c6 ♖dc8+ 24 ♔d7 ♘c5+
25 ♔d6 ♖b6 mate Ciocaltea

101 Schmidt-Pytel Poland 78
1 d4 e6 2 c4 ♘f6 3 ♘c3 ♗b4 4 g3 c5
5 ♘f3 b6 6 ♗g2 ♗b7 7 0-0 0-0!? 7 ..
cxd4 8 d5! ♗xc3 9 bxc3 exd5 10
♘h4 d6 10...♘c6 11 cxd5 ♘a5 12 e4
d6 13 ♘f5 ♘c4? 14 ♗g5 ♖fe8? 15
♕a4! ♘e5 16 f4 ♘g6 17 ♘xg7! ♔xg7
18 e5 +− Gralka-Judycki, Poland
76 11 cxd5 ♘bd7 12 e4 ♖e8 13
♖e1 b5? 13...♗a6!? 14 ♖b1!± ♗a6
15 ♘f5 ♘b6 16 ♗f1 ♘a4 16...♘xe4?
17 ♕g4 +− 17 ♕f3 ♘d7 18 ♗f4 18
♘xd6? ♘e5 ♕f6?! 19 ♖e3 ♘e5 20
♗xe5 ♕xe5 21 ♗xb5 21 ♕f4!± ♖ab8
22 c4 ♗xb5 23 cxb5 a6 24 ♕f4 ♕xf4
25 gxf4 ♖b6 26 e5 dxe5 27 fxe5
axb5 28 ♘d6 ♖eb8 29 ♖a3! c4?

29...f6!? 30 f4 fxe5 31 fxe5 c4! 32
♘xb5?=; 32 ♘e4!± 30 ♖xb5 ♖xb5
31 ♘xb5 +− ♘c5 32 ♘d6 g5 33 ♘xc4
g4 34 h3 ♖b4 35 ♘d6 ♘d7 36 e6
fxe6 37 dxe6 ♘f6 38 e7 ♖b1+ 39
♔g2 ♖e1 40 ♖e3 gxh3+ 41 ♔xh3
1-0 Pytel

Queen's Indian

102 Vaganian-Gulko Lvov 78
1 d4 ♘f6 2 c4 e6 3 ♘f3 b6 4 a3 d5
4...♗b7 5 ♘c3 ♗e7 (5...d5) 6 d5
exd5 7 cxd5 c5? (7...d6; 7...0-0)
8 d6 ♗f8 9 ♕d3 ♘a6 10 ♕e3+ ♗e7 11
♕xe7+ ♕xe7 12 dxe7 ♔xe7 13 ♗g5
1-0 Huss-Arnold, Lugano 78: 9...
♕c8 10 ♕e3+ ♘d8 11 ♘g5 ♗xd6
12 ♘xf7+ ♔c7 13 ♗b5+ +− 5 ♘c3
♗e7 6 cxd5 exd5 7 g3 0-0 8 ♗g2 c5
9 0-0 ♗b7 10 ♗f4 ♘a6 11 ♘e5 ♘e4?
12 ♘xe4 dxe4 13 dxc5! ♗xc5 14
♕c2! △ b4 ♖c8 14...f6 15 ♖fd1 ♕e8
16 ♘c4 15 ♖fd1 ♕e8 16 ♗h3! ♘e6
16...♖a8 17 b4 △ ♘d7; 16...♖c7
17 ♘g6; 16...f5 17 b4 ♘a6 18 ♕b3+
17 ♕b3 ♗xf4 18 gxf4 18 ♗xc8 ♘xe2+
19 ♔f1 ♘xg3+ 20 hxg3 ♗xc8 e3?!
19 ♗d7! exf2+ 20 ♔f1 ♕d8 21 ♗xc8
♕xc8 22 ♖d7 ♗c5 23 ♖xf7 ♖xf7
24 ♖d1! h6 24...♕e8 25 ♖d7 25
♕xf7+ ♔h7 26 ♕g6+ 26 ♖d7 ♗f8!
27 ♖xb7 ♕c1+ 28 ♔xf2 ♗c5+ ♔g8
27 ♘g4 ♕f8 28 f5! 28 ♘xh6 ♕h3+
♗e4 29 ♘xh6! gxh6 30 ♕f6+ 1-0

103 Malich-Gaprindashvili
Leipzig 77
1 ♘f3 ♘f6 2 c4 e6 3 d4 b6 4 ♘c3
♗b7 5 a3 ♗e7?! 5...♘e4 6 ♘xe4
♗xe4 7 ♘d2 ♗b7 8 e4 ♕f6 9 d5 ♗c5
10 ♘f3! ♕g6 11 b4 ♕xe4+∞ Tseitlin-
Zilberstein 77: 5...d5 6 cxd5 ♘xd5 7
e3 ♘d7!; 6...exd5 7 ♗g5 ♗e7 8 e3 0-0

9 &e2!? &bd7 10 0-0 &e4 11 &xe7 &xe7 12 &c1 &fd8!= Olafsson-Browne, Amsterdam 76 **6 d5 0-0 7 e4 d6 8 &d3 &bd7 9 0-0 &e8 10 &e1 &f8 11 &c2 &6d7!? 12 &d4 &f6 13 &a4 a6 14 &e3 &g6 15 &c1 &ge5 16 &e2** Δ f4, &f2± &g6 **17 &cd1** 17 b4!? &xd4 18 &xd4 &f4 19 &g4±; 17 f4? &xd4 18 &xd4 &xf4 &e7 18 b4 **&f8 19 &b3** Δ dxe6, c5 &h8 20 &h5?! **&ae8 21 &ce2 &xd4!** **22 &xd4** 22 &xd4 exd5 =+ &f6 **23 &h3** 23 &f3 &e5 24 &f4 &g6=; 24... &h5 25 &g5 &xg5 26 &xg5 h6 27 &c1 += &xe4 24 &c1 exd5! **25 f3** 25 cxd5 &d8 −+ dxc4 **26 &xc4 d5!** 26...&g5 27 &g3 &e6 28 &xe6 fxe6 29 &xe6 Δ &c5 +− **27 &f1?** 27 &d3!? **&c8?** Zeitnot 27...&g5 28 &g3 &e6 29 &b2 &g5? 30 &xe6 &xg3 31 &xg7+ &g8 32 hxg3 +−; 29...&d7! 30 &f5 f6 31 h4 &ef4 −+ **28 &h5 &f6 29 &xe7 &xh5 30 &xc7≈ &hf4 31 b5!** axb5 **32 &xb5 &e6? 33 &xe6 &xe6 34 &xd5 &e1+ 35 &f2 &e6 36 &d6** 36 &xe1 &xd5 37 &e3+± **&h1 37 h3?** 37 &xb6 &xh2 38 &g1 &h4 39 a4 +− **&b8 38 &f1 h5! 39 &e3? &a8 40 &c3 &e7! 41 &c1** 41 &xb6 &d5 42 &c5 &xb6 43 &xh5+ &g8 44 &xb6 g6 Δ &xa3= **&d5 42 &c2?!** 42 &d3 &c8 43 &d2 Δ g4, &g2 **h4! 43 &d2 &c8 44 &b2 &e3 45 &d8+ &xd8 46 &xd8+ &h7 47 &d3+ &f5 48 f4! &g6** 48...&h6 49 &h8+ &g6 50 &xh4 Δ &g4+ +−; 48...g6?? 49 &h8 mate; 48...&d1 49 &xf5+ +−; 48...f6 49 &d6 +− **49 &d6 b5 50 &b6 &d1 51 &e2 &g1 52 &e4 &h7! 53 &f2 &d1 54 &xb5 g6 55 &b8 &g7 56 a4?! &c4!! 57 a5?** 57 &f3? &f1+ 58 &e3 &f5+ 59 &e4 &e1+ −+; 59 &d2 &f2+ 60 &c3 &f1≈; 57 &b4 &a6 58 &xg7! &xg7 59 &b6±

&f1+ **58 &e3 &d1?** 58...&f5+ 59 &d2 &f2+ 60 &c3 &f1≈; 59 &xf5 gxf5 60 &h8+ &g6 61 &xh4 &b1 += 62 &c3!? Δ &a8, a6± **59 &xg7! +− &xg7 60 &b1 &xb1 61 &xb1 f5 62 &d3 &d5 63 a6 &xg2 64 &e2** Δ &f3 **1-0 Malich**

104 Balashov-Romanishin Lvov 78
1 d4 &f6 2 c4 e6 3 &f3 b6 4 &c3 &b4 5 e3 &b7 6 &d3 &e4 7 0-0 &xc3?! 7...&xc3 8 bxc3 f5 **8 bxc3 &xc3 9 &b1 &c6 10 &b3 &a5 11 e4± h6** 11...&e7 **12 d5 &e7 13 &b2 0-0 14 &e5 &g6 15 &g4 &e7 16 f4** Δ f5 **f5 17 exf5 exf5**

18 &xh6+!! gxh6 19 &h5 &h7 20 &xf5 &xf5 20...&g8 21 &h3 **21 &xf5 &f8 22 &c2 &c5+ 23 &h1 &xd5!? 24 &g3! &g8 25 f5 &f8 26 f6+ &g6** 26...&g6 27 f7 **27 &xg6 &xg6 28 f7 1-0 Pytel**

105 Ungureanu-Gheorghiu
Rumania 78
1 d4 &f6 2 c4 e6 3 &f3 b6 4 &c3 &b4 5 e3 &b7 6 &d3 0-0 7 0-0 d5 7...c5 8 &a4 cxd4 9 exd4 &e7 10 &b1 d6 11 b4∞ **8 a3 &d6 9 b4 dxc4 10 &xc4 a5! 11 b5 &bd7 12 &b2 e5 13 dxe5!?=** 13 &e1 e4 14 &d2 &e7 15

♗e2 ♖ad8 16 ♕c2 ♖fe8 17 f3 exf3 18 ♗xf3 ♗xf3 19 ♘xf3 ♘e4! Portisch-Petrosian, Lone Pine 78 **♘xe5 14 ♘xe5 ♗xe5 15 ♕xd8 ♖axd8 16 ♖ad1 h6!** =+ 16...♘e4? 17 ♘xe4 ♗xb2 18 ♘g5!± **17 ♖xd8 ♖xd8 18 ♖d1 ♖xd1+ 19 ♘xd1 ♗xb2 20 ♘xb2 ♘e4** =+ **21 ♘a4 ♘d6 22 ♗d3 ♗d5 23 ♘c3 ♗c4 24 ♗xc4 ♘xc4 25 a4 ♔f8 26 ♔f1 ♔e7 27 ♔e2 ♔d6 28 ♔d3 ♔c5 29 f4!=** ♘b2+ **30 ♔c2 ♘c4 31 ♔d3 ♘b2+ 32 ♔c2 ♘c4 33 ♔d3 f5 34 e4!** ♘b2+ **35 ♔c2 ♘c4 36 ♔d3 fxe4+ 37 ♘xe4+ ♔b4 38 ♘c3 ♘b2+ 39 ♔d4!! ♘xa4 40 ♘xa4 ♔xa4 41 ♔c4!=** ♔a3 **42 ♔c3 ♔a4 43 ♔c4!=** ½-½ Gheorghiu

106 Liutian-Chechelian USSR 78

1 d4 ♘f6 2 c4 e6 3 ♘f3 b6 4 ♘c3 d5 5 e3 ♗b7 6 ♗d3 dxc4 7 ♗xc4 ♗e7 8 0-0 0-0 9 ♕e2 c5 10 ♖d1 cxd4 11 exd4 += ♘c6 **12 a3 ♖c8** 12...♘d5!? **13 ♗a2 ♕c7 14 ♗g5 ♖fe8!? 15 ♖ac1 h6 16 ♗h4 ♘h5** 16...♕f4 17 ♗g3 ♕g4 18 h3 ♕h5 19 d5± **17 d5 exd5** 17...♘f4 18 ♕d2 exd5 19 ♗g3 ♗d6 20 ♘b5 ♘e2+ 21 ♕xe2 ♖xe2 22 ♘xc7 ♗xg3 23 hxg3 ♖xc7 24 ♗xd5 ♖d7= **18 ♘xd5**

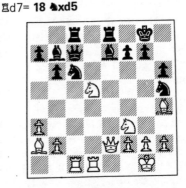

18...♘f4! 19 ♘xf4 19 ♘xe7+ ♘xe7! 20 ♕c4 ♕xc4 21 ♗xc4 ♘g6 =+; 20 ♕d2? ♕xc1! ♗g5? 19...♕xf4 20 ♗g3

♕f6= **20 ♘xg5 hxg5 21 ♕g4?!** 21 ♕h5 gxf4 22 ♕g6! +-; 21...gxh4 22 ♘g6 +- **♕xf4 22 ♕xg5±** 22 ♕xf4 gxf4 23 ♖d7 ♘e5! **♘d4! 23 ♗xf7+?!** 23 ♖xc8 ♖xc8 24 ♕xf4 ♘e2+ 25 ♔f1 ♘xf4 26 f3± **♕xf7 24 ♖xd4 ♖c5! 25 ♕d2 ♕g6 26 f3** 26 ♗g3?? ♕c6 -+ **♗xf3 27 ♖xc5 bxc5 28 ♖d8 ♖xd8 29 ♕xd8+ ♔h7 30 ♗g3?!** 30 ♕d2 += **♕b1+ 31 ♔f2 ♗e4** ½-½ Gufeld

107 N.Popov-Ornstein Albena 78

1 d4 e6 2 ♘f3 ♘f6 3 c4 b6 4 g3 4 ♗g5!?; 4 e3 **♗a6 5 b3** 5 ♕a4!? ♗e7 6 ♘c3 0-0 7 ♗g2 ♗b7 8 ♕c2! += Korchnoi-Spassky (17) 78 **♗b4+ 6 ♗d2 ♗e7 7 ♘c3 ♗b7** 7...c6 Δ d5 **8 ♗g2 c5?** 8...0-0 (Δ ♕c8!) 9 c5 Tal-Polugaevsky, Moscow 78 **9 d5!± exd5 10 ♘h4 0-0** 10...♘e4 11 ♘f5 **11 cxd5 d6 12 0-0 ♖e8 13 ♘f5 ♗f8 14 e4** 14 a4 ♘a6 Δ ♘b4 **b5 15 ♕c2 ♕b6 16 ♖fe1 ♘a6 17 ♖ad1 ♗c8?!** 17...♘c7!? **18 ♗g5! ♗xf5 19 exf5 ♗e7 20 ♖e3 h6 21 ♗h4 ♖d8** 21...♘c7 22 ♕e2 ♗d8 23 ♖xe8+ ♘fxe8 24 ♗xd8 ♖xd8 25 ♘e4± **22 ♖xe8+ ♘xe8 23 ♗xe8** ♗xd8 ♖xd8 **24 ♘e4! ♗b4 25 ♕e2 ♕a5 26 ♖d2 ♘c7?** 26...♕a3!?; 26...f6 27 g4 Δ h4, g5± **27 f6! ♘bxd5 28 ♕g4 g6 29 ♕h4** +- **h5 30 ♕g5** 30 g4! **♔h7 31 ♗h3! ♖e8 32 ♗f5 ♕xd2?!** Zeitnot 32...♖e5! 33 ♘xd6 ♖e1+ 34 ♔g2 ♘e3+! 35 ♔h3! ♕xd2 36 ♘xf7 +- **33 ♘xd2 ♖e5 34 ♕xh5+ ♔g8 35 ♕h6 ♗xf6 36 ♗xg6 ♘cd5 37 ♗c2 ♖e2** 37...♖h5!? 38 ♗h7+! ♔h8 39 ♕f8+ ♘xh7 40 ♕xf7+ +- **38 ♕g5+ ♔f8 39 ♔f1 1-0** Ciocaltea

108 Ivkov-Pokojowczyk Polanica 77

1 ♘f3 ♘f6 2 c4 e6 3 d4 b6 4 g3 ♗b4+ 5 ♗d2 ♗xd2+ 6 ♕xd2 ♗a6 7 ♘a3

c5! 7...0-0 8 ♗g2 c6 9 0-0 d6 10 ♖fd1 ♘bd7 11 ♖ac1 ♕e7 12 ♘c2! ♗xc4? 13 ♘b4 ♗b5 14 ♘xc6± **8 ♗g2 ♘c6 9 0-0 0-0 10 ♖fd1 ♖c8 11 ♖ac1 d5=** 12 cxd5 exd5 13 ♘c2 13 dxc5 bxc5 14 ♖xc5? ♘e4 −+; 14 ♘e1! ♖e8 14 e3 ♕d6 15 a3 ♘e4 16 ♕e1 c4!∓ 17 ♘d2 ♘f6 18 ♘b1 ♖cd8 19 ♘b4 ♗b7 20 ♘xc6 ♗xc6 21 ♕b4 ♕e6! 22 a4 ♘g4 23 ♖d2 23 ♘d2 △ ♘f3 ♕h6 24 h3 ♘f6 25 b3 ♗d7 26 bxc4 ♗xh3 27 cxd5 ♘g4 28 ♖c6

28...♖xe3!! 29 ♖dc2 29 fxe3 ♕xe3+ 30 ♔f1 ♘h2 mate; 29 ♗xh3 ♕xh3 30 fxe3 ♕xg3+ 31 ♔h1 ♕h3+ 32 ♔g1 ♕e3+; 29 ♖xh6 ♖e1+ **♖d3! 30 ♕e1 ♘f6! 31 ♗xh3 ♕xh3 32 ♕f1 ♕xf1+ 33 ♔xf1 ♖d1+ 34 ♔g2 ♖xb1 35 ♖c7** 35 ♖c8 ♖f8 **♖b4 36 ♖xa7 ♖xd4 37 ♖cc7 ♖4xd5 38 ♖xf7 ♖5d7 39 ♖fxd7 ♖xd7 40 ♖a6 ♖b7 41 ♔f3 0-1 Pytel**

109 Polugaevsky-Larsen
Reykjavik 78
1 d4 e6 2 c4 ♘f6 3 ♘f3 b6 4 g3 ♗b4+ 5 ♗d2 ♗e7 6 ♘c3 ♗b7 7 ♗g2 0-0 8 0-0 ♘a6?! 9 ♖c1 ♖e8 9...c5 10 d5 exd5 11 ♘h4 g6 12 cxd5 **10 ♕a4?!** 10 a3 c5 **♕c8 11 ♘e1 ♗xg2 12 ♘xg2 c5 13 d5 exd5 14 cxd5 ♘c7 15 e4 b5 16 ♕c2 d6?!** 17 **♘d1 ♕a6 18 ♘de3**

♗f8 19 f3 ♖ac8 20 ♘c3 ♘d7 21 b3 ♕b6 22 ♔h1 a5 23 ♕d2 a4 24 ♘f5 f6 25 g4 axb3 26 axb3 ♘e5 27 g5 g6 28 gxf6! ♘f7 29 ♘gh4! b4 30 ♗b2 ♖e5 31 ♖g1 ♘e8 32 ♗xe5 dxe5 33 ♘xg6 hxg6 34 ♖xg6+ ♔h7 35 ♖cg1 c4 36 ♕e1 ♗h6 37 ♘xh6 ♕xg1+ 37...♘xh6 38 ♖xh6+ ♔xh6 39 ♕h4 mate **38 ♖xg1 1-0**

110 Korsunsky-Margulev USSR 77
1 c4 c5 2 ♘f3 ♘f6 3 g3 b6 4 ♗g2 ♗b7 5 0-0 e6 6 ♘c3 ♗e7 7 d4 cxd4 8 ♕xd4 d6 9 b3 a6 10 ♖d1 ♘bd7 11 e4 ♕c7 12 ♗a3!? += ♘c5 13 e5! dxe5 14 ♕xe5 ♕c8?! 14...♕xe5 15 ♘xe5 ♗xg2 16 ♔xg2 ♖c8!?

15 ♘a4!± ♘cd7 16 ♕b2 ♗xa3 17 ♕xa3 b5 18 cxb5 axb5 19 ♘d4! bxa4 19...♗xg2 20 ♘xb5 +− **20 ♘b5 +− ♕c5 21 ♘d6+ ♔e7 22 b4 1-0 Gufeld**

111 Zhidkov-Donchenko USSR 77
1 ♘f3 ♘f6 2 g3 b6 3 ♗g2 ♗b7 4 c4 e6 5 0-0 c5 6 ♘c3 ♗e7 7 d4 cxd4 8 ♕xd4 d6 8...♘c6 9 ♕f4 0-0 10 ♖d1 ♕b8 11 e4 += **9 b3 0-0 10 ♖d1** 10 e4 ♘bd7 11 ♕e3 a6 12 ♘d4 ♕c7 13 ♗b2 ♖fe8 14 ♖ac1 ♗f8 15 h3 ♖ad8 16 g4 g6= **♘bd7 11 ♗b2 a6 12 ♕e3 ♕c7** 12...♕b8 13 ♘d4 ♗xg2 14 ♔xg2 ♕b7+

15 ♕f3 ♕xf3 16 ♘xf3 ♖fc8 17 ♘d4
♖ab8 18 ♖ac1 h6 19 e4 ♘e8 20 f4
♗f6 21 ♕f3 +=; 13...♖e8!? += **13**
♘d4 ♖fe8! 13...♖ad8? 14 ♘f5 **14**
♖ac1 ♗f8 15 h3?! 15 ♗xb7 ♕xb7 16
♕f3 += ♗xg2 16 ♔xg2 ♕b7+ 17 ♔g1?!
♗e5 18 ♗f3 18 f4? ♘g6 19 ♕f3 d5 =+
♗xf3+ 19 ♕xf3 ♕xf3 20 exf3 b5!
21 ♗e4 21 cxb5 axb5 22 ♘xb5 ♖xa2
23 ♗xf6 gxf6 24 ♘xd6 ♖b8 25 ♖b1
♖a3= **♗xe4 22 fxe4 ♖ec8 23 cxb5**
axb5 23...♖xc1 24 ♖xc1 axb5 25 a3
♗e7 26 ♖c6 ♗f6 27 ♘c1 +=; 25...d5
26 exd5 exd5 27 ♖d1 ♗xa3 28 ♘xa3
♖xa3 29 ♖xd5 ♔f8 30 ♖xb5± ; 27...
♖d8! 28 a4 bxa4 29 bxa4 ♖a8 30 ♖a1
♗c5= **24 ♖xc8 ♖xc8 25 a4! bxa4 26**
bxa4 ♖a8 26...♘c2 27 ♖b1 d5 28
exd5 exd5 29 a5 ♗c5 30 ♗d4! +−
27 ♖a1 ♗e7 28 a5 ♗f6? 28...♗d8!
29 a6 ♗b6 +=; 29 ♘c3 += **29 ♗xf6**
gxf6 30 a6± ♖a7 31 ♕f1 ♕f8 32
♔e2 ♔e7 33 ♖a5! ♔d7 34 h4 ♖a8
35 ♔f3 ♔c6 36 ♖h5! ♖h8 37 ♖h6
♔b6 **38 ♖xf6 ♖f8 39 ♔g4 ♔xa6**
39...♖g8+ 40 ♔h5 ♔g7 41 ♔h6 ♖g6+
42 ♖xg6 hxg6 43 g4 +−; 42...fxg6
43 ♔xh7 d5 44 exd5 exd5 45 ♔g6
d4 46 h5 d3 47 h6 d2 48 h7 d1♕
49 h8♕ ♕g4+! 50 ♔h6 ♕h3+ 51
♔g7 ♕d7+ 52 ♔f8 ♕c8+!=; 43 ♔g5
♔xa6 44 ♔f6 +− **40 ♔h5 ♔b5 41**
♔h6 d5 42 exd5 exd5 43 ♖d6 ♔c5 44
♖d7 ♔c6 45 ♖a7 d4 46 ♔xh7 ♖d8 47
h5 d3 48 ♖a1 ♖b5 48...♔d5 49 h6!
♔e4 50 ♔g7 ♔f3 51 h7 ♔xf2 52 g4!
♔f3 53 g5 ♔f4 54 ♖g1! +− **49 g4 ♔b4**
50 ♔g7 ♖d7 51 g5 d2 52 h6 ♔c3
53 h7 f6+ 54 ♔g6 1-0 Gufeld

112 Stefanov-Gheorghiu
Rumania 78

1 c4 c5 2 ♘f3 ♘f6 3 ♘c3 e6 4 g3
b6 5 ♗g2 ♗b7 6 0-0 ♗e7 7 d4 cxd4

8 ♕xd4 8 ♘xd4 ♗xg2= **d6 9 e4** 9 b3;
9 ♖d1 **0-0 10 ♕e3 a6 11 ♗d4 ♕c7 12**
b3 ♗bd7 13 ♗b2 ♖fe8!α 14 ♔h1
14 ♖ac1; 14 ♖ae1 **♗f8 15 f4 g6 16**
♖ae1 ♗g7 17 h3 △ e5; 17 e5? dxe5
18 fxe5 ♘g4 **e5! 18 ♘c2 exf4 19**
♕xf4 ♗c5! 19...♘e5 20 ♖d1α **20**
♗b4! ♗h5! 21 ♕f2 21 ♕e3? ♘xe4
22 ♘xe4 ♗xe4 23 ♗xe4 ♖xe4 24
♕xe4 ♘xg3+ −+ **♕d7!!∓ 22 ♘cd5**
22 g4 a5!∓; 22...♘f6∓ **♗xd5 23**
♗xg7 23 ♘xd5 ♘d3 −+; 23 exd5
♖xe1 24 ♖xe1 ♗xb2 25 ♕xb2 a5 26
♘c6 ♘d3∓ **♗xe4** △ ♕xh3+ **24 g4**
♗xg7 −+ 25 ♗xe4 ♖xe4 26 ♘d5 ♖e6
27 ♕f3 ♖b8 0-1 Gheorghiu

113 Vadasz-Rigo
Hungary Final 77

1 c4 ♘f6 2 ♘f3 e6 3 g3 b6 4 ♗g2
♗b7 5 0-0 ♗e7 6 ♘c3 0-0 7 d4 d5 8
♘e5 ♗a6 9 ♗e3!? c5 10 ♖c1 cxd4
10...♘e4! 11 cxd5 exd5 12 ♘xe4
dxe4 13 dxc5 ♗xc5 14 ♗xc5 ♘xc5
15 b4 ♘e6 16 ♘c6 ♕e8= Browne-
Tal, Las Palmas 77 **11 ♗xd4 ♘c5 12**
b4 ♘ce4 12...♘cd7 13 cxd5 ♘xe5
13 ♗xe5 ♘xd5 14 ♘xd5 ♗xd5 15
♗xd5 exd5 16 ♕b3 += **13 ♘xe4 dxe4**
13...♘xe4 14 c5 f6 15 c6 ♗c8 16
♘d3 e5 17 ♗e3 ♗e6 17 f4 += **14 c5**
bxc5 15 bxc5 ♕a5 15...♗d5! 16 ♕a4
♕c7 17 ♖fd1 ♖fc8 += **16 c6 ♗a6**
17 ♕c2 ♗a3 18 ♖b1 ♖fd8?

Diagram

19 ♘c4! ♗xc4 20 ♕xc4 ♘e8 21 ♗c3
♕h5 22 ♕xe4 ♖ac8 23 ♕a4 ♗c5
24 ♗f3 ♕g5 25 ♖fd1 ♗b6 26 ♗d4
♖xd4 27 ♖xd4 ♗xd4 28 ♕xd4 ♕a5
29 ♖b7 ♖d8 30 ♖d7 ♖b8 31 ♔g2
♕xa2 32 ♖d8 1-0 Vadasz

114 Sturua-Gedevanashvili
USSR 78
**1 d4 ♘f6 2 c4 e6 3 ♘f3 b6 4 g3 ♗b7
5 ♗g2 ♗e7 6 0-0 0-0 7 ♘c3 ♘e4 8
♕c2 ♘xc3 9 ♕xc3 c5 10 ♖d1 ♗f6?!**
10...d6 11 b3; 11 ♗f4 ♕c7 12 dxc5
bxc5 13 ♕d3 ♖d8 14 b4!? **11 ♕d3
♘c6 12 dxc5 bxc5 13 ♗f4** 13 ♕xd7!?
♕b6 14 ♗f4 += ♕b6 14 ♗d6 14 ♕x
d7!? **♖fe8 15 e4 e5 16 ♕d5 ♘a5** 16...
♗e7!? 17 ♘xe5 ♘xe5 18 ♕xe5 ♗xd6
19 ♕xd6 ♗xe4 **17 ♕xc5 ♕xc5 18
♗xc5** += ♖xe4 18...♘xc4 19 b3 +=
19 ♖ac1 ♖ec8 20 b4 d6!? 21 ♖xd6
21 ♗xd6 ♘xc4 22 ♗c5 ♗b2; 21 ♘d2
♗xg2 22 ♔xg2 dxc5 23 bxa5 e4!=
♘b7 22 ♖xf6! gxf6 23 ♗e3 a5 24 b5
24 a3 axb4 25 axb4 ♖a4∝ **♘d6 25
♘d2 ♗xg2 26 ♔xg2 ♘xb5 27 ♘e4!**
∝/+= **♘a3** 27...f5 28 ♘f6+ ♔g7 29
♘d7± **28 c5 ♖c6 29 ♘d6 ♖b8 30
♖c3 ♗b1 31 ♖c4 ♖b4 32 ♖c1 h5?!**
32...♘a3 33 ♘f5 ♖b7 34 ♔f3 ∝/+=
33 ♘f5± ♔h7 33...♔f8 **34 ♘e7 ♖e6 35
♘d5 ♖b8 36 c6 ♘a3 37 c7 ♖c8 38
♘b6 ♖xb6 39 ♗xb6 ♗b5 40 ♖d1 1-0
Gufeld**

115 Stean-Larsen Lone Pine 78
**1 c4 ♘f6 2 ♘f3 b6 3 g3 ♗b7 4 ♗g2
e6 5 0-0 ♗e7 6 ♘c3 0-0 7 d4 ♘e4 8**

♕c2 ♘xc3 9 ♕xc3 d6!? 9...♗e4; 9...f5;
9...c5!? **10 ♕c2 f5 11 d5** 11 ♘e1
e5 **12 e4 ♗c8!** 12...fxe4 **13 exf5**
13 ♘e1 f4 14 gxf4 exf4 15 e5 ♗f5
△ g5 ♗xf5 **14 ♕e2 ♘d7 15 ♘d2 ♗g5
16 ♘e4 ♗xc1 17 ♖axc1 a5 18 ♕e3
♕e8 19 b3 ♕g6 20 ♖fe1 h6 21 ♖cd1**
21 a3 ♘c5 22 b4 axb4 23 axb4 ♘xe4
24 ♗xe4 ♗xe4 25 ♕xe4 ♕xe4 26
♖xe4 ♖a2; 22 ♘xc5; 22 ♖c3 **♖f7 22
♖d2 ♖af8 23 ♕c3?!** 23 a3! **♕h5
24 ♕e3 ♗h3 25 ♕c3 g5 26 ♗h1 ♕g6
27 ♕e3 ♗g4 28 ♕c3 ♗f3 29 ♗xf3
♖xf3 30 ♖d3 ♖3f5 31 ♖d2 h5 32 ♕d3
g4 33 ♖e3 ♔g7 34 ♔g2 ♘f6 35 ♗xf6
♖8xf6 36 ♕e4 ♕g5 37 ♖ee2 h4 38
♔g1 ♖f3 39 ♖c2 ♕h5 40 ♖e1 hxg3
41 fxg3 ♕h3** 41...♕g6 **42 ♖g2 △ ♖f1+
♕f8 43 ♖b1 ♔e7 44 ♖e1 ♕d8 45
♖b1 ♕h5 46 ♖c2 ♔e7** 46...♖f8 △ ♕f7,
♖f1+/♖f2 **47 ♖e1 ♖f8 48 ♖d2 ♕f7
49 ♕e2** 49 ♖dd1? ♖xg3+ −+ **♕f5 50
♖b2 ♖f6 51 ♖c2 ♔f7 52 ♖d2 e4 0-1**
53 ♕xe4 ♖f1+ 54 ♔g2 ♕f2+ 55 ♖xf2
♖6xf2 mate; 53 ♖dd1 e3 54 ♖d3
♖f2 55 ♕xe3 ♖f1+; 54 ♖f1 ♕e4 55
♖de1 ♖xf1+ 56 ♖xf1 ♖xf1+ 57 ♕xf1+
♕f3; 56...♖f3

116 Zaltsman-Stean Lone Pine 78
**1 c4 b6 2 ♘f3 ♗b7 3 g3 ♘f6 4 ♗g2
e6 5 0-0 ♗e7 6 d4 0-0 7 ♘c3 ♘e4 8
♕c2 ♘xc3 9 ♕xc3 f5 10 b3 ♗f6 11
♗b2 ♕e7** 11...♘c6!? 12 ♖ad1 ♕e7
13 ♕d2 ♖d8∝ Miles-Korchnoi, Wijk
aan Zee 78 **12 ♕d2 d6** 12...♘c6 13
d5! ♘d8 14 ♘d4± **13 ♘e1! ♗xg2 14
♘xg2 ♘c6 15 ♘f4!± △ d5 ♖ae8 16
♖fe1 ♘d8 17 e4 fxe4 18 ♖xe4 ♗g5
19 ♖ae1 ♕d7**

Diagram

20 ♕e2! ♗xf4 21 gxf4 △ d5 ♖f5 22

d5 ♔f7 23 ♕g4 g6 24 ♕h3 h5 25
♕c3 +− e5 26 fxe5 ♖fxe5 26...dxe5
27 f4! **27 f4! 1-0 Shamkovich**

117 Sahovic-Spassov Trstenik 78

**1 d4 ♘f6 2 c4 e6 3 ♘f3 b6 4 g3 ♗b7
5 ♗g2 ♗e7 6 0-0** 6 ♘c3 ♘e4 7 ♗d2
0-0 7 ♘c3 ♘e4 8 ♗d2! 8 ♕c2= d5?!
8...♘xc3 9 ♗xc3 ♗f6; 9...♗e4 10 d5!±
9 cxd5 exd5 10 ♖c1 ♘d7 10...♘a6!?
**11 ♗f4 c5 12 dxc5 ♘xc3 13 ♖xc3
bxc5 14 ♘e5 ♘b6 15 ♖c2!± ♖e8 16
b3! ♗f8** 16...g5 **17 ♘d3 ♖c8 18
♗e3 ♗a6** 18...♘d7 19 ♗h3±; 19 ♕c1±
19 ♘xc5 +− ♗xc5 20 ♗xc5 ♖xc5
20...♗xe2 21 ♖xe2 ♖xc5 22 ♖xe8+
♕xe8 23 ♕d4 +− **21 ♖xc5 ♗xe2 22
♕d4 ♗xf1 23 ♔xf1! ♕e7 24 ♗f3
♕f8 25 a4 ♖c8 26 ♖xc8+ ♘xc8 27
♕xd5 ♕c7 28 ♕a8! ♕e7 29 ♕e4+
♕f8 30 ♕xh7 ♕c3 31 ♕h8+ ♕e7 32
♕h4+ ♕e8 33 ♕e4+ ♘e7 34 ♕a8+
1-0 Sahovic**

118 Grigorian-Korsunsky USSR 77

1 ♘f3 ♘f6 2 c4 b6 3 d4 3 g3 e6 4
g3 ♗b7 5 ♗g2 ♗e7 6 0-0 6 ♘c3 0-0
7 ♘c3 ♘e4 8 ♗d2 8 ♕c2= ♗f6 9 ♕c2
**♘xd2 10 ♕xd2 d6 11 e4 ♘d7 12
♖ad1 ♕e7 13 ♖fe1 ♖ad8?!** 13...g6;
13...♖fd8!? **14 ♘d5! += exd5 15
exd5 ♘e5 16 dxe5 dxe5 17 b4!±**
17 ♘xe5 ♗xe5 18 f4 ♕c5 **b5!?** 17...

♕d6 18 a3! △ ♕c2, c5± **18 ♘xe5
♗xe5 19 f4 bxc4 20 fxe5?** 20 ♖xe5
♕d6 21 ♕c3 c6 22 ♕xc4 cxd5 23
♕d4± **♗xd5 21 ♗xd5 c6 22 ♗xf7+
♕xf7** 22...♔xf7 23 ♕f4+ △ ♕xc4
23 e6 ♕f3! 23...♕e7 24 ♕e2 c3 25
♕c4+ △ ♖d7 **24 ♕xd8= ½-½ Gufeld**

Grunfeld

119 Hort-Gulko Polanica 77

**1 c4 g6 2 d4 ♘f6 3 ♘c3 d5 4 cxd5
♘xd5 5 e4 ♘xc3 6 bxc3 ♗g7 7 ♗c4
0-0 8 ♘e2 ♕d7!?** 8...b6 9 0-0 ♗b7
10 e5!? c5 11 e6 f5 12 dxc5 ♕c8
Pytel-Vadasz, Dortmund 77 **9 0-0**
9 h4? ♕g4 b6 10 ♗e3 ♗b7 11 f3 ♘c6
12 ♗b5! e6 12...a6 13 ♗a4 b5 14
♗b3 ♘a5 15 ♕c2 e6 16 ♖ac1 ♗c6!
17 ♕d2 ♘c4 18 ♗xc4 bxc4 19 ♗h6
♗xh6 20 ♕xh6 ♖ab8= Pytel-Jansa,
Stockholm 75; 16...♖ac8 17 ♖fd1
♖fe8 18 ♘f4 c6 19 ♘d3± Pytel-
Lekander, Malmo 75 **13 ♖b1! ♖ad8
14 ♗g5 f6 15 ♗h4 g5 16 ♗f2 f5 17
exf5 exf5 18 ♘g3 += ♕f7 19 ♖e1 ♘e7
20 ♗d3 ♕h8** 20...♘c8!? **21 ♕b3!±**
g4 **22 fxg4 fxg4 23 ♕xf7 ♖xf7 24
♘h5! ♖h6?** 25 ♗h4 +− ♗f8 26 ♗f6+
♕g8 27 ♗e5 ♘d5 28 c4 ♘b4 29 ♗e4
♗xe4 30 ♖xe4 ♗e7 31 ♖xg4+ ♕f8 32
♘g7 △ ♘e6+ ♖c8 33 ♖e1 33 a4 ♘xa2
34 ♖a1 ♘c3 35 d5 ♗f6 36 ♘e6+
♕e7 37 ♗xc3 ♗xc3 38 ♖xa7 ♕d6 39
♘g5 ♖e7? 40 ♘e4+ ♖xe4 41 ♖xe4
♗a5 42 ♖e6+ 1-0 Pytel**

120 Knaak-Uhlmann
DDR Final 78

**1 d4 ♘f6 2 c4 g6 3 ♘c3 d5 4 cxd5
♘xd5 5 e4 ♘xc3 6 bxc3 ♗g7 7 ♗c4
0-0 8 ♗e3** 8 ♘e2 b6 9 h4 ♘c6 10 h5?!
♘a5 11 ♗d3 e5 12 dxe5 ♗xe5 13 hxg6
fxg6 14 ♗h6 ♗g7 15 ♗xg7 ♕xg7 16

♕d2 ♕e7 17 ♖d1 ♗b7 18 f3 ♔g8≈ Mohring-Uhlmann, DDR Final 78; 10 ♗d5!? ♕d7 11 h5 ♘a6? 12 hxg6 hxg6 13 ♘f4!± Spassky-Timman (3) 77; 11...e6 **b6** 8...♘c6 9 ♘f3!? ♘a5 10 ♗e2 c5 11 ♖c1 cxd4 12 cxd4 b6 13 0-0 ♗b7 14 d5 += Knaak-Uhlmann, Halle 76 **9 h4 ♗b7 10 ♕f3 ♕d7 11 ♘e2 h5 12 ♗g5 ♘c6** 12...b5 13 ♗b3 c5 Knaak-Uhlmann, Groditz 75 **13 ♘f4! e6** 13...♘a5 14 ♘xg6; 13...♔h7 14 ♘xh5 gxh5 15 ♕xh5+ ♔g8 16 ♖h3± **14 ♖d1 ♘a5 15 ♗d3 c5?**

16 ♗xh5! gxh5 16...f6 17 ♘xf6+ ♖xf6 18 ♗xf6 ♖f8 19 ♕g4 ♖xf6 20 e5 +−; 16...f5 17 ♘f4 +− **17 ♗f6 ♗xf6 18 ♕xf6 ♕d8** 18...♖fc8 19 ♖h3 ♔f8 20 ♖f3 c4 21 ♘c2 ♖c7 Δ ♕d8∞; 19 ♕h6 e5! 20 d5 f5 =+ **19 ♕h6 f6?** 19...f5 20 ♕g6+ ♔h8 21 ♕xh5+ ♔g7 22 ♖h3 f4 23 e5 +−; 21...♔g8 22 exf5 exf5 23 ♕g6+ ♔h8 24 ♕h6+ ♔g8 25 ♗xf5!± **20 ♕g6+ ♔h8 21 e5 f5** 21...♕e7 22 ♕h6+ ♔g8 23 ♖h3 ♖f7 24 ♖g3+ ♖g7 25 ♕h7+ +− **22 ♕h6+ ♔g8 23 ♖h3 ♔f7 24 ♖g3 1-0 Malich**

121 Knaak-Heinig
DDR Final 78

1 d4 ♘f6 2 c4 g6 3 ♘c3 d5 4 cxd5 ♘xd5 5 e4 ♘xc3 6 bxc3 ♗g7 7 ♗c4 0-0 8 ♗e3 c5 9 ♘e2 cxd4 10 cxd4 ♘c6 11 0-0 ♘a5 12 ♗d3 b6 13 ♖c1 e6 14 ♕d2 ♗b7 15 h4 ♕e7 16 ♗g5 f6 17 ♗f4 e5 N 17...♖ac8 18 ♕e3 ♘c6 19 ♖fd1 ♖fd8 20 ♗b5 a6 21 ♗xc6 ♖xc6 22 d5 += Knaak-Malich, Halle 76 **18 dxe5 fxe5 19 ♗g5 ♗f6 20 ♘c3 ♗xg5 21 hxg5 ♖f4 22 ♖fd1!** ♖af8 22...♕xg5 23 ♘e2 ♖g4 24 ♕xg5 ♖xg5 25 f3 h5 26 g3! ♖f8 27 ♔g2±; 22...h6 23 gxh6 g5 24 ♘e2! Δ ♘g3+ **23 f3 ♔h8?!** 24 ♗f1 ♕c5+ **25 ♕f2 ♕xf2+ 26 ♔xf2 ♖4f7 27 ♘d5 ♗xd5** 27...♘c6 28 ♗c4± **28 ♖xd5 ♖e7** 28...♖e8? 29 ♗b5 ♖ee7 30 ♖c8+ ♔g7 31 ♖dd8 h5 32 ♖g8+ ♔h7 33 ♖h8+ ♔g7 34 ♖cg8 mate **28 ♗a6!** ♔g7 **30 ♔e3 h6 31 gxh6+ ♔xh6 32 g3 ♔g7?!** 32...g5; 32...♖f6 Δ ♘c6≈ **33 f4 exf4+ 34 gxf4 ♘b7 35 ♗xb7 ♖xb7 36 ♖g1 ♔h7 37 ♖dg5 ♖f6 38 ♖h1+ ♔g7 39 f5 ♔f8? 40 ♖h6 1-0 Malich**

122 Alburt-Ghinda Bucharest 78
1 d4 g6 2 c4 ♘f6 3 ♘c3 d5 4 ♘f3 ♗g7 5 cxd5 ♘xd5 6 e4 ♘d2 c5! 7 ♖c1 ♘xc3 7 bxc3 c5 7...0-0 8 ♗e2 b6!? 9 0-0 ♗b7 10 ♕d3 c5 11 ♗g5 h6 12 ♗h4 cxd4 13 cxd4 ♕d7 14 ♖ad1 += Alburt-Jansa, Decin 77 **8 ♗b5+** 8 ♗e2 0-0 9 0-0 cxd4 10 cxd4 ♘c6 11 ♗e3 ♗g4 12 d5 += Plachetka-Banas, Stary Smokovec 77; 8...♘c6!? **♗d7** 8...♕d7 9 0-0 0-0 10 a4 a6 11 ♗c4 ♕c7 12 ♕e2 b6 13 e5 e6 14 ♘g5 ♗b7 15 f4 += Stein-Karpov, USSR 72 **9 ♗xd7+ ♕xd7 10 0-0 ♘c6 11 ♗e3 cxd4 12 cxd4 0-0 13 d5! +=** **♘b4 14 ♗d4 ♗xd4 15 ♘xd4 ♖ac8 16 ♕b3 ♘a6 17 ♖fd1 ♖fd8 18 ♕e3 ♘c5 19 ♘f3 a6 20 h3 ♘a4 21 ♕h6±** f6 22 ♘d4 ♘c5 23 ♕e3 e5?! 24 dxe6 ♘xe6 25 ♕b3! ♔f7 26 f4 f5 26...♕e7 27 ♘f5+ 27 ♘f3! 1-0 Ciocaltea

123 Rajkovic-Giffard Trstenik 78
1 d4 ♞f6 2 c4 g6 3 ♞c3 d5 4 ♞f3
♗g7 5 e3 0-0 6 ♗d2 ♞c6 6...c5! 7 dxc5
♞a6! 8 cxd5 ♞xc5= **7 ♖c1 ♗g4 8 cxd5**
8 h3 ♗xf3 9 ♕xf3 dxc4 10 ♗xc4 e5
11 d5 ♞a5!∝ **♗xd5 9 h3 ♗xf3** 9...
♞xc3 10 bxc3 ♗f5 11 ♗e2 e5 12 0-0
+= **10 ♕xf3 ♞b6 11 ♗b5 e5! 12 ♗xc6**
12 d5 ♞e7 13 e4 f5∝ **bxc6 13 0-0!**
♞c4?! 13...exd4! 14 exd4 ♞c4 15
♗e3 ♕d7! 16 b3 ♞xe3 17 fxe3 ♖ad8∝
14 ♕xc6! ♞xd2 15 ♖fd1 exd4 16
♖xd2 ♕h4 16...♔g5!? 17 ♞e4 ♕h4
18 ♖e2 dxe3 19 ♖xe3 ♗h6? 20 ♖c4!±
17 ♞d5 dxe3 18 ♞xe3 ♕b4± 19
♖e2! 19 ♖dc2 ♕b6 **♕a5 20 b3 ♖ac8?**
20...♖fe8 21 ♕xc7 ♕xc7 22 ♖xc7
a5 23 ♖d2± **21 ♞d5 +- ♚h8 22 a4!**
Δ b4 **♖cd8 23 ♖c5 ♖xd5 24 ♖xa5**
♖xa5 25 ♕xc7 ♖a6 26 a5! ♛g8 27
b4 ♗d4 28 ♖e4 ♗f6 29 ♕b7 1-0
Rajkovic

124 De Villeneuve-Pytel
Montpelier 77/78
1 d4 ♞f6 2 c4 g6 3 ♞c3 d5 4 ♞f3
♗g7 5 ♗f4 0-0 6 ♖c1 c5 6...dxc4!
7 dxc5 ♗e6 8 ♞d4 ♞c6 9 e3?! 9
♞xe6 fxe6 10 e3 += **♞xd4 10 exd4**
dxc4!= 11 ♗e2 11 ♗e5 ♗h6 12 ♖a1
♞g4∓ **♕a5 12 0-0 ♖fd8 =+ 13 ♕a4**
13 ♕d2 ♞h5 14 ♗e3!; 13...♞g4!
♕xa4 14 ♞xa4 ♞d5 14...♖xd4 15
♗e3 += **15 ♗e5?** 15 ♗e3!? **♗xe5 16**
dxe5 b5 17 axb6 axb6 18 b3 b5 19
♞c5 ♞f4 20 ♗f3 ♗d5! -+ 21 g3
♗xf3 22 gxf4 ♖d4 23 bxc4 ♖xf4 24
h3 bxc4 25 ♚h2 ♖xa2 26 ♚g3 g5 27
♖c3 ♗c6 28 ♞b3 ♖a3 29 ♖fc1 cxb3
0-1 Pytel

125 F.Portisch-Georgiev
Hungary 78
1 d4 ♞f6 2 c4 g6 3 ♞c3 d5 4 ♞f3 ♗g7

5 ♗f4 0-0 6 e3 c5 7 dxc5 ♞e4 8
♖c1 ♞xc3 9 bxc3 ♕a5 10 cxd5 ♗xc3+
11 ♞d2 ♞d7 12 ♕c2! N ♗b4 13 ♗e2
♞xc5

14 0-0!± ♗xd2 15 ♕xc5 ♗f5 16 g4!
♗d7 17 ♕xe7 ♗xc1 18 ♗h6?! 18
♕xd7± ♕d2 19 ♗xf8 ♗a4? 19...♕xe2
20 ♕xd7 ♗xe3 21 ♞d6 += **20 ♚b4**
♕xe2 21 ♖xc1 ♗d7 22 ♗h6 ♕xg4+
22...♗xg4? 23 ♕d4 +- **23 ♕xg4**
♗xg4 24 ♖c7 ♖c8 25 ♖e7! ♗f3 26 e4
g5 27 h4! 27 ♗xg5? ♖c4! **f5 28 exf5**
♖c4 29 d6 1-0 Adorjan

126 Pytel-Ghinda Zabrze 77
1 d4 ♞f6 2 c4 g6 3 ♞c3 d5 4 ♞f3 ♗g7
5 ♗g5 dxc4!? 6 e4 6 ♕a4+ ♞bd7 7
♕xc4 0-0 8 e3 ♞b6 9 ♕b3 ♗f5 10
♗e2 ♞e4= Ostojic-Holmov, Havana
68; 6 e3 ♗e6 7 ♞d2 c5 8 dxc5 ♞d5
9 ♗xc4 ♞xc3 10 bxc3 ♗xc4 11 ♕a4+
♞c6 12 ♕xc4 0-0 13 ♞b3 ♞e5 14
♕e2 += Petrosian-Savon, USSR 69
0-0!? 6...♗g4 7 e5!?; 6...c5 7 d5 b5
8 e5± **7 ♗xc4 ♗g4 8 ♗e2!** 8 ♕d2
♞c6 9 0-0-0 ♞d7 10 d5 ♞e5 11 ♗e2
♞b6 12 ♞d4 c5 =+ Zilberman-
Liberzon, USSR 72 **♞fd7 9 0-0** 9
♗e3!? **♞b6 10 d5 h6!? 11 ♗e3 e6 12**
h3 ♗xf3 13 ♗xf3 exd5 14 ♞xd5 ♞c6
14...♗xb2 15 ♗xh6± **15 ♖c1! ♗xb2**
16 ♗xh6 ♗xc1 17 ♗xf8 ♞xd5 18

Grunfeld

exd5 18 ♕xc1!? **♞e5 19 ♝c5 ♝xf3+**
20 ♕xf3 ♝g5= ½-½ Pytel

127 Liavdansky-Grigorian USSR 78
1 d4 ♞f6 2 c4 g6 3 ♞c3 d5 4 ♞f3 ♝g7
5 ♝g5 dxc4!? 5...♞e4 6 cxd5 ♞xg5 7
♞xg5 e6 8 ♕d2 exd5 9 ♕e3+ ♔f8=;
8 ♞f3 exd5 **6 e4?!** 6 e3 **c5 7 d5 b5!**
8 e5 8 ♞xb5 ♞xe4∓ **b4 9 exf6 exf6**
10 ♕e2+ 10 ♝d2 bxc3 11 ♝xc3 0-0
12 ♝xc4 ♖e8+ =+ **♔f8 11 ♝e3 bxc3**
12 ♝xc5+ ♔g8 13 bxc3 ♞d7 14 ♝e7
14 ♕xc4? ♕e8+ 15 ♝e2 ♞xc5 16
♕xc5 ♝a6 17 ♕e3 ♕d7! 18 ♝xa6
♖e8 -+ **♕e8 15 d6 ♞b6 16 ♖d1** 16
g3 ♞d5 17 ♖c1 ♖b8 18 ♝g2 ♞xe7
19 dxe7 ♖b7∓ **♕b7 17 ♕b2 ♝f8 =+**
18 ♕b4?! 18 ♝e2 ♝xe7 19 dxe7
♕xe7 20 0-0 =+ **♝xf3 19 gxf3 ♝xe7**
20 dxe7 ♔g7 21 ♖d4 ♖b8!∓ 22 ♝e2
♞d5 23 ♕xc4 ♖b1+ 24 ♝d1 24 ♖d1
♖xd1+ 25 ♔xd1 ♕xe7 26 ♕xd5?
♖d8; 25 ♝xd1 ♕xe7 26 ♝e2 ♖e8∓
♕xe7+ 25 ♖e4 ♕b7 26 0-0 ♖c8 27
♕d4 ♞xc3 28 ♖e3 ♕b2 29 ♕d7 ♞c5
30 ♖e7 ♕xa2 31 ♕d4 31 ♖ee1 ♖d5!
♖g5+ 32 ♔h1 ♖xd1 33 ♖xd1 ♞xd1
34 ♕xd1 ♕xf2 35 ♖xf7+ ♔h6 0-1
Gufeld

128 Johannessen-Pytel
Fredrikstad 78
1 d4 ♞f6 2 c4 g6 3 ♞c3 d5 4 ♞f3 ♝g7
5 ♝g5 ♞e4 6 ♝f4?! 6 ♝h4 ♞xc3 7
bxc3 c5 8 e3 ♞c6 9 cxd5 ♕xd5 10
♝e2 0-0 10...cxd4 11 cxd4 ♕a5+
12 ♕d2 ♝e6!= **11 0-0 ♝f5?!** 11...
cxd4= **12 c4! ♕e4 13 d5 ♞d4!?**
13...♝xa1 14 ♕xa1± **14 ♞xd4 cxd4**
15 f3 ♕c2 16 e4 16 exd4 ♕c3 ♕xd1
17 ♖axd1 e5! 18 ♝g3?! 18 exf5 +=;
18 ♝c1!? **♝d7 19 f4 exf4! 20 ♝xf4**
♖fe8 21 ♝d3 ♖ac8 22 ♝d6 b6 23
a4?

23...f5!!∓ 23...♝xa4 24 ♖a1 +− **24**
exf5 ♝xf5 25 ♝xf5 gxf5 26 ♝g3 ♖xc4
27 ♖xf5 d3! 28 d6 28 ♖xd3 ♝d4+
♖d4 29 ♖f4?! 29 h4 ♖xd6 30 ♖f3
♖d4 31 ♖fxd3 ♖xa4 32 ♖d7 ♝f6
33 h4 ♖e7 34 ♖d8+ ♔f7 35 h5 ♖a1
36 ♖xa1 ♝xa1 37 ♔f2 ♝f6 38 ♖a8
b5 39 ♖b8 ♞d4+ 40 ♔f3 ♝b6 41
♝d6 ♖d7 0-1 Pytel

129 Ornstein-Mihaljcisin
Vrnjacka Banja 78
1 d4 ♞f6 2 c4 g6 3 ♞c3 d5 4 ♝f4
♝g7 5 e3 0-0 6 ♕b3 c6 7 ♞f3 ♕a5
8 ♞d2 ♞bd7 9 ♝e2 ♞h5 10 ♝xh5
dxc4 11 ♞xc4 ♕xh5 12 0-0 b5!?
12...e5 **13 ♞a5 e5 14 ♝g3!?** exd4
15 exd4 c5!? 15...♝xd4 16 ♞xc6
♝g7 17 ♞d5; 15...♝a6 16 ♞xc6 b4
17 ♕xb4 ♝xf1 18 ♖xf1 **16 ♕xb5**
cxd4 17 ♕xh5 gxh5 18 ♞d5 ♞f6
18...♞e5 19 ♝xe5 ♝xe5 20 ♞c6 ♝g7
21 ♞c7 ♝b7 22 ♞e7+; 20...♝d6 **19**
♞e7+ ♔h8 20 ♝e5! ♖e8 21 ♞ac6
d3 22 ♖fd1 ♝a6 23 b4?! 23 ♞f5!?
♖ac8 24 ♞ce7; 23...♖e6 24 ♞fd4
♞e4! 24 ♝xg7+ ♔xg7 25 f3?! 25
a4 ♞c3 26 ♖d2 ♞e4 27 ♖b2!? ♝c4
♞c3 26 ♖d2 ♔f6!? 26...♞b5 **27 a4**
♝c4? 27...♖xe7 28 ♞xe7 ♔xe7 29 b5
♝b7 30 ♖xd3 **28 ♔f2 ♞e2 29 ♞a5**
♝e6 30 ♞ec6 ♝f5 31 ♞b3 h4 32
b5 ♞f4 35 ♞bd4 ♖g8!? 33...♝g6 34 a5

♘e6 35 ♘xe6 ♖xe6 36 a6 ♖d6 37
♖b2 ♗f5 38 ♘xa7! d2 39 b6 +− **34**
♘xf5 ♖xg2+ 35 ♔e3 ♔xf5? 35...♖xd2
36 ♔xf4 ♖xh2 37 ♘e5!? **36 ♖xg2**
♘xg2+ 37 ♔xd3 ♘f4+ 38 ♔c4 ♘e6
39 ♖d1 ♘g5 40 ♖d7 ♔e6 41 ♖xa7
♖xa7 42 ♘xa7 ♘xf3 43 b6 ♘e5+
44 ♔b5 ♔d7 45 a5 f5 46 a6 f4 47
♘c6 ♘xc6 48 a7 1-0

King's Indian

130 Pytel-Bielczyk Zabrze 77
1 d4 ♘f6 2 c4 d6 3 ♘c3 ♘bd7 4 e4
e5 5 ♘ge2 c6 5...g6 6 f3 **6 g3** 6 f3
exd4! g6 7 **♗g2 ♗g7 8 0-0 0-0 9**
h3 ♕b6 10 d5 cxd5 11 cxd5 ♘c5
12 ♖b1 a5 13 ♗e3 13 b3! △ a3, b4
+= **♗d7 14 ♕d2 ♖fc8 15 b3 ♕b4 16**
♖fc1 ♘e8= 17 f3 f5 18 ♘d1 fxe4
19 fxe4 b6?! 20 ♘f2 ♘c7 21 ♘c3
♘b5 22 ♘xb5 ♗xb5 23 ♖c2!± ♖a7?
24 ♕c1 +− ♖cc7 25 a3 1-0 Pytel

131 Petrosian-Kochiev USSR 78
1 d4 g6 2 c4 ♗g7 3 ♘c3 d6 4 e4 e5
5 ♘ge2 ♘f6 6 f3 0-0 7 ♗g5 ♘c6 8 d5
♘d4 9 ♘xd4 exd4 10 ♕xd4 h6 11
♗xf6 ♗xf6 12 ♕d2 c6 13 ♗d3 ♕b6
14 0-0-0 a5 15 ♔b1 a4 16 a3 ♗g7
17 h4 ♕d4?! 18 ♕c2! cxd5

19 ♗f1!! △ ♖d5-b5± **♕c5 20 ♖xd5**

♕c6 21 ♖b5 ♗d7 22 h5 g5 23 ♘d5
♕h8 24 ♘b6 ♖a6 25 ♘xd7 ♕xd7
26 ♗e2 ♕c7 27 ♖d1 ♖d8 28 ♖dd5
♗e5 29 ♖b4 ♖d7 30 ♕d2 ♔g7 31
♗d3 ♖c6 32 ♖bb5 ♖c5 33 ♕b4 ♖xb5
34 ♖xb5 ♗d4 35 ♖a5 ♗e5 36 ♗c2
♕c6 37 ♖b5 ♗d4 38 ♗xa4 ♗e5 39
♖a5 1-0 Suetin

132 Gheorghiu-Fedorowicz
Lone Pine 78
1 d4 g6 2 c4 d6 3 ♘c3 ♘d7 4 ♘f3 e5
5 e4 c6 6 ♗e2 ♗g7!? 6...♘gf6 += **7**
d5! c5 8 g4! ♘f8 9 ♖g1 ♘f6 10 ♘d2!
10 h3 h6! △ g5, ♘g6∞ h6 11 h4 ♘g8!?
12 b4! 12 ♖h1? ♗f6!∞; 12 ♘f3 ♘f6∞
cxb4 13 ♕a4+ ♗d7 14 ♘b5 ♗f8
14...♘c5 15 ♕xb4 +=; 15 ♘xd6+
♔f8 16 ♘xb7!!± **15 c5 ♗xc5** 15...
dxc5? 16 d6! +− **16 ♘xd6+ ♔e7 17**
♘xc8+ ♔f6 18 ♕d1 18 ♕xb4?? ♘d3+
♖xc8 19 ♗b2 ♗d6 20 f4 ♔g7 21 g5
♘d7 22 ♖c1! 22 ♘c4 ♖xc4! 23 ♗xc4
♕e7∞; 22 ♘f3 ♖c3!∞ hxg5 23 hxg5
♖xc1 24 ♕xc1 ♕b6 25 ♖f1! ♕e3 26
♘c4! +− ♕g3+ 26...♕xc1+ 27 ♗xc1
♗b8 28 ♗b2 +− **27 ♔d1 ♗b8 28**
fxe5 ♖h4?! 28...♘xe5 29 ♕f4!± ;
29 d6± **29 e6+ ♗e5 30 exf7 ♘f6 31**
♗xe5 ♗xe5 32 f8♕+ ♔xf8 33 ♕c8+
♔g7 34 ♖xf6! ♖h1+ 35 ♔c2 1-0
Gheorghiu

133 Petursson-Sahovic
Lone Pine 78
1 c4 g6 2 d4 ♗g7 3 e4 d6 4 ♘c3 ♘f6
5 ♗e2 0-0 6 ♘f3 e5 7 dxe5 dxe5 8
♕xd8 ♖xd8 9 ♗g5 ♖e8 10 0-0-0
♘c6! N 10...♘a6 **11 ♘d5** 11 h3!?
♗xd5 12 cxd5 ♘d4= 13 ♘xd4 exd4
14 ♗d3 ♗d7 15 ♔b1 c5 16 dxc6 bxc6
17 ♖c1 ♗f8 18 ♗f6 c5 19 h4!? h5
20 f3 ♖ab8 21 g4 hxg4 22 h5 gxf3
23 e5! 23 hxg6? fxg6 24 e5 ♗f5 −+

97

♗f5 24 ♗xf5 gxf5 25 h6 ♔h7 26 ♖cg1 c4? 26...f2 27 ♖g2 f1♕+ 28 ♖xf1 ♗xh6 29 ♖h1 ♖g8 Δ ♖g6∓

27 ♖g8!= 27 ♖g7+ ♗xg7 28 hxg7+ ♔g6 29 ♖g1+ ♔h5 30 ♖g5+ ♔h4 31 g8♕ ♖xg8 32 ♖xg8+ ♔h3 −+ ♗e7 27...♔xg8?? 28 h7 mate 28 ♖g7+ ♔h8 ½-½ Sahovic

134 Mikaeljan-Zhidkov USSR 77
1 ♘f3 ♘f6 2 c4 g6 3 ♘c3 ♗g7 4 e4 0-0 5 d4 d6 6 ♗e2 c6 7 0-0 a6!? 8 ♖b1 8 e5!? ♘e8 9 ♗f4 f6 += b5 9 cxb5?! 9 b4 bxc4 10 ♗xc4 d5 11 ♗d3 dxe4 12 ♘xe4 ♘xe4 13 ♗xe4 ♗e6= axb5= 10 b4 ♘bd7 11 ♕b3 ♘b6 12 d5!? ♘a4! 12...cxd5 13 exd5 ♗f5 14 ♗xb5! ♗xb1 15 ♘xb1 ♘fxd5 16 ♗c6 += 13 ♗d2! 13 dxc6 ♘xc3 14 ♕xc3 ♘xe4 15 ♕c2 ♘c3∓; 13 ♘xa4 bxa4∓ ♗b7 13...♘xc3 14 ♗xc3 cxd5 15 exd5 ♗b7 16 ♖fd1= 14 dxc6 ♗xc6 15 ♗d3 15 ♗xb5 ♗xb5 16 ♘xb5 ♘xe4 =+ ♘xc3 16 ♗xc3 e5! 16... ♘xe4?? 17 ♗xg7 ♔xg7 18 ♕c2 +− 17 ♘d2 ♕b6 18 h3 ♗h6 18...♘h5 Δ ♔h8, f5 =+ 19 ♖be1 ♗f4 20 ♕b2 ♕b7 21 ♕b1 d5! 21...♕a6 22 ♘b3 ♕xa2 23 ♘a5 ♕xb1 24 ♗xb1α 22 ♘b3 dxe4 23 ♘c5 ♕c8!∓ 24 ♗xe4 ♘xe4 25 ♖xe4 ♗xe4 26 ♕xe4 ♖xa2 27 ♗xe5 27 g3 ♗xg3! 28 fxg3 ♕xh3

−+ ♗xe5 28 ♕xe5 ♖e8 29 ♕d5 ♕a8 30 ♕d7 ♖a1 31 ♕xb5 31 ♕xe8+! ♕xe8 32 ♖xa1 ♕e2∓ ♖xf1+ 32 ♕xf1 ♕a3 33 ♕c4 ♖b8 34 ♘d3 ♖d8 35 ♘c5 ♕a1+ 36 ♔h2 ♕e5+ 37 f4 ♕d4 38 ♕xd4 ♖xd4 39 b5 ♖xf4 40 b6 ♖b4 0-1 Gufeld

135 Slonimsky-Zhelnin USSR 78
1 d4 ♘f6 2 c4 g6 3 ♘c3 ♗g7 4 e4 d6 5 ♘f3 0-0 6 ♗e2 e5 7 0-0 ♘c6 8 d5 ♘e7 9 b4 ♘e8 10 c5 ♔h8!? 11 ♘d2 f5 12 cxd6 cxd6 13 a4? ♗h6! 14 ♘c4 ♗xc1 15 ♖xc1 f4 16 ♘b5 ♘g8 17 ♗g4 ♗xg4 18 ♕xg4 ♘gf6 19 ♕e2 a6 20 ♘ba3 g5 21 a5 g4!∓ 22 ♖c3 ♖g8 23 ♘b6 ♖b8 24 b5 f3! 25 ♕e3 ♘h5! 26 gxf3 ♕h4 27 f4 exf4 28 ♕d4+ ♗ef6 29 ♘d7 g3! −+ 30 fxg3 fxg3 31 ♖xg3 ♖xg3+ 32 hxg3 ♕xg3+ 33 ♔h1 ♖g8 0-1 Suetin

136 Miles-Vukic Bugojno 78
1 c4 ♘f6 2 ♘c3 g6 3 ♘f3 ♗g7 4 e4 d6 5 d4 0-0 6 ♗e2 e5 7 0-0 ♘c6 8 d5 ♘e7 9 ♘e1 ♘d7 10 ♘d3 f5 11 ♗d2 ♘f6 12 f3 f4 13 c5 g5 14 ♖c1 ♘g6 15 cxd6 cxd6 16 ♘b5 ♖f7 17 ♕c2 ♘e8 18 a4 h5 19 ♘f2 ♗f8

20 ♘xa7!? N ♖c7 21 ♗a5 ♖xc2 21... b6? 22 ♘c6 +− 22 ♗xd8 ♖xe2 23

♘xc8 ♖xa7 23...♖xb2 24 a5 += **24**
♘d3 += g4 25 ♖f2 ♖e3 26 ♘e1 ♖a8?!
27 ♖fc2 ♖b3 28 ♔f2 ♖a2 29 ♖b1
♔f7 30 ♔e2 ♗g7 31 ♘d3 ♗f6 32 ♖b6
♖a8 33 ♗f2 ♘h4 34 ♗g1 ♗d8 35 ♘c1±
♖b4 36 b3 ♖a3?! 37 ♖a2?! 37 ♘xd6+!
♘xd6 38 ♗c5 +− **♖a6 38 ♖c2 ♘h4 39**
♘a2 ♖xa2 39...♖b5 40 b4 ♖a4 41
♖bb2! △ ♘c3 +− **40 ♖xa2 ♘xg2 41**
♖a4! +− ♖xa4 41...♖b5 42 b4 △ ♘a7
+− **42 bxa4 ♘h4 43 ♖xb7+ ♔f8 44**
fxg4 hxg4 45 ♗b6 ♗xb6 46 ♘xb6
♘f3 47 ♘d7+ ♔g8 48 a5 ♘xh2 49 a6
1-0 49...g3 50 a7 f3+ 51 ♔d2 f2 52
♘f6+ **Miles**

137 Pinter-F.Portisch Hungary 78
1 d4 ♘f6 2 c4 g6 3 ♘c3 ♗g7 4 e4 d6
5 ♗e2 0-0 6 ♘f3 e5 7 0-0 ♘c6 8 d5
♘e7 9 ♘e1 ♘d7 10 f3 f5 11 g4 ♘f6 12
♘d3 c6 13 ♗e3 ♔h8!? N 13...b5 14
dxc6 bxc4 15 ♘b4 ♖b8? 16 ♗xc4+
♔h8 17 ♘b5 +− Pinter-Perenyi 78;
15...a5 16 c7!± **14 h3! b5?! 15 dxc6**
bxc4 16 ♘b4 ♖b8? 16...♗e6! **17 ♕a4!**
a5 18 ♘bd5 ♘fxd5 19 exd5 e4 20 fxe4
20 ♕xc4?? ♖b4 −+ **♖xb2 21 ♕xc4**
♖b4 22 ♕d3 fxe4 23 ♕d2! 23 ♘xe4?
♗a6 24 ♕xa6 ♖xe4 25 ♕d3 ♖xe3 26
♕xe3 ♘xd5 **♘g8 24 ♖ab1 +− ♖xb1 25**
♘xb1 h5 26 ♖xf8 ♕xf8 27 ♗d4 ♕e7
28 ♗xg7+ ♔xg7 29 ♕d4+ ♔h7 30 ♘c3
hxg4 **31 hxg4 ♕h4 32 ♕a7+! ♔h6 33**
♕f2 ♕g5 34 ♕f8+ ♔h7 35 ♕xc8 ♕e3+
36 ♔g2 ♕xc3 37 ♕d7+ ♔h6 38 g5+
♔xg5 39 c7 ♘f6 40 c8♕ ♕e1 1-0
Adorjan

138 Liebert-Knaak
DDR Final 78
1 ♘f3 ♘f6 2 c4 g6 3 ♘c3 ♗g7 4 d4
d6 5 e4 0-0 6 ♗e2 ♘bd7 7 0-0 e5 8
♖e1 c6 9 ♗f1 a5 10 ♖b1 exd4 11
♘xd4 ♖e8 **12 b3?** 12 f3; 12 ♗f4;

12 ♘c2 **♘g4! 13 ♕xg4** 13 f3 ♘xh2
14 ♔xh2 ♘e5+ 15 f4 ♕h4+ 16 ♔g1
♗xd4+ 17 ♕xd4 ♕xe1 18 ♗b2 c5
19 ♕d3 ♕h4 20 ♘d5; 13...♕b6? 14
♘ce2 ♘c5! 15 fxg4 ♖xe4 16 ♗b2
♗xg4∓/∞ **♗xd4 14 ♕g3 ♕f6** 14...
♕b6 15 ♗e3 **15 ♗b2 ♘c5 16 ♖bd1**
♗e5 17 ♕e3 g5 17...a4 18 b4 a3 19
♗a1 ♘a6 **18 ♕d2 a4** 18...♘e6 19
♘a4 **19 b4** 19 ♘xa4 ♗xb2 **♘e6 20**
♖e3 g4 20...♗f4 21 ♘d5 **21 a3 ♘g5**
22 ♕c2 ♕h6 23 ♖g3

23...♕g7! 24 ♘xa4?! ♖xb2 25 ♗xb2
♗xe4 26 ♖e3 ♗f5 27 ♗d3 ♖xa3!
28 ♖xe4 ♗xe4 29 ♗xe4 ♖c3! 29...
♖a2 30 ♖b1 d5 (30...♖xb2=) 31
♗d3 **30 ♕b1** 30 ♕e2 f5 31 ♗d5+
♔f8 32 ♗e6 ♕f6 33 ♖xd6 ♖c1+
34 ♘d1 ♖xe6 −+ **♖b3 31 ♖d2 f5 32**
♗xf5 ♕c3! 32...♖xb2? 33 ♗xh7+
♔h8? 34 ♖xb2; 33...♔f8 34 ♖xb2
♕xb2 35 ♕f5+ ∓/∞ **33 ♖d1 ♖xb2 34**
♕a1 ♖d2 35 ♗xg4 ♖xd1+ 0-1

139 Dorfman-Kochiev USSR 77
1 c4 g6 2 d4 ♘f6 3 ♘c3 ♗g7 4 e4 d6
5 ♗e2 0-0 6 ♘f3 e5 7 0-0 ♘bd7 8
♖e1 c6 9 ♗f1 a5 10 ♗e3 10 ♖b1!?
exd4 11 ♘xd4 ♖e8 12 ♗f4 ♘c5 13
f3 d5 14 exd5 ♖xe1 15 ♕xe1 ♘xd5
16 cxd5 ♗xd4+ 17 ♗e3 ♗xe3+ 18 ♕x
e3 += Tal-Grigorian, USSR 77 **exd4**

11 ♘xd4 ♖e8 12 f3 d5 13 cxd5 cxd5
14 ♘db5 dxe4 15 ♘d6 ♖f8 15...exf3?
16 ♘cxe4 16 f4!? ♘xe4 17 ♗xe4 a4
18 ♗d4 ♘f6 19 ♗c5 ♘xe4= 20 ♖xe4
♗xb2 21 ♖b1 a3 22 ♗xf8 ♕xf8 23
♖e2 ♗f5 24 ♖bxb2 axb2 25 ♖xb2
♕a3 26 ♖xb7 ♕xa2 27 ♕b3 ♕xb3
28 ♖xb3 ½-½ Gufeld

140 Kovacevic-Ivanovic
Jugoslavia Final 78

1 d4 ♘f6 2 ♘f3 g6 3 c4 ♗g7 4 ♘c3
0-0 5 e4 d6 6 ♗e2 ♘bd7 7 0-0 e5 8
♖e1 c6 9 ♗f1 ♖e8 9...a5 10 d5 ♕c7
11 ♖b1! 11 g3 ♘f8 12 a3 ♘g4 13
♘h4 a6 14 ♗d2 h5 15 h3 ♘f6 16 b4
a5 12 a3 ♗f8 13 h3 a4 14 ♗e3 14
♘xa4? ♘xe4 15 ♖xe4 ♖xa4 16 ♕xa4
♘c5 △ ♘xe4 ♕a5 15 ♗d3! ♖a6? 15...
♘c5 16 ♗xc5 dxc5 17 ♗c2; 15...c5
16 ♘b5! 16 g4 16 ♘d2 ♖a8 17 ♘d2
h5? 17...♘c5 18 ♗xc5 dxc5 19 ♗c2
h5!: 18 ♗c2 h5!: 18 ♗e2 ♗d7 18
♗e2! hxg4 19 hxg4 ♘c5 20 ♕g2 ♗d7
21 ♖h1 ♘h7 22 ♕g1 f6 22...♗g7 23
♕h2 ♘f8 24 ♗h6

23 ♖xh7! 23 ♖h3 ♗g7 24 ♕h2 ♘f8
25 ♗h6 ♖e7 26 ♗xg7 ♖xg7 27 ♖h8+
♔f7 28 g5 f5; 25 ♖h1 g5 ♕xh7 24
♕h2+ ♔g8 25 ♖h1 ♗g7 26 ♕h7+
♔f7 27 ♗h6 27 ♖h6 g5 28 ♕g6+
♔f8 29 ♖h7 ♖e7; 28 ♖g6 ♖g8 29

♘f3 ♕f8 30 ♗xg5 fxg5 31 ♘xg5 ♗e8
32 ♖xg7 ♖xg7 33 ♕h8+ ♔e7 34
♕xg7+ ♔d8; 28 ♖xf6+ ♔xf6 29 ♗xg5+
♔f7 30 ♘h6 ♖g8 31 g5 ♔e7!; 29
♕h5+ ♔e7 30 ♗xg5+ ♔f8 ♖g8 28 g5
fxg5 28...f5 29 ♘h5! gxh5 30 g6+
♔f6 31 ♖xh5 △ ♗g5 mate; 30...♔f8
31 ♗xg7+ ♖xg7 32 ♕h8+ ♖g8 33
♕f6+ ♔e8 34 ♕f7+ 29 ♘f3 ♕d8
29...g4 30 ♘g5+ ♔f6 31 ♗xg7+ ♖xg7
32 ♕h4 30 ♘xg5+ ♔f6? 30...♕xg5+!
31 ♗xg5 ♖h8 32 ♕xh8 ♖xh8 33
♖xh8 ♗xh8 34 ♗e3! cxd5 35 cxd5
△ ♗xc5, ♗b5; 32...♗xh8 33 ♖d1!
cxd5 34 cxd5 △ f3, ♗b5 31 f4! exf4
32 ♖f1 ♗f5 33 exf5 ♖xh6 34 ♕xh6
♕e7 35 ♘e6 ♗xe6 36 fxe6 1-0

141 Szekely-Honfi Hungary 77

1 ♘f3 ♘f6 2 c4 g6 3 ♘c3 ♗g7 4 e4
d6 5 d4 0-0 6 ♗e2 ♘bd7 7 0-0 e5
8 ♗e3 c6 N 9 ♕c2 ♘g4 10 ♗g5 ♕c7
11 ♖ad1 exd4 12 ♘xd4 ♘c5 13
♗c1?! 13 ♗h4 a5 14 h3 ♘f6 15 f4
♖e8 16 ♗f3≈ Gheorghiu-Honfi,
Bucharest 73; 13 h3?! ♗xd4 14 ♖xd4
♘e6 15 ♖d2 ♘xg5 16 hxg4 f6≈
♖e8 14 b4!? 14 h3; 14 f3 ♘h6 15 b4
♘e6≈ ♘a6 15 h3!? 15 a3!? d5 16
♗xg4 ♗xg4 17 f3 ♗e6 18 ♘xe6 fxe6≈
♘xb4!? 16 ♕b3 ♗xd4 17 ♖xd4 ♘f6
18 ♖fd1? 18 ♗f4? ♕b6 19 ♖fd1 ♘d7
20 ♗xd6 ♘c5≈ ♘a6 19 ♗g5 19 ♗f4
♘c5 20 ♕b1 ♕a5 21 ♗d2 ♕b6∓ ♘c5
20 ♕c2 ♖e6 21 f4 ♘e8 22 ♗g4

Diagram

22...f6! 23 f5 23 ♗xe6+ ♘xe6 24
♗h4 ♘xd4∓ fxg5! 24 fxe6 ♗xe6∓
25 ♕f2?! ♗xg4 26 hxg4 ♘e6 27
♖4d2 ♕g7 28 ♕e3 ♕e5 29 ♖b1 b6
30 ♕d3 ♖d8 31 ♖f1 ♘f6 32 ♕f3
♖f8 33 ♕h3 ♕c5+ 34 ♔h1 ♘f4 35

♕f3 ♕xc4 36 ♖xd6 ♞xg4! 37 ♖dd1
♞e6 38 ♕e2 ♕xe2 39 ♞xe2 ♞f2+
0-1 Honfi

142 Knaak-Bruggemann
DDR Final 78

1 d4 ♞f6 2 c4 d6 3 ♞c3 ♞bd7 4 e4
e5 5 ♞f3 g6 6 ♗e2 ♗g7 7 0-0 0-0 8
♗e3 c6 9 d5 c5 10 ♞e1 ♞e8 11 g4!?
11 ♞d3 f5 12 f4; 12 exf5 gxf5 13 f4
♔h8 11...f5 12 exf5 gxf5 13 gxf5
♖xf5 14 ♗g4; 13...♞df6 14 ♕c2±
12 ♞g2 b6?! 13 ♗d3 ♞df6 14 f3
♕e7 15 ♕d2 ♞g8 16 ♖ae1 ♗d7 16...
f5 17 exf5 gxf5 18 gxf5 ♗xf5 19
♗xf5 ♖xf5 20 ♞e4 17 ♞e2 ♞c7 18
♞g3 a5 18...b5 19 ♕a5 19 h4 b5 20
h5 bxc4 21 ♗xc4 h6 21...♖fb8 22
g5! hxg5 23 ♗xg5 ♗f6 23...f6 24
♞h4! ♗e8 25 ♗e3 24 f4! exf4 24...
♔g7 25 ♗xf6+ ♕xf6 26 ♞xf4 ♕g7
27 hxg6 fxg6 28 ♖e2 ♞f6 28...♞h6
29 ♖h2 ♔g8 30 ♞xg6; 29...♖f6 30
♞e6 29 ♖h2+ ♞h7 30 ♔g2 ♖f7 31
♖fh1 ♕f6 32 ♖h6 ♖g8 33 ♖f1! ♖e7
34 ♞e6 ♕e5 35 ♞xc7 ♗f5 36 ♕c3
♕xc3 37 bxc3 ♗xe4+ 38 ♞xe4 ♖xe4
39 ♞e6 1-0

143 Uhlmann-Knaak Leipzig 77

1 c4 g6 2 e4 ♗g7 3 d4 d6 4 ♞c3 ♞d7
5 ♗e2 e5 6 ♞f3 ♞gf6 7 0-0 0-0 8 ♗e3
8 ♖e1 c6 9 ♗f1 a5 10 ♖b1 exd4 11

♞xd4 ♖e8 12 f3?! d5 13 cxd5 cxd5
14 exd5 ♖xe1 15 ♕xe1 ♞b6= Malich-
Knaak, Leipzig 77; 14 ♞db5 dxe4
15 ♞d6 exf3 16 ♞xe8 ♞g4∞
Polugaevsky-Kochiev, USSR 77; 12
♗f4 ♞c5 13 f3 d5∞; 12 ♞c2!?; 10
♗e3!? Dorfman-Kochiev, USSR 77
♞g4 9 ♗g5 f6 10 ♗d2! c6 11 b4 f5
12 d5 f4! 13 ♗c1 c5!? 14 ♞b5 14
♞a3!? ♞df6 15 ♞g5 15 bxc5? ♞xe4
16 cxd6 ♞exf2 17 ♖xf2 ♞xf2 18
♔xf2 e4 19 ♞fd4 ♕h4+ 20 ♔g1 f3
21 gxf3 ♗e5∓ a6 16 ♞e6 ♗xe6 17
dxe6 axb5 18 ♗xg4 bxc4 19 bxc5
dxc5 20 ♖b1 ♕e7?! 20...♕xd1 21
♗xd1 ♞xe4 22 ♖xb7 ♞c3 23 ♗b2
♞xd1 24 ♖xd1 ♖xa2 25 ♖dd7 ♗f6∞;
23 ♗f3? e4∓; 23 ♗g4 h5!∞ 21 ♗e2!
♞xe4 21...♕xe6 22 ♕c2 c3! 23 f3
△ ♕xc3± 22 ♗xc4 ♞d6 22...♞c3?
23 ♕d7!; 22...♖fd8 23 ♖xb7! +− 23
♗d5 e4 24 ♖e1 24 ♗b2!? ♞d4 25
♗b2 ♗xb2 26 ♖xb2 ♖ad8 27 ♕c1
♖f5 28 ♕xc5 f3 28...e3 29 fxe3 fxe3
30 g3 += 29 g3? 29 ♖d2! ♞c8 30
♕c3! ♖fxd5 31 ♖xd5 ♖xd5 32 ♕xc8+
♔g7 33 ♕c3+ ♕f6 34 ♕c7+±; 29...
♕g5 30 e7+ ♔g7 31 ♕c3+ ♔h6 32
♕e3 ♖e8 33 ♗b3 ♞b5 34 ♖d7 +−
e3!! 30 ♕d4 30 ♖xe3 ♖c8 −+; 30
fxe3 f2+ 31 ♖xf2 ♖xf2 32 ♔xf2 ♞e4+
−+ b5? 30...♞e8! −+ 0-1 Malich

144 Uhlmann-Vadasz Tallinn 77

1 c4 g6 2 d4 ♞f6 3 ♞c3 ♗g7 4 e4 d6
5 ♗e2 0-0 6 ♗g5 ♞bd7 7 ♕d2 e5 8
♞f3 8 d5!? ♞c5? 9 ♗xf6! ♗xf6 10
b4 ♞d7 11 ♖c1 += F.Portisch-Sax 77
♕e8!? 9 0-0! 9 dxe5?! dxe5 10 0-0
b6 11 h3 ♞c5 12 ♕c2 ♞e6 13 ♗e3
♗b7 14 ♖ad1 ♞d7 15 ♞e1 ♞dc5 16
♞d5 c6 17 ♞c3 ♞d4 =+ Kluger-
Vadasz, Hungary Final 71 exd4 10
♞xd4 ♞xe4 11 ♞xe4 ♕xe4 12 ♞b5

101

♕c6 **13 ♗f3?!** 13 ♖ac1! a6 14 ♘c3
♘b6 15 b3 △ ♗f3 += **♕xc4 14 ♗e2**
14 a4!? c6 15 ♘xd6 (15 ♘c7 ♖b8
16 ♗e7 d5 =+) ♕e6 16 ♖fe1 ♘e5 17
♗e2 h6∝ **♕c6 15 ♖ac1 ♘c5 16 b4 a6
17 bxc5** 17 ♘c3 ♗xc3 18 ♕xc3 ♘e6
19 ♕f6 ♕d7 20 ♗h6 ♕d8 21 ♕b2
♖e8 22 ♘c4 ♕h4 −+ **axb5 18 ♗e7**

18...d5! 19 ♕b4 ♗d7 20 ♗xf8 ♗xf8
21 ♖fd1? b6! 22 ♕b3 bxc5 23 ♖xd5
♗e6 24 ♗f3 ♖b8 25 ♖d2 ♗xb3 26
♗xc6 ♗e6 27 ♖cd1 c4 28 a3 ♖b6
28...♗xa3! 29 ♖d8+ ♖xd8 30 ♖xd8+
♔g7 31 ♗xb5 c3 −+ **29 ♗d5 ♗xd5
30 ♖xd5 ♗xa3 31 ♖a1 ♗d6 32 ♖c1**
♕f8 **33** ♔f1 ♔e7 **34** ♔e2 ♔d7 **35**
g3 ♔c6 **36 ♖d2 ♖a6 37 ♖dc2 ♔c5
38 f4 ♗f8 39** ♔f2 ♗g7 **40** ♔e2 ♗d4
0-1 Vadasz

145 Lukacs-Uhlmann Bucharest 78
**1 d4 ♘f6 2 c4 g6 3 ♘c3 ♗g7 4 e4
d6 5 ♗e2 0-0 6 ♗g5 ♘bd7 7 ♕d2 e5
8 d5** 8 ♘f3 ♘c5 9 f3 h6 10 ♗e3
10 ♗xh6 ♘fxe4 11 fxe4 ♕h4+ −+
**a5 11 g4 h5 12 g5 ♘h7 13 h4 f5
14 0-0-0** 14 gxf6?! **b6 15 ♘h3 ♖f7 16
exf5 ♗xf5 17 ♘f2 ♘f8 18 ♘fe4 ♘fd7
19 b3** 19 ♘g3 ♕e7! **20** ♔b2 ♘b8! **21
♘g3?!** 21 a3 a4 22 b4 ♘b3 23 ♕c2
♘d4 **e4! 22 ♘xf5?** 22 fxe4 ♗xe4
23 ♖hf1 ♖xf1 24 ♖xf1 ♘bd7 25 ♗d4

♖e8 **♖xf5 23 f4** 23 ♖hf1 exf3 24
♗xf3 ♖xf3 25 ♖xf3 ♘e4 **♘ba6! 24
a3 ♘b4! 25 axb4** 25 ♗xc5 bxc5 26
♔b1 e3 27 ♕c1 ♗xc3 28 ♕xc3 ♕e4+
29 ♔b2 ♖xf4 (△ ♗f2) 30 axb4 axb4
31 ♕d3 ♕e5+ −+ **axb4 26 ♖c1?** 26
♗d4 ♘d3+ 27 ♗xd3 ♗xd4 −+ ♖a3!
0-1

146 Hort-Vogt Polanica 77
**1 d4 ♘f6 2 c4 g6 3 ♘c3 ♗g7 4 e4 d6
5 ♗e2 0-0 6 ♗g5 h6 7 ♗e3 e5** 7...c5!?
8 d5 c6 9 h4!± cxd5 10 cxd5 ♘bd7
10...h5 **11 h5 g5 12 g4! +− ♘c5 13
f3 a5 14 a4 ♘e8 15 ♗c4 ♕f6 16 ♘h3
♘c7 17 0-0 ♗d7 18** ♕e2 ♖fc8 19
♘f2 ♗f8 20 ♖fc1 ♗e7 21 ♔g2 ♘7a6
22 b3 ♗d8 23 ♘h1 ♗b6 24 ♘g3 ♘b5
25 ♖ab1 ♔h7 26 ♘b5 ♗xb5 27 ♗xb5
♕d8 28 ♘f5 ♗xf5 29 ♗xa6! ♖xa6
30 ♗xb6 ♕xb6 31 ♕b5 ♕xb5 32 axb5
♖xc1 33 ♖xc1 ♘c5 34 ♖c3 ♖d8 35
b6! ♖d7 36 ♔f2 a4 37 bxa4 ♘xa4
38 ♖c7 ♘xb6 39 ♖xd7 ♘xd7 40 ♘xd6
1-0 Pytel

147 Alexandria-Chiburdanidze (10) 77
**1 d4 ♘f6 2 c4 g6 3 ♘c3 ♗g7 4 e4 d6
5 f3 0-0 6 ♘ge2** 6 ♗e3; 6 ♗g5 **c5!
7 ♗e3 ♘bd7 8 ♕d2 a6 9 ♘g3?!** N 9
**0-0-0 cxd4 10 ♗xd4 ♘e5 11 ♗e2 ♗e6
12 ♘d5 b5! 13 ♘xf6+** 13 cxb5 axb5
14 ♗b6 ♕d7 15 ♘c7 ♖ab8 16 ♗xb5
♘c6∝ **♗xf6 14 cxb5 axb5 15 f4** 15
♗xb5 ♘xf3+ 16 gxf3 ♗xd4 17 ♕xd4
♕a5+∓ **♘c4 16 ♗xc4 ♗xc4 =+ 17
a3?!** 17 ♗xf6 exf6 18 a3 d5 =+ ♗xd4
18 ♕xd4 ♕a5+ 19 ♔f2 e5!∓

Diagram

20 ♕e3 ♕a7?! 20...exf4 21 ♕xf4 d5
22 ♖hd1 ♕b6+ 23 ♕e3 ♕f6+∓ **21
♕xa7 ♖xa7= 22** ♔e3 exf4+ **23** ♔xf4

♖b8 23...d5!= **24 ♖hd1 ♖a6?! 24...
b4!= 25 ♖d4 += ♔f8 26 ♘h1! ♗e6
27 ♖ad1 ♔e7 28 ♘f2 ♖c6 29 ♘d3
♖bb6 30 ♘b4 ♖c5 31 ♖1d2 ♖c1 32
♔e3 32 ♖c2!? ♖e1+ 33 ♔d3 ♗c4+
34 ♔c3? ♖e3+ 35 ♘d3 35 ♖2d3
♖e2 ♖a6 36 ♔c2 ♖c6! =+ 37 ♘b4
♗b3+ 38 ♔b1 ♖e1+ 39 ♖d1 ♗xd1
40 ♘xc6+ ♔d7 41 ♘e5+ ♔e6 42 ♘d3
♖g1∓ 43 ♘a2 ♗c2! 43...g5!?; 43...
♖xg2?? 44 ♘e1! 44 g3 g5 45 ♘b4
♗b1+ 46 ♔b3 ♖e1 47 ♘a6 ♗xe4 48
♘c7+ ♔e5 49 ♘xb5 ♗c6 50 ♖b4 f5!
-+ 51 ♘d4 ♗d5+ 52 ♔c3 f4 53 gxf4
gxf4 54 ♘c2 ♖c1 55 ♔d3 ♖d1+ 56
♔e2 ♖h1 57 ♘e1 ♖xh2+ 58 ♔f1 ♖h1+
59 ♔f2 ♖h2 -+ ½-½ Gufeld**

148 Sinjavsky-Gufeld USSR 77

**1 d4 ♘f6 2 c4 g6 3 ♘c3 ♗g7 4 e4 d6
5 f3 0-0 6 ♗e3 a6 7 ♘ge2** 7 ♗d3
♘c6 8 ♘ge2 e5 9 d5 ♘b4 10 ♗b1 a5
11 ♕d2 ♘e8 12 0-0 c6 13 dxc6 bxc6
14 a3 ♘a6 15 c5! += ½-½ Silva-Durao
(4) 78 **b6** 7...♘c6 8 ♕d2 c5 9 ♘h6
9 d5 ♗xh6! **10 ♕xh6 ♘c6 11 ♖d1
11 0-0-0∞ ♗d7! 12 h4 e5! 13 dxc5
dxc5 14 h5 ♕e7** 14...♘d4!? 15 ♘xd4
exd4 16 ♘d5 ♘xd5 17 hxg6?! ♘f6
18 g7 ♖e8∞/∓ **15 ♘d5 ♗xd5 16 exd5
♘d4 17 hxg6 fxg6 18 ♘xd4 exd4+
19 ♔f2 ♗f5 20 ♖e1 ♕f7 21 ♕d2 ♖ae8
22 ♗d3 ♗xd3 ½-½ Gufeld**

149 Reicher-Troys
Wijk aan Zee 78

**1 d4 ♘f6 2 c4 g6 3 ♘c3 ♗g7 4 e4 d6
5 f3 c6 6 ♗e3 a6 7 g4** N 7 c5 0-0 8
♘ge2 ♘bd7 9 ♘c1 b5 10 ♗e2 dxc5
11 dxc5 ♘e5 12 ♕c2 ♗e6 13 0-0 +=
Larsen-Byrne, Leningrad 73; 7...b5
8 cxd6 exd6 9 a4 ♗b7 10 ♘h3 0-0
11 ♗e2 ♘bd7= Korchnoi-Gheorghiu,
Moscow 71; 7 ♗d3 b5 8 e5 ♘fd7 9
f4 0-0 10 ♘f3 ♘b6 11 b3 ♘8d7 12
a4 bxc4 13 bxc4 c5!= Portisch-
Kavalek, Wijk aan Zee 75; 7...0-0 8
a4 a5 9 ♕d2 ♘a6 10 ♖d1 e5 11
♘ge2 += Rubinetti-Partos, Nice 74;
7 ♕d2 0-0 8 ♗d3 b5 9 ♘ge2 ♘bd7 10
0-0 e5 11 cxb5 axb5 12 b4 ♗b7 13
♖fd1 exd4= Ree-Sakharov, Sochi 76
b5 8 h4 h5 8...bxc4 9 h5 d5 10 e5
♘g8 11 ♕d2± **; 10...♘fd7 11 h6 ♗f8
12 f4± 9 g5 ♘fd7 10 ♕c2 e5 11
0-0-0 ♕a5 12 f4! b4 13 ♘a4 exd4 14
♗xd4 ♗xd4 15 ♖xd4 ♘c5 16 ♘xc5
dxc5 17 ♖d6 ♕xa2 18 ♘f3 ♘d7**
18...♔e7 19 ♘e5 ♗e6 20 ♖d1 Δ f5;
19...♔xd6 20 ♘xf7+ Δ ♘xh8± **19
♗g2 ♘b6 20 ♘e5 b3?** 20...♗e6!? 21
♘xg6 ♘xc4!? 22 ♖xe6 fxe6 23 ♘xh8
0-0-0 **21 ♕d3 ♕a1+?!** 21...♗e6!?
**22 ♔b1 ♕xb1+ 23 ♔xb1 0-0 24 ♖xc6
♖b8 25 ♖d1! ♖e8 26 ♖dd6 ♘a4
27 ♖c7 ♗e6 28 ♖a7!** 28 ♖xa6 ♘b6
29 ♗f1 ♖ed8 **♖ed8 29 ♖axa6 ♖xd6
30 ♖xd6 ♘b6 31 ♗f1 ♔g7 32 ♗d3
♘a4 33 f5 ♗xf5 34 exf5 ♖e8 35
f6+ ♔g8 36 ♖d5 ♘b6 37 ♖xc5 ♘d7
38 ♖b5! ♖xe5 39 ♖xe5 ♘xe5 40
♗e2 ♔f8 41 ♔c1 ♘c6 42 ♗d3 1-0
Ciocaltea**

150 Pachman-Ostermeyer
BRD Final 78

**1 c4 ♘f6 2 ♘c3 g6 3 e4 d6 4 d4 ♗g7
5 f3 0-0 6 ♗e3 b6 7 ♗d3 ♗b7 8 ♘h3**

c5 9 d5 e6 10 ♕d2 exd5 11 cxd5 ♖e8
12 ♘f2 12 0-0? ♘xd5 13 exd5 ♖xe3
△ ♗d4 ♘bd7 13 0-0 a6 14 a4 ♖c8?!
15 ♖ac1 ♕e7 16 ♖fe1 h5 16...♘e5
17 ♗e2 △ f4

17 ♕e2! ♖a8 18 f4 ♘h7 19 ♕f3 ♕f8
19...♗c8? 20 e5! dxe5 21 d6 △ ♕xa8
20 e5! dxe5 21 f5 gxf5 21...e4 22
♗xe4 ♘e5 23 ♕h3 ♗c8 △ ♖a7 22
♗xf5 ♘df6 23 ♘fe4 ♗h8 24 ♗xh7+
1-0 24...♖xh7 25 ♕xh5 ♗g7 26 ♖f1
♗c8 27 ♖f3 ♖a7 28 ♖g3 +−

151 Holm-Sznapik Zabrze 77

1 d4 ♘f6 2 c4 g6 3 ♘c3 ♗g7 4 e4
d6 5 f3 0-0 6 ♗e3 ♘c6 7 ♕d2 ♖e8 8
♘ge2 8 a3! a6 9 b4 ♖b8 9 h4 a6 10
♗h6 ♗h8 11 h5 e5 12 hxg6 fxg6
13 dxe5 ♘xe5 14 ♗f4 ♘f7!∓ 15 ♘fd5
c6 16 ♘xf6+ ♕xf6 17 0-0-0 b5 18
♗e3 b4 19 ♘b1 c5 20 ♗e2 ♗e6 21
f4 ♗c8! 22 ♗f3 ♗b7 23 e5?! dxe5
24 ♗xb7 ♖xb7 25 ♖hf1 exf4 26 ♗xf4
♖d7! 0-1 Pytel

152 Raskin-Gufeld USSR 78

1 d4 ♘f6 2 c4 g6 3 ♘c3 ♗g7 4 e4 0-0
5 ♗e3 5 e5?! ♘e8; 5 f3 c5!? d6 6 f3
♘c6 7 ♘ge2 a6 8 ♖c1 e5 9 d5 ♘d4
10 ♘1e2 10 ♘b3 c5!? 10...♘xe2 11
♗xe2 ♘h5 11 dxc6 ♘xc6 11...bxc6?!
12 ♘xd4 exd4 13 ♗xd4 α/± 12 ♘c1

♗e6= 13 ♘b3 ♖c8 14 ♖c1?! 14 ♕d2
♘a5 15 ♘xa5 ♕xa5 16 ♕a4? 16
♕xd6 ♖c6 17 ♕e7 ♘d7α ♕c7 =+
17 b3 17 ♘d5 ♗xd5 18 cxd5 ♕xc1+
19 ♗xc1 ♖xc1+∓ ♘h5 18 ♗e2 18
g3 f5 =+ ♘f4 19 ♕f2 f5 20 ♕b4 ♕e7
21 g3 ♘xe2 22 ♕xe2 ♖c6 23 ♖cd1
b5!∓ 24 cxb5 axb5 25 ♘xb5 ♕b7!
26 a4 fxe4 27 ♕xe4 ♗xb3 27...d5?
28 ♖xd5 ♗f5 29 ♕b4 28 ♖xd6 ♖c2+!
28...♗xa4?! 29 ♕xa4 ♖xd6 30 ♘xd6
♕xf3+ 31 ♔d2 ♕xh1 32 ♕c4+ ♔h8
33 ♘f7+ ♖xf7 34 ♕xf6 =+ 29 ♖d2
♖xd2+ 29...♗c4+! 30 ♔d1 ♖xd2+
30 ♔xd2 ♖d8+ 31 ♔c1 Zeitnot 31
♔e2! ♗d5 32 ♖d1!∓ ♗d5 32 ♕d3
♕c8+ 33 ♕c2 ♗xf3 34 ♖f1 ♕g4 −+
35 ♕b3+ ♗d5 36 ♕a3 ♕e2 37 ♖d1
♖c8+ 0-1 Gufeld

153 Gheorghiu-Rozran Rumania 78

1 d4 ♘f6 2 c4 g6 3 ♘c3 ♗g7 4 e4 d6
5 f3 0-0 6 ♗e3 e5 7 d5 ♘h5 8 ♕d2
f5 9 exf5 9 0-0-0 f4 10 ♗f2 ♗f6 11
♘ge2 += gxf5 10 0-0-0 ♘d7 11 ♗d3
♘c5 12 ♗c2 a5 13 ♘ge2 ♗d7

14 h3± △ g4 ♕h4 14...f4 15 ♗xc5
dxc5 16 ♘e4± 15 g4 ♘f4 15...♘g3 16
♗g5! ♘xe2+ 17 ♘xe2 ♕f2 18 ♖df1
+− 16 ♘xf4 exf4 17 ♗xf4 ♘f6 18
♗g5 ♕f7 19 ♗h6! f4 20 ♗xg7 ♕xg7
21 ♖he1 a4 22 ♕d4 +− ♕xd4 23

♖xd4 ♖f7 24 ♕d2 ♗g7 25 ♘e4! △
♘g5 h6 26 ♘xc5 dxc5 27 ♖de4 a3
28 b3 ♖a6 29 ♕c3 ♖d6 30 b4! +−
cxb4+ 31 ♕xb4 c6 32 ♕b3 cxd5 33
cxd5 h5 34 ♕c5 ♖ff6 35 ♖e7+ ♔f8 36
g5 b6+ 37 ♔d4 ♖f5 38 h4! 1-0
Gheorghiu

154 Pytel-Dobrzyinski Poland 78

1 c4 g6 2 ♘c3 ♗g7 3 d4 d6 4 e4 ♘d7
5 ♗e3 e5 6 d5 ♘gf6 7 f3 ♘h5 8 ♕d2
f5 9 0-0-0 0-0 10 ♗d3 f4 11 ♗f2 ♘f6
12 ♘ge2!? 12 ♕e1!± ♗h4 13 ♗g1?!
♕g5! 14 g4 fxg3 15 ♗e3 ♕e7 16 hxg3
♘xg3 17 ♖xg3 ♗xg3 18 ♘e2 ♖xf3
19 ♘g5?! 19 ♖h3 ♖xe3= ♕f7 20 ♘xg3
♘c5! 20...♖xg3? 21 ♖df1 ♖f3 22
♗e2 +− 21 ♗e2 ♖xg3 22 ♖df1 ♕e8
23 ♗f6!? 23 ♖h6 ♘xe4 24 ♕e1 ♗f5
△ ♕a4 −+ ♗h3!! 23...♘xe4 24 ♕h6
♘xf6 25 ♖xf6 ♕e7?? 26 ♖f8+ +−;
25...♖h3± 24 ♖xh3 24 ♕h6!? ♕d7
25 ♘g4!?! ♗xg4? 26 ♕xg6+ hxg6 27
♖h8+ ♔f7 28 ♖h7+ =; 25...♖xg4! −+
♖xh3 25 ♗g4 ♗xe4 26 ♕g2 ♗xf5
27 ♖xf6 ♖h4 28 ♗e6+ ♔g7 29 ♕f3
♖xc4+ 30 ♔b1 ♕d8 31 ♗f7+ ♔h6 −+
32 ♗g4 ♕h4 33 ♕e3+ ♖f4 34 ♗e2
♖g8 35 ♖xc7 ♕g7 36 ♖c1 ♖gf7 37
♗b5 ♕g7 38 ♕xa7 ♕f2 39 ♕a3 ♕b6
40 ♕d3 ♖f3 41 ♕e2 ♖f2 0-1 **Pytel**

155 Pytel-Gralka Poland 78

1 c4 g6 2 d4 ♘f6 3 ♘c3 ♗g7 4 e4 d6
5 f4 0-0 6 ♘f3 c5 7 d5 b5?! 8 cxb5
a6 9 a4! N 9 ♕c2 axb5 10 ♘xb5 ♘a6
11 a4 ♕b6 12 ♖a3 e6! 13 dxe6 fxe6
14 ♗e2 ♘c6 15 0-0 ♘b4 16 ♕b1 d5
17 exd5 exd5 18 ♘e5 ♗c8∞
Witkowski-Pytel, Poland 68; 9 bxa6
♕a5 10 ♗d2 ♖xa6 11 ♗e2 ♕b6 12
0-0 ♘bd7 13 ♗xa6 ♖xa6 14 ♕c2 c4
15 ♖ae1 ♘b6 16 h3 ♖fb8 17 a3 ♘fd7
18 e5 ♘a4 19 ♗c1 ♕b6 20 ♖f2 ♘xc3

21 ♕xc3 ♕c5 22 ♖d1 ♖b3 23 ♕c2
dxe5 ½-½ A.Zaitsev-Doda, Polanica 71
axb5 10 ♗xb5 ♗a6 11 0-0 ♘b4 12
e5 ♘e8 13 ♗c4! ♘c7 13...♗a6 14 b3!
14 ♗e3 ♗b7 15 ♕d2 ♖a5? 15...dxe5
16 ♖ad1 ♕a8 17 exd6! 17 ♗f2! ♖d8
18 ♗h4 dxe5 19 ♗xe7 exd6 18 f5!
♗c8!? 19 fxg6 hxg6 20 ♗h6 ♗f5 21
♗h4! ♗c2 22 ♖c1 ♕d8 23 ♗g5 f6 24
♗h6 g5 25 ♗xg7 ♔xg7 26 ♘f5+ +−
♗xf5 27 ♖xf5 ♖h8 28 ♖cf1 ♖h4 29
b3 ♕e7 30 ♖e1 ♕d8 31 ♘e4 ♕h8 32
♖xf6 1-0 **Pytel**

156 Lombardy-Westerinen Lone Pine 78

1 c4 ♘f6 2 ♘c3 g6 3 e4 d6 4 d4 ♗g7
5 f4 0-0 6 ♘f3 c5 7 d5 e6 8 dxe6
♗xe6!? 8...fxe6∞ 9 ♗d3 ♘c6 10 f5!
♗d7 11 0-0 ♘b4 12 ♗b1 ♗c6 13
a3 ♘a6 14 ♗g5! ♘c7 14...h6 15 ♗h4
g5 16 ♗g3± 15 ♕d2 ♕d7 16 ♗c2 b5
17 ♖ad1 ♘fe8 18 ♗h6! bxc4 19
♗xg7 ♔xg7 20 e5! +−

20...d5 21 f6+ ♔g8 22 h3 d4 23 ♘e4
♘e6 24 ♕h6 ♗xe4 25 ♗xe4 ♖ab8 26
♘h4!! △ ♘f5 d3 27 ♘f5 ♕h8 28 ♖f4
1-0 △ ♖h4 **Gheorghiu**

157 Sturua-Gufeld USSR 77

1 d4 ♘f6 2 c4 g6 3 g3 ♗g7 4 ♗g2
0-0 5 ♘c3 d6 6 ♘f3 ♘c6 7 0-0 a6

8 d5 8 h3!? ♖b8 9 ♗e3 b5 10 ♘d2 ♞a5 **9 ♘d2 c5 10 ♕c2 ♖b8 11 b3 b5 12 ♗b2 e5** 12...bxc4 13 bxc4 ♞h6 14 f4 e5 15 ♖ae1 exf4 16 gxf4 ♘h5 17 e3 ♗f5?! 18 ♘ce4 += Haritonov-Magerramov, USSR 77; 17...♗g7 18 ♘d1 ♗f5 19 ♕c1? ♗xb2 20 ♘xb2 ♕f6∓ Ivkov-Smejkal, Novi Sad 76; 19 ♗e4= **13 ♘d1** 13 dxe6 fxe6 14 cxb5 axb5 15 ♘ce4 += **♞h5!= 14 f4?!** 14 e4 f5 15 exf5 gxf5 16 f4 bxc4 17 bxc4 ♖xb2! 18 ♘xb2 exf4∓; 17 fxe5 **bxc4** =+ 14...exf4 15 ♗xg7 ♔xg7 16 gxf4 f5= **15 fxe5!?** 15 bxc4 ♖xb2! 16 ♘xb2 exf4 17 gxf4 ♗d4+ 18 ♔h1 ♕h4∓ **cxb3 16 axb3 dxe5** 16...♕b6!? 17 ♖a5? ♕xa5 18 ♘c4 ♕a2 -+; 17 exd6 c4 =+ **17 ♗c3 ♖b5=** 17...♗b7? 18 ♘c4± **18 ♕a2 ♗b7 19 ♘c4** 19 ♕xa6?! **♗d6 20 ♞xe5 ♖e8 21 ♘c4 ♞e4?** 21...♖b4!? 22 ♗xb4 cxb4 23 ♖c1 ♘b5∞ **22 ♗xg7 ♞xg7 23 ♗xe4 ♖xe4 24 ♘c3 ♖e8 25 e4±** 25 ♘xb5!? ♗h3 26 ♖f2?! 26 ♖fe1± ♖b4 27 e5 ♕b8 28 ♞e4 28 d6 ♕b7! += ♖xe5! 29 ♞f6+ 29 ♘xc5 ♖xd5 30 ♘xa6 ♕d8 31 ♘xb4 ♖d1+ 32 ♖f1 ♕d4+ 33 ♔h1 ♕e4+ 34 ♔g1 ♕d4+ = ♕h8 30 ♞xe5 ♕xe5 **31 ♕b2?** 31 ♕xa6! ♘f5? 32 ♕c8+ ♔g7 33 ♕g8+ ♔h6 34 ♕xh7+ ♔g5 35 ♖af1 ♗xf1 36 h4+ ♔xf6 37 ♕h8+ +-; 31...♖xb3?! 32 d6!± ♖d4 **32 ♕e2** Zeitnot **♖e4!?** Zeitnot 32...♖xd5!? **33 ♕d1** 33 ♘xe4 ♕xa1+ 34 ♖f1 ♗xf1 35 ♕xf1 ♕d4+∓ ♖e3! Δ ♖xg3+ **34 ♖c1 ♞f5 35 d6! ♕xf6** 35...♘xd6 **36 d7 ♕d8 37 ♖d2** 37 ♖xc5 ♕xd7! -+ ♖e5 38 g4? 38 b4! ♘e3! =+ ♞g7 39 ♕f3 ♗xg4 40 ♕xf7 ♗e6 41 ♕f4 ♖g5+ **0-1 Gufeld**

158 Portisch-Van der Sterren Wijk aan Zee 78

1 ♘f3 ♞f6 2 g3 g6 3 ♗g2 ♗g7 4 c4 0-0 5 d4 d6 6 ♘c3 ♞c6 7 0-0 a6 8 d5 ♞a5 9 ♘d2 c5 10 ♕c2 ♖b8 11 b3 b5 12 ♗b2 ♗h6 13 f4 bxc4 14 bxc4 e5 15 dxe6! 15 ♖ae1 exf4 16 gxf4 ♘h5 17 e3 ♖e8 18 ♘ce4! ♗f5 19 ♘c3 ♘b7 20 ♕a4 a5 21 ♖b1± Portisch-Petrosian, Santa Monica 66 **fxe6** 15...♗xe6 16 ♘d5!± Csom-Ghitescu, Moscow 77 **16 ♞ce4 ♞g4?** 16...♘xe4 17 ♗xe4 d5 18 ♗g2 ♖xb2 19 ♕xb2 ♗g7 20 ♕c2 ♗xa1 21 ♖xa1 dxc4≈ Adamski-Gralka, Poland Final 78

17 ♞b3!± ♞xb3 17...♘e3? 18 ♕c3 **18 axb3 ♗g7 19 ♗xg7 ♔xg7 20 ♕c3+ ♔g8 21 ♖fd1 +- ♗b7 22 ♖xd6 ♕e7 23 ♖ad1 ♖fd8 24 ♖xd8+ ♖xd8 25 ♖xd8+ ♕xd8 26 ♞d2 ♗xg2 27 ♔xg2 1-0 Pytel**

159 Petrosian-Adorjan Sochi 77
1 c4 g6 2 e4 e5 3 ♞f3 ♗g7 4 d4 exd4 5 ♗xd4 ♞f6 6 ♞c3 0-0 7 ♗d3!? d5!= 8 cxd5 c6! 8...♘xd5 9 exd5 ♗xd4 10 ♗e2 += **9 0-0 cxd5 10 exd5** 10 e5?! ♞g4 11 e6 ♘xf2 **♞xd5 11 ♗e4 ♞xc3 12 bxc3 ♕a5 13 ♕b3 ♞d7! 14 ♕a3 ♕xa3 15 ♗xa3 ♖e8 16 ♖fe1 ♗f8 17 ♗xf8 ♔xf8 18 ♗f3 ♖xe1+ 19 ♖xe1 ♞c5 20 ♖e5?!** 20 ♘b3= **♞e6 21 h4 ♖b8=+ 22 ♞b5?** 22 ♔f1= **a6 23 ♞d6 b6∓ 24 ♗e2 ½-½ Petrosian**

160 Beljavsky-Kochiev USSR 77

1 d4 ♘f6 2 c4 d6 3 ♘c3 e5 4 ♘f3
♘bd7 5 g3 c6!? 5...g6 6 b3!? ♗g7 7
dxe5 dxe5 8 ♗a3 += 6 ♗g2 6 b3?!
e4! g6 7 0-0 ♗g7 8 b3 0-0 9 ♕c2 ♖e8
10 ♖d1 ♕e7 10...♕c7 11 dxe5 dxe5
12 ♘g5 ♘f8 13 a4 e4 13...♗f5 14
♘ge4 += 14 ♗a3 ♕e5 15 ♘gxe4 ♗xe4
15...♗f5 16 f4! ♕e6 17 ♖d6! 16
♕xe4 16 ♘xe4 ♗f5 ♕xe4 17 ♘xe4
♗f5 17...♗xa1? 18 ♖xa1± 18 ♘d6
♖xe2 19 ♖e1 ♖c2 20 ♘xf5 20 ♖ad1
♖a2! 21 ♘xf5 ♖xa3 22 ♘xg7 ♔xg7=
gxf5 21 ♖ad1 ♗e6 22 ♕f1 ♗d4 23
♖e2 ♖xe2 24 ♕xe2 ♕g7 25 b4 ♕f6
26 f4 ♖c8 27 a5 b6 28 a6 ♕g6 29
♕d3 c5 30 b5 ♕f6 31 ♗d5 h5 32 ♕e2
h4 33 ♕f3 hxg3 34 hxg3 ♖h8 35
♔g2 ♕g6 36 ♗c1 ♘g7 37 ♗c6 ♕f6
38 ♖e1 ♘e6 39 ♗d2 ♖d8 40 ♖b1 ♕e7
41 ♖e1 ½-½ Gufeld

161 Liebert-Bodach
DDR Final 78

1 c4 ♘f6 2 ♘f3 g6 3 ♘c3 d6 4 d4 ♗g7
5 g3 0-0 6 ♗g2 c6 7 0-0 ♘bd7 8 e4
e5 9 h3 ♖e8 10 ♖e1 ♕c7 10...exd4
11 b3 ♘f8 12 ♗e3 ♘h5 13 ♖c1 ♕e7
14 ♔h2 h6 15 b4 exd4 16 ♘xd4
♗e6 17 b5 c5 18 ♘xe6 18 ♘f5 ♘xe6
19 ♕d2 ♔h7 20 ♖ed1 ♘d4 21 ♘e2
♘xe2 22 ♕xe2 ♘f6 23 ♕c2 ♖ad8
23...♘xe4 24 ♗xe4 ♕xe4 25 ♕xe4
♖xe4 26 ♖xd6 b6 24 ♖e1 ♘d7 24...
♘xe4 25 ♗d2 f5 26 f3 +- 25 e5!
dxe5 25...♘xe5 26 f4 ♘d7 27 ♗f2
26 ♗xb7 f5 27 ♗c6 ♖f8 28 ♖cd1
♘b6 29 ♖xd8 ♖xd8 30 a4 f4? 31
♗xf4 ♖d4 32 ♗d5! ♘xd5 33 cxd5
♖xd5 34 ♗e3 ♕d6 35 ♕c4 ♗f8 36
♖c1 ♕d7 37 a5 ♕g7 38 b6 axb6 39
axb6 ♕b7 40 ♖a1 ♖d7 41 ♖a7 ♕c6
42 ♖xd7+ ♕xd7 43 ♗xc5 1-0

162 Vogt-Uhlmann
DDR Final 78

1 ♘f3 ♘f6 2 c4 g6 3 ♘c3 ♗g7 4 e4
d6 5 d4 0-0 6 g3?! e5 7 ♗g2 ♘c6 8
d5 ♘d4 9 ♘xd4 9 0-0 ♗g4 =+ exd4
10 ♘e2 10 ♕xd4? ♘xe4∓ c5 11 dxc6
bxc6 12 ♘xd4 12 0-0 ♗g4! ♕a5+
13 ♗d2 ♕c5 14 ♗c3 ♕xc4 14...♘xe4?!
15 ♗xe4 ♖e8 16 0-0 ♖xe4 17 ♘b3!
15 ♕e2 ♕xe2+ 16 ♔xe2 ♖e8 16...
♗b7 17 ♘xc6 ♗b7 18 ♘a5 ♗a6+ 18...
♗xe4 19 f3 +=; 18...♘xe4 19 ♗xe4
♗xe4 20 ♖he1= 19 ♔d2 ♘xe4+ 20
♗xe4 ♖xe4 21 ♖he1 ♖ae8 21...♗xc3+
22 bxc3 ♖ae8 23 c4! 22 ♗xg7 ♔xg7
23 ♖xe4 ♖xe4 24 ♘c6 ♖e2+ 25 ♔c3
♖xf2 26 ♘xa7 ♖xh2 27 b4 ♖g2 28
b5 ♖xg3+ 29 ♔d4 ♗b7 30 a4 ♖g4+
31 ♔c3 ♖g3+ 32 ♔b4 h5 33 a5 h4 34
a6 ♗d5

35 b6? 35 ♘c6 h3 36 a7 h2 37 a8♕
♖g1 38 ♕a7! ♖xa1 39 ♕xa1+ ♔h7
40 ♘d8 ♔g8 41 b6 h1♕ 42 ♕x
h1+ ♗xh1 43 b7=; 37...♖g4+? 38
♔a5 ♖g1 39 ♔b6 h1♕ 40 ♖xg1 ♕xg1+
41 ♔c7± h3 36 ♘b5 36 b7? ♖b3+
37 ♔a4 ♖xb7! 38 axb7 ♗xb7 -+
♖g4+? 36...h2 37 b7 ♖g1 38 ♖xg1
hxg1♕ 39 b8♕ ♕c5+ 40 ♔a4 g5∓
37 ♔a5 h2 38 b7 ♖g1 39 ♖xg1 hxg1♕
40 b8♕ ♕a1+ 47 ♔b6 ♕g1+ 42 ♔c7
½-½ 42...♕c1+ 43 ♔d8 ♕g5+; 42...♕c5+

43 ♔d8 g5 44 ♘xd6 ♕a5+ 45 ♔e7
♕xa6 46 ♕f8+ ♔h7 47 ♔f6 **Vogt**

163 Lombardy-Sigurjonsson
Reykjavik 78
1 d4 ♘f6 2 c4 g6 3 ♘c3 ♗g7 4 ♘f3
d6 5 g3 0-0 6 ♗g2 ♘c6 7 0-0 a6 8
h3 ♖b8 9 ♗g5 b5 10 cxb5 axb5 11
♖c1 ♘a5?! 11...b4?! 12 ♗xf6 exf6
13 ♘d5 ♘e7 14 ♘xe7+ ♕xe7 15 d5±
Larsen-Timman 77; 11...♗d7 **12 b3!**
c6 13 e4! △ e5 b4?! 13...♘d7 △ f6,
e5 **14 e5 bxc3 15 exf6 exf6 16 ♗e3**
♗e6 17 ♖xc3 ♕d7 18 ♔h2 ♖b5! 19
♕d2 ♖fb8 20 ♖fc1?! ♘h5 20...♗xb3
21 ♘g1 ♖bb5 22 f3 ♖b8 23 g4 ♖hb5
24 ♘e2?! f5 25 ♘f4? 25 ♕d3 +=
♗xb3! 26 axb3 ♘xb3 27 ♖xb3 ♖xb3
28 ♘d3 fxg4 29 hxg4 29 fxg4 c5=
h5 30 ♘f2 ♕e7 31 ♗g5 ♗f6 32 ♗xf6
♕xf6 33 ♖xc6? 33 hxg5 ♕h4+ 34
♘h3= ♖b2 34 ♖c2 ♖xc2 35 ♕xc2
♕f4+ 36 ♔g1 ♕xd4 37 ♕e4 ♕c5
38 ♕e2? 38 gxh5 hxg4 39 fxg4 ♖b3∓
40 ♗f3 ♕c3! 41 ♔g2 ♖b2 42 ♕f1
♕e3 43 ♔g3 d5 44 ♔g2 ♖d2 45 ♔g3
♖a2 46 ♔g2 d4 47 ♗d5 ♖b2 48 ♗c4
♕f4 49 ♗e2 49 ♔g1 ♖c2 d3 50 ♗xd3
50 ♗f3 ♕xg4+ −+ 51 ♔f2 ♕d4+ 52
♔f3 ♖b5! 53 ♕c1 ♖f5+ 54 ♘f4 ♔g7
54...g5?? 55 ♕c8+ **55 ♕e3 ♕f6 56**
♔g3 ♖e5! 57 ♕d2 ♖e4 58 ♗f3 58
♘d3; 58 ♘g2 ♖d4 59 ♕e3 ♕d6!
△ g5 **60 ♔g4 f5+ 61 ♔g3 ♕f6!** △ g5
0-1 61...g5?? 62 ♕xd4+ ♕xd4 63
♘e6+ +− **Sigurjonsson**

164 Chechelian-Podgaets
USSR 77
1 ♘f3 ♘f6 2 c4 g6 3 g3 ♗g7 4 ♗g2
0-0 5 0-0 d6 6 d4 ♘bd7 7 ♕c2 e5 8
♘c3 ♖e8 8...exd4 9 ♘xd4 ♘b6!?
10 b3 c5= **9 ♖d1 c6 10 b3?!** 10
dxe5 dxe5 12 b3 += **e4! 11 ♘g5**

11...e3! 12 ♗xe3 ♖xe3 13 fxe3 ♘g4
14 ♘ge4 f5 15 ♘f2 15 ♘xd6 ♕e7 −+
♗xe3 16 ♕d2 ♗h6! **17 ♖db1 ♗f6 18**
♘cd1 ♖xd1 19 ♕xd1 19 ♕xh6 ♘xf2
−+ ♗e3 20 ♗f3 ♘g4! 21 ♕d3 21
♗xg4 fxg4 22 ♕d3 ♕e7 23 ♖f1 ♗f5
24 ♕c3 ♖e8 −+ ♗xf2+ 22 ♔g2 ♕f6
23 ♖d1 f4 24 ♗xg4 ♗xg4 25 ♔xf2
♖e8 26 ♖f1 ♖e3! 26...fxg3+ 27
♔xg3 ♕g5+ 28 h4! ♖e3+ 29 ♖f3 +−
27 ♕d2 ♖xe2+ 28 ♕xe2 ♕xd4+ 0-1
Gufeld

165 Peresipkin-Grigorian USSR 77
1 ♘f3 ♘f6 2 c4 g6 3 g3 ♗g7 4 ♗g2
0-0 5 0-0 d6 6 d4 ♘bd7 7 ♘c3 e5 8
♕c2 ♖e8 8...exd4 9 ♘xd4 ♘b6 10
b3 c5= **9 ♖d1 c6 10 e4 a6** 10...♕c7
11 h3 a5 12 ♗e3 exd4!? 13 ♘xd4
♘c5 **11 h3 b5!? N 12 c5!? exd4 13**
♘xd4 ♘xc5!?= **14 ♘xc6** 14 e5!?
dxe5 15 ♘xc6 ♕c7 16 ♘xb5 axb5
17 ♕xc5 e4! 18 ♗f4 ♕b7 19 ♘d8
♕e7 =+; 16 ♘e7+? ♕xe7 17 ♗xa8
♗f5! **♕c7 15 e5** 15 ♘b4 ♗b7 16
♗f4 ♖ad8 17 ♘bd5 ♘xd5 18 ♘xd5
♗xd5 19 ♖xd5 ♘e6 20 ♕xc7 ♘xc7
21 ♖xd6 ♗xb2 22 ♖b1 ♗e5= ♗f5

Diagram

16 ♕xf5 gxf5 17 exf6 ♗e4 17...♗xf6?
18 ♘d5 +− **18 ♘e7+ ♖xe7 19 ♘d5**

108

♖xf6! 19...♕c2?! 20 ♘xe7+ ♔f8 21
♘xg7+ ♔xe7 22 ♗e3 △ ♖ac1, ♗d4
20 ♘xc7 ♖xc7 21 ♖d5 ♖ac8 22 ♗f4?
22 ♖xf5 ♖xc1+ 23 ♖xc1 ♖xc1+
24 ♔h2 d5 25 ♗xe4 dxe4 26 ♖xf6
♖c2 27 ♔g2∞ ♗xb2 23 ♖e1 ♗e5 24
♗xe4 24 ♗xe5 ♖c1! 25 ♖xc1 ♖xc1+
26 ♔h2 dxe5 27 ♖xe5 ♘xf2 fxe4
25 ♖xe4 25 ♗xe5 ♖c1+ ♗c5! 26
♗d3 ♖c4 27 ♖ee3 ♗xf4 28 gxf4
♖8c6 29 ♖e8+ ♔g7 30 ♖g3+ ♔f6
31 ♖h8 ♖xf4 32 ♖xh7 ♖c1+ 33
♔g2 ♖c2 34 ♖h6+ ♔f5 −+ 35 ♖h5+
♔e4 36 ♖e3+ ♔d4 37 ♖f3 ♖xf3 38
♔xf3 ♖xa2 39 ♖h8 b4 40 ♖b8 a5 41
♖4 ♔e5 42 ♔g4 ♖xf2 43 ♖b5+ ♔d4 44
♖5 ♔c4 45 ♖xa5 b3 46 ♖a7 b2 47
♖b7 ♔c3 48 h6 ♖h2 0-1 Gufeld

166 Tukmakov-Suba Decin 77
1 d4 ♘f6 2 c4 d6 3 ♘f3 g6 4 g3 ♗g7
5 ♗g2 0-0 6 0-0 ♘bd7 7 ♘c3 e5 8 e4
♖e8 8...c6!?; 8...exd4!? 9 h3 9 d5!?
exd4 10 ♘xd4 ♘c5 11 ♖e1 a5 12
♖b1!? 12 ♘db5!? ♘fd7 12...c6 13
♗f4 13 ♗e3 ♘e5 14 ♕e2 14 ♗f1
♘c6; 14 b3 a4 15 b4 ♘c6 c6 15 ♖bd1
15 ♖ed1 ♕e7∞ ♕b6 16 f4 ♘ed7 17
♕c2 a4 18 ♗f2 ♕b4 19 ♗f1 19 ♘b1!?
♘b6 20 ♘a3∞ ♘b6 20 ♕c1!? ♘xc4!?
21 a3 ♕xb2 22 ♗xc4 ♕xc1 23 ♖xc1
♗xh3 24 ♖cd1 ½-½ 24...♘g4 25 ♗e2
♗xe2 26 ♖xe2∞ Tukmakov

167 Ftacnik-Ciocaltea
Bucharest 78
1 d4 g6 2 c4 c5 3 ♘f3 ♗g7 4 e4 ♘c6
4...cxd4!?; 4...♕a5+ 5 ♗d2 ♕b6 6
♘c3 (6 ♗c3!?) cxd4 7 ♘d5 ♕d8
8 ♗f4 d6 9 ♘xd4 e5 10 ♘b5 exf4 11
♘bd7+ ♔f8 12 ♘xa8 ♘a6≈
Christiansen-Beljavsky, Teesside 73;
4...d6?! 5 ♘c3 ♘c6?! 6 dxc5 ♕a5 7
cxd6 ♗xc3+ 8 bxc3 ♘f6 9 dxe7!
♘xe4 10 ♕c2 +− Filip-Planinc, Vrsac
71 5 d5 5 dxc5 ♕a5+ 6 ♘fd2!? ♘d4
6 ♘xd4 ♗xd4 7 ♗d3 d6 8 0-0 ♘f6!
9 ♘d2 ♘h5 9...0-0 10 ♘b3 10 ♘b3
♗g7 11 f4 11 g4 ♘f6 12 g5 ♘h5 13
♗e2 ♘h3 14 ♖e1 h6!? 0-0 12 ♕c2
e6 13 dxe6 fxe6! 13...♗xe6? 14 f5
14 ♗e3 b6 15 ♖ae1 ♗b7 16 f5 ♗e5!
17 g3 17 fxe6? ♗xh2+ 18 ♔xh2 ♕h4+
19 ♔g1 ♘g3 −+ ♕d7 18 fxg6 hxg6
19 ♘d2 ♕g7 20 ♘f3 ♗xb2 21 e5!
21 ♘g5 ♕xe5 22 ♖xf3 ♗xf3 23
♕xb2 dxe5 24 ♗g5 e4 25 ♕xg7+ ♔xg7
26 ♗xe4 ♗xe4 27 ♖xe4 ♖e8 27...
♔f7?! 28 g4 ♘g7 29 ♖f4+ ♔e8 30
♖f6=; 29...♔g8 30 ♖f6 ♔h7 31 ♖f7
28 ♖e3 ♘f6 29 ♖d3 ♖e7 30 ♔g2 e5
31 ♖d6! ♖f7 32 ♖e6 ♘e4 33 ♗e3!
33 ♖xe5 ♘d6∓ ♖f6 34 ♖e7+ ♖f7
35 ♖xe5?! 35 ♖e6!= ♘d6 36 ♗f4 ♘xc4
37 ♖e4 b5 38 ♖e8 a5 39 ♖c8 ♖f5
40 ♔f3 g5! =+ 41 ♖c7+ 41 ♔e4?
♖xf4+ 42 gxf4 ♘d6+; 41 ♔g4? gxf4
42 ♖c7+ ♖f7 −+ ♔g6 42 ♖c6+ ♖f6
43 ♖xf6+ ♔xf6 44 ♗b8! 44 ♗c1? g4+!
45 ♔xg4 ♘e5+ 46 ♔h5 b4 −+ ♔e6 45
h4 gxh4 46 gxh4 b4 47 ♔e4? 47
♗a7!! ♔d6 48 ♔e4 a4 49 ♔d3 b3 50
axb3 a3? 51 ♔xc4 a2 52 ♗xc5+ +−;
47...♔d5 48 ♔e2 a4 49 ♔d3 ♘e5+
=+ a4 48 ♗a7 b3! 49 axb3 axb3
50 ♔d3 ♘a3! 51 ♔c3 ♘b5+ 52 ♔xb3
♘xa7 −+ 53 h5 ♘c6 54 h6 ♘e5 55
h7 ♘f7 56 ♔c4 ♔d6 57 ♔c3 ♔d5 58

♕d3 c4+ 59 ♔c3 ♔c5 60 ♔c2 ♔d4 61 ♕d2 c3+ 62 ♔c2 ♔c4 63 ♔c1 ♔d3 64 ♕d1 ♘h8 65 ♔c1 c2 0-1 **Ciocaltea**

1 e4 b6

168 Jovcic-Sahovic Jugoslavia 78
1 e4 b6 2 d4 e6 3 ♘f3 ♗b7 4 ♗d3 c5 5 0-0 cxd4 6 ♘xd4 ♗c5 7 ♘b3 ♗e7 8 c4 d6 9 f4 ♘d7 10 ♘c3 ♘gf6 11 ♕e2 0-0 12 ♗d2 ♘e8! 13 ♖ae1 ♗f6= 14 ♔h1 a6 15 ♕g4?! 15 ♕e3 g6! 16 ♔h3 ♕e7 17 ♘c1 ♘c7 18 ♘1e2 b5 19 ♘g1 ♘c5 20 e5 dxe5 21 fxe5 ♗g7 22 ♘e4 ♘xd3 23 ♘f6+?! 23 ♕xd3 ♗xe5 ♗xf6 24 exf6 ♕d8! 25 ♕h6 ♘e8 26 ♖e3 ♗xf6 27 ♗c3 e5! −+ 28 ♖xd3 ♕xd3 29 ♖xf6 ♕e4 30 ♘f3 ♕b1+ 31 ♘g1 ♖ae8 32 h3 b4! 33 ♗xb4 ♕xb2 34 ♗d2 34 ♗xf8 ♕xg2 mate ♖d8 35 ♖f2 f6 36 ♗e3 ♕c3 37 ♗b6 ♖d1 38 ♗c5 ♖f7 39 ♖e2 ♕xc4 40 ♕e3 ♕d3 0-1 41 ♕f2 ♕xh3 mate **Sahovic**

169 Haik-Sahovic Trstenik 78
1 d4 b6 2 e4 ♗b7 3 ♗d3 3 f3!?; 3 ♘c3; 3 d5!? e6 3...f5!? 4 ♘f3 c5 5 0-0 cxd4 6 ♘xd4 ♘c6 6...♗c5 7 ♘b3 ♗e7 7 ♘xc6 ♗xc6 8 ♘d2 8 c4!? d6 9 ♕e2 ♘f6 10 f4 ♗e7 11 b3 0-0 12 ♗b2 ♘d7 Δ ♘c5 13 ♖ae1 13 b4 += ♘c5 14 ♕g4 g6! 15 f5 ♘xd3 16 cxd3 e5 17 ♖f3?! 17 ♘c4 b5! 18 d4 ♗f6 19 ♖ef1 ♗d7!∓ 20 dxe5 dxe5 21 ♕g3 ♕e7 22 ♔h1 ♖ac8 23 fxg6 fxg6 24 ♖3f2 ♖c2 25 ♘b1! 25 ♘f3? ♖xb2 26 ♖xb2 ♗h4 27 ♘xh4 ♖xf1 mate ♖xf2 26 ♖xf2 ♗c6 27 ♘c3 b4 28 ♘d5 ♗xd5 29 exd5 ♕c5 30 h3 30 ♖d2 ♗g5 −+ ♕xd5 31 ♕e3 a5 32 ♖d2 ♕c6 33 ♕a7! 33 ♗xe5 ♗xe5 34 ♕xe5 ♕c1+ −+ ♕b5 34 ♖f2 ♗g7 35 ♖xf8+ ♗xf8 36 ♕c7 e4 37 ♕f4 Δ ♕e5 ♕d5 38 ♗e5 ♗g7 Zeitnot

39 ♗xg7 ♕xg7 40 ♕c7+ ♔g8 41 ♕c8+ ♔f7 42 ♕c7+ ♔f6! −+ 42... ♔g8=; 42...♔e6=; 42...♔e8= 43 ♔g1 43 ♕xh7 e3! 44 ♕h4+ ♔e5 45 ♕g5+ ♔d4 46 ♕xd5+ ♔xd5 47 ♔g1 ♔e5 48 ♔f1 ♔f4 49 ♔e2 ♔g3 −+ ♕d4+! −+ 44 ♔f1 44 ♔h1 ♕a1+ 45 ♔h2 ♕e5+ −+ ♕a1+ 45 ♔f2 ♕xa2+ 46 ♔e3 ♕xb3+ 47 ♔xe4 ♕b1+ 48 ♔d4 ♕d1+ 49 ♔e4 ♕e2+ 50 ♔d4 ♕d2+ 51 ♔e4 ♕xg2+ 52 ♔d4 ♕f2+ 53 ♔e4 ♕f5+ 54 ♔d4 g5 55 ♕c6+ ♔g7 56 ♕g2 b3 0-1 **Sahovic**

Sicilian .

170 Mihalchishin-Psahis USSR 78
1 e4 c5 2 ♘f3 b6?! 3 d4 cxd4 4 ♘xd4 ♗b7 5 ♘c3 d6 6 ♗g5 ♘d7 7 ♗d5!? 7 ♗c4 a6 8 ♕e2 b5 9 ♗d5 ♕c8 10 0-0 ♘gf6 11 ♖ad1 e6 12 ♘xe6! fxe6 13 ♗xe6± Panchenko-Psahis a6 8 ♕f3 ♕c8 9 ♘f5 g6 9...e6 10 ♘de7 10 ♘dxe7 ♗xe7 11 ♘g7+ ♔f8 11...♔d8 12 ♕xf7 +− 12 ♘e6+ = ½-½ **Pytel**

171 Vaisman-Gheorghiu Rumania 78
1 e4 c5 2 ♘f3 e6 3 b4!? cxb4 4 d4 ♘f6 4...d5 5 e5∝ 5 ♗d3 d5 6 e5 ♘e4 7 0-0 ♗e7 8 ♕e2 ♘c3!?= 8...0-0 9 ♗xe4 dxe4 10 ♕xe4 ♘c6 11 c4!∝ 9 ♘xc3 bxc3 10 ♖b1 ♗c6 11 ♖b3 0-0 12 ♖xc3 f5! 13 exf6!∝ 13 ♗a3 ♗xa3 14 ♖xa3 b6 =+; 14...♘b4 =+ ♗xf6 14 ♗a3! ♘xd4!= 14...♖e8 15 ♘e5! ♘xd4 16 ♕h5! +−; 14...♖f7 15 ♘e5!± 15 ♘xd4 ♗xd4 16 ♖xc8?! 16 ♗xh7+ ♔xh7 17 ♕h5+ ♔g8 18 ♖h3 ♗f6 19 ♕h7+ ♔f7 20 ♕h5+ = ♕xc8! 17 ♗xf8 ♕xf8 18 ♗xh7 ♕e7! =+ 19 ♖d1 ♕c5 20 ♗f5 ♗xf2+!∓

Diagram

Sicilian

21 ♔h1 21 ♕xf2 ♕xf2+ 22 ♔xf2 exf5 23 ♖xd5 ♖c8! 24 ♖d2 ♖c3! Δ ♖a3∓; 22...♖f8∓ ♕e3 **22 ♕g4!** g5 23 ♗xe6 ♕xe6 24 ♕xg5+ ♔d7 25 ♖xd5+ ♔c6 26 ♖d1 ♖g8 27 ♕f4 ♗c5 28 h3 ♖f8 29 ♕a4+ b5 29...♔c7 −+ 30 ♕a6+ ♗b6 31 a4! ♕e2! 32 axb5 ♔c7 33 ♕a1 ♖e8 33...♖g8! 34 ♕c3+ ♔b8 35 ♕f3 ♕xf3 Δ ♖g3 −+ **34 ♕c3+ ♔b8 35 ♕d3 ♕e5!** Δ ♗c7 36 g3 ♖d8! −+ 37 ♕xd8+ ♗xd8 38 ♖xd8+ ♔c7 39 ♖d3 ♕e1+ 40 ♔g2 ♕e2+ 41 ♔g1 ♕xc2 42 ♖f3 ♔b6 **0-1 Gheorghiu**

172 Planinc-Velimirovic
Jugoslavia Final 78

1 e4 c5 2 ♘f3 ♘c6 3 ♘c3 g6 4 ♗c4!? ♗g7 5 0-0 e6?! 6 d4! cxd4 7 ♘b5 d5 7...d6 8 ♘fxd4 ♘xd4 9 ♘xd4 += **8 exd5 exd5 9 ♗xd5 ♘ge7 10 ♗xc6+ ♘xc6 11 ♗g5! ♕b6** 11...♕d7? 12 ♖e1+± **12 ♘d6+ ♔f8 13 ♗f4** Δ ♘g5 **h6 14 ♖e1 ♗e6 15 ♘h4** Δ ♘xg6+ **g5**

Diagram

16 ♖xe6 += fxe6 17 ♘g6+ ♔g8 18 **♕g4? ♘d8?** 18...♕xb2 19 ♕xe6+ ♔h7 20 ♖e1 ♕xc2 −+ **19 ♘e7+ ♔f8** 19...♔h7 20 ♕h5 ♖f8 21 ♕g6+ ♔h8 22 ♗e5! +− **20 ♘g6+ ♔g8= 21 ♖e1!?**

♔h7 21...gxf4? 22 ♘e7+ ♔f8 23 ♖xe6 (Δ ♕f5+) ♘xe6 24 ♕xe6 ♕c6 25 ♘g6 mate **22 ♗g3 ♕c6!** Δ ♕xc2 −+ 22...♔xg6 23 ♖xe6+!! ♘xe6 24 ♕f5+ ♔h5 25 ♕f7+ Δ h3 mate **23 c3** Δ ♘e7, ♕e4 mate **♖e8 24 ♗xe8 ♕xe8 25 ♘e5 dxc3 26 ♕e4+ ♔g8 27 bxc3** += **♖c8 28 c4 ♘f7 29 ♘g6 ♗f6 30 h4 ♕c6 31 ♕xe6 ♔g7 32 ♕f5** Δ ♘e7 **♖e8 33 ♘e5!± ♗xe5 34 ♗xe5+ ♔g8 35 hxg5 hxg5 36 ♖e3 ♖e6 37 ♗d4?** 37 c5! Δ ♗d4±; 37 ♖f3?! ♘xe5 38 ♕f8+ ♔h7 39 ♖h3+ ♖h6 40 ♕e7+ ♔g6 += **♖xe3 38 ♗xe3 ♕xc4** += **39 ♗xg5 ♕xa2 40 ♕g6+ ♔f8 41 ♗e3?!** 41 ♗f6± **♕a1+** = **42 ♔h2 ♕h8+ 43 ♔g3 ♕e5+ 44 ♗f4 ♕g7 45 ♕xg7+ ♔xg7 ½-½ Maric**

173 Malich-Adamski Leipzig 77

1 ♘f3 ♘f6 2 d4 e6 3 ♗g5 c5 4 e4!? 4 c3; 4 e3!? **cxd4!** 4...h6?! 5 ♗xf6 ♕xf6 6 e5 ♕d8 7 d5!±; 4...♕b6 5 ♘bd2 cxd4 6 e5 ♘d5 7 a3!? Δ ♘c4; 7 ♗c4!? **5 ♘bd2 ♘c6! 6 e5?!** 6 ♗b5!? **h6 7 ♗h4 g5 8 ♗g3 ♘h5** 8...♘d5∞ **9 ♗b5** 9 ♘e4 ♕a5+∓; 9 ♗d3 g4 10 ♗h4 ♗e7 11 ♗xe7 ♕xe7∓ **g4 10 ♗h4** 10 ♗xc6 dxc6 11 ♘e4 ♗b4+! 12 ♔f1 gxf3 13 ♕xf3 ♘xg3+ −+; 11...gxf3 12 ♕xf3 ♘xg3?? 13 ♘f6+ Δ ♕a3+ **♕b6** 10...♗e7? 11 ♗xe7 ♕xe7 12 ♗xc6 dxc6 13 ♘xd4±; 10...♕c7!

11 ♗xc6 dxc6 12 ♘xd4 ♕xe5+ 13
♘e2 ♘f4∓; 11...♕xc6 11 ♗xc6 11 a4
Δ 11...gxf3 12 ♕xf3 ♘g7 13 ♘e4
∝/+− ♗e7 14 ♗xe7 ♚xe7 15 ♕f6+ ♔f8
16 ♘d6 ♘d8 17 a5 ♕c7 18 ♗d3 Δ
♘b5/♗g6; 11...a6! ♕xc6 12 ♘xd4
♕xg2 13 ♖f1 ♕xh2 14 ♕xg4 ♕xe5+
15 ♔d1 ♗f6 15...♘f4?? 16 ♘2f3 ♕d6
17 ♗f6 +− 16 ♕f3 ♗e7 −+ 17 ♕d3
♕h5+ 18 ♘2f3 ♕g6 19 ♕b3 a6 20 c4
d6 21 ♖g1 ♕h5 22 ♘e2 b5 23 ♘g3
♕g4 24 ♕c3 ♗b7 25 ♔e2 ♕xc4+
26 ♕xc4 bxc4 27 ♖ac1 ♖c8 28 ♘d2
a5 29 ♔d1 ♘g4 30 ♗xe7 ♚xe7 31
♘xc4 ♖c5 32 ♘xa5 ♗f3+ 33 ♔d2
♖d5+ 34 ♔e1 ♖e5+ 35 ♔d2 ♖d5+
36 ♔e1 ♖c8 0-1 Bellin

2 c3/3 c3

174 Bondoc-Gheorghiu
Rumania 78
1 e4 c5 2 c3 d5 3 exd5 ♕xd5 4 d4
♘f6 5 ♘f3 e6 6 ♘a3 ♗e7 7 ♘b5 ♘a6!=
8 ♗e2 0-0 9 0-0 cxd4 10 ♕xd4 ♕xd4
11 ♘bxd4 ♘c5 12 ♗g5 h6 13 ♗h4 g5
14 ♗g3 ♘fe4 =+ 15 ♖fd1 ♘xg3 16
hxg3 ♗f6 17 ♘b3! ♘a4! 17...♘xb3?
18 axb3± 18 ♘d2 a6 19 ♖ad1 ♖b8 20
♘h2 b5 21 ♘g4 ♗g7 22 a3! ♗b7 23
♘e3 ♗a8 24 ♗f3 ♗xf3? 24...♖fc8! =+
25 gxf3 ♖fc8 26 ♔g2= ½-½ Gheorghiu

175 Oblamsky-Kapengut Minsk 78
1 e4 c5 2 c3 ♘f6 3 e5 ♘d5 4 d4 cxd4
5 ♘f3 ♘c6 6 cxd4 d6 7 ♗c4 ♘b6 8
♗b5 dxe5!? 9 ♘xe5 ♗d7 10 ♗xc6
10 ♘xd7 ♕xd7 11 ♘c3 e6 12 0-0 a6
13 ♗xc6 ♕xc6 14 ♕g4 h5 15 ♕g5
♖d8 16 f3 ♖h6 17 ♕e5 ♖g6 18 ♕xh5
♖xd4∓ Zhuravlev-Gutman, Riga 71;
15 ♕h4 ♗e7 16 ♕h3 ♖d8 17 ♗e3
♘d5 18 ♖ac1 ♘xc3 19 bxc3 ♕c4 20
♕g3 0-0 21 ♗h6 ♗f6= Sveshnikov-

Popov, Lvov 73; 14...g6?! 15 d5!?
♘xd5 16 ♘xd5 ♕xd5 17 ♖d1 h5
18 ♕a4+ ♕b5 19 ♕d4 e5 20 ♕e4
♗g7 21 ♖d5± Chekhov-V.Zilberstein,
Moscow 76; 12 ♕g4 h5 13 ♕f3 ♖c8
14 0-0 ♕xd4 15 ♗f4 ♗e7 16 ♖fd1
♕f6 17 ♘e4 ♕f5 18 ♗d3 ♕g4 19
♕xg4 hxg4∓ Platonov-Peshina, Vilnius
77 ♗xc6 11 ♘xc6 bxc6 12 0-0 g6
12...e6?! 13 ♕g4 ♗e7 14 ♕xg7 ♗f6
15 ♕g3 ♕xd4 16 ♘c3 ♘d5 17 ♗e3
♘xc3 18 bxc3 ♕e5 19 ♕f3± Gurieli-
Kislova, Tbilisi 76 13 ♘c3!? 13 ♖e1
♗g7 14 ♗g5 ♕xd4?! Izvozchikov-
Kirpichnikov, USSR 75; 14...♘d5!;
13 ♕c2 ♖c8 14 ♖d1 ♗g7 15 ♗f4 0-0
16 ♗e5 c5! 17 ♘c3 c4 18 ♗xg7 ♔xg7
19 d5 ♖c5 =+ Machulsky-Podgaets,
Beley 77 ♗g7 14 ♕f3 ♖c8 14...0-0!
15 ♕xc6? ♕xd4 =+; 15 ♖d1 ♗xd4?!
16 ♗h6 ♖e8 17 ♕xc6 ♖c8 18 ♕f3
e5 19 ♘e4 +=; 15...♕d7! 15 ♖d1 0-0
15...♗xd4? 16 ♗h6± 16 ♗g5 ♖e8 17
♖d3 h6 18 ♗f4 18 ♗e3? ♘c4 Δ ♘e5
♕d7 19 ♖ad1 ♕f5 20 g4?! ♕a5 21
♕h3 ♘c4!∓ 22 ♗c1 22 b4!? ♕xb4
23 ♖e1 ♕a5 24 ♗xh6 e5! =+ e5!
23 dxe5 ♘xe5 24 ♖d6 ♕b4 25 f3
♘c4 26 ♖d7 ♘xb2 27 ♗xb2 ♕xb2
28 ♘e4 ♕xa2! −+ 29 g5 h5 30 ♘d6
♗d4+! 31 ♔h1 ♕e2 32 ♖f1 32 ♖b1?
♕e1+ ♖cd8 33 ♘xe8 ♖xd7 34 ♘f6+
♗xf6 35 gxf6 ♖d6 0-1 Kapengut

176 Makropoulos-Bilek Athens 77
1 e4 c5 2 c3 g6!? 3 ♘f3 ♗g7 4 d4
4 ♗c4!? cxd4 5 cxd4 d5 6 exd5
6 e5 ♘c6 7 ♗b5 ♘h6 8 0-0 0-0 9
♘c3 ♗g4 10 ♗xc6 bxc6 11 h3 ♗xf3
12 ♕xf3 ♘f5 13 ♖d1 f6∝ Olsen-
Filipowicz, Gausdal 77 ♘f6 7 ♗b5+
♘bd7 8 d6 0-0!? 8...exd6 9 ♕e2+
+= 9 dxe7 ♕xe7+ 10 ♗e2 10 ♕e2 +=
♖e8 11 ♘c3 ♘e4! 12 ♗e3? 12 ♘xe4

♕xe4 13 ♗e3= ♘df6 13 ♗b5?

13...♘xf2!! −+ 14 ♔xf2 ♘g4+ 15 ♔g3 ♘xe3 16 ♕a4 ♗xd4! 17 ♗xe8 17 ♘xd4 ♕g5+ 18 ♔f2 ♕xg2+ 19 ♔e1 ♘c4+; 17 ♔f2 ♘c4+ 18 ♔f1 ♕e3 14 ♘d1 ♕xf3+ 15 gxf3 ♗h3 mate **♘f5+** 18 ♔h3 ♘h6+ 19 g4 ♗xg4+ 20 ♔g3 ♗xf3 21 ♖he1 ♕g5+ 22 ♔xf3 ♕g4 mate 0-1 Pytel

177 Kapengut-Terentiev Frunze 77
1 e4 c5 2 ♘f3 a6 3 c3 d5 4 exd5 ♕xd5 5 d4 ♘f6 6 ♗e2 e6 7 0-0 ♗e7 8 ♘bd2! N 8 ♗f4 ♘c6 9 ♘e5 ♘xe5 10 ♗xe5 0-0 11 ♗f3 ♕d8± Stein-Bolbochan, Stockholm 62; 8...0-0 9 ♘e5 cxd4 10 cxd4 ♖d8 Arseniev-Kushelman, USSR 62; 8 ♗e3 cxd4 9 ♘xd4 ♘bd7 10 ♘bd2 ♕d6 11 ♗g5 0-0 Geller-Taimanov, Tbilisi 67 **♘bd7 9 ♘c4** cxd4 10 ♘xd4! ♕c5 11 a4 0-0 12 a5 ♘d5 12...♕c7 13 ♗g5 13 ♕d3 ♕c7 14 ♕g3! ♕xg3 15 hxg3 ♗f6 16 ♖d1 ♘e5 17 ♘f3!± ♘c6 17...♘xc4 18 ♗xc4 ♖d8 19 ♗g5± 18 ♗g5 ♖b8 19 ♗xf6 gxf6 20 ♘fd2 ♘ce7 21 ♘e4 ♔g7 22 ♘c5 b6? 22...e5 23 ♘d6 ♖d8 24 ♘xc8 ♖bxc8 25 ♘xb7± 23 axb6 ♘xb6 24 ♖d2 24 ♘xb6 ♖xb6 25 ♖d2 +− ♘d5 25 ♖a3 ♖a8 26 b4 e5 27 ♘a5 f5 28 ♘c6! +− ♘xc3 29 ♘xe7 ♘b1 30 ♖da2 ♘xa3 31 ♖xa3

♖b8 32 ♗xa6 ♗xa6 33 ♘xa6 ♖b6 34 ♘xf5+ ♔f6 35 ♘e3 ♖d8 36 ♘c7 ♔g5 37 b5 ♖d4 38 ♖a6 ♖b8 39 ♖c6 ♖b4 40 ♖c5 f6 41 f4+ ♔g6 42 f5+ ♔f7 43 ♘ed5 ♖b1+ 44 ♔h2 1-0 Kapengut

178 Formanek-Gheorghiu
Lone Pine 78
1 e4 c5 2 ♘f3 e6 3 c3 d5 4 e5 4 exd5 ♕xd5∞ d4! 4...♘d7 5 d4 += 5 ♗d3!? 5 ♗b5+ ♗d7= ♘c6 6 0-0 ♘ge7 7 ♖e1 ♘g6! 8 g3 a6 8...♕c7 9 ♕e2 f6!?∞ 9 a4 b6 10 h4 ♕c7 11 ♕e2 ♗b7 12 ♘a3! 12 h5 c4!! 13 ♗xc4 ♘gxe5∓; 13 hxg6 cxd3∓ ♘a5 13 h5 ♘e7 14 ♗e4 ♘d5!∓ 15 ♘c2 ♘b3 16 ♖b1

16...♕d7?! 16...♖d8! 17 c4 ♘e3!!∓ 18 ♗xb7 ♘xc2; 18 ♕d3 ♗xe4 19 ♕xe4 ♘xc2 **17 c4 ♘e3??** 17...♘e7 18 ♗xb7 ♕xb7 19 ♕d3 ♘xc1 20 ♖exc1 ♘c6 =+ **18 ♗xb7 d3** 18...♘xc2 19 ♗xa8 +− **19 ♕xe3 dxc2 20 ♖a1!!** +− **♘xc1** 20...♘xa1 21 ♗xa8 **21 ♗xa8 ♘d3 1-0 Gheorghiu**

179 Lipski-Kruszynski
Poland Final 78
1 e4 c5 2 ♘f3 e6 3 c3 ♘f6 3...d5 4 e5 ♘d5 5 d4 cxd4 6 cxd4 d6 6...b6!? 7 a3 ♗e7 8 ♗d3 ♗d7 9 ♘c3 ♗xc3?! 9...♘c6 10 ♘e4 dxe5 11 dxe5 ♘d7! 10 bxc3 ♗c6 11 ♗f4 ♕c7? 11...dxe5

12 ♘xe5 ♘d7! **12 0-0 ♘d7 13 ♖e1 dxe5** 13...♗xf3!?; 13...0-0 **14 ♘xe5 ♘xe5 15 ♗xe5 ♗d6 16 ♕g4!± ♗xe5 17 ♖xe5 0-0-0 18 ♖b1 g6 19 ♖c5!!** △ ♗b5 h5 **20 ♕e2 ♖d5 21 ♖c4 ♖a5 22 ♗e4 ♖xa3 23 ♗xc6 bxc6 24 ♖cb4 ♖a5 25 c4! ♖a6 26 c5 ♖a5**

27 d5!! 27 ♖b8+? ♕xb8 28 ♖xb8 ♔xb8 29 ♕e5+ ♔b7 30 ♕xh8 ♖a1 mate **♖xc5** 27...exd5 28 ♖b8+! **28 ♕a6+ 1-0 Pytel**

2 ♘c3/2 d3

180 Spassky-Ljubojevic Bugojno 78

1 e4 c5 2 ♘c3 ♘c6 3 g3 ♖b8!? 4 f4!? 4 ♗g2 b5 5 ♘ge2 e6 6 ♘f4 ♘f6 7 0-0 ♗e7 8 ♖e1 d6∞ Hasenfuss-Barcza, Munich 36 **g6 5 ♘f3 ♗g7 6 ♗g2 b5 7 a3 ♕a5!** =+ **8 0-0 b4 9 ♘e2 9** ♘d5!? e6 10 ♘e3∞ **c4! 10 d4** 10 ♔h1 cxd3 **11 cxd3 ♕b6+ 12 ♔h1 bxa3 13 ♖xa3 ♗xb2! 14 ♗xb2 ♕xb2 15 ♕a1?! ♘f6 16 ♘ed4 ♘xd4 17 ♘xd4 a6∓ 18 ♖c1 0-0 19 ♕xb2 ♖xb2 20 ♖b3 ♖xb3 21 ♘xb3 ♗b7 22 ♖c7 ♖b8 23 ♘c5** 23 e5!? ♗c6 **24 h3 a5 25 g4 ♘e8! 26 ♖a7 d6 27 ♘d7 ♖b7! 28 ♖xb7 ♗xb7 29 ♘b6 ♗a6 30 d4 ♘c7 31 d5 ♗b5 32 ♗f3 a4 33 ♗d1 a3 34 ♗b3 ♘a6 35 e5 ♗b4 36 ♘c8 ♗a4 37 ♗c4**

dxe5 **38 fxe5 ♕f8 39 ♘b6 ♗b5 0-1 Pytel**

181 Spassky-Hort Bugojno 78

1 e4 c5 2 ♘c3 ♘c6 3 g3 g6 4 ♗g2 ♗g7 5 d3 d6 6 f4 e5 6...e6!; 6...f5!? **7 ♘h3! ♘ge7 8 0-0 d4 9 f5!? gxf5 10 ♕h5 h6** 10...♘xc2 11 ♖b1∞ **11 ♖f2 ♗e6 12 ♗e3 ♕d7 13 ♖af1 0-0-0 14 ♘d5! fxe4 15 ♘xe7+ ♕xe7 16 ♗xd4 cxd4**

17 ♖xf7! ♕e8! 18 ♗xe4 ♖f8 19 ♗f5!! += **♕xf7 20 ♕xf7 ♖xf7 21 ♗xe6+ ♖fd7 22 ♖f7 ♔c7 23 ♗xd7 ♖xd7 24 ♖xd7+ ♔xd7 25 ♔g2 ♔e6 26 ♔f3 d5?** 26...♔f6! += **27 ♔g4 ♔f6 28 ♕h5±** **♗f8** 28...b5! **29 ♘g1** 29 a4! **b5! 30 ♘e2 a5 31 g4 a4 32 h4 b4 33 b3 a3 34 ♘g3 e4! 35 g5+** 35 dxe4 dxe4 36 ♘xe4 ♔e5 △ d3, ♔d4, ♔c3, ♔b2 **hxg5 36 hxg5+ ♔e5 37 ♔g4 ♗g7??** 37...e3 **38 ♘h5 ♗f8 39 g6 e3 40 ♔f3 ♔f5 41 g7 1-0 Pytel**

182 Shaw-R.Jamieson Australia Final 78

1 e4 c5 2 ♘c3 ♘c6 3 g3 g6 4 ♗g2 ♗g7 5 d3 d6 6 f4 e5 7 ♘h3 7 ♘f3 ♘ge7 8 0-0 0-0 9 ♗e3 exf4 10 gxf4 f5 11 ♕d2 ♖b8 12 a3 Spassky-Minic, USSR-Jugoslavia 65 **exf4** 7...♘f6? 8 0-0 0-0 9 f5± **8 ♘xf4 ♘ge7 9 0-0 0-0 10 ♔h1**

10 ♘fd5 ♘xd5 11 ♘xd5 ♗e6 12 ♘f4
♗d7 13 c3 b5 14 a3 a5 15 ♗e3 ♘e5
16 h3= Bilek-Evans, Lugano 68 **♖b8
11 ♗e3 b5 12 ♕d2 b4 13 ♘d1 a5 14
c4 bxc3 15 bxc3 ♘e5 16 ♘f2 ♗a6
17 ♖ab1 ♕d7 18 ♕c2 ♗b5 19 ♖b2
♗a4 20 ♕d2 ♖b5 21 ♖fb1 ♖fb8 22
h3 ♖8b6 23 ♘d1 ♗xd1 24 ♖xb5
♖xb5 25 ♖xb5?** 25 ♕xd1 ♕b7 26
♖xb5 ♕xb5 26 ♕xd1 g5! 27 ♘h5!
27 c4 ♕b2∓ ♗xd3 28 ♘xg7 ♕xg7 29
♗f1 c4 30 a4 ♕d7 31 ♔g2 31 ♗xd3?
♕xh3+ −+ f6 32 ♗d4 ♕e6 33 ♗xd3
exd3 34 ♕xd3 ♕a2+ 35 ♔g1 ♕a1+
36 ♔h2? 36 ♕f1= ♕xa4 37 ♕f3 ♕a2+
38 ♔g1 ♕e6 39 c4 ♘c6 40 ♗c3 a4 41
♕e3 h6 42 c5 d5 43 g4 dxe4 44 ♗b2
♔g6 45 ♔f2 ♘b4 46 ♕d4 ♘d3+ 47
♔g2 h5 48 gxh5+ ♔xh5 49 ♔h2 ♘xb2
50 ♕xb2 e3 51 ♕c2 △ ♕h7 mate
♔h6 52 ♕c3 e2 53 ♕e1 a3 54 c6 a2
55 c7 ♕e5+ 56 ♔g2 ♕xc7 0-1

183 Ciocaltea-Cojocaru
Rumania 78
1 e4 c5 2 ♘f3 e6 3 d3 g6 3...d5 4
♘bd2 ♘c6 5 g3 g6; 5...♗d6!? 4 g3
♗g7 5 ♗g2 ♘c6 6 0-0 ♘ge7 7 ♖e1 0-0
8 c3 d6 8...e5 9 ♗e3 d6 10 ♘a3 9
d4 e5 9...cxd4!? 10 cxd4 e5 △ ♗g4
10 dxc5! dxc5 11 ♘a3! ♗g4 12 h3
♕xd1 13 ♖xd1 ♗xf3 14 ♗xf3 ♖fd8
15 ♗e3 b6 16 ♘b5!± ♗f8 17 g4 h6
18 h4 ♕g7 19 g5 h5 20 ♗e2 ♘c8 21
♘c7 ♖b8 22 ♗b5 ♖xd1+ 23 ♖xd1
♘8e7 24 ♖d7! ♔g8 24...♖d8? 25
♗xc6 ♘xc6 26 ♘e6+ +− 25 ♘d5 ♘xd5
26 ♖xd5 ♘e7 27 ♖d7! 27 ♖xe5?!
♖b7! △ 28...♗g7 ♘c8 28 ♗c4 28 ♖d8!
♗e7 28...♘d6 29 ♗d5 △ f4 +− 29
f4 +− ♔f8 30 fxe5 b5 31 ♗d5 b4 32
c4 1-0 Ciocaltea

3 ♗b5

184 Glek-Shirjaev USSR 78
1 e4 c5 2 ♘f3 ♘c6 3 ♗b5 ♘d4!? 3...
♘f6!? 4 e5 ♘d5 5 ♘c3 ♘c7 6 ♗xc6
dxc6 7 h3 g6 8 0-0 ♗g7 9 ♘e4 b6 10
♖e1 0-0 11 d3 ♘e6= Adorjan-
Sveshnikov, Sochi 76; 3...♕b6 4 ♗a4
g6 5 0-0 ♗g7 6 c3 e6 7 ♖e1 ♘ge7 8
♘a3! += 4 ♘xd4 4 ♗c4!? cxd4 5 0-0
5 c3!? a6 6 ♗e2 d5 7 ♕a4 ♗d7 8 ♕xd4
dxe4 9 ♕xe4 ♗c6 10 ♕g4 += g6!?
6 d3 ♗g7 7 ♗c4 e6 8 f4 += △ f5
♘e7 9 f5! gxf5 10 ♕h5 d5 11 ♗b3
h6 12 ♗d2!± dxe4 13 dxe4 ♗d7 14
♘a3 ♕c7 15 exf5 ♕c5 15...♘xf5? 16
♖xf5 +−

16 ♗b4!! +− ♕xb4 17 fxe6 0-0-0 18
exd7+ ♖xd7 19 ♖xf7 d3!? 20 c3
♕b6+ 21 ♔h1 ♗f6 22 ♕b5! ♕f2
22...♕d6 23 ♕c4+ △ ♕e6 +− 23 ♗e6
♖g8 24 ♕xd7+ ♔b8 25 ♗d5 1-0
Gufeld

185 Gipslis-Wirthensohn Dortmund 78
1 e4 c5 2 ♘f3 ♘c6 3 ♘c3 ♘f6 3...e5
4 ♗c4 g6 5 d3 h6 6 0-0 ♗g7 7 ♘e1!
d6 8 f4 ♘f6 9 ♘d5 ♘xd5 10 ♗xd5
exf4 11 ♗xf4± Matulovic-Evans,
Siegen 70 4 ♗b5 a6 4...e6 5 0-0
♗e7 6 ♗xc6 bxc6 7 d3 d5 8 ♗g5 +=
Lein-Lengyel, Cienfuegos 72; 4...g6
5 h3 ♗g7 6 e5 ♘g8 7 ♗xc6 dxc6 8
d3 ♘h6 9 g4!? f5 10 exf6 exf6 11

&e2+ &e7 12 &xe7+ &xe7 13 &e3±
Kuzmin-Timoshenko, Baku 77; 4...
&d4 5 e5! &xb5 6 &xb5 &d5 7 0-0
a6 8 c4! &b6 9 &c3 d5 10 d4 e6 11
&g5 &d7 12 cxd5 &xd5 13 &xd5
&xd5 14 dxc5 &xc5 15 &c2 0-0
16 &fd1± Sax-Sveshnikov, Hastings
77/8 **5 &xc6 dxc6 6 h3** N 6 0-0±
Dueball-Schiffer, Berlin 71 **g6 7 0-0
&g7 8 d3 0-0 9 &e3 &d7 10 &d2 e5
11 &h6 &e7** 11...f5?! 12 exf5 gxf5
13 &xg7 &xg7 14 &g5+ &xg5 15
&xg5±; 11...f6!? **12 &h2 &d8 13 &xg7
&xg7 14 f4** 14 &g4?! &f8 exf4 15
&xf4 &e5 15...&f8 16 &e3 &e6?!
17 &g4!±; 16...f5 17 &ae1± **16
&f3! &xf3+** 16...f6 17 &xe5 fxe5
18 &g3 &d7 19 &b1! △ &d2, &f3±,
&xe5; 17...&xe5 18 &xe5 fxe5 19
&a4 +− **17 &xf3 b5** 17...f6 18 &af1
&f8 19 e5! f5 20 &e4!±; 17...f5 18
exf5 &xf5 19 g4 &e6 20 &e5+ &g8
21 &e1! +− **18 &af1 &e6?** 18...&a7!?
19 &e2 △ &g3± **19 &e5+ &g8** 19...
&f8 20 &h8 mate

20 &xf7 1-0 20...&xf7 21 &xf7 &xf7
22 &xc5 +− Gipslis

186 Sax-Sveshnikov Hastings 77/78
**1 e4 c5 2 &f3 &c6 3 &b5 &f6 4 &c3
&d4 5 e5 &xb5 6 &xb5 &d5 7 0-0 a6
8 c4! &b6** 8...axb5 9 cxd5 d6 10 &e2!

9 &c3 d5 9...&xc4 **10 d4! e6 11 &g5**
&d7 12 cxd5 &xd5 13 &xd5 &xd5 14
dxc5 &xc5 15 &c2 0-0 16 &fd1 &c6
17 &ac1 &a7 18 &d2 &b5

19 &f6! h6 19...gxf6 20 &h6 fxe5
21 &g5 +− **20 &f4 &xb2 21 &g4**
&xf2+ 22 &h1 g6 23 &b4! △ &xf8+
&b6 24 &d2 &e3 25 &c3 a5 26 &xf8+
&xf8 27 &xe3 1-0

187 Ciocaltea-Biriescu
Bucharest 78

1 e4 c5 2 &f3 &c6 3 &b5 &f6 4 &e2!?
a6 5 &xc6 dxc6 6 h3 6 d3 g6 7 &d2
&g7 8 &c3 &g4!? 9 &bd2 0-0
Bronstein-Bannik, USSR 57 **g6 7 0-0**
&g7 8 a4 a5! 9 d3 0-0 10 &c3 &e8 11
&e3 b6 12 &e1! e5 13 f4 exf4 14
&xf4 &c7 15 &f3 &e6 16 &e3 f5 16...
&d4! **17 &ae1 f4 18 &f2 &g5!?** 18...
&d4! **19 e5! &e8 20 &xg5 &xg5 21**
&f3 &xe5 21...&xe5 22 &xc6 &xh3
23 &xe5! +− **22 &xc6 &b8 23 &c7**
&a8 24 h4 +− &f5 25 &xe5 &xe5
25...&xe5 26 &c6 &b8 27 &e1 &b7
28 &xb6± **26 &d8+ &g7 27 &e7+**
&g8 28 &e8+ &g7 29 &e1 &f6 30
&c6 &a7 31 &e4 &e7 32 &xb6 &b7
33 &xa5 f3 33...&xb2 34 &c3+ &f6
35 &xf6 &xf6 36 &e7+ **34 &c3+**
&g8 35 &g3 &f7 36 &e4 fxg2 37 &b3
&f3 38 &c4+ &g7 39 &c3+ &g8

40 ♘g3 1-0 Ciocaltea

188 Ciocaltea-Tratatovici
Rumania Final 77
**1 e4 c5 2 ♘f3 ♘c6 3 ♗b5 g6 4 0-0
♘f6 5 ♖e1 ♗g7 6 h3 0-0 7 c3 ♘e8**
N 7...e5!? 8 ♗xc6? dxc6 9 ♘xe5 ♖e8
10 f4 ♘xe4! 11 ♖xe4 f6 12 ♕b3+
♗e6 13 ♘c4 ♗d5!∓ Veingold-
Kapengut, USSR 75; 8 d4 cxd4 9
cxd4 exd4 10 e5!? **8 d4 cxd4 9 cxd4
♘c7 10 ♗a4 10 ♗f1!? d5 11 ♗xc6 bxc6
12 e5 ♘e6 13 ♘c3 ♗b7** 13...f6!? **14
♗a4 ♖c8 15 ♘g5! +– ♗xg5 16 ♗xg5
f6 17 ♗f4! c5 18 ♘xc5** 18 dxc5?!
d4 **♖xc5 19 dxc5 1-0 Ciocaltea**

189 Ciocaltea-Spirov Albena 78
**1 e4 c5 2 ♘f3 ♘c6 3 ♗b5 g6 4 0-0
♗g7 5 c3 ♕b6?!** 5...♘f6; 5...e5 6 ♘a3!
a6 7 ♗a4 e6? 7...♕c7!? **8 ♘c4 ♕c7 9
♗xc6! bxc6?!** 9...♕xc6 **10 e5! f6 11
d4 cxd4 12 cxd4 ♘e7 13 ♘d6+ ♔f8 14
b3! h6 15 ♗a3 +– ♕d8** 15...♔g8 16
exf6 ♗xf6 17 ♘e8 ♕f4 18 ♘d6! ♕f5
19 ♘xf6+ ♕xf6 20 ♗e5 +– **16 ♘h4
♖h7 17 ♘xc8 1-0 Ciocaltea**

5...e5

190 Honfi-Piasetski Subotica 78
**1 e4 c5 2 ♘f3 ♘c6 3 d4 cxd4 4 ♘xd4
♘f6 5 ♘c3 e5 6 ♘db5 d6 7 ♗g5 a6 8
♘a3 b5 9 ♗xf6 gxf6** 9...♕xf6? 10
♘d5 ♕d8 11 c4± **10 ♘d5 f5 11
♗xb5!? axb5 12 ♘xb5 ♖a4!? 13
♘bc7+ ♕d7 14 0-0 ♖xe4?!** 14...♘e7;
14...♕g5 **15 ♕h5 ♘e7 16 ♕xf7 ♕c6 17
c4! ♖g8** 17...♘xd5 18 cxd5+ ♔b7 19
♘e6+ ♕d7 20 ♕xf5±; 18...♔b6 19
♖fc1± **18 ♖fc1 ♖g7** 18...♖eg4 19
g3 ♖4g6 20 c5!! dxc5 21 ♖xc5+ ♔xc5
22 ♖c1+ ♔d6 23 ♘xe7 ♗e6 24 ♘xf5+
+–; 20...♘xd5 21 cxd6+ ♔xd6 22

♘b5 mate

**19 ♘e6! ♗xe6 20 ♕xe6 ♖eg4 21 g3
♖4g5 22 ♘b4+ ♔b7 23 c5 ♖5g6 24
c6+ ♔a8 25 ♕b3! 25** ♕d7! +– **♕b6
25...♕a5 26 c7 ♘c8 27 ♘d5 ♕a7 28
♖c4 +–; 25...♘c8 26 ♘d5 +– 26
c7 ♔b7 26...♘c8 27 ♖c6 ♕b5 28 a4
+– 27 ♕d5+! 1-0 Honfi**

191 Balashov-Geller USSR 77
**1 e4 c5 2 ♘f3 ♘c6 3 d4 cxd4 4 ♘xd4
♘f6 5 ♘c3 e5 6 ♘db5 d6 7 ♗g5 a6
8 ♗xf6 gxf6 9 ♘a3 b5 10 ♘d5 f5
11 ♗d3 ♗e6 12 c4!?** 12 c3! += **♕a5+
13 ♔f1 fxe4 14 ♗xe4 ♗g7! 15 cxb5**
15 ♘f6+ ♗xf6 16 ♗xc6+ ♔e7 17 ♗xa8
♖xa8∓; 16 ♕xd6 ♘e7! 17 ♗xa8 0-0
**axb5 16 ♖c1 ♖a6 17 ♕d3 ♗xd5 18
♕xd5 ♘e7 19 ♕xb5+ ♕xb5 20 ♘xb5
0-0 21 ♖c7 ♖xa2 ½-½ Pytel**

192 Banas-Plachetka
CSSR Final 78
**1 e4 c5 2 ♘f3 ♘c6 3 d4 cxd4 4 ♘xd4
♘f6 5 ♘c3 e5 6 ♘db5 d6 7 ♗g5 a6 8
♘a3 b5 9 ♘d5 ♗e7 10 ♗xf6 ♗xf6
11 c3 0-0 12 ♘c2 ♖b8** 12...♗g5
13 a4 bxa4 14 ♖xa4 a5 **13 ♗e2** 13
♗d3 ♗g5 14 0-0 g6 15 a4 bxa4 16
♘cb4 ♘xb4 17 ♘xb4 ♗d7 18 ♗xa6±
Levy-Day, Haifa 76; 13 a4 bxa4 14
♘cb4 ♘xb4 15 ♘xb4 ♗b7 16 ♕xa4

Banas-Novak, CSSR Final 78; 16...a5!
17 ♕xa5 ♕xa5 18 ♖xa5 ♗xe4 19 f3
♗h4+!= ♗g5 14 a4! += bxa4 15 ♘cb4
♘xb4 16 ♘xb4 ♗b7 17 ♕xa4 a5 18
♕xa5 ♖a8 19 ♗a6 19 ♘a6? ♖xa6 20
♗xa6 ♕xa5 21 ♖xa5 ♖a8 22 ♗xb7
♖xa5 △ ♖b5 −+ ♕f6?! 19...♖xa6
20 ♘xa6 ♕xa5 21 ♖xa5 ♖a8 22 0-0
♖xa6 23 ♖xa6 ♗xa6 24 ♖a1±; 19...
♗xe4!? 20 0-0 +=

20 ♗xb7!! ♖xa5 21 ♖xa5 ♗d2+! 22
♔e2 22 ♔xd2? ♕xf2+ △ ♕b6∓ ♕g5
23 ♖d1 ♗c1 24 ♘d3 24 b3? ♗b2∞
♕g4+ 25 ♔e1 ♗g5 26 g3 g6 26...f5
27 exf5 e4 28 ♖a4± 27 h4 ♗d8 28
♖a8 ♔g7? 29 ♘xe5 +− dxe5 30
♖dxd8 ♖xd8 31 ♖xd8 f5 32 exf5?!
32 ♖d7+!? ♔h6 (32...♔f6 33 ♗d5)
33 exf5 gxf5 34 ♖d3! f4 35 ♗f3 +−
gxf5 33 ♗d5? 33 ♖d2! f4 34 ♔f1 e4
(34...fxg3 35 fxg3 +−) 35 ♖e2! +−
♕a4 34 ♖b8? 34 ♖a8 ♕b5 35 c4 +=
e4= 35 c4 ♕f6 36 ♖b5 ♕c2 37 ♔f1
h5 38 ♔g1 ♕e2 39 b4? 39 ♖b6+ ♔e5
40 ♖b5= ♔d4? 41 ♗e6 +− ♕d1+ 40
♔g2 ♕f3+ 41 ♔g1 ♕e5 42 ♗f7+ ♔d4
43 ♖d5+ ♔c3 44 ♖e5 ♕d1+ 45 ♔g2
f4 46 ♖xe4?? −+ 46 gxf4 ♕f3+ 47
♔g1 ♕xf4 48 ♖e7 ♕f6 49 ♖xe4
♕xf7 50 ♖e3+ △ ♖g3, ♖e3, ♖g3=
f3+ 47 ♔h2 ♕e2 48 ♖e3+ ♔d2 49 ♔g1
♕xe3 50 fxe3 ♔e1 0-1 Banas

193 Kalinichev-Timoshenko USSR 78
1 e4 c5 2 ♘c3 ♘c6 3 ♘f3 e6 4 d4 cxd4
5 ♘xd4 ♘f6 6 ♘db5 d6 7 ♗f4 e5 8
♗g5 a6 9 ♘a3 b5 10 ♘d5 ♗e7 11
♗xf6 ♗xf6 12 c3 0-0 13 ♘c2 ♗g5 14
a4 bxa4 15 ♖xa4 a5 16 ♗b5!? 16
♗c4 ♖b8 17 b3 ♗e6 18 ♕a1 g6 19 0-0
♕d7 20 ♖d1 f5 Karpov-Sveshnikov,
USSR Final 73; 17...♔h8 18 0-0 f5
19 exf5 ♗xf5 20 ♘ce3 ♗e6
Zeliandinov-Timoshenko, USSR 74;
16...♔h8 17 0-0 f5 18 exf5 ♗xf5 19
♗d3 g6 ½-½ Estevez-Sveshnikov, Sochi
76; 19 ♕e2 ♖b8 20 ♘ce3 ♗e6 21
♖d1 ♕d7 22 ♖aa1 ♕f7 Geller-
Sveshnikov, USSR Final 77 ♗e7 17
♘cb4! N 17 ♘xe7+ ♕xe7 18 0-0 ♕b7
19 ♕d3 ♗e6 20 c4 ♗d8 21 ♕xd6 ♕xe4
Smyslov-Sveshnikov, USSR 77 ♗e6!?
17...♗b7 18 ♘xe7 ♕xe7 19 ♘d5 +=
18 ♘xe7+ ♕xe7 19 ♗c6 19 ♘d5 ♕b7
20 c4 f5! ♖ac8 20 ♖xa5

20...♖xc6!? 21 ♘xc6 ♕b7 22 ♕xd6?
22 ♘b4 ♕xe4+ 23 ♔f1 ♗c4+ 24 ♔g1≈;
22 h4! ♕xb2 23 hxg5 ♕xc3+ 24 ♕d2
♕xc6 25 f3 f5 26 gxf6±; 22...♕xc6
23 hxg5 ♕xe4+ 24 ♔f1 ±/∞ ♖d8!
−+ 23 ♖a7 23 ♕c5 ♖c8 24 ♕xe5 ♗f6
−+ ♖xd6 24 ♖xb7 ♖xc6 25 ♖b8+
♗c8 26 ♔e2 h5 27 ♖a1 ♔h7 28 ♖a5 f6
28 ♖d5 ♗a6+ 30 ♔e1 ♗c4 31 ♖dd8
♗e6 32 ♔e2 f5 33 ♖h8+ ♔g6 34 exf5+

♗xf5 35 ♖b5 ♖d6! 36 ♖xe5 ♗d3+
37 ♔e1 37 ♔f3 ♖f6+ 38 ♔g3 ♗f4+
−+ ♖a6 38 ♖xg5+ 38 f3 ♖a1+ 39
♔f2 ♗f4 40 ♖e1 ♖a2 −+ ♔xg5 39
♔d2 ♗f1 40 g3 ♖e6 41 ♖f8 ♖e2+
42 ♔c1 ♗h3 43 ♖f3 ♗g4 44 h4+ ♔g6
45 ♖f4 ♗f5 46 c4 ♖c2+ 47 ♔d1 ♖xb2
48 c5 ♗e6 49 ♖f3 ♗g4 50 ♔c1 ♗xf3
51 ♔xb2 ♔f5 52 ♔c3 ♔g4 53 ♔d4
♔h3 0-1 Kapengut/Artishevsky

194 Gaprindashvili-Szabo Leipzig 77
1 e4 c5 2 ♘f3 ♘c6 3 d4 cxd4 4 ♘xd4
♘f6 5 ♘c3 e5 6 ♘db5 d6 7 ♗g5 a6 8
♘a3 b5 9 ♘d5 ♗e7 9...♕a5+ 10 ♗d2
♕d8 11 ♗g5 ♕a5+ 12 ♗d2 ♕d8 13
♘xf6+ ♕xf6 14 ♗d3 ♕g6 15 ♕f3
♗e7 16 ♕g3 ♗e6= Gaprindashvili-
Bueno, Leipzig 77 **10 ♘xe7 ♘xe7 11
♗xf6 gxf6 12 ♕f3!? 12 ♕d2 ♘g6!?**
12...f5 ∝/± **13 0-0-0** 13 ♘b1 ♗e6 14
♘c3 ♖c8 =+ ♗e6 14 **♔b1 ♕e7 15 c4**
♕a5 16 ♖c1 ♖hc8 17 g3 17 ♗e2/d3?
♘f4 △ ♘xe2/d3, b4 −+ ♖c5 17...b4?
18 ♘c2 ♗xc4? 19 ♗xc4 ♖xc4 20
♘e3 +− **18 ♗d3 ♖ac8 19 cxb5 axb5**
19...♖xc1+ 20 ♖xc1 ♗xa2+ 21 ♔xa2
♖xc1 22 bxa6 ∝/± **20 ♖xc5 ♖xc5
21 ♕e2 ♗d7** 21...♗xa2+ 22 ♔xa2 b4
23 ♖a1! **22 ♘c2 b4 23 ♘e3 ♗e6 24
♗c4 ♗xc4 25 ♘xc4 ♕b5 26 b3 d5
27 exd5 ♖xd5 28 ♖d1 f5 29 ♖xd5
♕xd5=** 30 ♘e3 ♕h1+ 31 ♔b2 f4 32
gxf4 ♘xf4 33 ♕c4 ♕f6 34 ♘g4+
♔f5 35 ♕c8+ ♘e6 36 ♕g8 ♕c6 △
♕c3+ **37 ♘e3+** 37 ♘h6+ ♔f6 38
♕xf7+ ♔g5 39 ♘g8 ♕c3+ = ♔f6 38
♕h8+ ♘g7 39 ♕d8+ ♔e6 40 ♕d2
♕d6= 41 ♕c2 ♕d4+ 42 ♔b1 e4 43
♕c6+ ♔e5 44 ♕h6 ♘f5 45 ♕h5 ♕d3+
46 ♔c1 ♕c3+ 47 ♘c2 f6 48 ♕xh7
♕c5 49 ♕d7 ♕xf2 50 ♕c7+ ♔e6 51
♕c4+ ♔e5 52 ♕c7+ ♔e6 53 ♕c8+
♔e5 54 ♕c7+ ½-½ Bellin/Wicker

195 Ligterink-Petursson
Lone Pine 78
1 e4 c5 2 ♘f3 ♘c6 3 d4 cxd4 4 ♘xd4
♘f6 5 ♘c3 e5 6 ♘db5 d6 7 ♗g5 a6
8 ♘a3 ♗e6 8...b5 9 ♗xf6 gxf6 10
♘d5∝ 9 ♘c4 ♖c8 10 ♗xf6 gxf6 11
♘e3 ♗h6! 12 ♘cd5 ♗xe3 13 ♘xe3
♕b6!∓ 14 ♗d3 ♕b4+! 14...♕xb2
15 0-0 △ ♕h5∝ 15 ♕d2 ♕xb2 16
0-0 ♕d4 17 ♖ab1 b5 18 c3 ♕a4 19
♗c2 ♕a5 20 ♗b3 ♘d4!!∓

21 ♗xe6 fxe6 22 ♘g4 0-0 23 ♖be1
♕xc3 24 ♕h6 ♕c7! 25 f4 25 ♘xf6+
♔h8∓ ♕g7 26 ♕h3 ♖c2 27 ♔h1 f5
28 exf5 exf5 0-1 29 ♘h6+ ♔h8 30 fx
e5 dxe5 31 ♘xf5 ♕xf5 32 ♖xf5 ♖xf5
33 ♕xf5 ♕xg2 mate **Gheorghiu**

4...g6

196 Kurajica-Velimirovic Osijek 78
1 e4 c5 2 ♘f3 ♘c6 3 d4 cxd4 4 ♘xd4
g6 5 ♘c3 ♗g7 6 ♘b3!? ♘f6 7 ♗e2 0-0
7...d6 8 g4!?± 8 0-0 d6 9 ♔h1! a5
9...a6 10 f4 b5 11 ♗f3 += **10 a4 ♗e6
11 f4 ♕b6?!** 12 ♘d5 ♗xd5 13 exd5
♘b4 14 ♗f3 ♖ac8 15 c3 ♘d3 16 ♕xd3
♕xb3 17 ♖e1 += ♘d7!? 18 ♕e2 18
♖xe7? ♖fe8∓ ♘c5 19 ♖a3 ♕b6 20
♗e3 ♖fe8 21 b4! axb4 22 a5 ♕a6
22...bxa3!? 23 axb6 ♗xc3 24 ♖b1± **
23 cxb4 ♕xe2 24 ♖xe2 ♘a6 25 b5**

♘b4 26 ♖a4 ♘d3 27 a6± bxa6 28 bxa6 ♘b2 29 ♖xb2?! 29 ♖b4 ♗xb2 30 a7 ♖a8 31 h4 ♖ec8 32 ♗e2 ♖c3 33 ♗g1? Zeitnot 33 ♖b4 ♖xe3 34 ♖b8+ ♔g7 35 ♖xa8 ♖xe2 36 ♖b8 ♖e1+ 37 ♔h2± ♖c1 34 ♔h2 ♔g7?? 34...♖xg1 35 ♔xg1 ♖xa7= 35 ♗b6 +- e6 36 ♗a6 exd5 37 ♗b7 ♖xa7 38 ♗xa7 ♖c4 39 ♖a2 ♗c1 40 ♗xd5 ♖xf4 41 g3 ♖b4?! 42 ♖c2 1-0 **Kurajica**

197 Sorokin-Jusupov USSR 78
1 e4 c5 2 ♘f3 ♘c6 3 d4 cxd4 4 ♘xd4 g6 5 ♘c3 ♗g7 6 ♗e3 ♘f6 7 ♗c4 0-0 7...♕a5 8 ♗b3 d6 9 f3 9 h3!? ♘a5 10 0-0 a6 11 f4 ♕c7 12 ♘f3α Kurajica-Miles, Wijk aan Zee 77; 9...♗d7!? ♕a5! 9...♕b6? 10 ♘f5± 10 ♕d2 10 0-0 ♘xd4 11 ♗xd4 b5 ♘xd4 11 ♗xd4 ♗e6!? 11...b5?! 12 ♘d5± 12 ♗xe6 12 0-0 fxe6 13 h4?! ♖ac8 14 0-0-0 ♖c4! △ ♘xe4 15 ♕e3 15 ♕d3 ♖xd4!? 16 ♕xd4 ♘d5 17 ♕a4 ♗h6+ 18 ♖d2 ♗xd2+ 19 ♔xd2 ♕xa4 20 ♘xa4 ♘f4 =+; 15...♖fc8 ♖fc8∓ 16 ♖d3 e5! 17 ♗a7 ♖4c6 △ b6 -+ 18 ♘d5 ♘xd5 19 exd5 ♖xc2+ 20 ♔b1 e4 21 ♗d4! ♗xd4 21...exd3 22 ♕e6+ = 22 ♖xd4 ♕b6 23 b3 ♕c5 △ ♕a3 0-1 **Gufeld**

3 ♗b5+

198 Kuzmin-Dorfman Lvov 78
1 e4 c5 2 ♘f3 d6 3 ♗b5+ ♘c6!? 3... ♗d7= 4 0-0 ♗d7 4...a6?! 5 ♗xc6 bxc6 6 d4 cxd4 7 ♕xd4± 5 ♕e2 5 c3 ♘f6 6 ♖e1 a6 7 ♗a4 c4?! (7...b5=) 8 ♗c2 ♗g4 9 h3 ♗h5 += Suetin-Balashov, USSR 69; 7 ♗f1α g6 6 e5?! dxe5 7 ♘xe5 ♘xe5 8 ♕xe5 ♗xb5 8...♘f6 9 ♕xc5 ♖c8 10 ♗xd7+ ♕xd7 11 ♕xa7 ± 9 ♕xh8 ♗xf1 10 ♕xg8α ♗xg2!?

10...♗b5 11 d3! △ ♗h6± 11 ♕xg2 ♕d5+ 12 ♔g1 ♕g5+ 13 ♔f1 ♕h5 14 ♘c3 ♕xh2 15 ♘d1 ♖c8 15...♖d8!? 16 d3 c4 17 d4 ♕h1+ 18 ♔e2 ♕h5 19 f3 ♖c6 20 ♘f2 ♖e6+ 21 ♗e3 ♕h6 22 ♘g4 ♖xe3+ 23 ♔f2!? 23 ♘xe3 ♕h2+ 24 ♔e1 ♕g3+ 24 ♔d2 ♕f2+ 26 ♔c3 ♕xe3+α ♖xf3+ 23... ♕f4 24 ♘xe3 ♕h4+ 25 ♔g1 ♕xd4 26 ♖e1 h5 24 ♕xf3 ♕h3+ 25 ♕f4 f5?!

26 ♘f6+!! exf6 27 ♖e1+ ♔d7 28 ♕f7+ ♔c6 29 ♕xc4+ ♔d6 30 ♕e6+ ♔c7 31 ♕f7+ ♔c6 32 d5+ ♔b6 33 ♖e6+ ♔a5 34 ♕c7+ ♔a4 35 ♕c4+ ♔a5 36 ♕c7+ +- ♔a4 37 ♕c4+ ♔a5 ♕c3+ ♕xc3 39 bxc3 ♔b5 40 ♖xf6 ♗h6+ 41 ♔f3 ♗c5 42 c4 ♗g7 43 ♖e6 ♗f8 44 ♖e8 ♗d6 1-0 45 ♖c8+ ♔b6 46 a4 **Pytel**

Najdorf

199 Bruggemann-Okrajek DDR Final 78
1 e4 c5 2 ♘f3 d6 3 d4 cxd4 4 ♘xd4 ♘f6 5 ♘c3 a6 6 ♗c4 e6 7 ♗b3 ♗e7 ♕e2 ♘c6 9 ♗e3 0-0 10 0-0-0 ♘xd4! 10...♕a5; 10...♕c7; 10...♘a5 11 ♗xd4 ♕a5 12 f3?! ♗d7 13 ♔f2 ♗d8 14 g4 ♖c8 15 ♖hg1 ♗e8 16 g5 ♘d7 17 ♕h4? 17 f4 ♘e5 18 ♕g3 ♘c4 19 f4 b5 20 ♘f6! ♗b6!? 21 ♖g2 21 ♕h4? ♗xg1

22 Rxg1 Qb6 b4? 21...Ne3 22 Rdd2 Nxg2 23 Rxg2 b4 24 Nd1 Kh8 25 Qh4 gxf6 26 gxf6 △ Qh6

22 Qh4 Qh8 23 Rg3 bxc3 24 Rh3 cxb2+ 25 Bxb2! Be3+ 26 Kb1 Na3+ 27 Ka1 Nxc2+ 28 Bxc2 1-0

200 Filipenko-Fedorov USSR 78
1 e4 c5 2 Nf3 d6 3 d4 cxd4 4 Nxd4 Nf6 5 Nc3 a6 6 Be2 e5 7 Nb3 Be6 7...Be7! 8 f4 Qc7 8...Nc6 9 f5 Bxb3 10 axb3 d5!?∞ Veingold-Vitolins, USSR 76 9 0-0 9 g4! += Nbd7 10 Kh1 Be7 11 a4 0-0 12 Be3 Nb6!? 12...exf4 13 Rxf4 Ne5 14 a5 Rfe8 15 Nb6 Qc8!= Peters-Grefe, USA 77 13 f5 Nc4 13...Bc4? 14 Bxb6 +- 14 Bc1 Bd7 15 g4? 15 Nd5 Nxd5 16 Qxd5 Nb6 △ Bc6, d5 =+; 15 a5!? d5! 16 g5 16 Nxd5 Nxd5 17 Qxd5 Nb6 18 △ Rfd8 =+; 16 exd5!? Nxe4 17 Nxd5

Diagram

17...Bc6! 18 Bxc4 18 Nxc7? Nf2+ 19 Kg1 Nh3 mate Rad8∓ 19 Qd3 19 Kg1 b5! -+ Nc5! 20 Nxc5 Bxc5 21 a5 21 g6!? Qd6 22 c3 Qxd5+! 23 Bxd5 Rxd5 -+ 24 Qf3 Rd1! 25 Kg2 25 Qxc6 Rxf1 + 26 Kg2 Rg1+ Rxf1 0-1 Gufeld

201 Commons-Bogdanovic
Lone Pine 78
1 e4 c5 2 Nf3 d6 3 d4 cxd4 4 Nxd4 Nf6 5 Nc3 a6 6 Be2 e5 7 Nb3 Be7 8 0-0 0-0 9 a4 Nc6 9...Be6!? 10 f4 Qc7∞ 10 f4 Nb4 11 Be3 Be6 12 a5 12 f5! += Rc8 13 Bf3 13 f5 Bc4 exf4 14 Bxf4 d5!∞ 15 e5 Ne4 16 Nxe4 dxe4 17 Bxe4 Qxd1 18 Raxd1 18 Rfxd1 Nxc2∓ Nxc2! 19 Na1 19 Bxb7?? Bxb3 -+ Nb4!∓ 20 Bxb7 Rb8 21 Be4 Rb5 22 Nc2 Bc5+ 23 Nd4 Nd5! 24 Kh1 Bxd4 25 Rxd4 Nxf4 26 Rxf4 Rxa5∓ △ Rxe5 27 h3 Rxe5 28 Ra4 Rb8! 29 Nf3 29 Rxa6 g5! -+ Rxb2 30 Rxa6 g5! 31 Rd4 Bxh3! -+ 32 Nd5?? 32 gxh3 Re1 mate Rxd5 0-1 33 Rxd5 Bxg2+ Gheorghiu

202 Vogt-Enders
DDR Final 78
1 e4 c5 2 Nf3 d6 3 d4 cxd4 4 Nxd4 Nf6 5 Nc3 a6 6 Be2 e5 7 Nb3 Be7 7...Be6 8 f4 Qc7 9 g4 8 0-0 0-0 9 a4 Be6 10 f4 Nbd7?! 10...Qc7 11 Kh1 Rc8 12 f5 Bc4 13 a5 Bxe2? 13...h6 14 Qxe2 Nc5 15 Rd1? 15 Bg5± Nfxe4?? 16 Bxe7 Nxc3 17 Qg4 +- Rc6 16 Nxc5 Rxc5 17 Na4 Qxa5! 18 Nxc5 18 Bd2 Qb5!; 18 b4

Qb5 Rxa1 19 Nxb7 Rb8? 19...Qa4∓
20 Qc4 20 Nxd6? Bxd6 21 Bg5 Qxb2
22 Bxf6 gxf6 23 Rxd6 Qa1+ 24 Rd1
Rb1 -+ Bf8 21 Qc6 21 Qc7? Nxe4
22 Re1 Ra8 23 Bd2 Qxb2 24 Rxe4
Ra7∓ Ng4 22 Re1 Qb1 23 Nxd6
23 Qc7? Rxb7! 24 Qxb7 Nf2+ 25
Kg1 Qxc2 26 Rf1 Nd1 -+ Rxb2
24 Qe8 Rb8 25 Qxf7+ Kh8 26 Qd5
26 Ne8 Qb4 27 Bd2 Qe7 28 Qxe7
Bxe7 29 Nc6 Bd6= Bxd6 27 Qxd6
Nf2+ 28 Kg1 Nxe4 29 Qxa6 29
Qxe5?? 30 Qb6+ Be3 31 Qxe3+!
Qxc2 30 Qa7? 30 Qe2= Re8 31 Be3
Nf6 32 Rf1 Qe4 33 Bg5 Ra8 34 Qf2
Zeitnot Ng4 35 Qc5 h6! 36 Bd2 Ra2
37 Qb4 Qe2 38 Qf8+ Kh7 39 Qf7
Ra6 40 Bc1 Nxh2! 0-1 Vogt

203 Rorvall-Pytel
Fredrikstad 78
1 e4 c5 2 Nf3 d6 3 d4 cxd4 4 Nxd4
Nf6 5 Nc3 a6 6 Be2 e5 7 Nb3 Be7 8
0-0 0-0 9 f4?! 9 a4; 9 Be3 b5!? 10
Bf3 Bb7 11 Qe1 Nbd7= 12 f5?!
Rc8 13 a3 Nb6=+ 14 Na5 Ba8 15
Bg5 Na4!∓ 16 Nxa4 bxa4 17 b4?!
Rxc2 18 Bd1 Rc8 19 Bxf6 Bxf6 20
Bxa4 d5 21 Rc1?! 21 exd5 Qxd5 22
Qe2 Rc3 23 Rad1 Qe4∓ dxe4 22 Rx
c8 Qd4+! 23 Qf2 Rxc8 24 Rd1 e3 -+
25 Qe2 Qe4 Δ Bh4 26 Re1? Bh4
0-1 Pytel

204 Ghinda-Ungureanu
Bucharest 78
1 e4 c5 2 Nf3 d6 3 d4 cxd4 4 Nxd4
Nf6 5 Nc3 a6 6 Be2 e6 7 f4 7 0-0
Nbd7 8 f4 b5 9 Bf3 Bb7 10 e5 Bxf3
11 Nxf3 dxe5 12 fxe5 Ng4?! 13 Qe2
Qc7 14 Kh1± Hulak-Barczay,
Moscow 77; 12...b4! 13 exf6 bxc3
14 fxg7 Bxg7 15 bxc3? (15 b3!)
Qb6+ 16 Kh1 Bxc3 =+ Bangiev-

Fojgel, USSR 77 Qc7 7...Be7!? 8 0-0
0-0 9 Kh1 8 Be3 b5?! 8...Be7!? 9
Bf3 Bb7 10 e5 dxe5 11 Bxb7 Qxb7
12 fxe5 Nfd7 13 0-0 Nc6 13...b4!?;
13...Be7?! 14 Qg4 g6 15 Nf3± Vogt-
Bonsch, DDR 74; 15 Nxe6!? Nxe5
16 Qg3 Nbc6 17 Nxg7+ Kf8 18
Bh6 f6 19 Nh5+ Kf7 20 Nxf6! +-
Bradvarevic-Sines, Cateske Toplice 68
14 Nxc6 Qxc6 15 Qh5! g6 16 Qh4
Bg7 17 Bh6 Bxh6 18 Qxh6 b4 19
Nd1 Qc5+ 20 Kh1 Qxe5?! 21 a3!
Rc8 22 Ne3 bxa3 23 bxa3 Qc5 24
Rad1 Ne5 25 h3! 25 Qg7 Rf8 26
Nd5 Ng4! 27 h3 Rd8! Rf8 26 Rfe1!
Rd8 27 Qh4 Rxd1 28 Rxd1 f6 29
Qxh7 Qe7 30 Qh4 Qxa3 31 Nc4 Qc5
32 Nxe5 Qxe5 33 Qh7 Rf7 34 Qg8+
Rf8 35 Qxg6+ Be7 36 Qd3 Qb5 37
Qd6+ Kf7 38 Qc7+ Kg6 39 Rd3 +-
Qb1+ 40 Kh2 Qb8 41 Rg3+ Kf5 42
Qh7+ Ke5 43 Rb3 Qd6 44 Rd3 Qb6
44...Qb8 45 Qh4! Rd8 46 g3! +-
45 Qg7 Rc8 46 Qg3+ Ke4 47 Rd6
Qc7 48 Qg4+ 1-0 Ciocaltea

205 Bogdanovic-Polugaevsky
Lone Pine 78
1 e4 c5 2 Nf3 d6 3 d4 cxd4 4 Nxd4
Nf6 5 Nc3 a6 6 Be2 e6 6...e5 7 f4
Be7 8 Bf3 Qc7 9 0-0 0-0 10 Kh1
Nc6 11 a4 Bd7 12 Nb3 Na5 13 Nxa5
Qxa5 14 Qe1 Δ Nd5 Qc7 14...Kh8!α
15 Be3 Bc6 16 a5 Nd7 17 Qd2 Rac8
18 Rfd1 f5! 19 Qe2 19 exf5? Bxf3∓
fxe4 20 Bg4 Rf6 21 Nd4 Rg6 22
Nxe4 Bb5 22...Bxe4 23 Qxe4 Rxg4?
24 Qxe6+ +- 23 Qf3 Rf8 24 Bh3
24 Bh5 Rh6 25 Qg3 Nf6!∓ Qxc2!
25 Rd2 Qc6 26 Be3 Nc5 27 Bxc5
dxc5 28 f5 Rh6 29 f6 gxf6! 30 Qg4+
Kh8 31 Qxe6 Qxe6 32 Bxe6 f5 -+
33 Nc3 Rxe6 0-1 Gheorghiu

**206 Kruszynski-Schmidt
Poland Final 78**

1 e4 c5 2 ♘f3 d6 3 d4 ♘f6 4 ♘c3
cxd4 5 ♘xd4 a6 6 ♗e2 e6 7 0-0 ♗e7
8 ♗e3 0-0 9 f4 ♘c6 10 ♕e1 ♗d7 11
♕g3 ♘xd4 12 ♗xd4 ♗c6 13 ♖ae1 b5
14 a3 ♕d7 15 ♗d3 a5 16 e5 16 ♖f3 b4
17 ♘d5!? exd5 18 exd5 ♗xd5 19 ♖xe7
♕xe7 20 ♖e3 ♗e6 21 ♕h4 ♖fe8
22 f5 h6 23 fxe6 fxe6 24 ♖g3 e5 25
♗e3 e4 26 ♗b5 ♔h7∓ Bielczyk-
Schmidt, Poland 77; 19 ♗xh7+ ♔xh7
20 ♕h4+ ♔g8 21 ♖xe7 ♕g4 22 ♕xg4
♘xg4 23 ♖g3 ♗e6 24 h3 ♖fc8 25
hxg4 ♖xc2 26 f5 ♗d5= Bielczyk-
Schmidt, Poland 78 dxe5 17 ♗xe5
g6 18 f5! ♘h5 19 ♕h3 exf5 20 ♗xf5
♕b7 21 ♗e4 ♖ae8?! 21...♗xe4 22
♘xe4 f5 23 ♘d6 ♕d5 24 ♘xf5!; 21...
f5 22 ♗xf5 α/± 22 ♕f3 ♗xe4 23
♘xe4 ♕b6+ 23...f5?? 24 ♘f6+ ♗xf6
25 ♕xb7 +− 24 ♔h1 ♗h4?! 24...f5!?
25 ♗d6 ♗xe1 26 ♗xf8 f5 27 ♗h6±
♗h4 28 ♘c3 b4 29 axb4 ♕xb4?!
29...axb4 30 ♕d5+ ♔h8 31 ♕f7 ♖d8
31...♕b8 32 g3 ♗f6 33 ♖e1 ♕b8 34
♘d5 +− ♗e5 34...♗xb2 35 ♖e7 +−
35 c4 a4 36 c5 a3 37 bxa3 ♕b3?!
38 ♖xe5 ♕b1+ 39 ♔g2 ♕b2+ ½-½??
40 ♔h3 ♕xe5 41 ♗d2 +− Pytel

207 Perenyi-A.Schneider Hungary 78

1 e4 c5 2 ♘f3 d6 3 d4 cxd4 4 ♘xd4
♘f6 5 ♘c3 a6 6 ♗e3 e6 7 g4!? N e5
7...h6 8 ♕f3!? ♘bd7 9 ♕h3 ♘c5 10
f3 e5 11 ♘b3 ♗e6 12 ♘xc5 dxc5
13 ♕g3 ♗e7! 14 h4 ♕a5 15 ♕xe5
0-0-0 16 ♗c4! Sax-Tukmakov, Las
Palmas 78; 8...e5 9 ♘f5 g6 10 ♘xh6!?
♗xh6 11 g5; 10 0-0-0!? 8 ♘f5 g6 9
g5 gxf5 10 exf5 10 gxf6? f4 d5!
11 ♕f3! ♘e4? 11...d4 12 0-0-0 ♘bd7!;
12...♕c7?! 13 ♗xd4!≈ 12 ♘xe4 dxe4
13 ♕xe4 ♘c6 14 ♗c4 ♗d7 15 0-0-0

♕c7 16 ♖he1 f6? 16...0-0-0 17 ♗xf7±;
16...♘e7 17 f6 ♗f5 18 ♗b6!! +−; 17
♖xd7!!?

17 ♖xd7!! ♕xd7 18 gxf6 ♗d6 19 ♗e6
♕c7 20 f7+ ♔d8 21 ♖d1 ♖c8 22
♕xe5!! 1-0 Adorjan

208 Kapengut-Juferov Minsk 78

1 e4 c5 2 ♘f3 d6 3 d4 cxd4 4 ♘xd4
♘f6 5 ♘c3 a6 6 f4 ♕c7 7 ♗d3 g6 8
0-0 ♗g7 9 ♔h1 ♘bd7 9...0-0 10 f5
b5 11 ♗g5 ♘bd7 12 ♕e1 ♗b7 13 ♕h4
♖ae8 14 ♖ae1 e5 Kuzmin-Grigorian,
75; 12 fxg6 hxg6 13 ♕d2 ♗b7 14
♗h6 e6 15 ♖ae1 ♘e5 16 ♗xg7 ♔xg7
17 ♕g5 ♕d8! =+ Kapengut-Bangiev,
Yalta 76 10 a4 10 ♕e1 b5 11 ♘f3 e5
12 fxe5 dxe5 13 ♗g5 ♗b7 14 a4!
b4 15 ♘a2 a5 16 c3 += Tseshkovsky-
Savon, Sochi 75; 11 ♘f3 ♘c5 12
♕h4 e6? 13 f5! exf5 14 exf5 ♘xd3
15 cxd3 ♗xf5 16 ♗g5 ♘d7 17
♘d5± Tseshkovsky-Anikaev 75; 11
f5 b5 12 a3 ♗b7 13 ♕h4 ♘e5 14
♗h6 ♕b6 15 ♗xg7 ♔xg7 16 ♘f3 ♗c6
17 ♖ae1 b4 =+ Kapengut-Mikaelian,
Kiev 77 e5 10...0-0 11 f5 ♘e5 12
♗g5 e6 13 ♕d2 ♗d7 14 ♖ad1 ♖ac8
15 ♕f4!? ♕b6 16 ♘b3 ♘h5 17 ♕h4
♘xd3 18 ♖xd3± Kapengut-Gofstein,
France 77 11 ♘f3 0-0 12 ♕e2 ♘c5
13 fxe5 dxe5 14 ♗c4!? 14 ♗g5 ♗e6

123

15 ♘h4 ♘h5 16 ♘f5 ♘f4 17 ♗xf4
exf4 18 ♘xg7 ♔xg7 19 ♕f2?! (19
♕d2!) ♖ad8 20 ♖ad1 ♕e5 21 ♕xf4
♕xf4 22 ♖xf4 ♖d4 ≈ Tseshkovsky-
Bukic, Ljubljana 77; 15 ♘d2! ♗e6!
N 14...♗g4 15 h3 ♗xf3 16 ♕xf3 ♘e6
=+ Tseshkovsky; 15 ♗g5! ♘e6 16 ♗xf6
♗xf6 17 ♘d5 ♕d8 18 ♕e3! =+ 15
♗g5 15 ♗g5 ♘cxe4 16 ♗xe6 ♘xc3
17 ♗xf7+ ♖xf7 18 bxc3 e4! =+ ♗xc4
16 ♕xc4 ♖ac8 17 ♗e3 h6 =+ 18
♖xf6!? ♗xf6 19 ♘d5 ♕d6! 19...♕d8
20 ♘xc5 ♗xg5 21 ♕b4 ♖e8 22 ♘b6
♕d7 23 ♖d1 += 20 ♗xc5 ♖xc5 20...
♗xg5 21 ♗xd6? ♖xc4∓; 21 b4! 21
♘xf6+ ♕xf6 22 ♕xc5 hxg5 =+ 23
♖d1 ♕g7 24 ♕c4 ♖h8 25 ♖f1 ♖c8
26 ♕d3 ♕c6 27 ♕f3 ♕e6 28 c3 ♖d8
½-½ Kapengut

209 Shamkovich-Morales Mexico 78

1 e4 c5 2 ♘f3 d6 3 d4 cxd4 4 ♘xd4
♘f6 5 ♘c3 a6 6 f4 e5 7 ♘f3 ♕c7 8
♗d3 ♗e7 9 0-0 0-0 10 ♔h1 b5 10...
♘bd7 11 fxe5 dxe5 12 ♕e2 ♘bd7
12...b4? 13 ♘d5 ♘xd5 14 exd5 ♗d6
15 ♗xh7+!±; 14...♘d7 15 d6! ♕xd6
16 ♕e4 +−; 15...♗xd6 16 ♗xh7+!
13 ♘h4 ♖e8? 13...♘c5 14 ♗g5 ♗e6
15 ♘f5 += 14 ♘f5 ♗f8 15 ♕f3!± ♗b7
15...b4 16 ♘d5 ♘xd5 17 exd5 △ d6,
♘h6+ 16 ♗g5 △ ♘h6+ b4 17 ♘d1
♖e6 18 ♘de3 ♘c5

Diagram

19 ♘h6+ ♕h8 20 ♘d5 ♗xd5 20...
♘xd5 21 ♘xf7+ ♔g8 22 exd5 e4
23 ♕h3 ♖g6 24 ♗c4± 21 exd5 e4
21...♖d6 22 ♘f5 22 ♕h3! △ dxe6
♖b6 23 ♗c4! +− △ d6 ♘cd7 24
♘xf7+ ♔g8 25 ♗b3 △ d6 ♗d6 26
♘xd6 ♕xd6 27 ♗f4 ♘e5 27...♕f8
28 ♗c7 ♖b7 29 d6+ +− 28 ♕e6+!

♕xe6 29 dxe6 ♘g6 30 ♗g5 ♘g4
30...♘e8 31 e7+ ♔h8 32 ♖f8+ 31
♗d8! 1-0 Shamkovich

210 Kuzmin-Pokojowczyk
Polanica 77

1 e4 c5 2 ♘f3 d6 3 d4 ♘f6 4 ♘c3
cxd4 5 ♘xd4 a6 6 ♗g5 ♘c6 7 ♕d2 e6
8 0-0-0 h6 9 ♗f4 ♗d7 10 ♘xc6 1♥
♗g3!? ♗xc6 11 ♕e1 ♕a5 12 ♗c4 0-0-0
13 ♗b3 b5? 13...♗e7; 13...d5? 14
♘xd5! ♕xe1 15 ♘b6 mate 14 a3 ♕b7
15 f3!± ♗e7 16 ♕f2 ♖d7 17 ♖he1
♖hd8?

18 ♘d5 ♗xd5! 18...exd5 19 exd5 +−
19 exd5 e5 20 ♗d2 ♕b6 21 ♗e3 ♕a5
22 ♔b1 ♖c7 23 ♖e2 ♘d7? 24 ♗d2
♕b6 25 ♕e1! +− ♕a7 26 ♗a5 ♘b6
27 f4 ♗f6 27...f6 28 fxe5 ♗xe5 29
♖xe5! dxe5 30 d6 ♖cd7 31 ♕xe5
♕b8 32 ♗xb6 ♔xb6 33 ♕e3+ 1-0 Pyte

211 Katalymov-Gofshtein USSR 78
1 e4 c5 2 ♘f3 d6 3 d4 cxd4 4 ♘xd4
♘f6 5 ♘c3 a6 6 ♗g5 e6 7 ♕d3 b5 8
0-0-0 ♘bd7 9 f4 ♗b7 10 e5!? dxe5
11 fxe5 11 ♘dxb5 axb5 12 fxe5 b4
13 exf6 bxc3 14 fxg7 ♕xg5+ 15 ♔b1
♗d5!∓ **♘xe5 12 ♕g3 ♘ed7 13 ♘cxb5?**
13 ♗xf6 ♕xf6 14 ♕c7! ♘c8 15 ♘c6±;
13...gxf6 14 ♗e2= **axb5 14 ♗xb5**
♖xa2 15 ♔b1 ♕a8! 16 ♘b3 ♗d5 17
♗xf6

17...♖a1+! 17...gxf6 18 ♗xd7+ ♔xd7
19 c4 += **18 ♘xa1 ♕a2+ 19 ♔c1**
♕xa1+ 20 ♔d2 ♕a5+ 21 ♗c3 ♕xb5∓
22 ♖hf1 ♘f6 23 ♔c1 ♗e7 24 ♔b1
24 ♕xg7 ♖g8 25 ♕h6 ♘e4 −+ **♘e4**
25 ♕xg7 ♘xc3+ 26 ♕xc3 0-0 27 ♕g3+
♔h8 28 ♖f4 f5! 29 b3 ♗f6 30 c4
♕a5 31 cxd5 ♕a1+ 32 ♔c2 ♕b2+
33 ♔d3 ♖c8 34 ♖d2 ♖c3+ 35 ♔e2
♖xg3 36 hxg3 ♕xb3 37 dxe6 ♕xg3
38 ♖f2 ♕e5+ 39 ♔f1 ♕a1+ 40 ♔e2
♕a6+ 41 ♔e1 ♕xe6 42 ♖de2 ♕d5
0-1 Gufeld

212 Nasybullin-Liavdansky USSR 78
1 e4 c5 2 ♘f3 d6 3 d4 cxd4 4 ♘xd4
♘f6 5 ♘c3 a6 6 ♗g5 e6 7 ♕d3 ♘bd7
8 0-0-0 b5 9 f4 ♗b7 10 e5 dxe5 11
fxe5 ♘xe5 12 ♕g3 ♘ed7 13 ♗xf6
gxf6 14 ♗e2 b4 15 ♘h5 ♗h6+ 16
♔b1 ♔f8? 16...bxc3 17 ♘xe6 ♕b6 18

b3 ♘e5!∓; 18 ♕xc3 ♕xe6 19 ♖ae1
♘e5∓; 18 ♗xf7+ ♔xf7 19 ♖xd7+
♔xe6? 20 ♕h3+ f5 21 ♕xh6+ ♔xd7
22 ♕xb6±; 19 ♔e8!∓

17 ♖he1! bxc3 18 ♘xe6+ 18 ♖xe6
♘e5?! 19 ♖xe5 fxe5 20 ♕xe5 ♗g7
21 ♘e6+ fxe6 22 ♖xd8+ ♖xd8 23
♕c7±; 18...♕b8! 19 ♖e7! ♔xe7 20
♘f5+ ♔f8? 21 ♖xd7 ♗d5 22 ♕xc3
♕f4 23 ♕c5+ ♔g8 24 ♘xh6+ ♔xh6
25 ♕d5±; 20...♔e8!∓ **fxe6 19 ♖xe6**
♗d2! 20 ♕d6+ ♔g7 21 ♖e7+ ♔h6
22 ♖xd7 ♕f8 23 ♖xd2 ♕xd6? 23...
cxd2 24 ♕xd2+ ♔h5 25 ♕e2+ =
♔g6? 26 ♕g4+ ♔h6 27 ♖d3±; 25...
♔g5? 26 h4+ ♔g6 27 ♕g4+ ♔h6 28
♕f4+ ♔g6 29 g4±; 25...♕h6 26 ♕e3+
♔g6 27 ♕g3+ ♔f5 28 ♕h3+ ♔e5!
29 ♕e3+ ♗e4!∓ **24 ♖2xd6 += ♗c8**
25 ♗f3 ♖b8 26 ♖c7 ♖xb2+ 27 ♔c1
♖xa2 28 ♖xc3 ♖f8 29 ♖b6 ♖a1+
30 ♔b2 ♖e1 31 ♖b8 ♖ee8 32 ♖c7
♔g6 33 c4 ♗f5 34 ♖xe8 ♖xe8 35
♗d5 ♖e3 36 c5 a5 37 c6 ♖d3 38 ♗f3
38 ♗f7+ ♔h6 39 ♖a7 ♖d2+ 40 ♔b3
♖xg2 41 ♖xa5 ♗c8 42 c7 ♖xh2 43
♖a8 ♗f5= **a4 39 ♖a7 ♖b3+ 40 ♔a2**
♗e6 41 ♖e7! 41 ♔a1? a3 42 ♖e7
♖e3!∓ **♖xf3+** 41...♖e3+ 42 ♖xe6
♖xe6 43 c7 ♖e8 44 ♗b7± **42 ♖xe6**
♖c3 43 ♔b2 ♖c4 44 ♖d6 h5 45 g3
♔g5 46 ♖d5+ ♔g6 ½-½ Gufeld

213 Bogner-Rogalewicz corr. 78
1 e4 c5 2 &f3 d6 3 d4 cxd4 4 &xd4
&f6 5 &c3 a6 6 &g5 e6 7 f4 b5 8
e5 dxe5 9 fxe5 &c7 10 &e2 &fd7 11
0-0-0 &b7 12 &g4 &xe5 13 &d3 13
&e2!? h6 14 &h4 g5 15 &g3 &e3+
16 &b1 h5 17 &he1 &xe1 18 &xg5
&h6 19 &xh5 &e3 20 &xe6 &xe6
21 &e1 &xe1+ 22 &xe1 &g7 23 &g4
&f8! 23...0-0 24 &h4± 24 &g3 24
&e4 &h6 25 &b4+ &g8 26 &c3 &g6
27 &g5 &f6 28 &f4 &xg5 29 &xg5
&bd7 30 &f5 b4 31 &xb4 &e8≈
Lanka-Feldmann, corres 77; 24...
&xh2! 25 &b4+ &g8 26 c3 (26 a3
&h1+ 27 &a2 &d5+) &e5 27 &g3
&h1+ 28 &c2 &bd7 29 &d6 &xd3
30 &xd3 &e5 31 &g3 &d5 32 &c5
&h6 Δ &g6 −+ &f6 25 &b4+ &g8
26 a4 &xg2! 27 axb5 axb5 28 &xb5
&c6∓ 29 &d6? 29 &d2 &h6 30
&f4 &e8 31 &c5 &e6 32 &f2 &b4!

33 &xg2?? 33 &c4 &e1+ 34 &xe1
&a1+ 35 &xa1 &xc2+ Δ &xe1; 33
&f5 &ea6 34 &a3 &xa3!? 35 bxa3
&xa3 36 &c1 &f3 37 &d2 &a2 &a1+!
0-1 34 &xa1 &e1+ 35 &c1 &xc1 mate
Konikowski

214 Litvinov-Juferov Minsk 78
1 e4 c5 2 &f3 d6 3 d4 cxd4 4 &xd4
&f6 5 &c3 a6 6 &g5 e6 7 f4 &c7 8
&f3 b5 9 a3 9 &xf6!? &bd7 10 0-0-0
&b8 11 &xf6 &xf6 12 g4 12 e5!?
&b7 13 &h3 &d5 14 &e4 &xf4 15
&xd6+? &xd6 −+ Juferov-Litvinov,
Minsk 77; 13...dxe5 14 &cxb5
axb5? 15 &xb5+ &e7 16 fxe5
+− Kupreichik-Gutman; 14...&b6!
Boleslavsky b4 13 axb4 &xb4 14 g5
&d7 15 f5 &e5 16 &h3 &b6 17 &b3
&e7 18 g6!? fxg6 19 fxe6 &xb3 20
cxb3 &xb3 21 &g3 &xe6 22 &d5!? N
22 &e2 0-0 23 &xb3 &xb3 24 &d4
&f3 25 &b4 &g5+ 26 &b1 &d2+ 27
&a1 &c4 28 &f4 &xf1 29 &h3 &e3 30
&xc4 &xc4 31 &xg5 h6 −+ Bronstein-
Polugaevsky, Moscow 67 &xd5 23
&xd5 &b4 24 &xa6?! 24 &g2 0-0 25
&c3∞ 0-0 25 &e1 &b6 26 &b5 &a8 27
&c2 &g4 28 &c4 &h8 29 &b5 &d4
30 &b3 &a7?! 30...&f6 31 &a1! &c8
32 &c1 &e3 33 &e2∞ 31 &f1 &e3?
31...&a4+ 32 &c3 &f6+ 33 &d3 &e5+
34 &xe5 &xe5 =+ 32 &a1!± h5 33
&xa7 &xa7 34 &b8+ &h7 35 &g8+
&h6 36 &h1 &g5 37 &g1+ 37 &d5 Δ
&c3, b4 +− &f6 38 h3 &c7 39 &g3
&c2 40 &d5 &d4+ 41 &a2 g5 42
&b7?! += 42 b4± &xb7 43 &xb7
&e5 44 b4 &f4 45 &g1 g4 46 hxg4
hxg4 47 &c8 g3 48 &h3 &e2 49 &f1+
&xe4 50 &g2+ &d4 51 &b3 &f6 52
&f5 &e5 53 &g5 &e3 54 b5 &f4 55
&h5 &g4 56 &xe5!? dxe5 57 b6 &f4!=
58 b7 &xg2 59 b8& ½-½ **Kapengut**

215 Korsunsky-Konoval USSR 78
1 e4 c5 2 &f3 d6 3 d4 cxd4 4 &xd4
&f6 5 &c3 a6 6 &g5 e6 7 f4 &bd7 8
&f3 &c7 9 0-0-0 b5 10 &xb5 axb5
11 e5 11 &dxb5 &b8 12 e5 &a5!
Balashov-Polugaevsky, Manila 76 &b7
12 &dxb5 &c8!! N 12...&b6 13 &e2
dxe5 14 fxe5 &d5 15 &xd5 &xd5 16
&xd5 exd5 17 &d6+ ∞/± 13 &e2

dxe5 14 fxe5 &d5 15 &e4 15 ᗜxd5
&xd5 16 ᗜxd5 exd5 17 e6 ᗜf6 18
e7 ᗜe4∓ ♛c6? 15...ᗜa6!

16 ᗜxd5! h6 16...exd5 17 ᗜc7+♛xc7
18 ᗜd6+ +– **17 &bd6+ 1-0 Gufeld**

216 Petryk-Gadalinski Poland 77
**1 e4 c5 2 &f3 d6 3 d4 cxd4 4 &xd4
&f6 5 &c3 a6 6 &g5 e6 7 f4 &e7 8
♛f3 ♛c7 9 0-0-0 &bd7 10 &d3 b5 11
ᗜhe1 &b7?** 12 ♛g3 b4? 12...0-0-0
13 &d5! exd5 14 e5 dxe5 15 fxe5
0-0-0 16 &f5! &xe5 17 &xe7+♛xe7
18 ᗜxe5 ♛c7 19 &f4 ♛c5 20 ♛xg7
&d7 21 &f5 +– &c6 22 &xd7+ &xd7
23 ᗜexd5 ♛c4 24 ♛e5 **1-0 Pytel**

217 Parma-Bukic
Jugoslavia Final 78
**1 e4 c5 2 &f3 d6 3 d4 cxd4 4 &xd4
&f6 5 &c3 a6 6 &g5 e6 7 f4 &e7 8
♛f3 ♛c7 9 0-0-0 &bd7** 9...ᗜc6 10
ᗜxc6 ♛xc6 11 ♛g3 h6 12 &xf6 &xf6
13 e5!: 10...bxc6 11 e5; 9...0-0 10 &d3
ᗜc6 11 ᗜxc6 bxc6 12 e5; 9...h6 10
&h4 &bd7 **10 &d3** 10 g4 b5 11 &xf6
&xf6 12 g5 &d7 **h6** 10...b5 11 ᗜhe1
&b7 12 ♛g3 0-0-0 13 &xb5! axb5 14
ᗜdxb5 ♛b6 15 e5 **11 &h4** 11 ♛h3
&b6 12 ᗜhf1!? &d7 13 &h4 ᗜc8
14 ♛b1 Timman-Browne, Amsterdam
76 **g5!? 12 e5** 12 fxg5 ᗜe5 13 ♛e2

&fg4 14 &f3 hxg5 15 &xg5!? &xg5+
16 ᗜxg5 ♛c5 17 &f3!? **gxh4** 12...
dxe5 13 ᗜxe6! fxe6 14 &g6+ ♛f8
15 fxg5 hxg5 16 &xg5 ♛g7 17 ♛g3!
13 exf6 &xf6 13...&xf6 14 ᗜde2 Δ
ᗜe4, f5 **14 f5 e5 15 &de2 &d7 16
&e4** 16 &e4 &c6 17 ᗜd5 &xd5 18
&xd5 ᗜxd5 19 ᗜxd5 &g5+ 20 ♛b1
0-0-0! Stean-Garcia, Lublin 75 **d5!
17 &xf6+ &xf6 18 ♛xd5 &c6 19 ♛b3**
19 ♛c5 0-0-0 20 ᗜhg1 ᗜd5 Δ ᗜhd8,
e4 **0-0-0 20 &c4 &xg2** 20...&g5+ 21
♛b1 f6 **21 ᗜhg1 &g5+ 22 ♛b1 ᗜxd1+
23 ᗜxd1 ᗜd8 24 ᗜxd8+ ♛xd8 25
a4 h3! 26 &c3 &f4 27 &xf7 &xh2 28
&d5 &xd5 29 &xd5 &f4 30 f6** 30
ᗜxf4 h2 **h2 31 ♛f3 ♛b8 32 ♛e4**
32 ᗜxf4 ♛xf6 ♛a8 33 c4 ♛g8 34
♛a2 ♛f7 35 ♛g2 ♛a7 36 ♛f2+ ♛b8
37 ♛g2 ♛a7 38 ♛f2+ ♛b8 39 ♛g2
♛d7 40 ♛b3 ♛a7 41 ♛f2+ ♛b8 42
♛g2 ♛f5 43 ♛a2 &g3! 43...h5 44
♛g8+ ♛c8 45 f7 &h6 46 ♛e8 h1♛
47 ♛xe5+ ♛a7 48 ♛d4+ = **44 f7**
44 a5 h5 (Δ h4) 45 ♛xg3 h1♛ 46
♛g8+ ♛a7 47 &b6 ♛hb1+ **♛xf7**
44...♛a8! 45 ♛xg3 h1♛ 46 ♛g8+
♛a7 47 f8♛ ♛hb1+ **45 ♛xg3 h1♛
46 ♛xe5 ♛a7** 46...♛c8 47 ♛d6 Δ
&b6+ **47 ♛d4+ ♛b8 48 ♛h8+ ½-½**

218 Ivanovic-Bukic
Jugoslavia Final 78
**1 e4 c5 2 &f3 d6 3 &c3 a6 4 d4 cxd4
5 &xd4 &f6 6 &g5 e6 7 f4 &e7 8 ♛f3
♛c7 9 0-0-0 &bd7 10 &d3 h6 11 &h4
g5!? 12 fxg5 &e5 13 ♛e2 &fg4** 13...
ᗜh7 14 &f3 hxg5 15 &f2 &f8?! 16
&e3 ᗜg8 17 ᗜxe5 dxe5 18 ♛f2!
Hort-Bobotsov, Wijk aan Zee 70
14 &f3 14 ♛d2 ᗜg6 15 g3 ♛c5; 14
&g3 hxg5 15 ᗜhf1 &d7 16 &f3 b5!;
14 h3 hxg5 15 &g3 &f6 16 ᗜhf1
&d7 17 ♛b1 0-0-0 18 &f3 &h5 19

♗h2 ♗f6! **hxg5 15 ♗xg5!?** 15 ♘g3
♗d7 16 h3 ♘xf3 17 gxf3 ♘e5
Janosevic-Martinovic, Zagreb 77 18
♔b1 ♗f6! **♗xg5+ 16 ♘xg5 ♕c5 17
♘f3!?** 17 ♘h3 ♗d7 18 ♕d2 0-0-0 19
♗e2 ♘e3 Litvinov-Zidkov, USSR 73
♘f2 18 ♘xe5 18 ♘a4 ♘fxd3+ **dxe5?!**
18...♘xd1 19 ♘xf7 ♘xc3 20 ♕f3 ♖f8
21 ♖f1 ♘xa2+ 22 ♔b1 ♘b4 23 ♕f6
♕c7 24 ♕g6 ♕e7!; 23 e5 ♘xd3 24
♘xd6+ ♕xd6 25 ♕h5+ ♔d7 26 exd6
♖xf1+ 27 ♔a2 ♘c1+ 28 ♔a3 ♔xd6;
24 ♕xd3 ♖xf7 25 ♕g6 ♔d7!; 24 cxd3
♔d7 25 exd6 ♕f5! 26 ♕e2 ♖xf7
27 ♖xf5 ♖xf5 △ ♔xd6; 24 ♕f6 ♕c7
25 ♕g6 ♕xf7!! 26 ♖xf7 ♖xf7 27
♕g8 ♖f8 28 ♕g6+ ♔d8 29 ♕xd3 d5
30 c4 ♔c7! **19 ♘a4 ♕a7**

20 ♗b5+ axb5 20...♔e7? 21 ♕d2 **21
♕xb5+ ♔e7** 21...♔f8 22 ♕xe5 **22
♕b4+ ♔f6** 22...♔e8 23 ♕d6 ♘xd1
24 ♖xd1 f6 25 ♕d8+ ♔f7 26 ♕xh8
♕e3+ 27 ♔b1 ♖xa4 28 ♕h7+ ♔e8
29 ♕g8+ ♔e7 30 ♕xd8 ♖d4 31 ♕xb7+
23 ♘b6 23 ♖hf1 ♕g6 24 ♕e7 ♕e3+
25 ♖d2 ♖xa4 26 ♖fxf2 ♕e1+ 27
♖d1 ♕xf2 **♘xd1** 23...♘xh1 **24 ♖f1+
♔g6 25 ♕e7 f5 26 exf5+ exf5 27
♘c4?** 27 ♖f3 (△ ♖g3+) f4 (△ ♖h5)
28 ♘c4 ♕xa2 29 ♘xe5+ ♔f5 30
♘d3 ♖a4 31 ♕e5+ ♔g6 32 ♕xh8;
27...♘f2 28 ♕d6+ ♔g5 29 ♖a3 ♕xa3

30 bxa3 ♖a6 31 ♕d2+ ♔f6 32 ♕xf2
♗e6 33 ♕c5! △ ♕d6/♕c7; 29...♕b8
30 ♕e7+ △ ♖xa8; 29...♘e4 30 ♕e7+
♔g6 31 ♖xa7 ♖xa7 32 ♘xc8 ♖xc8.
33 ♕e6+; 28...♔h5 29 g4+!! ♘xg4
30 ♖h3+ ♔g5 31 ♖xh8 ♕xa2 32 ♘d5
♕xd5 33 ♕xd5 ♖a1+ 34 ♔d2 ♖d1+
35 ♔xd1 ♘e3+ 36 ♔d2 ♘xd5 37 ♖xc8;
32...f4 33 h4+ ♔f5 34 ♘e7+ ♔e4
35 ♕d3 mate; 31...♕a5 32 c3 ♖a6
33 ♕d8+ ♘f6 34 ♖g8+ ♔f4 35 ♕d2+
♔e4 36 ♖xc8; 29...fxg4 30 ♕xe5+;
29...♔xg4 30 ♖g3+ **b5! 28 ♘xe5+
♔h5 29 ♕f6 ♖g8** 29...♕h7 30 ♖f4
30 ♖f3 ♗f2 31 g3 ♕d4 32 g4+! fxg4
32...♖xg4? 33 ♕h8+ ♔g5 34 ♕g7+
♔h5 35 ♕h7+ ♔g5 36 ♕g6+ ♔h4
37 ♕h6 mate **33 ♕f7+ ♔h6 34 ♕f6+
♔h5 35 ♕f7+ ♔h6 36 ♖f6+ ♔g5 37
♘f3+ gxf3 38 ♕xg8+ ♔xf6 39 ♕h8+
♔f5 40 ♕xd4 ♘e4 41 ♕d5+ ♔f4 42
♕xa8 f2 43 ♕b8+ ♔f3 44 ♕xb5 ♔g2
45 ♕e2 ♗f5! 46 c4 ♔g1 47 ♕e3 ♔g2
48 ♕e2 ½-½**

Sicilian 4♘

219 Schneider-Rosenlund
Roskilde 78

**1 e4 c5 2 ♘f3 e6 3 d4 cxd4 4 ♘xd4
♘f6 5 ♘c3 ♘c6 6 ♘xc6 bxc6 7 e5
♘d5 8 ♘e4 ♕c7 9 f4 c5 10 c4 ♘b4
11 a3!** 11 g3 ♘c6 12 ♗d3 ♘d4 13
0-0 ♗b7 14 ♗e3 ♘f5 15 ♗f2 ♖d8?!
**16 ♕c2! d6 17 b4! dxe5 18 ♘xc5
♗xc5 19 ♗xc5 ♘d4 20 ♕a4+ ♖d7
21 fxe5 ♗c6 22 ♕a6 ♕xe5** 22...♗b7
23 ♕a4 ♗c6 24 ♕d1 ♕xe5∝ **23 ♖ae1
♕g5 24 ♗e4 ♗xe4 25 ♖xe4 ♘b3
26 ♗e3 ♕g6 27 ♕c8+ ♔e7**

Diagram

28 ♖xf7+ ♕xf7 29 ♗g5+ ♔d6 30

**♖d4+ ♔e5 31 ♕xd7 ♕g6 32 ♕d6+
♔f5 33 ♕f4 mate 1-0**

Sozin

220 Gusenov-Korsunsky USSR 78

**1 e4 c5 2 ♘f3 ♘c6 3 d4 cxd4 4 ♘xd4
e6 5 ♘c3 d6 6 ♗e3 ♘f6 7 ♗c4 ♗e7
8 ♕e2 a6 9 0-0-0 ♕c7 10 ♗b3 ♘a5
11 g4 b5 12 g5 ♘xb3+ 13 axb3 ♘d7
14 ♘f5?! exf5 15 ♘d5 ♕d8 16 exf5
♗b7 17 f6 gxf6 18 ♖he1 ♗xd5 19
♖xd5 ♖g8 20 gxf6** 20 ♗f4!? ♔f8
21 ♕h5 ♕a5 22 ♕e2 ♕d8=; 22...♖e8?
23 gxf6± **♗xf6 21 ♖f5 ♖b8 22 ♗a7
♖b7 23 ♗d4 ♘g4 24 h3** N 24 ♕f3
♕c8! **25 ♕d5 ♘h6 26 ♖h5 ♖g6 27 f4
♖c7 28 f5 ♖xc2+ 29 ♔b1 ♖gg2 30
♕e4 ♘xf5 31 ♖xf5 ♖ce2 32 ♖xe2
♖xe2 33 ♕f4 ♕c2+ 34 ♔a2 ♖e1 35
♖xf7 ♕b1+ 36 ♔a3 ♕e4 -+** Radulov-
Korsunsky, USSR 76; 24...♖d7 **♘e5
25 ♕e4 △ ♖h5**

Diagram

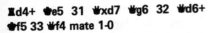

**25...♖g5!! 26 ♖xg5 ♗xg5+ 27 f4
♖e7! 28 ♖g1?!** 28 ♖f1!? f5 29 ♕d5
♘h6 30 ♗xe5 ♖xe5 31 ♕g8+ ♔d7
32 ♕xh7+ ♔e7 33 ♕xh6 ♖e1+ -+;
29 ♕xf5! ♖f7 30 ♕e6+ ♗e7 α/∓ **d5
29 ♕xh7 ♘f3! 0-1 Gufeld**

221 Yurtaev-Zhidkov USSR 78

**1 e4 c5 2 ♘f3 d6 3 d4 cxd4 4 ♘xd4
♘f6 5 ♘c3 ♘c6 6 ♗c4 e6 7 ♗e3 ♗e7 8
♕e2 ♘xd4 9 ♗xd4 0-0 10 0-0-0 ♕a5
11 f4?!** 11 ♔b1 ♗d7 12 f3 ♖fc8 13
g4 b5! 14 ♗xb5 ♖ab8 15 ♗xd7 ♘xd7
16 ♕d2 ♕a6 17 b3 ♘e5 18 ♗xe5
dxe5 19 ♕d3 ♕a3; 11 ♗b3 ♗d7 12
♔b1 ♘c6 13 f4 ♖ad8 14 ♖hf1 b5 15
f5! b4 16 fxe6 bxc3 17 exf7+ ♔h8
18 ♖f5 ♕b4 19 ♕f1!+= e5 **12 ♘d5**
12 ♗e3 ♗g4∓ **♘xd5 13 exd5 exd4!
14 ♕xe7 ♕c5!** 14...♗f5! 15 ♖xd4
♖ac8 16 ♕xd6 ♖xc4 17 ♖xc4 ♕xa2∓;
16 ♗b3 ♗xc2 17 ♗xc2 ♕xa2 18 ♖dd1
♕a1+ 19 ♔d2 ♕xb2 20 ♕e4 f5 21
♕d3 ♕b4+ 22 ♔c1 ♕xf4+ =+; 16
♕e1! ♕a4 17 ♕c3! b5 18 ♗b3 ♖xc3
19 ♗xa4 ♖c5 20 ♗b3 a5 21 c3 +=;
16...♕c5! 17 c3? b5 △ ♕xd4∓; 17
♕d2 b5 18 ♗b3 ♖e8! 19 ♖d1 ♗g4
△ ♖e2∓ **15 ♗d3 ♕xd5 16 ♕e4!** +=
16 ♗xh7+ ♔xh7 17 ♕xf8 ♕xa2 18
♕xd6 ♕a1+ 19 ♔d2 ♕xb2 =+ **♕h5
17 h3 g6 18 ♕xd4 ♗e6 19 ♖he1**
19 ♕xd6! ♗xa2 20 b3 ♕a5 21 ♔b2±
19...♕a5 20 a3 ♖fd8 21 ♕e5 += **♖ac8
20 a3 ♕c5! 21 ♗e4 d5 22 ♕xc5 ♖xc5
23 ♗f3 ♖fc8 24 c3 b6 25 ♖e5** 25
♖d4 ♖c4 26 ♖ed1 △ ♗e2 += **♖c4!
26 f5 ♗xf5 27 ♗xd5 ♖4c7 ½-½ Gufeld**

Richter-Rauzer

222 Beljavsky-Ubilava USSR 78
1 e4 c5 2 ♘f3 d6 3 d4 cxd4 4 ♘xd4
♘f6 5 ♘c3 ♘c6 6 ♗g5 ♗d7 7 ♕d2
♖c8 8 f4 8 ♗e2 ♘xd4 9 ♕xd4 ♕a5
10 ♗d2 a6 11 0-0 ♕c5 Lerner-
Ubilava, USSR 76 ♘xd4 9 ♕xd4 ♕a5
10 e5 dxe5 11 fxe5 e6 12 0-0-0 ♖xc3
13 ♗d2 ♕xa2 14 ♗xc3 g6 15 b4!
N 15 b3 ♗h6+ 16 ♖d2 ♘d5 17 ♕c5;
15...♘d5!; 15 ♔d2 ♗c5 16 ♕d3 ♘d5
17 b3 ♗e3+ 18 ♔e1 ♕a3 19 ♗d2
♗b6 20 c4 ♕b5 21 ♕e2 ♘b4∓ Kriz-
Markland, Reggio Emilia 72/3; 16
♕c4 ♕xc4 17 ♗xc4 ♘e4+ 18 ♔e2
♘xc3+ 19 bxc3 ♗c6 Klovan-Liberzon,
USSR 72 ♘d5 16 ♗c4 ♗h6+? 16...
♕a3+ 17 ♗b2 ♕e3+ 18 ♔b1 ♕xd4
19 ♗xd4 ♘xb4 20 ♗xa7 ♗c6± 17
♖d2 ♕a3+ 18 ♗b2 ♕xb4 19 ♗xd5
♗xd2+ 20 ♕xd2 ♕xd2+ 21 ♔xd2
exd5 22 e6 +− ♖f8 23 exd7+ ♔xd7
24 ♖e1 f5 25 ♗a3 ♖f7 26 ♖e5 f4
26...♔c6 27 ♖e6+ ♔b5 28 ♖e7 ♖xe7
29 ♗xe7 +− 27 ♖xd5+ ♔e6 28 ♖d3
h5 29 ♗d6 g5 30 ♗b8 a6 31 ♖d6+
♔f5 32 ♖d5+ ♔g6 33 h4! gxh4 34
♔e2 ♖f8 35 ♗e5 b5 36 ♔f3 ♖c8 37
c3 ♖c4 38 ♗d4 b4 39 cxb4 ♖xb4
40 ♔xf4 ♖b3 41 ♖g5+ ♔h6 42 ♗g7+
♔h7 43 ♗e5 ♔h6 44 ♔f5 ♖b1 45
♖g6+ ♔h7 46 ♖g7+ ♔h6 47 ♖a7 △
♗f4 mate 1-0 Kapengut/Artishevsky

223 A.Ivanov-Kondratiev USSR 77
1 e4 c5 2 ♘f3 d6 3 d4 cxd4 4 ♘xd4
♘f6 5 ♘c3 ♘c6 6 ♗g5 e6 7 ♕d2 ♗e7
8 0-0-0 ♘xd4 8...0-0 9 f4 ♘xd4 10
♕xd4 ♕a5 11 e5 dxe5 12 ♕xe5 ♕xe5
13 fxe5 ♘d5 14 ♗xe7 += Evans-
Santos, Portimao 75; 9...h6 10 ♗h4
e5 11 ♘f5 ♗xf5 12 exf5 exf4 13 ♔b1
d5 14 ♗xf6 ♗xf6 15 ♘d5 ♗e5 16

♗c4! += Gufeld-Tukmakov, Vilnius 75
9 ♕xd4 0-0 10 f4 10 e5 dxe5 11 ♕xe5
♗d7 12 h4 ♖c8 13 ♖h3 += h6 11 ♗h4
11 h4?! hxg5 12 hxg5 ♘g4 13 ♗e2
e5 14 ♕g1 exf4 15 ♗xg4 ♗xg5 =+
♕a5 12 ♗c4! 12 ♕d3=; 12 e5= e5
12...♖d8 13 ♖hf1 ♕h5 14 g3 △ f5±
13 fxe5 13 ♕d3? exf4 14 ♘b5 ♗g4
△ a6∓ dxe5 14 ♕d3 ♗g4 14...♕c5
15 ♗xf6 ♗xf6 16 ♕e2 += 15 ♖df1!?
15 ♗xf6! ♗xf6 16 ♖df1 ♖ac8 17
♖xf6! △ ♘d5± ♖fd8 15...♕e6!? 16
♗xe6 fxe6 17 ♕c4 ♕b6 18 ♗f2 ♕d6=
16 ♕g3! += ♖ac8 17 ♗xf6 ♗xf6 18
♗b3 18 ♕xg4 ♖xc4 19 ♖xf6 ♖xc3!=
♗e6! 19 ♗xe6 19 ♖xf6 ♗xb3! 20 cxb3
♖xc1! fxe6 20 ♔b1 ♖d6! 21 ♖f3
♗e7 22 ♕g6 ♗f8 23 ♖hf1± ♖b6 24
♖g3 △ ♖xf8+ +− ♕b4? 24...♖xc3!
25 ♖xf8+ ♔xf8 26 ♕xg7+ ♔e8 27
♕g8+ ♔d7 28 ♖g7+ ♔c6 28 ♕xc8+
△ ♕xc3 += 25 ♘d1 ♕d2 26 ♘e3?
26 ♖xf8+! ♔xf8 27 ♕xg7+ ♔e8 28
♕h8+ ♔d7 29 ♖d3+ +−

26...♖xb2+!! 27 ♔xb2? 27 ♔a1=
♗a3+! −+ 0-1 Gufeld

224 Matulovic-Ivanovic
Jugoslavia Final 78
1 e4 c5 2 ♘f3 ♘c6 3 d4 cxd4 4 ♘xd4
♘f6 5 ♘c3 d6 6 ♗g5 e6 6...h6 7 ♗xf6
gxf6 8 ♕d2 ♕b6 9 ♘b3 f5 10 ♘d5

♕d8 11 ♗b5! ♗g7 12 ♘d4 **7 ♕d2 a6 8 0-0-0 ♗d7 9 f4 ♗e7** 9...♖c8 10 ♘f3 ♕a5 11 ♔b1 b5 12 e5; 9...b5 10 ♗xf6 gxf6 11 f5!; 9...h6 10 ♗h4 ♘xe4 11 ♕e1 ♘f6 12 ♘f5 ♕a5 13 ♘xd6+ ♗xd6 14 ♖xd6 0-0-0 15 ♖d1! **10 ♘f3 b5 11 ♗xf6 gxf6** 11... ♗xf6 12 ♕xd6 ♗e7 13 ♕d2 b4 14 ♘e2 ♖a7 15 ♘ed4 ♕b6. 16 ♘xc6 ♕xc6 17 ♕d4! ♕c7 18 ♘e5 ♗c8 19 ♔b1 0-0 Vogt-Suetin, Budapest 76 **12 g3** 12 f5 ♕b6 **13 ♗h3 0-0-0 14 f5 ♕b8** 14...b4 15 fxe6! fxe6 16 ♘e2 **15 fxe6 fxe6** 15...♗xe6 16 ♗f5 △ ♘d5 **16 ♗e2** 16 ♔b1 ♗c8 17 ♕e1! ♗e5 **17 ♘fd4** 17 ♖hf1 ♘c4 △ ♘e3 ♗c4 **18 ♕d3 f5! 19 exf5 e5! 20 ♗e6** 20 ♘b3 ♗c6 21 ♖he1 d5 △ a5 ♖c8 **21 ♔b1** 21 ♘c3 ♕a5 ♗c6 **22 ♘c3 ♕a5! 23 ♖he1** 23 ♘d5 ♗xd5 24 ♕xd5 ♕b4; 23 b3 ♘a3+ 24 ♔b2 ♗xh1 25 ♖xh1 b4 **♕b4 24 b3 ♗b7! 25 f6** 25 ♖c1 ♘a3+ 26 ♔b2 ♖xc3 27 ♕xc3 ♘c4+ **♗xf6 26 ♘e4 ♘a3+ 27 ♔b2 ♖xc2+ 28 ♔a1 ♖xh2 29 ♘xf6 ♘c4!** 29... ♘c2+ 30 ♔b1 ♘xe1 31 ♘d7+ **30 ♘d7+ ♔a7 31 ♘xe5 dxe5 32 ♘c5 ♖xa2+ 33 ♔b1 ♖b2+ 34 ♔c1 ♕a3 35 ♗f5 0-1**

.225 Gufeld-Osnos
USSR 78

1 e4 c5 2 ♘f3 ♘c6 3 d4 cxd4 4 ♘xd4 ♘f6 5 ♘c3 d6 6 ♗g5 e6 7 ♕d2 ♗e7 8 0-0-0 0-0 9 f4 h6 10 ♗h4 ♗d7 11 ♘f3 ♘xe4!? N 12 ♘xe4 ♗xh4 13 ♕xd6 ♗e8 13...♘b8! 14 ♕a3 ♕c7 15 ♕d6 ♕d8 16 ♘xh4 ♕xh4 17 g3 ♕d8= 18 ♕xd8 ♘xd8 19 ♗g2 ♗c6 20 ♖hg1 ♖c8 21 ♘d6 ♖c7 22 ♗xc6 ♘xc6 23 ♘b5 ♖e7 24 ♘d4 ♘xd4 25 ♖xd4 ♖fe8 26 ♖dg1 e5 27 fxe5 ♖xe5 28 ♖d7 ♖8e7 29 c4 h5 30 ♖xe7 ♖xe7 ½-½
Suetin

Scheveningen

226 Malevinsky-N.Popov USSR 78
1 e4 c5 2 ♘f3 e6 3 d4 cxd4 4 ♘xd4 ♘f6 5 ♘c3 ♘c6 6 a3?! 6 ♘xc6!? bxc6 7 e5 ♘d5 8 ♘e4 +=; 6 g3 d5! 7 exd5 exd5=; 6 ♘db5 **d6** 6...♗e7 7 ♗e2 0-0 8 0-0 d5 9 exd5 ♘xd5 10 ♘xc6 bxc6 11 ♘e4∞ **7 f4** 7 ♗e2= **♗e7 8 ♘f3 a6 9 ♗d3 ♕c7 10 0-0 b5 11 ♕e1 ♗b7 12 ♕g3 g6** =+ **13 f5!? gxf5! 14 exf5 e5 15 ♗g5 ♖g8 16 ♕h4 ♘d4! 17 ♔h1** 17 ♗xf6 ♘xf3+ −+ **♗xf3 18 gxf3**

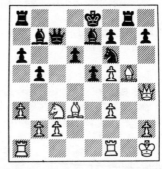

18...♖xg5! 19 ♕xg5 0-0-0∓ 20 ♕g7 d5! △ e4 **21 ♕xf7 e4 22 ♖ae1 ♖d7 23 fxe4 dxe4 24 ♘xe4 ♗d5! 25 ♕g7 ♕e5!** −+ **26 ♕g2 ♗c5 27 ♖e2 ♖d8 28 ♖fe1 ♖g8 29 ♕f3 ♖g4! 30 a4 ♗d6 31 axb5 ♘xe4 32 ♕xg4 ♘g3+** 32...♘f2+? 33 ♔g1 ♕xh2+ 34 ♔f1 ♘xg4 35 ♖xh2 ♘xh2+∞ **33 ♔g1 ♗c5+ 0-1 Gufeld**

227 Bodach-Mohring
DDR Final 78
1 e4 c5 2 ♘f3 e6 3 d4 cxd4 4 ♘xd4 ♘c6 5 ♘c3 ♘f6 6 ♗e2 d6 7 ♗e3 ♗e7 8 0-0 0-0 9 f4 ♗d7 10 ♕e1 10 ♘b3 a6 11 ♗f3 ♖b8 12 ♕e1 b5 13 g4? b4 14 ♘e2 e5!∓ Rye-Malich, DDR 77 **♘xd4 11 ♗xd4 ♗c6 12 ♕g3 g6 13 f5!?** 13 ♕e3 ♘d7? **14 ♖ad1! ♕a5 15**

♕d2 ♕c7 16 f5!± Rigo-Espig, Leipzig 77; 13...♕a5!? **e5 14 ♗e3 ♘xe4 15 ♘xe4 ♗xe4 16 ♗h6** 16 ♘d3!? **♕b6+ 17 ♔h1 ♖fc8** 17...♕xb2 18 ♗xf8 ♖xf8 19 ♘d3 ♘d5 20 c4 ♘c6 21 fxg6 fxg6 22 ♘xg6 hxg6 23 ♕xg6+≈ Liebert-Mohring, DDR Final 78 **18 ♗d3 ♗xd3 19 cxd3 ♗f8 20 ♗g5?!** 20 ♕h3 d5? 21 f6 +−; 20...♕d8 21 fxg6 hxg6 22 ♖xf7 ♔xf7 23 ♖f1+ ♔g8 24 ♕e6+; 20...♖c2 21 f6 ♕c6 22 ♖f3 ♔h8 23 ♖g1 +− **♖c2 21 fxg6?!** 21 h4!? ♖e8 22 h5 hxg6 **22 ♖xf7 ♔xf7 23 ♖f1+ ♔g8** 23...♔e8 24 ♗e3!≈ **24 ♗d8! ♕f2! 25** ♕xg6+ ♗g7 26 ♕e6+ ♔h7 27 ♕h3+ ♗h6 28 ♕d7+ ♔h8 29 ♕e8+ ♔h7 30 ♕d7+ ½-½ **Malich**

228 Sznapik-Knaak Zabrze 77

1 e4 c5 2 ♘f3 e6 3 d4 cxd4 4 ♘xd4 ♘f6 5 ♘c3 d6 6 ♗e2 ♗e7 7 0-0 0-0 8 f4 ♘c6 9 ♗e3 e5 10 ♘b3 exf4 11 ♗xf4 ♗e6 12 ♔h1! d5 13 e5 ♘e4 14 ♗d3 ♘xc3 15 bxc3 ♕d7 16 ♕h5 16 ♘d4!?± g6 17 ♕h6?! 17 ♕f3 Δ ♕g3, h4, h5 **♖fc8 18 ♖ae1 ♕d8!= 19 ♗c1** 19 ♘d4 d4 20 cxd4 ♘xd4 **21 ♖d1 ♗f8! 22 ♕f4 ♘xb3**

23 ♗xg6?! ♕e7 24 ♗xh7+ ♔xh7 25 axb3 ♖d8 26 ♖de1 ♗g7 =+ 27 ♖f3 ♖d5 28 c4 ♖a5! 29 ♖g3 ♖a1 30 ♕d4 ♖xc1!?∓ 31 ♖xc1 ♖d8 32 ♕e4+

♔h8 33 ♖f1 ♖d2 34 h3 ♕d8 35 ♖f4 ♔g8 36 ♖h4 ♗f5 37 ♕f4 ♖d1+ 38 ♔h2 ♕b6 39 c5? 39 ♕e3 ♕e6 −+ 40 ♖h5 ♗g6 41 ♖hg5 ♖d5 42 ♕g4 ♕xg4 43 ♖3xg4 ♗xe5+ 44 ♔g1 ♔h7 45 c6 bxc6 46 h4 ♔h6 45 ♖c4 c5 48 b4 cxb4 49 ♖xb4 a5 50 ♖c4 f6 51 ♖gg4 ♔h5 52 ♔f2 ♖d7 53 ♖a4 ♗c2 54 ♖ac4 ♗b3 55 ♖ce4 a4 0-1 **Pytel**

229 Larsen-Olafsson
Las Palmas 78

1 e4 c5 2 ♘f3 e6 3 d4 cxd4 4 ♘xd4 ♘c6 5 ♘c3 d6 6 ♗e2 ♘f6 7 0-0 ♗e7 8 ♔h1 0-0 9 f4 e5!? 10 ♘b3 10 ♘xc6!? bxc6 11 ♕d3 Δ ♕g3 a5 11 a4 ♘b4 12 ♗e3 ♗d7 13 ♖f2 ♕c7!? 14 h3! ♗xh3!? 15 f5 d5 16 ♗g5! d4 17 ♗xf6 ♗xf6 18 ♘a2 ♕xc2 19 ♘xb4 19 ♕xc2 ♘xc2 20 ♖g1? ♗h4!; 20 gxh3! ♘xa1 21 ♘xa1 ♖ac8 22 b3 += ♕xe4 20 ♘c5 20 ♕d3!? ♕h4 21 g3 ♕h6 22 ♖h2!? 21...♕g5∝ ♕h4 21 ♘bd3 ♗xf5+ 22 ♔g1 ♗g6 23 ♗f3∝ ♗g5 23...e4? 24 ♗xe4 24 ♘xe5 ♗e3 24...♗f4!? 25 ♘g4 ♗xf2+ 26 ♘xf2 d3 27 ♗xb7 ♖ad8 28 ♕d2 ♖fe8 29 ♗f3± ♖c8?! Zeitnot 30 ♘cxd3 ♖ed8 31 ♕e3 ♖b8 32 ♘e5 ♖e8 33 ♕c3 ♖ec8 34 ♘c6 ♔h8 35 ♖d1 h6 36 ♖d4 ♕f6 37 ♘g4 ♕e6 38 ♘ge5 +− ♖b3 39 ♕c4 ♖xb2? 40 ♕xe6 1-0 **Larsen**

230 Lukovnikov-Tivlin USSR 78

1 e4 c5 2 ♘f3 e6 3 d4 cxd4 4 ♘xd4 ♘c6 5 ♘c3 d6 6 ♗e2 ♘f6 7 0-0 ♗e7 8 ♗e3 0-0 9 f4 a6 10 ♕e1 ♘xd4 11 ♗xd4 b5 12 a3 12 e5!? ♗b7 13 ♗f3 ♕c7 14 ♕g3 ♖ad8 15 ♔h1 ♗c6 16 ♖ae1 a5!? 17 e5 dxe5 18 ♗xe5 ♕b7 19 f5 exf5 20 ♗xc6 ♕xc6 21 ♖xf5 g6! 22 ♖ff1 b4 23 axb4 axb4 24 ♕g5? bxc3 25 ♗xf6 ♖d5! 26 ♕h4 ♖d2

27 ♖5f3 ♗xf6 0-1 Suetin

231 Keene-Korchnoi England 78
1 e4 c5 2 ♘f3 ♘c6 3 d4 cxd4 4 ♘xd4
♘f6 5 ♘c3 d6 6 ♗e3 e6 7 f4 ♗d7 8
♕f3 ♘xd4 9 ♗xd4 ♗c6 10 0-0-0 ♕a5
11 ♗d3 ♗e7 11...b5?! 12 ♘xb5 ♗xb5
13 e5 ♘d5 14 ♘xd5 exd5 15 ♕xd5
△ exd6 **12 ♔b1 0-0-0?!** 12...0-0 13
♕h3 g6 14 ♕h4 ♘d5 15 ♕h6 **13**
♖he1 ♔b8 14 ♕g3 ♖hg8 15 e5! dxe5
16 fxe5! ♘h5 16...♖xd4 17 exf6+
♗d6 18 ♕e3 **17 ♕f2 f5 18 exf6** 18
♗c4 ♗d7 19 g4! gxf6 **19 ♖xe6** 19 g3
♖xg2 20 ♕f5 20 ♕e3 ♕xf5 21 ♗xf5
♖g7 22 ♖xe7 ♖xe7 23 ♗xa7+ ♔xa7
23...♔c7 24 ♘b6+ **24 ♖xd8 ♘g7 25**
♗h3 25 ♗xh7? ♘e6 26 ♖h8 ♘g5 -+
f5 26 ♔c1 f4 27 ♔d2 ♘e6 28 ♗xe6
♖xe6 29 ♖f8 f3 30 ♖f4 ♖g6 31 h4
h5 32 ♘e4 ♖g2+ 32...♖g4? 33 ♖xg4
hxg4 34 ♘g3 +- **33 ♔d3 ♖h2 34**
♘d2 += ½-½ **Keene**

232 Vogt-Malich DDR 78
1 e4 c5 2 ♘f3 e6 3 d4 cxd4 4 ♘xd4
♘f6 5 ♘c3 d6 6 f4 ♘c6 7 ♗e3 ♗d7
7...♗e7 8 ♕f3 ♘xd4 9 ♗xd4 ♗c6
10 0-0-0 ♕a5 11 ♔b1 11 ♗c4 0-0-0
12 ♘b3 ♗e7 13 ♖he1 += **♗e7 12 g4**
0-0 13 g5 ♘d7 14 h4 ♖fe8 14...e5
15 ♗e3 **15 h5 f5 16 gxf6 ♗xf6** 16...
♘xf6 17 ♗c4 d5 18 exd5 exd5 19
♗d3± **17 h6!** 17 ♗xf6 ♘xf6 18 ♖xd6?
♕b4∞ g6 18 ♗c4± ♗xd4 19 ♖xd4
♕c5 20 ♖hd1 ♘b6 21 ♗b3 ♖ad8

Diagram

22 f5?! 22 ♕g4! d5 23 f5 exf5 24
exf5 ♕d6 25 ♘e4 +-; 23...e5 24
♖xd5 +- **♕xf5 23 exf5 ♗xf3 24**
fxe6! d5 24...♗xd1 25 e7+ +- **25**
♖1d3 ♗g2 26 ♖g3 ♗f1 26...♗h1?

27 ♖d1 ♗e4 28 ♘xe4 dxe4 29 ♖xd8
♖xd8 30 e7+ +- **27 ♘xd5 ♔h8 28**
♖e3 ♗c4 29 ♗xc4 Zeitnot **♘xc4 30**
♖xc4 ♖xd5 31 b3 ♖h5 32 ♖ec3
♖e5 33 ♖c7 ♖5xe6 34 ♖xb7 g5
35 ♖g7! 35 ♖cc7 ♖xh6 ♖xh6 36
♖xg5 ♖he6 37 ♖c7 ♖6e7 38 ♖xe7
♖xe7 39 c4 h6 40 ♖g2 ♔h7 41 c5 +-
h5 42 c6 ♖c7 43 ♖c2 ♔g6 44 b4 h4
45 b5 h3 46 ♔b2 ♔f5 47 ♔b3 ♖c8
48 ♔b4 ♖h8 49 c7 ♖c8 49...h2 50
♖xh2 **50 ♔a5 h2 50...**♔e6 51 b6! +-
51 ♖xh2 ♖xc7 52 ♖e2 ♔f6 53 1-0
Vogt

233 Levitina-Belavenets USSR 78
1 e4 c5 2 ♘f3 e6 3 d4 cxd4 4 ♘xd4
♘f6 5 ♘c3 d6 6 ♗e3 ♗e7 6...a6 7
♗d3 b5 8 0-0 ♗b7 9 ♕e1 ♘bd7 10 f3
♗e7=; 6...♘c6 **7 f4 0-0 8 ♕f3 a6?!**
8...♕c7 **9 0-0-0 ♕c7 10 g4± ♘c6 11**
g5 ♘d7 12 h4 b5

13 g6! ♘xd4 13...hxg6 14 h5! +− **14 gxh7+ ♔h8 15 ♗xd4 ♗b7 16 ♖g1 e5 17 fxe5 dxe5 18 ♗e3 ♗f6 19 h5** +− **b4 20 h6! bxc3 21 hxg7+ ♗xg7 22 ♕g4 cxb2+ 23 ♔b1 ♗f6 24 ♗h6 1-0** 24...♔xh7 25 ♕h5 +− **Gufeld**

234 Plachetka-Jankovec
CSSR Final 78

1 e4 c5 2 ♘f3 e6 3 d4 cxd4 4 ♘xd4 ♘f6 5 ♘c3 d6 6 f4 ♘c6 7 ♘f3!? a6 8 ♗d3 ♕c7 9 0-0 ♗e7 10 ♕e1 ♘d7?! 10...0-0 11 a3 b5 12 b4!? Plachetka-Matulovic, Sarajevo 78 **11 ♕g3 ♗f6?** 11...0-0; 11...g6 **12 e5!± dxe5 13 ♘e4 g6** 13...exf4 14 ♗xf4! ♕b6+ 15 ♔h1 0-0 16 ♗h6 +−; **14 fxe5 ♗xe5 15 ♘xe5 ♘cxe5 16 ♗h6!** 16 ♗f4 0-0!∝ **f5 17 ♘g5 ♘f6 18 ♖ae1 ♘fg4**

19 ♔h1!! +− ♘xh6 20 ♖xe5 ♕b8 20...♕e7 21 ♘xe6; 20...0-0 21 ♖exf5! +− **21 ♘xe6 ♗xe6 22 ♖xe6+ ♔d7 23 ♕e3! ♘g4 24 ♕d4+ ♔xe6 25 ♗c4+ 1-0** 25...♔e7 26 ♖e1+ **Plachetka**

235 Velimirovic-Rajkovic
Jugoslavia Final 78

1 e4 c5 2 ♘f3 e6 3 d4 cxd4 4 ♘xd4 ♘c6 5 ♘c3 ♘f6 6 ♗f4 d6 7 ♘f3 7 ♗g3 ♘xd4 8 ♕xd4 ♘h5 9 ♗b5+ ♗d7 10 ♗xd7+! ♕xd7 11 ♗h4! += ♗e7 8 ♕d2

0-0 9 0-0-0 ♕a5! 10 ♗c4?! 10 ♗xd6 ♖d8 11 e5 ♘xe5 12 ♘d5∝; 10 ♔b1! ♖d8 11 ♗c4 ♗d7 12 ♖he1 ♗e8∝ **♘e5 11 ♗b3 b5! =+ 12 ♕e1** 12 ♘xe5 dxe5 13 ♗xe5 b4 14 ♗xf6 ♗xf6 15 ♘e2 ♕e5∓; 12 ♗xe5 dxe5 13 ♘xe5 ♗b7∓ **b4 13 ♔b1 ♗b7 14 ♘bd2 ♖fc8 15 ♔b1 ♕b5!?** 15...♕c7! 16 ♘d4 a5∓ **16 ♘d4 ♕e8 17 ♗g3! a5 18 f4 a4! 19 ♗d5?** 19 ♗xe6 fxe6 20 fxe5 dxe5 21 ♗xe5 ♖a5 22 ♗g3 ♖ac5∝ **♘c6!∓ 20 ♗xe6** 20 ♘xc6 ♗xc6 21 ♗xc6 ♕xc6 22 ♖c1 a3! −+ **fxe6 21 ♗xe6+ ♔h8 22 e5**

22...♘d4!! 23 ♘c4 23 exf6 ♗xf6 24 ♗xc8 ♕xc8 25 ♖c1 b3 26 cxb3 ♕f5+ 27 ♔a1 ♘xb3+! 28 ♘xb3 axb3 29 a3 ♖xa3 mate **♘xe6 24 exf6 ♗xf6 25 ♘xd6 ♕c6! 26 ♘xc8 ♖xc8 27 ♕xb4** 27 ♕d2 ♘d4 28 ♖c1 b3 29 cxb3 ♕e4+ −+ **♕xc2+ 28 ♔a1 ♘d4! Δ ♘b3+ 29 ♖b1 ♕xb1+! 0-1** 30 ♔xb1 ♗e4+ **Rajkovic**

236 Shamkovich-Gheorghiu
Lone Pine 78

1 e4 c5 2 ♘f3 e6 3 g3 ♘c6 4 ♗g2 ♘f6 5 ♘c3 d6 6 0-0 ♗e7 7 d4 cxd4 8 ♘xd4 ♗d7 9 ♘de2 a6 10 b3 0-0 11 ♗b2 ♕c7 12 ♕d2 12 h3 ♖fd8 13 g4 d5! 14 exd5 ♘e8 =+ **♖fd8 13 h3 ♗e8** Δ d5 Δ ♘b4∓ **14 a3 b5 15 ♕e3**

♖ac8 16 ♖fd1 ♕b8 17 ♖d2 ♘d7 18
♘d1 a5 19 ♘d4 ♘xd4 20 ♗xd4 ♘c5
21 ♘c3 b4∓ 22 axb4 axb4 23 ♘e2
e5 24 ♗b2 ♗c6 25 ♖e1 ♕b7 △ f5∓
26 f3 ♘d7 27 ♔h2 ♕b6 28 ♕xb6 ♘xb6
29 f4 f6! 30 ♖ed1 ♘d7 31 ♘c1 ♘c5
32 ♖e1 ♖a8 33 h4 ♗b5 34 ♗h3 ♔h8
35 ♗g2 ♖db8 36 ♗f3 ♖b6 37 ♖e3
♘e6 38 f5 ♘c5 39 g4 ♖c6?! Zeitnot
40 ♗e2!∝ ♗xe2 41 ♖exe2 ♖ac8
42 ♔g3 ♔g8 43 ♔f3 ♔f7 44 ♖g2 g6
45 ♘a2 ♖b6 46 ♖g1 ♖a8 47 ♘c1
♖d8 48 g5 gxf5 49 exf5 d5 50 g6+
♔g8 51 ♖dg2 ♗f8!!∓ 52 gxh7+ ♔xh7
53 ♖g8 ♖bb8 54 ♖8g6 ♘e4! 55 ♘d3!
♖bc8 56 ♖1g2 ♖d7 57 ♗c1 ♘d6
△ ♘xf5, e4+ 58 ♔g4 ♖g7! 59 ♖xg7+
♗xg7 60 ♘xb4 ♖g8! 61 ♔h3 d4∝
62 ♘d5 ♖c8 63 ♔g4 ♖c5 64 ♘e7
d3!∓ 65 c4

65...♘xc4! 66 h5 66 bxc4? ♖xc4+
△ ♖xc1 −+ ♘a5 67 ♗e3 ♖c2 68
♖g1 ♖e2?! 68...♖c7!! 69 ♘d5 ♖d7
70 ♘b6 ♖d8 71 b4 ♘b3 △ d2 −+
69 ♔f3 ♘xb3 70 ♘d5 =+ ♘d2+ 71
♗xd2 e4+ 72 ♔g4! 72 ♔f4 ♗h6+ −+
♖xd2 73 h6!!= ♗h8 73...♖xh6 74
♘xf6+ △ ♘xe4= 74 ♔f4 ♖h2 75 ♔xe4
d2 76 ♖d1 ♔xh6 77 ♔d3 ♔g5 78 ♘e3
♔f4 79 ♖xd2 ½-½ Gheorghiu

Boleslavsky

1 e4 c5 2 ♘f3 d6 3 d4 cxd4 4 ♘xd4
♘f6 5 ♘c3 ♘c6 6 ♗e2 e5 7 ♘f3!? h6!
7...♗e7 8 ♘g5! ♗e6 9 0-0 0-0 10 ♗xf6
♗xf6 11 ♘d5 += Smyslov-Hort,
Tilburg 77 8 0-0 ♗e7 9 b3! 0-0 10
♗b2 a6 11 ♖e1 11 ♘d2!? ♘d4 12
♗d3 b5 13 ♖e1 ♗b7 14 ♘e2 ♘e6
15 ♘g3 += Smyslov-Timman, Tilburg
77 b5 12 ♗d3 12 ♘d2!? ♗b7 13 a4
b4 14 ♘e2 ♖e8≈ 14...d5 15 exd5
♕xd5 16 ♘g3± 15 ♘g3 ♗f8 16 ♕e2
♕c7 17 ♖ad1 17 ♖ac1!? ♖d8 18 ♕d2
♕b6 19 c4! bxc3 20 ♕xc3 ♖c8 21
♗c4 ♘e6 22 a5 ♕c7 ½-½ Bellin

Dragon

1 c4 c5 2 ♘f3 ♘c6 3 ♘c3 ♘f6 4
d4 cxd4 5 ♘xd4 g6 6 e4 ♗g7 7 ♗e3
0-0 7...♘g4 8 ♗e2 d6 8...b6!? 9 0-0
♗b7 10 ♕d2?! ♘xd4 11 ♗xd4 e5!
12 ♗xe5 ♘xe4 =+ Geller-Bellon, Las
Palmas 76; 10 ♖c1? ♘xd4 11 ♗xd4
♗h6! =+; 10 f3! d6 11 ♕d2 ♕d7
12 a4! += Gheorghiu-Bellon, Las
Palmas 76 9 0-0 ♗d7 10 ♖c1 10 ♕d2
♘xd4 11 ♗xd4 ♗c6 12 ♗d3!? a6 13
♖fe1 += Rogoff-Larsen, Biel 76;
10 f3?! ♘xd4 11 ♗xd4 ♗c6 12 ♕d2
♘d7 13 ♗e3 a5 14 ♖ac1 ♘c5 =+
Cabrillo-Ivkov, Jugoslavia 76 ♘xd4
11 ♗xd4 ♗c6 11...a6!? 12 f3 a5!
12...♘d7 13 b4 ♗xd4 14 ♕xd4 ♕b6
15 ♕xb6 ♘xb6 16 e5!± Razuvaev-
Honfi, Cienfuegos 76 13 b3 ♘d7 14
♗xg7 14 ♗e3!? ♘c5 15 ♔h1 ♕b6 16
♘b5 ♖fc8 17 ♕d2 ♕d8 18 ♖fd1 b6
19 ♘c3 ♕d7 20 ♗d4 ♕b7 +=
Martinovic-Velimirovic, Jugoslavia 76
♔xg7 15 ♕d4+ ♔g8 16 ♖fd1!? N 16
♔h1 ♕b6= ♕b6 17 ♕xb6 ♘xb6 18
f4! += ♖fd8 19 ♘d5 ♗xd5 20 cxd5

♘d7 20...♖ac8 21 ♘g4± 21 ♖c7±
♖ab8 22 ♗b5 ♘f6 23 ♖xe7 ♕f8 24
♖c7 ♘xe4 25 ♖e1! f5 26 ♗d7 ♔g8
27 ♗e6+ ♔h8 28 g4 ♘d2 29 ♖e3 fxg4
30 ♗xg4 ♖e8 31 ♗e6 +− ♘b1 32
♖h3 h5 33 ♖g3 1-0 Gufeld

239 Gofshtein-Gufeld USSR 78
1 e4 c5 2 ♘f3 d6 3 d4 cxd4 4 ♘xd4
♘f6 5 ♘c3 g6 6 ♗e2 ♗g7 7 0-0 0-0
8 ♗g5 ♘c6 9 ♘b3 a6 9...♗e6 10 f4
10 ♔h1 b5 11 f4 ♗b7 12 ♗f3 ♔d7!
13 ♕e1 a5!∞ Tal-Gufeld, USSR 77;
10 a4!? b5 11 ♗f3 b4! 12 ♘a4 12
♘d5 ♘xd5 13 exd5 ♘a5! =+ ♗d7!
13 a3 13 e5 ♘e8 =+ ♖b8 =+ 14 axb4
♘xb4 15 ♔h1 15 e5 dxe5 16 ♘ac5
e4!?∞ ♕c7 15...♘b5 16 ♖e1 ♕c7 17
♘c3 ♗c4 16 ♘c3 ♗e6 17 ♘a5 17 ♘d4
♗c4 18 ♖e1 e5!∓ ♖fd8! 17...♘a2
18 ♘xa2 ♕xa5 19 ♘c3 ♕b6 20 ♖ab1
=+ 18 ♕e2 d5 19 exd5 19 e5 d4!∓
♘fxd5∓ 20 ♘xd5 ♘xd5 21 c3

21...♖b5! −+ 21...h6 22 ♗h4 ♖b5
23 ♗g3! 22 ♘c6 ♕xc6 23 c4 ♖xb2
24 cxd5 ♖xd5 25 ♕xe7 ♖c8 26 ♕e3
♗xf3 27 ♕xf3 ♕xf3 28 ♖xf3 ♖cc2 29
♖g1 0-1 Gufeld

240 Tal-Gufeld USSR 77
1 e4 c5 2 ♘f3 d6 3 d4 cxd4 4 ♘xd4
♘f6 5 ♘c3 g6 6 ♗e2 ♗g7 7 0-0 ♘c6

8 ♘b3 0-0 9 ♗g5 a5!? 9...♗e6 10 f4
10 a4!? b5 11 ♗f3 ♗b7 12 ♔h1 12
♘d5!? ♘d7 13 ♕e1 13 a3 ♘b6=
a5! 13...b4?! 14 ♘d5 ♗xb2 15 ♖d1
♗g7 16 e5! ∞/+= 14 ♘xb5 a4 15 ♘d2
h6 16 ♗h4 ♘c5! 16...♗xb2 17 ♖b1
a3 18 ♘xa3!; 16...♘b4 17 ♕b1!?
17 ♘c4 ♗a6 18 ♘ba3 ♘d4! ∞/=+
19 ♖f2 ♖c8? 19...d5!? 20 exd5 ♘xf3
21 gxf3 ♕xd5 22 ♘b6 ♕h5 ∞/=+;
19...♘xf3 20 gxf3 f5! 21 exf5 g5
22 fxg5 hxg5 23 ♗xg5 ♖xf5 ∞/∓;
21...♖xf5!? ∞/=+ 20 ♖d1 ♘xf3 21
gxf3 △ ♖xd6 ♕c7 22 b3± 22 b4?
♗xc4 23 ♘xc4 ♘e6! f5!? 23 exf5
g5 23...♖xf5 24 ♘e3! 24 fxg5 hxg5
25 ♗xg5 ♖xf5 26 ♕xe7 d5! 27 ♘d6
27 ♘e3 ♕xe7 28 ♗xe7 ♘e4∞; 28...
♖e5!? ∞/+= ♕xe7 27...♖xg5 28 ♕xg5
♕xd6 29 ♕xd5+ ♕xd5 30 ♖xd5∞;
28 ♘xc8 ♕f4! 29 ♕xc5? ♗e2! 30
♖df1 ♗xf1 31 ♖xf1 ♗d4 △ ♕xf3+!,
♖g1 mate; 29 ♘d6! ∞/± 28 ♗xe7
♘e4 29 fxe4 29 ♘xe4? dxe4∞ ♖xf2
30 ♘xc8 ♗xc8 30...dxe4?! 31 ♗c5 +−
31 exd5 axb3 32 axb3 ♗h3 33 ♗c5
♖e2

34 ♖d3? 34 ♘c4! ♖xc2 35 d6 ♗d7
36 ♗d4 ♗c6 37 ♔g1 +− ♖e1+ 35
♗g1 ♗f5 ∞/+= 36 ♖e3 ♖a1! 36...
♗e4+?? 37 ♖xe4 +− 37 ♘c4 ♗d4
38 ♖g3+ ♔h7 39 h4 ♖c1! 40 ♘d2

40 ♔h2 ♗e4! ♖xc2 41 d6 ♖d1! 42
♘c4 ♗f2! 42...♗xb3 43 ♖xb3 ♗xg1
44 ♖b7+ ♔h6 45 ♔g2± 43 ♖g4
43 ♖g2 ♗e4+ 44 ♔h2 ♗xg2 45 ♗xf2
♗d5= ♗xb3 44 ♘b2 ♗d5+ 45 ♔h2
♗xg1+ 46 ♖xg1 ♖d2+ 47 ♔g3 ♖xb2??
47...♗b3=; 47...♗e6= 48 d7 +− ♖b8
49 ♖d1 ♖g8+ 50 ♔f4 ♗e6 51 d8♕
♖xd8 52 ♖xd8 1-0 Gufeld

241 Hardicsay-Kilcsar Hungary 78
1 e4 c5 2 ♘f3 ♘c6 3 d4 cxd4 4 ♘xd4
♘f6 5 ♘c3 g6 6 ♗e3 ♗g7 7 ♗c4 ♕a5
8 0-0 0-0 9 ♘b3 ♕d8?! 9...♕c7 10
f4 d6 11 ♗e2 += 10 f4 d6 10...♘g4?!
11 ♕xg5 d5 12 ♕e2± 11 ♗e2 ♗d7
12 ♗f3 ♕c8 13 h3 ♗e6 14 ♘d5! ♖e8
15 c3! b6 16 ♕e2 ♘d7 17 ♖ad1 ♘c5
18 ♘d4 ♗xd5 19 exd5 ♘xd4 20 cxd4!
20 ♖xd4 += ♘d7 21 ♖c1 ♕b7 22 ♖c6
♖ac8 23 ♖fc1 ♘b8 24 ♖6c3 ♖xc3
25 bxc3 ♘d7 26 ♕b5! ♖c8 27 c4
♘f6 28 c5!? dxc5 29 dxc5 ♕c7! 30
c6 30 ♕xd7 ♘xd7 31 c6 ♘c5? 32
♖xc5! bxc5 33 ♗xc5 +−; 31...♘f6 Δ
♘e8 += ♕d6 31 ♕b3 e6! 32 dxe6 ♕xe6
33 ♕d3 ♗f8 34 a4 ♗d6 35 ♖d1 ♗c7
36 ♔h1 ♖e8 37 ♗c1 ♘e4 38 ♗xe4
♕xe4 39 ♕d7! ♕e7 39...♖d8? 40
♕xd8+ ♗xd8 41 ♖xd8+ ♔g7 42 c7
+− 40 ♔h2 ♕xd7 41 ♖xd7 41 cxd7!
♖d8 Δ ♗b2, ♗f6 +− ♖c8 42 ♔g3
Zeitnot 42 g3! (Δ ♔g2-f3-e4-d5 +−)
g5!? 43 ♔g4! ♗xf4 43...gxf4 44 ♗b2
♔f8? 45 ♗f6 +−; 44...a6!? 45 ♔f5 b5
46 axb5 axb5 47 ♔e4 +− 44 ♗xf4
gxf4 45 c7 ♔g7 46 ♔f5! +− a6 47
♔e5 b5 48 axb5 axb5 49 ♔d6 1-0
time Hardicsay

5 ♕xd4

242 Ciocaltea-Giuramia Rumania 78
1 e4 c5 2 ♘f3 d6 3 d4 ♘f6 4 ♘c3 cxd4

5 ♕xd4!? N a6 6 ♗g5 ♘c6 7 ♕d2 h6
8 ♗f4 8 ♗h4?! g5! 9 ♗g3 ♘h5= e5!
9 ♗e3 ♗e6 10 ♗e2 ♖c8?! 10...d5!=
11 0-0 ♗e7 12 ♖fd1!± g5? 12...0-0
13 ♘e1! b5 14 f3 ♘a5 15 b3 ♕c7
16 ♘d5 ♘xd5 17 exd5 ♗d7 18 ♖ac1
0-0 19 h4 f5 20 hxg5 f4 21 ♗f2 hxg5
22 ♘d3 ♗d8 23 ♘b4 ♕b7 24 ♘c6
♘xc6 25 dxc6 ♖xc6 26 c4 ♗b6 27
c5! ♗a7 28 b4 ♔g7 29 a4 ♔f6 30
axb5 axb5 31 ♗d3 ♗e6 31...d5 32
♗b1 Δ ♕d3, ♔f1, ♔e2, ♖h1 32 ♗e4
d5 33 ♗xd5 ♗b8 34 ♕d3 ♖h8 35
♕e4 ♗f5 36 ♕e2 ♕h7 37 ♔f1 ♕h1+
38 ♗g1 ♖h2 39 ♗xc6 ♖xg2 40 ♕xg2
♗h3 41 ♖c2 +− g4 42 fxg4 ♗xg2+
43 ♖xg2 ♔g5 44 ♗e4! ♕h8 45 ♖h2
♕g8 46 ♖d5 f3 47 ♗xf3 ♔f4 48
♔g2! ♕g6 49 ♖h5 1-0 Ciocaltea

243 Ciocaltea-J.Adamski Bucharest 78
1 e4 c5 2 ♘f3 d6 3 d4 ♘f6 4 ♘c3 cxd4
5 ♕xd4 N ♘c6 5...a6 6 ♗g5 ♘c6 7
♕d2 6 ♗b5 ♗d7 7 ♗xc6 ♗xc6 8 ♗g5
e6 9 0-0-0 ♗e7 10 ♖he1 0-0 11 ♔b1
♕c7! 11...♕a5?! 12 ♕d2! ♔h8 13 ♘d4
♖fd8 14 f4! h6?! 15 h4!± Ciric-Diaz,
Jugoslavia 76 12 ♕d2 ♖fd8 12...b5!?
13 ♘d4 a6 13...♖ab8! 14 f4 b5 15 a3
♖ab8 16 f5! ♗d7 17 g4 a5 18 ♘b3
b4 19 axb4 axb4 20 ♘a2 ♖dc8 Δ
♘xe4, ♗xg5, ♕xc2+ 21 h4 ♗c6?!
21...♗a4! 22 ♗xf6 ♗xf6 23 g5 ♗e5
24 ♘xb4! ♗a4 25 ♘d3! ♖a8 26 ♘xe5
♗xb3 27 cxb3 ♕a7 27...dxe5 28
♖c1± 28 ♘c4 ♕a2+ 29 ♔c2 ♖ab8!
30 ♕c3! 30 ♖e3? ♖xc4+! −+ ♖xb3!
31 ♕xb3 ♖xc4+ 32 ♕xc4 ♕xc4+
33 ♔b1± ♕b4 34 ♖e3 h6 35 g6!
♔f8 36 ♖c1 ♕b7 37 ♖f1! ♔e7 38
f6+! 38 fxe6?! f6! gxf6 38...♔f8 39
fxg7+ +− 39 g7 ♕a8 40 ♖g1 ♕g8
41 ♖b3 f5 42 exf5 e5 43 ♖b6 1-0
Ciocaltea

137

Kan

244 Kristiansen-Filipowicz
Roskilde 78

**1 e4 c5 2 ♘f3 e6 3 d4 cxd4 4 ♘xd4
a6 5 ♘c3 ♘c6 6 ♘xc6!?** 6 ♗f4!?
d6 7 ♘f3!?; 6 ♗e2 ♘ge7 7 ♗f4 ♘g6 8
♗g3 ♗e7 9 ♕d2 0-0? 10 h4!
Kupreichik-Taimanov, USSR 76 **bxc6
7 e5 ♕c7 8 ♗f4** 8 f4 f5 9 ♗e3 ♘h6
10 ♗e2 c5 11 0-0 ♗e7 12 ♘a4 ♗b7
13 c4 Hartston-Rath, Esbjerg 77
g5!? 9 ♗g3 ♖b8 10 ♗d3 10 b3??
**♗b4 -+ h5!? 11 h3 ♖xb2 12 0-0 g4
13 h4!** 13 hxg4 hxg4 14 ♕xg4 ♖b4
15 ♘e4±; 13...h4 14 ♘h2 h3 **d5 14
exd6 ♗xd6 15 ♘e4!** 15 ♗xd6 ♕xd6
16 ♘e4 ♕d4 17 c3 ♕e5∞ **♗xg3 16
fxg3 f5!? 17 ♘g5 ♗e7** 17...♕xg3?
18 ♗xf5 exf5 19 ♖fe1+ ♘e7 20
♕d4 ♖xc2 21 ♕xh8+ ♔d7 22 ♖ad1+
♔c7 23 ♕d8+ ♔b8 24 ♖b1+ +-;
19...♔f8 20 ♕d8+ ♔g7 21 ♕d4+ +-
18 ♕e1! △ ♕c3 e5 19 ♗c4! ♖xc2
**20 ♗f7+ ♔f8 21 ♘e6+ ♗xe6 22 ♗xe6
♕g7** 22...♕b6+ 23 ♔h1 ♕b2 24 ♖b1
+- **23 ♕e3! f4!? 24 gxf4 ♘d5! 25
♕e4! ♖c3! 26 fxe5!** 26 ♕f5 ♕b6+
27 ♔h1 ♕d8! 28 fxe5 ♕xh4+ 29 ♔g1
♖f3!!; 28 ♕f7+ ♔h6 29 fxe5 ♕xh4+
30 ♔g1 ♖f3!=; 28 ♕xe5 ♕f6=; 26...
♘xf4 27 ♕g5+ ♔f8 28 ♖ad1! ♘e8
29 ♖xf4! exf4 30 ♕g6+ ♔f8 31 ♖d8+!
+- **♖e3 27 ♕d4! ♕xe5 28 ♕a7+
♔h6 29 ♗xd5 cxd5 30 ♕f7?** 30 ♖ab1!
♖e8 31 ♕f7 ♕g7 32 ♖b6+ ♔h7 33
♕xh5+ ♔g8 34 ♖g6; 34...♖g8 31
♖b6+ ♖g6 32 ♖xg6+ +- **♖f3! 31
♕a7 ♖hf8** 31...♕e3+ 32 ♕xe3 ♖xe3=
**32 ♖fe1 ♖3f7 33 ♕xa6+ ♖f6 34 ♕d3
♕f5 35 ♕d2+ ♕f4 36 ♕xf4+ ♖xf4
37 a4 ♖a8 38 a5 ♖a6 39 ♖eb1 ♕g6
40 ♖b5 ♖f5 41 ♖ab1 ♖a7! 41...♖a8?
42 ♖b6+ ♖f6 43 ♖f1! ♖xb6 44 axb6

♖b8 45 ♖b1 ♖b7 46 ♔f2 ♔f5 47
♔e3 ♔e6 48 ♖b5± 42 ♖b6+ ♖f6 43
♖f1 ♖xb6 44 axb6 ♖b7 45 ♖b1
♕f5 46 ♔f2 ♔e4 47 ♖b4+ ♔d3 48
♔g3 ½-½**

245 Goliak-Tompa Leipzig 77

**1 e4 c5 2 ♘f3 e6 3 d4 cxd4 4 ♘xd4
a6 5 ♘c3 ♕c7 6 g3 ♗b4!? 7 ♘de2**
7 ♗d2 ♘f6 8 ♗g2 ♘c6 9 ♘xc6 bxc6
10 0-0 0-0 11 ♖e1 e5? 12 ♘d5±
Vogt-Honfi, Cienfuegos 76 **♘f6 8
♗g2 ♗e7 9 0-0 0-0 10 b3** 10 h3 ♘c6
11 f4 b5 12 ♗e3 ♗b7 13 g4 d5! =+
Tarjan-Gheorghiu, Los Angeles 74
♘c6 11 ♗b2 d6! 11...b5?! 12 ♘d5!
exd5 13 exd5 ♗b7 14 dxc6 dxc6
15 ♘d4 △ ♘f5 += **12 a4 ♗d7** 12...b6
**13 ♕d2 ♖fd8 14 ♖fd1 ♘b4 15 ♘a2
♘xa2 16 ♖xa2 ♗c6 17 ♗xf6** 17 c4
d5 **♗xf6 18 c4 b6 =+ 19 ♕e3 ♖ab8
20 ♖ad2 h6** 20...b5?! 21 axb5 axb5
22 c5 **21 h4 ♗e8 22 ♘d4 ♕f8** △ 23...
♕c5 24 ♘c2 ♔e7 23 **f4 ♕c5 24 e5?!
dxe5 25 fxe5 ♗e7** 25...♗xe5?? 26
♘xe6+ +- **26 ♕h2 ♕c7∓ 27 ♕e4
♗c5 28 ♘c6 ♖xd2 29 ♖xd2 ♖c8**
29...♗xc6 30 ♕xc6 ♕xe5 31 ♖d7∞
30 ♕h7? 30 ♘d4 ♖d8 31 ♘f3 ♖xd2
32 ♘xd2 ♕d7 33 ♘f3 ♔g8!∓ **♗xc6
31 ♕h8+ ♔e7 32 ♕xg7 ♗xg2 -+ 33
♖xg2 ♕e8 34 ♖e2 ♗f8 35 ♕f6 ♖d8
36 g4 ♖d1 37 g5 ♕c6 38 ♖g2 ♕e4
39 gxh6** 39 g6 ♗e7! 40 gxf7+ ♔d7
41 f8♕ ♗xf8 -+ **♖d4 40 ♔h3 ♕e3+
41 ♖g3 ♕xh6 0-1 Tompa**

246 Hardicsay-Piasetski Hungary 78

**1 e4 c5 2 ♘f3 e6 3 d4 cxd4 4 ♘xd4
a6 5 ♗d3 ♘e7!? 6 f4 N ♘bc6 7 ♘f3
d5 8 e5 ♕b6** 8...♘g6 △ f6 += **9 ♘bd2!
♗f5 9**...♕e3+? **10 ♗e2 ♕xf4 11 ♘c4
+- 10 ♘b3 a5 11 a4 ♗d7 12 ♕e2
♗e7 12**...♗b4+ 13 ♔f1!? △ g3, ♔g2±

13 Bxf5 exf5 14 Be3 Qb4+? 14...
Qc7 15 Nfd4 +- 15 Qf2 Qc4 16 Rhd1
Nb4 17 Nfd4 Rd8 18 c3 Na6 19 Nd2
Qxe2+ 20 Qxe2 Nc5!? 20...Nc7 +-
21 Nxf5 Bxa4 22 Nd6+ Qf8 23
Ra2 b5 24 Bd4 Nb6 25 Nb7 Nc4 26
Nf3 Bc7 27 Bc5+! Qe8 28 b3 Nb6
29 Nd6+ Bxd6 30 Rxb6 Be7 31 Rxa5
+- Rc8 32 Bd4 Bc6 33 Ra7 h5 34
b4! Bd7 35 Rda1 Rh6 36 Rb7 Bc6
37 Rb6 Bd8 38 Rba6 Rg6 39 Qf2 h4
40 Bc5 Rg4 41 Be3 Bd7 42 R1a3
Bf5 43 Ra8 Rxa8 44 Rxa8 Qd7 45
g3 Zeitnot **hxg3+ 46 hxg3 Bc7 47**
Nd4 Bd3 48 Ra7 Qc8 49 Nc6 f6 1-0
time **50 Kf3 Rg6 51 Ne7+ +-**
Hardicsay

247 Stoica-Gheorghiu Rumania 78
1 e4 c5 2 Nf3 e6 3 d4 cxd4 4 Nxd4
a6 5 Bd3 Nf6 6 0-0 d6 7 Kh1 Be7
8 c4 0-0 9 Nc3 b6!= 10 b3 Bb7 11
Bb2 Nc6 12 Nxc6 Bxc6 13 Qe2 Nd7
14 f4 Re8 15 Rad1 Qb8 Δ b5 **16**
Rfe1 Qh4 17 Rf1 Be7= ½-½ **Gheorghiu**

248 Westerinen-Larsen
Las Palmas 78
1 e4 c5 2 Nc3 e6 3 Nf3 a6 4 d4 cxd4
5 Nxd4 b5 6 Bd3 Qc7 7 0-0 Nf6 8
Qe2 b4!? 8...Bd6?? 9 Ndxb5; 8...d6
9 a4; 8...Nc6 9 Nxc6 dxc6 +=; 9...
Qxc6 10 a4 b4 11 Nd5 += **9 e5!?** 9
Nd5!? **bxc3 10 exf6 gxf6 11 bxc3**
Bb7 12 Rb1 Nc6∞ 13 Bf4?! Qxf4
14 Rxb7 Nxd4 15 cxd4 Bd6 16
g3 Qxd4 17 Bxa6 Qe7 18 Rd1 Qc5
19 Qb5 Rhd8 20 Qxc5 Bxc5 21 Rb5
Ra7 =+ 22 Rxa7 Bxa7 23 c4 d6 24
a4 Bb6 25 Rb1 Rb8 26 Qf1 Ba5 27
Qe2 f5 28 Rd1 h5 29 Rd4 Bc3 30
Rd3 Bb4 31 Rb3 Ba5 32 Rd3 Rh8
33 Rb3 Qf6 34 Rd3 Rd8 35 Rb3
h4 36 gxh4 Rh8 37 Rh3 Qg6 38

h5+ Qh6 39 Rd3 Rd8 40 Rh3 f4?!
41 Qf3 e5 42 Qg4! Bb6 43 Rf3 Rg8+
43...Qg7!? **44 Qf5 Rg2** 44...Rg5+!?
45 Qf6 Rg2 **45 Be8 Bxf2 46 Bxf7**
Bc5 47 Rb3 Rg5+ 48 Qe4 Rg7 49
Rb7 Qg5 50 Bd5 Rxb7 51 Bxb7
Qxh5 52 a5 Qg5 ½-½ **Larsen**

Taimanov

249 Ivanovic-Kurajica
Jugoslavia Final 78
1 e4 c5 2 Nf3 Nc6 3 d4 cxd4 4 Nxd4
Qc7 5 Nc3 e6 6 Be2 a6 7 0-0 Nf6
8 Kh1!? Bb4 8...d6 9 Bg5 **9 Nxc6**
bxc6 10 Qd4 Bd6 11 f4 e5=; 10 f4!?
d5 11 e5 Nd7 12 Na4 Nb6 13 c4 +=
Bxc3 10 Bxf6 gxf6 11 bxc3 Ne7!
11...b5?! 12 a4 += **12 Qd2 d5 13**
Qh6!? N 13 exd5 Nxd5 14 c4 Nf4
15 Bf3 0-0 =+ **dxe4 14 Qxf6 Ng6**
Δ Qe7 **15 f3 e5!** 15...e3? 16 f4±
16 Nf5 Bxf5 17 Qxf5 e3= 18 Rad1
0-0 18...Qxc3!? **19 Rd3 Rac8 20**
Rxe3 Qb6 21 Re4 Rxc3 22 Bc4?!
22 Bd3 **Qg7 23 Bb3** 23 h4 Qf6 24
Qg4? h5!∓ **Rc7 24 Rd1 Qf6 25 Qg4**
h6 Δ Qg5 **26 Rb4? h5! =+ 27 Qe4**
27 Qxh5 Rh8 28 Qg4 Rh4 -+ **Rd8**
28 Rxd8 Qxd8 29 h4 Qf6 30 g3?
30 Rxb7= **b5 31 Bd5? Qe7 32 c4 Rd7**
33 Rb3 bxc4 34 Bxc4 Nf5 35 Qe1
Nd4 36 Rd3 Nxf3 37 Qd1 Rxd3 38
Qxd3 a5 39 Bd5 Nd4 40 Qg2 Qd6
41 Qc4?? Nf5 -+ 42 Qf3 Qa3+ 0-1
Kurajica

250 Kavalek-Olafsson Tilburg 77
1 e4 c5 2 Nf3 Nc6 3 d4 cxd4 4 Nxd4
e6 5 Nc3 a6 6 g3 Qc7 7 Bg2 b5?!
8 0-0 Bb7 9 Re1 9 Nxc6 Qxc6 10
Re1 Bc5 11 Nd5 Ne7 Timman-
Olafsson, Reykjavik 75 **Ne5?!** N 9...d6
10 a4 b4 11 Nd5!±; 9...Rc8 10 Nd5!

♕b8 11 a4! ♘xd4 12 ♕xd4 ♖c4 13
♕d3± Ciric-Janosevic, Titovo Uzice
66 **10 ♗f4 f6** 10...d6 11 a4 b4 12
♘a2± **11 a4 b4 12 ♘a2 h5?!** 12...♖c8
13 c3 bxc3 14 ♘xc3 ♘e7 15 ♖c1
♕b8 += **13 c3 g5 14 ♗e3 bxc3 15
♘xc3± ♕b8** 15...♘e7 16 ♘db5 **16 a5
♗e7 17 ♘a4 ♘c8 18 ♖c1 h4 19 ♕b3
hxg3 20 hxg3 ♗c6?** +- 20...♗e7 **21
♘b6 ♘xb6 22 axb6 ♗e7** 22...♕b7 23
f4 △ ♘xc6, ♕xe6+; 23...♗xe4 24
♖c7 +-; 22...♗b7 23 ♘xe6! dxe6 24
♕xe6+ ♗e7 25 ♖c7 +- **23 ♘xc6 ♘xc6
24 b7 ♖a7 25 ♖xc6 ♖xb7 26 ♖b6
♖xb6 27 ♕xb6 ♕xb6 28 ♗xb6 ♔f7
29 ♗d4 ♖c8 30 ♗c3 ♗c5 31 ♖a1 1-0
Bellin**

251 Korsunsky-Sideif-Zade USSR 78
**1 e4 c5 2 ♘f3 e6 3 d4 cxd4 4 ♘xd4
♘c6 5 ♘c3 a6 6 g3 ♘ge7 7 ♘b3 7
♗g2?!** ♘xd4 8 ♕xd4 ♘c6= **d6** 7...♘a5
8 ♕h5!? += **8 ♗e3 ♗d7 9 ♕e2!?** +=
△ 0-0-0; 9 ♕xd6 ♘d5 -+ **♘c8 10
♗g2 ♗e7 11 f4** += **b5?! 12 e5! d5**
12...dxe5? 13 0-0-0 ♕c7 14 ♖xd7!
♕xd7 15 ♖d1 ♕c7 16 ♕f3 +- **13
0-0-0± ♘b6** 13...b4 14 ♘xd5! exd5
15 ♖xd5 ♕c7 16 ♖xd7!; 15...♘b6 16
♖xd7! **14 f5! b4** 14...0-0 15 f6!?
gxf6 16 ♗xb6 ♕xb6 17 ♕g4+ ♔h8
18 ♘xd5 exd5 19 ♕xd7±; 14...♗g5
15 ♗f4± **15 fxe6 fxe6** 15...bxc3
16 ♗xb6 +- **16 ♗xb6 ♕xb6**

Diagram

17 **♘xd5! exd5** 17...♕d8 18 ♘f6+
+- **18 e6 ♗c8 19 ♕h5+** +- **♔d8**
19...g6 20 ♕xd5 +- **20 ♕xd5+ ♔c7
21 ♘d4 ♖d8** 21...♘xd4 22 ♖xd4
♗b7 23 ♕xb7+ ♕xb7 24 ♖d7+ +-
**22 ♕xc6 ♕xc6 23 ♘xc6 ♗g5+ 24
♔b1 ♖xd1+ 25 ♖xd1 ♗xe6 26 ♘xb4**

♖e8 **27 ♘xa6+ ♔b6 28 ♖d6+ 1-0
Gufeld**

252 Gallmayer-Lengyel
Denmark 78
**1 e4 c5 2 ♘f3 e6 3 d4 cxd4 4 ♘xd4
♘c6 5 ♘c3 a6 6 g3 ♘ge7!? 7 ♗g2 7
♘de2!?** ♘xd4 8 ♕xd4 ♘c6 9 ♕d1
d6 10 a4 ♗e7 11 0-0 ♕c7= 12 ♗f4
0-0 13 ♕d2 ♖d8 14 ♖ad1 ♗e5 15
b3 ♗d7 16 ♘e2 b5 17 axb5 axb5
18 ♘d4 ♖ac8 =+ 19 ♕b4 ♘g6 20
♗d2 ♕b8 21 c3 ♕b7 22 ♕a3 d5 23
b4 dxe4 24 ♖fe1 f5 25 f3!? e5 26
fxe4 ♕b6 27 ♗e3 exd4 28 ♗xd4 ♕c7
29 exf5 ♗xf5 30 ♕a2+ ♔h8 31 ♕f7
♗f6 32 ♕xc7 ♖xc7 33 ♗xf6 ♖xd1!
34 ♖xd1 gxf6 0-1

Caro-Kann

253 Durao-Silva (3) 78
**1 e4 c6 2 ♘c3 d5 3 ♘f3 ♗g4 4 h3
♗h5!? 5 g4 ♗g6 6 exd5 cxd5 7 ♘e5
♘c6 8 ♗b5 ♖c8 9 d4 e6 10 h4?!** 10
♕e2 ♗b4 11 h4 ♘ge7 12 h5 ♗e4
13 f3 0-0 14 ♗xc6 ♘xc6 15 ♘xc6
♖xc6 16 0-0 ♗xc3 17 bxc3 ♖xc3 18
♗d3 ♖xc2 19 fxe4 dxe4 ½-½ Durao-
Silva (5) 78 **f6 11 ♘xg6 hxg6 12
♕d3 ♔f7 13 h5 gxh5 14 gxh5 ♘ge7
15 ♗e3 ♘f5 16 ♗xc6 ♖xc6 17 0-0-0**
17 ♘e2∓ Fischer-Smyslov, Jugoslavia

1 e4 c6 2 d4 d5 3 ♘c3 dxe4 4 ♘xe4 ♘d7/♗f5

59 ♗b4 18 ♘e2 ♕a5 19 a3 ♗d6 20
♗f4? 20 ♘g3! ♕a6 21 ♕f3? 21 ♕xa6∓
♕c4 22 ♖d2 ♗xf4 23 ♘xf4 ♘xd4 −+
24 ♕g4 ♘b3+ 25 ♔d1 ♗xd2 26 ♕g6+
♔e7! 27 ♕xg7+ ♔d6 28 ♕xh8 ♕xc2+
0-1

254 Chiburdanidze-Kushnir (4) 78
1 e4 c6 2 d4 d5 3 ♘d2 dxe4 4 ♘xe4
♘d7 5 ♗c4 ♘gf6 6 ♘g5 e6 7 ♕e2 ♘b6
8 ♗d3 h6 9 ♘5f3 c5 10 dxc5 ♘bd7
10...♗xc5 11 ♘e5 ♘bd7 12 ♘gf3
♘xe5 13 ♘xe5 0-0 14 0-0 b6 15
♖d1 ♕e7 16 b4 ♗d6 11 ♘e5 ♘xe5
12 ♕xe5 ♘d7 12...♕a5+ 13 ♗d2 ♕xc5
14 ♘f3 ♕xe5+ 15 ♘xe5 ♗c5 16 ♗e2
♘e4 13 ♕e2 ♘xc5 14 ♗b5+ ♗d7 15
♗xd7+ 15 ♗d2 ♗xb5 16 ♕xb5+ ♕d7
17 ♕e2 ♕d5! ♕xd7 16 ♘f3 ♗d6 17
0-0 0-0 18 b3 ♖fd8 19 ♗b2 ♕c6 20
♖ad1 ♕e4 21 ♕xe4 ♘xe4 22 ♖d4
f5?! 22...♘f6 23 ♖fd1 ♖dc8

24 c4! 24 ♖xd6 ♘xd6 25 ♖xd6
♖xc2 26 ♖d2 ♖ac8! ♖c6 25 ♘e5!
♖a6 26 f3! ♗xe5 27 ♖d8+ ♖xd8 28
♖xd8+ ♔f7 29 ♗xe5 ♘f6 30 ♖b8!
♖xa2 31 ♖xb7+ ♔g6 32 ♖e7 32 c5
♖c2 33 b4 ♖a3 33 c5 ♖xb3 34 c6
♖b1+ 35 ♔f2 ♖c1 36 c7 f4! 36...
♘d5 37 ♖xg7+ ♔h5 38 ♔g3! Δ ♔h3,
g4+ 37 ♗xf4 ♖c2+ 38 ♔e1 38 ♔f1
♘d5 39 ♖e8 ♘xc7 40 ♖c8 ♖c4! 41

♘g3 ♘d5! ♘d5 39 ♖e8 ♘b6? 39...
♘xc7 40 ♖c8 ♖c4! 41 ♗g3 (41 ♗xc7?
a5) e5! 42 ♗xe5 ♖c5 43 ♗d6 ♖d5
44 ♗xc7 ♖c5; 39...♗xf4 40 c8♕
♖xc8 41 ♖xc8 ♘xg2+ 42 ♔f2 ♘f4
40 ♗e5 ♔f7 41 ♖b8 g5 42 ♖h8 ♔g6
43 ♖f8 ♖c6 44 g4! h5 45 ♖f6+ ♔h7
46 gxh5 ♔g8 47 ♖h6 1-0 47...a5 48
♖h8+ ♔f7 49 h6 ♖c5 50 ♗d6 ♖c6
51 h7 ♔g6 52 c8♕ +−; 47...♖c5 48
♖h8+ ♔f7 49 ♗d6 ♖c6 50 h6 ♖xd6
51 ♖d8 +−

255 Larsen-Rogoff
Lone Pine 78
1 e4 c6 2 d4 d5 3 ♘c3 dxe4 4 ♘xe4
♘d7 5 ♘f3 ♘gf6 6 ♘xf6+ ♘xf6 7 ♘e5
♘d7 7...♗f5 8 c3 e6? 9 g4 ♗g6 10
h4 h5 11 g5 ♘d5 12 ♘xg6 fxg6 13
♕c2 Karpov-Hort, Bugojno 78 8
♗f4 ♘xe5?! 9 ♗xe5 ♕b6 10 ♗d3!
f6 10...♕xb2? 11 0-0 e6 12 ♕e2!
11 ♗g3 ♗e6 11...♘f5 12 ♗xf5 ♕a5+
13 ♕d2 ♕xf5± 12 ♕e2 ♗f7 13 0-0
e6 13...♕xb2 14 ♖ab1 ♕xd4 15 ♖fd1
14 c3 0-0-0 15 ♗c4 ♖e8 16 b4 h5 17
h4 ♖g8 18 ♕f3 ♗e7 19 a4 g5 20 a5
♕d8 21 a6 gxh4 22 axb7+ ♔xb7 23
♖xa7+ 1-0 23...♔xa7 24 ♕xc6 +−

256 Tal-Vukic Bugojno 78
1 e4 c6 2 d4 d5 3 ♘d2 dxe4 4 ♘xe4
♗f5 5 ♘g3 ♗g6 6 ♗c4 e6 7 ♘1e2 ♘f6
8 h4 8 ♘f4 ♗d6 9 ♗b3 ♕c7 10 ♕f3
♘bd7 11 h4 e5!= h6 9 ♘f4 ♗h7
10 0-0 10 ♕e2!? ♗d6 11 ♗e3 ♘bd7 12
♘gh5 ♘xh5 13 ♘xh5 ♖g8 14 g4
♕c7!= ♗d6 11 ♘xe6?! fxe6 12 ♗xe6
♕c7!? 12...♘bd7 13 ♖e1 ♕c7 14
♗g8+ ♔f8 15 ♗xh7 ♖xh7 16 ♘f5
g6 17 ♗xh6+ ♔g8 18 ♘xd6 ♕xd6
19 ♗g5 ♖e7 20 ♕d3 ♔g7 21 ♕g3
♖xe1+ 22 ♖xe1 ♕xg3 23 fxg3 ♖f8!∓
Tal-Botvinnik 60

1 e4 c6 2 d4 d5 3 ♘c3 dxe4 4 ♘xe4 ♗f5

13 ♘h5? 13 ♖e1!? ♘bd7; 13...♗xg3? 14 fxg3 ♕xg3 15 ♗c8+ +− **♖f8 14 c4 ♗g6!∓ 15 ♘g3 ♘bd7 16 c5 ♗xg3 17 fxg3 ♘d5 18 ♖e1** 18 ♗xd5? cxd5 19 ♕g4 ♖xf1+ 20 ♔xf1 ♘f8 −+ **0-0-0 19 ♕g4 ♗f7 20 ♗xd5 ♗xd5 21 ♗f4 h5! 22 ♕g5** 22 ♕xh5? ♖xf4! **♕a5** 22...♖xf4! 23 gxf4 ♘f6 24 ♖e5 ♕d7 −+ **23 ♖e2 ♕a4 24 ♖d2 ♖de8 25 ♕xg7 ♕c4?** 25...♖e4! △ ♖g8 **26 ♕g6 ♖e2 27 ♕d6! += ♖xf4 28 ♕xf4 ♗xg2** 28...♘xc5? 29 b3! ♕c3 30 ♖xe2 ♕xa1+ 31 ♔h2 ♘e6 32 ♕f6 +− **29 b3 ♕e6 30 ♖xe2 ♕xe2 31 ♕f2 ♕xf2+ 32 ♔xf2 ♗h3 33 ♖e1 ♕d8 34 ♔f3 ♗f8 35 ♖e5 ♗g4+ 36 ♔e4 ♘h7 37 ♔f4 ♕d7 38 d5 cxd5 39 ♖xd5+ ♔c6 40 ♔e5 ♘f8 41 b4 ♘d7+ 42 ♔d4 ♔b5 43 a3 ♘b8** 43...♔a4? 44 c6! bxc6 45 ♖a5+ **44 ♔g5 ♘c6+ 45 ♔c3 a5 46 ♖g7 axb4+ 47 axb4 ♘d8 48 ♖h7 b6!= 49 cxb6 ♔xb6 50 ♔c4 ♘c6 51 ♖g7 ♗e2+ 52 ♔c3 ♗f3 53 ♖g6 ♗d1 54 ♖g5 ♗e2 55 ♖c5 ♗g4 56 ♖c4 ♘e7 ½-½ Vukic**

257 Spassky-Larsen
Bugojno 78
1 e4 c6 2 d4 d5 3 ♘c3 dxe4 4 ♘xe4 ♗f5 **5 ♘g3 ♗g6 6 ♘f3 ♘d7 7 ♗d3 ♕a5+ 8 ♗d2 ♕c7 9 ♗xg6 hxg6 10 ♕e2 e6 11 ♘e4 0-0-0?** 11...♘gf6 **12 g3 c5 13 ♗f4 ♕c6 14 0-0-0 c4 15 ♘c3 ♘h6 16 d5! exd5 17 ♖xd5 ♗c5 18 ♖hd1 f6**

19 ♖d6! ♗xd6 20 ♖xd6 ♕c5 21 ♖d5 1-0

258 Ivanovic-Vukic
Jugoslavia Final 78
1 e4 c6 2 d4 d5 3 ♘c3 dxe4 4 ♘xe4 ♗f5 5 ♘g3 ♗g6 6 ♘f3 ♘d7 7 h4 h6 8 h5 ♗h7 9 ♗d3 ♗xd3 10 ♕xd3 e6 11 ♗d2 ♕c7 12 ♕e2 ♘gf6 13 0-0-0 **♗d6 14 ♘f5 ♗f4** 14...0-0 15 ♘xd6 ♕xd6 16 ♗c3 b5! Beljavsky-Bagirov, USSR Final 77 **15 ♗xf4 ♕xf4+ 16 ♘e3 b5?!** N 16...♘d5 **17 ♖dg1?! 0-0-0** 17...♘d5 18 c4 += a6 19 ♔b1 ♔b7 20 ♖c1 ♖c8 21 a4! bxa4 22 c5!± ♘d5 23 ♖c4 ♖a8 24 ♖h4 ♕f6 25 ♖xa4 ♖hb8 26 ♕d2!! △ ♘c4-d6± ♕c8 27 ♘xd5 exd5 27 cxd5 ♖f4 28 ♕e7 29 ♕d3 a5 30 ♕h7 ♕f8 31 ♖g4 +− **28 ♖a3! ♕f5+ 29 ♔c2 ♕f6 30 ♖e3 ♖b5 31 g3 ♖ab8 32 ♖f4 ♕d8** 32...♖xb2+ 33 ♔xb2 ♖xb2+ 34 ♔xb2 +− **33 ♖xf7 +− ♖8b7 34 ♖ee7 ♘f6 35 ♕f5+ ♔b8 36 ♘e5 ♖xb2+ 37 ♔c1 1-0 Maric**

142

259 Kavalek-Andersson (7) 78

1 e4 c6 2 d4 d5 3 ♘d2 dxe4 4 ♘xe4 ♘f6 5 ♘xf6+ exf6 6 c3 6 g3!? **♗d6 7 ♗d3 0-0** 7...c5 8 ♘e2 ♘c6 9 ♗e3 ♕e7 10 dxc5 ♗xc5 11 ♗xc5 ♕xc5 12 ♕c2 ♗e6 13 0-0 += Gurgenidze-Holmov, USSR Final 67 **8 ♘e2** 8 ♕c2; 8 ♔h5 ♖e8 8...♕c7? 9 ♕c2 g6 10 h4 ♗e6 11 h5 f5 12 ♗h6 ♖e8 13 0-0-0 ♘d7 14 hxg6 fxg6 15 g4± Suetin-Andersson, Sochi 73; 8...♘d7 9 0-0 ♖e8 10 ♘g3 ♘f8= **9 ♕c2 g6 10 h4 ♘d7** 10...c5!? 11 h5 f5 12 hxg6 hxg6 13 g4 ♕c7? 14 ♗g5± **11 h5 ♘f8 12 ♗h6** 12 hxg6 fxg6 13 ♔b3 ♗e6 14 ♕xb7 ♗d5 15 ♔f1= Szabo-Flohr, Groningen 46; 13 ♗h6 ♗e6 14 0-0-0 f5 15 ♔b1 b5 16 ♘c1 ♕f6 17 f4 ♗d5 18 ♖h3 ♘e6∝ Pilnik-Golombek, Amsterdam 51 **♕c7 13 0-0-0 ♗e6 14 c4 ♖ad8 15 hxg6 fxg6 16 c5 ♗e7 17 ♘f4 ♗f7 18 ♗c4 ♖d5 19 ♖de1 ♖ed8 20 ♗xd5 cxd5 21 ♖e3 ♖d7 22 ♖he1 g5 23 ♗xf8 ♗xf8 24 ♖h1 h6 25 ♘g6 ♗xc5 26 ♖c3** 26 dxc5 d4 △ d3, ♗xg6 **♗d6 27 ♖xh6 ♕g7 28 ♘f8** △ ♕h7+ **♕xf8 29 ♖h8+ ♕e7 30 ♕e2+ ♗e6 31 ♖h7+ 1-0**

260 Gaprindashvili-Andersson
Dortmund 78

1 e4 c6 2 d4 d5 3 ♘c3 dxe4 4 ♘xe4 ♘f6 5 ♘xf6+ exf6 6 ♗c4 6 c3 ♗d6 7 ♗d3 0-0 8 ♕c2 g6 9 h4± ♕e7+ 6... ♗e7 7 ♘e2 0-0 8 0-0 ♘d7 9 ♗b3 ♖e8 10 ♘f4± **7 ♕e2** 7 ♘e2?? ♕b4+ —+ **♗e6 8 ♗xe6** 8 ♗b3!? ♕xe6 9 ♗f4 ♘a6 **10 c3** 10 0-0-0 0-0-0 11 ♕xe6+ fxe6 12 ♘e2 ♘b4 13 c3 ♘d5 14 ♗g3= Shmit-Bronstein, Moscow 70 **0-0-0 11 ♕xe6+ fxe6= 12 ♘e2 c5 13 ♗e3 ♗d6 14 0-0-0 ♖he8 15 ♕c2 ♗f8** 15...c4? 16 b3± **16 ♖he1 b6 17 dxc5 ♘xc5 18 ♖xd8+ ♕xd8** 18...♖xd8 19

♘f4! e5 20 ♗xc5 ♗xc5 21 ♘e6!± **19 ♘d4 a6 20 b4! ♗d7** 20...♘a4?! 21 ♔b3 b5 22 c4!± **21 a4 e5 22 ♘b3 ♕c7 23 ♖d1 f5 24 f3 ♖e6 25 ♘d2 ♗e7** 25...♖g6 26 g3 **26 ♘c4 g6 27 ♔b3 ♗f8 28 a5! b5 29 ♘b6** 29 ♘a3 ♖d6!= **♖d6 30 ♖xd6 ♗xd6 31 ♘d5+ ♔c6 32 c4! e4! 33 f4 ♗f8** 33...bxc4+!? 34 ♔xc4 ♘f8 △ ♘e6, ♘c7=

34 cxb5+! ♔xd5?? Zeitnot 34...♔xb5! 35 ♘c3+ ♔c6 36 ♔c4 ♘e6! 37 g3 ♘c7=; 37 b5+? axb5 38 ♘xb5 ♗xf4∓ **35 bxa6 +−** ♘e6 35...♔c6 36 b5+ ♔c7 37 b6+ ♔c6 38 a7 ♔b7 39 a6+ +−; 36...♔xb5 37 a7 △ a8♕ +− **36 a7 ♘c7 37 b5 1-0** 37...♘a8 38 b6 ♔c6 39 a6! +− **Gipslis**

261 Westerinen-Rosenlund
Roskilde 78

1 e4 c6 2 d4 d5 3 ♘c3 dxe4 4 ♘xe4 ♘f6 5 ♘xf6+ gxf6 6 ♗c4 ♗f5 7 ♗f4 e6!? 8 ♕f3 ♗d6 9 ♗g3 ♕c7 10 ♕e2!? 10 ♘h4! ♗g4 11 0-0-0 ♘d7 12 d5! cxd5 13 ♗xd5 ♗f4+ 14 ♔b1 ♗xg3 14...0-0-0? 15 ♗xb7+! **15 hxg3 0-0-0? 16 ♗xb7+ ♕xb7 17 ♕c4+ ♔b8 18 ♕xg4 ♕b6 19 ♕g7 ♕xf2 20 ♖d2!** 20 ♖xd7?! ♕xg2 21 ♖hd1 ♕xf3! **♕e3 21 ♖xd7 ♖xd7 22 ♕xh8+ ♔b7 23 ♕xf6 ♕e2 24 ♘d4 1-0**

1 e4 c6 2 d4 d5 3 ♘c3 g6/3 ♗d2 g6

262 Pribyl-Pajdla CSSR 78

1 e4 g6 2 d4 c6 3 ♘c3 3 c4!? d5 4
e5 ♗g7 5 ♘c3± **d5 4 ♘f3 dxe4?**
4...♗g7; 4...♗g4 5 h3 ♗xf3 6 ♕xf3
e6 7 ♗f4 ♗g7 8 exd5 exd5 9 0-0-0
♘e7 10 g4± **5 ♘xe4 ♘bd7 6 ♗c4 ♘gf6
7 ♘eg5 ♘d5** 7...e6?! 8 0-0 ♗g7 9
♗xe6! +− **8 0-0 ♗g7 9 ♕e2 0-0 10 ♖e1
♘7f6 11 ♘e5!±** h6 12 ♘gf3 ♘g4 13
h3 ♘xe5 14 dxe5! e6 15 a4! b6 16
♖a3 a6? 16...♗b7 **17 h4!±** ♗b7 18
h5 c5 19 ♕e4 +− gxh5 20 ♗d3 f5
20...♖e8 21 c4 +− **21 exf6 ♖xf6
22 ♕h7+!?** 22 c4 ♕c7 23 cxd5 exd5±
♔f8 23 ♘e5! ♘e7 24 ♗g6 △ ♗xh6
♕d4 24...♕d5 25 ♖g3! h4 26 ♖g4
+− **25 ♖ae3! ♖d8 26 c3! ♕f4 27
♖3e2!** 27 ♗f3? ♕xe5! 28 ♖xe5 ♗xf3∞
♕h4 **28 ♗xh6 ♗xh6 29 ♕xh6+ ♔g8
30 ♗h7+ ♔h8 31 ♘f7+!** 31 ♘g6+!?
♘xg6 32 ♗xg6+ ♔g8 33 ♕h7+ ♔f8
34 ♕h8+ ♔e7 35 ♕g7+ ♔d6 36 ♕xb7
+− **♖xf7 32 ♗g6+ ♔g8 33 ♗xf7+
♔xf7 34 ♕xe6+ 1-0** 34...♔f8 35 ♕h6+
♔g8 36 ♖xe7 +− **Pribyl**

263 Tomic-Andersson
Dortmund 78

1 e4 c6 2 ♘c3 d5 3 ♘f3 g6 3...♗g4!
**4 d4 ♗g7 5 h3 dxe4 6 ♘xe4 ♘d7 7
♗f4 ♘gf6 8 ♘xf6+ ♘xf6 9 ♗e5** 9
♗c4! **0-0 10 ♗c4 b5 11 ♗b3 a5?!**
11...a6 △ ♗b7 **12 a3 ♗b7 13 0-0
♕b6 14 c4?** 14 c3 bxc4 15 ♗xc4
c5 16 dxc5 ♕xc5 17 ♕d4 ♕xd4 18
♘xd4 ♖fc8 19 ♗b5? 19 ♗e2 △ ♗f3
♖c5 20 ♖fe1 ♖d8 21 ♖ad1 e6 22 b4?
22 f4 axb4 23 axb4 ♖xe5 24 ♖xe5
♘e4? 24...♘h5! **25 f4 ♗xe5 26 fxe5
♘c3 27 ♖c1 ♖xd4 28 ♖xc3 ♖xb4
29 ♗f1?** 29 ♗e2 ♖e4 30 ♗f3! ♖e4
0-1 Andersson

264 Kavalek-Andersson (9) 78

1 e4 c6 2 d4 d5 3 ♘d2 g6 4 h3 4 e5
♗g7 5 ♗d3 c5 6 c3 ♘c6 7 ♘e2 ♕b6 8
0-0 ♗g4 9 dxc5 ♕xc5 10 ♘b3 ♕b6
11 e6!? ♗xe6 12 ♘f4 ♘f6 13 ♘xe6
fxe6 14 ♗e3≈ Geller-Botvinnik, USSR
Final 64; 4 c3; 4 ♘gf3; 4 ♗d3 **♗g7
5 ♘gf3 ♘h6** 5...dxe4 6 ♘xe4 ♘d7
7 ♗c4 ♘gf6 8 ♘xf6+ ♘xf6 9 0-0 +=
6 ♗d3 0-0 7 0-0 f6 7...a5 8 a4 ♘a6
9 ♖e1 c5 10 e5 cxd4 11 ♘xd4 ♘c5
12 ♘2f3 ♘f5 13 ♗d2 ♘xd4 14 ♘xd4
f6 15 ♗f4 ♕b6 += Tukmakov-Spassky,
Moscow 71 **8 c4** 8 ♖e1 ♘f7 9 c4 e6
10 ♘f1 dxe4 11 ♗xe4 c5 12 dxc5
♕xd1 13 ♖xd1 f5 14 ♗c2 ♘a6 15 ♖b1
♘c5 16 b4± Vasyukov-Gurgenidze,
USSR 73 **dxe4 9 ♘xe4 ♘f5 10 ♗c2
♘a6 11 ♖e1 ♗d7 12 ♗f4 ♖e8 13
g4 ♘h6 14 ♗d2 ♗xd2 15 ♕xd2 ♘d6
16 b3 ♘f7 17 ♖e2 ♗d7 18 ♖ae1 b6
19 ♘g3 e6 20 ♕f4 ♖c7**

**21 h4 e5 22 dxe5 fxe5 23 ♘xe5 ♘e6
24 ♕d2 ♘xe5 25 ♖xe5 ♘f4 26 ♖e7
♗xg4** 26...♘h3+ 27 ♔h1 ♖xf2 28
♕h6 +− **27 ♕c3 ♘h3+ 28 ♔h1 ♖f7
29 ♖xf7 ♔xf7 30 f3 ♗e6 31 ♕e5
♕f6 32 ♕xf6+ ♔xf6 33 ♘e4+ ♔e7
34 ♘g5 ♗xg5 35 hxg5 ♖d8 36 ♖e2
♖d7 37 ♔g2 a5 38 ♗e4 ♖d6 39 ♔g3
♔d7 40 ♔f4 ♖d1 41 ♔e5 b5 42
cxb5 cxb5 43 ♖c2 a4 44 ♖c5 ♗xb3**

144

45 axb3 a3 46 ♖c2 b4 47 ♖h2 ♛e8 48 ♗d5 1-0

265 Pokojowczyk-Kuligowski
Poland Final 78
1 e4 c6 2 d4 d5 3 exd5 cxd5 4 c4 ♘f6 5 ♘c3 e6 6 ♘f3 ♗b4 7 ♗d3!? dxc4 8 ♗xc4 0-0 9 0-0 b6 10 ♛e2!? ♗b7 11 ♗g5 ♗xc3! 12 bxc3 ♘bd7 13 ♖ac1 ♛c7 14 ♗d3 14 ♘h4 ♗xf3 **15 gxf3 +=** ♘g4! **15 ♗e4 ♘xe4 16 ♛xe4 ♘gf6 17 ♛e2** 17 ♛d3 ♖ac8 18 c4 ♛b7 19 ♖c2 ♖c7 20 ♖fc1 ♖fc8 21 ♛b3 ♛a6 =+ ♖ac8 **18 c4 ♛b7 19 ♖fe1! h6 20 ♗f4 ♖c6 21 ♘e5! ♘xe5 22 dxe5 ♘h7 23 ♖c3 ♖fc8 24 ♛g4 ♔h8 25 ♖g3? g5∓ 26 h4? h5! −+ 27 ♛xh5 gxf4 28 ♖g4 ♖xc4 29 ♖d1 ♛e7 30 ♖d3 ♖g8 31 ♖xg8+ ♔xg8 32 ♛d1 ♛xh4 33 ♖h3 ♛g5 34 ♖xh7 f3! 0-1 Kuligowski**

266 Banas-Meduna
CSSR Final 78
1 e4 c6 2 d4 d5 3 exd5 cxd5 4 c4 ♘f6 5 ♘c3 e6 6 ♘f3 ♗e7 7 cxd5 ♘xd5 8 ♗d3 ♘c6 9 0-0 0-0 10 ♖e1 ♘f6 11 a3 b6 12 ♗g5 12 ♗c2 ♗a6!? **♗b7 13 ♗c2 ♖c8 14 ♛d3 g6 15 ♖ad1 ♘d5 16 ♗h6 ♖e8** 16...♘xc3?! 17 bxc3 ♖e8 18 c4!± **17 h4** 17 ♗a4 a6?! 18 ♘xd5 ♛xd5 19 ♛e3 ♗f6 20 ♗b3 ♛h5 21 d5 +− Smyslov-Karpov, USSR 71; 17...♘xc3!? 18 bxc3 ♗xa3 19 ♖a1 ♗f8 20 ♗xf8 △ ♗xc6, ♖xa7=; 19 c4 ♗f8!∓ **♘xc3 18 bxc3**

Diagram

25 ♘xh7?= 25 ♘e4! fxe4 26 fxe4!± **♖xh7 26 ♛g5 ♘f7 ½-½** 27 ♛xg6+ ♔h8 28 ♛f6+ ♔g8 29 ♛g6+ = **Banas**

Scandinavian

267 Kapengut-Shereshevsky
Minsk 78
1 e4 d5 2 exd5 ♘f6 3 d4 ♘xd5 4 ♘f3 ♗g4 5 h3 5 c4 ♘b6 6 c5!? ♘d5! 7 ♛b3 b6? 8 ♘e5 1-0 Timman-Bakkali; 6...♗xf3 7 ♛xf3 ♘d5 8 ♛b3! b6 9 ♗g5! ♛d7 10 ♘e3± Suetin-Shamkovich, USSR 64; 6...♘bd7 7 ♛b3 ♘c6 8 ♗e3 ♗xf3 9 gxf3 e5 10 ♛xb7 ♖xd4 11 ♗xd4 exd4 12 ♘h3 ♗xc5 Szilagyi-Salan, Hungary 72 **♗h5 6 c4** 6 g4 ♗g6 7 ♘e5 ♘d7 8 ♘xg6 hxg6 9 ♗g2 c6 10 c4 ♘5b6 11 ♛e2 ♘f6 += Razuvaev-Gipslis, USSR 72; 7...♘c6 8 ♘xc6 bxc6 9 ♗g2 ♛d6 10 ♘a3 h5 Alexandria-Gaprindashvili, Tbilisi 76 **♘b6 7 ♛b3!** N 7 c5 ♘6d7 8 ♛b3 ♘c6 9 d5 ♗xf3 10 ♛xf3 ♘d4 11 ♛e4 e5 12 dxe6 ♘xe6 13 ♛xb7 ♗xc5 Klovan-Gutman, Riga 72 **♗xf3 8 ♛xf3 ♛xd4 9 ♛xb7 e5 10 ♘c3** 10 c5 ♗xc5 11 ♗b5+ = **♗b4 11 ♗d2 0-0 12 0-0-0 ♛xf2?!** 12...♗xc3 13 ♗xc3 ♛xf2 14 ♗d3 += **13 ♘d5!± ♘xd5** 13...♗xd2+ 14 ♖xd2 ♛e1+ 15 ♖d1 ♛a5 16 ♘xc7+ **14 ♛xa8 ♘e3 15 ♗xe3 ♛xe3+ 16 ♔b1 e4 17 ♛b7± c5 18 h4 h6 19 a3 ♗d2**

20 ♕d5 ♗a5 21 ♖h3 ♕f4 22 ♕xc5 ♗b6 23 ♕d6 ♕f2 23...♕g4 24 ♖g3 ♕xh4 25 ♕e5! g6 26 ♖d6 ♔h7 27 ♔a2 ♘c7 28 ♖h3 +− 24 ♕e7 e3? +− 24...♕f5 25 ♕b7± 25 ♖f3 ♕g1 26 ♕e4 ♘a6 27 b4 e2 28 ♗xe2 ♕xg2 29 ♗d3 1-0 Kapengut

Spanish

268 Tunik-V.Zhuravlev USSR 78
1 e4 e5 2 ♘f3 ♘c6 3 ♗b5 a6 4 ♗a4 d6 5 d4 5 0-0 ♗d7 6 c4 ♘f6 7 ♘c3 ♗g4 8 h3 ♗xf3 9 ♕xf3 += Romanishin-Smyslov, Hastings 76/77; 5 c4!?; 5 ♗xc6+ bxc6 6 d4 f6 7 ♘c3 ♘e7 8 ♗e3 ♗e6!? 9 ♕d2 ♕b8 10 dxe5! fxe5 11 ♘g5 △ 0-0-0 += Ciocaltea-Tatai, Torremolinos 77 b5 5...exd4 6 ♘xd4 ♘e7 += 6 ♗b3 ♘xd4 7 ♘xd4 exd4 8 ♗d5!? 8 a4=; 8 c3!? dxc3 9 ♘xc3 ♘f6 10 0-0 ♗e7 11 ♖e1 △ ♗g5≈ ♖b8 9 ♕xd4 9 ♗c6+ ♗d7 10 ♗xd7+ ♕xd7 11 ♕xd4 ♘f6 12 ♘c3 ♗e7 13 0-0 ♗d7 9...♘f6=; 9...♗b7!? 10 c3 ♘f6 11 0-0 11 ♘g5 ♗e7 12 ♗b3= ♗e7= 12 h3!? N 12 ♗b3= ♘xd5 13 exd5 0-0 14 ♗e3 ♗f6 15 ♕d2 15 ♕d3 ♕c8!? ♖e8 16 ♘a3! △ ♘c2, ♗d4 += b4 16...♗f5 17 ♘c2 ♗xc2 18 ♕xc2 ♕d7= 17 cxb4 ♖e4 18 ♘c2 ♗xb2 19 ♖ae1 ♖c4 19...♗b5 20 ♘d4!

20 ♗a7! ♖b7 21 ♕e2 += ♗b5 22 a4! ♖xc2 23 ♕xc2 ♗xf1 24 ♕c6! ♔f8 25 ♕xb7 ♗d3 26 ♗b8 +− ♗d4 27 ♗xc7 ♗xf2+!? 28 ♔h1 28 ♔xf2 ♕h4+ 29 ♔f3 ♕xe1 30 ♘xd6+ +− 1-0 Gufeld

269 Kruszynski-Pytel Poland 78
1 e4 e5 2 ♘f3 ♘c6 3 ♗b5 a6 4 ♗a4 d6 5 0-0 ♗d7 6 c3 ♘f6 7 ♖e1 g6 8 d4 ♕e7 9 d5 9 c4!? Parma-Pytel, Dortmund 75 ♘d8!? 10 c4 ♗g7 11 ♘c3 0-0 12 ♗xd7 12 b4! ♘xd7 13 ♖b1 f5 14 b4 ♘f7 15 exf5?! gxf5 16 ♘d4 ♘d8 17 ♕h5 ♕f6! 18 ♘de2 18 ♗g5 exd4 19 ♗xf6 ♘xf6 20 ♕h4 dxc3∓ ♕g6 19 ♕xg6 hxg6∓ 20 c5?! ♖f7! 21 ♘a4 ♗f8 22 cxd6 ♗xd6 23 ♗e3 b6 24 f4 ♘b7 25 ♘ac3 ♖e8 26 fxe5 ♘xe5 27 ♘f4 ♘c4 28 ♘e6 ♗e5 29 ♘d1 ♖d7 30 ♗f2 ♘d2 31 ♖c1 ♘e4 32 ♘e3 ♘d8! 33 ♘xd8 ♖dxd8 34 h3 ♗c3 35 ♖e2 ♗xb4 36 ♖xc7 ♗c5 37 ♗h4 g5 38 ♔h1 gxh4 39 ♘xf5 ♘g3+ 39...♘f2+ 40 ♖xf2 ♗xf2?? 41 ♘h6+ =; 40...♖e1+ △ ♗xf2 40 ♘xg3 hxg3 0-1 Pytel

270 Honfi-Szegi Subotica 78
1 e4 e5 2 ♘f3 ♘c6 3 ♗b5 a6 4 ♗a4 ♘f6 5 d4 exd4 6 0-0 ♗e7 7 ♖e1 b5 8 ♗b3 8 e5!? d6 9 ♗d5 ♘xd5?! 9...♗d7 10 ♗xc6 ♗xc6 11 ♘xd4 ♗d7= 10 exd5 ♘e5 11 ♘xd4 0-0 12 a4! 12 f4? ♘g4 13 ♕d2 ♘g6∓ ♗d7 12...♗b7?? 13 axb5 ♗xd5? 14 ♘f5 ♗e6 15 ♘xe7+ ♕xe7 16 f4 +−; 12...bxa4± 13 ♘c3 b4 14 ♘e4 a5 15 ♘g3 ♖e8 15...♘c4? (△ ♘b6) 16 ♕e2! 16 b3 c5?! 16...♗f6! 17 ♘e4! ♗g4 18 f3 ♘xf3+! −+; 17 ♗b2!± 17 dxc6 ♘xc6 18 ♘b5 ♘e5 19 ♗b2 19 ♘xd6? ♗xd6 20 ♕xd6 ♘f3+ −+ ♗xb5?! 19...♗c6 20 axb5 ♕c7 21

♞f5 ♗f8 22 ♔h1 22 f4?! ♕c5+ 23 ♗d4
♘f3+ 24 ♕xf3 ♕xf5= g6 23 ♞e3 ♗g7
24 ♗d4± 24 f4? ♘g4 ♕b7 25 b6 f6?
25...♖e6 26 ♕d2± 26 ♕e2! ♞c6 27
♕c4+ ♔h8 28 ♕d5 ♖eb8 29 ♞c4
♞xd4? 30 ♖e8+ ♖xe8 31 ♕xb7 ♗xc2
32 ♖d1 a4 33 bxa4 b3 34 ♞xd6
♖eb8 35 ♕d5 h5 36 ♕xb3 1-0 Honfi

271 Grunberg-Vogt DDR 78
1 e4 e5 2 ♞f3 ♞c6 3 ♗b5 a6 4 ♗a4
♞f6 5 d4 exd4 6 0-0 ♗e7 7 ♖e1
7 e5 0-0 8 e5 ♞e8 8...♘d5 9 ♗f4 b5
10 ♗b3 d5 11 c3 ♗g4 12 h3 ♗h5 13
g4 ♗g6 14 ♞xd4 14 cxd4 ♘b4 15
♘g3 a5 16 a3 ♘d3 17 ♖e2 c5 18 dxc5
♘c7= ♞xd4 15 cxd4 15 ♕xd4 c6=
c6 15...f5 16 ♗e3 f5 17 f4 ♞c7 18
♞c3 ♕d7 19 ♕f3 ♔h8 20 ♖ad1 ♞e6
21 ♖f1 21 ♘xd5? fxg4 22 hxg4 ♘g5
−+ ♖ad8 22 ♕g2 h6 23 ♞e2 ♗h7 24
♞g3 24 g5 g6 25 gxh6 ♖g8 △ g5,
♗f8 g5! 25 ♗c2 25 gxf5 ♗xf5 26 ♘xf5
♖xf5 27 ♗c2? ♖xf4∓ gxf4 26 ♗xf4
fxg4 27 ♗xh6 ♖xf1+ 28 ♖xf1 ♗g5!

29 ♗xg5? 29 ♗xh7 ♕xh7 30 ♗xg5
♘xg5 31 hxg4 ♘h3+ 32 ♔h1 ♘f2+ =;
29...♗xh6 30 ♗f5± ♞xg5 30 ♗f5
♕a7 31 ♗xg4 ♕xd4+ 32 ♕f2 ♕xe5
33 ♕f6+ ♕xf6 34 ♖xf6 d4 35 ♖xc6
d3 36 h4 ♞e4?! 36...♘f7 37 ♗d1 ♘e5

38 ♖xa6 ♘c4 39 ♞f1 ♘xb2 40 ♞e3
=+ 37 ♞xe4 ♗xe4 38 ♖h6+! ♗h7 39
♔f2 ♖d4 ½-½ 40 ♗d1 ♔g7 41 ♖xa6
♖xh4= Vogt

272 Marjanovic-Honfi Subotica 78
1 e4 e5 2 ♞f3 ♞c6 3 ♗b5 a6 4 ♗a4
♞f6 5 d4 exd4 6 0-0 ♗e7 7 e5 ♞e4
8 ♞xd4 0-0 9 ♞f5 d5 10 ♗xc6 bxc6
11 ♞xe7+ ♕xe7 12 ♖e1 ♖e8 13 f3
♞d6 14 b3 N 14 ♗f4= f6 15 ♗b2
♞f7 16 f4 fxe5 17 fxe5 ♗f5 18 ♔h1
♕h4 18...♕c5?! 19 ♘d2! 19 ♞d2 ♖e6
20 ♞f3 ♕h5 21 ♞d4 ♗g4 22 ♕d3
♖h6 22...♘xe5? 23 ♕g3 ♖e7 24
♖e3 c5 25 ♖ae1 += 23 ♕g3 c5! 24 e6!
24 ♘f3? ♗xf3 25 gxf3 ♘g5 26 ♗c1
♕xh2+ 27 ♕xh2 ♖xh2+ 28 ♔xh2
♘xf3+ −+; 26 ♖f1 ♖f8 27 ♗c1 ♘e4
−+ ♞d6 25 ♞c6 ♖e8 26 ♖e5 ♞f5
27 ♖xf5 27 ♕f4?? g5 −+ ♕xf5 28
♕xc7 ♕f8!? 28...d4!? 29 ♞e7+ ♖xe7
30 ♕xe7 ♖xe6 =+ 29 ♕f7+! 29 e7?
♕f7 30 ♞e5 ♕f4! −+ ♕xf7 30 exf7+
♔xf7 31 ♞e5+ ♖xe5 32 ♗xe5 ♖e6
33 ♖e1 d4∓ 34 b4 cxb4 35 ♖f1+ ♔g6
36 ♗xd4 ♖e2?! 36...♗c6∓ 37 h3?
37 c3! bxc3 38 ♗xc3 ♖xa2 39 ♖a1=
♗f5 38 ♖f3 38 c3 ♗e4 39 ♖g1 bxc3
40 ♗xc3 ♖e3 −+ ♗xc2 39 ♖g3+
♔f5 40 ♖xg7 ♗e4 41 ♔g1 ♖xa2 42
♖xh7 ♖xg2+ 43 ♔f1 ♖d2 44 ♗e3
44 ♗h8 ♔f4 △ ♔e3 −+ ♗d3+! 45
♔g1 ♖e2 46 ♗d4 b3 47 ♖d7 ♔e4 48
h4 b2 49 ♗xb2 ♖xb2 50 h5 ♔e3 51
♖d6 a5 52 h6 ♗e4 0-1 Honfi

273 Tseshkovsky-Beljavsky Lvov 78
1 e4 e5 2 ♞f3 ♞c6 3 ♗b5 a6 4 ♗a4
♞f6 5 0-0 b5 6 ♗b3 ♗b7 7 d4 ♞xd4
8 ♞xd4 exd4 9 e5 9 c3 ♞e4 10 c3
dxc3?! 10...d3 11 ♕f3 ♕e7 12 ♘d2
♘c5 13 ♗d5 ♗xd5 14 ♕xd5 c6 11
♕f3 11 ♘xc3 ♞xc3 12 bxc3 ♕h4!

147

d5 **12 exd6 ♕f6!** N 12...♘xd6? 13 ♗xf7+± **13 ♖e1 0-0-0 14 dxc7 ♖d7?** 14...♖d3 15 ♕xd3? ♕xf2+; 15 ♕xf6 gxf6 16 ♘xc3 ♘xc3 17 bxc3 ♖g8 18 g3 ♗c5 19 ♗xf7 ♖g7 20 ♗f4!; 14...♔xc7 15 ♕xf6 ♘xf6 16 ♘xc3 ♗c5 17 ♗xf7 ♖hf8

15 ♕xf6 ♘xf6 16 ♘xc3 ♗d6 17 ♗g5 ♔c7 18 ♖ac1 ♔b6 18...♔b8 19 ♖cd1 (Δ ♖xd6, ♗f4) 19...♔a8 20 ♗xf6 gxf6 21 ♗xf7 **19 ♗e3+ ♔a5 20 h3! ♖c8 21 a3 b4 22 ♘a4 ♖xc1 23 ♖xc1 ♗d5 24 ♘d1 ♗e7** 24...bxa3 25 bxa3 ♗xa3 26 ♖a1 **25 axb4+ ♗xb4 26 ♘c3 ♗xc3 27 bxc3 ♗b7 28 ♖b1 1-0** 28...♘d5 29 ♗d2

274 Kupreichik-Shereshevsky
Minsk 78
1 e4 e5 2 ♘f3 ♘c6 3 ♗b5 a6 4 ♗a4 ♘f6 5 0-0 ♘xe4 6 d4 b5 7 ♗b3 d5 8 dxe5 ♗e6 9 c3 ♗c5 10 ♘bd2 0-0 11 ♗c2 ♘xf2 12 ♖xf2 f6 13 exf6 ♗xf2+ 14 ♔xf2 ♕xf6 15 ♘f1 15 ♔g1 ♘e5 16 ♗e3 ♖ae8 16...♘xf3 17 gxf3 ♖f7 18 ♔g2 ♖e8 19 ♗d4 ♕h4 20 ♔h1! ♘h3 21 ♗d3 ♕f4 22 ♘d2 ♖fe7 Medina-Moecte, corr. 74 **17 ♗c5** 17 ♔g1 ♘xf3+ 18 ♕xf3 ♕xf3 19 gxf3 ♖xf3 20 ♖e1? ♘h3 0-1 Edwards-Horner, England 72; 17 ♗d4 ♕h4+ 18 ♔g1 ♘xf3+ 19 gxf3 ♗f5 20 ♗xf5

♖xf5 21 ♕d2 ♖xf3∓ O'Connell ♗xf3 17...♖f7 18 ♘g3 ♗g4 19 ♕xd5 ♘xf3 20 gxf3 ♗xf3 21 ♕f5 ♕xf5 22 ♘xf5 ♗d5 23 ♖e1 ♖e6! 24 ♖xe6 ♗xe6 25 ♔e3 ♖xf5 26 ♗xf5 ♗xf5 27 a4 ½-½ Wittmann-Esualo, corr. 74; 18 ♘1d2 ♗f5 19 ♔g1 ♘d3? 20 ♘d4 ♕d6 21 ♕b1 ♕g6 22 ♘h4 ♖e1+ 23 ♕xe1 ♘xe1 24 ♖xe1! +- Liberzon-Rosino, Venice 74 **18 gxf3 ♖f7 19 ♔g2 h5 20 ♕d3** 20 ♘e3! Δ ♕d3 O'Connell **♕g5+ 21 ♔h1 ♗f5 22 ♕xd5 c6 23 ♕xc6 ♗d7**

24 ♕g6!± N 24 ♕d6 ♖e6 25 ♕d4? ♖e2! 26 ♘e3 ♗c6 27 ♗e4 ♗xe4 28 fxe4 ♖xh2+! -+ Maly-Samarian, corr. 65/66 **♕xc5 25 ♗b3 ♖ee7 26 ♘g3! ♕e3 27 ♕xh5 ♗e6 28 ♘f5 ♖xf5 29 ♕xf5 ♗xb3 30 axb3 ♕e2** 30...♖f7 31 ♕e4 ♕xf3+ 32 ♕xf3 ♖xf3 33 ♔g2 ♖d3 34 b4!±; 30...♕d2! **31 ♕d5+ ♔h7 32 ♕h5+ ♔g8 33 ♕d5+ ♔h7 34 ♖g1! ♖e5?** 34...♕xb2 35 ♕d3+ ♔g8 36 ♕d8+ ♔f7 37 ♖xg7+! +-; 34...a5 35 h3 a4 36 bxa4 bxa4 37 ♖g2± **35 ♕f7 1-0 Kapengut**

275 Geller-Gild.Garcia
Bogota 78
1 e4 e5 2 ♘f3 ♘c6 3 ♗b5 a6 4 ♗a4 ♘f6 5 0-0 ♘xe4 6 d4 b5 7 ♗b3 d5 8 dxe5 ♗e6 9 c3 ♗c5 10 ♘bd2 0-0 11

Spanish 9...♘a5

♗c2 f5 12 ♘b3 ♗b6 13 ♘fd4 ♘xd4
14 ♘xd4 ♗xd4 15 cxd4 15 ♕xd4!
f4 16 f3 ♘g3 17 ♖f2 17 hxg3 fxg3
18 ♕d3 ♗f5 19 ♕xf5 ♖xf5 20 ♗xf5
♕h4 21 ♗h3 ♕xd4+ = ♕h4 18 ♗d2!?
N 18 ♕d3 ♖f5 19 ♗xf4 ♖xf4 20 hxg3
♕xg3 21 ♕xh7+ ♔f7 22 ♕h2= ♖ae8
19 ♗b4 ♖f7 20 a4! ♗c8 21 axb5
♖e6 22 bxa6?? 22 h3 ♖h6 23 bxa6
♗xh3 24 gxh3 ♕xh3 25 ♖g2± ♕xh2+!
0-1 23 ♔xh2 ♖h6+ 24 ♔g1 ♖h1 mate
Sigurjonsson

276 Kurajica-Diesen Osijek 78
1 e4 e5 2 ♘f3 ♘c6 3 ♗b5 a6 4 ♗a4
♘f6 5 0-0 ♘xe4 6 d4 b5 7 ♗b3 d5 8
dxe5 ♗e6 9 ♕e2 ♗e7 9...♗c5 10 ♖d1
0-0 11 c3!? 11 c4 bxc4 12 ♗xc4 ♕d7
13 ♘c3 ♘xc3 14 bxc3 f6 += ♕d7
12 ♗e3 f5 13 ♘bd2 13 exf6!? ♘a5
14 ♘d4 c5 15 ♘xe6 ♕xe6 16 f4 +=
♖ad8 17 ♘xe4 fxe4 18 ♕f2! ♘xb3
18...♕c6? 19 f5± 19 axb3 d4 20
cxd4 ♕xb3 21 ♔h1 21 h3? ♗h4∓
cxd4 22 ♖xd4 ♖xd4 23 ♗xd4 ♖d8
24 h3± a5 25 f5 ♕d5 26 f6 ♗f8
26...♕xd4?? 27 fxe7 +- 27 ♗b6 ♖b8
28 ♖xa5 ♕xe5 29 ♗d4 e3 Zeitnot
29...♕c7 30 ♖a1 gxf6!; 30 fxg7 ♕xa5
31 gxf8♕ ♖xf8 32 ♕g3+ ♔f7 33 ♕g7+
♔e8 34 ♕e5+ ♔d7 35 ♕d5+ +-;
30...♗xg7 31 ♖a7 ♖b7 32 ♖xb7
♕xb7 33 ♕g3 +- 30 f7+ +- ♔h8
31 ♕xe3 ♕xe3 32 ♗xe3 ♖b7 33
b4 h6 34 ♖a8 ♖xf7 35 ♗c5 ♔g8 36
♖b8 g5 37 ♔g1 ♔g7 38 ♖xb5 ♖d7
39 ♔f2 ♖d2+? 40 ♔e3 ♖d7 41 ♔e4
♗e7 42 ♗xe7 ♖xe7+ 43 ♖e5 1-0
Kurajica

277 Silva-Durao (2) 78
1 e4 e5 2 ♘f3 ♘c6 3 ♗b5 a6 4 ♗a4
♘f6 5 0-0 ♗e7 6 ♖e1 b5 7 ♗b3 d6 8
c3 0-0 9 h3 ♘a5 10 ♗c2 c5 11 d4 ♕c7

12 ♘bd2 ♘c6 13 dxc5 dxc5 14 ♘f1
♖d8 14...♗e6 15 ♘e3 ♖ad8; 14...
♗d6; 14...h6!? 15 ♕e2 ♗e6 15...♘h5;
15...♖b8 16 ♘e3 c4 16...g6 17 ♘g5
♗c8 18 ♘d5± 17 ♘f5 17 ♘g5?! ♗c5
18 ♘xe6 fxe6 19 b3 ♗xe3 20 ♗xe3
♘d4!= Matanovic-Pilnik, Stockholm
52 h6! 17...♘d7 18 ♘g5 ♗xg5 19
♗xg5 f6 20 ♗e3±; 18...♘c5? 19
♘xg7 +- Torre-Loheac-Amoun,
Siegen 70 18 ♘3h4 ♗f8 19 ♕f3 ♘d7
20 ♗e3 20 a4!? ♕h7 21 g4 g6 22 g5
h5 22...gxf5 23 exf5 +- 23 ♘g3 ♘e7
24 ♔h2 ♗g7 25 ♘hf5 ♘c5 26 ♖g1
♘d3 Δ ♘f4 27 ♘xg7 ♔xg7 28 ♕f6+
♔f8! 29 ♗xd3 ♘g8! 30 ♕h8 ♖xd3
31 a4 bxa4! 32 ♖xa4 ♗xh3

33 ♔xh3?! 33 ♗c1!! ♗d7 34 b3!
♗xa4 35 ♗a3+ ♖d6 36 ♖d1! ♖ad8
37 ♕xe5; 35...♔e8 36 ♕xg8+ Δ
♕xa8 ♖xe3! 34 fxe3 ♕d7+ 35 ♔h2?!
35 ♘f5!? gxf5 36 g6; 36 ♖b4!? ♕xa4
36 ♕xe5 ♕b5 37 ♕d6+ ♘e7 38 ♖f1?
h4? Zeitnot 38...♕xg5 39 ♘e2 ♕xb2
40 ♕d1 ♔e8 41 ♔h3 ♖d8 ½-½ 42
♘d4!? ♕xc3 43 ♕f3 ♔d7 44 e5 ♔c7
45 e6

278 Tanner-Falkenstein
Switzerland 78
1 e4 e5 2 ♘f3 ♘c6 3 ♗b5 a6 4 ♗a4
♘f6 5 0-0 ♗e7 6 ♖e1 b5 7 ♗b3 0-0

149

8 c3 d6 9 h3 ♞a5 10 ♝c2 c5 11 d4
♛c7 12 ♞bd2 ♞c6 13 dxc5 dxc5 14
♞f1 h6 14...♝e6; 14...♖d8 15 ♞e3
♝e6 16 ♞h2 ♖ad8 17 ♛e2 ♛c8 18
♞hg4 ♝xg4 19 hxg4 b4 20 ♝b3 a5
21 ♞f5 ♞h7 22 ♝c4 ♝f6 22...♞g5 23
♝xg5 hxg5 24 ♞d5 ♝xd5 25 exd5
♖xd5?? 26 ♛e4+ 23 g3 ♝xf5 24
gxf5 ♞e7 25 ♚g2 g5 26 ♖h1 26
fxg6+?! ♞xg6 ♚g7 27 ♛h5 ♞g8 28
♝e3 ♛b7 29 ♛g4 ♞e7? 29...♛e7 30
♖xh6! +- ♚xh6 31 ♝xg5+ ♝xg5
31...♚g7 32 ♞xf6+ ♚xf6 33 ♛h4+
♚g7 34 ♛g5+ ♞g6 35 f6+ ♚g8 36
♛xg6+ +- 32 ♖h1+ ♚g7 33 ♛xg5+
♞g6 34 f6+ 1-0

279 Westerinen-Rajna Roskilde 78

1 e4 e5 2 ♞f3 ♞c6 3 ♝b5 a6 4 ♝a4
♞f6 5 0-0 ♝e7 6 ♖e1 b5 7 ♝b3 d6 8
c3 0-0 9 h3 9 d4 ♝g4 10 d5 ♞a5
11 ♝c2 c6 12 h3 ♝xf3 13 ♛xf3 cxd5
14 exd5 ♞c4 15 ♞d2 ♞b6 16 ♞f1
♞bxd5 17 ♞g3 ♞a5 10 ♝c2 c5 11
d4 ♛c7 12 ♞bd2 cxd4 13 cxd4 ♝d7
14 ♞f1 ♖ac8 15 ♞e3 15 ♞d3 ♞c6
16 ♝e3 ♞b4 17 ♖c1 ♛b8 Rabar-
Pirc 49; 15 ♖e2 ♖fe8 16 ♞g3 ♖fe8
16 b3 ♞c6 17 ♝b2 ♝d8 18 ♖c1 ♛a7
19 dxe5 dxe5 20 ♞d5 h6 21 a3 ♞h7
22 b4 ♞g5 23 ♝b3 ♝e6 24 ♞xe5 ♞xe5
25 ♝xe5 ♖xc1 26 ♛xc1 ♝xh3 27
♛b2 27 ♛c3 ♝b6 ♛d7 28 ♖e3 ♝xg2
28...♛g4 29 f3 29 ♚xg2 ♛g4+ 30
♝g3 ♖xe4 31 ♛c3 h5 32 ♖xe4 ♛xe4+
33 f3 ♛e2+ 34 ♝f2 h4 35 ♛e3 h3+
36 ♚g3 ♛f1 37 ♛e8+ ♚h7 38 ♝c2+
g6 39 ♞f4 ♝c7 40 ♝xg6+ ♚g7 41
♝d4+ f6 42 ♝xf6+ 42 ♛e7+ ♚g8 43
♛xc7 ♛xf3+ 44 ♚h2 ♛xf6 43 ♛f8+
♚e5 44 ♛e7+ ♞e6 45 ♛xe6+ ♚d4 46
♛e4+ ♚c3 47 ♛c2+ ♚d4 48 ♛c5
mate 1-0

280 Kuzmin-Smejkal
Leningrad 77

1 e4 e5 2 ♞f3 ♞c6 3 ♝b5 a6 4 ♝a4
♞f6 5 0-0 ♝e7 6 ♖e1 b5 7 ♝b3 d6 8
c3 0-0 9 h3 ♞b8 10 d4 ♞bd7 11
c4 c6 12 ♞c3?! b4 13 ♞a4?! N 13
♞b1; 13 ♞e2 c5 14 dxc5 dxc5 15
♝c2 ♛c7 16 b3 ♝b7 17 ♝b2 g6 18
♛d2 ♞h5= 19 ♖ad1 ♖ad8 20 ♛c1
f6 21 ♞h2 ♞b8 22 ♞g4 ♖xd1 23
♛xd1 ♖d8 24 ♛c1 ♝f8 25 ♛e3 ♞c6!

26 ♞xc5 ♞d4 27 ♞xb7 ♞xc2 28 ♛c1
♞xe1 29 ♞xd8 ♞d3 30 ♞e6 ♛c6 31
♛d2 ♛xe4 32 ♚h2 ♚f7 33 f3 ♛f5
34 ♞e3 ♛xe6 35 ♛xd3 ♞f4 36 ♛e4
♛d7 37 ♝c1 ♞d3 38 ♝d2 ♞c5 39
♛d5+ ♛xd5 40 ♞xd5 a5 41 ♝e3 ½-½
Suetin

281 Geller-Romanishin USSR 78

1 e4 e5 2 ♞f3 ♞c6 3 ♝b5 a6 4 ♝a4
♞f6 5 0-0 ♝e7 6 ♖e1 b5 7 ♝b3 d6 8
c3 0-0 9 h3 ♞b8 10 d4 ♞bd7 11 ♞bd2
♝b7 12 ♝c2 ♖e8 13 ♞f1 13 b4 ♝f8
14 a4 ♞b6 15 a5 ♞bd7 16 ♝b2 ♖b8
17 ♛b1 ♞h5!?= Ljubojevic-Karpov,
Manila 2 76 ♝f8 14 ♞g3 14 ♝g5 h6
15 ♝h4 c5?! 16 dxe5 dxe5 17 ♞3h2
♛c7 18 ♛f3 += Tal-Smejkal, Biel 76;
15...g5 16 dxe5 ♞xe5 17 ♞g3 ♞ed7=
Romanishin-Kraidman, Hastings 76/7
g6 14...c5 15 dxe5 dxe5 16 ♞f5 +=

15 a4 c5 16 d5 16 b3?! d5! 17 ♘xe5
♘xe4 18 ♘xe4 dxe4 19 ♗f4 cxd4
20 cxd4 f6 =+ Westerinen-Timman,
Reykjavik 76 **♖b6** 16...c4 17 ♗g5
♖b8 18 ♕d2 ♘c5 19 ♘h2 ♗c8 20
axb5 axb5 21 h4!? += Ljubojevic-
Portisch, Milan 75; 19 axb5 axb5
20 ♘h2!? ♗c8 21 ♖f1! += Tal-
Portisch, Varese 76; 17 ♗e3 ♘c5!
18 ♕e2 ♘fd7!= Karpov-Portisch,
Milan 75 **17 ♕e2! ♗xa4** 17...bxa4
18 c4 ♗c8 19 ♘d2 ♗h6!? Ljubojevic-
Gligoric, Manila 75 **18 ♗xa4 bxa4
19 ♖xa4 ♗c8** 19...♗g7 20 c4 ♗c8
21 ♗d2 ♖b8 22 ♖b1 ♖e7 23 ♘e1
+= Karpov-Gligoric, Milan 75; 19...
♘d7! 20 c4 ♘b6 21 ♖a3 a5∝; 20
♖a3!? ♘b6 21 ♘h2!? ♗g7 22 ♘g4
♗c8 23 c4 ♗xg4 24 hxg4 a5!= Torre-
Gligoric, Bad Lauterberg 77 **20 ♗g5!**
N 20 b3 ♖b8 21 ♖a3 ♖e7 22 c4 ♖eb7
23 ♕c2 ♘e8 Δ ♘g7, ♘f5= Karpov-
Smejkal, Moscow 77 **h6 21 ♗e3 ♖b8
22 ♖ea1** += **♘h7 23 ♕c2! h5 24 ♘d2
♗e7 25 ♘c4 ♗g5?! 26 ♕d2! h4 27
♘f1 ♔g7**

28 ♘xd6!± ♕xd6 28...♗xe3? 29
♘xe8+ +− **29 ♗xg5 ♘xg5 30 ♕xg5
♖xb2 31 ♕xh4 ♕b6 32 ♕g5** 32 ♘e3!?
♖b1 33 ♕d2 ♗d7 34 ♖4a2! ♖b8
35 c4 ♕b3 36 ♖xb1 ♕xb1 37 ♕c2!
♕e1 38 ♕e2 ♕xe2 39 ♖xe2 ♖b4?!

39...a5!?± **40 ♖c2 ♗a4 41 ♖c1 a5 42
♘d2 f5 43 ♖a1! +−** fxe4 **44 ♖a2 ♔f8
45 ♔f1 ♗d1 46 ♖xa5 ♗c2 47 ♔e2
♔e7 48 ♔e3 ♔d6 49 ♘xe4+ 1-0**
49...♗xe4 **50 ♖a6+** Δ ♔xe4 +−
Gufeld

282 Ghinda-Lukacs Bucharest 78
**1 e4 e5 2 ♘f3 ♘c6 3 ♗b5 a6 4 ♗a4
♘f6 5 0-0 ♗e7 6 ♖e1 b5 7 ♗b3 0-0
8 c3 d5 9 d4?!** 9 exd5!? **exd4 10
e5** 10 exd5 ♘xd5 11 cxd4 ♗g4 12
♘c3 ♘b6!? =+ Levenfish-Nejmetdinov,
USSR 50 **♘e4 11 cxd4** 11 ♘xd4
♘xe5 12 f3 c5 13 fxe4 cxd4 14 cxd4
♗g4 =+ **♗g4 12 ♘c3 ♗xf3 13 gxf3
♘xf2?** 13...♘xc3! 14 bxc3 f5; 14...
♕d7 **14 ♔xf2 ♗h4+ 15 ♔e3 ♗xe1
16 ♕xe1 ♘e7 17 ♗c2 c5 18 ♘e2 ♘c6
19 ♕g3 ♕e7 20 ♔f2! cxd4 21 ♗h6
g6** 21...f6 22 exf6 ♕xf6 23 ♗g5 +−
**22 ♗xf8 ♖xf8 23 f4 ♘b4 24 ♗d3 f6
25 exf6 ♖xf6 26 a3 ♖e6 27 axb4
♖e3 28 ♕g5! ♕xg5 29 fxg5 ♖xd3
30 ♘f4 +− ♖d2+ 31 ♔g3 ♖xb2 32
♘xd5 ♔f7 33 ♖xa6 d3 34 ♖f6+ 1-0**
Ciocaltea

283 Schrancz-Hardicsay
Hungary 78
**1 e4 e5 2 ♘f3 ♘c6 3 ♗b5 a6 4 ♗a4
♘f6 5 0-0 ♗e7 6 ♖e1 b5 7 ♗b3 0-0
8 d4** 8 a4; 8 c3 d5!? **d6 9 c3 ♗g4 10
d5** 10 ♗e3 d5!? =+ **♘a5 11 ♗c2 c6
12 h3 ♗c8!?** 12...♗xf3; 12...♗d7 **13
♘xe5 13 dxc6 ♕c7 14 a4** 14 ♘bd2
Δ ♘f1, ♘g3 **♗e6 15 axb5 axb5 16
♘g5 ♕xc6! 17 ♘xe6 fxe6 18 ♘bd2
♖fc8 19 ♗d3 ♕b7!** Δ b4 =+ **20 b4
♘c4 21 ♖xa8 ♕xa8 22 ♘xc4 bxc4
23 ♗b1 ♕a1! 24 ♕c2 ♖a8 25 f4?!**
25 ♗b2= **♘d7! 26 f5 exf5 27 exf5
d5! 28 f6 ♗xf6 29 ♖xe5 ♗xb4 30
♗g5 ♗c5+ 31 ♔h2 ♖b8 32 ♗xf6 ♕xb1**

33 ♕xb1 ♖xb1 34 ♖g5 ♗f8 35 ♗d4
♖b5 −+ 36 ♔g3 g6 37 ♔f3 ♔f7 38
♖g4 ♗d6 39 ♖h4 h5 Zugzwang 40
♗h8 ♖b8! 41 ♗d4 0-1 41...♔e6 42 g3
♗e7 43 ♖f4 ♗g5 −+ Hardicsay

284 P.Toth-Perenyi Hungary 77
1 e4 e5 2 ♘f3 ♘c6 3 ♗b5 a6 4 ♗a4
♘f6 5 0-0 ♗e7 6 ♖e1 b5 7 ♗b3 0-0
8 d4 d6 9 c3 ♗g4 10 ♗e3 d5! 11
exd5 exd4 12 ♗g5? 12 dxc6 dxe3
13 ♖xe3 ♗c5 14 ♕xd8 ♖fxd8 15
♖e1 ♗xf3 16 gxf3 ♖ab8 =+; 12 ♗xd4
♘xd4 13 ♕xd4 ♗xf3 14 gxf3 ♘d7! 15
♘d2 ♗c5 16 ♕g4 f5! 17 ♕g2 ♗d6 18
♘f1 ♘e5 19 ♖e2 ♘d3 −+; 13 cxd4
♗b4 14 ♘c3 += Gulko-Geller 78

12...♘xd5!! N 12...dxc3 13 ♘xc3
♘a5 14 ♗c2 += 13 ♗xd5 ♕xd5 14
♗xe7 14 ♖xe7 ♗xf3 15 ♕xf3 ♘xe7
16 ♗xe7 ♕e5 −+ ♗xf3 15 ♕xf3 15
gxf3 ♘xe7 16 ♖xe7 ♕g5+ −+ ♕xf3
16 gxf3 ♖fe8 17 cxd4 ♗xe7 18 ♘d2
♘f5 19 ♘b3 ♘h4 20 ♖xe8+ ♖xe8 21
♖c1 g5! 22 f4? 22 ♔f1 =+ gxf4 23
♔f1 ♖e7 24 ♖c3 ♔g7 25 ♘c5 a5 26
♘a6 f3! 27 ♘xc7 b4 28 ♖c1 28
♖c2 ♘g2 −+ ♖e2 29 d5 ♘f5 30 ♘b5
♖d2 31 a3 ♖xd5 32 ♘c7 ♖d2 33
axb4 axb4 34 ♖b1 ♗d6 35 ♘a6 ♘e4
36 ♘xb4 ♖xf2+ 37 ♔g1 ♖g2+ 0-1
Adorjan

285 Katoma-Bouwer Corr. 77/78
1 e4 e5 2 ♘f3 ♘c6 3 ♗b5 a6 4 ♗xc6
bxc6 5 d4 5 ♘c3 d6 6 d4 f6 7 ♗e3
♘e7 8 ♕d3± exd4 6 ♕xd4 ♕f6 7 e5
♕g6 8 0-0 ♕xc2 8...♗b7!? 9 ♘bd2
0-0-0 10 ♘b3 c5 11 ♔c3 f6= Krogius-
Lutikov, Leningrad 55; 9 e6? fxe6 10
♘e5 ♕xg2+! 9 ♘c3 ♗b7?! 9...♘e7 10
♖e1 += Alekhine 10 ♗f4 c5 11 ♕e3
♘h6? 12 ♗xh6 gxh6 13 ♘h4! +−
△ ♖ab1, ♖fc1 ♗c6 13...♗e7 14 ♖ac1
♕xb2 15 ♖b1 ♕a3 16 ♖b3 ♕a5 17
♖xb7 ♗xh4 18 ♘d5! +− 14 ♖ab1
♗b5 15 ♖fd1 ♗e7 16 ♖d2 ♗g5 17
♖xc2 ♗xe3 18 ♘xb5 1-0 Tompa

286 G.Honfi-Hardicsay Hungary 78
1 e4 e5 2 ♘f3 ♘c6 3 ♗b5 a6 4 ♗xc6
dxc6 5 0-0 ♕d6 6 d4 6 d3; 6 ♘a3!?
exd4 7 ♘xd4 ♗d7 8 ♗e3 0-0-0 9
♘d2! ♕g6 10 ♕e2 ♘h6 11 f3 ♗d6
11...♖e8! △ f5= 12 ♘c4! ♖he8 13
♘xd6+ cxd6 14 ♕f2 f5!? 15 ♗h5
15 exf5 ♘xf5 16 ♘xf5 ♗xf5 17 c3
+= ♕xh6! 16 ♗xf5 ♗xf5 17 exf5
♕f6! 18 b4? 18 c3=; 18 g4 ♕xb2=
♕xf5 19 a4 ♖e5! −+

20 ♖fe1 ♖de8 21 c3 ♕d3 22 ♖xe5
♖xe5 23 ♕d4 ♕xd4 24 cxd4 ♖d5!
25 ♖d1 a5 26 bxa5 ♖xa5 27 d5
c5 28 ♖e1 c4! 29 ♖c1 ♖xa4 30 ♔f2
b5 31 ♔e3 ♔c7 32 ♔d4 ♖a2 33 ♖e1

♖d2+ 34 ♔c3 ♖xg2 35 ♖e8 ♖f2 36 ♖e7+ ♔b6 37 ♖xg7 ♖xf3+ 38 ♔c2 ♖h3 0-1 **Hardicsay**

287 Gonzalez-Geller Bogota 78

1 e4 e5 2 ♘f3 ♘c6 3 ♗b5 a6 4 ♗xc6 dxc6 5 0-0 f6 6 ♘e1!? N **6 d4 ♘e7 6...♗c5!? 7 d3 ♘g6 8 ♘c3 ♗e6 9 ♘e2!? ♕d7 9...♘d6= 10 ♔h1 0-0-0 11 ♗e3 h5!? 12 f4 exf4 13 ♗xf4 ♗g4?!** 13...♘xf4 **14** ♗xf4 ♗d6 **14 ♘f3 ♗xf4 15 ♗xf4 g5 16 ♗e3 h4** 16...♖g8; 16...♗d6 **17 ♕d2 h3 18 g3** += **♗e7 19 ♖f2 c5** 19...♕e8!? **20 b3 ♖hf8 21 ♖af1 b6 22 ♔g1 ♔b7 23 ♘e1 ♕e6 24 c4!± ♕d7 25 ♔c1 ♗e6 26 e5! fxe5 17 ♗xg5 ♖xf2?!** 27... ♖g8 **28 ♖xf2 ♗xg5 29 ♕xg5 e4!? 30 dxe4 ♕d1 31 ♔f1 ♕b1??** Zeitnot 31...♗g4 **32** ♕e3± **32 ♕xd8 1-0 Gufeld**

288 Baer-Snyder Corr. 78

1 e4 e5 2 ♘f3 ♘c6 3 ♗b5 ♗c5 4 c3 f5?! 4...♘f6 **5 exf5?!** 5 d4 fxe4 6 ♗xc6 dxc6 7 ♘fd2! ♗d6 8 dxe5 e3 9 exd6! N exd2+ 10 ♘xd2 ♕xd6 11 0-0 ♗e6 12 ♕h5+ g6 13 ♕g5± Stern-Snyder, corr. 78 **e4 6 d4 exf3 7 dxc5 ♕e7+** 7...fxg2 8 ♖g1 ♕e7+ 9 ♕e2!± **8 ♗e3 fxg2 9 ♖g1 ♘f6 10 ♕f3 0-0 11 ♘d2 d6 12 0-0-0** 12 cxd6 cxd6 13 0-0-0 ♘e5 14 ♕xg2 ♗xf5 =+ Vasjukov-Arseniev, USSR 62 **♘e5 13 ♕xg2 ♗xf5= 14 ♘c4?** 14 ♖de1 ♕f7; 14 f4 ♘g6 **♘d3+ 15 ♖xd3 ♗xd3 16 cxd6 cxd6 17 ♘xd6 ♗g6!∓ 18 ♗c4+ ♔h8 19 ♗c5** 19 ♘b5 ♖ac8 20 ♘b3 ♕d7! **♕e5! 20 ♕g5** 20 ♘f7+ ♖xf7 21 ♗xf7 ♕xc7 22 ♗xg6 hxg6 23 ♕xg6 ♕e7 −+ **♘d7 21 ♕xe5 ♘xe5 22 ♗e2 b6 23 ♗d4 ♘c6 24 ♗e3 ♖ad8 25 ♖d1 ♖f6 26 ♘c4** 26 ♘b5 ♖xd1+ 27 ♗xd1 ♗f7 28 ♗b3 ♔g8 29 ♘d2 ♗xb3

30 axb3 ♖f5! 31 ♔c2 ♘e5 −+ 32 ♘e4 ♘g4 33 ♗d4 ♘xh2 34 ♘d6 ♖d5 35 ♘c8 ♖d7 36 ♘xa7 ♖xa7 37 ♗xb6 ♖b7 38 ♗e3 h5 0-1 **Snyder**

289 Dorfman-Gulko (2) 78

1 e4 e5 2 ♘f3 ♘c6 3 ♗b5 ♗c5 4 c3 ♘f6 5 0-0 0-0 6 d4 ♗b6 7 ♗g5 h6 8 ♗h4 8 ♗xf6 ♕xf6 9 ♗xc6 ♕xc6 10 ♘xe5 ♕xe4 11 ♘d2 ♕f5= **d6 9 ♕d3** 9 a4 a5 10 ♖e1 ♗g4 11 ♗xc6 bxc6 12 dxe5 dxe5 13 ♘bd2 += **♕e7 10 ♘bd2 ♗d7** 10...♘b8!? 11 ♖fe1 c6 12 ♗c4 ♖d8 13 ♘f1 ♘bd7 14 ♕c2 ♘f8 15 ♘e3 ♘g6 =+ Lein-Suetin, Harkov 63; 12 ♗a4 ♘bd7 13 ♘c4 ♗c7 14 ♘e3 ♖e8 15 ♘f5 ♕f8= Wade-Redolfi, Munich 58 **11 a4** Δ ♗xc6, a5 **a6 12 dxe5 ♘xe5** 12...dxe5 13 ♗xf6 ♕xf6 14 ♕xd7 axb5 15 axb5 **13 ♘xe5 dxe5 14 ♗xf6 ♗xb5**

15 axb5 15 ♗xe7! ♗xd3 16 ♗xf8 ♗xf1 17 ♗xg7 ♗xg2 18 ♗xe5 ♖d8 19 ♗f4 ♘h3 20 ♗xh6 ♔h7 21 ♗f4 +=; 18...♘h3 19 a5 Δ ♗xc7; 16...♗xf8 17 ♖fe1 += **♕xf6 16 bxa6 ♖xa6 17 ♖xa6 bxa6 18 ♘c4 ♖d8 19 ♕e2 ♕e6 20 h3** 20 g3 f6 21 ♖a1 ♗a7 22 ♔g2 ♕c6 23 ♘a5 ♕b6 24 b4 ♔h7 25 ♖a2± Stein-Van Geet, Hamburg 65 **f6 21 ♖a1 ♗a7 22 h4 h5 23 ♘a5 ♕b6 24 g3 g6 25 ♔g2 ♔g7** 25...♖d7! 26

b4 c5 **26 ♖a2** 26 b4 c5 27 bxc5 ♕xc5
28 ♘b7 ♕xc3 29 ♘xd8! ♕xa1 30
♕c4 += ♔h8 31 ♕f7 ♕d4 32 ♕xf6+
♔h7 33 ♕f7+ ♔h8 34 ♘e6 ♕xe4+
35 ♔h2 **♖d7 27 ♘c4 ♕c6 28 ♖a5
♖d8 29 b3** 29 ♘a3!? ♖d6 30 ♘c2
♕b6 31 b4 **♔h7 30 ♖a4 ♕b7 31 ♖b4
♕c6 32 ♕f3 ♗b6 33 ♖a4 ♗a7 34 ♖a2
♔g7 35 ♖a5 ♕b7 36 ♖a4** 36 b4 +=;
36 ♖a3 += **♕xb3 37 ♖xa6 ♖f8 38 ♘a5
♕b8 39 ♖e6** 39 ♘c6 ♕b5 40 ♖xa7
♕xc6= **♖f7 40 ♕d3?** 40 ♘c6 ♕c8 41
♖e7= **♕b2! 41 ♕f1** 41 ♕f3 ♕a2 42
♖a6 ♗b6 **♕c2 42 ♖a6 ♗c5 43 ♘c6
♖d7 44 ♘b4 ♕xe4+ 45 ♔h2 ♖d2
46 ♖a2 ♖xa2 47 ♘xa2 ♕f3 48 ♕g2
♕xf2 0-1**

290 Kurajica-Klaric Porec 78
**1 e4 e5 2 ♘f3 ♘c6 3 ♗b5 ♘ge7 4
c3 a6 5 ♗a4 b5?!** 5...d6 6 d4 ♗d7 +=
6 ♗b3 d5 7 d4! N exd4 7...dxe4?
8 ♘g5± **8 exd5 ♘xd5 9 0-0 ♗e6** 9...
♗e7 10 ♘xd4 ♘xd4 11 ♕xd4± **10
♗g5! ♗e7 11 ♗xe7 ♕xe7 12 ♖e1**
12 ♗xd5 ♗xd5 13 ♖e1 ♗e6 14 cxd4
♖d8 15 ♘c3 ♗b4 += ♕d6?! 12...♖d8
13 ♘bd2!± 0-0 13...dxc3? 14 ♘e4
+- **14 ♘e4 ♕f4 15 ♘c5 ♕d6 16 ♘xe6
fxe6 17 ♘g5 +- e5** 17...♕f4 18 ♘xe6
♕xf2+ 19 ♔h1 ♘e3 20 ♘xf8 +-;
17...♖ae8 18 ♕d3 **18 ♕d3 g6 19 ♕h3
♖f7** 19...h5 20 ♘e4 ♕d8 21 ♕e6+
+- **20 ♘xf7 ♕xf7 21 ♕f3+ +- ♕e6
22 ♖ad1 ♕c5 23 cxd4 ♘xd4 24
♕xd5+ ♕xd5 25 ♖xd4 1-0 Kurajica**

291 Sax-Sanz Las Palmas 78
**1 e4 e5 2 ♘f3 ♘c6 3 ♗b5 ♘ge7 4 0-0
g6 5 d4 5** c3!? exd4 **6 ♘xd4 ♗g7
7 ♗e3 0-0 8 ♘c3 d6 9 f4** 9 ♕d2!?
f5!= **10 ♕d2 fxe4 11 ♘xe4 ♘f5!?
12 ♘xc6 ♕e8 13 ♘xa7 ♕xe4 14
♗f2!? Δ** ♖ae1 **♗h6! 15 ♘xc8 ♖axc8**

16 g3??

16...♘h4!! 17 gxh4 ♖xf4 18 ♕c3
18 ♕e2 ♖g4+ 19 ♘g3 ♗e3+ 20 ♖f2
♖f8 21 ♖f1 ♖f3 -+ **♖g4+ 19 ♗g3
♗e3+ 20 ♖f2 c6??** 20...♗xf2+ 21
♔xf2 ♕f5+ 22 ♕f3 ♖f8 -+ **21 ♗c4+!
1-0** 21...d5 22 ♗xd5+! **Larsen**

**292 Sax-O.Rodriguez
Las Palmas 78**
**1 e4 e5 2 ♘f3 ♘c6 3 ♗b5 f5 4 ♘c3
♘d4 5 ♗c4 c6 6 ♗xg8?! ♖xg8 7
0-0 ♕f6 8 exf5 ♘xf3+?** 8...d5! 9
♘xe5 ♘xc2!α **9 ♕xf3 ♗e7** 9...d5
**10 ♘xd5! 10 d4 d5 11 dxe5 ♕xf5
+= 12 ♕e2 ♗e6 13 ♗e3?!** ♕xe5 14
**♖ae1 ♕f7 15 f4 ♕f5 16 ♔h1 h5α
17 ♕f2 h4 18 ♘e2!?** 18 ♗d4 h3 19
g3 ♗f6; 18 ♗xa7 h3 19 g3 d4 **♕xc2**
18...h3? 19 ♘d4 hxg2+ 20 ♕xg2 ♕h3
21 ♘xe6 ♕xg2+ 22 ♔xg2 ♔xe6 23
♗c5+ **19 f5 ♗d7 20 ♕f3 ♗f6 21 ♕g4
♖h8 22 ♗d4 ♖h6 23 ♗xf6 ♖xf6 24
♘d4 ♕c4 25 ♖e7+? ♕xe7 26 ♕xg7+
♖f7 27 ♖e1+ ♔d6** 27...♔d8!? **28
♕xf7 ♕xd4 29 ♕f8+ ♔c7 30 ♕xa8
♕f2 31 ♖g1 h3 32 ♕g8?** ♗xf5 -+;
**32 ♕f8! =+ 28 ♕e5+ ♔c5 29 ♕e3
♖e8?? 29...♕b6!∓ 30 ♘e6+ ♔b4 31
a3+ ♔b5 32 b3! +- ♕f1+ Zeitnot;**
32...♕c2 33 ♘c7+ ♕a5 34 ♕xa7 mate
33 ♖xf1 ♖xe6 34 ♕d3+ ♔b6 35

fxe6 ♖xf1+ 36 ♕xf1 ♖xe6 37 h3 d4
38 ♕f2 ♖d6 39 ♕xh4 d3 40 ♕b4+
♔c7 41 ♕d2 1-0 Larsen

293 Vitolins-Lanka USSR 77

1 e4 e5 2 ♘f3 ♘c6 3 ♗b5 f5 4 ♕e2!?
4 ♘c3 fxe4 5 ♘xe4 ♘f6 6 ♘xf6+
♕xf6 7 0-0 ♘d4!? 8 ♘xd4 exd4 9
♖e1+ ♗e7 10 ♕e2= Adorjan-Parma,
Moscow 77 fxe4 5 ♕xe4 ♘f6 6 ♕e2
♗d6! 6...d6 7 d4 e4 8 d5± 7 d4
7 ♗xc6 dxc6 8 ♘xe5 0-0 9 d4 ♖e8
10 ♗e3 ♗xe5 11 dxe5 ♖xe5 =+
Kozlov-Tseitlin, USSR 76 e4 8 ♘g5
♕e7 9 c3 h6 10 ♘h3 0-0 10...g5! =+
11 ♘d2 a6 12 ♗a4 b5 13 ♗c2 ♗b7
14 ♘f1 ♘a5∞ 15 ♘g3 △ ♘f5 ♕e6 16
0-0 ♘c4 17 a4 ♗d5!? 18 a5 e3? 18...
♖ae8 19 b3? 19 ♗xe3± ♘g4? 19...
exf2+ 20 ♖xf2 ♗xg3 △ ♕xe2, ♘d6=
20 f3 ♘xh2? 21 ♔xh2 ♗xg3+ 22 ♕xg3
♕d6+ 23 f4 +- g5 24 bxc4 ♗xc4
25 ♗d3 1-0 Gufeld

294 Tal-Romanishin Leningrad 77

1 e4 e5 2 ♘f3 ♘c6 3 ♗b5 ♘f6 4
0-0 ♘xe4 5 d4 ♘d6 6 ♗xc6 dxc6 7
dxe5 ♘f5 8 ♕xd8+ ♔xd8 9 ♘c3 h6
10 b3 ♗e6 11 ♘e2 ♗d5 12 ♘d2 a5
N 12...c5 13 c4 ♗e6 14 ♘f4 a4!

15 ♗b2 ♗b4 16 ♘f3 ♔c8!? △ a3
17 a3 ♗e7 18 ♘xe6 fxe6 19 g4 19

b4= ♘h4 20 ♘xh4 ♗xh4 21 b4 c5!
22 b5 ♗e7 22...c6= 23 f4 g6= 24
♖ad1 c6! 25 f5 gxf5 26 gxf5 exf5
27 e6 ♖d8 28 ♖xd8+ ♔xd8 29 bxc6
bxc6 30 ♖xf5 ♖b8 31 ♗f6 ♗xf6 32
♖xf6 ♔e7 33 ♖xh6 ♖b3 34 ♖h5 ♔xe6
35 ♖xc5 ♔d6 36 ♖a5 ½-½ Suetin

295 Lanka-Asanov USSR 78

1 e4 e5 2 ♘f3 ♘c6 3 ♗b5 ♘f6 4 0-0
♘xe4 5 d4 ♗e7 6 dxe5 0-0 7 ♕d5
♘c5 8 ♗e3 a6 8...♘e6!? 9 ♗xc5 axb5
10 ♗xe7 N ♕xe7 11 ♘c3 b4 12 ♘b5
♖a5 13 a4! ♘a7 13...b6 14 ♘d2!
♕d8 15 ♘c4 ♖a6 16 ♕d2 ♗b7 17
b3 ♘a5 18 ♘e3 c5 19 ♖ad1±
Mochalov-Amans, Corr. 74/76; 14...
♘xe5 15 ♖fe1 c6 16 ♖xe5 ♕f6 17
♘e4 cxd5 18 ♘xf6+± 14 ♕c4 c6
14...♘xb5!? 15 axb5 ♖xa1 16 ♖xa1
c5 17 ♖d1± 15 ♘d6 c5 16 ♕g4
♕e6 17 ♘f5± g6 18 ♘h6+ ♔g7 19
♕h4 f6 20 ♖fe1 ♘c6 21 ♘g4 ♘xe5
22 ♘fxe5 fxe5 23 ♖xe5 ♕g8 24 ♖e7+
♖f7 25 ♕f6+ ♔f8 26 ♖xf7+ ♕xf7 27
♕d8+ 1-0 Gipslis

4♘

296 Byrne-Shamkovich
USA Final 78

1 e4 e5 2 ♘f3 ♘c6 3 ♗b5 ♘f6 4 ♘c3
♘d4 5 ♗a4 ♗c5 6 ♘xe5 0-0 7 ♘d3
♗b6 8 e5 ♘e8 9 0-0 d6 10 exd6 ♘xd6!
10...♕f6!? 11 d7 ♗xd7 12 ♗xd7
♕xd7 13 ♘e1 ♖ae8≈; 13 ♘f4!? 11
♘e1 11 ♔h1 c6 12 ♘e2 ♘xe2 13
♕xe2 ♕h4; 12 ♘f4 ♗c7!? 13 d3
b5 14 ♗b3 a5 =+ c6 12 d3 ♖e8 13
♗f4 ♕f6 14 ♗xd6 14 ♕d2 ♗a5! △ ♖e2;
14 ♗g3 ♘6f5∓ ♕xd6 15 ♘e4 ♕g6 16
c3 ♗g4 17 ♕d2 ♘e2+ 18 ♔h1

Diagram

18...♖ad8? 18...♖xe4! 19 dxe4 ♖d8 20 ♕c2 ♕h5! △ ♖d6, ♕xh2+; 20 ♘d3 ♕xe4 21 ♗c2 ♕d5! **19 ♕g5! ♕xg5 20 ♘xg5 += ♘f4 21 f3 ♗f5 22 d4 ♖e2 23 b4 ♘d5!** △ ♘xc3 **24 ♗b3 ♗g6 25 ♘e4** 25 ♖c1 ♘e3 26 ♖g1 h6 27 ♘h3 ♗c7!∞; 27 ♘e4? ♗xe4 28 fxe4 ♘g4!∓ **♘e3 26 ♖f2 ♖xf2 27 ♘xf2 ♘d5 28 ♗xd5** 28 ♖c1 ♖e8 **cxd5 29 ♘ed3 f6 30 ♔g1?** 30 g3 += ♖c8 **31 ♘c5** 31 ♖c1? ♗xd3 32 ♘xd3 ♖xc3! **♗xc5 32 dxc5 b6 33 ♖d1** 33 cxb6 axb6 34 ♖c1 ♖a8= **bxc5 34 ♖xd5 cxb4 35 cxb4 ♗f7 36 ♖d2 ♖c1+ 37 ♘d1 ♗xa2 38 ♖xa2 ♖xd1+ 39 ♔f2 ♖b1 ½-½ Shamkovich**

297 Bellon-Lukacs Bucharest 78

1 e4 e5 2 ♘f3 ♘c6 3 ♘c3 ♘f6 3... g6 4 d4 exd4 5 ♘xd4 ♗g7 6 ♗e3 ♘f6 7 ♘xc6 bxc6 8 e5 ♘g8 9 f4! f6 10 ♕d2 fxe5 11 fxe5 ♗xe5 12 0-0-0± Sabanov-Vorotnikov, USSR 77; 6... d6 7 ♕d2 ♘f6 8 0-0-0 ♗g4 9 ♘xc6 bxc6 10 ♗d4 ♗xd4 11 ♕xd4 ♕f6= Bellon-Karpov, Las Palmas 77 **4 d4 ♗b4** 4...exd4 5 ♘d5 ♗e7 6 ♗f4 d6 7 ♘xd4 0-0 8 ♘b5 ♘xd5 9 exd5 ♗g5?! 10 ♗xg5 ♕xg5 11 ♕d2! ♖e8+? 12 ♔d1!± Bellon-Pomar, Las Palmas 75; 5...♘xd5 6 exd5 ♘b4 7 ♘d4 ♘xd5 8 ♘f5!± Bellon-Jamieson, Wijk aan Zee 77 **5 ♘xe5 ♕e7 6 ♕d3 ♘xe5 7**

dxe5 **♕xe5 8 ♗d2 0-0 9 0-0-0 ♗xc3** 9...d6 10 f3 ♗d7 11 g4 +=; 10 f4!? **10 ♗xc3 ♕f4+** 10...♕xe4 11 ♕g3! **11 ♖d2!** 11 ♔b1? ♘xe4 12 g3 ♘xc3+ 13 ♕xc3 ♕xf2∓ Drimer-Portisch, Hastings 69/70 **d5?!** 11...♘xe4 12 ♕d4! +–; 11...♕xe4 12 ♗xf6 ♕xd3 13 ♖xd3 gxf6 14 ♖f3 += Miagmasuren-Bisguier, Tallinn 71 **12 exd5 ♖e8 13 b3 ♗f5** 13...♘e4 14 ♕d4 ♕h6 15 ♗b5!± **14 ♕f3 ♖e1+ 15 ♔b2 ♕g5 16 h4 ♕g6 17 d6! ♘e4 18 ♖d5! ♗e6** 18...♘xc3 19 ♕xc3 +– **19 ♖e5 ♗g4**

20 d7! ♘f6 21 ♕xb7 1-0 Ciocaltea

298 Hartoch-Timman Leeuwarden 78

1 e4 e5 2 ♘c3 ♘f6 3 ♘f3 ♘c6 4 d4 exd4 5 ♘d5 ♘xe4 5...♘b4 6 ♘xd4 ♘xe4 7 ♘f5 c6 8 ♘xb4 ♗xb4+ 9 c3 ♕f6∓ Tal-Averbakh, USSR 54; 5...♘b6 6 ♘xd4 ♘xe4 7 ♘b5 ♗c5 8 ♕g4± Radojcic-Gligoric, Jugoslavia 45; 5... ♘xd5?! 6 exd5 ♗b4+ 7 ♗d2 ♕e7+ 8 ♕e2 ♗xd2+ 9 ♔xd2 ♕xe2+ 10 ♗xe2 ♘e7 11 d6 cxd6 12 ♘xd4± Trajkovic-Radojcic, Jugoslavia 45 6...♘b4 7 ♗c4 ♕e7+ 8 ♔d2 ♗c5 10 ♖e1+ ♗e7 10 ♕e2± Karaklaic-Janic, Jugoslavia 45; 5...♗e7!? **6 ♕e2 6 ♘c ♗f5 7 ♗f4 7 g4? ♘e7! 8 gxf5 ♘xd5 9 ♕xe4+ ♕e7∓; 7...♔f7 8 gxf5 ♗c5 =**

Gutnikov-Tal, USSR 51; 7 ♘d2
d3! 8 ♕xd3 ♘b4 9 ♘xb4 ♗xb4 10
c3 ♗c5 11 ♘xe4 ♕e7 =+; 7 ♘g5
d3 8 cxd3 ♘d4 9 ♕h5+ g6 10 ♕h4
c6 11 dxe4 cxd5 12 exd5 ♕a5= **d6**
8 0-0-0 ♗e7 8...♗e6 9 ♘xd4 ♘xd4
10 ♖xd4 Sopkov-Kamisov, USSR
50; 10...c3!∓ **9 ♗xe7 ♖xe7 10 g4 c5**
11 ♗h3 fxg4 12 ♕xe4 d5 13 ♕e5
0-0 14 ♖hg1 ♗f6 15 ♕h5 gxf3 16
♖g3 ♗h4 17 ♗xc8 ♖xc8 18 ♗g5 ♗xg5+
19 ♖xg5 ♕e8 20 ♕h6 ♖f7 21 ♖dg1
♖cc7 22 ♖xd5 ♖ce7 23 ♔d1 ♖e5
24 ♖xe5 ♕xe5 0-1

2♘

299 Nunn-Crouch London 78
1 e4 e5 2 ♘f3 ♘c6 3 ♗c4 ♘f6 4 d3
♗c5 4...d5=; 4...♗e7 **5 c3 d6** 5...d5
6 exd5 ♘xd5 7 0-0 0-0 8 ♖e1 ♗b6
9 ♘xe5 ♘xe5 10 ♖xe5 ♗xf2+ 11
♔h1 ♘f6 12 ♗g5 += Steinbuehler-
Steinitz, Manchester 1874 **6 b4**
6 ♘bd2 a6= Unzicker **♗b6 7 a4 a5**
7...a6!?= Unzicker **8 b5 ♘b8 9 0-0**
0-0 10 ♘bd2 h6 11 ♗a2 ♘bd7 12
d4 ♘h7 13 ♘c4 ♕f6 14 ♘e3 exd4
15 cxd4 ♘g5 16 ♘xg5 ♕xg5 17 f4
♕e7 18 ♗b1 ♖e8 19 ♔h1 ♕d8 20
♖a3 ♘f6 21 e5 dxe5 22 fxe5 ♘h7
23 ♗a2 23 ♗xh7+ ♔xh7 24 ♖xf7
♕xd4 25 ♖d3 ♕xe5 ♘g5 24 ♘d5
♗e6 25 ♘xb6 cxb6 26 d5 +− ♗d7
27 ♕d4 ♕e7 28 ♖e3 ♖ac8 29 ♗a3
♕d8 30 h4 ♘h7 31 e6 ♗xe6 32 dxe6!
1-0

300 Stein-E.Kristiansen
Gausdal 78
1 e4 e5 2 ♘f3 ♘c6 3 ♗c4 ♘f6 4 ♘g5
♗c5!? 5 ♗xf7+ ♕e7 6 ♗d5! ♖f8 7
♘f3 ♕e8!? N 7...d6 8 c3 +=; 7...♘d4?!
8 c3 ♕h5 9 0-0 9 d4 exd4 10 ♗xc6

bxc6!∝ **d6 10 d4 ♗g4!?** 10...♘b6 11
♕d3 +=; 10...exd4 11 ♗xc6± **11**
♗xc6?! 11 dxc5!? ♘xd5 12 exd5
♖xf3 13 cxd6+ cxd6 14 dxc6 bxc6
+− **bxc6 12 dxc5 ♘xe4 13 cxd6+**
cxd6 14 ♕d3?? 14 ♕e2! d5! 15
♘bd2 ♘xd2 16 ♕xe5+ ♔d7! 17
♗xd2 ♗xf3 18 ♕xh5 ♗xh5 += **♗xf3**
15 ♘d2 15 gxf3? ♕g6+ 16 ♔h1 ♘xf2+
♘xd2 16 ♕xd2

16...♖f4! −+ 17 gxf3 ♕xf3 18 ♖e1
♖g4+ 19 ♔f1 ♖f8! 20 ♕e3 ♕g2+ 21
♕e2 ♖e4 22 ♖g1 ♕xf2+ 0-1 Pytel

Scotch

301 Tatai-Kraidman
Beersheva 78
1 e4 e5 2 ♘f3 ♘c6 3 d4 exd4 4 ♘xd4
♗c5 5 ♘b3 ♗b6 6 ♘c3 d6 7 ♕e2?
7 a4! ♘ge7 8 ♗e3 0-0 9 0-0-0 f5
10 exf5 ♗xf5 △ ♘xe3∓ **11 ♗xb6**
axb6 12 f4 ♔h8 13 ♔b1 ♕f6 14 ♘d5
♕f7 15 c4

Diagram

15...♘fe7!! 16 ♘xc7? ♗f5+ 17 ♔a1
♘b4 18 a3 ♘ec6 19 ♘xa8 ♘c2+
20 ♔a2 ♘6b4+! 21 axb4 ♖xb4+
22 ♔a3 ♘c2+ 23 ♔a2 ♖xa8+ 24 ♘a5
♖xa5+ 25 ♔b3 ♖b5+! 0-1 26 ♔a4

Rb4 mate; 26 ♔a2 ♕g8! 27 b3 ♕a8+ 28 ♔b2 Rxb3+ 29 ♔xb3 ♕a3 mate; 26 ♔c3 ♕f6+ 27 ♔d2 ♕d4+ 28 ♔c1 ♕xb2+ 29 ♔d2 ♕d4+ 30 ♔c1 Rb1+! 31 ♔xb1 ♕a1 mate **Keene**

302 Wiese-Jurczynska Poland 78
1 e4 e5 2 ♘f3 ♘c6 3 d4 exd4 4 ♘xd4 ♗c5 5 ♘b3 ♗b6 6 ♘c3 6 a4! ♕f6 6...♘f6 7 ♗g5 h6= **7 ♕e2 ♘ge7 8 ♗e3** 8 ♘d5 ♘xd5 9 exd5+ ♘e7 10 h4 h6 11 g4 d6 12 g5 ♕f5 13 gxh6 gxh6= ♘d4 8...0-0 9 0-0-0 **9 e5** 9 ♕d2! ♘xb3 10 axb3 += **♕xe5?** 9...♘xe2!? 10 exf6 ♘xc3 11 fxg7 Rg8∝ **10 ♗xd4 ♗xd4 11 ♘xd4 ♕xd4 12 Rd1 ♕c5** 12...♕b4 13 a3! **13 Rd5 ♕b4 14 Re5 c6 15 a3 ♕h4 16 ♘e4 ♕h6 17 ♘g5 0-0 18 ♘xh7! ♕c1+ 19 ♕d1 ♕xd1+ 20 ♔xd1 Re8** 20...♔xh7 21 Rxe7± **21 ♗d3 f6 22 Re3 ♗f7 23 g4! d5 24 g5 ♗g4+?** 24...♗d7 **25 f3 ♗h5 26 Rhe1 f5 27 g6+! ♗xg6** 27...♗xg6 28 ♘g5+ ♔f8 29 ♘e6+ △ ♘c7; 28...♔f6 29 h4! **28 ♘g5+ ♕f8 29 ♘e6+ ♕g8 30 Rg1 f4?** 30...d4 **31 Ree1 ♗xf3+ 32 ♔d2 ♘f8 33 Rxg7+ ♕h8 34 Reg1! ♗e4 35 ♗xe4 dxe4 36 Rg8+ 1-0 Konikowski**

303 Stupina-Vilner USSR 78
1 e4 e5 2 ♘f3 ♘c6 3 d4 exd4 4 ♘xd4 ♗c5 4...♕h4?! 5 ♘b5 ♗b4+ 6 ♗d2!

♕xe4+ 7 ♗e2 += Sveshnikov-Barle, Bucharest 76; 4...♕f6!? **5 ♘b3** 5 ♗e3 ♕f6 6 c3 ♘ge7 7 g3!? d5 8 ♗g2 dxe4 9 ♘b5!?∝ Sveshnikov-Geller, Sochi 76; 7...d6?! 8 ♗g2 ♘e5 9 h3 ♗d7 10 ♕e2 += **♗b6** 5...♗b4 6 c3 ♗e7 7 g3 += **6 a4** 6 ♘c3 ♕f6 7 ♕e2 ♘ge7 8 ♗e3! 0-0 9 0-0-0 d6 10 h4 += Kupreichik-Sakharov, USSR 76 **a5 7 ♘c3 ♕f6 8 ♕e2 ♘ge7** 8...♘b4 9 ♘b5! △ c3 += **9 ♗d5!?** N 9 ♗e3 ♘b4 10 0-0-0 0-0 11 g3 += **♘xd5 10 exd5+ ♘e7 11 h4! h6 12 g4 d6 13 ♗g2 ♗d7 14 c3 0-0-0 15 ♗e3 ♗xe3 16 fxe3 ♕e5 17 0-0-0!± ♗xa4**

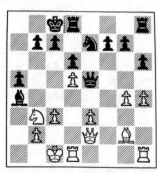

18 ♘xa5! ♗xd1 19 Rxd1 ♕g6 20 Rd4 △ ♘xb7! +- Rhe8 **21 ♕b5! ♕xe3+ 22 ♔b1 ♘e5 23 ♘xb7 Rd7 24 ♕a6 +- ♕b8 25 ♘a5 c5 26 dxc6 Ra7 27 c7+ 1-0 Gufeld**

Philidor

304 Vogt-Mohring DDR 78
1 e4 d6 2 d4 ♘f6 3 ♘c3 ♘bd7 4 ♘f3 e5 5 ♗c4 ♗e7 6 0-0 0-0 7 a4 c6 8 ♕e2 exd4 8...a5 9 Rd1 ♕c7 10 h3 h6 11 dxe5 dxe5 12 ♘h4± Kavalek-Najdorf, Manila 73 **9 ♘xd4 Re8** 9...♘xe4? 10 ♘xe4 d5 11 ♘f5 dxc4 12 ♗h6 +- **10 a5** 10 ♗a2 ♗f8 11 ♕f3 ♘e5 12 ♕d1± **d5!?** 11 exd5

cxd5 11...♗c5 12 ♘e6 fxe6 13 dxe6
♔h8 14 ♖d1± **12 ♗xd5 ♗d6** 12...
♗b4? 13 ♗xf7+ +− **13 ♕b5 ♖e5?**
13...a6 14 ♕c4 ♘xd5∞ **14 f4** 14
♘f3 ♖h5 15 ♗xf7+ ♔xf7 16 ♘g5+
♖xg5 17 ♗xg5± **♖h5??**

15 ♗xf7+! ♔xf7 16 ♕c4+ ♔e8 16...
♔g6 17 f5+ +−; 16...♔e7 17 ♕e6+ +−;
16...♔f8 17 ♘e6+ +− **17 ♖e1+ ♗e7 18
♘e6 ♘e5 19 ♕c7+ ♔d7 20 fxe5 1-0**
20...♕xc7 21 ♖d1+ +− **Vogt**

305 Sigurjonsson-Gonzalez
Bogota 78

**1 e4 e5 2 ♘f3 ♕e7?! 3 ♗c4 c6 4 0-0
d6 5 d4 ♗g4 6 c3 ♘f6 7 ♖e1 g6?!**
7...♘bd7 **8 dxe5! dxe5 9 h3 ♗xf3**
9...♗e6 10 ♘xe5; 9...♗d7; 9...♗c8
10 ♕xf3 ♘bd7 11 a4 ♘h5 △ ♕f6
12 ♖d1! ♖d8 12...♕f6 13 ♗xf7+
**13 ♗g5 f6 14 ♗e3 ♘b6 15 ♖xd8+
♔xd8 16 ♗f1 ♔c7 17 ♘d2 ♘g7 18
b4 ♘e6 19 b5 c5 20 a5 ♘c8 21 ♗c4∓
♔b8 22 ♘b3 b6 23 axb6 axb6 24
♕e2 ♘c7 25 ♕a2 ♕d6 26 ♗d5** +−
f5 27 f3 △ ♗c6, ♘d2-c4xb6 **♘xd5**
27...♘xb5 28 ♕a8+ ♔c7 29 ♘xc5
bxc5 30 ♕b7+ △ ♕xb5 **28 ♕a8+ ♔c7
29 exd5 ♗e7 30 ♗xc5! bxc5 31 ♖a6
♖d8** 31...♕d7 32 b6+ ♔d8 33 b7
+−; 32...♘xb6 33 ♖a7+; 31...♕d8 32
♕c6+ ♔b8 33 ♖a8 mate **32 ♖xd6**

1-0 Sigurjonsson

Latvian Gambit

306 Meshkov-Sukhin USSR 77

1 e4 e5 2 ♘f3 f5 3 ♘xe5 3 ♗c4!?
♘f6 **4 d4 fxe4 5 ♘xe5 d5 6 0-0±
♘c6!?** 3...♕e7 **4 ♕h5+ g6 5 ♘xg6
♕xe4+ 6 ♗e2± 4 ♕h5+!?** N **4** ♘xc6
△ ♘c3± **g6 5 ♘xg6 ♘f6 6 ♕h4** 6
♕h3! += **♖g8 7 ♘xf8 ♖g4! 8 ♕h6
♖xe4+ 9 ♗e2 ♕e7 10 ♘c3 ♘d4! 11
♘xe4 ♕xe4 12 0-0 ♘xe2+ 13 ♔h1
♘g4 14 ♕h5+! ♔xf8 15 f3?!** 15
d3! += **♕f4 16 ♕xh7 d6 17 d3 ♘xc1
18 ♖axc1 ♘f2+! 19 ♔g1 ♕e3= 20
♕h8+ ♔f7 21 ♕h7+ ♔f8 22 ♕h8+
♔f7 23 ♕h7+ ♔f8 ½-½ Gufeld**

Petroff

307 Eolian-Haritonov USSR 78

**1 e4 e5 2 ♘f3 ♘f6 3 ♘xe5 d6 4 ♘c4!?
♘xe4 5 ♕e2** N 5 d3 ♘f6 6 d4 ♗e7
7 ♗d3 0-0 8 0-0 ♘c6=; 5 d4 d5 6 ♘e3
♗e6 7 ♗d3 f5; 5 ♘c3!? ♘xc3 6 bxc3
g6 7 d4 ♗g7 8 h4 0-0 9 ♗g5∞ **♕e7
6 b3!? ♘c6 7 ♗b2 d5! 8 ♘e3 ♗e6=
9 g3 0-0-0 10 ♗g2 ♕d7 11 ♘c3 f5
=+ 12 0-0 ♖g8?** 12...♗e7 =+ **13 ♘exd5
♗xd5 14 ♘xd5 ♕xd5 15 d3 ♕b5 16
c4 ♕a5 17 dxe4 ♖d2**

French 3 ♘c3 ♗b4 4 ♘e2/4 e5 b6/4 e5 c5

18 ♕h5! ♖xb2 19 ♕xh7 ♞e7 20 exf5
+− △ ♗d5 ♕d2 20...♖d2 21 ♖ad1 +−
21 ♗d5 1-0 Gufeld

308 Wiese-Jurczynska Poland 78
1 e4 e5 2 ♞f3 ♞f6 3 ♞xe5 d6 4 ♞f3
♞xe4 5 d4 d5 6 ♗d3 ♗e7 7 0-0 ♞c6 8
♖e1 ♗g4 9 ♗xe4 9 c3!?; 9 c4 dxe4
10 ♖xe4 ♗xf3 11 ♕xf3 11 gxf3?
f5 12 ♖f4 0-0 13 d5 ♗g5 14 ♖a4
♗xc1 15 ♕xc1 ♕xd5∓ ♞xd4 12 ♕c3
♞e6 13 ♞d2 0-0 14 ♞f3 ♕d6 15 ♗d2
♗f6 16 ♕c4 b6 17 c3 c5 18 ♖ae1
♖ad8 19 ♗c1 ♕d5 20 ♕a4 ♕d7 21
♕b3 ♕d5 22 ♕a4 ♕d7 23 ♕a6 ♕c6
24 h3 ♞c7 25 ♕e2 ♖fe8 26 ♗g5 ♖xe4
27 ♕xe4 ♕xe4 28 ♖xe4 ♗xg5 29
♞xg5 ♖d7 30 b4? cxb4 31 cxb4 f6
32 ♞f3 ♞b5 33 ♖e1 ♔f7 34 a4 ♞c3
35 a5 bxa5 36 bxa5 ♞b5 37 ♖b1 a6
38 ♔f1 ♔e6? 38...♖d5! 39 ♖e1+ ♔f7
40 ♖c1 ♔e7 41 ♔e2 ♞d4+?! 42
♞xd4 ♖xd4 43 ♖c7+ ♖d7 44 ♖xd7+
½-½

French

309 Bleuel-Frey Switzerland 78
1 e4 e6 2 d3 b6 3 g3 ♗b7 4 ♗g2 f5
5 ♞e2 fxe4 6 dxe4 ♞f6 7 ♞bc3 ♗c5
8 0-0 0-0 9 ♞d4 9 ♗g5 ♞c6 10 ♗e3
10 ♞xc6 ♗xc6 11 ♕e2 ♞e5 11 ♖e1
11 h3 ♞fg4 12 h3 12 ♗f4 ♕f6 ♞xe3
13 ♖xe3 ♕f6 △ ♗xd4, ♞f3+ 0-1

310 Stoica-Uhlmann
Bucharest 78
1 e4 e6 2 d4 d5 3 ♞c3 ♗b4 4 ♞e2
dxe4 4...♞f6 5 ♗g5 dxe4 6 a3 ♗e7 7
♗xf6 gxf6 8 ♞xe4 b6 9 ♕d3 ♗b7 10
0-0-0 ♞d7 11 ♔b1 f5 Pilnik-Planinc,
Mar del Plata 71 5 a3 ♗e7 5...♗xc3+
6 ♞xc3 ♞c6 7 ♗b5 ♞e7 8 ♗g5 f6 9
♗e3 0-0 10 ♕d2 += Pachman-

Bondarevsky, Moscow 47 6 ♞xe4
6 g4 ♗d7 7 ♞g3 ♗c6 8 ♗g2 h6 9
♗e3 ♞f6 10 ♕e2 ♞bd7 11 0-0-0 ♞b6
Planinc-Ivkov, Jugoslavia 75 ♞c6 6...
♞f6 7 ♞2g3 ♞bd7 8 ♗c4 ♞xe4 9
♞xe4 ♞f6 10 ♞xf6+ ♗xf6 11 c3 +=
Mestrovic-Ivkov, Banja Luka 74 7
♗f4 7 g4 e5 8 d5 ♞d4 9 ♞2c3 f5 10
gxf5 ♗xf5 Keres; 7...b6 8 ♗g2 ♗b7
9 c3 ♞f6 10 ♞2g3 0-0 11 g5 ♞xe4
12 ♞xe4 ♔h8 13 ♕h5 Alekhine-
Euwe 35 ♞f6 8 ♕d3 0-0 9 0-0-0
9 g3!? b6 10 ♞2c3 ♞d5!? 11 ♞xd5
exd5 12 ♞c3 ♗f6 13 ♕f3 ♗e6 14
♗e3 ♞e7 15 g4 c5 16 ♗g2?! 16 h4
♞c6 17 dxc5 ♞e5; 17 ♞e2!? ♖c8
17 ♞e2 ♞c6 18 h4 ♕d7 19 ♗h3 cxd4
20 ♞xd4 ♞xd4 21 ♗xd4 ♗xh4?
21...♕a4! 22 b3 ♕xa3+ 23 ♔b1 ♗xd4
24 ♖xd4 −+

22 ♕e3 ♖fe8 23 ♕d2 ♕c7 24 f4
24 g5 ♗xg5! ♗d7 25 ♔b1 ♗g3 26
♗e5 ♖xe5 27 fxe5 ♗a4 28 ♖c1 28
b3 ♗f4! 29 ♕d3 ♗b5! ♕xe5 28...
♗xe5!? 29 g5 ♖d8 30 ♖cf1 g6 31
♖f3 ♖e8 32 ♖hf1 ♖e7 33 ♕b4 ♖c7?
33...♖e8 34 ♕xa4 1-0 Ciocaltea

311 Kurajica-Nikolac Jugoslavia 78
1 e4 e6 2 d4 d5 3 ♞c3 ♗b4 4 e5 b6
5 ♕g4! 5 a3 ♗xc3+ 6 bxc3 ♕d7 7
♞h3 += ♗f8 6 a4 6 ♗g5 ♞c6 6...♗a6

160

7 ♘b5 c6?? 8 ♘d6+ +− **7 h4 ♕d7 8
h5 f5 9 ♕d1 ♗b7 10 ♘b1?!** △ c3, b4
**♘h6 11 c3 ♘a5 12 b4 ♘c4 13 ♗xh6!?
gxh6 14 g4 ♕f7** 14...fxg4 15 ♕xg4
0-0-0 16 ♘h3 ♖e8 17 ♘e2± **15 gxf5
♕xf5 16 ♗d3 ♕f4!** 16...♕f7?! 17
♕f3 += **17 ♘h3 ♕f7 18 ♕e2 c5! 19
bxc5 bxc5 20 0-0 cxd4 21 cxd4
♗b4!= 22 ♔h2 0-0-0 23 f4 ♖hg8 24
♖a2 ♕e7 25 ♕f2 ♖g7** 25...♕f7=
**26 ♖g1 ♖dg8 27 ♖xg7 ♖xg7 28 ♖c2
♔b8 29 ♘c3 ♕e8 30 f5! exf5 31
♘f4∝ ♖g5** 31...♗xc3 32 ♖xc3 ♕xa4
33 ♗xc4 dxc4 34 d5± **32 ♗e2** △ ♗f3
♘xe5?? Zeitnot **33** dxe5 ♗a5 33...
♕xe5 34 ♘b5 +− **34 ♘cxd5 +− ♕xa4
35 ♕c5 ♖g8 36 ♖b2 ♔a8** 36...♕a1
37 ♖xb7+ ♔xb7 38 ♗a6+! ♔xa6 39
♕c6+ ♗b6 40 ♘c7+ ♔a5 41 ♕b5 mate
**37 ♗f3 ♕a1 38 ♖xb7 ♕a2+ 39 ♘g2
1-0 Kurajica**

312 Durao-Eslon Spain 78
**1 e4 e6 2 d4 d5 3 ♘c3 ♗b4 4 e5 c5
5 a3 ♗xc3+ 6 bxc3 ♘e7 7 ♘f3 ♗d7
8 a4** 8 dxc5 ♕c7 9 ♗d3 ♗a4 10 ♖b1!
Spassky-Korchnoi (10) 77 **♕a5 9 ♗d2**
9 ♕d2 △ ♗a3 **♘bc6 10 ♗e2 f6!?**
10...c4; 10...♕c7 **11 c4 ♕c7 12 exf6
gxf6 13 cxd5 ♘xd5 14 c4** 14 dxc5
0-0-0 15 0-0 e5 16 c3 ♖hg8 17 ♔h1
♘f4 18 ♗c4 ♖xg2 19 ♗xf4 ♖g4 20
♕e2 ♖xf4 21 ♘d2 ♘a5 22 f3 ♘xc4
23 ♘xc4 ♕xc5 24 ♘d2 ♗f5 25 ♘e4
♕c6 26 ♖ae1 ♗e6 27 ♖g1 f5 28 ♘g5
♗d5 29 ♖g3 h6 0-1 Lederman-
Korchnoi, Beersheva 78; 14 c3 0-0-0
15 0-0 ♖hg8 16 ♖e1 e5! 17 c4 ♘h3
18 ♗f1; 18 ♘g5!? **♘de7 15 ♗c3** 15
dxc5 0-0-0 16 ♗c3 e5 17 ♕d6 ♘f5!
18 ♕xc7+ ♔xc7 19 0-0 ♘fd4 20
♘xd4 ♘xd4 21 ♗d1 ♔c6 22 ♗xd4?∓
Timman-Korchnoi, Leeuwarden 76;
22 f4! ♔xc5 23 fxe5 fxe5 24 ♖e1

0-0-0 16 0-0 cxd4? 16...♘e8 17 d5
17 ♘xd4 ♗e8? 17...a6 **18 ♘xe6 ♖xd1
19 ♖fxd1** 19 ♘xc7? −+ **♕b8 20
♗xf6 ♘g6 21 ♗g4 ♗d7 22 ♖xd7 ♔xd7
23 ♘g7+ ♔d6** 23...♔c7 24 ♘e6+ ♔d7
25 ♘g7+ = **24 ♖d1+ ♔c5 25 ♘e6+
♔b4 26 ♖b1+ ♔xc4 27 ♖c1+ ♔b4
28 ♗c3+ ♔xa4 29 ♗d1+?** 29 ♖b1!
△ ♗d1+/♘c5+ **♔b5 30 ♗e2+ ♔b6 31
♖b1+ ♘b4 32 ♖xb4+ ♔c6 33 ♖d4
♖f8 34 ♘xf8 ♕xf8 35 ♗f3+ ♔c7 36
♗a5+ b6 37 ♗b4 ♕f6 38 ♖c4+ ♔d8
39 ♗c3 ♕f5 40 ♗e4 ♕e6 41 ♖d4+
♔e8 42 ♗d5 ♕f5 43 ♗e4 ♕c5 44 ♖d3
a5 45 ♖e3 ♔d7 46 ♖d3+ ♔c7 47
♗b2 ♕b4 0-1**

313 Banas-Prandstetter
CSSR Final 78
**1 e4 e6 2 d4 d5 3 ♘c3 ♗b4 4 e5
c5 5 ♕g4 ♘e7 6 ♘f3 ♘bc6!** 6...cxd4
7 ♘xd4 ♕c7 8 ♗b5+ ♘bc6 9 0-0±
Spassky-Uhlmann, Manila 76 **7 dxc5?!**
d4 8 ♗b5 ♕a5 8...♔f8 9 ♗xc6 ♘xc6
10 a3 ♕a5 11 ♖b1∝ **9 ♗xc6+ bxc6**
9...♘xc6? 10 ♕xg7 ♖f8 11 ♗h6 ♗xc5
12 0-0-0 dxc3 13 ♖d6 +− **10 ♕xd4
♘f5!** N 10...♗a6?! Keres 11 ♗d2±
11 ♕c4 11 ♕d2? ♗a6 △ ♖d8 −+ **♗a6
12 ♕b3 ♕b5**

13 ♔d1! ♕xc5 14 ♗d2 ♗c4= 14...
♕xf2 15 ♕xb4 ♕xg2 16 ♖e1 ♕xf3+

17 ♔c1 ♕f2! 18 ♘e4 ♕b6 19 ♘d6+ ♘xd6 20 ♕xd6 ♖d8 21 ♕a3 ♖b8 22 ♗e3; 14...0-0-0 15 ♔c1! **15 ♕a4** 15 ♘e4 ♗xb3 16 ♘xc5 ♗xc5 17 axb3 ♗xf2∓ **♗xc3 16 ♗xc3 0-0 17 ♘d2** **♖fd8 18 ♔c1** 18 ♕b4 ♕xf2 19 ♕xc4? ♘e3 −+ **♗d5 19 ♕f4 ♗xg2 20 ♖g1 ♗d5 21 ♘b3 ♕c4 22 ♕xc4** 22 ♕g5 ♕h4!= ½-½ **Banas**

314 Kuzmin-Kogan USSR 78

1 e4 e6 2 d4 d5 3 ♘c3 ♗b4 4 e5 ♘e7 5 ♕g4 0-0 5...c5 6 ♕xg7 ♖g8 7 ♕h6 cxd4 8 a3 ♗xc3+ 9 bxc3 ♕c7 10 ♘e2α Sigurjonsson-Uhlmann, Hastings 75/6; 6 ♘f3!? cxd4 7 ♘xd4 ♕c7 8 ♗b5+! ♘bc6 9 0-0 ♗xc3 10 bxc3 ♗d7 11 ♗xc6 bxc6 12 ♗a3± Spassky-Uhlmann, Manila 76; 5...♘f5! 6 ♘f3 ♘c6 7 ♗b5 ♗d7 8 ♗g5 h5!= **6 ♗d3!?** N 6 a3 **c5 7 dxc5 ♘bc6 8 ♘f3** △ ♗xh7+! **f5 9 exf6 ♖xf6 10 ♕h5 h6 11 0-0 ♗xc5 12 ♗e3!? ♗b6** 12... ♗xe3?! 13 fxe3 △ ♘d4 +=; 12...♗d6!? **13 ♗xb6 ♕xb6! 14 ♕e8+ ♖f8 15 ♗h7+ ♔xh7 16 ♕xf8 ♕xb2 17 ♘e2** e5!α 17...♕xc2 18 ♘ed4!± **18 ♘g3 e4 19 ♖ab1 ♕f6! 20 ♕xf6 gxf6 21 ♘d2 f5 22 ♘h5 b6 23 ♖fd1 ♗a6** △ ♗e2 **24 ♘f4 ♖d8 25 ♘b3?!** 25 ♖b3!? ♘g6 26 ♘xg6 ♔xg6 27 ♖a3!α **♗c4!** =+ **26 ♖d2 ♖d6 27 ♖e1 ♘g6 28 ♘xg6 ♖xg6 29 ♘d4 ♗xd4 30 ♖xd4 b5 31 f3! ♖a6 32 g4! ♖a3!∓ 33 gxf5 ♖xf3 34 a4! bxa4?** 34...a6!∓ **35 ♖exe4!= dxe4 36 ♖xc4** ½-½ **Gufeld**

315 Ermenkov-Velikov Albena 77

1 e4 e6 2 d4 d5 3 ♘c3 dxe4 4 ♘xe4 ♗d7 5 ♘f3 ♗c6 6 ♗d3 ♘d7 6...♗xe4 7 ♗xe4 c6 8 ♕e2 ♘f6 9 ♗d3 g6 10 0-0 += Rajkovic-Ciric, Jugoslavia 76 **7 ♕e2** 7 0-0 ♘gf6 8 ♘g3 ♗e7 += Balashov-Suba, Moscow 77 **♘gf6 8 ♗d2 8 ♗g3!? ♗d5 9 0-0 c5 10 ♗e3 ♕b6 11 c3** += Parma-Forintos, Maribor 77; 8 0-0 ♘xe4 9 ♗xe4 ♗xe4 10 ♕xe4 c6 11 c4 ♗e7 12 b3 += Parma; 8 ♘eg5!? ♗xf3 9 ♘xf3 += Sahovic-Ciric, Jugoslavia 76 **♘xe4 9 ♗xe4 ♗xe4 10 ♕xe4 c6 11 c4 ♗e7 12 0-0-0 0-0 13 ♔b1 ♕c7 14 ♘g5 ♘f6 15 ♕c2 ♖ad8 16 ♗c3 ♕f4 17 h4 h6 18 d5 ♕f5! 19 ♕xf5 exf5 20 d6** =+ ½-½ **Ciocaltea**

316 Chikovani-Liutian USSR 78

1 e4 e6 2 ♘f3 d5 3 ♘c3 ♘f6 4 e5 ♘fd7 5 d4 c5 6 ♗b5 6 dxc5 a6 6... ♘c6!? **7 ♗xd7+ ♗xd7 8 ♗e3!** 8 0-0?! ♘c6 **♘c6?!** 8...cxd4 9 ♕xd4 ♘c6 10 ♕f4 ♕c7!?; 9 ♘xd4 ♘c6 10 f4 += **9 dxc5! += ♕c7 10 0-0 ♘xe5 11 ♖e1** 11 ♘xe5 ♕xe5 12 ♖e1 ♗e7≈ **♘xf3+ 12 ♕xf3 ♗c6 13 ♗d4 ♕d7 14 ♕h3!± h5 15 b4** 15 ♔h1!? △ b4 **♖h6 16 f4 b6! 17 ♖ab1 bxc5 18 bxc5 ♗e7 19 f5** += ♔f8

20 ♖b8+! ♖xb8 21 ♕g3 g5 22 ♕xb8+ ♕d8 22...♕e8!? **23 ♖b1** 23 ♖b1 Zeitnot **exf5** Zeitnot **24 ♕a7 ♗f6! 25 ♖b8 ♗xd4+ 26 ♔f1 ♕xb8 27 ♕xb8+ ♔g7 28 ♕b3** += **♖e6?** 28... ♗e5!? += **29 ♘xd5± ♖e5 30 c4 ♗xc5 31 ♕b8 +− ♗d4 32 ♕d8 ♖e6 33 ♘c7 ♖e4 34 ♕xg5+ 1-0 Gufeld**

317 Arbakov-Gurevich USSR 78

1 e4 e6 2 d4 d5 3 ♘c3 ♞f6 4 ♗g5
♗b4 5 e5 h6 6 ♗d2 ♗xc3 7 bxc3
♞e4 8 ♛g4 g6 9 ♗c1 c5 10 ♗d3 ♞xc3
11 dxc5 ♛a5 12 ♗d2 ♛a4 13 h3
♞e4 14 ♞e2!? N ♞xc5 15 ♛f3 ♛d7
16 0-0 b6 △ ♗a6 17 a4!? ♗a6 18 a5
♗xd3 19 cxd3 ♞b3!? 20 ♛f6! ♜g8 21
axb6!? 21 ♗xh6! ♞xa1 22 ♖xa1≈
♞xd2 22 ♖fc1! △ ♖c7 ♞b3 22...♞c6
23 ♞d4!± 23 ♖cb1! 23 ♖c7 axb6!
24 ♖xd7 ♖xa1+ 25 ♔h2 ♞xd7 −+
♞c5 23...♛xa1? 24 b7 +− 24 d4!
♞e4 25 b7 ♛xb7 26 ♖xb7 ♗xf6
27 exf6 ♞d7 28 ♖c1! ♗xf6 29 ♖cc7
♖g7 30 ♞f4 ♖h7 31 ♞xe6 fxe6 32
♖xh7 ♞xh7 33 ♖xh7 ♖c8 34 ♖xa7
♖c1+ 35 ♔h2 ♔f8 36 ♖a3? 36 ♔g3
♖c4 37 ♔f4 ♖xd4+ 38 ♔e5= ♖d1!∓
37 ♖f3+ ♔e7 38 ♖f4 g5 39 ♖g4 ♔f6
40 f4 ♔f5 41 fxg5 hxg5 42 ♔g3
♖c1! △ ♖c4, e5 43 ♔f3 ♖c4 44 ♔e3
e5! 45 ♔d3 ♖a4 45...e4+ 46 ♖xe4
46 ♔e3 e4 47 ♖g3 ♖a2 48 ♖g4 48
h4 g4 49 h5 ♖a3+ 50 ♔f2 ♖xg3 51
♔xg3 e3 −+ ♖a3+ 49 ♔f2 ♖d3 0-1
Gufeld

318 Lanka-Arhipkin USSR 77

1 e4 e6 2 d4 d5 3 ♞d2 a6!? 3...b6?!
4 ♞gf3 dxe4 5 ♞xe4 ♗b7 6 ♗b5+!
+= Balashov-Kovacevic, Vinkovci 76;
3...g6!? 4 ♗d3 ♗g7 5 c3 ♞e7 6 ♞gf3
♞d7 7 0-0 0-0 8 ♖e1 c5 9 e5 ♞c6=
Eslon-Czerniak, Biel 76 **4 ♗d3!?**
4 e5 c5 5 c3 ♞c6 6 ♞df3 ♛a5 7
♞e2=; 6...c4!?; 4 ♞gf3 c5 5 dxc5
♗xc5 6 ♗d3 ♞f6 7 0-0 0-0 8 ♛e2 ♞c6
9 e5 += Hulak-Raicevic, Jugoslavia
76 **♞f6?!** 4...c5 5 dxc5! ♗xc5 6
♞gf3 += 5 e5 ♞fd7 6 f4 c5 7 c3
♞c6 8 ♞df3± b5 9 ♞e2 ♛b6 10 0-0
♗b7 11 ♔h1 △ f5 h6 12 f5! 0-0-0
13 fxe6 fxe6 14 ♞f4! cxd4?! 14...

♞e7± 15 ♞xe6 ♖e8 16 ♞exd4 ♞cxe5
17 ♗f5! ♛b8 18 a4 +− ♗d6 19 axb5
axb5 20 ♗f4 ♞c5 21 ♞xe5 ♗xe5 22
♛g4! ♗xf4 23 ♛xf4+ ♛c7 24 ♛f2!?
24 ♛xc7+ △ ♞xb5+ +− ♞c6 25 ♞xc6+
♛xc6 26 ♛g3+ 1-0 26...♛c7 27 ♖a8+
+−; 26...♔b7 27 ♛xg7+ △ ♛a7 mate

319 Skrobek-Pytel Poland 78

1 e4 e6 2 d4 d5 3 ♞d2 a6 4 ♞gf3
c5 5 e5 5 exd5! ♞c6= 6 ♗d3 ♞d7 7
dxc5 ♗xc5 8 a3 a5 9 0-0 ♞ge7 10
c4 ♞g6!? 11 ♞b3 ♗b6 12 ♖e1 a4?!
13 ♗g5 ♛b8 14 cxd5 exd5 15 ♗xg6
hxg6 16 ♞bd4 0-0 17 e6 fxe6 18
♞xe6 ♖f5! 19 g4? ♗xf2+

20 ♔g2 20 ♔xf2!? ♛xh2+ 21 ♔e3!∝
♖xf3! 21 ♛xf3 ♗xe1 22 ♖xe1??
22 ♛xd5! ♛e5! =+ ♗xe6 23 ♖xe6 ♞d4
−+ 24 ♛xd5 ♞xe6 25 ♛xe6+ ♔h7
26 h4 ♖a5 27 ♗d2 ♖e5 28 ♛c4 ♛e8
29 ♔f3 b5 30 ♛d3 ♛c6+ 31 ♔f2
♖d5 32 ♛c3 ♛d7 0-1 **Pytel**

320 Shamkovich-Filguth

Lone Pine 78

1 e4 e6 2 d4 d5 3 ♞d2 c5 4 ♞gf3
♞c6 5 ♗b5 a6 5...cxd4 6 ♞xd4 ♗d7
7 ♞b3!?; 5...♞f6 6 exd5 **6 exd5 axb5**
7 dxc6 c4!? 7...bxc6 8 dxc5 ♗xc5
9 0-0 ♞f6 10 ♛e2 ♗e7 Radulov-
Byrne, Leningrad 73, 11 c4! 0-0 12

b3 += **8 cxb7 ♗xb7 9 0-0 ♘f6 10 ♖e1 ♘d6** 10...♗e7 **11 c3 0-0 12 ♘f1 ♘d5 13 ♘g3 ♕c7** 13...b4!? **14 ♘e4 ♗e7 15 ♕c2** △ ♘eg5 f6 16 ♗d2 ♖a6? 16...b4! **17 a3!± ♘b6 18 ♖e2 ♘d5 19 ♖ae1 ♘d7 20 ♗c1 ♕b8 21 ♘g3 ♘d6?** 21...♘d8 △ ♗c7

22 ♖xe6! ♗xe6 23 ♖xe6± ♖d8 23...♖e8 **24 ♕e4**; 23...♖b6!? **24 ♕f5!** 24 ♗f4 ♘f8 25 ♖xd6 ♖axd6 26 ♘f5 ♖xd4! −+ **♘f8 25 ♖e4 ♗xg3 26 hxg3 ♕b7 27 g4!** ♕d7 27...g6 28 ♕f4 ♘e6 29 ♕e3 **28 ♕xd7 ♘xd7 29 g5! fxg5** 29...♔f7 30 gxf6 gxf6 31 ♖h4± **30 ♗xg5 ♖f8 31 ♔f1 ♖g6 32 ♗h4 h6 33 ♗g3 ♔f7 34 ♘e5+ ♘xe5 35 ♖xe5 ♖b6 36 ♖c5 ♖e8 37 ♗e5 +− ♖b7 38 ♔e2 ♖e6 39 ♖c6+ ♔f5 40 f3** △ g4+ h5 **41 ♔e3 ♖ee7 42 ♖c8 ♖bd7 43 ♖h8 ♔g6 44 ♖b8 ♖b7 45 ♖c8 ♖bd7 46 ♖c6+ ♔f5 47 ♖c5 ♖b7 48 ♔f2** △ ♗d6+ ♔g6 49 ♗f4! **♖f7 50 ♖g5+ ♔h6 51 ♔g3! ♔h7** 51...h4+ 52 ♔g4 ♔h7 53 ♖h5+ **52 ♖xh5+ ♔g6 53 ♖g5+ ♔f6 54 ♖c5 ♖fd7 55 ♖c6+ 1-0** 55...♔f7 56 ♗e5 △ ♔f4-e4 **Shamkovich**

321 M.Tseitlin-Feishter USSR 78
1 e4 e6 2 d4 d5 3 ♘d2 c5 4 ♘gf3 ♘c6 5 ♗b5 cxd4 5...a6 6 exd5 axb5 **7 dxc6 cxd4 8 cxb7 ♗xb7 9 0-0 ♘f6**

10 ♘b3∝ **6 0-0!?** N 6 ♘xd4 ♗d7 7 ♘xc6 ♗xc6?! 8 ♘xc6+ bxc6 9 c4 += **♗d6 7 ♖e1 ♘ge7 8 e5 ♗c7 9 ♘xd4 ♗d7?!** 9...0-0 **10 ♘xc6 bxc6** 10...♗xc6 11 ♗d3 += **11 ♗d3 ♘g6 12 ♘f1** c5 12...0-0 13 ♘g5! h6? 14 ♘xf7± **13 c4 ♗c6** 13...0-0 14 ♘g5 dxc4 15 ♕h5!; 13...dxc4 **14 cxd5 ♕xd5 15 ♕c2 ♘xe5** 15...0-0 16 ♖d1 ♖ad8 17 ♘g5 +−; 15...♖d8 16 ♗e4 ♕d7 17 ♘g5 +− **16 ♗e4 ♘xf3+ 17 ♗xf3 ♕d7** 17...♕d6 18 ♗f4 +− **18 ♖d1 ♗d5 19 ♗xd5 exd5 20 ♕xc5 0-0-0 21 ♗e3 ♕d6 22 ♕xa7 ♕xh2+ 23 ♔f1 ♕h1+ 24 ♔e2 ♕h5+ 25 f3 ♔g8 26 ♔f1 ♕c6 27 ♖ac1 ♕b5+ 28 ♔g1 ♕b7 29 ♖xc7+ 1-0 Gufeld**

322 Geller-Vaganian Lvov 78
1 e4 e6 2 d4 d5 3 ♘d2 c5 4 ♘gf3 ♘c6 5 exd5 exd5 6 ♗b5 ♗d6 7 dxc5 ♗xc5 8 ♘b3 ♗d6 9 0-0 ♘e7 10 ♖e1 0-0 11 c3 ♗g4 12 ♗g5 h6 13 ♗h4 ♕c7 14 ♗g3 ♗xg3 15 hxg3 ♖ad8 16 ♕d3 ♗xf3 17 ♕xf3 ♕b6 18 ♗xc6 18 ♗d3 a5 **♘xc6 19 ♖ad1 ♕a6!? 20 ♘c5** 20 a3 ♕b6; 20 ♘c1 d4 ♕c4 21 ♕e3 ½-½**

323 Peters-Ervin USA 78
1 e4 e6 2 d4 d5 3 ♘d2 c5 4 ♘gf3 ♘c6 5 exd5 exd5 6 ♗b5 ♗d6 7 dxc5 ♗xc5 8 0-0 ♘ge7 9 ♘b3 ♗d6 10 ♖e1 0-0 11 ♗g5 ♗g4 12 h3 ♗h5 13 ♗xc6 bxc6 14 ♘bd4 ♖c8 15 c4 h6 16 ♗xe7 ♗xe7 17 g4 ♗g6 18 ♘e5 ♗c5 19 b4! 19 ♘exc6 ♕b6 20 ♘e7+ ♔h7 21 ♘xc8 ♖xc8 22 ♘f3 ♗xf2+ ♗xd4 **20 ♕xd4 dxc4 21 ♕xc4 ♕h7 22 ♖ad1 ♕h4 23 ♔g2 f5 24 ♘xg6 ♔xg6 25 gxf5+ ♔h5** 25...♔g5?? 26 ♖d4 ♕h5 27 ♖g4+ ♔xf5 28 ♕e6 mate **26 ♖d4 ♕g5+ 27 ♖g4 ♕xf5 28 ♕e2! ♕b5** 28...♕d5+ 29 ♔g3 ♕d6+ 30 f4

Δ ♖g5+ +-

29 ♖g5+! 29 ♖h4+ ♔g6; 29 ♕d1 ♕d5+
♔xg5 30 ♕g4+ ♔f6 31 ♕e6+ ♔g5
32 f4+! ♖xf4 33 ♖e5+ ♕xe5 34
♕xe5+ ♖f5 35 h4+ ♔g4 36 ♕e4+
♖f4 37 ♕g6+ ♔xh4 38 ♕g3+ ♔h5
39 ♕xf4 +- ♖d8 40 ♕f3+ ♔g6 41
♕xc6+ ♔h7 42 a4 ♖d2+ 43 ♔f3
♖b2 44 ♕c3 ♖a2 45 a5 1-0

324 Ehrenfeucht-Pinkas
Bialystok 78

**1 e4 e6 2 d4 d5 3 ♘d2 ♘f6 4 e5 ♘fd7
5 ♗d3 c5 6 c3 ♘c6 7 ♘e2 cxd4 8
cxd4 f6 9 exf6 ♘xf6 10 ♘f3** 10 f4
♗d6 11 0-0 ♕c7 12 ♘c3 a6 13 ♗g5
♘g4?!** 13...0-0 14 ♗h4 ♗d7 15 ♖e1
♔h8 16 ♗g3 ♗xg3 17 hxg3 ♕b6 18
♘a4 ♕a7 19 ♗b1 Balashov-Vaganian,
USSR 76 **14 h3 ♘f6 15 ♖e1 0-0 16
♖c1 ♗d7 17 ♘e5 ♕d8** 17...♖ae8 18
♗xf6 ♖xf6 19 ♕h5 g6 20 ♗xg6 **18
♗b1 ♕e8 19 ♕d3 ♗b4 20 ♕e3 ♗c8
21 f4 h6 22 ♗g6 ♕d8 23 ♗h4 ♘c6
24 ♗b1** 24 g4! **♕b6 25 ♖ed1 ♘h5
26 g3** 26 ♘e2 ♘xf4 27 fxe5 ♗xe5 27 fxe5
g5 **28 ♗xg5 hxg5 29 ♕xg5+ ♘g7
30 ♕g6! ♖f3 31 ♕h7+ ♔f8 32 ♗g6
♖xg3+ 33 ♔h2 ♖xg6 34 ♕xg6 ♘xd4
35 ♕f6+ ♔g8 36 ♕f2!** ♗gf5 37 ♖g1+
37 ♘e2! ♕xb2 38 ♖xd4 ♘xd4 39
♖g1+ +- **♔f7 38 ♕g2 ♔e7 39 ♔h1

♘c6 39...♗d7 40 ♕g5+ ♔e8 41 ♕g8+
♔e7 42 ♕h7+ ♔d8 43 ♖g8+ ♔c7 44
♘xd5+ +- **40 ♖cf1! ♕c5 41 ♖xf5
exf5 42 ♘xd5+ ♔d7 43 ♕g7+ ♘e7
44 ♘xe7 ♔c7** 44...♕xe7 45 ♖d1+
♔e8 46 ♕g8+ ♕f8 47 ♖d8+ +- **45
♘xc8+ ♕xc8 46 ♕g8+ ♔c7 47 ♕xa8
♕d5+ 48 ♖g2 ♕f3 49 ♕a7! 1-0**

325 Foigel-Mouin USSR 77
**1 e4 e6 2 d4 d5 3 ♘d2 ♘f6 4 e5
♘fd7 5 f4 c5 6 c3 ♘c6 7 ♘df3 ♕b6
8 ♘e2?!** 8 g3 ♗e7 8...f6 9 g3?! cxd4
10 cxd4 ♗b4+ =; 10...fxe5 11 fxe5
♗b4+ 12 ♔f2? 0-0 13 ♗e3 ♘dxe5!
14 dxe5 ♖xf3+! 15 ♔xf3 ♘xe5+
Whitehead-Maroczy, London 23; 12
♘c3!; 9 a3! ♗e7 10 b4 cxd4 11 cxd4
0-0 Enevoldsen-Koch, Helsinki 52
9 g3 cxd4 9...0-0 10 ♗h3 ♕a6 11 0-0
cxd4 12 cxd4 ♘b6 13 g4 Haag-Farago
65 **10 cxd4 f6 11 ♗h3 fxe5 12 fxe5
0-0! 13 ♗xe6+?!** 13 ♘f4 ♗b4+ 14
♔e2 (14 ♗d2 ♘xd4) 14...♔h8 15
♘xe6 ♘dxe5! **♔h8 14 ♗xd5 ♘dxe5!
-+ 15 dxe5 ♘xe5 16 ♘fd4** 16 ♘xe5?
♗b4+ 17 ♗d2 ♕f2 mate **♗b4+ 17
♘c3 ♗g4 18 ♕d2 ♖ae8 19 ♘de2
♖f2! 0-1 Kapengut**

326 Sanz-Mariotti
Las Palmas 78

**1 e4 e6 2 d4 d5 3 ♘c3 ♗b4 4 exd5
exd5 5 ♗d3 ♘c6 6 a3!?** 6 ♘e2 ♘ge7
Δ ♗f5 ♗e7?!** 6...♗xc3+ 7 bxc3 ♘ge7
8 ♕f3!?; 8 ♕h5!? **7 ♘ce2?!** 7 ♘f3!
♗g4 8 h3! ♗h5 9 ♗f4! += **♗f6! 8 c3
♘ge7 9 ♘g3?!** g6 10 ♕f3?! ♗g7 11
♗g5 h5 12 ♕f4?** 12 ♗f6 ♕d7! **13 ♔f1!?
♘d8** 13...f6 14 ♖e1α **14 ♗f6 ♘e6
15 ♕h4? g5! 16 ♗xg5 ♘g6 17 ♗xg6
♕b5+∓ 18 ♘1e2 fxg6 19 ♗f6? ♕xb2
20 ♖e1 ♔f7! 21 ♗xg7 g5 -+ 22 ♗xh8
22 ♕h3 ♘xg7 ♗xh4 23 ♗xh5 ♗d7 24

♗e5 ♗b5 25 f4 ♖g8 26 ♖g1 ♕xc3 27 ♘f6 ♗xf4 28 ♗xf4 ♔xf6 29 ♔f2 ♗xe2 30 ♗e5+ ♔e6 31 ♔xe2 c5 0-1 Larsen

327 Mestel-Botterill London 78
1 e4 e6 2 d4 d5 3 e5 c5 4 c3 ♘c6 5 ♘f3 ♕b6 6 a3 c4 7 g3 f6 8 exf6 ♘xf6 9 ♗g2 9 ♗h3 ♘a5 10 ♘bd2 ♗d6 11 0-0 0-0 12 ♖e1 ♔h8 13 ♘e5? ♗xe5 14 ♖xe5 ♘c6 15 ♖e1 e5! 16 ♗xc8 ♖axc8 17 ♘f3 ♘e4∓ Goichberg-Botterill, London 78; 13 ♗xe6 ♗xe6 14 ♖xe6 ♖ae8 15 ♖xe8 ♖xe8∞ 16 ♘f1 ♘b3 17 ♖b1 ♘e4 18 ♘1d2 ♗xa3! ♗d6 10 0-0 0-0 11 ♕e2 ♔h8 12 ♘e5 ♗xe5 12...♘a5 13 ♘d2 ♗xe5 14 ♕xe5! += 13 dxe5 ♘d7 14 ♗e3 ♕c7 14...♘c5 15 ♘d2 ♕a5 16 f4 ♗d7 17 ♗xc5 ♕xc5+ 18 ♔f2 ♕xf2+ 19 ♖xf2 g5!? Alexander-Uhlmann, Munich 58; 17 ♘f3!? ♖ae8! △ ♖e7, ♗e8 15 f4 ♘a5 16 ♘d2 ♘c5 17 ♗xc5 ♕xc5+ 18 ♔f2 ♕xf2+ 19 ♔xf2! ♗d7 19...g5? 20 ♔e3± 20 ♔e3 ♖ae8 21 ♘f3 21 ♖ae1! ♖e7 22 f5!? exf5 23 ♗xd5 ♖xe5+ 24 ♔d4 ♖xe1 25 ♖xe1±; 22...♖xf5 23 ♖xf5 exf5 24 ♔d4 ♘c6+ 25 ♔xd5 ♗e6+ 26 ♔d6± ♘b3 22 ♖ab1 ♖e7 23 ♘d4 ♘c5 24 ♔d2 ♗e8 25 f5 25 g4 a6 26 h4!? (△ h5) h5! exf5= 26 ♗d5 ♖xe5 27 ♗xc4 ♗f7 ½-½ Botterill

328 N.Zhuravlev-Korsunsky USSR 78
1 e4 c5 2 c3 e6 3 d4 d5 4 e5 ♘c6 5 ♘f3 ♕b6 6 ♗e2 cxd4 7 cxd4 ♘ge7 8 b3 ♘f5 9 ♗b2 ♗e7 9...♗b4+ 10 ♔f1 h5 10 0-0 0-0 11 ♔h1 f6!? 12 g4?! 12 ♘c3 ♘h6 13 exf6 ♖xf6 14 g5 ♖xf3 15 ♗xf3 ♗xg5 ∝/=+ 16 ♘a3?! 16 ♘c3 ♕xd4 17 ♕xd4 ♘xd4 18 ♗g2 ∝/=+ ♗d7!? 16...♘f5 17 ♘c2

♗f6 17 ♘c2 ♖f8 18 ♗g2 ♗f4 19 ♕e2 19 ♗c1!? ♕d8 20 ♘e1

20...♗xh2!∓ 21 ♕h5 21 ♔xh2 ♕h4+ 22 ♔h3 e5?! 23 ♕d3 ♘g4+ 24 ♔g1 ♘xf2 ♗f4 22 ♗h3 e5?! 22...g6 23 ♕f3 ♗c1 24 ♗xc1 ♖xf3 25 ♘xf3∓ 23 dxe5 g6 24 ♖g1 ♔h8 25 e6+ d4 26 ♕d5?! 26 ♕f3! ♘e5? 27 exd7 ♘xf3 28 ♗xf3 ♘f5 29 ♘xd4 ♗e5 30 ♘e6 ♕h4 31 ♗xe5+ ♔g8 32 ♔h2! +-; 26...♗e8 △ ♘e5, ♗c6 =+ ♕h4 27 ♔g2 27 ♗xd4+? ♘xd4 28 ♕xd4+ ♔g8 -+ ♗e3 27...♘g4! 28 ♗xg4 ♕h2+ 29 ♔f1 ♗e3 -+; 28 ♘d3 ♘e3+! -+ 28 ♘d3 ♗xf2 29 ♔h2 ♘f5! 30 ♘xf2 ♕f3 ♗xg1+ 31 ♖xg1 ♗e6 -+ ♗e3 31 ♗xd4+ ♘xd4 32 ♕e5+ ♔g8 33 ♕xe3 ♖xf2+ 0-1 Gufeld

329 Botterill-Ligterink London 78
1 e4 c5 2 ♘f3 e6 3 c3 d5 4 e5 ♕b6 5 d4 ♘c6 6 ♗e2 ♘h6!? 6...cxd4 7 cxd4 ♘ge7 8 ♘c3 ♘f5 9 ♘a4 ♕a5+ 10 ♗d2 ♗b4 11 ♘c3 b5 12 a3 ♗xc3+ 13 ♘xc3 b4! =+; 8 ♘a3! 7 b3?! 7 ♗xh6!? ♕xb2? 8 ♗e3! ♕xa1 9 ♕c2 +-; 7...gxh6 8 ♕d2∝ cxd4 8 cxd4 ♘f5 9 ♗b2 ♗b4+ 10 ♔f1 0-0! Nimzovich! 10...h5 11 ♘c3 ♗xc3 12 ♗xc3 ♗d7∓ Holmov-Petrosian, USSR 49 11 g4 ♘h6 12 ♖g1 f6! 13

exf6 **Xxf6** 14 g5 **Xxf3!** 15 gxh6 **Xf7**
16 **Ad3** e5 17 **Wh5** e4 18 **Ae2 Ae6** 18...
g6∓ 19 **Ac3 Axc3** 20 **Axc3 Axd4!?**
21 **We5! Af5** 21...Xxf2+? 22 **Ce1!!**
+− 22 **Ah5 Xe7** 23 **Ag4** ½-½ Zeitnot
23...**Wc7** 24 **Wxc7 Xxc7** 25 **Axg7**
Cf7 26 **Ae5 Xd7** 27 **Axf5 Axf5** 28
Xg7+ =; 23...d4! (Δ **Ac4+**) 24 **Ce1**
Af7 25 **Wxf5** dxc3 26 **Wg5 Wf6** 27
Wxf6 gxf6 28 **Af5+** =; 24...e3!! 25
f4 **Af7** 26 **Wxf5** dxc3∓ **Botterill**

330 Wagman-Bukal Italy 78
1 e4 e6 2 d4 d5 3 e5 c5 4 c3 **Ac6** 5
Af3 Age7 6 a3 cxd4 7 cxd4 **Af5**
8 **Ac3 Ae7** 9 **Ae2 Ad7** 10 **Wf1?!** 0-0
11 h4 f6! 12 g4?!

12...**Afxd4!** 13 **Axd4** fxe5 14 **Af3**
14 **Axc6 Axc6** Δ d4 e4 15 **Ag5 Ac5**
16 **Axd5 Xxf2+** 16...exd5 17 **Wxd5+**
17 **Ce1 Xxe2+** 18 **Wxe2** 18 **Cxe2**
Ad4+ exd5 19 b4 **Ad4** 20 **Ab2 Wf6**
0-1 21 **Axd4 Axd4** Δ **Ac2+** −+; 21
Xb1 Axb2 22 **Xxb2 Ae5** Δ **Ad3+/**
Axg4/h6

331 Sax-F.Portisch
Hungary Final 78
1 e4 e6 2 d4 d5 3 e5 c5 4 c3 **Ac6** 5
Af3 Age7 6 **Aa3 Af5** 7 **Ac2** cxd4
8 cxd4 **Ae7** 9 **Ad3** 0-0 10 0-0 f6 11
Axf5 exf5 12 **Xe1** fxe5 13 dxe5 f4!
13...**Ae6** 14 **Acd4** 14 h3 **Ac5** 15 a3
a5 16 **Xb1 Ch8** 16...d4? 17 b4 d3

18 bxc5 dxc2 19 **Wxc2 Af5** 20 **Wb3+**
17 b4 axb4 18 axb4 **Wb6** 19 **Xe2**
Af5 20 **Xb2** 20 **Axf4 Axf2+** 21 **Xxf2**
Axc2 22 **Wxc2 Xxf4 Ae7!** 21 **Wxd5**
Xad8 22 **Wb3 Xd1+** 23 **Xe1 Axc2**
24 **Wxc2 Xxe1+** 25 **Axe1 Axe5** 26
We4 Ag6 27 **Af3 Wc6!** 28 **Wxc6** bxc6
29 **Ad2 Xb8** 30 **Ad4** c5 31 **Ac6 Xb5**
32 **Xa2** cxb4 33 **Xa8+ Af8** 34 **Axb4**
Wg8 35 h4?! 35 **Ae7+ Cf7** 36 **Axg6**
Axb4 37 **Axf4 Ad6 Cf7** 36 **Ad8+**
Cf6 37 **Ac3+ Cf5** 38 h5 **Ae5** 39 f3
Ac5+ 40 **Ch2 Af2** 41 **Xa5 Ag3+** ½-½

332 Gonzales Mestres-Marovic
Spain 77
1 e4 **Af6** 2 e5 **Ad5** 3 c4 **Ab6** 4 c5
Ad5 5 **Ac4** e6 5...c6 6 **Ac3** d6 7 cxd6
exd6 8 **Wb3** dxe5 9 **Axd5** cxd5 10
Axd5 Wc7= Dubinin-Kopilov, USSR
46 6 d4 b6!? 6...d6 7 cxb6 axb6
8 **Af3 Aa6** 9 **Axa6 Ab4+** 10 **Ad2**
Axd2+ 11 **Abxd2 Xxa6** 12 0-0 **Ac6**
13 a3 0-0 14 **Ae4** f5 15 exf6 gxf6!?
15...**Axf6** 16 **Axf6+ Wxf6** 17 d5
16 **Wd2 We8** 17 **Ac3 Ace7** 18 **Axd5**
Axd5 19 a4 **Wa8** 20 b3 b5 21 **Xa2**
bxa4 22 **Xfa1** a3 23 **Wc1 Wb7** 24
Xxa3 Xxa3 25 **Xxa3 Xb8** 26 h4
Wb4 27 **Wa1 Cf7** 28 **Xa8 Wxb3** 29
Xxb8 Wxb8 30 **Wa4 Wb1+** 31 **Ch2**
We7 32 **Wa3+** d6 33 **Wa8 Wg6** 34 **Wc6**
We4 35 **Wb7 Wc2** 36 **Wg3** f5 −+
37 **Wa8** f4+ 38 **Ch2 Af6** 39 **Wh8 Ag4+**
40 **Ch3 Axf2+** 41 **Ch2 Ag4+** 42
Ch3 Ae3 43 **Wg7+ Cd8** 44 h5 0-1

333 Kurajica-Fraguela Spain 77
1 e4 **Af6** 2 e5 **Ad5** 3 d4 d6 4 c4 **Ab6**
5 exd6 exd6 6 **Ae2 Ae7** 7 **Af3** 0-0 8
Ac3 Af5 8...**Ag4** 9 b3?! c5 10 **Ae3**
Ac6 11 **Xc1** f5 12 dxc5 dxc5= Minic-
Smyslov, Palma 70; 9 0-0!?; 8...**Ac6**

9 ♗e3 ♗g4 **9 0-0 ♗f6 10 h3 c6** 10...
♗g6 11 b3 ♘c6 12 ♗e3 a5 13 ♖c1
a4 14 ♘xa4 ♘xa4 15 bxa4 ♖e8 16
♖e1 ♕d7 17 ♕b3 ♗e4≈ Nicevski-
Hort, Athens 69 **11 ♗f4 ♘a6 12 g4
♗e6 13 b3 ♘c7 14 ♕d2 ♗e7 15 ♗d3
f5**

**16 g5 ♗f7 17 ♖fe1 ♗h5 18 ♘h4 g6
19 ♕e3 ♖e8 20 ♕g3 ♕d7 21 d5
♗f8 22 dxc6 ♕xc6 23 ♗f1 ♕d7 24
c5 ♘c8 25 ♖xe8 ♘xe8 26 ♗b5 ♕d8
27 ♖e1** 27 ♘xe8? ♕xe8 28 cxd6 ♕c6
♘g7 28 ♘d5 ♔h8 29 ♗c4 a5 30 ♕c3
♘a7 31 ♕f6 ♕xf6 31...♕d7 32 ♘e7 △
♕f7 +− **32 gxf6 ♘e8 33 f7 ♘g7
34 ♘c7** △ ♖e8 **1-0**

334 Hertzog-Grun
Hastings 2 77/78
**1 e4 ♘f6 2 e5 ♘d5 3 d4 d6 4 ♘f3
♗g4 5 ♗e2 c6 6 ♘g5 ♗f5 7 ♗d3 ♗xd3
8 ♕xd3 dxe5 9 dxe5 h6** 9...e6 10 c4
(10 ♘xh7) ♘b4 11 ♕xd8+ ♔xd8 12
♘xf7+ ♔e8 13 ♘xh8 ♘c2+ **10 ♘f3**
10 ♘xf7!? ♔xf7 11 c4 ♕a5+ 12
♗d2 ♘b4 13 ♕f5+ ♔g8 14 a3 c5
e6 11 0-0 ♘d7 12 c4 ♘b4 13 ♕e2
a5 14 ♘c3 ♘c5 14...♕c7 15 ♗f4 ♗e7
16 ♘e4 **15 ♖d1 ♕c7 16 ♗f4 ♖d8**
16...♗e7 17 a3 ♘ba6 18 b4!; 16...
♘ba6 17 ♘d2 **17 ♖xd8+ ♕xd8 18
♖d1 ♕c7 19 a3 ♘ba6 20 ♘d2!** f5?!

20...♗e7 21 ♕g4!

21 ♘de4! 21 exf6?! ♕xf4 22 ♕h5+
♔d7 **♘xe4** 21...fxe4 22 ♕h5+ ♔e7
23 ♕g6! a4 24 ♗g3 ♘d3 25 ♗h4+
♔d7 26 ♕f7+ ♗e7 27 ♘xe4; 23...
♘d3 24 ♗g3 ♔d7 25 ♘xe4; 23...♘d7
24 ♗g3 ♔d8 25 ♗h4+ +− **22 ♘xe4
fxe4 23 ♕h5+ ♔e7 24 ♕g6!** △ ♗g3-h4
mate **♘c5 25 ♖d6** 25 ♗g3?! ♘d3 26
♗h4+ ♔d7 27 ♕f7+ ♗e7 a4 **26 ♗g3 1-0**

335 Ciocaltea-Suba
Rumania 77
**1 e4 ♘f6 2 e5 ♘d5 3 d4 d6 4 ♘f3
♗g4 5 ♗e2 e6 6 0-0 ♗e7 7 c4 ♘b6
8 ♘c3 0-0 9 ♗e3 d5 10 c5** 10 cxd5!?
♗xf3 11 gxf3!? ♘c8! 11...♘6d7?!
12 b4 12 f4!? ♗h4 13 ♗d3 g6 14 f5!±
Pokojowczyk-Schmidt, Poland 76;
12...c6 13 ♗d3 g6? 14 b4±
Gurgenidze-Suba, Varna 75; 12...g6
13 ♔h1 ♔h8 14 b4± Bojkovic-Vukic,
Novi Sad 75 **b6** N 12...f6 13 f4 fxe5
14 fxe5 ♕e8 15 ♗d3 ♗d8 16 ♕g4±
Matanovic-Vukic, Jugoslavia Final 75
**13 ♖b1! f5 14 f4 ♖f7 15 ♔h1 c6
16 a4** += **♗f8 17 ♕d2 a5 18 b5!±
bxc5 19 dxc5 ♘d7 20 bxc6 ♘xc6
21 ♖fc1!** ♘b6 21...♘e4 22 ♘xe4
fxe4 23 ♗g4 ♕e8 24 ♖b7 **22 ♘b5
♘bxa4 23 ♘d6! ♗xd6 24 exd6 ♕xd6
25 ♗b5** △ ♕a2 **♘e4 26 ♕d4 ♘ac3**

27 ♖xc3 ♘xc3 28 ♕xc3 +− a4 29
♕c5 ♕xc5 30 ♗xc5 a3 31 ♖a1 a2
31...♖a5 32 ♖xa3 ♖xb5 33 ♖a8+ +−
32 ♗d6 ♖fa7 33 c7 ♕f7 34 ♗d7
♖xc7 35 ♗xc7 ♖a7 36 ♗e5 ♖xd7
37 ♖xa2 h6 38 ♔g2 g5 39 ♔f3 ♖b7
40 ♖c2 ♔g6 41 ♖c6 ♖b3+ 42 ♔g2
♔f7 43 ♖c7+ ♔g6 44 ♖e7 ♖b6 45
h3! △ 46 ♖g7+ ♔h5 47 fxg5 hxg5
48 ♗f6 g4 46 ♖g7+ ♔h5 47 hxg4+
fxg4 48 ♖f7! 1-0 Ciocaltea

336 Stoica-Alburt Bucharest 78
1 e4 ♘f6 2 e5 ♘d5 3 d4 d6 4 ♘f3
♗g4 5 ♗e2 e6 6 0-0 ♗e7 7 h3 ♗h5 8
c4 ♘b6 9 ♘c3 0-0 10 ♗e3 d5 11 cxd5
11 c5 ♘xd5 11...exd5 12 ♗d3 ♘c6
13 g4 ♗g6 14 ♗f5 ♕e8! 15 ♘e2 f6
16 ♘g3 fxe5 17 ♘xe5 Gulko-
Bagirov, USSR 77 12 ♕b3 ♘b6 12...
♘xe3 13 fxe3 b6 14 d5 ♗c5 15 dxe6
♗xe3+ 16 ♔h1 fxe6 17 ♕xe6+±
Georgadze-Alburt, Tbilisi 77; 14 ♗d3
♘c6 15 ♗e4 ♘a5 16 ♕c2 ♗g6 17 ♗xg6
hxg6 18 ♖ad1± Pytel-Bohm, Le
Havre 77 13 ♖fd1! 13 a4 a5 14 ♖ad1!
♘c6 15 d5!± Gligoric-Vukic, Novi
Sad 76 c6 13...♕c8 14 d5 15 ♘xd5
exd5 16 ♖xd5 ♗g6? 17 ♘d4!±
Sznapik-Schmidt, Polska 77; 16...♘c6
+= 14 a4 ♕d7 14...a5 15 d5! ♘xd5
16 ♕xb7 ♘d7 17 g4, 18 ♕xc6 15
♖ac1 ♘a6 16 a5 ♘d5 17 ♘xd5 exd5
18 ♗d2 18 e6 ♕xe6 19 ♕xb7 ♘b4!;
18...fxe6? 19 ♘e5 ♕e8 20 ♗xh5
♕xh5 21 ♕xb7 ♖ab8 19 ♕e3 ♘c7
20 ♗d3 ♗g6 21 ♖e1 f5?! 22 f4 ♘e6?!
22...♘h5!? 23 ♗e2 b6 24 b4 bxa5
25 bxa5 ♖fc8 26 ♘d3 ♖b3 27 ♕f2
♗h5?! 28 ♗xh5 ♖xd3 29 ♗e3 ♖xd1+?!
30 ♗xd1± c5 31 dxc5! d4 32 ♗d2
♖xc5 33 ♗b3! ♕f7 34 ♕e2 △ ♕h5+
♖xc1+ 35 ♗xc1 g6 36 ♕c4 ♗c5?? 37
♕xc5 1-0 Ciocaltea

337 Olafsson-Larsen Reykjavic 78
1 e4 ♘f6 2 e5 ♘d5 3 d4 d6 4 ♘f3
g6 5 ♗c4 ♘b6 6 ♗b3 ♗g7 7 ♘g5
7 ♘bd2 Spassky-Fischer (13) 72
d5 7...0-0? 8 e6 8 0-0 ♘c6 9 c3 ♗f5
9...h6 10 ♘f3 ♗g4 11 h3 ♗xf3 12
♕xf3 e6 △ ♕d7 += 10 g4! ♗xb1 11
♕f3 0-0 12 ♖xb1 ♕d7 13 ♗c2 ♘d8
14 ♕h3 h6

15 f4!! hxg5 16 f5! ♘e6 16...f6
17 fxg6 ♖e8 18 ♗xg5! ♘e6 19 ♕h7+
♔f8 20 ♗h6 △ ♕h8 mate; 16...e6
17 f6 ♗h8 18 ♕h6 △ ♖f3-h3 +−
17 fxe6 ♕xe6 18 ♗xg5 c5 19 ♔h1
cxd4 20 cxd4 ♖fc8 21 ♗f5! +−
gxf5 22 gxf5 ♕c6 23 ♖g1 ♕c2 23...
♔f8 24 f6 exf6 25 exf6 ♗xf6 26
♗h6+ ♔e7 27 ♖be1+ +− 24 ♖be1
♔f8 25 f6 1-0

338 Hardicsay-K.Honfi Hungary 78
1 e4 ♘f6 2 e5 ♘d5 3 ♘f3 d6 4 d4
g6 5 ♗c4 ♘b6 6 ♗b3 ♗g7 7 ♘g5
7 a4 += e6 N 7...d5 += 8 f4?! 8 exd6
+= dxe5 9 fxe5 c5 10 c3 cxd4 11
0-0 0-0 12 cxd4 ♘c6 13 ♘f3 f6!
14 exf6 ♕xf6 14...♗xf6 △ ♔h8, e5
15 ♗e3 ♘d5 16 ♗f2 ♔h8 16...♘f4!
△ ♘h3+/♕f5, ♕g4= 17 ♘c3 ♘xc3
18 bxc3 ♗d7? 18...e5 19 d5 e4!?=
19 ♗g3! +− ♕e7 20 ♖e1 ♘a5 21 ♘e5!
♗e8 22 ♕g4 ♘xb3 23 axb3 ♖f5 24

♕e4 a6 25 ♘c4! ♖b5 26 ♖ab1 ♗d7
27 ♗e5! ♖c8 28 ♗xg7+ ♚xg7 29 d5
♕c5+ 30 ♔h1 exd5 30...♕xd5 31
♕xd5 ♖xd5 32 ♘b6 +− 31 ♕e5+ ♔g8
32 ♘d6 ♕xc3 33 ♕e7 ♗f5 34 ♕f7+!
♔h8 35 ♘xc8 1-0 Hardicsay

Pirc

339 Gulko-Petrosian
USSR Final 77

1 d4 g6 2 e4 ♗g7 3 ♘c3 d6 4 ♘ge2
c6 4...♘d7 5 g3 e5 6 ♗g2 ♘e7 7 0-0
0-0 8 a4 ♘c6 9 ♗e3 exd4 10 ♘xd4
♘de5 11 ♘de2 ♗g4 12 h3 ♗f3 +=
Gulko-Muratov, USSR 74; 4...a6?!
5 a4 ♘d7 6 g3 c5?! 7 dxc5 ♘xc5 8
♗g2 ♘f6 9 0-0 ♗d7 10 ♗e3 +=
Buljovcic-Ivkov, Sombor 68 5 a4
5 g3 e5 6 ♗g2 ♘e7 7 0-0 0-0 8 a4! +=
Matulovic-Czerniak, Bucharest 66 e5
6 ♗e3 ♘f6 7 dxe5 dxe5 8 ♕xd8+
♔xd8 9 h3 ♗e6 10 ♘g1 ♘bd7 11 ♘f3
h6 12 ♘d2 ♔c7 13 ♗c4 ♖he8 14
0-0-0 ♗f8 15 f4 ♗c5 16 ♗xc5 ♘xc5
17 fxe5 ♘fd7 18 ♗xe6 ♖xe6 19
♘f3 ♘xe5 20 ♖hf1 ♖f8 21 ♘d4 ♖e7
22 b3 ♘ed7 23 ♖f4 a5 24 ♖df1 h5
25 ♖d1 ♘b6 26 ♖df1 ♘cd7 27 ♘f3
f6 28 g4 hxg4 29 ♖xg4 g5 30 h4
gxh4 31 ♖xh4 ½-½

340 Kurajica-Planinc
Jugoslavia Final 78

1 e4 g6 2 d4 ♗g7 3 ♘c3 d6 4 ♗e3
c6 5 h3!? 5 ♕d2 b5 6 f3 ♘d7=; 5...♘f6
6 f3 b5 7 g4 += b5 5...♘f6 6 f4 6 a3
♗b7 7 f4 ♘d7 8 ♘f3 a5?! 8...a6 Δ
c5 9 e5± ♘h6 9...b4 10 ♘e4 c5 11
dxc5! dxe5 12 ♘b5 +− 10 ♗d3 0-0
11 0-0 c5? 11...♘b6 12 dxc5 b4 13
♘a4 ♗xf3 13...dxe5 14 ♘xe5 ♘xe5
15 fxe5 ♕d5 16 ♕d2± 14 ♕xf3 dxe5
15 ♖ad1 exf4 15...♕c7 16 ♘b6!

♘xb6 17 cxb6 ♕b8 18 b7 +− 16
♕xf4 e5? 16...♕c8 17 ♕h4 ♕c6 18
♘b6? ♘xc5; 17 axb4± 17 ♕f2
♕c7 18 ♕h4 +− e4 19 ♗b5 ♘e5 20
♗xh6 ♗xh6 21 ♕xh6 ♘f3+?? 22 gxf3
1-0 Kurajica

341 Levicki-V.Volko USSR 77

1 e4 d6 2 d4 g6 3 ♘c3 ♗g7 4 ♗e3 ♘f6
5 f3 0-0 5...c6!? 6 ♕d2 c6 6...e5?!
7 d5 ♘e8 8 g4! Δ h4±; 6...♘c6 7 0-0-0
e5 8 d5 ♘d4 9 ♘ge2 c5 10 dxc6 bxc6
11 ♘xd4 exd4 12 ♗xd4 ♗e6 13
♘a4!± 7 ♗h6 7 h4 ♘bd7 8 ♗h6 e5
9 dxe5 Δ 0-0-0 +=; 7 0-0-0!? Δ g4,
h4 b5! 7...♗xh6 8 ♕xh6 ♕a5 9 ♗d3
♘bd7 10 ♘h3!? b4 11 ♘e2 c5=
Beljavsky-Hort, Moscow 75; 7...♕a5
8 h4! b5 9 ♗xg7 ♔xg7 10 h5 +=
Gliksman-Angelov, Varna 76 8 ♗xg7
8 0-0-0 ♗e6!? 9 d5 cxd5 10 exd5
b4 11 ♗xg7 ♔xg7 12 ♘e4 ♘xd5 13
♗c4≈ ♔xg7 9 ♗d3 ♗d7?! 9...b4;
9...♗e6!? 10 e5! ♘g8 10...♘e8 +=
11 ♘ge2 += ♕b6 12 h4! dxe5 13 dxe5
♖d8 14 h5 ♗f5 15 hxg6 fxg6 16 ♘f4
♘a6? 16...c5!? 17 g4± ♗xd3

18 ♘e6+ ♔h8 19 0-0-0! Δ ♖xh7+!
+− ♗f1!? 20 ♘xd8 ♗c4 21 ♘e4 ♔g7
22 ♘g5 h6 23 ♘ge6 ♗xe6 24 ♘xe6
♔f7 25 ♖xh6!! +− ♘xh6 26 ♕xh6
♖g8 27 ♘g5+ ♔e8 28 ♕h7 ♕e3+

29 ♔b1 1-0 Gufeld

342 Ciocaltea-Hazai Albena 78
1 e4 d6 2 d4 ♘f6 3 ♘c3 g6 4 f3 c6
5 ♗e3 ♘bd7 5...♗g7 6 ♕d2 b5 7 ♗h6
♗xh6 8 ♕xh6 ♕a5 9 ♘d3 ♘bd7 10
♘h3 b4 11 ♘e2 c5= Beljavsky-Hort,
Moscow 75 **6 ♕d2 b5 7 ♘h3** 7 h4!?
h5 8 ♘h3 △ ♘g5 += e5 7...♘b6 8
♘f2 a5 9 a4 b4 10 ♘d1 ♗g7 11 ♗e2
♗a6 12 ♗xa6 ♖xa6 += **8 ♘f2 ♗b7 9
♗e2 b4 10 ♘cd1 exd4 11 ♗xd4 c5 12
♗e3 ♕e7** 12...d5 13 ♗b5! += dxe4
14 ♘xe4 ♗xe4 15 fxe4 ♕a5 16 ♗xd7+
♘xd7 17 0-0 **13 a3 a5 14 axb4 axb4
15 ♖xa8+ ♗xa8 16 0-0 ♗g7 17 ♗f4!
♘e5** 17...d5 18 e5! ♘xe5 19 ♗b5+;
18...♘h5 19 ♗g5 ♕xe5 20 ♗b5 **18
♗b5+ ♔d8** 18...♘fd7 19 ♘e3 0-0 20
♖d1 **19 ♘e3 ♕c7 20 ♖a1 ♗b7** 20...
♘h5? 21 ♖xa8! **21 c3 b3** 21...♘h5
22 ♗xe5 ♕xe5 23 ♘c4! bxc3 24 bxc3
♕e6 25 ♕b2! **22 ♗c4 ♖a8 23 ♖xa8
♗xa8 24 ♗xb3 ♘h5 25 ♗xe5 ♗xe5
26 g3! 1-0 Ciocaltea**

343 Mednis-Soltis
USA Final 78
1 e4 g6 2 d4 ♗g7 3 ♘c3 d6 4 ♘f3
a6 5 ♗c4! b5 6 ♗b3 ♘c6!? N 6...♘f6?!
7 0-0 0-0 8 e5! dxe5 9 dxe5 ♕xd1
10 ♖xd1 ♘g4 11 ♗f4± Shamkovich-
Goodman, Lone Pine 77 **7 0-0 ♘a5**
7...♗g4? 8 ♗xf7+ **8 h3 ♘xb3** 8...c6!?
9 axb3 ♗b7?! 9...c6!? **10 ♕e2 ♕c8**
10...♘h6? 11 ♗xh6 ♗xh6 12 ♘xb5!
+- **11 ♖e1! e6 12 e5 ♘e7 13 ♗g5?!**
13 ♘e4!± ♘f5 **14 ♖ad1** 14 d5 0-0!=
h6 15 ♗f6 ♗xf6 16 exf6 ♕d8!

Diagram

17 d5 17 ♘xb5? ♗xf3 -+; 17 g4!?
♗xf3 18 ♕xf3 ♘h4 19 ♕c6+ ♔f8

20 ♖d3α **♕xf6 18 ♘xb5! 0-0! 19
♘xc7 ♖ac8** 19...♖a7?! 20 g4 +-
20 ♘xa6 ♕xb2? 20...♗xd5 21 c3!
♗xb3 22 ♖a1= **21 ♘b4 ♕c3 22 ♕d2±
♗xd5 23 ♘xd5 exd5 24 ♕xc3 ♖xc3
25 ♖e2** 25 ♖xd5! ♖xc2 26 g4±
**♖fc8 26 ♘e1 ♖3c5 27 ♖ed2 ♘e7 28
♖a1 ♔f8 29 ♔f1 ♔e8 30 ♔e2 ♘c6
31 ♔d1 ♘e5 32 ♖a4 ♔d7 33 ♖a7+**
33 ♖ad4!± **♖8c7! 34 ♖xc7+ +=
♔xc7 35 ♖d4** 35 ♘d3! += **♖a5 36
♔d2 ♔c6 37 ♖b4 ♖a1 38 ♖b8 h5
39 ♖f8 ♔d7! 40 ♖b8 ♔e6 41 ♖b4
f6 42 ♖a4 ♖b1! 43 ♖a8 += ½-½
Mednis**

344 Sanz-Larsen Las Palmas 78
1 e4 g6 2 d4 ♗g7 3 ♘f3 d6 4 ♘c3 ♘f6
5 ♗e2 0-0 6 0-0 a5?! Smyslov-Larsen,
Dortmund 60! **7 a4?! ♘a6 8 ♗e3
♘b4 9 ♘d2 e5= 10 dxe5 dxe5 11 ♗c5
♖e8 12 ♘c4 ♕xd1 13 ♖axd1 ♗d7**
13...♘xc2 14 ♘b5 ♘xe4 15 ♘xc7
♘xc5 16 ♘xe8 ♘d4 17 ♘b6!± ♘xe2+?
18 ♔h1 ♖b8 19 ♖d8 **14 ♘e3 ♗c6 15
♗b5!= ♘h6 16 ♗xb4 axb4 17 ♘cd5
♘xd5 18 ♘xd5 ♗xd5 19 ♗xe8** 19
exd5? ♖ed8∓ **♗xe4!?** 19...♗c4 20
♗b5 ♗xf1 21 ♔xf1 += **20 ♗b5 ♗f5**
20...♗xc2? 21 ♖d7 **21 ♖fe1 ♗f8 22
♖xe5?** 22 ♘d3 ♗d6= **♗xc2 23 ♖de1
c6 24 ♗f1 ♖xa4∓ 25 ♖e8 ♔g7 26
♖b8 ♖a7 27 g4!?** △ g5, ♖ee8 **h6 28**

♗g2 b3 29 ♖bd8 ♗b4 30 ♖f1 ♖a5 31 ♖d7 ♖b5 32 ♗f3 ♗c5 32...♗c3!? 33 h3 33 ♗d1 ♖b4 34 ♗xc2 ♖xg4+ 35 ♔h1 bxc2 36 ♖d2 ♖b4 37 ♖xc2 ♗d4 38 ♖b1 ♖b3 –+ ♖b4 34 ♗d1 ♗d4 35 ♗xc2 bxc2 36 ♖c1 ♖xb2 37 ♔g2 c5 38 ♕f3 b5 39 ♔e2 b4 40 ♕d2 b3 0-1 Larsen

345 Christiansen-Seirawan USA 78
1 ♘f3 g6 2 e4 ♗g7 3 d4 d6 4 ♘c3 ♘f6 5 ♗e2 0-0 6 0-0 ♘c6 7 d5 ♘b8 8 ♗g5 8 ♗e3 c6 9 ♕d2 a5 10 ♖ad1 ♕c7 11 ♖fe1 a4 12 a3 ♘bd7 13 h3 ♖e8 14 ♗f1 ♘b6 15 ♗h6 15 dxc6 bxc6 16 ♗f4 cxd5 16 ♗xg7 ♔xg7 17 exd5 17 ♘xd5 ♘bxd5 18 exd5 ♗d7 18 ♖e3 ♖a5 19 ♖d3 ♘c4 20 ♕c1 ♖c5 21 ♗g5 ♘xa3 22 ♖d4 h6 23 ♘ge4 ♘xe4 24 ♖xe4 ♘c4 25 ♖dd4 ♘b6 25...♘e5 26 f4 f5 27 fxe5 fxe4 28 e6 26 ♖h4 ♖h8 27 ♕e1 ♖e8 27...g5 28 ♗d3 g5? 28... ♖h8 29 ♕xe7 ♖e8

29 ♖xh6! ♔xh6 30 ♖h4+ ♔g7 30... gxh4 31 ♕e3+ ♔h5 32 ♕f3+ ♔g5 33 ♕xf7; 31...♔g7 32 ♕g5+ ♔f8 33 ♕h6+ ♔g8 34 ♕h7+ ♔f8 35 ♕h8 mate 31 ♖h7+ ♔f6 31...♔f8 32 ♕d1 32 ♖h6+ ♔g7 33 ♖h7+ ♔f6 34 ♘e4+ ♔g6 35 ♕d1 35 ♘xc5 f5 g4 35...♔xh7 36 ♕h5+ ♔g8 37 ♕xg5+ ♔f8 38 ♕h6+ ♔g8 39 ♘f6+ +– 36 ♕d2 ♖xd5 36...

♔xh7 37 ♘f6+ +– 37 ♕h6+ ♔f5 38 ♖xf7+ ♔e5 39 ♕g7+ ♔e6 40 ♖f6+ ♔e5 41 ♖xd6+ ♔f4 42 g3+ 1-0 42...♔f3 43 ♘d2 mate; 42...♔f5 43 ♕g5 mate

346 Shamkovich-Mednis
USA Final 78
1 e4 d6 2 d4 ♘f6 3 ♘c3 g6 4 ♘f3 ♗g7 5 ♗e2 0-0 6 0-0 ♗g4 6...c6; 6...♘c6 7 a4!? N 7 ♗e3 ♘c6 8 ♕d2 e5 9 d5 ♘e7 10 ♖ad1 ♗d7∞ Karpov-Timman, Tilburg 77 ♘c6 8 d5 8 a5!? ♘b4! 8...♗xf3 9 ♗xf3 ♘e5 10 ♗e2 c6 11 a5 += 9 a5 ♘d7 9...c5!= 10 a6 ♘xa6 11 ♗xa6 bxa6 12 ♘d4 += ♕c8 13 ♕d3 c6 14 dxc6 ♗xc6 15 ♘xc6 ♕xc6 16 ♖xa6 ♕b7 17 ♖a3 ♖fc8 18 ♗d2 △ ♖fa1 ♖ab8 18...♕xb2?? 19 ♖b3 +– 19 ♖b3 ♕c7 20 ♖xb8 ♖xb8 21 b3 △ ♘d5 ♖c8 22 h3 e6 △ ♘d7 23 ♖c1 △ ♘b5 ♕c6

24 ♖a1!± ♘e8 24...♘xe4? 25 ♖a6! 25 ♖a6 ♕b7 25...♕c7 26 ♖a4 26 ♖a4 ♖c6 27 ♘d1! ♘f6 28 ♘e3 ♘d7 △ ♘c5 29 b4 ♘e5 30 ♕a3 ♖c7 △ ♕xe4; 30...a6 31 f4 ♘d7 32 ♕d3± 31 f3 h5 32 ♕b3 ♗h6 33 b5! ♖c5 34 c4 +– d5!? 35 exd5 exd5 36 ♕a3! ♗xe3+ 36...♖c7 37 ♕d6! 37 ♕xe3 ♘d7 38 ♕e8+ ♘f8 39 ♗e3 ♖c8 40 ♕e5 dxc4 41 ♗d4 1-0 Shamkovich

347 Geller-Kuzmin Lvov 78
**1 e4 d6 2 d4 ♘f6 3 ♘c3 g6 4 ♘f3
♗g7 5 ♗e2 0-0 6 0-0 ♗g4** 6...♘bd7?
14/693; 6...c6 14/735,737,690,691;
6...♘c6 7 ♗g5?! 14/692 **7 ♗e3 ♘c6**
7...♘bd7 14/694 **8 ♕d2 e5 9 d5 ♘e7
10 ♖ad1 ♘d7** 10...♗d7! 11 ♘e1
♘g4 12 ♗xg4 ♗xg4 13 f3 ♗d7 14
f4 ♗g4 15 ♖b1 c6 += Karpov-Timman,
Tilburg 77 **11 ♘e1 ♗xe2 12 ♕xe2
f5 13 f4 exf4 14 ♗xf4 ♗xc3! 15 bxc3
fxe4 16 ♕xe4 ♘c5 =+ 17 ♕c4 ♕d7
18 ♘d3 ♕a4! 19 ♕xa4 ♘xa4 20 c4**
Yurtaev-Karasev, USSR 77 **♖ae8 21
♖de1 ♘f5 22 c5 ♘c3 23 ♖xe8?** 23
cxd6! cxd6 24 ♖xe8 ♖xe8 25 g4
♘d4 26 ♗xd6 ♘xd5= **♖xe8∓ 24 g4
♘d4 25 cxd6 ♘de2+! 26 ♔h1 ♘xf4
27 ♘xf4 cxd6 28 ♖f3 ♖c8 29 a3 b5
−+ 30 ♔g1 a5 31 ♔f1 b4 32 axb4 a4!
33 ♘e2 ♘b5 34 ♔e1 ♖xc2 35 ♖e3
a3 36 ♖e8+ ♔f7 37 ♖a8 a2 0-1**
Ciocaltea

348 Alexandria-Chiburdanidze (6)
USSR 77
1 d4 ♘f6 2 ♘f3 g6 3 ♘c3 ♗g7 3...d5
4 e4 d6 5 ♗e2 0-0 6 0-0 ♗g4 7 h3
7 ♗e3 ♘c6 8 ♕d2 e5 9 d5 ♘e7 10
♖ad1 += **♗xf3 8 ♗xf3 ♘c6=** 9 **♘b5!?**
**a6 10 ♘a3 e5 11 c3 exd4 12 cxd4
d5!? 13 exd5** 13 e5 ♘e4= **♘xd5 14
♕b3 ♘b6 15 ♘c2 ♗xd4 16 ♗f4** 16
♖d1 ♕f6; 16 ♗xc6 bxc6 17 ♘xd4
♕xd4 18 ♗h6 ♖e8≈; **♗e5! 17 ♗xe5**
17 ♘xc6 ♗xf4 18 ♘xb7 ♖ab8 19 ♗xa6
♕f6≈; 18...♖a7 **♘xe5 18 ♗xb7 ♖b8
19 ♗xa6 ♘d5 20 ♕g3 ♕f6** 22...♖xb2
23 ♕xe5 ♖xc2 24 ♖fd1± **21 ♖fe1**
21 b3 ♖fe8≈ **♘f4 22 ♖e4!** 22 b3?
♕xa6 −+ **♕xa6 23 ♕xf4 ♖xb2 24
♘b4 ♕d6** 24...♕b5 25 a4 ♕a5=; 24...
♖xb4 25 ♖xb4 ♘d3 26 ♖a4 +−
25 ♖d4 ♕e6 26 ♘d5 c5?! 26...c6=

27 ♖dd1 +=♘c6? 27...c4? 28 ♕d4±;
27...♔g7 **28 ♘f6+± ♔g7 29 ♘g4?!**
29 ♘d7 ♖b4? 30 ♘xf8 +−; 29...♖d8
30 ♘xc5 ♖xd1+ 31 ♖xd1 ♕xa2?
32 ♖d6! ♕a1+ 33 ♔h2 ♖b6 34 ♘e6+!
+−; 31...♕e5! 32 ♕xe5 ♘xe5 α/±
♖b4!= 30 ♕h6+ ♔g8 31 ♖ac1 31
♖e1!? **♘e5! =+ 32 ♘e3?** 32 ♘xe5
♕xe5 =+ **♖d4! 33 ♕g5 f6 34 ♕g3
♖fd8∓ 35 ♖f1 ♘d3 36 ♖c2 f5! 37
♕c7 ♖8d7 38 ♕b8+ ♔g7 39 ♖e2?**
Zeitnot **♘f4 39...f4 −+ 40 ♖c2 ♘d3
41 ♖e2??** 41 ♕b3 ♕e4 f4 42 ♔h1 **0-1**
Gufeld

349 Janosevic-Petrosian
Lone Pine 78
**1 e4 g6 2 d4 ♗g7 3 ♘c3 d6 4 f4 c6
5 ♘f3 ♗g4 6 ♗e3 d5** 6...♕b6 **7 ♕d2!±
7 ♗e2!?** 7 e5 dxe4 8 ♘xe4 ♘f6 8...
♘bd7 9 ♘e5± **9 ♘xf6+ ♗xf6 10 ♘e5
♗e6** 10...♗xe2 11 ♕xe2 += **11 0-0
♘d7 12 c4 ♘b6 13 b3 ♘c8 14 ♗g4!
♗xg4 15 ♕xg4 ♘d6 16 ♖ad1 ♕c8 17
♕f3 0-0 18 g4 ♗g7 19 d5! c5** 19...cxd5
20 ♖xd5 +=; 20 ♕xd5 **20 ♘d3 b6 21
f5! ♔h8 22 ♔h1 ♕d7 23 ♗g5 gxf5!?
24 gxf5 ♗f6 25 ♗h6** 25 ♗xf6+ exf6 +=
**♖g8 26 ♕f4 ♗d4 27 ♘e5 ♗xe5 28
♕xe5+ f6 29 ♕e6! ♕xe6**

30 dxe6? 30 fxe6 ♖g6 31 ♗f4! ♖d8 32
♖g1± **♖g4! 31 ♖d5 ♖ag8 32 ♗f4**

♟e4∓ 33 ♖dd1 33 h3!∓ ♖g1+!! 0-1
34 ♖xg1 ♘f2 mate **Gheorghiu**

350 Nagy-Breitenfellner
Corr. 76/78
1 e4 g6 2 d4 ♗g7 3 ♘c3 d6 4 f4 c6
5 ♘f3 ♗g4 6 ♗e3 d5 7 e5 e6 8 h3
♗xf3 9 ♕xf3 += h5 10 0-0-0 h4
11 ♗d3 ♘d7 12 g4! hxg3 13 ♖dg1!
♘f8 13...♘e7 14 ♖xg3 ♘f5 15 ♗xf5
exf5 16 e6 **14 ♖xg3 ♖h5 15 f5!? exf5
16 ♕xh5!? gxh5 17 ♖xg7 ♘e7 18
♘e2 ♘e6 19 ♖h7 ♔d7 20 ♖g1! ♕a5
21 c3!?** 21 ♔b1 ♕xa2 22 ♖xf7 △
♗xf5, ♖gg7 **♖f8** 22...♔e8 23 ♖h7
**23 ♖xf8 ♗xf8 24 ♘f4 a5 25 ♖g7
a4 26 ♗xf5+ ♔e8 27 ♗b1 ♕a1 28
♗d2 a3 29 bxa3 ♘f5?** 29...♕xa3+ 30
♔c2 ♕a4+ 31 ♔d3 ♕b5+ = **30 ♖xb7
♘e3?!** 31 ♖b8+ ♔e7 32 ♗e1! ♕xa3+
**33 ♔d2 ♘c4+ 34 ♔d1 ♔d7?! 35 ♗f5+
♔e7** 35...♔c7 36 ♖xf8 ♕xf8 37 ♘e6+
+- **36 ♗h4+ ♔f7 37 e6+ 1-0**

351 Gipslis-Seifert
Hradec Kralove 77/78
1 e4 g6 2 d4 ♗g7 3 ♘c3 d6 4 f4 ♘c6
5 ♗e3 ♘f6 6 ♗e2 0-0 7 ♘f3 ♘g4!?
7...♗g4 8 ♗g1 e5 9 d5! ♘b8 9...♘e7
10 h3 ♘f6 11 fxe5 dxe5 12 ♗h2±
10 h3 ♘f6 11 fxe5 dxe5 12 g4?!
12 ♗h2! c6! **13 ♕d2 cxd5 14 exd5
♘bd7?** 14...e4! 15 ♘g5 ♖e8 △ h6;
15 ♘h2 ♖e8 16 g5 ♘h5 17 ♗xh5
gxh5; 16 0-0-0 a6 17 ♗e3 b5 **15
0-0-0 a6** 15...e4 16 ♘d4! **16 ♗h2
♖e8?!** 16...e4 17 ♘d4! **17 g5! ♘h5
18 ♘e4 b5** 18...♘f4 19 h4 **19 ♔b1
♘b6** △ ♗f5 **20 d6 ♘f4 21 h4 ♗f5
22 ♗d3 ♘c4 23 ♕e1!** 23 ♗xc4 ♗xe4+!;
23 ♕b4 a5! 24 ♕c5 ♖c8 25 ♕xb5?
♘a3+!

Diagram

23...♖c8? 23...♘xd6? 24 ♘xd6 ♘xd3
25 ♖xd3!; 23...a5 **24 ♘f6+ ♗xf6
25 ♗xf5 ♘xb2 26 ♗xc8 ♘xd1 27 ♕xd1
♕a5 28 ♕d2 ♕a3 29 d7 ♖d8 30 gxf6
♕xf3 31 ♖e1 ♘d5 32 ♗xe5 1-0**

352 Sampouw-Hon Jakarta 78
1 e4 d6 2 d4 ♘f6 3 ♘c3 g6 4 f4 ♗g7
5 ♘f3 c5 6 ♗b5+ ♗d7 7 e5 ♘g4 8 e6
♗xb5 9 exf7+ ♔f8 9...♕d7 10 ♘xb5
♕a5+ 11 ♘c3 cxd4 12 ♘xd4 ♗xd4
13 ♕xd4 ♘c6 14 ♕d1! ♕h5 15 ♕f3
♖hf8 16 ♗d2 ♘f6! =+ **10 ♘xb5 ♕a5+
11 ♘c3 ♘c6 12 d5 ♘d4 13 ♘g5 ♘h6
14 0-0 ♗xf7 15 ♘ce4 h6 16 ♗xf7
♔xf7 17 c3 ♘b5 18 ♕g4 ♘c7 19
f5 1-0**

353 Klovan-Karasev USSR 77
1 e4 d6 2 d4 ♘f6 3 ♘c3 g6 4 f4
♗g7 5 ♘f3 0-0 6 ♗d3 ♘a6 7 e5 ♘d7
7...♘e8 8 ♘e4 N 8 ♘e2!? += c5 9 c3
cxd4 10 cxd4 dxe5 11 fxe5 ♘b4!
**12 ♗b1 ♘b6 13 0-0 ♗g4 14 ♘eg5
♘c6 15 h3 ♗xf3 16 ♘xf3 ♕d7=**
17 ♗e3 ♖ad8 18 ♕e2 18 ♗e4!? f6
**19 ♗c2 ♘d5 20 ♗f2 ♗h6! 21 ♖ae1
♔g7 22 ♗e4 f5!** =+ **23 ♗b1 e6 24
♗h4 ♖c8 25 ♕f2 ♔h8 26 a3 ♘a5 27
♗a2 ♘c4 28 ♗g5 ♗xg5 29 ♘xg5 h6?**
29...b5 += **30 ♗xc4 ♖xc4? 30...hxg5=
31 ♘e4 += ♕c6 32 ♘d6 ♖c2 33 ♖e2
♖xe2 34 ♕xe2 ♔g7 35 ♕d2 ♖d8**

36 ♖c1± ♕b6 37 b4 ♘e7?! 37...
**♕a6!? 38 ♖c5 a6 39 ♕c3 ♘d5 40
♕c4 g5?** Zeitnot **41 ♘xf5+** 41 ♘c8
+− ♔h7 **42 ♘d6 ♖f8 43 ♔h2 ♕d8 44
♖xd5! +− exd5 45 ♕xd5 ♕e7 46
♕xb7 ♕xb7 47 ♘xb7 ♖e8** 47...♔g6
48 d5 ♔f5 49 d6 ♖f7 50 e6 +−; 49...
♔xe6 50 ♘c5+ +− **48 ♘c5 ♔g6 49
♘xa6 ♖d8 1-0** Gufeld

354 Hofmann-Muller DDR 78

**1 e4 d6 2 d4 ♘f6 3 ♘c3 g6 4 f4 ♗g7
5 ♘f3 0-0 6 ♗d3 ♘c6 7 e5 dxe5 8
fxe5 ♘g4** 8...♘d5 9 ♘xd5 ♕xd5 10
c3 ♗e6 11 ♕e2 ♖ad8 **9 ♗e4 f6 10
h3 ♘h6 11 ♗d5+** 11 exf6 exf6 12
0-0 ♘e7 ♔h8 **12 0-0 ♘f5 13 ♖e1!
♘fxd4 14 ♘xd4 ♘xd4 15 ♕xd4 c6
16 ♗f4 cxd5?** 16...♗e6

**17 e6! ♕a5 18 ♘xd5 ♖d8 19 c4 b5
20 ♕c5** 20 ♗c7 ♕xc7 21 ♘xc7 ♖xd4
22 ♘xa8 ♗b7 23 ♖d1 f5; 23 ♘c7
♖d2 **24 ♘d5 bxc4 25 ♘e3 f5 26
♖ad1 ♖xd1 27 ♖xd1 ♗xb2 ♗b7 21
♗c7 ♖dc8 22 ♕xe7 ♕d2 23 ♖ad1
♕xb2 24 ♕d7 bxc4 25 e7 ♖e8 26
♗d8 1-0**

355 Chandler-Torre Jakarta 78

**1 e4 d6 2 d4 ♘f6 3 ♘c3 g6 4 f4 ♗g7
5 ♘f3 0-0 6 ♗d3 ♘c6 7 0-0 ♗g4 8
e5** 8 ♗e3; 8 ♗g5; 8 ♘e2; 8 ♕e1!?

dxe5 8...♘e8 9 ♗e3 ♘b4 10 ♗e2 c6
11 a3 ♘d5 12 ♘xd5 cxd5 13 h3 ♗xf3
14 ♖xf3± Hindle-Gheorghiu,
Vrnjacka Banja 67 **9 dxe5 ♘d5 10
h3!?** 10 ♘xd5; 10 ♗d2 ♘xc3?! 10...
♗f5!= Moles **11 bxc3 ♗f5 12 ♗xf5**
12 ♗e3± **gxf5** 12...♕xd1 13 ♖xd1
gxf5 14 ♘d4 ♖fd8 15 ♗e3 ♘xd4 16
cxd4 e6 17 g4 += Parma-G.Garcia,
Camaguey 74 **13 ♗e3 e6 14 ♕e2 ♕d5
15 ♖fd1** 15 ♘d4 ♕a5 16 ♘xc6 bxc6
=+ **♕a5 16 ♕c4 ♖fd8 17 ♖xd8+ ♖xd8
18 ♖b1 ♖b8 19 ♘d4 ♘xd4 20 cxd4
c6 21 g4 fxg4 22 hxg4 ♕d5 23 ♕xd5
cxd5 24 ♖b3 ♗f8 25 ♖c3 ♗e7 26
♖c7 ♔f8 27 f5 ♔e8 28 f6 ♗d8 29
♖c3 ♗a5 30 ♖a3 b6 31 ♔h6 31 c3
♖c8 32 ♗d2 Δ ...♔d3, ♖b3-b1-h1
♖c8 32 ♖h3 ♖xc2 33 ♗e3 ♗d2 34
♗xd2 ♖xd2 35 ♖xh7 ♖xd4 36 ♖h8+
♔d7 37 ♖g8 ♖f4 38 ♖g7 ♔c6 39
♖xf7 d4 40 ♖f8 ♔d5 41 g5 ♔xe5 42
f7 d3 43 g6 ♖g4+ 44 ♔h2 ♖xg6
45 ♖d8 ♖f6 46 f8♕ ♖xf8 47 ♖xf8
♔e4 48 ♖d8 e5 49 ♔g3** 49 ♔g2 ♔e3
50 ♔f1 d2 Δ b5-b4, a5-a4, b3 −+
**♔e3 50 ♔g4 d2 51 ♔f5 ♔e2 52 ♔xe5
d1♕ 53 ♖xd1 ♔xd1 54 ♔d5 ♔c2 55
♔c6 ♔b2 56 a4 ♔b3 57 ♔b5 a5 0-1**

356 Balashov-Timman Bugojno 78

**1 e4 d6 2 d4 ♘f6 3 ♘c3 g6 4 f4 ♗g7
5 ♘f3 0-0 6 ♗e3 c5 7 dxc5 ♕a5 8
♗d3 ♘g4 9 ♗d2 ♕xc5 10 ♕e2 ♘f6**
10...♘c6 11 h3 ♘h6 12 g4 f5 13 gxf5
gxf5 14 ♖g1 ♘d4 **11 a3?!** 11 ♗e3
♗g4 12 h3 ♗xf3 13 ♕xf3 ♘c6 14
♗e3 ♕a5 15 0-0 ♘d7 16 ♗d2 ♕b6+
17 ♔h1 ♘c5 18 ♖ab1 ♘xd3 19 cxd3
e6 20 ♘e2 ♖fe8 21 ♗c3 ♖ac8 22 ♕g3
22 f5 exf5 23 exf5 ♕e3; 22 d4 ♘xd4
23 ♘xd4 ♗xd4 24 f5 exf5 25 exf5
♖e3 26 ♕d5 **f5 23 h4 d5 24 ♗xg7
♔xg7 25 h5 ♘e7 26 e5 ♘g8 27 hxg6**

hxg6 28 ♕g5 ♖e7 29 ♘g1 ♛f8 30 ♘h3
♖c2 31 ♖f3 ♖h7 32 ♖g1 ♖h6 33
d4 ♚e8 34 ♖c3 ♛xb2 35 ♖xc2 ♛xc2
36 ♔h2 ♛d7 37 ♖f1 ♛c3 38 ♖f3
♛xd4 39 ♖b3 b6 40 ♕g3 ♘e7 41
♖d3 ♛a4 42 ♖f3 ♖h5 43 ♕f2 ♖h8
44 ♖c3 ♖c8 0-1

357 Romanishin-Balashov
USSR Final 77
1 d4 g6 2 e4 d6 3 ♘c3 ♘f6 4 ♗g5 ♗g7
5 ♕d2 h6 6 ♗h4 c6 7 f4 0-0 7...♗e6
8 ♘f3 d5 9 ♗d3 dxe4 10 ♘xe4 ♘xe4
11 ♗xe4 ♗d5 12 ♕e2 += Fuderer-
Pirc, Opatija 53 8 ♘f3 ♗g4 9 ♗e2 d5
10 e5 ♘e4 11 ♕e3 ♕d7 12 0-0-0
♘a6 13 h3 ♗f5 14 ♘d2 ♘xc3 15
♕xc3 c5 16 ♗xa6 cxd4 17 ♕xd4
bxa6 18 g4 ♗e6 19 ♖hg1 ♖ac8 20
c3 ♕c7 21 ♖de1 ♖fe8 22 f5 ♗d7
22...gxf5 23 gxf5 ♗xf5 24 ♖xg7+
♔xg7 25 e6+ ♔h7 26 exf7 △ ♖g1/
♖xe7 +− 23 fxg6 fxg6 24 ♛xd5+
♔h7 25 ♘b3 ♗a4 26 ♕e4 ♗c6 27
♕c4 ♛b6 28 ♕e6 ♖f8 29 ♗xe7 ♖ce8
30 ♕d6 ♖f3 31 ♗f6 ♗f8 32 ♕d4 ♖xh3
33 ♕c4 ♗g7 34 ♗xg7 ♔xg7 35 ♖gf1
♗f3 36 e6 ♕d8 37 ♘d4 ♕f6 38 ♔b1
h5 39 gxh5 g5 40 ♕a1 ♔h6 41 ♕c6
1-0

358 Pribyl-Swic Lodz 78
1 e4 d6 2 d4 ♘f6 3 ♘c3 g6 4 ♗g5 h6
4...c6 5 ♗e3! c6 5...♘g4? 6 ♗c1!
+= Parma ♗g7 7 f3 ♘f6 8 ♗e3 +=
Freidstein; 6 ♗f4 ♗g7 7 ♘f3 ♘c6 8
♗g3 e5 9 dxe5 ♘gxe5= 6 ♗e2!? N 6
f3 ♗g7 7 ♕d2 ♛a5 8 ♘ge2 b5 9 g3
♘bd7 10 ♗g2 ♗b7 11 0-0 a6 12 a3
♕c7 13 ♔h1 c5 14 d5 += Liberzon-
Etruk, USSR 68; 6 ♗d3 b5 7 ♕d2
♘g4 8 ♗f4 e5 9 dxe5 dxe5 10 ♗g3
h5 11 ♘f3 h4 (11...♗g7 12 h3 h4 13
hxg4 hxg3 14 ♖xh8+ ♗xh8 15 ♕h6

gxf2+ 16 ♔e2! += Tal-Gufeld 68) 12
♗xe5 ♘xe5 13 ♘xe5 ♕f6 14 f4 +=
♗h6 15 ♘e2! ♛xe5 16 fxe5 ♗xd2+
17 ♔xd2 += Liberzon-Torre, Nice 74
♗g7 7 ♘f3!? ♛b6!? 7...0-0 8 h3!
♛b6 9 0-0 ♛xb2 10 ♕d2± 8 0-0!
♛xb2 9 ♕d2! ♛a3 9...♘g4? 10 ♖fb1
♛a3 11 ♘b5!! cxb5 12 ♖b3 +− 10
h3!± ♛a5?! 11 a4! ♘bd7 12 ♗c4 0-0
12...♘b6 13 ♗b3 ♗e6 14 ♗xe6 fxe6
15 ♕d3±

13 ♗xh6!! ♗xh6? 13...♘xe4 14 ♘xe4
♛xd2 15 ♗xd2 d5 16 ♗d3 dxe4 17
♗xe4 ♘f6 18 ♗d3± 14 ♛xh6 d5!
15 ♗d3!! ♛xc3 15...dxe4 16 ♘xe4
♘xe4 17 ♗xe4 ♘f6 18 ♗d3 ♛h5 (18...
♗f5? 19 ♕g5!) 19 ♕xh5 ♘xh5 20
♖fe1± 16 e5 ♘h7 17 ♖ae1! c5 18
♖e3! △ ♗xg6 ♛a5?! 18...cxd4 19
♗xg6 fxg6 20 ♖xc3 dxc3 21 ♕xg6+
♔h8 22 ♘g5 ♘xg5 23 ♕xg5 +− 19
♘h4! +− cxd4 20 ♘f5!! 1-0 20...gxf5
21 ♖g3+ ♔h8 22 ♕g7 mate Pribyl

359 Honfi-Todorcevic Subotica 78
1 e4 g6 2 d4 ♗g7 3 c3 d6 4 ♗c4
♘f6 5 ♕e2 0-0 6 ♘f3 c6 7 e5 ♘d5
8 h3 ♘a6 9 0-0 ♘ac7 10 ♖e1 ♗f5
11 a4 a5 12 ♘a3 ♖b8 13 ♗g5 ♕d7
13...h6? 14 exd6! +− 14 ♘c2 f6 15
♗h4 ♔h8 16 ♗g3 ♖bd8 17 ♗b3 △ c4
♘e6 18 ♗xd5 cxd5 19 exd6 exd6 20

♘e3 ♗e4 21 ♘d2 f5 22 f3 f4 23 fxe4 dxe4! 24 ♘xe4 d5 25 ♗h4!? 25 ♘xd5 ♕xd5 26 ♗h4 g5 27 ♗f2 f3∞; 25 ♘c5 ♘xc5 26 dxc5 d4∞ dxe4 26 ♗xd8 f3! 27 ♕f2 ♘f4?! 27...♕xd8!? 28 g3 += 28 ♗h4! 28 ♗g5? ♘d3 −+ fxg2 29 ♕g3 g5 29... ♘xh3+ 30 ♔xg2 ♖f2+ 31 ♔h1 +− 30 ♗xg5 ♘xh3+ 31 ♔xg2 ♘xg5 32 ♕xg5 ♗f6 33 ♕h6 ♖g8+ 34 ♔h1 ♗g5 35 ♕h5! ♖g6 36 ♘g4 e3 37 ♘e5 ♕d5+ 38 ♕f3 ♕e6 39 ♕f8+ 1-0 Honfi

24 ♖xf7! ♗h8 24...♘xd2 25 ♖xg7+ ♔h8 26 ♖xa7+ ♔g8 27 ♘e7+ 25 ♘e7+ 1-0 25...♖xe7 26 ♖g7 mate

360 Godes-Kuznetsov USSR 78

1 ♘f3 g6 2 e4 ♗g7 3 d4 d6 4 c3 ♘f6 5 ♘bd2 0-0 6 ♗e2 c5 7 dxc5 dxc5 8 0-0 ♘c6 9 ♕c2 ♕c7 10 a4 += b6 11 ♖e1 ♗b7 12 ♗f1 ♖ad8 13 ♘c4 ♘g4 14 a5 ♘ce5 15 ♘fxe5 ♘xe5 16 axb6 axb6 17 ♕b3 ♘xc4 18 ♗xc4 ♖a8 19 ♖xa8 ♗xa8 20 g3 h6 21 ♗d5!± e6 22 ♗xa8 ♖xa8 23 ♕b5 ♔h7 24 ♗f4 e5 25 ♗e3 ♖d8 26 ♖a1 f5 27 exf5 gxf5 28 ♕c4 ♕d7 29 ♕h4 f4 30 gxf4 ♖g8 31 ♕h5 ♕d3 32 ♖a7 ♔h8 33 h3 exf4 34 ♗xf4 ♗e5+ 35 ♗g3 ♕b1+ 36 ♔g2 ♖xg3+ 37 fxg3 ♕xb2+ 38 ♔f3 ♕xc3+ 39 ♔e4 ♕e1+ 40 ♔f5 1-0 Suetin

361 Portisch-Bilek Hungary 78

1 d4 g6 2 e4 ♗g7 3 c3 d6 4 f4 ♘f6 5 ♗d3 e5 6 ♘f3 exd4 6...exf4 7 ♗xf4 0-0 8 0-0 c5!? 9 ♘bd2 cxd4 10 cxd4 ♘h5! 7 cxd4 0-0 8 ♘c3 ♘c6 9 0-0 ♘h5?! 9...♗g4 10 ♗e3 ♖e8 Δ ♘xe4 10 ♗e3 ♖e8 11 ♕d2 ♗g4 12 d5! ♘b4 13 ♗b1 ♗xf3 14 ♖xf3 c6 15 a3 ♘a6 16 dxc6 bxc6 17 ♗a2 ♘f6 17... ♘xc3 18 ♕xc3 ♖xe4 19 f5 d5 20 ♕xc6 18 f5! ♖b8 19 fxg6 hxg6 20 ♖af1 d5 21 exd5 cxd5 22 ♗d4 ♖e6 23 ♘xd5! ♘e4 23...♘xd5 24 ♗xg7 +−

362 Sveshnikov-Romanishin USSR Final 77

1 e4 g6 2 d4 ♗g7 3 ♘c3 c5?! 4 dxc5 ♕a5 5 ♘f3 ♘f6 5...♕xc3+ 6 bxc3 ♕xc3+ 7 ♗d2 ♕xc5 8 ♗d3 Δ ♕c1≈ 6 ♗d3 6 e5 ♘e4 7 ♕d4 ♘xc3 8 ♗d2 ♘b5 9 ♕e3 ♕a4 10 b3 ♘a3∞; 6...♘g4 7 ♕d4 h5 8 ♗b5!± ♕xc5 6...♘a6 7 0-0 ♘xc5 8 e5 ♘g4 9 ♗g5 += 7 ♗e3 ♕a5 8 ♕d2 ♘c6 9 0-0 0-0 10 h3 d6 11 a3 ♗e6 12 ♘g5 d5!? 12...♗d7 13 f4± 13 exd5 ♗xd5 13...♘xd5 14 ♘xe6 fxe6 15 ♘d1± 14 b4 ♕d8 15 ♖ad1 e6? 15...♘e5! 16 ♘xd5 ♘xd5 17 c4 += 16 ♘ge4! ♘xe4 17 ♘xe4 f5 18 ♘c3

18...♗xg2!? 19 ♔xg2 f4 20 ♗xf4!

20 ♘c5? f3+ △ ♕g5/♕h4 −+ ♗xc3
21 ♕e3 ♕f6 22 ♗g5 ♕e5 23 ♗c4±
♖ae8 24 ♖d3 ♗b2 25 f4? 25 ♖e1
♕xe3 26 ♖dxe3 ♗d4 27 ♖xe6 ♖xe6
28 ♖xe6 ♖xf2+ 29 ♔g3± ♕xe3 26
♖xe3 ♔g7! 27 ♖d1 27 ♖b1 ♗d4 28
♖e4 e5 += ♘d4! 28 ♖e4 28 c3! ♘f5
29 ♖d7+ ♖f7 30 ♖xe6 ♖xe6 31 ♗xe6
♖xd7 32 ♗xd7 += ♘f5 29 ♖d7+ ♖f7
30 ♖xe6 ♖xe6 31 ♗xe6 ♖xd7 32
♗xd7 ♗xa3 33 b5 ♘e3+ 34 ♔f3 ♘xc2
35 ♔e4 ♔f7 36 ♔d3 ♘e1+ 37 ♔e2
♗b4 38 f5 ½-½ Sveshnikov

363 Acers-Soltis USA 78

1 d4 g6 2 e4 ♗g7 3 e5!? N d6 3...c5
4 ♘f3 cxd4 5 ♕xd4 ♘c6 6 ♕e4∞;
4 c3!? 4 exd6 cxd6 5 ♘f3 ♘h6 6
♗c4 d5 6...0-0 7 ♗b5+ ♗d7 7...♘c6 8
♘e5! += 8 ♗xd7+ ♘xd7 9 0-0 0-0 10
♖e1 ♘f5 11 c3 e6 12 ♗f4 ♕b6 13
♕b3 ♖fc8 14 ♕xb6 14 g4! ♘xb6 15
♘a3! ♗f8 16 ♘c2 16 ♘b5 a6∓ ♘a4 17
♖ab1 ♖c6 18 g4! ♘d6 19 ♘e5 ♖c7
20 ♘e3 △ g5 f6 21 ♘d3 g5 22 ♗g3
♖c6?! 22...a5 23 ♗xd6 ♗xd6 24
♖e2 += ♔f7 25 ♖be1 ♖h8?! 25...a5;
25...b5 26 ♔g2! h5 27 gxh5 ♖xh5
28 ♘g4 ♖h4?! 28...♖h8 29 h3 ♗f4?!
30 ♖h1 ♗b8 31 ♖he1 a5 32 ♖c2?
32 ♖e3± △ ♖f3 +− ♖h8 33 ♖ec1?!
Zeitnot ♖hc8 34 ♖e1 b5 △ b4∓
35 ♖ce2 ♖b6? 35...♘b6!= 36 ♖e3!
+= △ ♖f3 +− ♔f4! 37 ♖f3 f5 38 ♘ge5+
38 ♘xf4?? fxg4 −+ ♗xe5 39 ♘xe5+
♔e7 40 ♖g3!± ♗xb2 41 ♖xg5 ♘c4!
41...♖xc3 42 ♖xf5 exf5 43 ♘c4+
♔d7 44 ♘xb6+ ♔c6 45 ♖xe6+ 42
♖g7+ ♔f8 42...♔d6 43 ♖d7 mate;
42...♔f6 43 ♖f7+ ♔g5 44 h4+!! +−
43 ♖h7!! 43 ♖a7? ♘xe5 44 ♖xe5
♖xc3 45 ♖xa5 ♖c4∓ ♔g8 44 ♘xc4!
♖xc4 45 ♖a7 ♖xc3 46 ♖g1 46 ♖e3
♖c4= ♔f8 47 ♔h2 ♖c2 48 ♖gg7

♖xf2+ ½-½ Acers

364 Chiburdanidze-Kushnir (6) 78

1 e4 g6 2 d4 ♗g7 3 ♘f3 c6 4 ♗d3 d6
5 0-0 ♗g4 6 c3 ♘f6 7 ♘bd2 0-0 8 h3
♗c8 9 a4 b6 10 ♕e2 a5 11 ♖e1 ♖a7
12 ♘f1?! 12 e5! ♕c7 13 e5 ♘d5 14
♘g3 dxe5 15 ♘xe5 ♘d7 16 ♘xd7
♗xd7 17 ♕f3 ♗e6 18 ♗d2 ♕d7 19
♘e4 h6 20 ♖ad1 ♗f5 21 ♘g3 ♗xd3
22 ♕xd3 ♖aa8 23 c4 ♘b4 24 ♕e4
e6 24...♕xd4?? 25 ♕xd4 ♗xd4 26
♗xb4 +− 25 ♗f4 ♖ad8 26 ♕e2 ♕e7
27 ♗e3 ♕h4 28 d5 28 ♕d2 ♗xd4 29
♗xd4 c5; 28 ♕g4 ♕xg4 29 hxg4
♘c2 −+ cxd5 29 ♗xb6 ♖b8 30 ♗c7
♖b7 31 ♗d6 ♖d8 32 c5 ♖c8 33 b3
♕f6 34 ♖c1 ♕b2 35 ♕d1 ♘a2 36 ♖b1

36...♘c3! 37 ♖xb2 ♘xd1 38 ♖a2
♘c3 39 ♖a3 h5 40 ♔f1 h4 41 ♘e2
♘e4 42 ♖a2 ♘xd6 43 cxd6 ♗e5 44
♖c1 ♖xc1+ 45 ♘xc1 ♗xd6 46 ♖c2
♗a3 47 ♔e2 ♔g7 48 ♖c3 d4 49 ♖c4
e5 50 ♘d3 e4 51 ♘c5 ♗xc5 52 ♖xc5
♖xb3 53 ♖xa5 ♖b2+ 54 ♔e1 d3 55
♖e5 f5 56 a5 ♖e2+ 57 ♔f1 ♖a2 58
♔e1 ♔f6 59 ♖d5 ♔e6 60 ♖b5 f4
61 ♖b8 ♖xa5 62 ♖e8+ ♔d5 63 ♖d8+
♔c4 64 ♖c8+ ♔d4 65 ♖d8+ ♔d5 66
♖g8 e3 67 fxe3+ fxe3 68 ♔d1 ♖a5
0-1

365 Rumens-Schlenker
Hastings 2 77/78

1 e4 g6 2 ♘c3 ♗g7 3 f4 c6 4 ♗c4 d5
5 exd5 b5 6 ♗b3 b4 7 ♘ce2 cxd5
8 ♘f3 ♘f6 9 0-0 0-0 10 a3 ♘c6 11 d4
♘a5! 12 ♗a4 12 axb4 ♘xb3 13 cxb3
♕b6 bxa3 13 b3!? ♗e4 13...a2!?
14 ♖xa2 14 ♗xa3 ♗a6! 14...♕c7
15 ♕d3! 15 ♗b4 15 ♖e1 ♕c7 △
♗xe2, ♘c3xa4, ♘c4 ♖b8 16 ♗e1
16 ♗xa5 ♕xa5 17 ♗c6 ♕b6 18 ♗xd5
♗xe2 19 ♕xe2 ♘c3 20 ♕c4 ♘xd5
21 ♕xd5 ♖fd8 22 ♕e4 ♖xd4!= ♕b6
17 ♔h1 ♗b7 △ ♗xe2 18 c3 ♘bd6!?
18...f6! △ ♘bd6-f5, e5 19 ♘e5!
♗xe5!? 20 fxe5 ♘b5 21 c4! ♘c7 22
♕c2 f5 23 exf6? 23 c5 ♕b7 24 ♖f3!
(△ ♗d7) ♘b5 25 ♖c1 ♖fc8; 23 ♖f3
dxc4! 24 bxc4 ♕b2! ♖xf6 24 ♗h4
24 ♖xf6 ♕xf6 25 cxd5 ♗xe2 26
♕xe2 ♘xd5∓ g5! 25 ♖xf6 25 cxd5
♗xe2! 26 ♕xe2 (26 ♖xf6 ♕xf6)
♕xd4! 27 ♖xf6 ♘xf6 28 ♖c1 gxh4
29 ♖xc7?! ♕a1+ −+; 27 ♖fd1 ♕e5!
28 ♖e1 (28 ♗e1 ♘ge+) gxh4 29
♕xe4?! ♖f1+; 27 ♖ad1 ♘c3!
♖xd4 ♘xe2 29 ♖xf6 ♘xd4 −+; 25...
♖bf8?! 26 ♖xf6 ♕xf6 27 ♕xe4 gxh4∞
♕xf6 26 ♗g3 ♖f8! 27 ♗xc7? 27 cxd5
♘xg3+ 28 ♘xg3 ♘xd5 ♘f2+ 28 ♔g1
♘h3+ 29 gxh3 29 ♔h1 ♕f1+ ♕f2+
30 ♔h1 ♕f3+ 31 ♔g1 ♕e3+ 32 ♔h1
♖f2! 0-1

1 ♘f3

366 Vokoun-Gross CSSR 78

1 ♘f3 c5 2 b3 ♘f6 3 c4 e6 3...g6
4 g3 ♗e7 5 ♗b2 0-0 6 ♗g2 ♕c7 7 0-0
♖d8 7...b6 8 ♘c3 a6 9 ♖c1 d6 10
d4 cxd4 11 ♘xd4 ♗d7 12 ♖c2 ♗e8
13 e4 ♘bd7 14 f4! ♖ac8 15 g4 ♘f8
16 g5 ♘6d7 17 h4 ♘b6 18 ♘ce2
♕c5 19 f5! ♘bd7 19...e5 20 f6 20

♔h1 e5? 21 f6! gxf6 22 ♘f5 ♘g6 23
♘xe7+ ♘xe7 24 gxf6 ♘g6 25 h5
♘gf8 26 ♕d3 △ ♕g3+ ♘e6 27 ♕g3+
♕f8 28 ♗c1! ♘xf6 29 ♖xf6 ♕e7 30
♘c3 ♗c6 30...♔xf6 31 ♘d5+ ♕xd5
32 exd5 31 ♖cf2 ♖f8 32 ♘d5+ ♕e8
33 ♖xe6+ 1-0 33...fxe6 34 ♖xf8+
♔xf8 35 ♗h6+ ♔e8 36 ♕g8+ ♗d7 37
♕f7+ ♔d8 38 ♕e7 mate

367 Barczay-Swic Lodz 78

1 ♘f3 g6 2 g3 ♗g7 3 ♗g2 ♘f6 4 b3 0-0
5 ♗b2 c5 6 c4 ♘c6 7 0-0 d6 8 d4 a6
9 ♘c3 ♗d7 10 dxc5 dxc5 11 ♘a4
b6 12 ♘e5 ♗xe5 13 ♗xe5 ♖a7 14 ♕c2
♘e8 15 ♗xg7 ♘xg7 16 ♖ad1 ♕c7
17 ♘c3 ♗c6 18 ♗xc6 ♕xc6

19 ♖d5 ♘e8 20 ♖fd1 ♘f6 21 ♖5d2
21 ♖d8?! ♕e6 22 ♘d5 ♘xd5 23
♖xd5± ♖c7 24 h4 ♖c6 25 ♕d2 ♖e8
26 h5 gxh5 27 ♖g5+ ♔h8 28 ♖xh5
♕f6 29 ♕d7 ♖g8 30 ♖f5 1-0

368 Liebert-Bruggemann
DDR Final 78

1 c4 ♘f6 2 ♘f3 g6 3 b3 ♗g7 4 ♗b2
d6 5 g3 0-0 6 ♗g2 ♘bd7 7 0-0 c6 8
♘c3 e5 9 ♕c2 ♖e8 10 ♖ad1 ♕e7 11
e3 ♘f8! 12 e4 ♗g4 13 h3 ♗xf3 14
♗xf3 ♘e6 15 ♘e2 c5 16 d3 ♗h6 17
♗g2 ♘h5 18 ♕c3 ♖ab8 19 f4? ♘d4!
20 ♘xd4 cxd4 21 ♕e1 exf4 22 gxf4

179

22 g4? ♘g3 23 ♖f3 ♕e5 24 ♕f2 ♗g7!
25 ♖xf4?? ♕xf4 23 ♗xd4 ♕g5!
24 ♖xf4 ♕xf4 25 ♕e2 ♗g7 25...b6!?
26 ♖f1 ♕g5 27 ♕f2 ♕e7 26 ♗e3 ♕g3
27 ♗f2 ♕g5 28 ♗xa7 ♖a8 29 ♗f2!
29 ♗e3? ♖xa2! 30 ♕xa2 ♕xe3+
31 ♕f2 ♕xf2+ 32 ♔xf2 ♘d4+ 33 ♔e2
b6 ♖a3?! 29...f5 **30 ♖d2 f5 31 ♖c2**
fxe4 32 h4 ♕f4 33 ♖xe4 ♔h8 34 h5?
34 ♕f3! ♕e5 35 ♗xb7 ♕a1+ 36 ♔g2
♖xa2 37 ♖xa2 ♕xa2 38 b4∞ ♖a5
35 hxg6 ♖g5+ 36 ♔f1 ♖xg6 37 ♕e3
♕f6 38 ♕c1 ♖g4 39 ♗xb7 ♖f4 40 ♗e4
♖f8 41 ♕e3 ♕d4! 42 ♕e1 ♕c5 43 ♔g2
♖g4+ 44 ♔f1 ♗d4 45 b4 ♕g5 0-1

369 Trincardi-Sala
Italy 78
1 ♘f3 d5 2 g3 ♘f6 3 ♗g2 c6 4 0-0
♗f5 5 d3 h6 6 ♘bd2 e6 7 b3 ♗e7 8
♗b2 0-0 9 c4 a5 10 a3 ♘bd7 11 ♖c1
♗h7 12 ♖c2 ♖e8 13 ♕a1 ♗f8 14 ♖h3
♕e7 15 ♖e1 g5 16 ♗g2 e5 17 cxd5
♘xd5 18 e4 ♘5b6 19 d4 ♗g7 20
♗h3 ♖ad8 21 ♗f5 f6

22 ♗xh7+ ♔xh7 23 ♗c3 a4 24 bxa4
♘xa4 25 ♗b4 ♕e6 26 ♘c4 ♕g4 27
♔g2 exd4 28 h3 ♕h5 29 ♘d6 c5 30
♘xb7 cxb4 31 ♘xd8 ♖xd8 32 axb4
d3 33 ♖c7 ♘ab6 34 ♕a5 ♕e8 35 ♕f5+
♔g8 ½-½

370 Augustin-Tichy
CSSR Final 78
1 ♘f3 d5 2 g3 ♗g4 3 ♗g2 ♘d7 4 d4
4 d3; 4 c4 e6 5 0-0 ♘gf6 6 c4 c6 7
♘bd2 ♗e7 8 b3 0-0 9 ♗b2 a5 10
♘e1? a4 11 f3 ♗h5 12 ♘d3 c5 13
♘f4 a3! 14 ♗c3 cxd4 15 ♗xd4 e5!
16 ♘xh5 exd4 17 ♘xf6+ ♗xf6 18
♕c2 ♖e8 19 ♔h1 ♖c8 20 ♕d3 ♗b4
21 ♖ad1 ♗c3 22 ♘b1 ♖e3 23 ♕c2
♗b2 24 ♖d3 ♕e7 25 ♖xe3 ♕xe3
26 f4 ♘e4 △ ♘f2+ 27 ♗f3 b5 28
♔g2 bxc4 29 bxc4 ♖xc4 30 ♕d3 ♕xd3
31 exd3 ♖c2+ 32 ♔g1 ♘c3 33 ♖e1
g6 34 g4 ♘xa2 35 ♗xd5 ♖c1 36 ♔f1
♘b4 0-1

371 Csom-Hamann Hungary 78
1 c4 c6 2 b3 d5 3 ♗b2 ♘f6 4 g3 ♗g4
5 ♗g2 e6 6 ♘f3 ♗d6 7 0-0 ♘bd7 8
d4 0-0 9 ♘bd2 ♗e7?! 10 ♖e1 h6 11
a3 b5 12 c5 a5 13 b4 axb4 14 axb4
♖xa1 15 ♕xa1 ♕a8 16 ♘b3! ♕b7?
16...♗xf3!

17 ♘e5! ♘xe5 18 dxe5 ♘d7 19 e4±
♖a8 20 ♕c1 ♕c7 21 h3 ♗h5 22 f4 ♖a4
23 ♕d2 ♗g6 24 exd5 exd5 25 g4
♗h4 26 ♖e2 f5 27 ♘d4 +- fxg4
28 hxg4 ♔h7 29 ♕c3 ♗e7 30 ♔h1
30 f5!? ♘xc5 31 bxc5 ♖c4 32 ♕d2
♗xc5 33 f5 ♗f7 34 ♗f3 ♕b6 35 ♗c2
b4 36 e6 ♗e8 37 ♘e3 ♗xe3 38 ♖xe3

1 ♘f3; c3/1 ♘f3; ♘c3

♖c2 **39 ♕xc2 ♕xe3 40 ♔g2** 40 f6+? ♗g6 **d4 41 ♕f2 1-0**

372 Andersson-Kavalek (10) 78

1 ♘f3 ♘f6 2 d4 d6 3 g3 ♘bd7 4 ♗g2 e5 5 0-0 g6 6 b3 ♗g7 7 c4 0-0 8 ♕c2 ♖e8 9 ♘c3 c6 10 e3 a6 11 dxe5 dxe5 12 ♗b2 ♘c5 13 ♖fd1 ♕c7 14 ♘d2 ♗g4 15 ♗f3 ♗xf3 16 ♘xf3 e4 17 ♘e1 a5 18 ♖d2 ♕c8 19 ♘e2 ♕f5 20 ♔g2 ♘g4 21 ♘d4 ♕h5 22 h3 ♘e5 23 ♕d1 ♕h6 24 ♖b1 ♘cd3 25 ♘xd3 ♘xd3 26 ♗a1 26 ♖xd3!? **♖ad8 27 ♘e2 ♕h5 28 g4 ♕h4 29 ♘g3 ♗xa1 30 ♖xa1 ♕f6** Zeitnot 30...♘xf2 31 ♔xf2 ♖xd2+ 32 ♕xd2 ♕f6+ △ ♕xa1 **31 ♘xe4 ♕e5 32 f3 f5 33 gxf5 gxf5 34 ♖xd3 ♖xd3 35 ♕xd3 ♕xa1 36 ♘d6 ♕b2+ 37 ♔f1 ♖d8 38 c5 ♕c1+ 39 ♔e2 ♕xc5 0-1**

373 Knezevic-Velimirovic
Jugoslavia Final 78

1 ♘f3 c5 2 c3 ♘f6 3 d4 e6 4 ♗f4 cxd4!? 4...♕b6 5 ♕b3≈ ♘c6 6 e3 ♕xb3 7 axb3 b6 8 h3 ♗e7 9 dxc5 bxc5 10 ♗b5 ♗b7 11 ♘bd2 a6 12 ♗a4 ♘d5 13 ♔h2 ♘b6 14 ♘c4 ♘xc4 15 bxc4 += Bronstein-Farago, Moscow-Budapest 71 **5 cxd4 b5!? 6 e3 a6** 6...♕b6!? **7 ♗d3 ♗b7 8 ♘bd2 ♘c6 9 h3** 9 e4!? += ♕b6 **10 0-0 ♗e7 11 ♘e5** 11 ♘e4 ♘xe4 (11...♘b4) 12 ♗xe4 ♘b4=; 11 a4 0-0 12 axb5 axb5 13 ♕e2 ♗a6≈ **♘b4!?** 11...♘xe5 12 ♗xe5 d6=; 12 dxe5 ♘d5 13 ♗e4≈; 13 ♔h2? ♘xe3! -+; 13 ♕g4 ♗xf4 14 ♕xf4 (14 exf4 ♕d4 -+) d6≈ **12 ♗b1 d6 13 ♘d3 ♘c6 14 a3=** 0-0 14...♘b8!? △ ♘bd7 **15 ♗g5 ♘a5?!** 15...e5 16 ♗xf6 ♗xf6 17 ♘e4 ♗e7 18 dxe5 dxe5 19 b4≈; 15...♕d8!? △ ♘d7/♘d5/ ♘e4 **16 ♗f4** △ ♘h5; 16 e4!? ♘c6 17 e5 ♘d5 18 ♗xe7 ♘cxe7 19 exd6 ♕xd6

20 ♘e4≈; 16...♕xd4?? 17 ♗e3 +- g6 16...h6 17 ♗xf6 ♗xf6 18 ♕c2± **17 ♘e4?!** 17 ♗a2! += △ b4, d5 **♕d8 18 ♘c3 ♖c8 19 ♕e2?!** 19 ♔h6 ♖e8 20 ♕e2 e5; 19 ♗a2 ♘d5 **20 ♖h6** 20 ♗xe7 ♘xc3 21 ♗xd8 ♘xe2+ 22 ♘xe2 ♖fxd8 23 ♗d3 ♘b3 =+ **♘xc3 21 bxc3 ♖e8 22 ♕g4 ♔h8 23 ♗a2** 23 ♘e2∓ **♖xc3 24 ♗xe6 fxe6 25 ♗g7+ ♔g8 26 ♘xg6 ♔xg7! -+ 27 ♘f4+** 27 ♘xe7+ ♔h8 -+; 27 ♘e5+ ♗g5 -+ **♔h8 28 ♘xe6 ♖g8 29 ♘xd8 ♗xd8! 30 ♕xg8+ ♔xg8 31 ♖fc1 ♖c4 32 ♖xc4 bxc4 33 ♖c1 ♗e4 34 f3 ♗d3 35 ♔f2 ♘b3 36 ♖d1 ♗a5 37 g4 ♗d2 0-1 Bellin**

374 Gulko-Gutman USSR 78

1 ♘c3 c5 2 ♘f3 d6 3 g3 g6 4 ♗g2 ♗g7 5 0-0 ♘c6 6 e3 ♘h6 7 d4 cxd4 8 exd4 ♘f5 9 d5 ♘e5 10 ♘g5 h5 10...h6 **11 h3 ♗d7 12 a4 ♖c8 13 ♘e2 ♕b6** 13...♕c7 **14 ♖a2 ♕a6 15 b3 b5 16 ♗d2 bxa4 17 ♘c3 ♘d4 18 ♘xa4 ♕e2 19 f4**

19...♗xa4 19...♘xh3 20 ♘xh3 ♘ef3+ 21 ♔h1 ♘xd2 22 ♖e1 +- **20 fxe5 ♗xe5 21 bxa4** 21 ♖xa4 ♖xc2 **♕c4 22 ♖a3! ♘e2+ 23 ♔h1 f6** 23...♘xg3+ 24 ♖xg3 ♗xg3 25 ♕f3 +- **24 ♘e4 f5 25 ♖e1 1-0** 25...♘d4 26 ♖c3 ♕a6 27 ♖xc8+ ♕xc8 28 ♘c3 fxe4 29 ♗xd4 +-

181

375 Mista-Smetana
CSSR 78

1 c4 e6 2 ♘f3 d5 3 g3 dxc4 4 ♕a4+ ♗d7 5 ♕xc4 ♗c6 6 ♗g2 ♘bd7 7 0-0 ♘b6?! 8 ♕c2 ♘f6 9 d3 ♗e7 10 ♘c3 0-0 11 e4 ♗e8? 12 d4 c5? 13 dxc5! ♗xc5 14 e5 ♘fd7 15 ♘g5 g6 16 ♘ge4 ♗d4 17 ♗h6 ♗xe5 18 ♗xf8 ♕xf8 19 ♖fd1 ♕c7 20 ♖ac1 ♖c8 21 f4 ♗g7 22 ♘d6 ♘c4 23 ♘xc8 ♘e3 24 ♕d2! ♘c4 24...♘xd1? 25 ♘xd1 25 ♕e2 ♕xc8 26 ♘e4 ♘db6 27 b3 ♗b5 28 bxc4 ♘xc4 29 ♕d2 f5 30 ♕b4+ 1-0

376 Kapengut-Timoshenko
USSR 78

1 c4 e6 2 ♘f3 d5 3 g3 ♘f6 4 ♗g2 dxc4 5 ♘a3 c5 6 ♘e5 a6 7 ♘axc4 ♖a7 8 a4 b6 9 d3 ♗b7 10 e4 ♘c6 11 f4 ♘d4 12 ♗e3 ♗e7 13 0-0 0-0 14 ♖f2 ♗a8 15 a5 b5 16 ♘b6 ♖c7 17 ♖c1 ♗b7

18 b4 ♗d6 19 ♖b2 ♗xe5 20 fxe5 ♘d7 21 ♗xd4 ♘xb6 21...cxd4 22 ♖xc7 ♕xc7 23 ♖c2 ♕d8 24 ♘xd7 ♕xd7 25 ♕c1 ♖c8 26 ♖c5 22 ♗xc5 ♘a4 23 ♖bc2 ♘xc5 24 d4 ♖d7 25 ♖xc5 ♖xd4 26 ♕e1 ♖xe4 27 ♕c3 27 ♗xe4 ♕d4+ ♕g5 28 ♗xe4 ♗xe4 29 ♖c8 g6 30 ♕d4 ♗f5 31 ♖xf8+ ♔xf8 32 ♖c8+ ♔g7 33 ♕c5 ♔h6 34 ♕c1 1-0

377 Djindjihashvili-Fedorowicz
Hastings 77/78

1 ♘f3 ♘f6 2 g3 d5 3 ♗g2 c6 4 c4 dxc4 5 ♘a3 g6 6 ♘xc4 ♗g7 7 0-0 0-0 8 d3 ♘bd7 9 ♗d2 ♘d5 10 ♕c2 a5 11 a3 b5 12 ♘e3 ♘xe3 13 ♗xe3 ♗b7 14 ♘d4± ♖c8 14...♕c7?? 15 ♘xb5 15 ♘b3 ♗a8 16 ♘c5 ♘f6 17 ♖ad1 ♘e8 18 ♗d2 ♕c7 19 ♗c3 ♘f6 20 b4 axb4 21 axb4 ♗b7 22 ♕b2 ♘h5 23 ♖a1 ♖a8 24 ♗f3 ♘f6 25 ♗e5 ♕c8 26 ♖xa8 ♗xa8 27 ♖a1 ♘e8 28 ♖a7 1-0

378 Kuzmin-Beljavsky Kiev 78

1 ♘f3 ♘f6 2 c4 e6 3 g3 d5 4 ♗g2 dxc4 5 0-0 a6 6 ♘c3?! b5?! 7 d3! cxd3 8 ♘e5 ♖a7 9 ♗e3 c5 10 ♕xd3! ♕c7 11 ♖fd1 ♗e7 12 a4 0-0 13 axb5 ♕xe5 14 ♗f4 ♕h5 15 ♗xb8 ♖d7 16 ♕c4 axb5 17 ♕xb5 ♕g6 18 ♖xd7 ♗xd7 19 ♕b7 ♕c2? 20 ♗e5 ♖d8 21 ♗xf6 ♗xf6 22 ♗e4 ♗c8 23 ♕b5 ♕d2 24 ♖d1 ♕xd1+ 25 ♘xd1 ♖xd1+ 26 ♔g2 ♖d8 27 ♕xc5 ♗xb2 28 ♗xh7+ ♔xh7 29 ♕c2+ ♔g8 30 ♕xb2 ♗d7 31 ♕b7 ♗e8 32 h4 ♖d7 33 ♕b8 ♖e7 34 g4 f6 35 f4 ♔f7 36 h5 ♗c6+ 37 ♔f2 e5 38 ♕d6 ♗d7 39 g5 fxg5 40 fxg5 1-0

379 Chiburdanidze-Alexandria (9) 77

1 ♘f3 c5 2 g3 ♘c6 3 ♗g2 d5 4 0-0 e6 5 c4 d4?! 5...♘f6 6 e3 += e5 7 exd4 exd4 8 d3 ♘f6 9 ♖e1+ ♗e7 10 ♘e5! ♘xe5 11 ♖xe5 0-0 12 ♘d2 ♕c7 13 ♖e1 ♖b8 14 ♘e4! ♘xe4 15 ♗xe4 ♗d6 16 ♕f3± b5 17 cxb5 17 b3± ♖xb5 18 b3 a5 19 ♗d5! a4 20 bxa4 20 ♗c6?! ♖b6 21 ♗xa4 ♗b7α ♖b4?! 20...♖a5 21 a5 ♗a6 22 ♗g5! ♖a4?! 22...♗b7! 23 ♖e4! ♖a3 24 ♖d1 ♗e5 24...♗b7 25 ♗f6 ♗xd5 26 ♕g4! g6 27 ♕h4 h5 28 ♕g5 ♔h7

29 ♖h4 ♗f3 30 g4 △ ♖xh5+ +−;
27...♗xe4 28 ♕h6; 27...♖b8 28 ♕x
h7+! +− 25 ♕f5 ♗d6 25...♗xd3
26 ♕xe5 +−; 26 ♖xd3 ♖xd3 27
♖xe5 +−

26 ♗f6! +− ♖b8 26...g6 27 ♕xg6+
hxg6 28 ♖h4 +− 27 ♕g5 ♗f8 27...
g6 28 ♕xg6+ 28 ♗xg7 ♗xg7 29 ♖g4
♕f8 30 ♕xg7+ 30 ♖e1 f6 31 ♕xf6+!
+− ♕e8 31 ♕g8+ ♕d7 32 ♕xf7+
1-0 Gufeld

380 Suetin-Kupreichik
USSR 78
1 ♘f3 d5 2 c4 d4 3 g3 ♘c6 4 ♗g2 e5
5 d3 ♗b4+ 6 ♗d2 a5 6...♗e7; 6...
♗xd2+; 6...♕e7 7 0-0 ♘f6 8 e3 0-0
9 exd4 exd4 10 ♘a3 ♗f5 11 ♗f4
h6 12 ♘b5 ♖c8 13 ♘e5

13...g5 14 ♗xc6 bxc6 15 ♘xc6 ♕d7

16 ♗e5 16 ♘e5? ♕e7 17 ♘c6 ♕c5 −+
♕xc6 16...♘g4 17 ♕f3 17 ♗xd4 ♕d7
18 ♗xf6 ♗g4 19 f3 ♗h3 20 ♘c2
20 ♖f2 ♗c5 21 ♘c2 △ d4 ♕f5 21
♗d4 ♗xf1 22 ♕xf1 ♖fd8 △ ♖xd4 −+
23 ♔g2 c5 24 ♗f2 ♗d2 24...♖xd3
25 ♘e3 ♕g6 26 ♘d5 ♖e8 27 ♘f6+
♕xf6 28 ♕xd3 25 ♖d1 ♖xd3 26
♕e2 ♖cd8 27 ♕e4 ♕xe4 28 fxe4 ♗b4
29 ♖xd3 ♖xd3 30 a3 ♗d2 31 ♗xc5
♗c1 32 ♔f1 ♖d2 33 ♘d4 ♖xb2 34
♘b5 ♖c2 35 ♘d6 ♖xh2 36 ♔e1 ♖a2
37 ♘b5 ♖c2 38 ♘d6 ♖c3 39 g4 ♗xa3
40 ♗xa3 ♖xa3 41 ♔d2 ♔f8 42 c5
♔e7 43 ♘f5+ ♔d7 44 ♘xh6 ♖f3 45
♘f5 ♖f4 0-1

381 Zilber-Djindjihashvili
Israel Final 78
1 ♘f3 ♘f6 2 g3 c5 3 ♗g2 ♘c6 4 0-0
e5 5 d3 d5 6 ♘bd2 ♗e7 7 e4 0-0 8
c3 d4 9 ♘c4 ♕c7 10 cxd4 cxd4 11
a4 ♗e6 12 b3 ♘d7 13 ♗a3? ♗xa3
14 ♖xa3 f6 15 ♕d2 ♖ac8 16 ♖c1
♘a5 17 ♘e1 ♖xc4!∓ 18 bxc4 ♘c5
19 a5 f5 20 exf5 ♖xf5 21 ♘c2 ♖cf8
22 ♖f1 ♕d6! 23 ♘b4 ♖5f7 24 f3 h5
25 ♖a2 h4! 26 gxh4 ♖f4 27 ♕e1 b5!
28 axb6 ♕xb6 29 ♖a3 ♖8f6 30
♘d5 ♗xd5 31 cxd5 ♕d6! 32 ♕b4
♖xh4 33 f4? exf4 34 ♕xd4 ♖g6
35 ♖xa7? 35 ♖a2 ♖hg4 −+ ♖xg2+!
0-1

382 Chiburdanidze-Alexandria (7) 77
1 ♘f3 d5 2 g3 c5 3 ♗g2 ♘c6 4 0-0 e6
5 d3 ♗d6 6 e4 ♘ge7 7 ♘bd2 0-0 8
♖e1 ♗c7 9 c3 b6 10 ♕c2?! 10 exd5
a5 11 a4 ♗a6= 12 h4 dxe4? 12...
♕d7 13 dxe4 += ♕d7 13...♗d3 14
♕b3 △ ♗f1 += 14 ♗f1 14 h5?! h6
15 ♗f1 ♗b7 △ ♕e8, f5∞ ♗xf1 15
♘xf1 ♖fd8 16 ♗e3 ♕d3? 17 ♕xd3
♖xd3 18 ♖ad1± ♖ad8 19 ♖xd3 ♖xd3

1 ♘f3 ♘f6

20 ♘1d2 20 h5!? **♘g6 21 ♔f1 h5!**
22 ♘c4 ♘e5 23 ♘fxe5 ♗xe5 24 ♘xe5?
24 ♘a3 △ ♗f4± ♗xe5 25 ♕e2 +=
♖d7 26 ♖d1? 26 ♖b1 += ♖xd1 27
♕xd1 ♕f8 28 ♕c2 ♕e8 29 ♕d3 29
b4 ♗d6 30 ♔b3 ♔d7 31 ♔c4 ♔c6=
♕d7 30 ♔c4 ♔c6= 31 ♗d2 ♗c7 32
♗e1 ♗d8 33 ♗d2 ½-½ Gufeld

383 E.Vladimirov-Vaganian
USSR 78

1 ♘f3 c5 2 g3 d5 3 ♗g2 ♘f6 4 0-0
♘c6 5 d3 e5 6 ♗g5 ♗e7 7 ♘fd2 0-0
8 ♘c3 ♗e6 9 e4 dxe4?! 9...d4 10
♗xf6 ♗xf6 11 dxe4 ♕d7 11...♘e7 12
♘d5 ♗d8 13 ♘c4± b5 14 ♘ce3 ♖b8
15 c3 c4 16 a4 a6 17 ♕h5! f6 18
♖fd1 ♕b7 19 ♗h3 ♗f7 20 ♕e2 ♗b6
21 ♘f5 ♗c5

22 ♘xf6+! +− gxf6 **23 ♖d7 ♕b6** 23...
♕xd7 24 ♕g4+ ♘g6 25 ♘h6+ ♔g7 26
♕xd7+ ♔xh6 27 ♕xc6 +− **24 a5!**
♘xa5 **25 ♘h6+ ♔g7 26 ♕h5 ♖b7 27**
♘f5+ ♔h8 28 ♕h6 ♖g8 29 ♖d6!
♗xf2+ 29...♖xd6 30 ♕xf6+ +− 30
♔g2 ♗g6 31 ♖xb6 ♗xb6 32 ♘d6 ♖bb8
33 ♗f5 △ ♘f7+ ♖g7 34 ♗xg6 ♖xg6 35
♕h3 ♘b3 36 ♖xa6 ♖gg8 37 ♕h6 ♖g6
38 ♖xb6! ♖xh6 39 ♖xb8+ ♔g7 40
♘f5+ ♔g6 41 ♖g8+ 1-0 Ilic

384 Plachetka-Augustin
CSSR Final 78

1 ♘f3 ♘f6 2 g3 b6 3 ♗g2 ♗b7 4 0-0
e6 5 d3 c5 6 e4 d6 7 ♘h4 ♕c7 7...
♗e7? 8 e5 +− 8 f4 ♗e7 9 ♘d2 d5
10 e5 ♘fd7 11 ♘hf3 ♘c6 12 ♖f2 b5
13 c3 a5 14 ♗f1 a4 15 a3 ♘a5 16
♗e3 ♘b3 17 ♖b1 g6 18 d4 △ 19
dxc5! ♘dxc5 20 ♘d4± b4 18...c4!?
△ 0-0-0 19 cxb4 cxb4 20 axb4 ♗a6!?
20...♗xb4 += 21 g4! h6 21...h5 22
f5! hxg4 23 fxe6 fxe6 24 ♘g5 +− 22
f5± ♘b6 23 fxg6 fxg6 24 ♘3d2
♗d3? 25 ♘xb3 ♗xb1 26 ♘c5! 26
♕xb1?! axb3 27 ♕xg6+ ♔d7 28 g5
(△ 29 ♕xe6+! ♔xe6? 30 ♗h3 mate)
hxg5 29 ♖f7 ♖ag8!∝ ♗e4 27 ♗xe4
dxe4 28 ♘xe6 ♕c4 29 d5! +− ♖b8
29...♘xd5 30 ♕xd5 30 ♗xb6 ♖xb6
31 ♕xa4+ 1-0 Plachetka

385 Hartston-Vehi Spain 78

1 g3 ♘f6 2 ♗g2 d5 3 ♘f3 b6 4 0-0
♗b7 5 d3 e6 6 ♘bd2 ♗c5 7 e4 0-0
7...dxe4 8 ♘g5 8 e5 ♘fd7 9 ♕e2 ♗e7
10 h4 c5 11 ♖e1 ♘c6 12 ♘f1 ♕c7
13 ♗f4 ♘d4 14 ♘xd4 cxd4 15 ♘h2
♖fc8 16 ♖ac1 ♘f8 17 h5± ♕c5 18
♕g4 f5 19 exf6 ♗xf6 20 h6 ♕e7 21
♗e5 ♗xe5 22 ♖xe5 ♕f6 23 ♕xg7+
+− ♕xg7 24 hxg7 ♔xg7 25 ♘f3 1-0

386 Hesse-Bruggemann
DDR Final 78

1 ♘f3 g6 2 g3 ♗g7 3 ♗g2 d6 4 d3
♘d7 5 e4 e5 5...c5; 5...♘gf6 6 0-0
♘h6 7 ♘bd2 0-0 8 c3 ♘b6 9 ♘e1
♗e6 10 f4 exf4 11 gxf4 ♕h4 12 ♕f3
f5 13 ♕g3 ♕xg3 14 hxg3 ♖ae8 15
♘c2 ♘a4 16 ♘e3 ♘c5 17 d4 ♘xe4
18 ♗xe4 fxe4 19 ♗xe4 ♘c4 20 ♗d2
20 ♘xc4 ♖xe4 21 ♘e3!?; 20 ♗d5+
♗xd4 21 cxd4 ♖xe4 22 ♘xc4 ♖xd4
23 b3 b5 24 ♘xd6 24 ♘c3 ♖d3 cxd4
24...♖xd6? 25 ♗b4 +−; 24...♖xd2?

25 ♘xb5 **25 Rfd1 Re8 26 Be1 Rxd1
27 Rxd1 Re2 28 a4 bxa4 29 bxa4
♞g4 30 Bb4 Re4 31 Rb1 a5 32 Bxd6
Rxa4 33 Rb7 Ra2 34 Ra7 h5 35
Bc5 a4 36 Bd4 ♔f8 37 Bc5+ ♔e8 38
♔f1 ♞f6 39 Re7+ ♔d8 40 Rg7 ♞e4
41 Bb6+ ♔c8 42 Rxg6 a3 43 Bd4
Rd2 44 Be5 a2 45 Rg7 ♔d8 46 ♔g1
♔e8 47 g4 h4 48 Rh7 ♞g3 49 Rxh4
♞e2+ 50 ♔f1 ♞xf4 51 Rh8+ ♔f7 52
Ra8 ♞d5 53 ♔e1 Rg2 54 Ra4 ♞b6
55 Ra7+ ♔e6 56 Bh8 ♞c4 57 Bc3
♔d5 58 g5 ♞e4 59 Ra5 ♔d3 60 Bf6
Re2+ 61 ♔f1 ♞d2+ 62 ♔g1 ♞e4 63
Rd5+ ♔e3 64 Rd1 ♞d2 0-1** 65 g6¦
♘f3+ 66 ♔f1 Rf2 mate; 66 ♔h1 Rh2
mate; 65 Rxd2 Rxd2 66 g6 a1♕
67 Bxa1 Rd1+ 68 ♔g2 Rxa1 69 g7
Ra8 −+

1 f4

387 Klausman-Bauer
CSSR 78

**1 ♞f3 ♞f6 2 b3 d5 3 Bb2 Bf5 4 c4
e6 5 e3 Be7 6 Be2 h6 7 0-0 0-0 8 ♞e5
♞bd7 9 f4 c6 10 h3 Bh7 11 d3 ♕b6
12 Rf3 Rad8 13 ♕h2 ♞e8 14 ♞c3?**
14 ♘d2 **♞xe5 15 fxe5 dxc4 16 ♞a4
♕c7 17 bxc4 Bf6!** 17...b5 18 cxb5
cxb5 19 Rc1 ♕b8 20 ♘c5 **18 ♔h1
Bxe5 19 ♕b3 Bxb2 20 ♞xb2 ♞f6
21 g4?! ♞d7 22 Rg1 ♞e5 23 Rfg3
g5 24 h4 Rd7 25 Rh3 Rfd8 26 e4**
26 d4 Be4+ 27 ♔h2 ♘xg4 mate **♞g6
27 hxg5 hxg5 28 Rh5 ♕e5 29 ♕c2
♞f4 30 Rh2 Bg6** 30...Bxe4+ 31 dxe4
Rd2 −+ **31 c5? ♞xd3! 32 ♞xd3** 32
Bxd3 Rxd3! 33 ♘xd3 Bxe4+ 34 Rgg2
♕a1+ 35 ♕c1 ♕xc1+ 36 ♘xc1 Rd1
mate; 34 Rhg2 ♕h8 mate **Bxe4+ 33
Rgg2 ♕a1+ 34 Bd1** 34 ♕c1 ♕xc1+
35 ♘xc1 Rd1+ 36 Bxd1 Rxd1 mate
Rxd3 0-1

388 Taylor-Rogoff
Lone Pine 78

1 f4 ♞f6 1...c5 2 ♘f3 ♘c6 3 g3 g6 4
Bg2 Bg7 5 0-0 d6 6 d3 Rb8 7 e4 b5
8 f5 ♘f6 9 ♕h4 0-0 10 g4 b4 11 a3 a5
Taylor-Ligterink, Lone Pine 78; 1...g6
2 ♘f3 Bg7 3 g3 d6 4 Bg2 e5 5 d3
♘e7 6 0-0 ♘bc6 7 c3 0-0 8 ♘a3
Re8 9 e4 Bg4 10 h3 Bxf3 11 ♕xf3
f5 Taylor-Arnason, Lone Pine 78
**2 ♞f3 d5 3 g3 g6 4 Bg2 Bg7 5 0-0
0-0** 5...b6 6 d3 Bb7 7 c3 0-0 8 a4 c5
9 e4 dxe4 10 ♘g5 ♕d7 11 ♘xe4 Rd8
12 ♕e2 ♘c6 Pelikan-Portisch, Mar
del Plata 66; 5...c5 6 d3 ♘c6 7 ♘c3
d4 8 ♘a4 ♘d7 9 c4 a6 10 Bd2 0-0 11
♕c2 ♕c7 12 a3 b6 13 b4 Lombardy-
Langeweg, Wijk aan Zee 69 **6 d3 ♞bd7**
6...c5; 6...b6; 6...c6; 6...♞c6 **7 ♞c3
♞c5 8 Bd2 c6 9 ♕e1 d4 10 ♞d1 ♞e6
11 c4 a5 12 b3 Ra6 13 Rb1 b6 14
f5 ♞c7 15 fxg6 hxg6 16 ♞e5 c5 17
♞c6 ♕e8 18 e3 dxe3 19 ♞xe3 Bd7**
19...Bb7?? 20 ♘xe7+ ♕xe7 21 Bxb7
+− **20 ♞e5 Be6 21 Rd1 ♕c8 22 Bc3
Bh3 23 ♞c6 ♞e4 24 ♕f2 Bxg2 25
♞xg2 ♕d7 26 ♞xe7+ ♕xe7 27 Bxf6
Bxf6 28 ♕xf6 ♕xf6 29 Rxf6± ♞e6
30 Rdf1 Re7 31 ♞e3 a4 32 ♞d5 Rb7
33 b4 cxb4 34 ♞xb4 Ra5 35 a3 Rc5
36 ♞d5 ♔g7 37 R6f2 b5 38 Rb1 Rd7
39 Rb4 ♞d4 Δ ♞c6 40 ♞f6 Re7 41
♞e4 Rxe4** 41...Rce5 42 cxb5 ♘xb5
43 Rxa4 +− **42 dxe4 bxc4 43 Rxa4
c3 44 Rxd4 c2 45 Rxc2 +− Rxc2
46 Rd3 ♔f6** 46...Re2 47 a4 Rxe4 48
Ra3 +− **47 Rf3+ ♔e6 48 Rf2 Rc1+
49 Rf1 Rc4 50 Ra1 Ra4** 50...Rxe4
51 a4 ♔d5 52 a5 +− **51 ♔f2 ♔e5
52 ♔f3 g5 53 h3 f6 54 Ra2 ♔d4 55
Rd2+ ♔e5 56 Rd5+ ♔e6 57 Rd3
♔e5 58 Rb3 Ra8 59 h4 gxh4 60
gxh4 Ra5 61 h5 f5 62 h6 fxe4+
63 ♔g4 ♔f6 64 Rh3 Ra8 1-0**

185

Games Index